Charts

OF

Cults, Sects, &
Religious Movements

ZondervanCharts Books in the Series

Charts of Ancient and Medieval Church History (John D. Hannah)

Charts of Christian Theology and Doctrine (H. Wayne House)

Charts of Cults, Sects, and Religious Movements (H. Wayne House)

Charts of the Gospels and the Life of Christ (Robert L. Thomas)

Chronological and Background Charts of Church History (Robert C. Walton)

Chronological and Background Charts of the New Testament (H. Wayne House)

Chronological and Background Charts of the Old Testament: Revised and Expanded (John H. Walton)

Chronological and Thematic Charts of Philosophers and Philosophies (Milton D. Hunnex)

Taxonomic Charts of Theology and Biblical Studies (M. James Sawyer)

Timeline Charts of the Western Church (Susan Lynn Peterson)

Charts

OF

Cults, Sects, & Religious Movements

H. Wayne House

Research Assistance
by Rich Abanes, Dan Chatham,
and Richard Featherstone

ZONDERVAN™

GRAND RAPIDS, MICHIGAN 49530 USA

ZONDERVAN™

Charts of Cults, Sects, and Religious Movements
Copyright © 2000 by H. Wayne House

Requests for information should be addressed to:

Zondervan, *Grand Rapids, Michigan 49530*

Library of Congress Cataloging-in-Publication Data

House, H. Wayne.
    Charts of cults, sects, and religious movements / H. Wayne House.
        p.   cm. — (ZondervanCharts)
    Includes bibliographical references and index.
    ISBN 0-310-38551-2 (softcover)
      1. Christian sects—United States—Doctrine Outlines, syllabi, etc.   2. Cults—United States—Doctrines Outlines,
syllabi, etc.   3. United States—Religious Outlines, syllabi, etc.   4. Christianity Apologetic works.   I. Title.
II. Series.
BR516.5.H68   2000
239'.9—dc21   99-42552
                                                                        CIP

Interior design by Sherri L. Hoffman

Printed in the United States of America

---

03 04 05 06 07 08 09 10 / ❖ VG / 10 9 8 7 6 5 4

In appreciation to
Bob and Gretchen Passantino
Longtime friends and fellow apologists for Christianity

Contents

Abbreviations

For Books of the Bible

Ge	Genesis
Ex	Exodus
Lev	Leviticus
Nu	Numbers
Dt	Deuteronomy
Jos	Joshua
Jdg	Judges
Ru	Ruth
1Sa	1 Samuel
2Sa	2 Samuel
1Ki	1 Kings
2Ki	2 Kings
1Ch	1 Chronicles
2Ch	2 Chronicles
Ezr	Ezra
Ne	Nehemiah
Est	Esther
Job	Job
Ps/s	Psalm/s
Pr	Proverbs
Ecc	Ecclesiastes
SS	Song of Songs
Isa	Isaiah
Jer	Jeremiah
La	Lamentations
Eze	Ezekiel
Da	Daniel
Hos	Hosea
Joel	Joel
Am	Amos
Ob	Obadiah
Jnh	Jonah
Mic	Micah
Na	Nahum
Hab	Habakkuk
Zep	Zephaniah
Hag	Haggai
Zec	Zechariah
Mal	Malachi
Mt	Matthew
Mk	Mark
Lk	Luke
Jn	John
Ac	Acts
Ro	Romans
1Co	1 Corinthians
2Co	2 Corinthians
Gal	Galatians
Eph	Ephesians
Php	Philippians
Col	Colossians
1Th	1 Thessalonians
2Th	2 Thessalonians
1Ti	1 Timothy
2Ti	2 Timothy
Tit	Titus
Phm	Philemon
Heb	Hebrews
Jas	James
1Pe	1 Peter
2Pe	2 Peter
1Jn	1 John
2Jn	2 John
3Jn	3 John
Jude	Jude
Rev	Revelation

Bible Versions

KJV	*King James Version*
NASB	*New American Standard Bible*
NIV	*New International Version*
NKJV	*New King James Version*
NRSV	*New Revised Standard Version*

Preface

This project on various cults, sects, and religions has been a long time coming to completion. The original idea began in 1989 with the encouragement of Len Goss, an editor with Zondervan. The first conception was a volume similar to my ZondervanCharts books on the New Testament and church doctrine. This more simple approach of those books eventually gave way to a more detailed approach in which the original statements of the various groups are accompanied by a biblical response.

The volume includes two kinds of groups. Some cults, sects, or religions tend to reflect a dependence on historic Christianity but deviate in some way theologically from the historic doctrines of the church. Others are influenced by Eastern religion yet usually use some Christian terminology or have minor dependence on Christian thought. I have endeavored not to create straw men but to accurately reflect the beliefs of these groups. Each of the statements of a group's belief is substantiated by a direct quotation from primary sources of that group. Then a response is given either to affirm the view stated or to provide a biblical or theological corrective. The reader should be aware that most of this volume was completed in 1995 and so certain information may not be current, though I have attempted to update any serious change in the group discussed. Regardless, the doctrinal deviations of the various groups are still consistent with each group discussed.

In two appendices I have provided a summary of biblical doctrines discussed in the charts, and I have also included several important creeds of the Christian church. These are provided so that readers may consult various doctrines or supporting passages as they read the responses I have offered to the different errors or offered in my attempts to correct understandings of a group. The bibliography is divided into two parts. First there is the listing of general works used on cults, sects, and religious movements. Then there is a listing for each group that includes specific works cited in the charts. Readers need to be aware that many of these groups do not have their publications in standard book form or magazine format, so that often the citation refers only to a pamphlet or a paper privately published by a group; often these are not even available to the public. Often these do not have regular publication information or page numbers; however, each quotation is based on photocopies of sources that are in the possession of the author.

My desire is that readers will be able, through these pages, to defend the faith once for all delivered to the saints (Jude 3) and be strengthened in the most holy faith and the Scriptures. Moreover, I pray that in confronting this book, many who have been deceived by unbiblical teachings may be reclaimed to the truth of Jesus Christ or be brought to a saving knowledge of Him.

—H. Wayne House

Soli Deo Gloria!

Note: The reader should realize that there is not one accepted definition for the term *cult,* or even *sect,* as mentioned in the title of this book. I have sought to use them only in reference to doctrinal deviations from orthodox Christianity and not in reference to sociological or psychological characteristics. In brief, then, a cult may be defined as a group of people who, though claiming to be Christian, accept one or more central tenets of belief that run contrary to historic Christianity. A sect is a group that has broken away from a larger religious organization, usually differing in a doctrinal manner from that original organization. "Religious movement" is a generic term covering a religious ideology shared by many people that has no formal structure. I purposely have not tried to suggest in the book which groups fits into which category; readers can make their own judgment in that regard. Some may be difficult to classify. Note, however, that all the groups deviate in some significant way from orthodox doctrine and historic Christianity, and that is the basis for their being included in this book.

Acknowledgments

The saying that no man is an island has surely been my experience in the production of this book. Many people have had a hand in its research and writing. Due to myriad facts and details, I have sought out a number of specialists in different religions and cults to provide for me the latest and best of research data. I then sought them again for checking the accuracy of the information included in this work. I have attempted to be complete in giving acknowledgments. If I have missed anyone, please let me know so I might correct that oversight in future printings. I wish to thank the students of my various theology classes at Dallas Theological Seminary, especially the following who rendered special assistance in the production of these charts: Mark Allen, Rod Chaney, Kathie Church, Larry Gilcrease, Alan K. Ginn, Casey Jones, Mike Justice, Johann Lai, Randy Knowles, Toni Martin, Doreen Mellott, Steve Pogue, Greg Powell, Brian Rosner, David Seider, Brian Smith, Gayle Sumner, and Larry Trotter. I give a special thanks to Richard Greene, Greg Trull, Steve Rost, and Gordon Carle, student research assistants and friends who labored with me on this project and others as a service of love to a fellow brother in Christ.

My thanks to the following who have provided information on the various groups presented in this book and have checked the charts for accuracy. First, I would like to thank persons who helped in a general way or worked on charts that did not make their way into the book: Philip Arn, Watchman Fellowship (Arlington, TX); Christian Research Institute (CRI) (Rancho Santa Margarita, CA) for use of their library and files; Desmond Ford, president of Good News Unlimited (Auburn, CA); Jim Koran (Chicago, IL); and Bob and Gretchen Passantino, directors of Answers and Action (Costa Mesa, CA), friends who gave critiques at different stages of the project. Second, I wish to express to people who gave of their time to correct and offer criticisms of individual groups included in the book: James Beverley (Toronto, Ontario): Unification Church; Jeff Drauden (Charlotte, NC): Reorganized Church of Jesus Christ of Latter-day Saints (RLDS); Todd Ehrenborg, pastor of the United Methodist Church, Yorba Linda (Yorba Linda, CA): Mind Sciences; Carol Eskridge, coordinator of Christian Liberty Outreach (Independence, MO): RLDS; John Juedes (Highland, CA): The Way International; David Johnson (Charlotte, NC): Church of Jesus Christ of Latter-day Saints; Kevin Johnson (Mt. Carmel Outreach, Rockford, IL): United Pentecostal Church (UPC), Christian Identity Movement, and New Age Movement; Ron Johnson: Christian Identity Movement; Duane Magnani, national director of Witness, Inc. (Clayton, CA): Jehovah's Witnesses; Pat Minichello (Brooklyn, NY): Unification Church; Bill McKeever, founder-director of Mormonism Research Ministry (El Cajon, CA): LDS; B. J. Oropeza, research associate for CRI (Rancho Santa Margarita, CA): UPC; Eric Pement, Jesus People U.S.A. (Chicago, IL): A Course in Miracles, RLDS, and Urantia Foundation; Ed Priebe: The Family; and Eldon Winkler: Freemasonry.

I want to thank Joseph and Barbara Gaziano for their considerable help in organizing the quotations in the charts and the original sources used for these quotes and checking each quote for accuracy against the original source material.

Special appreciation must be given to my primary researcher for this book, Richard Abanes. Also, I wish to thank Richard Featherstone and Daniel Chatham for their assistance in checking the manuscript and finding sources. Also my thanks to Dan Tarabek for assistance at the final stage of the project.

The responsibility for any errors of fact contained in this book lies at my feet and not at the feet of those skillful assistants, named above, who provided materials and reviews.

Thanks are due to Stan Gundry and Jim Ruark of Zondervan for invaluable help on the project. Also my thanks go to my former editor, Ed van der Maas, for his encouragement in the earlier stages of the book, and to Len Goss, formerly of Zondervan, who provided the idea for the book.

Finally, I wish to thank my wife, Leta, for her continued support in all my writing projects and my ministry in general for more than thirty-two years.

1

Alamo Christian Ministries

FACTS AND HISTORY

Facts	
Topic	*Current Facts*
Membership	During the late 1970s and early 1980s Alamo Christian Ministries (a.k.a. Tony & Susan Alamo Christian Foundation, Music Square Church, Holy Alamo Christian Church, Holy Alamo Ministries) was well on its way to becoming one of the largest and wealthiest churches to emerge from the Jesus People movement. Growth of the multimillion-dollar religious organization was brought to a stop, however, when its founder Tony Alamo (a clothing designer best known for the rhinestone studded denim jackets he sold to numerous celebrities) began having legal troubles.
	Although membership figures of several thousand have been reported, the group's high turnover rate has kept its numbers to fewer than 700 at any given time. As of 1994, Alamo followers had fallen under 300 and all of his holdings, except for three churches (one in Arkansas, one in Florida, and one in New York), had been sold.
	The ongoing significance of this small group lies in its recent anti-government publications that have been used by groups such as Scientology and the Family (a.k.a. Children of God) in an effort to garner support for "persecuted" religious sects.
Worship	Church and worship services have varied throughout the years. In the group's early days there were eight services a week (one each night Monday through Friday and two on Sunday) open to the public. There were also six "house meetings." Members were required to attend at least one service a day.
	Worship consisted of about 10 minutes of loud music (old-time gospel hymns) followed by some 10 minutes of "pop" testimonies. After another two or three songs (often solos), there would be a 15-minute sermon and altar call.
	Because Alamo no longer has control over a commune-church environment (see History chart), services are now held mostly in homes scattered throughout the country.
Leaders of the Holy Alamo Christian Church	1969—Tony & Susan Alamo. Susan died in 1982 of a brain tumor at Oral Roberts's City of Faith. Two years before her death, she claimed that she had been healed of the cancer that had spread through her body.
Publications	The group produces a vast array of tracts that are passed out on the street, in hospitals and convalescent homes, left on parked cars, and mailed throughout the country. One such tract declares, "Alamo literature circulation is more than *USA Today, The New York Times, L.A. Times* and many other national publications combined" (*CONSPIRACY*, p. 1).
	Tony Alamo is best known for his sensationalistic and highly inflammatory anti-Catholic literature, scathing anti-government pamphlets, and conspiratorial theories (see Interesting and Distinctive Beliefs charts).

Topic	Current Facts (cont.)
General statement of beliefs	The religious doctrines held by Alamo and his group are extremely difficult to document. According to ex-members, most of the church's beliefs about God, Christ, the Holy Spirit, salvation, sin, and the nature of man are spread primarily by "word of mouth." Former followers also state that many teaching tapes made by Alamo, as well as written materials dealing with doctrine, have been destroyed over the years under Alamo's orders. Based on the testimony of former members and the literature that remains, it appears that Alamo teaches many orthodox Christian doctrines, yet deviates on a few key issues such as salvation by grace alone.

History

Topic	History
Susan Alamo, 1969—1982	Until her death in 1982, Susan Alamo (born Edith Opal Horn in Arkansas in the 1920s) was the undisputed leader of the Alamo Christian Foundation. Her path to leadership began when she moved to California to begin a singing career under the name Susan Fleetwood. After her musical efforts failed, she married her first husband (Sol Lipowitz), converted to Christianity, and began teaching the Bible to the hippies and social outcasts on the streets of Hollywood. After a divorce, Susan married Tony Alamo in 1966 and continued her evangelism efforts with him by her side. According to Tony, this was when, where, and how the Jesus Movement began: "One evening, coming home from a service, she delivered an ultimatum to me. She was going out into the streets to the hippies and I could go or stay.... So we went to the streets.... here is where the Jesus Movement began.... I can tell you about it. Many people have tried to take the credit for the great revival that has swept the world, but believe me, there was no one else in the streets when Susan and I first went out there" (*Signs of the Times*, p. 6).
Tony Alamo, 1982—	On September 20, 1934, Bernard Lazar Hoffman was born to a Jewish family in Joplin, Missouri. During his youth he moved to California. There "Bernie" eventually changed his name to Tony Alamo and became a talent manager/promoter in Hollywood (*Signs of the Times*, p. 2). He converted to Christianity because during a 1964 business meeting, he allegedly heard a voice say, "'I AM THE LORD THY GOD. STAND UP ON YOUR FEET AND TELL THE PEOPLE IN THIS ROOM THAT JESUS CHRIST IS COMING BACK TO EARTH, OR THOU SHALT SURELY DIE'" (*Signs of the Times*, p. 3). The voice repeated the message until Alamo obeyed.

After the meeting ended, Alamo claims, he went to several churches, but found no one preaching the "powerful message" he had been given. He eventually found a Bible, from which he learned the plan of salvation and was saved. Alamo then asked Susan Fleetwood, whom he had known for some time, to be his Bible teacher. They eventually fell in love, got married, and spread the gospel on the streets. In 1969 they started the Tony and Susan Alamo Christian Foundation, which between 1970 an 1979 saw its yearly contributions soar from $46,000 to $1.3 million. Problems arose as the Alamos began owning and operating multiple businesses, using church members as workers. Tax and labor-law concerns, plus charges that the group had become a manipulative cult, brought numerous lawsuits from both the government and former followers. In 1976 the U.S. Department of Labor filed a complaint against the Foundation, and nine years later the group's tax-exempt status was revoked. (That same year the net worth of the ministry was placed at $60 million.) When charges of felony child abuse were filed against Tony Alamo in October 1988, he fled and eluded the FBI until July 1991. In June 1992 Alamo agreed to pay $5 million in restitution to ex-members for unpaid work. Five weeks later he filed for bankruptcy, and his businesses, land, cash, and property were seized by the government and auctioned off in order to pay back taxes and the numerous multimillion-dollar judgments that had been awarded in lawsuits against him.

Alamo's remaining followers meet mostly in private homes and receive instruction through tracts and selected teaching tapes. As of May 1994, Alamo was awaiting trial for felony child-abuse charges in California. Although the sect's future is uncertain, there are indications that other groups (such as Scientology and The Family/The Children of God) are distributing Alamo literature. |

THEOLOGY

The Doctrine of Revelation

Position	Support	Orthodox Response
The Bible is the Word of God and is to be believed. To doubt the Word of God means damnation.	". . . the Bible is the inspired Word Of God, for unaided man is neither capable of writing nor fulfilling such a literary wonder" (*The Messiah According to Bible Prophecy*, p. 3). "Calling the truth of the Word of God to question endangers the soul to an everlasting hell" (*The Set Up*, p. 15).	The statement is correct in stating that the Bible is God's inspired Word, but damnation lies not merely in questioning any statements of the Bible (though this writer accepts the inerrancy of the original writings) but also in failing to believe the gospel. Christ states that it is failure to believe who He is (Jn 8:24) and the message He brings of salvation that brings damnation (Jn 3:18).
Although the Bible is the Word of God, the truths preached at Alamo's churches stem from revelations Alamo received directly from God through a number of supernatural experiences.	". . . if it were not for the abundance of my supernatural experiences with the Lord (signs, visions, dreams, and wonders, which include a face-to-face talk with the Lord Jesus Christ Himself), I too might feel obliged to believe the current pipe dream [global peace through the UN]" (*Cult Protection Racket*, p. 1). "Tony didn't write them [tracts]. It was the Lord that wrote the tracts" (*4/5/94 interview with Alamo Christian Ministries representative*).	Although professing absolute reliance on the Bible, Alamo considers his revelations as the basis of his theology, rather than the Bible alone. Why should others without these revelations, then, be able to trust the Bible or him? Tony Alamo puts his tracts on a level with the inspiration of the Bible. This is a rejection of Sola Scriptura, the reformational and biblical concept that only Scripture is inspired.

The Doctrine of God—*The Trinity*

Position	Support	Orthodox Response
There is only one God.	". . . *the God of the Bible is the only true God*" (*The Messiah According to Bible Prophecy*, p. 84).	This is an orthodox statement.
The one true God exists as three persons: Father, Son, and Holy Spirit.	"God is One God, existing in Three Persons—Father, Son (Messiah) and Holy Spirit" (Ibid., p. 79).	This is an orthodox statement.
Since we are made in God's image, God must have a body with hands, arms, legs, eyes, etc. In other words, God the Father is a man.	"God is a man. We look like him . . ." (*4/5/94 interview with Alamo Christian Ministries representative*)	The Bible says just the opposite, that God is not a man (Nu 23:19), though the emphasis of this passage is God's veracity. Jesus says that God is a spirit (Jn 4:24), and He says elsewhere that a spirit does not have flesh and bones (Lk 24:39). Any biblical references to body parts for God (e.g., Ex 9:3; 33:11; Ps 71:2; Isa 65:3) are known as anthropomorphisms. These figures of speech put God in human terms so that we, as humans, can better understand and identify with God.

The Doctrine of Jesus Christ—*The Deity of Christ*

Position	Support	Orthodox Response
Jesus was, and is, God manifested in the flesh.	"Christ is presented as the SON OF GOD—yes, GOD HIMSELF in the flesh" (*The Messiah According to the Bible Prophecy*, p. 72). ". . . the Bible reveals Messiah (Christ) to be GOD MANIFEST IN THE FLESH" (Ibid., p. 74).	These are orthodox statements.

The Doctrine of Jesus Christ—*The Humanity of Christ*

Position	Support	Orthodox Response
Jesus was fully God and fully man. As a man, He never sinned.	"He [Jesus] is very God and perfect man; rather, He is the God-man, God and man in one, indivisible personality" (*The Messiah According to Bible Prophecy*, p. 74).	This is an orthodox statement.
Jesus was born of a virgin.	"Turning to the New Testament, we find that Jesus indeed was born of a virgin" (*The Messiah According to Bible Prophecy*, p. 21).	This is an orthodox statement.

The Doctrine of Jesus Christ—*The Resurrection of Christ*

Position	Support	Orthodox Response
Jesus physically rose from the dead after three days. He was truly resurrected.	"The New Testament of course bears abundant evidence that though Christ died, forsaken by God and man, yet **God raised Him from the dead on the third day**" (*The Messiah According to Bible Prophecy*, p. 53).	This is an orthodox statement.

The Doctrine of the Holy Spirit

Position	Support	Orthodox Response
The Holy Spirit is the life force from which all things living draw life. (Since God creates all life, the Holy Spirit can still be called God by Alamo.) It is actually a substance that fills the Bible (Word) and Jesus (Word).	"God's Holy Ghost is the Spirit of Life (John 6:63). God's Holy Spirit is the only life in the entire universe. All life is derived from the Holy Spirit, and God's will is that you daily drink from His well of life" (*Spiritual War*, p. 3). "The Spirit of God is life and is the spiritual seed, the life-giving substance within the inspired Word, spoken by God to Moses. . . . The spiritual life . . . is only to be found in the Word (Christ)" (Ibid., p. 1).	Alamo is correct in saying that the Holy Spirit is life, but this is also true of the Father and the Son (Jn 5:26). All this is true because God Himself is life (Jos 3:10; Ps 84:2; Ac 14:15; 1Ti 3:15).

The Doctrine of Man and Sin

Position	Support	Orthodox Response
Man was originally created with the same kind of godly nature possessed by Jesus Christ. When man sinned, he lost that nature and received the nature of Satan. When a person repents, the satanic nature departs and the godly nature is restored.	"Man was made good till he disbelieved and disobeyed God and believed and obeyed Satan and thus lost the Godly nature of Christ Jesus, the Light of God's Word, and because of it, took on the wicked nature of Satan. This satanic nature will depart upon repentance. The Godly nature will be restored by humbly coming to Christ.... You shall receive salvation and the nature of the Lord by sincerely asking God for repentance" (*The Preacher*, p. 11).	It is difficult to understand exactly what Alamo means by humans' having a "Godly nature" before the Fall and after repentance. Jesus, being God, has an absolutely holy nature. Even Adam and Eve, though having a nature without sin, nonetheless had the capacity to sin. God, by contrast, is holy in His essential character, totally separated from sin (Lev 11:44, 45; Isa 6:3; 40:25; 1Jn 1:5).
The unsaved, who have the nature of Satan, are alienated from God. Consequently, they need a Savior.	"The unsaved are alienated from God" (*The Weapon*, p. 3). "Sin left man in spiritual darkness.... so, man needs a Savior" (*The Messiah According to Bible Prophecy*, p. 66).	These are orthodox statements.

The Doctrine of Salvation

Position	Support	Orthodox Response
Salvation is obtained by placing one's faith in Jesus and accepting His death on the cross as an atonement for sin.	"... in Christ Jesus God has given us His perfect HIGH PRIEST, who offered the perfect offering to atone for the sins of the race, and thereby give eternal life to all who accept Him as their Substitute and Saviour" (*The Messiah According to Bible Prophecy*, p. 68). "... salvation of man's soul depends entirely on trusting Christ and what He did on the cross as the Redeemer for one's eternal salvation" (Ibid., p. 84).	These statements are essentially correct though there may be an emphasis on faith being the *reason* for salvation rather than the means through which salvation is received (Eph 2:8).
One obtains salvation purely by grace apart from works.	"Here [Is. 53:11] we are given a forecast of the tremendous truth, so fully developed by Paul in the New Testament, of JUSTIFICATION BY FAITH, salvation by grace—because Christ died for our sins and purchased a full redemption for all. This truth of justification by faith is the grand, central truth of the New Testament" (*The Messiah According to Bible Prophecy*, p. 64).	This is an orthodox statement. But the statement that "faith is the grand, central truth of the New Testament" misses the point that the central truth of the New Testament is the coming of God in the person of Jesus Christ. Faith is one of the primary truths relating to reception of God's work in Christ.
At the point of salvation all past sins are forgiven.	"God will forgive and forget your atrocities, all of your sins, if you'll just simply confess to God that you've been wrong, that you've sinned, and acknowledge Him as Lord, God, and Saviour" (*The Set Up*, p. 15).	This is an orthodox statement.

The Doctrine of Salvation (cont.)

Position	Support	Orthodox Response
Christ only made it possible for God to excuse our sins if we, through the power of the Holy Spirit, go and "sin no more" after being forgiven.	"God gives us eternal life through Christ by our willingness to reunite with Him by accepting His one and only method so long as afterward we walk in the power (the grace) provided to us by God, which is Christ living in us through faith by the Holy Ghost" (*Serpent*, p. 5). "Because Christ made peace for us, offering up His sinless self, He makes it possible for God to excuse our sinful selves if we go and sin no more" (Ibid., p. 6).	This error is similar to that taught by certain Galatians against whom Paul wrote. Paul rejected a view that would acknowledge beginning in the Spirit but ending in works (Gal 3:1–2). Moreover, such teaching makes current forgiveness based on the unforeseen future. Since we do not know the future, our salvation can never bring us peace and security because we would never know if we would be eternally saved.
Although eternal life is initially obtained by grace through faith, it is retained by keeping all of God's law and never sinning again. Sinning again would mean loss of salvation forever.	". . . God's Law, is not to ever be broken. Not even God could escape its penalty if He were to take our place as the condemned one. . . . All redeemed souls must be taught to know the necessity to go and sin no more. Sinning again after salvation is penalized by God's Law as double jeopardy without mercy, without forgiveness, because there remaineth no more sacrifice for sins (Hebrews 10:26)" (Ibid., p. 4). "Faith in God, God's Son (the Word of God), His death, His resurrection, as the substitute for our sins . . . so that everyone could, if they wish to escape eternal hell, receive these truths, repent, then go and sin no more, keeping all of God's commandments (the Law, highly exalted) through the new given power by the acceptance of the power of the now indwelling Christ by the Holy Ghost" (Ibid., p. 2). "He is the true rough and tough Jesus of the real Bible Who hates sin, renounces and condemns all unrepentant sinners, Who also condemns those of the redeemed who refuse to go and sin no more. The real Jesus of the real Bible states that all these shall spend eternity in an eternal burning hell" (*Serpent*, p. 5).	This teaching flies directly in the face of Scriptures that indicate that salvation is only by grace through faith and not works. Alamo has made the law a means to salvation, directly contrary to the gospel preached by Paul (Ro 10:9; 1Co 15:1–4; Gal 1:6–8). Also, Scripture teaches that believers do sin; there is no sinless human but Christ (1Jn 1:7–10; 2Ch 6:36).
Breaking even the slightest aspect of the law would mean loss of salvation.	"For a person to break the law, even one jot or tittle, after they have been saved, it is to be considered the ultimate of sins because this type of person uses the same bloody weapon (sin) that caused Christ to come to this world and die" (*The Heavenly Pharmacy*, p. 5).	Again, Alamo places salvation with the fragile ability of Christians never to sin after initial forgiveness. This is contrary to biblical teaching and our personal experience. Paul assured believers that even where sin abounds, grace abounds all the more (Ro 5:20–21).

The Doctrine of Salvation (cont.)

Position	Support	Orthodox Response
Because baptism is a commandment, one must also be baptized in order to keep salvation.	"Now that you are saved it is a commandment to be fully submerged, baptized in water in the name of the Father and in the name of the Son and in the name of the Holy Ghost. Follow all of God's commands and live" (*The Authorities*, p. 6).	Baptism is not given as an additional requirement to faith as a means of securing eternal life. The New Testament posits no "work" but believing in Christ (Jn 6:29). Salvation is based solely on the grace of God and is freely received through the agency of faith (Eph 2:8–9). No additional acts of baptism, penance, good works, or similar works are needed for salvation.
One must also "suffer" through serving God in order to retain salvation.	"We are told that if we believe in the Lord Jesus Christ we have eternal life. This is true. But if the Bible reader will continue reading . . . he will see a hitch—a contingency in the acquiring of eternal life. . . . We must prepare our hearts to suffer all things that we might gain eternal life. . . . Christ commands this spiritual sacrifice every moment of our lives. . . . This is the seal or up-to-date stamp of approval for qualification from God in His account book. . . . The chief commandment and provision Jesus makes to all is to do the work of suffering" (*The Arrangement*, pp. 1–2).	Again, Alamo adds a Christian's works to God's undeserved favor. Suffering with Christ refers to our reign with Him in the future, not to eternal life (2Ti 2:12).

The Doctrine of Rewards and Punishment

Position	Support	Orthodox Response
All those who achieve eternal life will dwell for all eternity in heaven.	"All those who will spend eternity in Heaven must first become righteous and holy through God's plan of salvation" (*The Authorities*, p. 5). "Turn yourself over to the great Physician [Jesus]. . . . This means salvation for your soul, escape from hell, and everlasting life in heaven" (*The Heavenly Pharmacy*, p. 5).	Alamo views salvation as a human achievement rather than the gift of God through faith in Christ's finished work on the cross. Alamo believes that a person must become righteous to be able to go to heaven. Under this requirement, none will go to heaven. Rather, our righteousness must be the imputed rightousness of Christ, not what is produced in our lives (Ro 3:21–26; 4:22–25).
All unbelievers (and those who lose their salvation) will be cast into the lake of fire for all eternity.	"You may accept Christ and be spared from an everlasting hell by taking God up on His offer to save your soul" (*Judge or be Judged*, p. 5). "Avoid hell's everlasting torments by accepting the Lord Jesus Christ as your Lord, your King, and Saviour" (*Give Caesar Tribute?* p. 11).	Generally, orthodox believers accept the doctrine of eternal punishment. However, evangelicals differ among themselves as to whether or not a believer can cease to believe in Jesus and finally be damned forever as though he or she had never believed in the first place.

INTERESTING AND DISTINCTIVE BELIEFS

Position	Support	Orthodox Response
Polygamy is a perfectly acceptable practice. It should not be practiced, however, by unbelievers (sinners).	"The Holy Scriptures proclaim polygamy to be righteous" (*The Polygamists*, p. 9). "Anyone who would believe that polygamy, according to God's Holy Scripture, is dead, would believe that God is dead, and that the Bible is meaningless" (Ibid., p. 1). "Polygamy is not meant for sinners because sinners' hearts and intentions are not godly" (Ibid., p. 7).	Although polygamy is allowed by God in the Hebrew Scriptures, nonetheless, it is never stated to be a superior practice to monogamy. Instead, Jesus states the original intention of marriage as one man and one woman (Mt 19:4–6; Mk 10:6–8). If polygamy were God's intention for marriage, there would be no restriction of the practice to unbelievers because marriage is a creation ordinance, not a redemption ordinance (Ge 1:27; 2:23–24).
Polygamy is a divine fulfillment of the curse pronounced on women (through Eve) after the Fall. This is why men are allowed more than one spouse while woman may have only have one husband.	"Why are godly men allowed to have two or more spouses and women allowed only one? The answer . . . dates back to God's curse on men and women from the garden of Eden. . . . The woman's desire, her longing, shall be toward him (her husband), because of God's curse on the woman from the days of Eden, her husband may be called by God to be a polygamist if he be holy. Thus the woman's desire would be for her husband to be exclusively her own. Thus the fulfillment of the curse (Genesis 3:16)" (*The Polygamists*, pp. 9–10).	Genesis 3:16b does not speak of a woman's desiring her husband to be exclusively hers. The passage teaches that a woman, due to the curse, would desire the position of authority over her husband. By giving attention to her role as mother a woman may be delivered from the tendency of taking authority over a man; this may be the apostle's teaching in 2 Timothy 2:15. Other than this, the woman's curse is pain in childbearing that she would not have had (Ge 3:16a).
Anyone who condemns or complains about the practice of polygamy will be damned for not accepting God's words.	"Jesus said, 'Whosoever therefore shall be ashamed of me and of my words (which includes the law of polygamy) . . . of him also shall the Son of man be ashamed" (*The Polygamists*, p. 13). "For a woman to be contentious about these commands from God's Word is worse than ever for her, because of what she has already done, and there is nothing more for her to look forward to but an eternity in the everlasting destruction of hell. And what if a woman object? What if anyone objects to God's law? They go to hell. . . . God doesn't care if you like it or not. Polygamy is scripturally sound because it has always been directed by God. Those who would object would fall into the same category as all the wicked men and women documented in the Bible who opposed God's words" (Ibid., pp. 17–18).	Christ gave no teaching in the Gospels on the practice of polygamy. This is reading into the text the teachings of Alamo rather than finding favorable teaching on polygamy in the words of Christ. Although Scripture reveals that God allowed polygamy, there is no evidence that it was promoted by God, the prophets, or the apostles. The teachings of Alamo here seem to be an attempt to subjugate women to a role never required of them by God, using intimation and threats of eternal punishment to do it.
Polygamy is actually a picture of the church.	"As the Lord and His bride (the true, spiritual church of God) is composed of many millions of redeemed souls, so also some godly men and their godly brides could be composed of two or more godly wives" (*The Polygamists*, p. 10).	One cannot use an analogy of Christ and His body, the church, to teach polygamy. The Scripture never does so, and analogies emphasize one point, not a number.

Position	Support	Orthodox Response
Neither Jesus, John the Baptist, nor Paul ever condemned polygamy.	"... the ungodly Sadducees came to catch Jesus in His words regarding the Levirate law (a woman getting married to her deceased husband's brother).... Jesus only addressed the issue of there being no one in heaven that is married.... If polygamy were illegal, or the law had been changed or today made void, Jesus certainly would have mentioned it at that point, but He never condemned godly polygamy.... He condemned divorce" (*The Polygamists*, pp. 6–7). "When John the Baptist reproached Herod, the tetrarch, it was for his sin of adultery ... not for the non-sin of polygamy.... Herod was a polygamist, but the Baptist never reproved Herod for it, because John knew the law, that polygamy is not a sin. Herod was married to another man's wife.... this is adultery" (Ibid., pp. 14–15). "Paul knew also that they [Romans and Greeks] were strictly monogamous (having one wife), but that sinful adultery was common among them.... Paul's attitude was, when in Rome and Greece, do as the Romans and Grecians do (as far as their monogamous rules of marriage were but not adultery). Paul didn't want the bishops and deacons of his churches to be stumbling blocks in the area. He wanted them to become all things to all men.... When the Apostle Paul tells the bishops and deacons to have only one wife, this amplifies and makes it clear that other strong men of God other than bishops and deacons in the church are implicitly allowed to have more than one wife" (Ibid., p. 15).	This is orthodox teaching. The New Testament does not condemn polygamy but neither does it teach polygamy as a desirable practice for the Christian man. It simply does not address the issue, unless 1 Timothy 3:2 does so, a position that most scholars do not accept.
Only the strongest and godliest men will be called by the Lord into polygamy.	"In the animal kingdom, the strongest animal leads the pack and has many wives.... when ordained by God, the strongest men of God have many wives.... A weak, cowardly Christian cannot handle the job (of THE POLYGAMIST). This job of godly shepherding can be handled only by a real man, the spiritual man" (*The Polygamists*, p. 15).	Those in the Old Testament who practiced polygamy were not uniformly the godliest and strongest believers. Certainly Abraham was, and Jacob became this way, and David, in general was a godly man. By contrast, polygamy was practiced by many of the ungodly kings of Israel and Judah and by Solomon, who fell into idolatry at the urging of his many wives. Yet Isaac had one wife, Rebekah, as did the various prophets whose wives are mentioned. Monogamy was not widely practiced in the first century A.D., and the apostles do not appear have been polygamous.
A woman will be more thankful for a godly polygamous marriage than for an ungodly monogamous marriage.	"The main benefactors from plurality will be women.... true godly women will always prefer a tenth share of a first-rate, godly, Christian man ... than the exclusive possession of a second- or third-rate ungodly one" (*The Polygamists*, p. 17).	Alamo has posed false options. The option not mentioned is a godly monogamous man. Moreover, polygamy is tolerated in the Old Testament, not specifically sanctioned by God. Alamo's statement presupposes that a polygamous man is godly. This makes his argument null and void.

Position	Support	Orthodox Response
The word "allelluia" is satanic.	"The original Hebrew word meaning 'praise the Lord' is **Hallelujah**,' not 'alleluia.' The word 'alleluia' is meaning-less.... Satan first sowed this great error into the churches and the world through the Catholic cult.... This mockery to God's praise satisfies Satan because the Christian praises to God become null and void, having no effect, by the use of the word 'alleluia'.... how can I or anyone receive strength from the Lord if the praises we give are null and void by our use of the satanic word 'alleluia?' The anger of the Lord is kindled against all using the word 'alleluia' whether in igno-rance or not" (*Let's Sing It Right*, p. 1).	Alamo has created a false issue in charging that the Latin word "alleluia" is satanic. The English word "Hallelujah" is a translit-erated of a Hebrew word (that is, a Hebrew word is made into an English word rather than being translated as "praise Yahweh"). This is possible because English and Hebrew have the same sounds needed for this word. Moreover, the use of *-jah* rather than *-yah* reflects influence from the German, in which "j" is pronounced "y." The Latin language did not have an "h" to transliterate so it is not used at the beginning of the Hebrew word "hallelu-yah." This was also true in the Greek language; Greek has only a weak "h" or aspirant, at the beginning of words, but it does not occur in the oldest manu-scripts (uncials, or all capitals).
The King James Ver-sion of the Bible is the only Bible con-taining God's truth.	"... faith comes by hearing, reading, and obeying the uncontaminated Word of God, the King James Version of the Bible" (*Ser-pent*, p. 5). "... The complete knowledge and under-standing of the will of God can **ONLY** be found in the **KING JAMES VERSION OF THE BIBLE**..." (*Fugitive Pope*, p. 7). "All faith can be attained by studying the holy, original writings of the Bible, which are the same in the original King James Version" (*The Polygamists*, p. 12).	If, as Alamo says, the King James Version of the Bible alone contains God's Word, then no believer prior to A.D. 1611 had God's Word, not even the early church and apostles. Their Bible was in Hebrew, Aramaic, and Greek. Moreover, no lan-guage group by the English-speaking world would have God's Word today. This specious argument does not hold up to careful research of manuscript transmis-sion and history of translation.
Homosexuality is caused by demon possession.	"God says that homosexuality is a demon possession.... I repeat, God says that it is a demon possession, not a third sexual preference" (*Guilty by Association*, p. 5).	Though it is true that homosexual acts are sinful and explicitly forbidden by the Scripture (Ro 1:26–27), nowhere is this sin presented as being caused by demon pos-session. This is true of other works of the flesh.
Women are not equal to men and should be com-pletely dominated, utterly controlled, and led by their husbands.	"The woman was man's equal before the crime, the sin, the transgression, the fall. But, after the fall, God makes it extremely clear that the woman is no equal to the man anymore, but is under subjection to her one and only husband. She is to be totally dominated, ruled through and by the godly man through the Word of God (positively no more equal rights, ladies)" (*The Polygamists*, p. 9).	Though women have been given a posi-tion of submission to their husbands (Eph 5:22; 1Pe 3:1–7; 1Co 11:3; Tit 2:5) and in the church (1Ti 2:11–14), the Scripture is equally clear that women are equal per-sons with men (1Co 11:11–12), sharing both the same creation image (Ge 1:27) and equal participation in the grace of God (Gal 3:26–29; 1Pe 3:7–8). The harsh attitude presented by Alamo has caused much sorrow to many women and the destruction of families.

Position	Support	Orthodox Response
The Roman Catholic Church is secretly setting up a satanic one-world government and church that will usher in the anti-Christ.	"... the Bible points out clearly that the Vatican is the head of today's one-world government and church.... the Vatican, the one-world government and church, are spiritually powered by 'that old serpent, called the Devil'" (*Conspiracy*, p. 5).	The vitriolic attack on the Roman Catholic Church fails to show proper appreciation for the many good things preserved over the centuries by the Roman Church even if we recognize many problems and errors perpetrated by this body. Despite the persecution of Protestants during certain periods of Christian history, this is historically not the general practice.
This diabolical scheme has spawned some of the most sensational and horrific deeds in recent history such as the Nazi holocaust, the Manson murders, the Jonestown massacre, the assassinations of John F. Kennedy and Abraham Lincoln, and the Branch Davidian tragedy. These and other infamous events have all been carried out by secret agents of the Vatican.	"The master plan for the Vatican rule of the world included the Jewish holocaust" (*Conspiracy*, p. 4). "Hitler, Mussolini, and Franco were all Catholics, financed by the Vatican to win the world for Romanism, Vaticanism, Catholicism" (*Tony Alamo's Answer to Rabbi Nuri*, p. 4). "... the Catholic termites murdered President Abraham Lincoln, and President John F. Kennedy" (*"Tony Alamo is Right!!!"* p. 8). "Jim Jones, a Roman Catholic Jesuit deacon posing as a Christian, was sacrificed" (*The Pope's Secrets*, p. 2). "... narcotics, prostitution, pornography, booze and black market—every filthy thing—can be traced right back to the Vatican" (Ibid., p. 6).	Alamo is making scurrilous charges without providing serious evidence to substantiate these claims. His charges have the ring of sensationalist conspiracy theories, which can be readily discredited by objective research.
The Pope (who is demon-possessed) is directing this world takeover.	"... the Vatican created and started World War II, in order to justify the United Nations.... What a diabolical plot, to develop a one world nation so the Pope could dictate through it ... and now send ambassadors to every nation, and ambassadors from every nation are sent to the diabolical demon possessed Pope" (*"Tony Alamo is Right!!!"* p. 8). "The criminally insane Pope John Paul II... is completely possessed with the devil himself" (*Fugitive Pope*, p. 4). "By knowing the Bible, we know who you are, pope. Here is a quote about you from the Bible: '**How art thou fallen from heaven, O Lucifer**'" (*You Be the Judge*, p. 3).	See comment immediately above.

Position	Support	Orthodox Response
Virtually all American institutions, agencies, high-ranking officials, world leaders, and media organizations are Vatican-controlled.	"I liken the White House and today's government to be nothing more than a Roman rat infested tenement. They believe that they must destroy the world in order to save it. This kind of thinking adds up only to the Catholic's 'new world order,' and the Waco burn-out is but the first of their final plans of open Christian extermination in this country" (*Intolerance*, p. 2). "This cult (the Vatican) is very close to replacing our U.S. Constitution with her one-world satanic canon laws of death to the 'heretic' (anyone that is not Roman Catholic)" (*The Pope's Secrets*, p. 1).	Viewing the Roman Catholic Church as responsible for controlling America and instrumental in the assassinations and tragedies listed by Alamo (see above) is ludicrous and entirely unsubstantiated by him. This is a conspiracy plot that cannot be demonstrated and requires one to draw broad conclusions by weaving together tenuous threads.
At present, the U.S. government is hardly more than a Vatican-run Nazi state that is systematically taking away religious freedom in order to annihilate all Christians one day.	"'. . . (the Vatican's centuries old plan) proceeds as follows: Stage one: to terminate . . . (. . . kill in cold blood) all disrupters [non-Catholic Christians] who are publicly interfering with "Operation Cablesplice." (. . . the plan to combine all municipal, county, and state governments into one federal government and then into a one world government).' . . . 'Stage two: the federal government law enforcement will arrest . . . all disruptors who jeopardize Operation Cablesplice simply because of their harmless religious lifestyles. . . . Some stage two disruptors will have to be terminated as they can't be rehabilitated [meaning they will not join the Catholic cult].' . . . 'Stage three . . . This includes the confiscation of all of the Christian's wealth and property. . . . Stage one is under implementation now'" (*Intolerance*, pp. 9–10).	These charges are entirely unprovable and seem to confuse reality and fantasy.
Everything and everyone is controlled by Rome.	"Because of her age-old desire to control the world government and church, the serpent-like Vatican has infested the world and the U.S. government with so many of her zealous highly-trained and dedicated Jesuit devotees, that she now controls the **United Nations** . . . **White House**; **Congress**; every state, federal, civic, and social government agency including the **U.S. Department of Labor** . . . **IRS** . . . **FBI**, **Supreme Court**, judicial systems, the armed forces; state, federal, and other police; also the international banking and federal reserve systems . . . labor unions, the **Mafia**, and most of the heavy-weight news media" (*The Pope's Secrets*, p. 1). "The government media's job is to slander Christians and exalt the Vatican's one-world satanic government, their church, and its cult leader, the Pontiff" (*Intolerance*, p. 8).	Again, Alamo's claims are broad-brushed without any proof. This kind of argumentation merely incites emotions and fails to recognize that the Roman Catholic Church has authority only over church affairs.

Position	Support	Orthodox Response
. . . continued	"NBC, CBS, ABC, Newsweek, Time, Life, People magazine, the L.A. Times, New York Times . . . and thousands of others are controlled by Rome" (*Duped?* p. 3). ". . . the Vatican secretly has even more control and dictates policy even a little bit more in the Soviet Union than it secretly does here in America" (*Genocide*, p. 1).	
The battle of Armageddon is the current conflict between God and Satan.	"Currently we are living in the war of Armageddon, the battle between God and Satan" (*"Tony Alamo is Right!!!"* p. 6).	Most Christians believe that the battle of Armageddon lies in the future, at the second coming of Christ (Joel 3:2; Zec 14:2; Eze 38:7ff.; 39:2; Rev 16:14–16).
When the Catholic Church takes over, it will force everyone to receive the "mark of the beast" (the computer chip/bar coding system) and convert to the satanically energized one-world religion: Roman Catholicism.	"The Bible calls the one-world government that we live in today the Beast. . . . The church that is given power by the dragon [the devil] is the Vatican. Satan's church uses the one-world government to destroy every church other than itself. . . . Eventually, the demonic pope, government, and churches will compel everyone to take a mark of allegiance on his or her forehead or hand" (*Fugitive Pope*, p. 6). "We are at the end of time. Final prophecy is moving as rapidly as jet aircraft. The mark of the beast is here now" (*Cult Protection Racket*, p. 4). "The Vatican's UN Global 2000 satanic world cult religion with its bar code mark is Satan, the Beast. . . . Satan's global 2000 government religion says, 'Let us put the federal I.D. number on you' (the mark of the Beast)" (Ibid., pp. 2, 3–4). ". . . if you allow yourself or your loved ones to receive this mark, whether by computer chip, laser or whatever, your soul literally will be damned to hell" (*What is Truth?* p. 4).	This is pure speculation.
Alamo Christian Ministries has been harassed and attacked for 25 years because it has sought to expose the Vatican and its plan of world domination.	"The only ones now that this new Satanic government puts on trial are people that expose Satan's Church and government, such as . . . the Holy Alamo Christian Church" (*Did You Know that Satan Needed a Church and Government?* p. 2). "Catholic Nazi harrassment has been going on against myself and our churches for over 25 years" (*Fugitive Pope*, p. 5).	It is doubtful whether Alamo's organization of a few hundred followers has even received the attention of the Roman Church. He holds a high opinion of his importance on the world scene.

Position	Support	Orthodox Response
No other church has done as much as Alamo's church.	"Hundreds of thousands of people are now Christians and are completely rehabilitated and are living decent, honest, Christian lives because of this ministry" (*Tony Alamo: My Side of the Story*, p. 4). ". . . our church and myself have helped millions to find the living God" (*Government Subversion Against Alamo*, p. 7). "The Holy Alamo Christian Church gets more people off of narcotics and drugs, away from lives of crime and other abuses to people's bodies, minds, and their souls, through the Gospel of the Lord Jesus Christ than all other churches in the world combined . . . has won more souls to Christ, than all the other churches in the world combined . . . has informed more people of the truth than all the other churches in the world combined. . . . feeds, clothes, and houses without cost more people than any other church on a world-wide basis" (*Duped?* p. 5). "Reverend Alamo and our church have been the greatest asset to America and the world" (*Nailed!!* p. 8).	On the basis of numbers alone, Alamo's church has had minimal impact on the conversion of the lost or discipling of the saved in comparison with many major evangelical denominations such as the Southern Baptists, Assemblies of God, and the Evangelical Free Church, to mention only a few.
Only the churches having their tax-exempt status revoked are true Christian churches. (Alamo's status was revoked in 1987.)	"The gestapo I.R.S. is busy taking away all tax exempt status from churches alien to Satan's church and government" (*Did You Know that Satan Needed a Church and Government?* p. 2). "Satan knew that our church is their [Catholic church's] only enemy because we are the exact opposite of him" (*Duped?* p. 8).	This seems to be a defensive ploy by Alamo in response to the several court battles he has faced regarding charges of financial misconduct. NOTE: If all Christian churches (those "alien to Satan's church") are having their tax-exempt statuses revoked, but most Protestant churches are remaining tax-exempt, then the number of Christian churches is quite small. Alamo refers to his church as being Satan's *only* enemy. In other words, only Alamo's group is a true Christian church.
Because Alamo and his group preach the Holy Word of God, anyone criticizing them will be committing blasphemy of the Holy Ghost, a sin for which there is no forgiveness.	"Calling those that are preaching the Holy Word of God and the Word that they preach 'cultish' or 'brainwashed' is blasphemy of the Holy Ghost and is never forgiven. . . . Do you choose to call God's Word 'brainwash' and the people that preach it 'brainwashers,' and 'cultists' and instead receive the anti-Christ as your Lord and wind up forever in hell" (*Nailed!!* p. 8).	This is a ploy often used by those whose doctrines and practices will not stand up to scrutiny. "Touch not the Lord's anointed" will not pass muster. Even Paul, the great apostle, welcomed the scrutiny of the Berean Christians who judged everything by the Word of God (Ac 17:11).

2

Association for Research and Enlightenment

FACTS AND HISTORY

<table>
<tr><td colspan="2" align="center">Facts</td></tr>
<tr><td align="center">Topic</td><td align="center">Current Facts</td></tr>
<tr>
<td>Membership</td>
<td>The Association for Research and Enlightenment (A.R.E.) offers two different memberships: (1) Associate ($40 annually); and (2) Sponsor ($60 annually). As of 1994, paid membership in A.R.E. was nearly 40,000.</td>
</tr>
<tr>
<td>Worship</td>
<td>A.R.E. is more of an educational foundation than a church. The organization stresses that it is not a religion. Consequently, the group does not conduct church or worship services.

Teachings are spread "through nationwide lecture programs, publications, a Braille library, a camp and an extensive Study Group Program" (Edgar Cayce on Religion and Psychic Experience, p. 264).

A.R.E. also offers materials through a mail-order service and has its own publishing house, A.R.E. Press. The Edgar Cayce Foundation, which is related to A.R.E., serves as the archive for all materials produced by the organization's founder, Edgar Cayce.

Atlantic University, an affiliate of A.R.E., disseminates Cayce's teachings through courses on a wide range of metaphysical subjects, such as holistic healing, dream interpretation, and psychic powers.</td>
</tr>
<tr>
<td>Leaders</td>
<td>Edgar Cayce   1932–1945
Hugh L. Cayce   1945–1982
Charles T. Cayce 1982–</td>
</tr>
<tr>
<td>Publications</td>
<td>A.R.E. produces two bimonthly publications for members: Venture Inward and A.R.E. Community. Both have a circulation of about 35,000.</td>
</tr>
<tr>
<td>General statement of beliefs</td>
<td>A.R.E. is an organization that combines Christian concepts, Eastern metaphysical thought, and occultism.

In place of orthodox Christian doctrines such as the Trinity, the deity of Christ, and salvation by grace through faith, A.R.E. teaches pantheism, reincarnation, and other teachings received by Edgar Cayce during self-induced trances. These trances produced "well over 14,000 documented stenographic records of the telepathic-clairvoyant statements he had given for more than six thousand different people over a period of forty-three years" (Edgar Cayce on Religion and Psychic Experience, p. 10).

According to Cayce, the tenets of Christianity are perverted remnants of pure doctrines that existed long ago in the ancient mystery religions of the world: "The system of metaphysical thought which emerges from the readings of Edgar Cayce is a Christianized version of the mystery religions of ancient Egypt, Chaldea, Persia, India, and Greece" (There Is a River: The Story of Edgar Cayce, p. 305).

". . . complex symbology employed by the mystery religions has survived fragmentarily in Christianity. . . . It is interesting to speculate on the fact that Edgar Cayce was raised in strict nineteenth century Bible tradition, and suffered the greatest mental and emotional shock of his life when he discovered that in his psychic readings he declared the truth of the mysteries" (Ibid., pp. 305–6).</td>
</tr>
</table>

History	
Topic	*History*
Edgar Cayce, 1877–1945	A.R.E. identifies itself as an organization "interested generally in parapsychology and its spiritual dimensions and interested specifically in making practical use of Edgar Cayce readings" (*There Is a River: The Story of Edgar Cayce*, p. 377).
	Cayce founded A.R.E. after a long history of involvement with the occult that included numerous paranormal experiences and a grandfather who, through psychic abilities, was reportedly able to speak with the dead, find water underground (dowsing), and "make brooms dance and tables rise by concentrating on them" (*A Seer Out of Season: The Life of Edgar Cayce*, p. 269).
	Although he was raised in Christian churches, Cayce began following in his grandfather's footsteps at a young age: "At the age of six or seven he told his parents that he was able to see and talk to 'visions,' sometimes of relatives who had recently died" (*Edgar Cayce on Religion and Psychic Experience*, p. 9).
	Paranormal experiences such as these continued as Cayce matured. One occasion involved "a vision, a figure of radiant light," who asked Cayce what he sought. Cayce responded that he wanted to help others. The being of light responded: "'Thy prayers are heard. You will have your wish'" (*A Seer Out of Season: The Life of Edgar Cayce*, p. 277).
	At about age twenty-three, Cayce fell ill and lost his voice. Doctors were unable to help him. He turned to a hypnotist for help, who in turn placed him in several trances. He eventually learned to put himself into a trance. In one of these self-induced trances he diagnosed and healed his malady. Soon he began to use his trances to diagnose other people's illnesses.
	In time, Cayce gained great popularity and expanded his activities to include dream interpretation, prophetic speculation, and contact with the dead and other spiritual entities.
	Cayce formed A.R.E., a nonprofit organization, in 1931 for the purpose of carrying on "psychical research" (*Edgar Cayce's Story of Jesus*, p. 350). The organization reportedly possesses "one of the largest metaphysical, parapsychological libraries in the country" (*Edgar Cayce On Religion and Psychic Experience*, p. 264).
Hugh L. Cayce, 1945–1982	Hugh L. Cayce assumed leadership of A.R.E. when Edgar, his father, died in 1945. Under the younger Cayce, A.R.E. continued to gain steady popularity.
Charles T. Cayce, 1982–	When Hugh L. Cayce passed away in 1982, his son Charles T. Cayce gained the leadership of A.R.E.

The Doctrine of Revelation

Position	Support	Orthodox Response
The teachings promoted by A.R.E. come from Edgar Cayce's trances, in which he received "truths" from an unknown source in the spirit world. Some of these "truths," especially about Jesus, came through Cayce's alleged ability to read the "Akashic Record."*	"The celebrated 'sleeping clairvoyant' was a Sunday School teacher who found that the psychic information he received in trances appeared to supplement the teachings of the Bible without contradiction" (*Edgar Cayce on Religion and Psychic Experience*, back cover). "Readings"—the statements Cayce made while in his trances—"constitute one of the largest and most impressive records of psychic perception ever to emanate from a single individual. Together with their relevant records, correspondence and reports, they have been cross-indexed under thousands of subject headings" (Ibid., p. 10). "His family and staff. . . . distinguished carefully between what was said by the waking Cayce and what was said by 'the information,' as they called the unknown source or sources of his trances" (Ibid., p. 21). "His own readings said that in such counsel he was inspecting and interpreting objective 'records written on time and space,' or 'Akashic records'" (*A Seer Out of Season: The Life of Edgar Cayce*, p. 150).	The Bible teaches that God spoke to Moses and other prophets and revelators after him. Later prophets must perfectly harmonize with the revelation of God that came through the writings of Moses. Any revelations that are not in accord with Scripture cannot be accepted or trusted. Capital punishment was the penalty for false prophecy (see Dt 13:6–10). The Pentateuch must judge the writings that follow it in the OT, and the OT must judge the NT. Deuteronomy 29:29 states that what is revealed belongs to us, but what is hidden belongs to the Lord. This means that God is never taken by surprise by the machinations of Satan. The spirit world is by its very nature hidden—that is, "occult"— from our direct inspection. The hidden nature of Cayce's source thus arouses suspicion; his "source" is tantamount to another god. As we will see, his revelations are faulty because they contradict the claims and teachings of the Bible (see Dt 18:17–22; 1Co 14:29–32).
The Bible is like any other great religious work or biography. Its main purpose is to provide spiritual "truths" and rules of living that, when followed, give hope and comfort.	". . . one could set his mind to remember, in times of stress, the faith of others in distress. . . . for this purpose the study of the Bible was man's best resource, though every great life or biography might carry assurances—as the Cayce readings often referred to Woodrow Wilson, and at other times to such figures as the Buddha, Lao Tse, Swedenborg, or the founder of Zoroastrianism" (*Edgar Cayce on Religion and Psychic Experience*, pp. 115–16).	The Bible portrays itself as the authoritative revelation of God and unlike any other work because of Him who is the ultimate Source of its writing (see Isa 44:6 9). It has proven itself through more than 300 prophecies about the first coming of Jesus alone. Accurate prophecy of the future has substantiated its claims over and over again, and this sets it in stark contrast with any other religious or so-called spiritual body of writings.

* New Age expert Ron Rhodes explains: "Occultists believe the physical earth is surrounded by an immense spiritual field known as 'Akasha' in which is impressed every impulse of human thought, will, and emotion. It is therefore believed to constitute a complete record of human history" (*Christian Research Journal*, Fall 1989, p. 18).

The Doctrine of Revelation (cont.)

Position	Support	Orthodox Response
The correct meaning behind many biblical passages concerns psychic truths brought to light through Cayce's reinterpretation of the verses.	"Paraphrasing Paul, the readings insisted in literally hundreds of passages that 'His Spirit is ever ready to bear witness with our spirits'; something quite literal was meant, including psychic quickenings and confirmations as well as heightenings of psychokinetic energy" (*Edgar Cayce on Religion and Psychic Experience*, p. 62).	In Romans 8:16 Paul states that the Spirit bears witness with our spirit that we are God's children. The intent of this passage is to affirm that the Spirit is the agent of assurance to believers that they are accepted by God. Cayce's interpretations must be evaluated according to more than two thousand years of biblical hermeneutics. The Bible interprets itself, speaking plainly about its main subject matter and the meaning it is to hold for those who read it. Moreover, the Bible affirms that no person will be given final say or carte blanche in its ultimate interpretation: "Above all, you must understand that no prophecy of Scripture came about by the prophet's own interpretation" (2Pe 1:20).

The Doctrine of God—*The Trinity*

Position	Support	Orthodox Response
The view of God held by A.R.E. is pantheistic (that is, all is God, God is all).	"... in the beginning there was a sea of spirit.... It withdrew into itself ... that which had filled it was shining from its center.... This was the individuality of the spirit.... this was God. God desired to express Himself.... Therefore, He projected from Himself the cosmos and souls" (*There Is a River: The Story of Edgar Cayce*, pp. 306–7). "Each person is a corpuscle in the body of that force called God" (Ibid., p. 320). "The cosmos was built with the tools which man calls music, arithmetic, and geometry: harmony system and balance. The building blocks were all of the same material, which man calls the life essence.... everything moved, changed, and assumed its design in various states of form and substance. Activity was begun and maintained by the law of attraction and repulsion: positive and negative, attracting each other and repelling themselves, maintained the form and action of all things. All this was a part of God, an expression of His thought" (Ibid., pp. 307–8).	Biblical descriptions of God always show His unique singularity in His person and essence (see Dt 6:4; Ex 15:11; Zec 14:9). God is also unique in His character in that the Bible says "God is not a man" who would lie or repent (Nu 23:19). The difference between God and man appears throughout the Bible. In pantheism, God is in essence what Christians would call His creation, including mankind. This means, contrary to the orthodox position, that no final or absolute distinction can exist between God and physical beings. The NT declares that the work of creation is accomplished by the Word of God (Jn 1:3). Moreover, despite the idea that some impersonal force, the law of attraction and repulsion, is responsible for the continuation of the cosmos, Colossians 1:16–17 declares that it is the personal work of Jesus Christ that maintains all creation (see also Jn 5:17).

The Doctrine of God—*The Trinity (cont.)*

Position	Support	Orthodox Response
According to Cayce, the concept of a Tri-une God (Father, Son, and Holy Spirit) is only accurate insofar as it symbolizes the "three-ness" that exists within man's nature: body, mind, and soul. In other planes of existence, a different explanation of God is necessary.	"The Cayce source never wearied of saying that the formula of 'Father, Son, and Holy Spirit' had come to the human mind and stayed there because it so well corresponded to three-dimensional existence—while on other planes perhaps six or seven dimensional existence would require different types of symbolism. On earth the primal symbolism of the Trinity was parallel with human three-ness: The Father was like the body of man; the Son ... was like the mind of man, while the Spirit was like the spiritual or soul realm of man's experience. ... So long as man had to contend with these three overlapping realms of reality, all drawn from the One, he would find Trinitarian thought helpful to him" (*Edgar Cayce on Religion and Psychic Experience*, p. 241).	Because God is a nonanalogous being, there are no human formulations of speech that can provide either an unlimited analogy or metaphor that will adequately define God. Nothing in creation completely corresponds to His attributes or essence. God exists as three persons sharing one being or divine essence. Nowhere apart from the Bible do we find a divinity revealed as three self-conscious persons existing in total harmony while sharing the same essence. Scripture shows God to be an objective reality and not a symbolic formulation. These distinctions in the Godhead are eternal (see Jn 1:1; 17:5; Php 2:6).

The Doctrine of Jesus Christ

Position	Support	Orthodox Response
Jesus was not God in the flesh. He was a man with whom the "Christ Consciousness" had joined. Jesus, like other avatars (a spiritual teacher appointed to a given age), served as a pattern to follow.	"He, Jesus, triumphed over death and the body, became the way, laying down the ego of the will, accepting the crucifixion, returning to God. He is the pattern we are to follow" (*There Is A River: The Story of Edgar Cayce*, p. 316).	"In the beginning was the Word, and the Word was with God, and the Word was God ... [and] the Word became flesh and made his dwelling among us" so states the Holy Spirit of God in the first chapter of the Gospel of John. His pattern of selfless love is to be followed but no one else can lay claim to being the Word become flesh and no one else can duplicate His redemptive work on the cross.
Jesus experienced many lives through reincarnation.	"The trance counsel described past lives for Jesus" (*A Seer Out of Season: The Life of Edgar Cayce*, p. 156).	Jesus was very God from all eternity: "He is the same yesterday today and forever" (see Heb 13:8). This means that what He was in His essential nature as God was not abridged or heightened in any way during His incarnation.

The Doctrine of Jesus Christ—*The Deity of Christ (cont.)*

Position	Support	Orthodox Response
Jesus became the Christ because the "Christ Consciousness" entered him. The "Christ Consciousness" is a soul that returned to God after it completed its experience in creation. It now periodically comes to dwell in various people. The person known as Jesus of Nazareth was the incarnation of a person who had already lived many lives.	"The race of man was fostered by a soul which had completed its experience of creation and returned to God, becoming a companion to Him and a cocreator. This is the soul man knows as the Christ. The Christ soul was interested in the plight of its brother souls trapped in earth.... it took form itself, from time to time, to act as a leader for the people.... The Christ soul helped man as Enoch, as Melchizcdek.... He was born as Joseph, again as Joshua, again as Jeshua ... and finally as Jesus" (*There Is a River: The Story of Edgar Cayce*, pp. 316–17).	The name "Christ" comes from the Greek *Kristos,* which parallels the Hebrew word *Moshiach* (English: Messiah). Its meaning is that of "anointed one"—anointing symbolizing the setting apart of a person or place for a specific purpose of God. Jesus was set apart, before the world was created, to be the atoning sacrifice for all sin. Since His going forth was from all eternity (see Isa 9:6; Mic 5:2) and He was the Creator of all things and therefore infinite in wisdom, knowledge, power, and love (see Jn 1:3), it does not follow logically that He would need to live many lives or be involved in any reincarnative "evolvement" of His divine spiritual self.
Jesus did indeed rise from the dead, but not due to the power of the Triune Christian God. Rather, He rose from the dead through a healing of his cells that occured in reaction to the power of Cayce's pantheistic God.	"The quiet voice of the entranced Cayce observed without reservation that the claim of the One risen from the tomb was factual" (*A Seer Out of Season: The Life of Edgar Cayce*, p. 117).	It is essential to biblical and orthodox Christianity that not only the "factual" or "historical" nature of Jesus' resurrection be clearly affirmed but also the nature of the power that accomplished this. It was the power of the infinite, personal, living God, not an impersonal pantheistic force, that brought Jesus out of the grave.

The Doctrine of Man and Sin

Position	Support	Orthodox Response
Man is merely an extension of God.	"Souls were created for companionship with God. The pattern used was that of God Himself. . . . In building the soul there was spirit, with its knowledge of identity with God; there was the active principle of mind; and there was the ability to experience the activity of the mind separately from God. Thus a new individual, issuing from and dependent upon God ... came into being" (*There Is a River: The Story of Edgar Cayce*, p. 308).	Cayce correctly asserts that a new person issued forth from God and remained dependent on God. He seems to assert—and this view would be incorrect—that man is merely an extension of God. In fact, God is separate and distinct from His creation. Creation itself, including the substance that man sprang from, was brought into being *ex nihilo,* "out of nothing." God did not "scoop" a portion of Himself and refashion it into creation. Genesis 1 states that God formed man out of the dust of the ground and breathed the breath of life into him. At that point, man became a living soul.

The Doctrine of Man and Sin (cont.)

Position	Support	Orthodox Response
A soul lives numerous times as different people. This process is known as reincarnation.	"The view of reincarnation in the readings, I knew, was not that of lives completed and left behind like beads on a string. Instead, the major values and dynamics from each life carried right into the present" (*A Seer Out of Season: The Life of Edgar Cayce*, p. 211).	Reincarnation is not scriptural. The Bible states that "man is destined to die once, and after that to face judgment" (Heb 9:27). This clearly shows that there is only one lifetime granted to man. The same truth is expressed in the account of the rich man and Lazarus (Lk 16:20–25), which indicates that while there is ongoing existence after physical death, people are forbidden to return to earthly life once they have departed. Moreover, reincarnation equates the soul with human existence, but the Bible makes clear that being fully human requires both body and soul. See, e.g., 1 Corinthians 15:35–49 (1Co 6:20, 1Th 5:23, Jas 2:26).

The Doctrine of Salvation

Position	Support	Orthodox Response
Sin is a lack of attunement with the One God that permeates the universe.	"Without such attunement, any soul could expect to slip into 'selfish aggrandizement,' the precise Cayce definition of sin" (*Edgar Cayce on Religion and Psychic Experience*, p. 64).	If Cayce were talking about the God of the Bible and not some pantheistic notion of his own, his definition of sin, though imprecise, would be compatible with the biblical understanding of man's "self-aggrandizing" sin nature.
Salvation is not obtained through the atoning sacrifice of Jesus Christ, but through health and wholeness of mind and body that is achieved through embracing spiritual truths. Our advancement toward salvation depends on self-discipline and self-training.	"Growing as a person was not left by the readings to accident and impulsive self improvement.... The task of self-training was presented not as collecting merit badges, but as a process of larger importance.... The self-training, while essential, was not a burden to be borne alone. Again and again the readings insisted that the help of Christ was available.... He was ever there as Elder Brother, offering both pattern and the vitality to keep it. What was required in self-discipline, then, was hungering and thirsting for His way, not simply learning skills and laws" (*A Seer Out of Season: The Life of Edgar Cayce*, pp. 222–23). "Redemption occurred to get man back on to this track [becoming a co-creator with God]" (*Edgar Cayce on Religion and Psychic Experience*, p. 176).	Acts 4:12 states, "Salvation is found in no one else, for there is no other name under heaven given to men by which we must be saved." This explicitly says that Jesus is essential and unlike any other in His role as Savior of mankind.

The Doctrine of Salvation (cont.)

Position	Support	Orthodox Response
Acceptance of Jesus as Savior is not crucial to obtaining salvation.	"Even though the Cayce source insisted that Jesus had demonstrated the reality of direct, personal relations between man and God . . . there was no insistence that each person go through a conversion experience or turning-point revelation to find the Oneness" (*Edgar Cayce on Religion and Psychic Experience*, p. 242).	Jesus told Nicodemus that a man must be "born again" in order to enter the kingdom of God (Jn 3:3–8). "If anyone is in Christ, he is a new creation; the old has gone, the new has come" (2Co 5:17). Jesus said, "for if you do not believe that I am He, you will die in your sins" (Jn 8:24 NKJV). These words directly contradict Cayce's view of the role of Jesus in salvation.

The Doctrine of Rewards and Punishment

Position	Support	Orthodox Response
The ultimate reward is absorption back into the spirit of God and the ceasation of reincarnation.	"When a soul returns to God it becomes aware of itself not only as a part of God, but as a part of every other soul, and everything" (*There Is a River: The Story of Edgar Cayce*, p. 309).	God is a transcendent Being who is separate from His creation. As high "as the heavens are higher than the earth," so are His ways and thoughts higher than our ways and thoughts (Isa 55:9). The human soul was never part of God, but rather a created entity. Genesis 2:7 states, "The LORD God formed the man from the dust of the ground and breathed into his nostrils the breath of life, and the man became a living being." As regards the "ultimate reward," there could be nothing like having sins forgiven and living in the presence of God for eternity. Individual rewards are given to believers at the judgment seat of Christ and are based on how they lived.
A person's sins are dealt with through karma and reincarnation. Karma is "the law of cause and effect on a moral plane. Often refers to the debt accumulated against a soul as a result of actions during his earthly life or lives" (*Handbook of Today's Religions*, p. 543).	"Always the thrust of Karma was toward soul growth, not mere retribution or reward. . . . Someone blind to the needs of others in a medieval town was now back blind. A man who had gossiped about homosexuals . . . was now back as an uncontrollable homosexual. . . . A woman who misused her power in the turmoil after the French Revolution had returned as a widow with a child. . . . 'We must pay every jot and tittle for that done which is destructive to others and to self'" (*A Seer Out of Season: The Life of Edgar Cayce*, p. 231).	The Bible says there is one ultimate punishment for sin: being eternally separated from God (see Mt 25:41), who is the Giver of "every good and perfect gift" (see Jas 1:17). Jesus paid for all sins committed by every human being, past, present, and future (Heb 10:10; 13:8; 1Jn 2:2).

The unrighteous are moving toward the day of ultimate judgment (2Pe 2:4–6). There is no biblical support for the idea that sins can be worked off by suffering in this life or a future life. Suffering for one's own sins for a period of time would not be adequate to satisfy the righteous nature of God. A belief in reincarnation is an attempt to provide a means of self-justification so that humans can become their own savior. The Scriptures state that faith in Jesus is the only means of justification (Ro 3:21–26). |

INTERESTING AND DISTINCTIVE BELIEFS

Position	Support	Orthodox Response
Sometimes smoking in moderation can be healthy. Cigarettes are better than other types of smoking.	"Smoking in moderation for this body would be helpful. To excess it's very harmful. The smoking of cigarettes is better than most types" (*Venture Inward* 3539–1 M.59 1/6/44).	The Bible says that the body is the temple of the Holy Spirit (see 1Co 6:19). We are to take care of our bodies. Modern science has shown conclusively the link between smoking and disease; therefore it would be very unwise to indulge in smoking.
The mind is able to transfer thoughts to others through telepathy and can move objects through techniques such as telekinesis.	"There may be specific tests in mind reading, telepathy, thought transference, moving of objects even; yet these when presented out of their realm of activity, dealing with the individual for a helpful experience in the seeking, become channels that are of an entirely different nature" (Ibid., 1135–6 M.36 11/11/36).	The Bible states that the "secret [or hidden] things belong to the LORD our God" (Dt 29:29) and that "Man looks at the outward appearance, but the LORD looks at the heart" (1Sa 16:7). The Bible may not say all there is to say about latent abilities of the soul—even any that may perhaps have been resident in man before the Fall—it indicates that God does not usually allow the curtain to be drawn back on the unseen world. The possibility of demonic involvement increases when people try to do things that are considered occultic.
Human beings are co-creators with God.	"The soul of each individual is a portion then of the Whole, with the birthright of Creative Forces to become a co-creator with the Father, a co-laborer with Him" (Ibid., 1549–1 F.55 3/11/38).	The Bible states clearly that God alone is the Creator and a personal God who communicates as a person. God states that He alone is responsible for creating the universe (Isa 44:24).

3

Christadelphians

FACTS AND HISTORY

Facts	
Topic	*Current Facts*
Membership	Christadelphians fall into one of two groups: (1) Amended Christadelphians; and (2) Unamended Christadelphians. The split came in 1898, when a prominent Christadelphian church in Birmingham, England, accepted an amended version of the statement of faith that until then was being adhered to by all Christadelphians. The controversial portion of the statement pertained to the resurrection. A Christadelphian tract has accurately stated: "Christadelphians are nowhere numerous. Few of their congregations can be described as large" (*CHRISTADELPHIANS*, "The Way Leaflet No. 8," back page). As of 1992, the Amended Christadelphians had a total membership of about 50,000 worldwide, with some 4,000 members in the United States. That same year the Unamended Christadelphians numbered only around 2,000 in North America. Very few Unamended Christadelphians live outside the United States and Canada.
Worship	Christadelphian churches are called "ecclesias" after the New Testament Greek word *ecclesia* ("called-out ones"), which is translated in the Bible as "church." The ecclesias usually meet in private homes, rented rooms, or rented halls. A Christadelphian "church" building *per se* is rare. All ecclesias meet for a weekly celebration of the "Breaking of Bread" (communion) and are run autonomously, with no central administration or headquarters. Other church activities include Sunday school, public meetings on Bible truths, Bible study classes, and preaching campaigns conducted by Christadelphian youths during holidays. Members are addressed as "Brother" and "Sister" and have equal responsibility for the welfare of the church. Each congregation, instead of having paid clergy, elects members to perform various tasks.
Leaders	1844–1871 John Thomas 1871– No central leadership
Publications	Amended Christadelphians produce a variety of materials through independent publishing houses—most notably, *The Sunday School Journal* (Meridian, CT), *Christadelphian Tidings* (Franklin, MI), and *The Watchman* (Austin, TX). The most visible of the Unamended Christadelphian publications is *The Christadelphian Advocate*. Christadelphian literature has a very small circulation.
General statement of beliefs	Christadelphians openly deny almost every essential doctrine of historic Christianity, including the Trinity, the deity of Christ, salvation by grace through faith, and the substitutionary atonement of Christ. They also deny the immortality of the soul and the reality of eternal conscious punishment for the wicked. Despite their rejection of orthodox Christian doctrines, they claim to be the one true church, the remnant of faithful disciples left over from a partial apostasy: "The Bible predicted that the time would come when the original faith of the Gospel would be obscured by error, and this came to pass in the fourth century after Christ.... there always have been those 'few' (Luke 12:32) from the days of the Apostles to the present age, who have kept the light of truth shining.... Each little group, down through the ages, like links in a chain, connect the testimony of the Apostles with the teaching of Christadelphians today" (*Introducing the Christadelphians*, pp. 6–7).

	History
Topic	**History**
John Thomas, 1844–1871	Christadelphian origins can be traced to John Thomas, a physician in Richmond, Virginia, who, after coming to America from England in 1832, became associated with Alexander and Thomas Campbell, founders of the Disciples of Christ. Soon, however, Thomas found himself at odds with the Campbells over various doctrines, including the immortality of the soul and the reality of hell as a place of eternal conscious punishment. Eventually Thomas's private Bible studies and public debates "forced him to the conviction, not only that current Christianity was not founded upon true Bible teaching, but that its very teaching destroyed the hope of salvation in those who embraced it" (*Introducing the Christadelphians*, p. 10). Although Thomas met with considerable opposition, he continued to proclaim what he believed to be the truths of Scripture and soon gained a following. Thomas broke completely from the Campbellites in 1844 and began a monthly magazine called *The Herald of the Future Age*. Four years later he published *Elpis Israel*, a book setting forth what he had discovered in his Bible studies. In 1864 Thomas named his followers "Christadelphians" after a compound of the two words "Christ" and *"adelphos"* (Greek for "brother"). Christadelphians consider themselves "Brethren of Christ." Thomas died in 1871.
Christadelphian leadership, 1871–	After Thomas died, Christadelphian congregations became autonomous (self-governing) and were only loosely tied by common beliefs. A rift occurred in 1898 when a congregation in Birmingham, England, affirmed that some people would be resurrected to face judgment even though they had not been justified by Christ's blood. Such a teaching went against the standard Christadelphian belief that only individuals "in Christ" would be resurrected. The schism led to formation of the Amended Christadelphians (who embraced the new view of the resurrection) and the Unamended Christadelphians (who retained the standard view).

THEOLOGY

The Doctrine of Revelation

Position	Support	Orthodox Response
The Bible is God's Word and must be looked to as the sole authority over one's life and beliefs.	"THE BIBLE is the inspired and infallible Word of God, the only authoritative source for the saving truth of the Gospel" (*Introducing the Christadelphians*, p. 8). ". . . the book currently known as the Bible . . . is the only source of knowledge concerning God and His purposes at present extant or available in the earth, and that the same were wholly given by inspiration of God in the writers, and are consequently without error in all parts of them" (*The Constitution of the Glendale Christadelphian Ecclesia*, p. 11). "We reject the doctrine—that the Bible is only partly the work of inspiration—or, if wholly so, contains errors which inspiration has allowed" (Ibid., p. 18).	There are orthodox statements of inspiration, inerrancy, and authority overall.

The Doctrine of God—*The Trinity*

Position	Support	Orthodox Response
There is only one God.	"There is ONE GOD" (*Introducing the Christadelphians*, p. 8). "There is only one eternal, immortal God" (*Answering Your Questions about the Christadelphians*, inside cover).	These are orthodox statements.
God is not omnipresent. He is located in one place—heaven.	"God, Himself, is localised in heaven" (*God is One Not Three*, p. 15).	Numerous Bible passages demonstrate that this statement rejecting the omnipresence of God is false. Scripture reveals that the infinite God is unlimited in location (2Ch 2:6; Ps 139:7–10; Jer 23:24).
The Trinity is not a true doctrine.	"We reject the doctrine—that God is three persons" (*The Constitution of the Glendale Christadelphian Ecclesia*, p. 18). "Christadelphians teach that the doctrine of the Trinity is false; that God is one only" (*God is One Not Three*, p. 2). ". . . the doctrine of the Trinity is contradictory, incomprehensible, and unscriptural" (Ibid., p. 3).	Although the Trinity doctrine was not formally stated in the creeds until after the second century, the doctrine has been a cardinal teaching of Christianity from the church's beginning. To believe in the Trinity is not to accept more than one God, nor is the doctrine contradictory if one understands that, according to the Trinity doctrine, there is only one true God who exists in three persons. This doctrine may be beyond our full understanding, but it is not incomprehensible. In other words, finite individuals may not understand all the "how's" of God's being or works, but He has revealed to us many "what's," including that God is three in one.

The Doctrine of God—*The Trinity (cont.)*

Position	Support	Orthodox Response
The Trinity doctrine came from pagan religions. The word "Trinity" is not even in the Bible.	"The Bible nowhere teaches that God is a triune Being" (*God is One Not Three*, p. 4). "The word 'Trinity' is not found in the Bible, but is a title manufactured to serve the cause of theology" (*Herald of the Coming Age*, vol. 21, no. 1, "Why We Proclaim Jesus Did Not Pre-Exist!" p. 2). "The Trinitarian concept is found alike in the pagan mythology of Rome, Greece, Babylon, and Egypt; but not in the Bible" (*God is One Not Three*, p. 6).	Although the ancient world had several deities that existed in triads, they were in no way "trinities" in the same manner as the Christian Trinity. The fact that the word "trinity" is not found in the Bible in no way invalidates the truth of the doctrine any more than the absence of the phrase "virgin birth" invalidates this doctrine. The word "Trinity" simply describes a truth about God that comes to light when comparing hundreds of Bible verses.
Only the Father is God.	"The true God (i.e. the Father) is alone to be worshipped" (*God is One Not Three*, p. 4). "What do Christadelphians stand for? . . . They believe in the Eternal God, the Father" (*CHRISTADELPHIANS*, "The Way Leaflet No. 8," inside back cover).	The early church practiced worship of Christ as God (Mt 2:11; 14:33; 28:9, 17; Jn 9:38; 20:28). Even God's angels worshiped Christ (Heb 1:6). The Holy Spirit, too, was thought of as God (2Co 3:17).

The Doctrine of Jesus Christ—*The Deity of Christ*

Position	Support	Orthodox Response
Jesus did not exist until He was miraculously begotten of the Virgin Mary by the Holy Ghost. Jesus is not co-eternal with the Father.	"Jesus had no existence prior to his birth in Bethlehem, 1900 years ago" (*Herald of the Coming Age*, vol. 21, no. 1, "Why We Proclaim Jesus Did Not Pre-Exist!" p. 2). "We reject the doctrine—that the Son of God was co-eternal with the Father" (*The Constitution of the Glendale Christadelphian Ecclesia*, p. 18).	Jesus Himself declared that He was with the Father before the world began (Jn 17:5, 24). John explicitly identifies the pre-existent Logos of John 1:1–3 with Jesus (Jn 1:14). The Son was not only given to the world (Jn 3:16), but He was the creator of the world (Jn 1:3; Col 1:16). Consequently, He must have existed before the incarnation (Jn 1:30).
John 1:1 does not prove that Jesus pre-existed.	"The Greek term translated 'word' is *Logos*. It signifies the outward form of inward thought or reason. . . . in the very beginning, God's purpose, wisdom or revelation had been in evidence. It was 'with God' in that it emanated from him; it 'was God' in that it represented Him to mankind. . . . A similar expression is used by Christ in Matthew 26:28: 'This is my blood'—that is, this represents my blood" (*Herald of the Coming Age*, vol. 21, no. 1, "Why We Proclaim Jesus Did Not Pre-Exist!" p. 13). "This Word, Wisdom, or Doctrine found its reality, its substance, its confirmation (Romans 15:8) in the person of the Lord Jesus Christ" (Ibid.).	The Christadelphian doctrine does considerable injustice to the context, grammar, and word meanings of John 1:1. To argue that "with God" means only emanation from God betrays a careless reading of the preposition *pros* (with). It speaks of movement toward God in relationship, not movement from God as an impersonal emanation. Moreover, the text in John 1:1 speaks of an eternal relationship, not Christ's relationship to humans in time to represent God. There were pre-incarnate revelations of Christ, called Christophanies (see Ex 23:20–32:34; Isa 63:9), and He was finally revealed in the incarnation (Jn 1:14, 18), but this passage addresses a time before the world began. Seeking to use "is" in John 1:1 with the same meaning as Matthew 26:28 is faulty because John 1:1

The Doctrine of Jesus Christ—*The Deity of Christ (cont.)*

Position	Support	Orthodox Response
. . . continued		has straightforward language of Christ's person and is not trying to communicate some other truth to the disciples by means of a physical symbol.
Jesus was not God, yet He was still divine. By being begotten by the Holy Spirit, Jesus received within Him the very pattern of God's nature and character. Thus God the Father was in Him, making it proper to speak of Christ as being God manifested in the flesh (as long as it is remembered that Jesus was not God in and of Himself).	"It is sometimes claimed that Christadelphians reject the divinity of the Lord Jesus. This is incorrect" (*God is One Not Three*, p. 8). "He [Jesus] was human because he was the Son of Mary; but divine because he was begotten of the Holy Spirit: from that Spirit he derived his wisdom; and the pattern of the character which he possessed. Jesus was thus a manifestation of God in human flesh" (*The Christadelphian Instructor*, p. 11). **"Jesus Christ . . . must be considered from two points of view, one *Deity*, and the other *Man*. The man was the Son, whose existence dates from the birth of Jesus; the Deity dwelling in him was the Father"** (*God is One Not Three*, p. 9). "From his mother, he [Jesus] derived the nature common to all mankind, but from his Father he inherited latent spiritual proclivities that strengthened him to conquer the flesh, and manifest divine qualities" (*Herald of the Coming Age,* vol. 21, no. 1, "Why We Proclaim Jesus Did Not Pre-Exist!" p. 2).	Trying to distinguish between Christ as deity and divine is quibbling with words. Either Christ was God of very God or He was no God at all. The use of "divine" to speak of persons with "sparks" of divinity falls terribly short of the biblical teaching about being the same essence as the Father (Heb 1:3) and being in very nature God (Php 2:6–7). If the indwelling of God in man is divinity, then each Christian is as much divine as Christ except for not being born at birth indwelt by the Spirit.

The Doctrine of Jesus Christ—*The Humanity of Christ*

Position	Support	Orthodox Response
Jesus was born of the Virgin Mary by the power of the Holy Spirit.	"Jesus of Nazareth was the Son of God, begotten of the Virgin Mary by the Holy Spirit" (*The Constitution of the Glendale Christadelphian Ecclesia*, p. 11).	This is an orthodox statement.
Although Jesus was sinless, the only thing that really made Him different from others was His divine conception and predilection toward spirituality.	"Jesus was sinless" (*Answering Your Questions about the Christadelphians*, inside back cover). ". . . where Jesus differed from all before or since, was in his Divine conception, and his exceptional predilection for spiritual things" (*Herald of the Coming Age,* vol. 21, no. 1, "Why We Proclaim Jesus Did Not Pre-Exist!" p. 3).	It is true that Jesus was sinless (1Pe 1:19), but this is only one way in which Christ differed from other humans. The second person of the Trinity did not begin with the humanity of Christ, as our personhood begins with our human existence, but instead joined deity and humanity: one person who is fully God and fully man.

The Doctrine of Jesus Christ—*The Humanity of Christ (cont.)*

Position	Support	Orthodox Response
Jesus' fully human nature included the sinful desires common to all men. But because He had the Father's nature and character dwelling within Him, He was able to live a sinless life and become an example of how we should live. By dying sinless, Jesus redeemed Himself from His own sinful nature.	"Jesus, as a representative man, who bore in his nature the same flesh-promptings as all other men but conquered them (1 Pet. 2.21–24), was in need of redemption from that nature (not from actual sin for he never committed any) as are all mankind. He obtained this by his own offering" (*Herald of the Coming Age,* vol. 18, no. 5, "Christ's Death and Your Salvation," p. 76). "Jesus saved himself from endless death—that was the first result of his sacrifice" (Ibid.).	Christ had no sinful nature or propensities as we do. We are born with a sinful tendency, the guilt of Adam, and we commit personal sins. Not only did Christ not sin, but also He had no sin, neither nature nor guilt (1Pe 1:19; 3:18; Heb 7:26).
Jesus had the same nature as all men. He was only able to live a sinless life because the Father's nature was indwelling Him, thereby giving Him an "edge," for lack of a better expression, over sin.	"There is only one man who has never sinned: he is the Lord Jesus Christ. . . . From whence did Jesus derive the strength to accomplish that which no other person had done: render perfect obedience unto God? He received it from God Who tabernacled in him by His spirit. . . . Jesus' nature was the same as our own" (*Herald of the Coming Age,* vol. 18, no. 5, "Christ's Death and Your Salvation," pp. 69–70).	It is true that Jesus possessed our human nature (1Ti 2:5), but it is also true that He possessed His own divine nature (Jn 20:28).

The Doctrine of Jesus Christ—*The Resurrection of Christ*

Position	Support	Orthodox Response
Jesus was raised physically from the dead.	". . . the Bible shows that the bodily resurrection of Jesus is absolutely fundamental to the purpose of God. . . . What did God raise from the dead? Obviously that which had been buried, or laid in the sepulchre—the literal body of the Lord" (*Herald of the Coming Age,* vol. 20, no. 3, "Jehovah's Witnesses Refuted by the Bible!" p. 36).	This is an orthodox statement.

The Doctrine of the Holy Spirit

Position	Support	Orthodox Response
The Holy Spirit, rather than being a person, is actually God's power or divine energy.	"We reject the doctrine—that the Holy Spirit is a person distinct from the Father" (*The Constitution of the Glendale Christadelphian Ecclesia*, p. 18). "The Holy Spirit is the energy or power of God by which all creation came originally into being, and by which it is sustained.... This God-derived energy is the substratum of all creation.... the Holy Spirit has frequently been personified in Scripture, identifying it with God, and so it is personified as *he*" (*God is One Not Three*, p. 15).	The Scripture attributes to the Holy Spirit all the major characteristics of personhood so that there is no reason to deny that He is a person.

The Doctrine of Man and Sin

Position	Support	Orthodox Response
Man does not *have* a soul; he *is* a soul, a natural body of life.	"The first man was formed by God from the dust of the ground, animated by the breath of life, and became 'a living soul' or living creature" (*The Christadelphian Instructor*, p. 6).	In Matthew 10:28 man is described as an immaterial spirit or soul (*psyche*) completely united with a physical or material body (*soma*).
Because man is a soul (body plus life), he ceases to have consciousness when he dies. At death he goes completely out of existence.	"Man has no existence of any kind in death. He is dead, and knows no more than if he had never been born" (*The Christadelphian Instructor*, p. 7).	Conscious life continues beyond the grave. Jesus said that those who believe in Him "will never die" (Jn 11:25–26). The apostle Paul reported that "to be absent from the body is to be present with the Lord" (Php 1:21–23; 2Co 5:8). Jesus spoke to Moses and Elijah on the Mount of Transfiguration long after they had departed normal existence on earth (Mt 17:13).
God originally created man perfect, but Adam disobeyed God and brought death—physical and spiritual—to the human race. The sin nature was also passed on to all humanity.	"Adam, our first father, sinned, and was sentenced to death. Death began with him, and came to us through him. We inherit the nature that he had after he was condemned to die. Besides this, we are all sinners ourselves, and thus personally under the sentence of death" (*The Christadelphian Instructor*, pp. 7–8).	This is an orthodox statement.
Sin is the same thing as Satan (the devil). In other words, Satan is not a personal entity.	"**Sin in its various manifestations, is the devil of the Bible**" (*Herald of the Coming Age,* vol. 19, no. 5, "Can A Divided Christendom Save?" p. 78). "We set forth the proposition, sustained by Scripture, that man's greatest adversary (satan) is his own fleshly desires" (*Herald of the Coming Age,* vol. 13, no. 5, "The Devil Defined," pp. 66–67).	Satan is a sinful angelic adversary of God. He is shown to have all the characteristics of a self-aware intelligent being throughout the Old and New Testaments. A classic example of this is found in the very personal verbal exchange between God and Satan over a third (human) party in the book of Job (Job 1–2). The dialogue between Jesus and Satan also identifies Satan as a personal being (Mt 4:1–11).

The Doctrine of Salvation

Position	Support	Orthodox Response
Jesus' death did not atone for our sins.	". . . the common doctrine of the Atonement, which sets forth Jesus as a substitute sacrifice, does not reveal God as just. This doctrine suggests that Jesus died instead of others; that he paid a debt of death that they had incurred but to which he was not associated. . . . Jesus did not die instead of others; he died as a representative of humanity . . . in need of redemption from that death-doomed state as much as anybody else" (*Herald of the Coming Age*, vol. 18, no. 5, "Christ's Death and Your Salvation," pp. 70–71).	Scripture teaches that Jesus did indeed die in the place of others (1Pe 2:24; 3:18). Furthermore, Jesus Himself did not need redemption because He was without sin (1Pe 1:19), and it is sin that brings death (Ro 6:23).
Christ's death openly showed the effects of sin to the world while at the same time demonstrating the holiness of God through Christ's perfect life. Through this demonstration of good and evil, men now can see how they should live. Looking to Christ's life and recognizing these truths, coupled with a lifelong attempt to emulate Christ, provides the way to salvation.	". . . Jesus Christ, son of Adam . . . was of the same flesh and blood nature . . . and, as such, under the same sentence. . . . and the righteousness he manifested came from denying the flesh, not obeying it. But, God also raised him from the dead, because His justness made it impossible that one manifesting complete righteousness 'should be holden of death'. . . . It is comforting to recognise this, for it shows that virtue will never go unrewarded. . . . He [God] realises that flesh is weak and prone to sin, and that unless one is Divinely strengthened, he must inevitably succumb to it. Therefore, having sacrificially illustrated this principle in His only begotten Son, He is prepared to offer forgivenenss of sins to those acknowledging it, and seeking forgiveness" (*Herald of the Coming Age*, vol. 18, no. 5, "Christ's Death and Your Salvation," p. 71).	The apostle Paul wrote, "For by grace you have been saved through faith; and that not of yourselves, it is the gift of God; not as a result of works, that no one should boast" (Eph 2:8–9 NASB). Salvation comes through trusting in Christ and His all-sufficient atoning sacrifice on the cross as payment for sin culminating in His resurrection for our justification (Ro 6:8–9; 2Ti 2:12). To add anything else as a requirement for salvation like a "lifelong attempt to emulate Christ" is to insult the Spirit of grace and invite God's condemnation (Ro 4:4–5). Man's pride would like to obligate God to save him, but He will have none of it. He requires only simple childlike trust or faith in His Son in order to enter the kingdom of God (Mk 10:15 NASB).
Salvation is by works of righteousness in response to Christ's perfect life set as a model to follow.	**"What else is necessary for salvation besides faith?** 'Works'—that is obedience to God's commands as taught by Jesus" (*The Christadelphian Instructor*, p. 39).	Christ's is certainly the perfect exemplary life we should seek to emulate, but it is pure folly to think that we can merit salvation by good works. Obedience to the law has never imparted life (see Gal 3:21–25). Jesus said that to "work the works of God" one must believe on Him (see Jn 6:28–29 NASB).
Baptism is also necessary for salvation.	"Belief, baptism, and obedience (in that order) are the essential steps to salvation" (*Baptism Essential to Salvation*, p. 2).	Adding any works religious (such as baptism) or otherwise (good morality) to Christ's finished work on the cross will not lift God's condemnation. Only faith in Christ will alleviate God's judgment and impart eternal life (Jn 3:16; Ro 10:9).

The Doctrine of Rewards and Punishment

Position	Support	Orthodox Response
All of the wicked will be annihilated. There is no conscious eternal punishment.	"Death, annihilation, is the punishment of the unredeemed, a merciful oblivion" (*What Your Decision for Christ Demands*, p. 12).	The Bible plainly teaches that those who die without Christ will continue to exist in a state of conscious torment (Job 21:30–34; Isa 14:9–11; 2Pe 2:9). This is shown in the story Jesus told of the rich man and Lazarus (Lk 16). The rich man suffered both physical and mental anguish and was totally aware of who he was and of what his life had been on earth.
Saved persons who receive eternal life will live on earth. There is no such thing as heaven.	"**HEAVEN AS THE REWARD OF THE RIGHTEOUS: One will search the Bible in vain for this teaching. . . . It is contrary to the express declaration of the Lord that 'the meek will inherit the earth' (Matt 5:5)**" (*Herald of the Coming Age,* vol. 19, no. 5, "Can a Divided Christendom Save?" p. 77).	The exact identification of "heaven" is debated. Will it be an actual place, or is it a descriptive term describing a state of existence rather than a location? Will heaven, whatever it is, consist of earth as we now know it or an earth that has been glorified? The bottom line seems to be that wherever Jesus will spend eternity will be where Christians spend eternity (Jn 12:26; 14:2–3; 1Th 4:17).
Those who inherit eternal life will receive glorified, immortal bodies. Eventually they may become equal unto the angels ("gods"). **Although "gods" is a term used by Christadelphians for angels, further reading seems to indicate that their becoming equal unto "gods" means actually becoming a true God (like Christ) and not just an angel.**	"It was the ambition of Adam and Eve that they might become 'equal unto the gods' (i.e. the angels); it is the hope of the redeemed that by obedience to the will of God, they may attain unto that state, and become 'equal unto the angels' (Luke 20:36). . . . These expressions testify to the great hope set before believers. They can attain unto the 'glory of God,' 'divine nature,' the 'name of God,' and complete 'oneness with Him.' The Lord Jesus attained unto all this, and thus had the name of God bestowed upon himself, a name that he promises all true believers . . . (Rom 8:17)" (*God is One Not Three*, p. 14).	The redeemed will be graciously given immortal bodies like Jesus' (1Co 15:51–52; 1Jn 3.2). The redeemed will actually judge the angels (1Co 6:2–3) as well as be like them (Mt 22:30; Mk 12:25). It is wrong to equate the infinite and eternal Creator with angels, who are finite creatures (Heb 1:5–8). It is equally wrong for us to aspire to "godhood" or to engage in the vanity of imagining that it is even possible to aquire God's attributes such as omniscience, omnipresence, and omnipotence. A limited, finite creature will never experience being infinite in thought or essence. Christ could, for He is the Eternal I Am or YAHWEH. Furthermore, God has explicitly stated that He will not share His glory with others (Isa 42:8; 48:10–11).

4

Christian Identity Movement

FACTS AND HISTORY

Facts	
Topic	*Current Facts*
Membership	The Christian Identity Movement is just that—a movement. It represents a loose-knit confederation of various small groups and sects that are bound together primarily by their commonly held myths of racial origins. The groups are usually very secretive and suspicious of outsiders, so it is difficult to get an exact or reliable figure of total membership.
Worship	The worship services are generally nonliturgical in the "high church" sense but may include recitation of oaths and creeds. Corporate worship resembles revivalist-oriented church services found in the Pentecostal, Wesleyan, or Baptist traditions, embracing hymn-singing and personal testimonies. Coming to a true understanding of racial purity is emphasized as a common theme in the testimonies.
Leadership	A number of leaders speak or have written tracts, booklets, newsletters, and books on the subject. Some of these are Lt. Colonel Jack Mohr, Sheldon Emry, Thom Arthur Robb, Dan Gayman, Bertrand L. Comparet, Roy Mansker, Raymond Capt, Richard Butler, and "Pastor" Arnold Murray.
Publications	Books and booklets have played a major role in building cohesion in the ranks. The 19th-century book *Identification of the British Nation With Lost Israel* by Edward Hine is one of the staples still in use. *Foundations—Biography of Aryan Nations* by Richard Butler is a book offered as an explanation of their beliefs by the Church of Jesus Christ Christian Aryan Nations. Booklets abound such as *The Seven Big Lies of Religion* by Dan Gayman and *Heirs of the Promise* and *Who Killed Christ?* by Sheldon Emry.
General statement of beliefs	The Christian Identity Movement's core belief is that the true descendants of God and Adam came through Abraham, Isaac, and Jacob and that the identity of their descendants known as the "lost tribes of Israel" are the Teutonic peoples that include white citizens of Germany, England, and Scandanavia. Historically this ethnocentric belief system has been known as British-Israelism or Anglo-Israelism. In the modern theory it is emphasized that all nonwhite races are not only inferior but inherently evil, as they are literally the physical children of the devil. The groups are different from one another in regard to which orthodox doctrines they embrace, and they are eclectic in the ongoing evolution of their belief systems. Some have adopted the "Holy Name" movement's insistence on the use of Yahweh and Yahshua (*sic*) as the names for God and Jesus; others have adopted the heretical Oneness Pentecostal view of the Godhead; still others blend New Age ideas and revere Edgar Cayce and his views. The race issue is truly the "tie that binds." We will examine the doctrines and views of two of the groups known as *The Christian Identity Church* and *The Aryan Nations* along with various authors such as Sheldon Emry and Dan Gayman.

History

Topic	History
The early Victorian roots of the movement—fertile soil for racism via Darwin	The false doctrine of British-Israelism goes back to post-Elizabethan England. One of its main proponents in early times was Richard Brothers (1757–1824). The 19th century saw the rise of Darwinianism, which, in propounding naturalistic evolution, conflicts with the biblical teaching about human origin, namely, that God created mankind from "one blood" (see Ac 17:26 NASB) and that all people are equal before God in having a common ancestry in Adam and Eve. Thus, by the latter half of that century, many people were inclined to consider it scientifically trustworthy to believe that the races represent different and separate strains of evolutionary development. This attitude served as justification of the racist views of white supremacist groups such as the Ku Klux Klan.
A 19th-century British export to the United States	The modern Anglo-Israelite movement was born in 1870 through the efforts of the Rev. John Wilson. It was brought to the United States from England that same year by Edward Hine. In more recent times it was championed by James Lovell of Fort Worth, Texas, and Howard Rand of Destiny Publishers. It was Rand who first coined the term "Identity" in addressing the supposed caucasoid inheritors of "the covenant." Another major advocate of British-Israelism was the late Herbert W. Armstrong, the founder of the Worldwide Church of God. Although he and his church were not a part of the Identity movement, they helped to keep alive the notion of the otherwise declining and discredited Anglo-Israelism theory.
The 20th-century Nazi connection	The bonding of Anglo-Israelism and 19th-century racism can be attributed to Wesley Swift, who later became associated with the Nazism of Hitler's Germany. Swift was a member of the Ku Klux Klan in 1946 when he founded the Identity Church of Jesus Christ Christian. He then converted Richard Butler, who later inherited the leadership of Swift's church. Butler founded the Aryan Nations Compound located near Hayden Lake, Idaho, where he has been known to hold annual gatherings composed of Klan members, neo-Nazi groups, and Skinheads.
Opportunistic hate-mongering through taking advantage of economic ills and racial-ethnic animosity	In recent times the movement has taken advantage of social and civil unrest and economic turmoil in the United States and Germany (and to some extent the rest of Europe) to advance its cause. Hard times in American agriculture, which precipitated such events as the massive "Farm Aid" concerts, also served as a spring board for the Identity Movement to blame "Jewish bankers" for the ills of the farmer. The celebrated Randy Weaver case, in which his Montana compound was attacked by federal authorities (August 21, 1992), provided the movement with a martyr in that Weaver was recognized as an Identity adherent. An influx of Turkish immigrants and other nationalities in Germany during the 1980s and 1990s, like the farm crisis in America, resulted in a proliferation of the pro-white ethnic message. Conspiracy theories of Jewish plans for world conquest abound, and the United States government is referred to as ZOG (Zionist Occupation Government) as a way of decrying that the Jews are in control.
Names of groups involved in the overall movement	It is beyond the scope of this book to relate the history of all the small groups involved in this movement, but it is appropriate to mention the larger groups that would find a significant portion, if not a predominance, of their membership believing this false teaching. Their names are Aryan Nations, The Covenant, Sword and Arm of the Lord, Posse Comitatus, Christian Identity Church, Israel World Federation, Neo Nazism, Skinheads, the Ku Klux Klan, and British Israel World Federation.

THEOLOGY

Position	Support	Orthodox Response
The Bible is the inspired, inerrant word of God.	"We believe the entire Bible, both Old and New Testaments, as originally inspired, to be the inerrant, supreme, revealed Word of God.... All scripture is written as a doctrinal standard for our exhortation, admonition, correction, instruction and example; the whole counsel to be believed, taught and followed (II Tim. 3:16, Act. 20:27)" (Doctrinal Statement, Christian Identity Church, *Encyclopedia of American Religions*, 1st ed., p. 624).	This is an orthodox statement.
The Bible is written for physical descendants of Adam who are elect first because they are Adam's white physical progeny. Although the Christian Identity Church doesn't insist that all whites go to heaven, it would say that being white is a prerequisite for salvation.	"The history, covenants, and prophecy of this holy book [the Bible] were written for and about a specific elect family of people who are children of YHVH God (Luke 3:38; Psalm 82:6) through the seedling of Adam (Gen 5:1)" (Doctrinal Statement, Christian Identity Church, *Encyclopedia of American Religions*, 1st ed., p. 624). "Adam is the father of the white race only" (*This is Aryan Nations*).	The Bible is God's revelation to His children in Christ and those who will become His children who are still in Adam. The elect family of God are those who are spiritually born into the family of God (see Jn 3:6–7) by grace through faith (see Eph 2:8–9). "Faith comes from hearing, and hearing by the word of Christ" (Ro 10:17 NASB). This word is for all people groups to hear and be saved by. "God is now declaring to *men* that *all everywhere* should repent" (Ac 17:30, NASB emphasis added). Clearly, members of all races may come to a saving knowledge of Jesus and enter into God's spiritual family through faith in His revealed gospel.

The Doctrine of God—*The Trinity*

Position	Support	Orthodox Response
The groups in general affirm the deity of the Father, the Son, and the Holy Spirit.	"We believe in YHVH the one and only true and living eternal God (Isa. 44:6); the God of our fathers Abraham, Isaac and Jacob (Exo. 3:14–16); the Creator of all things (1 Cor. 8:6) who is omnipotent, omnipresent, unchangeable and all-knowing; the Great I Am who is manifested in three beings: God the Father, God the Son, and God the Holy Spirit, all one God (Deut. 6:4)" (Doctrinal Statement, Christian Identity Church, *Encyclopedia of American Religions*, 1st ed., p. 626).	This is an orthodox statement. It would be more appropriate to say that there exists three persons in one Being and better to omit the word "manifested," as it may give the impression of Sabellianism. Not all the Identity groups are in agreement with the Trinitarian view of God and would be Sabellianist or Arian in their denial of the Trinity due to the influence of some of the "Holy Name" groups on their theology.

The Doctrine of Jesus Christ—*The Deity of Christ*

Position	Support	Orthodox Response
Jesus Christ is God the Son who died for the remission of sins and was raised the third day and now rules from heaven.	"We believe God the Son, Yahshua the Messiah (Jesus Christ), became man in order to redeem His people Israel (Luke 1:68) as a kinsman of the flesh (Heb. 2:14–16; Rom. 9:3–5); died as the Passover Lamb of God on the Cross of Calvary finishing His perfect atoning sacrifice for the remission of our sins (Matt. 26:28). He arose from the grave on the third day, (1 Cor. 15:4) triumphing over death and ascended into heaven where He is now reigning at the right hand of God (Mark 16:19)" (Doctrinal Statement, Christian Identity Church, *Encyclopedia of American Religions*, 1st ed., p. 625). "We believe Yahshua the Messiah (Jesus Christ) to be our only High Priest (1 Tim. 2:5; Heb. 3:1, 6:20, 7:17, 24–25) and Head over His Body of called-out saints, the Church (Romans 12:5; 1 Cor. 12:12, 27; Eph. 1:22–23, 4:12, 5:23, 30; Col. 1:18, 24)" (Ibid.).	These are orthodox statements if understood apart from the movement's racial teachings.

The Doctrine of Jesus Christ—*The Humanity of Christ*

Position	Support	Orthodox Response
Jesus Christ is God incarnate. **Jesus was born miraculously of a virgin.** **Jesus Christ is eternal.**	"We believe Yahshua the Messiah (Jesus the Christ) to be the only incarnate begotten son of God, the Word made flesh (John 1:14), born of the Virgin Mary in fulfillment of divine prophecy (Isa. 7:14; Luke 1:27) at the appointed time, having had His eternal existence as one with the Father before the world was (John 17:5, 21–22)" (Doctrinal Statement, Christian Identity Church, *Encyclopedia of American Religions*, 1st ed., p. 624).	This is an orthodox statement if viewed apart from the racial implications of other teachings on this matter.
Jesus Christ died as a perfect sacrifice in order to bring remission of sins.	"We believe God the Son, Yahshua the Messiah (Jesus Christ), became man in order to redeem His people Israel (Luke 1:68) as a kinsman of the flesh (Heb. 2:14–16; Rom. 9:3–5); died as the Passover Lamb of God on the Cross of Calvary finishing His perfect atoning sacrifice for the remission of our sins" (Doctrinal Statement, Christian Identity Church, *Encyclopedia of American Religions*, 1st ed., p. 625).	This is an orthodox statement.

The Doctrine of Jesus Christ—*The Resurrection of Christ*

Position	Support	Orthodox Response
Jesus physically rose from the dead.	"He arose from the grave on the third day, (1 Cor. 15:4) triumphing over death and ascended into heaven where He is now reigning at the right hand of God (Mark 16:19)" (Doctrinal Statement, Christian Identity Church, *Encyclopedia of American Religions*, 1st ed., p. 625).	This is an orthodox statement.

The Doctrine of the Holy Spirit

Position	Support	Orthodox Response
The Holy Spirit is part of the Triune Godhead who reveals to the spirit of natural man the things of God; who indwells the children of God and empowers them with specific gifts; who sets a seal of identity on the members of the body of Christ.	"We believe in the personally revealed being of God the Holy Spirit, the Comforter (John 15:26, 16:7), who was sent by God the Son to glorify Him (John 16:14) and teach us all truth (John 14:26, 16:13; 1 Cor. 2:10–12) according to promise (Ezek. 36:25–27; Acts 2:33; Eph. 1:13–14). The Holy Spirit is sent to dwell in (1 Cor. 3:16; John 14:17) the members of the body of Christ, giving unto each different gifts (1 Cor. 12) empowering them to witness (Acts 1:8) of sin, of righteousness, and of judgment (John 16:8–11). Natural man can not know the things of the Spirit (John 14:17; 1 Cor. 2:14), which God sent forth to His sons (Gal. 4:6), thus identifying the children of Israel (Isa. 44:1–3, 59:20–21; Haggai 2:5; Rom. 8:16) in this world" (Doctrinal Statement, Christian Identity Church, *Encyclopedia of American Religions*, 1st ed., pp. 624–25).	This is an orthodox statement if viewed apart from the racial implications of other teachings.

The Doctrine of Man and Sin

Position	Support	Orthodox Response
Sin is the transgression of God's law.	"We believe sin is transgression of God's law (1 John 3:4; Rom. 3:31, 7:7) and that all have sinned (Rom. 3:23)" (Doctrinal Statement, Christian Identity Church, *Encyclopedia of American Religions*, 1st ed., p. 626).	This is basically an orthodox statement, although the Bible also equates lack of faith in God with sin. Romans 14:23 states, "Everything that does not come from faith is sin." Transgressions of God's commands ultimately stem from this lack of faith.
White caucasoid people (and not the black, yellow, red, or brown peoples of the earth) are God's chosen race.	"<u>WE BELIEVE</u> that Adam-man of Genesis was the placing of the white race upon this earth. All races did not descend from Adam. Adam is the father of the white race only" (*This is Aryan Nations*).	The apostle Paul states clearly that the flesh profits nothing when it comes to salvation. God is no respecter of a person's social, racial, or ethnic status. While man looks on the outward appearance, God looks on the heart. Romans 9:8 says, "It is not the natural children who are God's children, but it is the children of the promise who are regarded as Abraham's offspring." Merely being born of a particular race profits nothing. "And He made from *one blood* every nation of mankind to live on all the face of the earth, having determined their appointed times, and the boundaries of their habitation, that they should seek God, if perhaps they might grope for Him and find Him, though He is not far from each one of us" (Ac 17:26–27 NASB). Moreover, science testifies to the truth of this statement. All races share basic blood types and are able to receive blood tranfusions from each other. In addition, studies at the University of Hawaii have traced the chromosomes of all racial groups back to a common female ancestor. The apostle Paul said in Athens, "God is now declaring to *men* that *all everywhere* should repent" (Ac 17:30 NASB, emphasis added).

The Doctrine of Salvation

Position	Support	Orthodox Response
The Jew is the enemy of God. Only members of the white race can come to salvation.	"<u>WE BELIEVE</u> the Jew is the adversary of our race and God, as is attested to by all secular history as well as the word of God in scripture" (*This is Aryan Nations*). "<u>WE BELIEVE</u> there is a battle being fought this day between the children of darkness (today known as Jews) and the children of light (God), the Aryan race, the true Israel of the Bible" (Ibid.).	Scripture makes a strong distinction between the physical children of Abraham, Isaac, and Jacob and those who are "grafted in" and made spiritual sons of Abraham through faith in Christ. The apostle Paul states that this distinction should not produce animosity and shows that the natural seed (the Jews) will be saved en masse by God's sovereign act at some future date (see Ro 9; 11:17–24).
The church, the Bride of Christ, is Israel; Israel is the church.	"His bride, the wife of the Lamb, is the twelve tribes of the children of Israel (Isa. 54:5; Jer. 3:14; Hosea 2:19–20; Rev. 21:9–12)" (Doctrinal Statement, Christian Identity Church, *Encyclopedia of American Religions*, 1st ed., p. 625).	Revelation 21:9–12 does not say that the bride of Christ is the 12 tribes of Israel. Rather, it simply shows that the descendants of Abraham, Isaac, and Jacob will be held in high esteem in the heavenly city.
Only the physical descendants of Adam through Abraham, Isaac, and Jacob alone will be the heirs of salvation.	"Each individual Israelite must repent, putting off the old corrupt man, and become a new creature (Eph. 4:22–24; II Cor. 5:17) walking in the newness of life (Rom. 6:4). This spiritual rebirth (John 3:3–6; I Pet. 1:23) being necessary for a personal relationship with our Savior" (Doctrinal Statement, Christian Identity Church, *Encyclopedia of American Religions*, 1st ed., p. 625). "<u>WE BELIEVE</u> that Adam-man of Genesis was the placing of the white race upon this earth. All races did not descend from Adam. Adam is the father of the white race only" (*This is Aryan Nations*). "<u>WE BELIEVE</u> that the true, literal children of the Bible are the 12 tribes of Israel which are now scattered throughout the world and are now known as the Anglo-Saxon, Celtic, Scandinavian, Teutonic people of this earth" (Ibid.).	Revelation 7:9 gives us a clear picture of the redeemed in heaven: "After this I looked and there before me was a great multitude that no one could count, from every nation, tribe, people and language, standing before the throne and in front of the Lamb. They were wearing white robes and were holding palm branches in their hands. And they cried out in a loud voice: 'Salvation belongs to our God, who sits on the throne, and to the Lamb.'" Obviously, all races are included among the redeemed. Since Celtic, Teutonic, Scandinavian, and Anglo-Saxon peoples represent only a few of the tribes of the earth and because the Word of God makes it plain that all ethnic groups are represented in heaven, it is certain that this teaching is wrong.

The Doctrine of Rewards and Punishment

Position	Support	Orthodox Response
Only the white race, descended from Adam through Abraham, is destined for rewards and its members are all known as Israelites. In this context individual Israelites may be lost if they refuse to accept Jesus as Savior.	"We believe individual Israelites are destined for judgement (II Cor. 5:10; Heb. 9:27) and must believe on the only begotten Son of God, Yahshua the Messiah (Jesus Christ), in whom only there is salvation (Acts 4:12), that they be not condemned (John 3:18; Mark 16:16)" (Doctrinal Statement, Christian Identity Church, *Encyclopedia of American Religions*, 1st ed., p. 625). "Adam and his descendants can know YHVH God as their Father not merely as their Creator. Adamic man is made trichotomous, that is, not only of body and soul, but having an implanted spirit giving him a higher form of consciousness and distinguishing him from all the other races of the Earth" (Ibid., p. 626).	Second Corinthians 5:10 refers to all believers, Jews or Gentiles—that is, by implication, all races—as having to face the judgment seat of Christ. In view of their definition of "Israelites," the movement's statement could as easily be understood to say, "We believe individual Germanic, Teutonic, white Caucasians are destined for judgment and must believe on the only begotten Son." This, of course, leaves out all other people as unworthy of salvation solely on the basis of race. The Scriptures state that all people came from the same parentage, namely Adam and Eve. "And He made from *one blood every nation of mankind* to live on all the face of the earth, having determined their appointed times, and the boundaries of their habitation, that they should seek God, if perhaps they might grope for Him and find Him, though He is not far from each one of us" (Ac 17:26–27 NASB, emphasis added).
Jesus Christ will return physically to this earth to rule the nations of the world.	"We believe in the literal return to this Earth of Yahshua, the Messiah, (Jesus Christ) in like manner as He departed (Acts 1:11), to take the throne of David (Isaiah 9:7; Luke 1:32) and establish His everlasting Kingdom (Daniel 2:44; Luke 1:33; Rev. 11:15). Every knee shall bow and every tongue shall confess that He is King of kings and Lord of lords (Phil. 2:10–11; 1 Tim. 6:14–15)" (Doctrinal Statement, Christian Identity Church, *Encyclopedia of American Religions*, 1st ed., p. 625).	This is an orthodox statement.
Believers are to keep and teach the laws of God on a personal and national basis.	"We believe God gave Israel His laws for their own good (Deut. 5:33). Theocracy being the only perfect form of government, and God's divine Law for governing a nation being far superior to man's laws, we are not to add to or diminish from His commandments (Deut. 4:1–2). All present problems are a result of disobedience to the laws of God, which if kept will bring blessings and if disregarded will bring cursings (Deut. 28)" (Doctrinal Statement, Christian Identity Church, *Encyclopedia of American Religions*, 1st ed., p. 626).	The New Testament teaches that believers in Christ are "not under law, but under grace" (Ro 6:14). The 613 laws of Moses were given to the physical descendants of Abraham, Isaac, and Jacob and were tied to the land covenant given to Abraham. Genesis 15 tells us this land is mostly found in what is known today as Eretz Yisrael, or the nation of Israel in the Middle East, not America! The Jews are the only people who were ever obliged to keep the Mosaic covenant. The rest of the nations are under the Noahic covenant (see Ge 9:1–18).

INTERESTING AND DISTINCTIVE BELIEFS

Position	Support	Orthodox Response
Interracial marriages are wrong and sinful in God's eyes. Mixing races should be punishable by death.	"We need today, ministers of God, who will stand up for righteousness, who will not be afraid to 'tell it like it is' that race-mixing is wrong, it's **SIN**" (Thom Arthur Robb, untitled pamphlet, p. 7). "Our nation needs to turn back to God's laws and outlaw race-mixing, with the death penalty being the judgment of doing so" (Ibid.). "<u>WE BELIEVE</u> in the preservation of our race individually and collectively as a people as demanded and directed by God. We believe a racial nation has a right and is under obligation to preserve itself and its members" (*This is Aryan Nations*).	God's prohibitions in the Mosaic Law that His earthly people, the Jews, not marry into other nations was concerned with the ungodly pagan practices of those nations, not their racial makeup. Race or genetic lineage per se was not an issue for separation. Rahab the harlot was a Canaanite from pagan Jericho and Ruth was a Moabitess, yet both are found in the lineage of Jesus. Each converted to a true understanding of Judaism and the worship of the God of Israel and was allowed to marry a descendant of Abraham, Isaac, and Jacob.
The Jews are literally Satan's children and the enemies of Adam's white descendants.	"We believe that the Man Adam (a Hebrew word meaning: ruddy, to show blood, flush, turn rosy) is father of the White Race only" (Doctrinal Statement, Christian Identity Church, *Encyclopedia of American Religions*, 1st ed., p. 626). "Adam is the founder of the white race only" (*This is Aryan Nations*). "We believe in an existing being known as the Devil or Satan, and called the Serpent (Gen. 3:1; Rev. 12:9) who has a literal 'seed' or posterity in the earth (Gen. 3:15) commonly called Jews today (Rev. 2:9; 3:9; Isa. 65:15)" (Doctrinal Statement, Christian Identity Church, *Encyclopedia of American Religions*, 1st ed., p. 625). "<u>WE BELIEVE</u> the Jew is the adversary of our race and God . . ." (*This is Aryan Nations*).	Genesis 3:15 does not teach that Satan had sexual relations with Eve. Nowhere does the Bible teach that there are any men who are not descendants of Adam and Eve. Furthermore, the Bible does not teach that Adam (a Hebrew word that simply means "clay") was white. We don't know for certain what shade of "clay" Adam was. All children of God were formerly "creatures of wrath" or "children of the devil." Even the apostle Paul says that in his old nature dwelled "no good thing." Second Corinthians 5:17 says, "If *anyone* is in Christ, he is a new creation" (emphasis added). Moreover, Paul's statement in Romans 11:28 clearly limits the Jews' so-called adversary status: "As far as the gospel is concerned, they are enemies on your account; but as far as election is concerned, they are loved on account of the patriarchs." Verse 31 states further, "So they too have now become disobedient in order that they too may now receive mercy as a result of God's mercy to you." This God-ordained mercy to the Jews is notably absent from Christian Identity theology.

Position	Support	Orthodox Response
The Jews are a different race from those known as Israelites.	"WE BELIEVE that the true, literal children of the Bible are the 12 tribes of Israel which are now scattered throughout the world and are now known as the Anglo-Saxon, Celtic, Scandinavian, Teutonic people of this earth" (*This is Aryan Nations*). "We believe an existing being known as the Devil or Satan, and called the Serpent (Gen. 3:1; Rev. 12:9) who has a literal 'seed' or posterity in the earth (Gen. 3:15) commonly called Jews today (Rev. 2:9; 3:9; Isaiah 65:15)" (Doctrinal Statement, Christian Identity Church, *Encyclopedia of American Religions*, 1st ed., p. 625). "Jews will not become Christians" (Sheldon Emry, *Who Killed Christ?* p. 18).	The term "Jew" was already in use in Jesus' day as a reference to all descendants of the twelve tribes of Israel because of the prominence of the tribe of Judah and the derivative name Judea given to the land. The apostle Paul called himself both an Israelite and a Jew. In writing about God's election he stated, "And He did so in order that He might make known the riches of His glory upon vessels of mercy, which He prepared beforehand for glory, even *us*, whom he also called, not from among *Jews* only, but also from among Gentiles" (Ro 9:23–24 NASB, emphasis added). In the same passage, Paul also referred to himself as an Israelite: "I could wish that I myself were cursed and cut off from Christ for the sake of my brothers, those of my own race, the people of Israel" (Ro 9:3–4).
The United States of America is the Promised Land.	"We believe that the United States of America fulfills the prophesied (II Sam. 7:10; Isa. 11:12; Ezek. 36:24) place where Christians from all the tribes of Israel would be regathered" (Doctrinal Statement, Christian Identity Church, *Encyclopedia of American Religions*, 1st ed., p. 626).	There is only one land that God has promised to the physical descendants of Abraham and only one place they will return to. Its geographic boundaries are given in Genesis 15:18–21 with landmarks and rivers that exist only in the Middle East. All prophecies of a regathering of the people of Israel must be viewed with this promised land in mind.
Being in Adam or a descendant of Adam is the deciding factor in spirituality.	"Adam and his descendants can know YHVH God as their Father not merely as their Creator. Adamic man is made trichotomous, that is, not only of body and soul, but having an implanted spirit giving him a higher form of consciousness and distinguishing him from all the other races of the Earth" (Doctrinal Statement, Christian Identity Church, *Encyclopedia of American Religions*, 1st ed., p. 626).	Adam is not exalted in Scripture in that he is presented as the federal head of a fallen race of creatures. When people repent of their sins and ask Jesus to be their Savior, they are considered by God to be in Christ (see 2Co 5:17), not Adam (see Gal 3:26; 4:21–31). The apostle Paul states in Romans 5:12 and 6:11, "Therefore, just as sin entered the world through one man [Adam], and death through sin, and in this way death came to all men, because all sinned.... Count yourselves dead to sin but alive to God in Christ Jesus" (emphasis ours). Those who are in Christ are reckoned dead to the old man (the Adamic nature) and are considered alive in Christ. Thus the elect are those who are so by spiritual rather than physical birth.

Position	Support	Orthodox Response
The modern Jew is not the same as ancient Israel because the ten tribes of the northern kingdom became the Northern Europeans after being taken captive by Assyria. Millions of Jews were removed from Israel during the Assyrian invasion of the northern kingdom, and these make up the ancestors of white Europe.	"What happened to the millions of Israelites who were dispersed out of old Canaanland seven centuries before Christ, and who never returned? *They migrated onto the continent of Europe and were the ancestors of the white, European race*" (Sheldon Emry, *Heirs Of The Promise*, p. 19). "So the two conquests of Assyria would have removed the vast majority of the Israelites into Assyria and out of the land of Palestine. The number removed would have been in the millions" (Ibid., p. 11).	"Not all of the northern tribes went into captivity in 721 B.C. Archaeology has confirmed this fact, which is so clearly taught in Chronicles. Excavations have revealed that the population of Judah rapidly increased after the fall of the northern kingdom as a result of the many refugees mentioned in 2 Chronicles 11:14–16. Furthermore, archaeologists have uncovered the annals of the Assyrian king Sargon, in which he tells of carrying away only 27,290 people and fifty chariots." (*Biblical Archeologist*, vol. 6, 1943, p. 58, as quoted in *Can Israel Survive In A Hostile World?* by David Allen Lewis, New Leaf Press).
The term "Gentile" as applied to all who are not Jews is a bad translation from the Greek and Hebrew. This leads people to believe that white Europeans are not the "children of promise" but that the modern Jew is.	"The teaching of the Satanic doctrine that the Jew is God's chosen people is one of the most diabolical lies ever passed off for the truth in the history of the world.... There is no such word as Gentile. It is a word that was supplied by the KJV translators many hundreds of years after the last book of the New Testament was written" (Dan Gayman, *The Seven Big Lies of Religion*, p. 6).	The Israelites continued to maintain their identity as Israelites throughout their captivity, as witnessed by Daniel's persistence in prayer to the one true God. After the Assyrians were conquered by the Babylonians, and they in turn by the Persians, all the Israelite captives were mingled together. The fact that they were called Jews upon their release by Cyrus, and on into the Roman and then modern eras, is because they returned to Judea, named after the most prominent tribe of Israel—Judah.
Those who have been historically understood as being the physical descendants of Israel known as the Jews are not really the Jews but are themselves non-Jews or Gentiles because they are descendants of Ishmael or came from the Khazar empire of southern Russia that existed in the 8th and 9th centuries A.D.	"But what happened to the other tens of millions of Israelites who never returned to Jerusalem?" (Sheldon Emry, *Heirs Of The Promise*, p. 12). "Jesus Christ who knows the end from the beginning, knew that the scribes and Pharisees and the chief priests to whom He was talking were NOT ISRAELITES, BUT WERE THE DESCENDANTS OF ISHMAEL OR ESAU" (Sheldon Emry, *WHO KILLED CHRIST?* p. 18).	In Matthew's gospel, the lineage of Jesus is traced back to Abraham, who is considered a Jew. In Acts 22:3, Paul states that he is a Jew. In several places the Pharisees are also called Jews (see Jn 3:1; Mk 7:3). Paul mentions that in his day there continued to be an advantage in being a physical descendant of Jesus— that is, they were given the oracles of God. This, of course, is a reference to the Old Testament. Those who have historically been considered Jews are the ones who received those Scriptures.

Position	Support	Orthodox Response
The modern Jews of Israel and Europe are not really the descendants of Abraham, Isaac, and Jacob but are descended from the Khazar dynasty.	"Modern scholarship, however, has begun to question whether all who consider themselves Jews are in fact Jews at all. There is mounting evidence that the great majority of Jews today (the Ashkenazim or eastern European Jews) are not the off-spring of Abraham but descendants of the ancient central European nation of Khaz-aria, converted to Judaism in A.D. 740. There are many aspects of the darker side of Judaism which Jews do not mind know-ing as long as Gentiles are not in on the secret. The ghost of Khazaria is not one of them. The Khazar origin of most Jews today is one secret in a religion of secrets which even they cannot entertain" (Theodore Winston Pike, *Israel Our Duty/Our Dilemma*, p. 297, 303). [Although Pike cannot be said to be a CIM spokesman, his Khazar theory is accepted by some adherents to the Christian Identity Movement.]	It is complete nonsense to argue that the present-day Jews derive from the Khazars. For one, only the Russian Jews, if any, could possibly derive from the Khazars . . . because we know nothing of a migration of Jews out of Russia into the West after the Khazar episode about A.D. 800. All Jewish movements after that time, until the 19th century, were into Russia, not out of it. But even in the 19th century, the vast majority of Jews lived outside Russia, and therefore could not derive from the Khaz-ars, and the Jews which settled in Pales-tine were mostly other than Russian. But if there is any Khazar blood in Russian Jewry, it is so little as to be practically neg-ligible. Only the king and some of the nobles became Jews. Most of the people did not become Jews and were no doubt absorbed by other Turkish tribes after the dynasty fell in the 10th century. In fact, after the 11th century, the Khazars are mentioned in Arabic sources as Muslims. . . .
The Yiddish lan-guage is of Khazar origin.	"Yiddish is the mother tongue of the Khaz-ars, or self-styled Jews originally from East-ern Europe" (Stan Rittenhouse, *For Fear of the Jews*, p. 67). [Rittenhouse is another author who speaks on the Khazar theory but to our knowledge is not an adherent to the Christian Identity Movement or a spokesperson for it.]	"The language of the Khazars is described as being related to Bulgarian, which means the Turkish dialect the Bulgars spoke before they adopted a Slav lan-guage in their new Balkan home. There are no Jews whatsoever in Russia who speak or spoke a Turkish dialect. . . . All other Jews of Russia spoke Yiddish, which is a form of German originally spoken in the area of the middle Rhine and the Main around Frankfurt, and their customs and culture are those of medieval German Jews" (from a letter by Professor Chaim Rabin to Benjamin Jaffe in Jerusalem, as published in the book *Can Israel Survive in a Hostile World?* by David Allen Lewis).

5

Church of Jesus Christ of Latter-day Saints

FACTS AND HISTORY

Facts	
Topic	*Current Facts*
Membership	In 1994 the Church of Jesus Christ of Latter-day Saints (LDS) reported 9,024,569 members in 2,008 stakes, 21,774 wards and branches, and 303 missions worldwide. There were 47,311 full-time missionaries (*Salt Lake Tribune*, April 2, 1995, p. A1). The LDS church "expects to have 12 million members by the end of the century and 157 million by 2050" if the church growth rate of the 1980s is sustained (*Salt Lake Tribune*, April 4, 1992, p. A12).
Worship	Mormon members in good standing attend a variety of services or meetings during a three-hour time period on Sundays. Men attend a Priesthood Meeting; women attend four Relief Society Meetings. The men's meeting includes a spiritual "lesson," announcements, and discussion of relevant subjects such as changes in the church and the excommunication or disfellowshiping of particular members. Women's meetings cover spiritual living, culture and refinement, inspirational issues, and homemaking. LDS Sunday school classes have a four-year cycle for teaching the New Testament, the Book of Mormon, the Pearl of Great Price, and Doctrine and Covenants (other Mormon Scriptures).* The Sacrament Meeting is a very formal, planned service that always begins with two or three songs followed by announcements, the passing of the sacrament (communion), and individual "talks" (talks lasting from five to 30 minutes, covering any subject from the Bible to personal experience to practical information). Former members claim that attending all Sunday meetings is an unspoken requirement.
	*Mormons do not italicize the titles of their Scriptures.
Presidents of the church	Joseph Smith, Jr. 1830–1844 Brigham Young 1844–1877 (officially installed as president in 1847) John Taylor 1877–1887 (officially installed as president in 1880) Wilford Woodruff 1887–1898 (officially installed as president in 1889) Lorenzo Snow 1898–1901 Joseph F. Smith 1901–1918 Heber J. Grant 1918–1945 George Albert Smith 1945–1951 David O. Mckay 1951–1970 Joseph Fielding Smith 1970–1972 Harold B. Lee 1972–1973 Spencer W. Kimball 1973–1985 Ezra Taft Benson 1985–1994 Howard W. Hunter 1994–1995 Gordon B. Hinckley 1995–
Publications	The church has several publications: (1) *Deseret News*, a daily newspaper; (2) *The Ensign*, a magazine for adults; (3) *New Era*, a magazine for teenagers; (4) *The Friend*, a magazine for children; and (5) *The Church News*, a newspaper that covers religious and church issues.

Facts (cont.)	
Topic	**Current Facts**
General statement of beliefs	Mormons believe that their church is "'the only true and living church upon the face of the whole earth' (D&C 1:30), the only organization authorized by the Almighty to preach his gospel and administer the ordinances of salvation, the only Church which has power to save" (*Mormon Doctrine*, 1977 ed., p. 136). Mormons either deny or pervert every essential doctrine of historic Christianity, including the uniqueness of God, the virgin birth, the Trinity, the authority of Scripture (by relegating it to a position below their other sacred writings), and salvation by grace through faith.

History	
Topic	**History**
Joseph Smith, Jr., 1830–1844	Joseph Smith, Jr., born in 1805, founded the Church of Jesus Christ of Latter-day Saints (originally named the Church of Christ) in 1830. This occurred after several years of supernatural experiences that allegedly began in 1820 when, at the age of 14, after retreating to a secluded spot in the woods, he had a vision of God the Father and Jesus Christ. (Conflicting versions of this vision have been published by the church but only one is prominent today.) Jesus allegedly told Smith that the Christian churches "were all wrong" and that he should join none of them. In 1823 he reportedly had a second vision, in which an angel calling himself Moroni appeared to him. He later claimed that the angel was a personage named Nephi (Pearl of Great Price, 1851 ed., p. 41), and this story also has evolved over the years. Mormons currently identify the being of light as the angel Moroni. The angel allegedly appeared to Smith and revealed the existence of some golden plates inscribed with an account of the former inhabitants of North America. These plates supposedly contained "the fullness of the everlasting gospel."
	After four years of visitations from the angel, Smith retrieved the golden plates from their resting place in 1827. According to Smith, they contained Reformed Egyptian (a language for which there is no known archaeological evidence). He claims to have translated the plates with the Urim and Thummin (sometimes described as a seer stone placed in a hat). The product of his occult "translation" was the Book of Mormon. Smith founded his new church soon after the translation was published.
	Smith's group grew rapidly in number and soon came into conflict with neighboring communities over religious and social issues. A series of violent confrontations forced the Mormons to relocate several times. The tensions between Mormons and society culminated in the arrest and subsequent murder of Joseph Smith while he was awaiting trial in Carthage, Illinois, on charges of riot and treason.
Brigham Young, 1847–1877	A power struggle after the death of Smith left Brigham Young, a high-ranking Mormon, in control of the sect. Young is best known for leading the Mormon people from Nauvoo, Illinois, to the great Salt Lake Valley during a trek that lasted from February 1846 until July 1847. Young was president of the church during the infamous Mountain Meadows Massacre of 1857 in which Indians and Mormons murdered approximately 100 immigrants in a wagon train passing through Utah.
Taylor to Hunter, 1880–1995	During the 100 years that followed Young's death, Mormonism grew at a rapid rate. The church, which had a rather negative image during the 19th century, has become much more popular in the 20th century. It attracts new members partly by advocating family values and partly by not disclosing all the church's doctrines until converts are well within the fold.
	Ezra Taft Benson, who once served as a cabinet member in the federal government, was president of the church from 1985 to 1994. He was succeeded by Howard W. Hunter, who died after seving less than nine months—the shortest term in the church's history.
Gordon B. Hinckley 1995–	In 1995 Gordon B. Hinckley succeeded Howard W. Hunter as president.

THEOLOGY

The Doctrine of Revelation		
Position	*Support*	*Orthodox Response*
The church has four "Standard Works" that it views as authoritative and inspired Scripture: the Bible, the Book of Mormon (BOM), Doctrine and Covenants (D&C), and the Pearl of Great Price (PGP). Speeches and writings of the current president of the church are also authoritative.	"By the *standard works* of the Church is meant the following four volumes of scripture: The Bible, Book of Mormon, Doctrine and Covenants, and Pearl of Great Price.... These four volumes of scripture are the standards, the measuring rods, the gauges by which all things are judged. Since they are the will, mind, word, and voice of the Lord.... they are true.... When the living oracles speak in the name of the Lord or as moved upon by the Holy Ghost, however, their utterances are then binding upon all who hear ..." (*Mormon Doctrine*, 1977 ed., pp. 764–65).	The initial revelation of God is limited to the 39 books of the Old Testament. Jesus indicated these were authoritative by quoting from them (see, for example, Mt 5:27, 43; 7:23; 9:13; 10:35; 12:29, 40; 13:14–15, 43; 15:8–9; 19:5; 26:31; Luke 4:18–19; 23:30; John 13:18).
		The authoritative writings of the New Testament era are limited to (1) those written by apostles who were with Christ when He was on earth, and (2) those written by men recognized as authoritative by the apostles. This would exclude writings after the first century A.D.
		Even if God were to give additional revelations, they would have to be consistent with any prior revelations. This principle would eliminate Mormon writings, since they stand in direct opposition to the divine revelation that has already been given by God in the Bible.
The King James Bible is the most accurate translation and is used above all other versions.	"... the King James Version is by all odds the greatest of the completed English translations.... It is no wonder that the King James Version has been and remains the official version of the Church ..."(*Mormon Doctrine*, 1977 ed., pp. 422–23).	The King James Version of 1611 is an accurate translation of the Bible, yet it is not to be held in esteem over English translations that often reflect readings nearer to the original manuscripts.
The Bible is relegated to a position far below the other Standard Works because it is full of errors.	"... acceptance of the Bible is coupled with a reservation that it is true only insofar as translated correctly.... The other three, having been revealed in modern times in English, are accepted without qualification" (*Mormon Doctrine*, 1977 ed., p. 764). "As all informed persons know, the various versions of the Bible do not accurately record or perfectly preserve the words, thoughts, and intents of the original inspired authors" (Ibid., p. 383).	What is the standard? The Bible can be said to contain errors, but only if another work or works is said to be more authoritative. For all practical purposes, the Mormon statement implies that the Bible is always wrong whenever and wherever it conflicts with established LDS doctrine. This is unacceptable because it effectively places all Mormon writings in a position above Scripture. For all intents and purposes, the LDS church has made the Bible worthless. Scripture itself, however, assures us that it is profitable for teaching, reproof, correction, and training in righteousness (2Ti 3:16).

The Doctrine of Revelation (cont.)

Position	Support	Orthodox Response
Those who say the Bible should be the only source of authority are foolish.	"... many of the Gentiles shall say: A Bible! A Bible! We have got a Bible, and there cannot be any more Bible.... Thou fool, that shall say: A Bible, we have got a Bible, and we need no more Bible.... because that ye have a Bible ye need not suppose that it contains all my words; neither need ye suppose that I have not caused more to be written" (BOM, 2 Nephi 29:3, 6, 10).	The canonicity of the Old and New Testaments is dependent on the inspiration of the Holy Spirit through the prophets and apostles. A few works in the New Testament were recognized as inspired even though not written by an apostle but by a colleague of an apostle who wrote the work under the authority of that association. The church councils did not make books canonical but only recognized the authority inherent in the books based on apostolic authority and the inspiration of the Holy Spirit. No one has demonstrably occupied these offices since the time of the New Testament; the canon is closed.
The Book of Mormon, Doctrine & Covenants, and the Pearl of Great Price cover a wide range of subjects and are directly from God. They restore many truths that were taken away from the Bible.	"BOOK OF MORMON: One of the standard works of the church that has an account of God's dealings with the people of the American continents from about 2200 [B.C.] ... to 421 [A.D.].... It was translated from gold plates by Joseph Smith and contains the fulness of the gospel" (*Gospel Principles*, 1992, p. 375).	The Book of Mormon, which is said to be translated from gold plates, has been investigated by scholars in linguistics. It has been discovered that the supposed Reformed Egyptian characters that Joseph Smith copied from the Book of Mormon plates are gibberish. There is no existing evidence of a "Reformed Egyptian" language. Nor is there any evidence that the following words are Egyptian or Semetic: Shazar (1 Nephi 16:13–14), Irreantum (1 Nephi 17:5), deseret (for "bee," Ether 2:3), Liahona (Alma 37:38), or other words unique to the BOM. Moreover, although the Book of Mormon was written in the 19th century, it is written in King James English, which dates from the late 16th century. Does this indicate an attempt to authenticate the Book of Mormon by writing it to compare with the language of the KJV? As for the issue of authority, the Bible has stood the test of time concerning archaeological discoveries, while the Book of Mormon has not. Some scholars have left the church because they find discrepancies between Mormon claims and the historical record. Some of the more untenable aspects of the Book of Mormon are as follows: **Language Problems:** 1 Nephi 1:2 and Mosiah 1:4 say that the Hebrew native language from 600–91 B.C. was Egyptian and Mormon 9:32 says it was Reformed Egyptian by A.D. 400. Both assertions are incorrect. According to well-established history, the Hebrews spoke Hebrew in 600 B.C. Then, as a result of the Babylonian captivity (560–538 B.C.), the Hebrew language was spoken only by the scribes, priests,

The Doctrine of Revelation (cont.)

Position	Support	Orthodox Response
... continued		and rabbis while the rest of the people adopted Aramaic. In A.D. 70, when Titus forced them from Palestine, the Jews adopted the languages of the nations to which they were scattered. **Geographical Problems:** 1 Nephi 17:5 describes Arabia as "bountiful because of its much fruit and also wild honey." 1 Nephi 18:1 indicates that Arabia contained ample timber. Yet Arabia has never, in recorded history, had ample or bountiful supplies of timber, fruit, or honey. Arabia is only plentiful in supplies of sunshine, sand, and petroleum. • 1 Nephi 2:6–9 speaks of a river named Laman flowing continually to the Red Sea. In reality, there has been *no river at all* in Arabia in recorded history. **Zoological Problems:** 1 Nephi 18:25 asserts that North America had cows, oxen, asses, horses, and goats "for the use of man" in 600 B.C. The fact is that there were no such animals in North America until the Europeans brought them over many hundreds of years later. • 2 Nephi 21:6–8 plagiarizes Isaiah 11:6–8 from the KJV and applies it to North America (see also 2 Nephi 30:12–14). But North America had no sheep, lions, leopards, or two snakes (asps and cockatrices) at the time indicated by the BOM.
	"Doctrine and Covenants: One of the standard works of the church, containing revelations given to Joseph Smith and other latter-day Presidents of the Church" (*Gospel Principles,* 1998, p. 376). "The Pearl of Great Price contains the Book of Moses, the Book of Abraham, and some inspired writings of Joseph Smith" (Ibid., 1992, p. 54). "*Book of Moses*— ... Moses personally is the author of the Pentateuch or first five books of the Old Testament. ... these five books no longer contain many of the teachings and doctrines originally placed in them. ... by direct revelation in modern times the Lord has restored through the Prophet many of the great truths lost from the Mosaic Scriptures" (*Mormon Doctrine,* 1977 ed., p. 563). "*Book of Abraham*—This work was translated by the Prophet from a papyrus record taken from the catacombs of Egypt. ... Abraham was originally the	Like the BOM, the Doctrine and Covenants could hardly have come from God. This volume, first published in 1833 as the "Book of Commandments" and reprinted in 1835, allegedly contains revelations given by God to Joseph Smith and subsequent prophets of the Mormon church. But D&C has been changed numerous times throughout the years. For instance, what was originally a 141-word revelation in section 6 of the 1833 edition ended up as a 252-word revelation in section 7 of the 1835 edition. Section 19 gained an additional 64 words, section 20 received 388 more words, and section 28 (originally a mere 93 words in the 1833 edition) grew to 649 words in the 1835 edition. The 1935 edition also took several revelations—such as sections 17–21, which took place at the same place and time—and blended them into one continuous revelation. The Pearl of Great Price has also been shown not to live up to the claims made

The Doctrine of Revelation (cont.)

Position	Support	Orthodox Response
. . . continued	author, and the scriptural account contains priceless information about the gospel, pre-existence, the nature of Deity, the creation, the priesthood . . . which is not otherwise available" (Ibid., p. 564). "*Writings of Joseph Smith*—Three extracts from the Prophet's writings are here included: one, an extract from the Inspired Version of the Bible [a translation of the Bible done by Joseph Smith]; the second, extracts from the history of Joseph Smith; and the third, the statement of belief now called the Articles of Faith" (Ibid.). "Vision of the Redemption of the Dead is a vision given to President Joseph F. Smith, 3 October 1918 . . . sets forth the doctrine of the redemption of the dead" (*Gospel Principles*, p. 51).	for it. The number of facts that discredit this book are too numerous to mention here, but one particularly interesting example deserves mention. The *Book of Abraham* is allegedly Joseph Smith's translation of some Egyptian papyri. The actual papyri used by Smith was long thought to have been destroyed in a Chicago fire, but in 1967 it was discovered in New York City's Metropolitan Museum. Egyptologists and other scholars, after examining the texts, have confirmed that the scrolls are nothing but common Egyptian funeral texts belonging to the *Book of Breathings*, and what they say bears no resemblance to the *Book of Abraham*.
The Bible is only valuable when read and interpreted in light of the other LDS scriptures.	"When the Bible is read under the guidance of the Spirit, and in harmony with the many latter-day revelations which interpret and make plain its more mysterious parts, it becomes one of the most priceless volumes known to man" (*Mormon Doctrine*, 1977 ed., p. 83).	Again, this is an issue of authority. If other works are said to be more authoritative than the Bible, anything in the Bible can be called into question.

The Doctrine of God—*The Trinity*

Position	Support	Orthodox Response
There are many gods.	"How many Gods there are, I do not know. But there never was a time when there were not Gods" (Brigham Young, *Journal of Discourses* 7:333).	There is only one God (Dt 6:4; 33:26–27; Isa 43:10; 44:6; 45:5, 21; 46:9; 1Ti 2:5).
The Trinity is composed of three separate gods.	"Many men say there is one God; the Father, the Son, and the Holy Ghost are only one God! I say that is a strange God anyhow—three in one and one in three. . . . It would make the biggest God in all the world. He would be a wonderfully big God—he would be a giant or a monster" (Joseph Smith, Jr., *History of the Church* 6:476). "I have always declared God to be a distinct personage, Jesus Christ a separate and distinct personage from God the Father, and the Holy Ghost was a distinct personage and a Spirit: and these three constitute three distinct personages and three Gods" (Ibid., 6:474).	If we understand that there is more than one god, then there is really no sovereign God. God, if He is to be God at all, by necessity is all powerful, all knowing, and in complete control of the universe. If there were two or more gods, one would possess power and knowledge not held by the other or the many—an idea that negates either as God. The Mormon belief in many gods demonstrates what can happen when one accepts biblical passages that speak of God's plurality, but denies verses that set forth God's unity. The Trinity of orthodox Christians, which takes into consideration the full counsel of God, is the only logical way to reconcile both kinds of verses.

The Doctrine of God—*The Trinity (cont.)*

Position	Support	Orthodox Response
God the Father is an exalted man (a man who has progressed to godhood) with a body of flesh and bones.	"God himself was once as we are now, and is an exalted man.... I say, if you were to see him today, you would see him like a man in a form—like yourselves in all the person, image, and very form as a man" (*Teachings of the Prophet Joseph Smith*, 1973 ed., p. 345). "The Father has a body of flesh and bones as tangible as man's; the Son also" (D&C 130:22).	The Bible is most explicit in stating that God is not a man (Nu 23:19; 1Sa 15:29; Hos 11:9). God the Father, the eternal God, is Spirit (Isa 55:8–9; 6:1–5; 57:15; Pss 90:2; 113:5–6; 123:1; Jn 4:24; 8:23). Jesus said that a spirit does not have flesh and bones (Lk 24:39).
Neither the Father nor the Son nor the Holy Ghost is omnipresent.	"The Holy Ghost as a personage of Spirit can no more be omnipresent in person than can the Father or the Son" (*Mormon Doctrine*, 1977 ed., p. 752).	God is immanent, everywhere (Ps 139:7–12; Jer 23:24; Mt 28:19–20; Ac 1:8).
God the Father also has a father.	"The Prophet also taught... that there is 'a god above the Father of our Lord Jesus Christ.'... if Jesus had a Father, can we not believe that *he* had a Father also?" (*Mormon Doctrine*, 1977 ed., p. 577).	God the Father has always existed as the Father. He had no beginning; He had no father. The term "Father" implies that the Son is subordinate to the Father in function rather than implying that the Father conceived the Son (Isa 44:6; Rev 1:8; 21:6; 22:13). The term "Father" is also used to describe our relationship with God. Scripture often compares our relationship with our perfect Heavenly Father to the way we relate to our earthly, physical fathers (Lk 11:11–13). It must always be kept in mind, however, that the term "Father" is not indicative of gender. God is spirit; hence, He can be neither male nor female.
God the Father became a God after learning truth, aggressively pursuing godhood, and being obedient to the laws of the gospel.	"God undoubtedly took advantage of every opportunity to learn the laws of truth and as He became acquainted with each new verity He righteously obeyed it.... As He gained more knowledge through persistent effort and continuous industry, as well as through absolute obedience, His understanding of the universal laws continued to become more complete... until He attained the status of Godhood.... He became God by absolute obedience to all the eternal laws of the Gospel" (*The Gospel Through the Ages*, pp. 114–15).	God the Father has always existed as such (Dt 33:27; Isa 43:10; 44:6; 45:5, 21; 46:9; Mal 3:6; 1Co 8:4; 1Ti 2:5; Rev 1:8; 21:6; 22:13). As Psalms 90:2 and 93:2 state, God has been God "from eternity to eternity."
God the Father has a wife, through whom he procreates spirit children.	"Implicit in the Christian verity that all men are the spirit children of an *Eternal Father* is the usually unspoken truth that they are also the offspring of an *Eternal Mother*. An exalted and glorified Man of Holiness (Moses 6:57) could not be a Father unless a Woman of like glory, perfection, and holiness was associated with him as a Mother" (*Mormon Doctrine*, 1977 ed., p. 516).	The Godhead determined to make man in their image, not to procreate spirit children (Ge 1:26). Nowhere does Scripture even hint at the existence of an Eternal Mother.

The Doctrine of God—*The Trinity (cont.)*

Position	Support	Orthodox Response
God is not a uniquely eternal being. All spirit is self-existent matter and is eternal (without beginning or end). Such "matter" (called intelligences) sometimes becomes "organized" into a spirit being through birth to celestial parents. Then that spirit is born through human parents on earth. Like all people, God took this course and eventually reached Godhood.	". . . *spirit element* has always existed; it is co-eternal with God. . . . It is also called *intelligence*. . . . portions of the self-existent spirit element are born as spirit children, or in other words . . . is organized into intelligences" (*Mormon Doctrine*, 1977 ed., p. 751). "Abraham used the name *intelligences* to apply to the spirit children of the Eternal Father. . . . Use of this name designates both the primal element from which the spirit offspring were created and also their inherited capacity to grow in grace . . . until such intelligences . . . become like their Father, the Supreme Intelligence" (Ibid., p. 387; see also D&C 93:29, 33; *Abraham* 3:18–23).	God is not God unless He is all-powerful, all knowing, absolutely in charge. If God exists only as God because of support given from other intelligent forms, He is not God at all (Isa 44:6; Ro 3:4; Rev 1:8; 21:6; 22:13). Mormons rely heavily on extrabiblical revelations to substantiate their concept of God. In this quote from *Mormon Doctrine,* for example, Abraham is said to have spoken of spirit children and eternal spirit matter called "intelligences." These words come not from the Bible, but from LDS writings (specifically the *Book of Abraham,* which we have shown to be a fraud) that are allegedly restored truths that were either lost or intentionally removed from the Bible. Such assertions, which serve to undermine the authority of Scripture, have no basis in fact and cannot be proven.
God would stop being God if intelligences stopped supporting Him as God.	". . . the universe is filled with vast numbers of intelligences. . . . Elohim is God simply because all of these intelligences honor and sustain Him as such. . . . if He [God] should ever do anything to violate the confidence or 'sense of justice' of these intelligences, they would promptly withdraw their support, and the 'power' of God would disintegrate" (Former BYU Prof. W. Cleon Skousen, *The First 2000 Years*, p. 355).	God is unchangingly omnipotent, and no purpose of His can be thwarted. He is not overruled by anyone (Ge 17:1; Job 36:22–23; 42:2; Isa 14:26–27; 40:13–14; Jer 32:27; Mt 19:26; Lk 1:37; Ac 17:24–25; Rev 19:6).

The Doctrine of Jesus Christ—*The Deity of Christ*

Position	Support	Orthodox Response
Jesus, properly spoken of as being only one god among many gods, is Jehovah of the Old Testament (OT). Elohim is the name the OT gives to God the Father.	"Christ is *Jehovah*; they are one and the same Person" (*Mormon Doctrine*, 1977 ed., p. 392). "Elohim . . . is also used as the exalted name-title of God the Eternal Father" (Ibid., p. 224).	This is a contrived distinction that is impossible to support by the Old Testament Scriptures. The names "Yahweh" (Jehovah) and "Elohim" are used dozens of times in the same passage to refer to the same Being, not to two distinct persons (Ex 3:15; Dt 6:4; Pss 95:3–7; 99:6; 100:3; Jer 7:28; 10:10). In Psalm 83:18, Yahweh (not Elohim) is called the Most High over all the earth, and this was prior to the incarnation, death, and resurrection of Christ.
Jesus is not God the Son, the second person of the Trinity, who is equal to the Father.	"Jesus is greater than the Holy Spirit, which is subject unto him, but his Father is greater than he!" (Joseph Fielding Smith, *Doctrines of Salvation*, 1:18).	Jesus is God the Son, the second person of the Trinity, who is equal with the Father and the Spirit. Although they are different in function, they are equal in sharing the same nature (Jn 1:1–18; 8:58; 10:31–38; 20:28; Ac 20:28; Ro 9:5; Tit 2:13; 2Pe 1:1; Mt 28:19–20).

The Doctrine of Jesus Christ—*The Humanity of Christ*

Position	Support	Orthodox Response
Before becoming a man, Jesus existed in the spirit world as the eldest of many spirit children born to God the Father.	"He [Jesus] was the most intelligent, the most faithful, and the most Godlike of all the sons and daughters of our Heavenly Father in the spirit world" (*The Gospel Through the Ages*, p. 21). "Among the spirit children of Elohim the firstborn was and is Jehovah or Jesus Christ" (*Articles of Faith*, p. 472).	Jesus has existed for all eternity as God the Son, with God the Father and God the Holy Spirit. He did not come into existence after the Father (Mic 5:2; Ps 90:2; Jn 1:1; Col 1:17).
Jesus, who was appointed in eternity past to save mankind, is the spirit-brother of Lucifer in a historical sense as spirit children of the Heavenly Parents, but not in an ethical sense. (That is, Christ is morally opposed to everything that Lucifer represents.)	"The holy Scriptures give an account of a great council which was held in the spirit world before man was placed on the earth. This meeting . . . was presided over by God our eternal Father; and those in attendance were His sons and daughters. . . . Eternal Father explained to the assembled throng . . . the great 'Gospel plan of salvation.' . . . The appointment of Jesus to be the Savior of the world was contested by one of the other sons of God. He was called Lucifer. . . . this spirit-brother of Jesus desparately tried to become the Savior" (*The Gospel Through the Ages*, pp. 12–15).	Jesus cannot possibly be the "spirit-brother" of Lucifer because, as God the Son, Jesus is Lucifer's creator. If Jesus was the agent of creation, then He could not be Lucifer's peer. Lucifer is a fallen angel (Jn 1:1–3; 1Co 8:6; Col 1:16–17; Heb 1:2; Lk 10:18), whereas Jeus is consistently described as God's only-begotten (*monogenes*, Gr.), or one of a kind, Son. The Mormon view is also impossible because, for it to be true, many other Mormon doctrines—such as God's existence as an exalted man, the reality of an Eternal Mother, and Jesus' origin as a spirit baby—would have to be true. These doctrines, however, are false.

The Doctrine of Jesus Christ—*The Humanity of Christ (cont.)*

Position	Support	Orthodox Response
Jesus was not miraculously begotten by the Holy Spirit or born of a virgin. He was begotten through sexual intercourse between Mary and God the Father.	"CHRIST NOT BEGOTTEN OF HOLY GHOST.... Christ was begotten of God. He was not born without the aid of Man and *that Man was God*" (Joseph Fielding Smith, *Doctrines of Salvation*, 1:18). "Christ was begotten by an Immortal Father in the same way that mortal men are begotten by mortal fathers" (*Mormon Doctrine*, 1977 ed., p. 547). "The birth of the Saviour was as natural as are the births of our children; it was the result of natural action. He partook of flesh and blood—was begotten of his Father, as we were of our fathers" (Brigham Young, *Journal of Discourses* 8:115). "I was naturally begotten; so was my father, and also my Saviour Jesus Christ. According to the Scriptures, he is the first begotten of his father in flesh, and there was nothing unnatural about it" (Apostle Heber C. Kimball, *Journal of Discourses* 8:211).	Jesus was miraculously begotten by the Holy Spirit. Mary was a virgin at the time and remained a virgin until after Jesus was born (Mt 1:18–20; Lk 1:26–38).
Jesus was a polygamist who was married to at least Mary Magdalene, Mary the sister of Lazarus, and Martha. Jesus also had children through His multiple marriages. This doctrine, taught by early LDS leaders, is minimalized today but not denied.	"...there was a marriage in Cana of Galilee; and on careful reading of that transaction, it will be discovered that no less a person than Jesus Christ was married on that occasion.... Object not, therefore, too strongly against the marriage of Christ" (Brigham Young, *Journal of Discourses* 4:259–60). "When Mary of old came to the sepulchre... she saw two angels.... 'And they say unto her, Woman why weepest thou? She said unto them, Because they have taken away my Lord,' or husband" (Apostle Orson Hyde, *Journal of Discourses* 2:81). "I said, in my lecture on Marriage, at our last Conference, that Jesus Christ was married at Cana of Galilee, that Mary, Martha and others were his wives, and that he begat children" (Ibid., 2:210).	Jesus was never married, let alone a polygamist. The Bible in no way alludes to the idea that Jesus was married. John 2:2 says Jesus was invited to the wedding feast. A bridegroom is not invited to his own wedding. Jesus' relationship with Mary Magdalene was a result of Jesus' forgiveness of her sin. She was involved in worshiping the Lord. Jesus' relationship with Mary the sister of Lazarus was surely that of friendship with the entire family. Again, what we see here are doctrines that come not from the BIble, but from the darkened minds of LDS leaders.

The Doctrine of Jesus Christ—*The Resurrection of Christ*

Position	Support	Orthodox Response
Although Jesus rose from the grave with an immortalized body, His resurrection did not destroy death and sin. It only ensured that all men would be resurrected (brought back to life) with a permanently joined body and soul.	"The facts of Christ's resurrection from the dead are attested by such an array of scriptural proofs that no doubt of the reality finds place in the mind of any believer in the inspired records" (*Articles of Faith*, pp. 385–86). "The resurrection of Christ brings to pass the resurrection of all men" (*What the Mormons Think of Christ*, p. 26).	The death of Jesus satisfied the holiness and justice of the Father in relation to the sin of mankind and the punishment for sin. Christ is the propitiation for our sins (1Jn 2:12). Our transgressions are forgiven in light of God's having taken away the certificate of debt and nailing it to the cross (Col 2:13–15). Peace with God is possible through Jesus Christ because sin and death have been dealt with completely on the cross (Ro 5:1).

The Doctrine of the Holy Spirit

Position	Support	Orthodox Response
The Holy Ghost is a spirit man, the third god in the Trinity. The Holy Spirit is an impersonal influence that proceeds from the Father. (This distinction is drawn from the KJV use of both terms.)	"The Holy Ghost is an individual personage, the third member of the Godhead; the Holy Spirit, in a distinctive sense, is the 'divine essence' by means of which the Godhead operates upon man and in nature" (*Articles of Faith*, p. 488).	There is no distinction between the Holy Spirit and the Holy Ghost in the Bible. These are simply synonyms for the same Greek expression. The Holy Spirit is the third person of the Trinity, is fully God, and has intellect, emotion, and will. He has the same attributes as the other two persons of the Trinity, yet is distinguished from them (Mt 28:19; Mk 3:28–29; Jn 14:26; 16:7–14; Ac 5:3–4; Ro 15:30; 1Co 2:10–13; 12:11; Eph 4:30).

The Doctrine of Man and Sin

Position	Support	Orthodox Response
Man is an eternal being like God because he originally came from eternal spiritual matter. After God reached the status of Godhood, He and His celestial wife procreated spirit children.	"Man was also in the beginning with God. Intelligence, or the light of truth, was not created or made, neither indeed can be" (D&C 93:29). "Life, intelligence, mind, the 'light of truth,' or whatever name one gives to the center of the personality of man, is an uncreated, eternally existent, indestructible entity.... In the first stage, man was an eternally existent being termed an intelligence.... The next realm where man dwelt was the spirit world.... eternally-existing intelligences were clothed with spirit bodies.... numerous sons and daughters were begotten and born of heavenly parents into that eternal family in the spirit world" (*The Gospel Through the Ages*, pp. 126–27).	Man is a finite being, not an eternal one. The first man Adam was created at a specific point in time (Ge 1:26–27; 2:7; 1Co 15:45–49). Man did not exist in the beginning when God was creating the universe, for if he had, God's question to Job would have made no sense (Job 38:4). Man was created lower than the angels, so that David wondered why God is even mindful of him (Pss 8:3–5; 144:3). Not a single verse in the Bible suggests that God has a wife, but Isaiah 44:24 explicitly says that the Lord made all things by Himself. Moreover, several passages in Isaiah indicate that there is only one God and there is none beside Him (44:8; 45:6) or like Him (46:9).

The Doctrine of Man and Sin (cont.)

Position	Support	Orthodox Response
Jesus came into existence in the same way all men did. Consequently, He is *literally* our elder brother. Everyone lived a life with Jesus in heaven before coming to earth.	"... these spirit children were organized, possessing divine, eternal, and godlike attributes, inherited from their Heavenly Father and Mother. There in the spirit world they were reared to maturity, becoming grown spirit men and women prior to coming upon this earth" (*The Gospel Through the Ages*, p. 127). "Jesus is man's spiritual brother. We dwelt with Him in the spirit world as members of that large society of eternal intelligences, which included our Heavenly Parents and all the personages who have become mortal beings upon this earth or who ever shall come here to dwell.... Jesus was the 'firstborn,' and so He is our eldest brother" (Ibid., p. 21).	Jesus was and is Almighty God from everlasting to everlasting. He is the creator of all that exists and is "firstborn" over all creation in the sense that He is the preeminent originator of life and the universe (Mic 5:2; Ps 90:2; Jn 1:1–3; Ac 3:14–15; Col 1:16–17; Heb 1:2). This meaning for the word "firstborn" can be understood by comparing Genesis 41:51–52, which states that Manasseh was Joseph's "firstborn" son while Ephraim was the second, with Jeremiah 31:9, where God calls Ephraim the "firstborn." Obviously, "firstborn" does not always mean the one literally born first.
After being raised in the spirit world, the spirits come to earth in "tabernacles of flesh" (human bodies). They are made to forget their pre-earthly existence.	"Following his stay in the spirit world, man comes on earth in a probationary state prepatory to the eternal existence beyond the mortal confines of this world [in preparation for life after they die on earth].... It is true that when we are born into mortality a veil is drawn over our minds, so that we have forgotten our pre-mortal life" (*The Gospel Through the Ages*, p. 128).	Man has no pre-earthly existence. The body and soul of each person is formed in his mother's womb (Pss 119:73; 139:13–16; Job 10:8–12; 31:15; Zec 12:1) . Although the Scripture says that God "knew" Jeremiah before He formed him in the womb, this does not indicate pre-existence but rather God's foreknowledge and omniscience, as He "calls those things which do not exist as though they did" (Ro 4:17 NKJV).
Eventually each person dies and awaits the resurrection and judgment, when they will be given either rewards or punishments.	"... mortal death comes upon all. The eternal spirit goes to the spirit world to await resurrection and judgment" (*The Gospel Through the Ages*, pp. 128–29).	This is an orthodox statement.
Death and sin came through the fall of Adam and Eve. But their deed was not actually a "sin." It was really a blessing because it enabled man to continue progressing on toward eternal life.	"They [the Christian world] have been long taught that Adam and Eve were great transgressors.... We, the children of Adam ... should rejoice with them, that through their fall and the atonement of Jesus Christ, the way of eternal life has been opened up to us" (*Articles of Faith*, p. 476).	Rejoicing is hardly the proper response to Adam's sin. Because of that sin, both Adam and Eve died spiritually and their physical bodies began to deteriorate. Eve was given pain and sorrow in child-bearing, Adam was required to work and sweat in order to eat, the entire creation was cursed, they were thrown out of the Garden forever, and the entire human race was destined to be born dead in sins and children of God's wrath by nature (Ge 3:16–24; Ro 3:23; 5:12–15, 17–19; 8:19–22; Eph 2:1–5; 1Jn 3:4).

The Doctrine of Salvation

Position	Support	Orthodox Response
Christ's death on the cross (the atonement) canceled the penalty of death imposed on all men through Adam's sin, thereby ensuring that all men would be redeemed—resurrected and given immortality (the reuniting of spirit with body)—as a gift.	"If there had been no atonement, temporal death would have remained forever, and there never would have been a resurrection. The body would have remained forever in the grave" (*Mormon Doctrine*, 1977 ed., p. 63). "Redemption from death, through the sufferings of Christ, is for all men, both the righteous and the wicked" (Ibid., p. 65). "Immortality is a free gift which comes by grace alone without works on man's part" (Ibid., p. 377).	Not everyone is blessed through Christ's crucifixion. Only those who accept His sacrifice and surrender themselves to Him (Ro 10:9) will receive the benefit of Jesus' death and resurrection, which is forgiveness of sins (Ac 10:43) and salvation (Ro 3:24). Eternal life "in Christ," and not just simply eternal existence through resurrection, is the gift offered by God to humanity (Ro 6:23). This gift is obtainable only by grace through faith (Eph 2:8–10). Jesus' death serves to reconcile all believers to God (Ro 5:10). In dying, Jesus broke down the wall of separation between us and God that was present through man's disobedience to the Law (Eph 2:11–22).
Christ's death cannot remove personal sins. It can only provide for people an opportunity to remove their own sins and achieve salvation (eternal life).	"**The Individual Effect of the Atonement** makes it possible for any and every soul to obtain absolution from the effect of personal sins, through the mediation of Christ; but such saving intercession is to be invoked by individual effort as manifested through faith, repentance, and continued works of righteousness. . . . the blessing of redemption from individual sins, while open for all to attain, is nevertheless conditioned on individual effort" (*Articles of Faith*, p. 89). ". . . redemption from personal sins can only be obtained through obedience to the requirements of the gospel, and a life of good works" (Ibid., pp. 478–79). ". . . individual salvation or rescue from the effects of personal sins is to be acquired by each for himself, by faith and good works" (Ibid., p. 476).	Jesus paid the price for all our personal sins (1Co 15:3; 1Pe 3:18). Paul declares that Jesus gave himself "for our sins" (Gal 1:4; Heb 9:28; 10:12). Jesus actually "bore our sins in his body" (1Pe 2:24). The truth presented here cannot be made any clearer: Jesus paid for our sins as well as for the sin of Adam. We cannot be justified by works. Any who try to do so will actually have their good works counted against them as debt (Ro 4:4). Those who believe in Him, apart from works, are the ones justified (Ro 4:5).
Salvation (eternal life) must be earned. It is not a gift of God.	"*Eternal life* is the reward for 'obedience to the laws and ordinances of the Gospel'" (*Mormon Doctrine*, 1977 ed., p. 62). ". . . it is by grace that we are saved, after all we can do" (BOM, 2 Nephi 25:23).	As previously indicated, eternal life is a gift (Ro 6:23; Eph 2:8–10), not a reward.

The Doctrine of Rewards and Punishment

Position	Support	Orthodox Response
The first phase of the afterlife is known as "spirit prison." In a general sense it is the realm of the dead where deceased individuals await the resurrection and judgment. Righteous spirits wait in Paradise while unrighteous spirits wait in hell. Christ bridged the gulf between the two places so that those in Paradise and hell could freely mingle. This enables unrighteous spirits to repent and gain salvation through the gospel preached to them by the righteous spirits.	". . . the whole spirit world (including both paradise and hell) is a *spirit prison*. . . . In a more particular sense, however, the *spirit prison* is hell, that portion of the spirit world where the wicked dwell. . . . Before Christ bridged the gulf between paradise and hell—so that the righteous could mingle with the wicked and preach them the gospel—the wicked in hell were confined to locations which precluded them from contact with the righteous in paradise. . . . Now that the righteous spirits in paradise have been commissioned to carry the message of salvation to the wicked spirits in hell. . . . Repentance opens the the prison doors to the spirits in hell; it enables those bound with the chains of hell to free themselves from darkness, unbelief, ignorance, and sin. As rapidly as they can overcome these obstacles—gain light, believe truth, acquire intelligence, cast off sin, and break the chains of hell—they can leave the hell . . . and dwell with the righteous in the peace of paradise" (*Mormon Doctrine*, 1977 ed., p. 755). "The wicked and ungodly will suffer the vengeance of eternal fire in hell until they finally obey Christ, repent of their sins, and gain forgiveness therefrom" (Ibid., p. 816).	Hebrews 9:27 states that it is appointed for a man to die once, after which will come the judgment. There is no open door left for people to hear the gospel preached to them in some kind of spirit prison. Paul declared that "now is the day of salvation" (2Co 6:2). Is this fair? Some may be tempted to answer no. What about those who live in remote parts of the world and have never heard the gospel? But who are we to decide what is fair and what is not? We are created beings who have an extremely limited perspective that is itself filtered through a multitude of sin-tainted thoughts and feelings. God, by contrast, is absolutely holy and unencumbered by our limitations. He is wholly righteous and full of truth (Ps 96:12–13). As such, we can rest aassured that God will judge fairly on the last day (Ps 19:9). As one missionary to the Mormons has aptly stated: "The Lord will make a way for the desiring heart to hear the Gospel regardless of geographical barriers" (Bill McKeever, *Answering Mormons' Questions*, p. 90).
There are three degrees of glory, corresponding to kingdoms of the same name: the telestial glory/kingdom; the terrestrial glory/kingdom; and the celestial glory/kingdom. **"General salvation," which involves obtaining a position in one of the first two glories/kingdoms (that is, telestial or terrestrial), is achieved by nearly everyone (non-Mormons and "lukewarm" Mormons).**	". . . there are in eternity *kingdoms of glory* to which all resurrected persons (except the sons of perdition) will eventually go . . . *celestial, terrestrial,* and *telestial*" (*Mormon Doctrine*, 1977 ed., p. 420). "Most of the adult people who have lived from the day of Adam to the present time will go to the *telestial kingdom*. . . . They will be the endless hosts of people . . . who have been carnal, sensual, and devilish; who have chosen the vain philosophies of the world rather than accept the testimony of Jesus; who have been liars, thieves, sorcerers and adulterers, blasphemers and murderers" (Ibid., p. 778). "To the *terrestrial kingdom* will go: 1. Accountable persons who die without law. . . . 2. Those who reject the gospel in this life and who reverse their course and accept it in the spirit world [see explanation that follows]; 3. Honorable men on earth who are blinded by the craftiness of men and who therefore do not accept and live the gospel law; and 4. Members of The Church [LDS] . . . who are not valiant, but who are instead lukewarm in their devotion to the Church and to righteousness" (Ibid., p. 784).	This LDS doctrine can be seen as a radical misinterpretation of 1 Corinthians 15:40–41, supplemented by D&C 76. It comes from the many extrabiblical writings Mormons have adopted as authoritative. Scripture presents only two ultimate destinations for human beings, apart from works: (1) eternal life with God (salvation); and (2) eternal separation from God (the Lake of Fire).

The Doctrine of Rewards and Punishment (cont.)

Position	Support	Orthodox Response
Those who do not go to one of the kingdoms of glory are termed "sons of perdition." **Sons of Perdition include Satan and all his angels, any who have willingly rejected LDS teachings, apostates from the LDS Church, and extremely evil people. All these will be assigned to the outer darkness for all eternity.**	"Those in this life who gain a perfect knowledge of the divinity of the gospel cause ... and come out in open rebellion, also become sons of perdition. Their destiny ... is to be cast out with the devil and his angels.... their torment is as a lake of fire and brimstone" (*Mormon Doctrine*, 1977 ed., pp. 746, 759). "Those who have committed the unpardonable sin ... will be cast out as sons of perdition to dwell with the devil and his angels in eternity.... To commit this unpardonable crime a man must receive the gospel, gain from the Holy Ghost by revelation the absolute knowledge of the divinity of Christ and then deny 'the new and everlasting covenant by which he was sanctified, calling it an unholy thing.' ... This is the case with many apostates of The Church of Jesus Christ of Latter-day Saints" (Ibid., pp. 816–17).	This teaching would appear to be nothing less than an attempt to silence critics of the Mormon church. Scripture describes the Lake of Fire simply as the destination for those who reject Jesus Christ (Mt 7:21–23; 25:46; Rev 20:15). The word *as* is their loophole (in "as a lake of fire ..."), that is, outer darkness is torment, but without flames.
Only life in the celestial kingdom is considered heaven. This celestial kingdom itself has three degrees/heavens/ glories. The highest degree is known as exaltation, or eternal life in the truest sense of the words. This is the reward for which Mormons are working. Only Mormonism offers such salvation. **The whole process of obtaining "salvation" (exaltation/ eternal life) is known as eternal progression. It is the same process God the Father went through in order to become God. Mormons hope to receive the same reward—godhood.**	"In its most important sense, *heaven is the celestial kingdom of God*" (*Mormon Doctrine*, 1977 ed., p. 348). "In the celestial glory there are three heavens or degrees" (D&C 131:1). "*Salvation* in its true and full meaning is synonymous with *exaltation* or *eternal life* and consists in gaining an inheritance in the highest of the three heavens within the celestial kingdom.... It is the salvation which the saints seek.... There is no salvation outside The Church of Jesus Christ of Latter-day Saints" (*Mormon Doctrine*, 1977 ed., p. 670). "... the ultimate goal of eternal progression is to receive eternal life, i.e., to become as God is" (*The Gospel Through the Ages*, p. 106). "... those who gain eternal life receive exaltation.... They are gods" (*Mormon Doctrine*, 1977 ed., p. 237). "Those who have been born unto God through obedience to the Gospel may by valiant devotion to righteousness obtain exaltation and even reach the status of godhood" (*Articles of Faith*, p. 470). "That exaltation which the saints of all ages have so devoutly sought is *godhood* itself. Godhood is to have the character, possess the attributes, and enjoy the perfections which the Father has. It is to do what he does, have the powers resident in him, and live as he lives" (*Mormon Doctrine*, 1977 ed., p. 321).	It has been shown that Scripture teaches there is only one God. In Isaiah 43:10, God declares, "Before me no God was formed, nor will there be one after me." God would surely know if there were any other Gods in existence. Also, God asks in Isaiah 44:8, "Is there any God besides me?" His answer is clear: "I know not one." The result is that no matter how sincere they may be, Mormons will never achieve godhood.

The Doctrine of Rewards and Punishment (cont.)

Position	Support	Orthodox Response
We can become gods because we are the literal offfpring of beings who were once like us and progressed to godhood.	"... since mortal beings are the spirit children of Heavenly Parents ... the ultimate possibility is for some of them to become exalted to Godhood" (*The Gospel Through the Ages*, p. 104).	Mormon arguments in favor of man's eventual godhood are flawed because they are built on faulty premises—namely, other LDS doctrines.
	"God the Eternal Father was once a mortal man who passed through a school of earth life similar to that through which we are now passing. He became God—an exalted being—through obedience to the same eternal Gospel truths that we are given opportunity today to obey" (Ibid.).	The church teaches that it is only natural for the spirit children of Heavenly Parents to grow up into gods like their parents. But what if there are no Heavenly Parents to begin with?
	"'*As man is, God once was; as God is, man may become*'" (Lorenzo Snow, *Millennial Star* 54:404, as quoted in *The Gospel Through the Ages*, pp. 105–6).	Mormons also teach man's eternal progression to godhood since God Himself—who is simply a man like us (only more advanced)—traveled along a similar course to godhood. But what if God is not a man like us and has not had to advance to godhood at all?
	"Here, then, is eternal life—to know the only wise and true God; and you have got to learn how to be Gods yourselves.... the same as all Gods have done before you,—namely, by going from one small degree to another.... To inherit the same power, the same glory and the same exaltation, until you arrive at the station of a God, and ascend the throne of eternal power" (Joseph Smith, Jr., *Journal of Discourses* 6:4).	Unfortunately, Mormons customarily, perhaps out of wishful thinking, lean on the church's doctrines rather than the Bible.

INTERESTING AND DISTINCTIVE BELIEFS

Position	Support	Orthodox Response
Mormons have buildings called "temples" in which secret and sacred ceremonies take place. Only Mormons in good standing, after meeting several requirements, can attend these secret services.	"Certain gospel ordinances are of such a sacred and holy nature that the Lord authorizes their performance only in holy sanctuaries.... Except in circumstances of great poverty and distress, these ordinances can be performed only in temples" (*Mormon Doctrine*, 1977 ed., p. 779).	Much of what comprises secret temple ceremonies can be traced directly back to Joseph Smith's involvment with Freemasonry. Only six weeks after his initiation into Masonry on March 15, 1842, Smith instituted the secret temple endowments based on what he had experienced there.

Jesus, in contrast to Joseph Smith, did nothing in secret: "I have spoken openly to the world . . . I said nothing in secret" (Jn 18:20). |
| **One temple ordinance (ceremony), "baptism for the dead," is the practicing of baptizing living persons for dead persons who accept the gospel in the Spirit world. It is an ordinance of salvation. Other temple ordinances further the exaltation process for living Mormons.** | "Baptism for the dead, an ordinance opening the door to the celestial kingdom to worthy persons not priviledged to undergo gospel schooling while in mortality, is . . . an ordinance of salvation. All other temple ordinances—washings, anointings, endowments, sealings—pertain to exaltation within the celestial kingdom" (*Mormon Doctrine*, 1977 ed., p. 779). | According to Luke 16:26, those who die in unbelief have no means of crossing over to where believers dwell, especially through any form of baptism by proxy performed by people still living on earth. The only biblical passage that mentions "baptism" for the dead—1 Corinthians 15:29—clearly indicates that Paul is referring to individuals who were baptizing for the dead while at the same time denying the resurrection. His point was simply to show the self-contradiction: "Else what shall they do which are baptized for the dead, if the dead rise not at all?" (KJV). Note that Paul, by using the word "they," apparently distinguished himself from the people who were baptizing for the dead. |
| **One temple ordinance necessary for exaltation is marriage because Mormons believe that after death couples remain married and produce children. People who die unmarried will never be able to continue in a family unit or procreate spirit children. Consequently, these people will never obtain godhood (exaltation/salvation).** | "Marriages performed in the temples . . . are called *celestial marriages*" (*Mormon Doctrine*, 1977 ed., p. 117).

"Celestial marriage is the gate to *exaltation*, and exaltation consists in the continuation of the family unit in eternity" (Ibid., p. 257).

". . . by definition exaltation consists in continuation of the family unit in eternity.... *The most important things that any member of The Church of Jesus Christ of Latter-day Saints ever does in this world are: 1. To marry the right person, in the right place, by the right authority*" (Ibid., pp. 117–18). | Marriage is a temporal blessing for earth, not heaven. Jesus said that in the resurrection people neither marry, nor are they given in marriage (Mt 22:29–30). Romans 7:1–4 states that death releases people from their marriage commitment. Moreover, we cannot be married in heaven because all believers together—the entire church—will constitute the bride of Christ (2Co 11:2; Rev 19:9). |

Position	Support	Orthodox Response
Only Mormon men can hold what is termed the Priesthood. It is the power and authority to act on behalf of God for the salvation of men.	"... priesthood is the power and authority of God delegated to man on earth to act in all things for the salvation of men. It is the power by which the gospel is preached; by which the ordinances of salvation are performed ... by which men are sealed up unto eternal life.... 'There are, in the church, two priesthoods, namely, the Melchizedek and Aaronic, including the Levitical Priesthood'" (*Mormon Doctrine*, 1977 ed., pp. 594–95).	The Bible describes the priesthood as a position that allowed one to act on behalf of other people in matters pertaining to God (Heb 5:1).

Furthermore, the Old Testament priesthood has been changed (Heb 7:11–16). There is now only one high priest (Jesus) who represents us (1Ti 2:5) and lives forever after the order of Melchizedek (Heb 7:17, 21). Even if the OT priesthoods were still in effect, Mormons could not fill such positions because they would have to be literal descendents of Aaron (Nu 3:10).

The only priesthood available to Christians is the one shared by all believers—the royal priesthood belonging to those washed of their sins through the shed blood of Christ (1Pe 2:5–6; Rev 1:5–6). |
| **Since its founding, the church has taught that African people are "inferior" spirits who were cursed by God because of their conduct during the pre-earth life. The mark of their curse, black skin and a flat nose, was placed on Cain (the son of Adam and Eve), from whom they all sprang. Because of this curse, persons of African descent were not allowed to hold the priesthood until June 1978 when, after mounting social presssure, members of the Negro race were admitted.** | "Those who were less valiant in pre-existence ... are known to us as the *negroes*. Such spirits are sent to earth through the lineage of Cain ... are denied the priesthood ... are not equal with other races where the receipt of certain spiritual blessings are concerned.... this inequality is not of man's origin. It is the Lord's doing ..." (*Mormon Doctrine*, 1977 ed., p. 527).

"You see some classes of the human family that are black, uncouth, uncomely, disagreeable, and low in their habits, wild, and seemingly deprived of nearly all the blessings of the intelligence that is generally bestowed upon mankind.... Cain slew his brother ... and the Lord put a mark upon him, which is the flat nose and black skin" (Brigham Young, *Journal of Discourses* 7:290).

"Not only was Cain called upon to suffer, but because of his wickedness he became the father of an inferior race" (Joseph Fielding Smith, *The Way to Perfection*, p. 101).

"Shall I tell you the law of God in regard to the African race? If the white man who belongs to the chosen seed mixes his blood with the seed of Cain, the penalty, under the law of God, is death on the spot. This will always be so" (Brigham Young, *Journal of Discourses* 10:110).

"From the days of the Prophet Joseph even until now, it has been the doctrine of the Church, never questioned by any of the Church leaders, that the Negroes are not entitled to the full blessings of the Gospel. Furthermore, your ideas, as we understand them, appear to contemplate the intermar- | Any system of religious beliefs that includes racism is incompatible with the Christian doctrine of love. God is no respecter of persons (Ac 10:34–35). There are absolutely no racial distinctions in God's economy (Gal 3:28). This is because we are all related to one another through our common ancestors Adam and Eve (Ge 3:20).

The fact that the LDS church has finally admitted the black race to the priesthood in no way erases the racism that was so blatantly promoted by Mormonism for 140 years, especially as a matter of revelation to the church. |

Position	Support	Orthodox Response
. . . continued	riage of the Negro and White races, a concept which has heretofore been most repugnant to most normal-minded people. . . . there is a growing tendency. . . . 'toward the breaking down of race barriers in the matter of intermarriage between whites and blacks, but it does not have the sanction of the Church and is contrary to Church doctrine' " (*Letter of LDS Presidency to Dr. Lowery Nelson*, July 17, 1947, as quoted in *Mormonism and the Negro*, pp. 46–47). "Had I anything to do with the negro, I would confine them by strict law to their own species" (Joseph Smith, Jr., *History of the Church*, 5:217–18).	
The Garden of Eden was originally located in Jackson County, Missouri. In fact, remnants of an altar built by Adam himself were still in existence during Joseph Smith's day.	". . . the Garden of Eden was located in what is known to us as the land of Zion, an area for which Jackson County, Missouri, is the center place. . . . Our revelations recite: 'Three years previous to the death of Adam, he called Seth, Enos, Cainan, Mahalaleel, Jared, Enoch, and Methuselah . . . and there bestowed upon them his last blessing.' . . . 'At that great gathering Adam offered sacrifices on an altar built for the purpose. A remnant of that very altar remained on the spot down through the ages.' On May 19, 1838, Joseph Smith and a number of his associates stood on the remainder of the pile of stones at a place called Spring Hill, Davies County, Missouri" (*Mormon Doctrine*, 1977 ed., pp. 20–21).	No one knows the exact location of Eden, but it certainly was not located in the vicinity of present-day Missouri. Genesis 2:11–14 names four rivers that were near Eden: the Pishon, the Gihon, the Tigris, and the Euphrates. This would place Eden somewhere in the Middle East. Mormon Scriptures contradict each other on this point. The Doctrine & Covenants places Adam in the Americas (107:53; 116:1; 117:8) while the Pearl of Great Price places him in the Old World (*Book of Moses* 3:10–13).
Mormonism has never denied the principle of polygamy (having more than one wife) and practiced it until pressure from the United States government forced the church to abandon its "plural marriage" doctrine in 1890. Mormons claim plural marriages stopped because of a revelation given to Wiford Woodruff, president of the church at the time.	"*I have constantly said no man shall have but one wife at a time, unless the Lord directs otherwise*" (*Teachings of the Prophet Joseph Smith*, p. 324). ". . . as part of the promised restitution of all things, the Lord revealed the principle of *plural marriage* to the Prophet" (*Mormon Doctrine*, 1977 ed., p. 578). "After Brigham Young led the saints to the Salt Lake Valley, plural marriage was openly taught and practiced until the year 1890. At that time conditions were such that the Lord *by revelation* withdrew the command to continue the practice. . . . the holy practice will commence again after the Second Coming of the Son of Man and the ushering in of the millennium" (Ibid., p. 578).	God created Eve to be Adam's helper, not Eve, Sally, Gina, and Annette. Genesis 2:24 outlines God's perfect plan for marriage: one woman and one man (see also Mt 19:5 and Mk 10:7–8). "The singular wife is used in every case, never wives" (Bill McKeever, *Answering Mormons' Questions*, p. 97). Paul the apostle similarly spoke of every man having his own *wife* and of every woman having her own *husband* (1Co 7:2). He also directed that church leaders have only one wife (1Ti 3:2). Although we indeed find Old Testament figures in polygamous relationships, this does not constitute an endorsement of the practice any more than the biblical account of David's experiences with Bathsheba thereby suggests that we should commit fornication, adultery, and murder. As another example, Abraham is several times caught in a lie, but this does not imply that we should imitate his bad habit. Polygamy, like these other ungodly acts, was never at any point in Scripture sanctioned by God.

Position	Support	Orthodox Response
Church members must abstain from alcohol, tobacco, coffee, and tea. This practice is called the "Word of Wisdom."	"Word of Wisdom is the common title for a revelation that counsels Latter-day Saints on maintaining good health.... 'The practice of abstaining from all forms of ALCOHOL, TOBACCO, COFFEE, and TEA... derives from this revelation" (*Encyclopedia of Mormonism*, p. 1584).	Jesus said that what defiles a man is not what goes into his mouth, but what comes out of it (Mt 15:11). Paul seemed to express the same sentiment when he discussed foods offered to idols. In short, Paul said that whatever is received with a clean conscience is permissible. His only restriction was not to eat if so doing would offend a weaker fellow believer (Ro 14:20–23).
In the Garden of Gethsemane Jesus took upon himself the sins of the world and atoned for man—not on the cross.	"There [in Gethsemane] He suffered the pains of all men.... It was in Gethsemane that Jesus took on Himself the sins of the world.... His pain was equivalent to the cumulative burden of all men" (*Teachings of Ezra Taft Benson*, p.14).	Jesus bore the sins of the world on the cross (1Pe 2:24). Peace between God and us was accomplished through the blood Jesus shed on the cross (Col 1:20), not while in Gethsemane.
There are some sins that Jesus' blood cannot cleanse. These are sins for which people must spill their own blood. This doctrine, known as the doctrine of "blood atonement," is rarely discussed publicly by Mormons.	"There are sins that men commit for which they cannot receive forgiveness... if they had their eyes open to see their true condition, they would be perfectly willing to have their blood spilt upon the ground, that the smoke thereof might ascend to heaven as an offering for their sins; and the smoking incense would atone for their sins.... there are transgressors, who, if they knew... the only condition upon which they can obtain forgiveness, would beg of their brethren to shed their blood.... It is true that the blood of the Son of God was shed for sins... yet men can commit sins which it can never remit" (Brigham Young, *Journal of Discourses* 4:53–54). "I replied, I was opposed to hanging, even if a man kill another, I will shoot him, or cut off his head, spill his blood on the ground, and let the smoke thereof ascend up to God" (Joseph Smith, Jr., *History of the Church* 5:296). "Suppose you found your brother in bed with your wife, and put a javelin through both of them, you would be justified, and they would atone for their sins.... There is not a man or woman, who violates the covenants made with their God, that will not be required to pay the debt. The blood of Christ will never wipe that out, your own blood must atone for it" (Brigham Young, *Journal of Discourses* 3:247). "... there are men and women that I would advise to go to the President immediately, and ask him to appoint a committee to attend to their case; and then let a place be selected, and let that committee	It is unbiblical to say that Jesus' shed blood, or His death, could not atone for some of our sins. It is the height of blasphemy to say that where Jesus' death fails, ours will succeed. The Bible consistently affirms that Jesus' death and shed blood covers all our sins (Ro 11:27; 1Co 15:3; 2Co 5:15; Gal 1:4; 2Ti 2:11; Heb 8:12; 9:14, 28; 1Pet 3:18; 1 Jn 1:9; 2:2, 12; 3:5; 4:10; Rev 1:5). The doctrine of blood atonement completely cancels out any need for a savior. If our own blood can cleanse us from sins too terrible for Jesus' blood to take care of, then our blood (or our death) must be of more value than His and as such would be able to take care of any lesser sins as well. All of us, for all intents and purposes, would be able to die for ourselves as a means of cleansing us entirely from our sins. This, of course, is an absurd notion.

Position	Support	Orthodox Response
... **continued**	shed their blood" (Apostle J. M. Grant, *Journal of Discourses* 4:49).	
	"... suppose that he [a saint] is overtaken in ... a sin he knows will deprive him of that exaltation which he desires ... and also knows that by having his blood shed he will atone for that sin.... is there a man or woman in this house but would say, 'shed my blood that I may be saved and exalted with the Gods'? ... This is loving our neighbor as ourselves; if he needs help, help him; and if he wants salvation and it is necessary to spill his blood on the earth in order that he may be saved, spill it" (Brigham Young, *Journal of Discourses* 4:219–20).	

6

Church Universal and Triumphant

FACTS AND HISTORY

	Facts
Topic	*Current Facts*
Membership	It is against the Church Universal and Triumphant's policy to report its membership figures. However, religion chronicler J. Gordon Melton estimates that C.U.T. has somewhere between 30,000 and 50,000 members (*Church Universal and Triumphant: In Scholarly Perspective*, p. 20).
Worship	The individual worship process includes the "science of the spoken word," a combination of prayer, meditation, and visualization. During this religious process members are encouraged to chant the phrase, "I AM THAT I AM."
	In addition to the 28,000-acre ranch in Montana that serves as its international headquarters, C.U.T. also has a number of teaching centers around the world that offer weekly services and lectures.
Leaders	David L. Prophet, 1958–1973
	Elizabeth Clare Prophet, 1973–
Publications	The primary means of spreading their beliefs is the periodical *Pearls of Wisdom*, which has been published every week since 1958 and includes messages from the Ascended Masters, and *Heart to Heart*, a monthly newsletter.
	The group also distributes books and tapes that explain their basic beliefs.
	The basic text used by C.U.T. members is entitled *Climb the Highest Mountain*; other prominent books are *The Lost Years of Jesus*, *The Human Aura*, and *The Lost Teachings of Jesus*.
General statement of beliefs	The religious tenets of Church Universal and Triumphant are strongly linked to Christian Science, Buddhism, and Gnosticism. An emphasis is placed on the need to perfect one's karma through continual reincarnation. Most docrines of orthodox Christianity are denied or distorted by C.U.T.
	This group also proclaims that all people should strive for the "initiation of the ascension" that takes place after the soul has become purified in the fullness of the Christ Consciousness. Once this initiation takes place, the soul returns to the Divine Source and is freed from the cycle of Karma and rebirth. The essential mission of Church Universal and Triumphant is to teach people how to attain ascension.

History	
Topic	*History*
Mark L. Prophet, 1918–1973	The husband of Elizabeth Clare Prophet, Mark Prophet was the leader of Church Universal and Triumphant until his death in 1973. Born in Chippewa Falls, Wisconsin, Mark Prophet claimed to commune with angels and nature spirits from a very young age. He also claimed to have received all nine gifts of the Holy Spirit before finishing high school.
	Mark was influenced by his mother's involvement with the Unity School of Christianity, and he later associated himself with the Eastern mysticism propounded by Francis K. Ekey.
	In 1958 Mark Prophet founded Summit Lighthouse, which is the original name of Church Universal and Triumphant. Located in Washington, D.C., Summit Lighthouse focused on publishing *Pearls of Wisdom*, the supposedly blessed teachings of the Ascended Masters ("Immortal, God-free beings" who have attained ascension).
	Mark Prophet married Elizabeth Clare Wulf in 1963.
Elizabeth Clare Prophet, 1939–	Born Elizabeth Clare Wulf in Red Bank, New Jersey, Elizabeth Prophet is the spiritual leader of the Church Universal and Triumphant. Claiming to have recollections of past lives, she became involved with the Christian Science Church at a young age. Not completely satisfied with her metaphysical studies, Elizabeth continued her search for truth. She claims to have been visited by an Ascended Master, El Morya, in 1961. El Morya is supposed to have told her to go and receive training under Mark Prophet.
	After her marriage to Mark Prophet in 1963, Elizabeth began delivering prophetic messages from the Ascended Masters to the congregation. She and her husband moved to Colorado Springs in 1966, where they founded a Montessori school to teach others their beliefs.
	After Mark's death, Mrs. Prophet held control of C.U.T. and soon moved the organization to California. In 1981 she married Edward L. Francis, who is the business manager for C.U.T. The organization left California in 1986 and established its new headquarters in Montana.
	Elizabeth Clare Prophet is called "Guru Ma" by her followers.

The Doctrine of Revelation

Position	Support	Orthodox Response
The Bible is full of not only error, but also unreliable scribal insertions. Consequently, Scripture does not accurately represent what Jesus and His disciples taught.	"Ancient Tibetan manuscripts say that Jesus spent 17 years (age 12 to 29) in the East as both student and teacher" (*Profile: Elizabeth Clare Prophet—Teachings of the Ascended Masters*, p. 7). "Apart from intentional deletions by the authors, we know that the Gospels have been edited, interpolated, subjected to scribal errors, garnished by additions and plagued by subtractions" (*The Lost Teachings of Jesus,* vol. 1, pp. l–li).	This betrays a major misunderstanding of the nature of both manuscript evidence and manuscript transmission. The New Testament is historically more reliable than any ancient piece of literature. The entire NT, except possibly John's writings, were written within a generation of the life of Christ or were contemporaneous with the events, issues, and persons they discuss. Portions of exant copies of the NT date to within a generation of the actual writing. Scholars are in general agreement that the manuscripts have no major deviations that invalidate any biblical doctrine and that almost all the scribal errors concern minor details such as spelling or word order. The Greek text of the NT is considered 99.9 percent accurate. The actual writings of the apostles and their companions were verbally inspired by God and without error. The few scribal problems in no way detract from this truth
Many writings of Jesus and His disciples were lost, destroyed, or purposefully done away with by early Church leaders.	"... Many Of Jesus' Teachings Were Altered, Deleted, Or Never Recorded" (*The Lost Teachings of Jesus,* vol. 1, cover page).	John 20:30–31 clearly states that it would have been impossible to record every event in the life of Christ. The Gospels claim to contain the "Good News" about Jesus, therefore preserving the teaching of Christ necessary for eternal life.
The Bible contains many esoteric teachings. Only those who are initiated into its secret teachings can really understand it.	"... certain teachings were withheld deliberately by Jesus and his apostles themselves. For, as we shall see, they did have a mystery teaching and they did intend to keep it secret" (*The Lost Teachings of Jesus,* vol. 1, p. xl). "... Paul speaks of veiled truths reserved for those who are "perfect," or "mature," that is, among those who are initiated into the deeper mysteries Jesus taught, which, as far as the canon goes, are simply not there" (Ibid., p. xliv).	The idea of "secret teaching" is mentioned several times in the NT (cf. Mk 4:11–12; Ro 16:25–26; 1Co 2.6–7). In each of these passages the truth that is hidden is the message of Christ and His kingdom. It is hidden and not understood from those who are without faith or from the previous ages before the time of Christ. Paul, in contrast, warns believers about deceptive philosophies that do not depend on Jesus Christ (cf. Col 2:8).

The Doctrine of Revelation (cont.)

Position	Support	Orthodox Response
The Bible does not contain the truth about where Jesus was from ages 12 to 30. According to various accounts believed by C.U.T., Jesus was in India during those years.	"Jesus . . . is generally thought to have learned everything from Moses and the prophets and was otherwise God-taught. And yet *The Life of Saint Issa* and other jewels from the heart of Asia say just the opposite—i.e., that he went east 'with the object of perfecting himself in the Divine Word and of studying the laws of the great Buddhas'" (*The Lost Years of Jesus*, p. 397).	Isaiah 40:13–14 correctly asks the question, "Who could enlighten the LORD?" John 1:1–14 precludes the question whether the eternal Word would have need of instruction from any person or perfection in the Divine Word. Luke 2:40, 52 attributes the wisdom of Jesus to a grace from God. In Matthew 7:28 the crowd recognizes the difference in the teaching of Jesus—that is, that it had authority and was not merely the reciting of what He had learned from others.
The Gnostic Gospels provide additional information about Jesus and His life. These Gospels were wrongfully suppressed by early church leaders.	"The early Christian Gnostics whose writings were suppressed by orthodoxy, taught . . . [that] Jesus said, 'I am not your Master. . . . He who will drink from my mouth will become as I am: I myself shall become he'" (*Profile: Elizabeth Clare Prophet—Teachings of the Ascended Masters*, p. 8).	It is true that the early church did not recognize certain writings as Scripture because they were inconsistent with the teachings of Christ. The suppression of false teachers such as the Gnostics, who denied either the divinity or humanity of Christ, began in the apostolic period. Second John says such teachers are deceivers and should not be given the support of believers.
Elizabeth Clare Prophet continues to receive revelations of truth from various Ascended Masters.	"Elizabeth Clare Prophet is the messenger for the Ascended Masters in the tradition of the Old Testament prophets who delivered the Word of the Lord to his people" (*Profile: Elizabeth Clare Prophet—Teachings of the Ascended Masters*, p. 10). "The Ascended Masters are part of a heirarchy of beings known as the Great White Brotherhood, a spiritual order of Western saints and Eastern masters. . . . They are our elder brothers and sisters on the path of personal Christhood who have graduated from earth's schoolroom, ascending as Jesus did at the conclusion of his early mission" (Ibid., pp. 10–11).	The claim to be "in the tradition" of the Old Testament prophets is a claim to speak the very words of God. Yet Elizabeth Clare Prophet claims to be the messenger for the Ascended Masters. There is no connection between the concept of Ascended Masters and the OT understanding of speaking the very words of God. There is no scriptural support for the idea of intermediaries, whether saints or not. Hebrews 4:14–5:10 states that Jesus is our great and only High Priest. He is the only intermediary between the Father and humanity.

The Doctrine of God—*The Trinity*

Position	Support	Orthodox Response
God is all, and all is God. Ultimately we are all one with God and originate from the same spirit sub- tance.	"We are one with the Word as the Word is one with us. We can be separated neither from the creative Sound nor from the cre- ative Source. So we contain all our begin- nings and our endings—and even the Origin of our origin" (*The Lost Teachings of Jesus,* vol. 1, p. 27). "So you see, you have all of the shining qualities of God, of the Creator of a living soul which has the real potential—the realizable potential—of the Spirit. *Qualita- tively* you can become God. But *quantita- tively* you will always be the all within the All" (Ibid., p. 56).	The Bible distinguishes the creation of God from God Himself, and humans are part of the creation. God is infinite, whereas humans are finite, or limited. Genesis 1:1 says that God created the heavens and the earth, but nowhere indi- cates that He is identified with this cre- ation; that is, He and the creation are not the same. Whenever the Bible speaks of God and creation, He is never seen to be a part of it nor it a part of Him (Ne 9:6; Ps 19:1–2; Ac 17:24, 26; Rev 4:11; 14:7). Jesus is also presented in Scripture as perform- ing the work of creation, in that He is God (Jn 1:1–3; Col 1:16–17; Heb 1:2).

The Doctrine of Jesus Christ—*The Deity of Christ*

Position	Support	Orthodox Response
Jesus was not God. He was a disciple.	"Jesus did not claim that he was born a god. He saw himself as a disciple" (*Profile: Elizabeth Clare Prophet—Teachings of the Ascended Masters,* p. 7).	Many passages of Scripture indicate that Jesus self-consciousnessly saw Himself as God. John 8:58 should be viewed as a claim of divinity; that is what Christ's immediate audience understood His words to mean. At the least the passage points to the preexistence of Christ. In John 10:30–39 and 14:8–13 Jesus claims to be one with the Father. Once again His immediate audience understood this as a claim to deity. Jesus also takes divine pre- rogative in the forgiveness of sins (Mk 2:5–7), the judgment of humanity (Mt 25:31–46), and the redefining of the law of God (Mk 2.27 28). Moreover, Jesus does not rebuke or correct those who attribute divinity to Him (Mt 26:63; John 20:28).
Jesus was not the exclusive Son of God.	"Jesus never said that he was the exclusive Son of God. When in John 3:16 he spoke of the 'only begotten Son,' he was refer- ring to the universal Christ whose Body is individualized (broken) for each of us as our personal inner Teacher" (*Profile: Eliza- beth Clare Prophet—Teachings of the Ascended Masters,* p. 7).	There is no doubt that John 3:16, in con- nection with John 20:31, states that those who believe in Jesus as the unique Son of God are promised eternal life. All four canonical Gospels record the declaration of Jesus as God's Son during His baptism (Mt 3:17; Mk 1:11; Lk 3:22; Jn 1:34). The Scrip- tures record Jesus' claim of complete unity with the Father (Jn 10:30–39; 14:8–13) and make numerous references to Jesus as God's Son (Mt 4:3, 6; 11:27; 16:16; Mk 1:1; 14:61–62; Lk 1:32; 22:70; Ro 8:3, 32; Col 1:13; 1Th 1:10; Heb 1:3; 4:14; 1Jn 4:15). Also, the possibility of our being adopted as children of God rests on the work of the unique Son of God (Gal 4:5–6).

The Doctrine of Jesus Christ—*The Deity of Christ (cont.)*

Position	Support	Orthodox Response
Christ was a great teacher, an avatar, just like Buddha and other religious leaders in history.	"Why, then, did Christ, Buddha, and all the avatars put everything around God?" (*The Lost Teachings of Jesus*, vol. 1, p. 67).	In John 14:6 Jesus claims the unique title of "the way" and states that no one can come to the Father except through Him. Therefore it is impossible to blend Christ's teaching and the teaching of other religious figures, because Jesus claims to be the only way to God. Either Jesus Christ is exactly who He claimed to be, the unique Son of God and the only way to be reconciled to God, or He was the greatest, most presumptuous fraud in history.

The Doctrine of Jesus Christ—*The Humanity of Christ*

Position	Support	Orthodox Response
Jesus was not born of a virgin.	"[Elizabeth Clare Prophet] does not believe that the conception of Jesus by his father Joseph, as the agent of the Holy Spirit, in any way detracts from the divinity of his soul or the magnitude of the incarnate Word within him" (*The Lost Years of Jesus*, p. 428).	Matthew 1:18–25 and Luke 1:26–38 both clearly record that the conception of Jesus was miraculous and took place while Mary was a virgin. Matthew 1:19 reveals that Joseph was not involved, in that he was surprised to learn that Mary was pregnant. The conception of Jesus by the virgin Mary has been an important belief to orthodox Christians because it points to the unique nature of Jesus as fully God and fully man and to His sinless nature.
Jesus was not the Christ. The Christ is a separate entity that possessed and empowered the man Jesus.	"Churches have changed it all around. They think of Jesus Christ as the only begotten Son of God without understanding that this is the matrix from which we were all made. Christ is the Universal Reality from which we all sprang. . . . For Jesus attained the epitome of that Christhood to which we, therefore, can aspire. We forget that sometimes" (*The Lost Teachings of Jesus*, vol. 1, p. 79).	Scripture teaches just the opposite of this claim. John said he wrote his book for the purpose of demonstrating that Jesus was the Christ (Jn 20:31), not *a* Christ, or one in whom Christ dwelled. Moreover, one who denies that Jesus is the Christ is an antichrist (1Jn 4:1–3; 5:1). Throughout the NT, Jesus is identified with the Christ, or OT Messiah (Mt 16:16), so that "Christ" actually became part of His name and more than a title (Ro 1:1). The NT speaks of many false christs (Mt 24:24; 1Jn 2:18), but never more than one true Christ, and that is Jesus, the Son of God.

The Doctrine of Jesus Christ—*The Resurrection of Christ*

Position	Support	Orthodox Response
Jesus taught for many years after He was resurrected. The ascension story in the Bible is incorrect.	"There was a tradition during the sub-apostolic age and the second century of a long interval between the resurrection and the ascension. Evidence of it appears not only in the writings of the eminent Church Father Irenaeus, who held that Jesus suffered in his thirtieth year but taught until he was forty or fifty years old, but also in a number of Gnostic works which likewise deal with an extended post-resurrection stay on earth" (*The Lost Years of Jesus*, p. 429).	The Gospel writer Luke records that Jesus appeared to the disciples for forty days (Lk 24:50–53; Ac 1:3). The truth of a short period of resurrection appearances follows from Jesus' words in John 16:5–7. There Jesus states that He is going back to the One who sent Him and that after He is with the Father He will send the other comforter. This promise is fulfilled on the Day of Pentecost.

The Doctrine of the Holy Spirit

Position	Support	Orthodox Response
The Holy Spirit is the violet flame of God, and its primary function is to remove karmic debt.	"The violet flame is the gift of the Holy Spirit known to mystics throughout the ages but introduced at large by Saint Germain early in this century. When invoked and visualized in the giving of dynamic decrees, this seventh-ray aspect of the sacred fire transmutes the cause, effect, record, and memory of negative karma and misqualified energy that result in discord" (*Profile: Elizabeth Clare Prophet—Teachings of the Ascended Masters*, p. 9). "The saturation of their auras by the violet flame was and is the means whereby the avatars have held the balance of world karma. By the amplification of the violet flame through the seat-of-soul chakra, they have engaged in planetary transmutation of Darkness by Light and they have survived as pillars of fire midst the planetary weight of Evil" (*The Lost Teachings of Jesus*, vol. 1, p. 72).	The Bible teaches that the Holy Spirit is personal. To call the Holy Spirit a "function," an "aspect," or an "essence," using the pronoun "It," denies the personhood of the Spirit. Jesus described the Holy Spirit as "another Counselor," using the Greek word *allos*, meaning "another of the same kind" (Jn 14:16). Since Jesus is a personal being, the Holy Spirit must also be essentially personal and deity. According to Jesus, the purpose of the Holy Spirit is to testify of Jesus (Jn 14:23) and to convict the world about sin, righteousness, and judgment (Jn 16:8). If there were such a thing as "karmic debt," it would have been paid by the blood of Jesus Christ.

The Doctrine of Man and Sin

Position	Support	Orthodox Response
We all have a divine spark and can realize the Christ within, in the same way Jesus did. Such a teaching was suppressed by the church fathers.	"... all sons and daughters of God have a divine spark which is their potential to become, or realize, the Christ within and ascend to God as Jesus did.... This concept [was] either destroyed or obscured by Church Fathers" (*Profile: Elizabeth Clare Prophet—Teachings of the Ascended Masters*, p. 7). "Your Divine Self is a permanent gift, but you have to externalize that gift daily by renewing your determination to do it" (*The Lost Teachings of Jesus*, vol. 1, p. 21).	People are not naturally sons and daughters of God. The Bible says, "We are his offspring" (Ac 17:28), but sonship occurs only for those who have believed in Jesus Christ: "For ye are all the children of God by faith in Christ Jesus" (Gal 3:26 KJV). Also, Christians have Christ living within them (Gal 2:20), but they are never told to "sanctify Christ as Lord in your hearts" (1Pe 3:15 NASB). The Bible never tells us to sanctify ourselves *as* Christ. The claim that "self Christhood" was suppressed by the church fathers has no historical basis.
Sin is merely "vibrational patterns of misqualified energy" that go against cosmic laws of the universe.	"You see, the so-called Ôsin' that Jakob Boehme was talking about as hiding God was the vibrational patterns of misqualified energy.... let's try to realize what the Master Jesus and the Master Saint Germain are talking about when they talk about changing our vibrations.... They want us to transmute by the violet flame the records of so-called sin, or karma" (*The Lost Teachings of Jesus*, vol. 1, pp. 136–37).	The Bible defines sin as the transgression of God's law (1Jn 3:4). Sin is described in legal terms as a debt we owe to God ("the wages of sin is death"—Ro 6:23) and as a judicial violation that brings a penalty ("Let no one deceive you with empty words, for because of such things God's wrath comes on those who are disobedient"—Eph 5:6). This has to do with personal, individual actions, not "vibrational patterns."
Man possesses a dual essence: an evolving, impermanent soul and a permanent, divine Spirit.	"Your soul is the nonpermanent aspect of being which is made permanent through the ritual of the ascension" (*Profile: Elizabeth Clare Prophet—Teachings of the Ascended Masters*, p. 11). "[Soul] means the essence of self as the evolving self contrasted with the permanent atom of being which we call the Spirit, with a capital 'S,' or the I AM THAT I AM which was revealed to Moses" (Interview in *Heart* magazine, n.d., p. 59). "Man ... was born a manifestation of the duality of God—a being of both Spirit and Matter. We speak of the two parts of man's duality as his Higher Self and his lower self—as the Changeless and the changing. ... One with his Creator, he is omnipresent, omniscient and omnipotent.... Whereas the soul is the living potential of God which man ... can immortalize, the Spirit is that permanent atom of Being" (Mark and Elizabeth Prophet, *Climb the Highest Mountain*, pp. 121–22).	Although Christians disagree whether humans are bipartitite (body and soul/spirit) or tripartite (body, soul, and spirit) beings, they agree that the immaterial components, like the material, are created by God and are not essentially divine (see Isa 42:5; 57:16). Moreover, the Bible does not imply that the soul of man contains "impermanent" aspects that will later become permanent. Nor does it ever portray the human spirit as omnipresent, omniscient, and omnipotent. These are attributes of God alone and not mankind.

The Doctrine of Salvation

Position	Support	Orthodox Response
Reincarnation	"We've sown in previous lives and we reap in this life" (Interview in *Heart to Heart*, n.d., p. 59). ". . . reincarnation is the means by which we have the opportunity to regain our point of origin-oneness with God" (*The Lost Teachings of Jesus*, vol. 1 p. 47).	Second Peter 2:4–6 is quite clear that the unrighteous are moving toward the day of ultimate judgment. There is no biblical support for the idea that sins can be worked off by suffering in this life or even in the future life. Merely suffering for ones own sin for a period of time would not be adequate to satisfy the righteous nature of God. Reincarnation is a meager attempt to provide a means of self-justification in order that man can become his own savior.
We are cleansed from sin (that is, our karmic debt is paid) by entering into and relying on the violet flame—the all-consuming fire of God.	". . . through the grace of Jesus Christ, a true entering into the Word and Work of the Lord, and the violet flame—the all-consuming fire of God which cleanses us from sin, i.e., transmutes karma—all can balance their negative karma, accomplish their unique mission and fulfill the requirements for the ascension" (*Profile: Elizabeth Clare Prophet—Teachings of the Ascended Masters*, p. 8). "Therefore, we must watch and pray for world transmutation of world karma (by the Holy Spirit's violet flame) as well as the records of our own past misdeeds, which do come full circle for redemption in order that we may fulfill every jot and tittle of the law of our personal Christhood—both here and hereafter" (*The Lost Teachings of Jesus*, vol. 1, pp. 114–15).	The Bible states that "without the shedding of blood there is no forgiveness" (Heb 9:22). Specifically, this refers to the blood Jesus Christ shed on the cross in payment for the sins of mankind . . . *but if we walk in the light, as he is in the light, we have fellowship with one another, and the blood of Jesus his Son, purifies us from all sin* (1Jn 1:7). The only one who could ever "fulfill every jot and tittle of the law" was Jesus Christ, who perfectly satisfied its demands during His earthly life. "Therefore no one will be declared righteous in his sight by observing the law; rather, through the law we become conscious of sin. But now a righteousness from God, apart from law, has been made known. . . . This righteousness from God comes through faith in Jesus Christ to all who believe" (Ro 3:20–22).
Through suffering, some people can take on the sins (bad karma) of the world in the same way Jesus did.	"For some [cancer victims] it is old karma falling due; for others, it is their soul's sacrifice on the altar of the world community: They have made a vow to God to take unto themselves—even into their very flesh and blood, their brain cells and the marrow of their bones—the karma of world hatred, bearing the sins of the world as Christ did" (*The Lost Teachings of Jesus*, vol. 1, p. 110).	The Bible teaches that every person is responsible for his or her own sin. "The son will not share the guilt of the father, nor will the father share the guilt of the son. The righteousness of the righteous man will be credited to him, and the wickedness of the wicked will be charged against him" (Eze 18:20). There is no need for us to bear the world's "karma," because Jesus has already borne it all.
One specific goal is to experience our own Christhood.	"And the Word is made flesh over and over again, because his Light Body, the universal Corpus Christi, was fragmented—like the infinite drops of the infinite ocean—so that you could experience the Person of Christ in your very own being" (*The Lost Teachings of Jesus*, vol. 1, p. 119).	The Bible teaches that the Word (that is, Jesus Christ) never stopped being flesh. He continues even now to have a glorified body of flesh and bone. "For in Christ all the fullness of the Deity lives [present tense] in bodily form" (Col 2:9). See also 1 John 4:3; 2 John 1:7.

The Doctrine of Rewards and Punishment

Position	Support	Orthodox Response
Heaven and hell do not exist. People are not punished for sins. Nor is there a heavenly reward based on accepting salvation through the person and work of Jesus.	"Therefore, you see, just because you make one mistake doesn't mean you're going to burn forever, and just because you've experienced your conversion, doesn't mean you've achieved your divine inheritance" (*The Lost Teachings of Jesus*, vol. 1, p. 33). "They have not reckoned with those unregenerate spirits who have spawned a Luciferian theology.... they bind the faithful to doctrine and personality through their satanic lies of hellfire and damnation" (*Climb the Highest Mountain*, p. 349).	Jesus taught more about hell than anyone else in the New Testament, including the apostle Paul (see, for example, Mt 10:28; 13:40–42; 18:8; 25:41–46; Mk 3:29). In contrast, eternity holds something much different in store for believers as attested to in both the Old and New Testaments (see Da 12:2; Mt 13:43).
All religions are simply different paths back to oneness with God. Some paths, however, are more tedious than others. The straightest line is the way of the Ascended Masters.	"So here we are searching for our Maker and all of these religions stand before us. And they're all supposed to be ways to God.... And I quite agree, except that some of these ways are more circuitous than others.... I do believe that the shortest distance between any two points is a straight line—not a devious line or a circle or a zigzag. And so we need to understand what the Teachings of the Ascended Masters are all about" (*The Lost Teachings of Jesus*, vol. 1, pp. 38–39).	Biblical Christianity teaches that there is one way to eternal life as attested to by Jesus Christ. "I am the gate; whoever enters through me will be saved. He will come in and go out, and find pasture.... the man who does not enter the sheep pen by the gate, but climbs in by some other way, is a thief and a robber" (Jn 10:9, 1).
Qualitatively we can all become God. Our eventual reward is to return to our God-state.	"So you see, you have all of the shining qualities of God, of the Creator of a living soul which has the real potential—the realizable potential—of the Spirit. Qualitatively you can become God" (*The Lost Teachings of Jesus,* vol. 1, p. 56). "As we joyfully, wholeheartedly go about our Father's business, offering Christ's Lost Teaching 'without money and without price,' we shall return to our God-estate of divine Being—just being creatures reborn in Christ returning unto Elohim" (Ibid., p. 67).	The God of the Bible says He is unique. "Before me no god was formed, nor will there be one after me" (Isa 43:10). The God of the Bible is by definition uncreated and triune. For us to become God would mean that God would change in His fundamental make-up, adding components that are essentially mortal and created. Further, God would cease to be tri-personal and become multi-personal and open-ended; therefore some members of the "godhead" (that is, humans) would be finite. The idea of restoring Christ's lost teaching denies His sovereign protection over His own word. In contrast, Jesus prophesied, "Heaven and earth will pass away, but my words will never pass away" (Mk 13:31).

INTERESTING AND DISTINCTIVE BELIEFS

Position	Support	Orthodox Response
C.U.T. members change the world around them by making divine decrees in accordance with what they term the Science of the Spoken Word.	"Students of the Ascended Masters give dynamic decrees to direct God's light for the solving of personal and planetary problems, including crime, pollution, drugs, child abuse, the economy, AIDS, and the threat of nuclear war" (*Profile: Elizabeth Clare Prophet—Teachings of the Ascended Masters*, p. 9).	The Bible says that no one is God's counselor (Ro 11:34). No matter how much we ask (much less decree) that something occur, it will not happen unless the mind of God has been sovereignly decided and results in His decreeing that it will happen. "This is the confidence we have in approaching God: that if we ask anything according to his will, he hears us" (1Jn 5:14). If what we ask is not according to His will, we will not receive an answer from Him that conforms to our wishes.
St. Germaine stands before "the Lords of Karma as an advocate for mankind."	"St. Germaine stands forth this day before the Lords of Karma to plead the cause of mankind! He stands reading that petition which he has also written from his heart, pleading for time, pleading for energy, as he has done for hundreds and thousands of years. "St. Germaine is a familiar face to the Lords of Karma. He is that one, that advocate for mankind, who frequents our chambers most often on behalf of mankind" (Elizabeth Clare Prophet, *The Great White Brotherhood in the Culture, History, and Religion of America*, p. 152).	The Bible knows nothing of the "Lords of Karma," and the only "Advocate" it speaks of in cosmic proportions is Jesus Christ. "My little children, these things write I unto you, that ye sin not. And if any man sin, we have an advocate with the Father, Jesus Christ, the righteous" (1Jn 2:1 KJV).

7

A Course in Miracles

FACTS AND HISTORY

Topic	Current Facts
Membership	*A Course in Miracles* has no membership because it is neither a church nor a religious group. The Course is a three-volume set of books containing about 1,200 pages of channeled information received and transcribed by the late Jewish psychologist Helen Schucman from 1965 to 1973 (*New Age Almanac*, p. 53). The "inner voice" that dictated the Course to Schucman claimed to be none other than Jesus Christ (*A Course in Miracles: Manual for Teachers*, vol. 3, p. 56).
	As of 1991, more than 500,000 copies of the Course (first published in 1975) had been sold. The three-volume set is currently available in both hardbound and softcover editions. The Course has been translated into Spanish, Portuguese, and German.
	Two Course initiates whose books contain Course-related material, beliefs, and teachings are psychologist Jerald Jampolsky, author of the best-seller *Love Is Letting Go,* and Marianne Williamson, author of several best-sellers. Williamson's followers include Hollywood personalities Elizabeth Taylor, Oprah Winfrey, Raquel Welch, Cher, Leslie Ann Warren, and Kim Basinger (*People*, "The Divine Miss W," 9 March 1992, p. 35).
Worship	Meetings that center around the Course have no worship time. The gatherings, often referred to simply as study groups, resemble informal Bible studies in that they involve discussion of the teachings of the Course.
Leadership	There is no central leader or teacher to whom pupils of the Course look for guidance. "A teacher of God," according to the Course, "is anyone who chooses to be one. His qualifications consist solely in this; somehow, somewhere he has made a deliberate choice in which he did not see his interests as apart from someone else's. Once he has done that . . . He has entered an agreement with God even if he does not yet believe in Him. He has become a bringer of salvation. He has become a teacher of God" (*A Course in Miracles: Manual for Teachers*, vol. 3, p. 3).
	The only site that could be considered a headquarters is the Foundation for Inner Peace in Glen Ellen, California, the publisher of the Course. Although this organization is dedicated to disseminating the Course, it has made no attempts to organize students formally. The Unity School of Christianity, however, which has been a long-time advocate of the Course, sponsored a national festival on *A Course in Miracles* in Honolulu, Hawaii, in fall 1986 (*New Age Almanac*, p. 54).
General statement of beliefs	Many people regard the doctrines presented in *A Course in Miracles* as Christian. The Course often speaks of Jesus Christ, God, the atonement, sin, and other concepts reminiscent of Christianity. When closely examined, however, it becomes apparent that the meanings given to the Christian terminology reflect beliefs consistent with the New Age movement.
	The language used in *A Course in Miracles* implies that the communication originated from Jesus Himself.

THEOLOGY

The Doctrine of Revelation

Position	Support	Orthodox Response
Revelations come from "Jesus." In other words, Jesus allegedly communicated directly with Schucman.	"Revelations are indirectly inspired by me [Jesus]" (*A Course in Miracles*, vol. 1, p. 5). "This course has come from him [Jesus] because his words have reached you in a language you can love and understand" (Ibid., vol. 3, p. 56).	Although the Bible teaches that Jesus can speak to Christians (Jn 10:27; see also, e.g., Jn 10:3–4; 14:21; Ro 8:14–16; 1Co 2:10–14; Col 2:6; Rev 3:20, etc.), it is equally a biblical teaching that *authoritative* and *inspired* revelation that is intended for compilation as Scripture and dissemination to all people everywhere (canonical Scripture) must be composed by an apostle or with apostolic approval. Jesus made special promises to the apostles that He did not make to His followers generally (e.g., Jn 15:27; 16:13–15). The apostles had to have seen Jesus' resurrection (Ac 1:22), and their direction guided the early church at critical points (Ac 15:1–35). But even if the canon of Scripture were open (which orthdox Christians deny), the true Jesus would not reveal anything contradictory to Himself. *A Course in Miracles* contradicts Jesus' own words in many places, so it cannot come from the Jesus of the Bible.
Revelations are completely subjective and do not have to correspond to another person's revelations because all that we see is illusory.	"Revelation is intensely personal and cannot be meaningfully translated" (*A Course in Miracles,* vol. 1, p. 5). The Course "is but one version of the universal curriculum. There are many others.... They all lead to God in the end" (Ibid., preface).	Although revelation is subjectively *experienced,* it must be objectively *testable.* Paul's statement "Do not treat prophecies with contempt. Test everything. Hold on to the good" (1Th 5:20–21) recognizes that a purported prophecy isn't necessarily from God. Jesus commended the church at Ephesus because "you have tested those who claim to be apostles but are not, and have found them false" (Rev 2:2). Not all people who claim to be sent from God are to be trusted. If the Course is of God at all, it will agree with what Scripture says. "To the law and to the testimony! If they do not speak according to this word, they have no light of dawn" (Isa 8:20). Because the Word of God is "very pure" and "truth" (Ps 119:140, 142 NASB), a message that contradicts it cannot be from God. The claim that there are "many other" teaching courses and that they "all lead to God in the end" is an immediate danger sign. Jesus said, "Make every effort to enter through the narrow door, because many, I tell you, will try to enter and will not be able to" (Lk 13:24). "All who ever came before me were thieves and robbers, but the sheep did not listen to them. I am the gate; whoever enters through me will be saved" (Jn 10:8–9).

The Doctrine of Revelation (cont.)

Position	Support	Orthodox Response
Biblical Scriptures sometimes err.	"The statement 'For God so loved the world that He gave His only begotten Son, that whosoever believeth in Him should not perish but have everlasting life' needs only one slight correction to be meaningful in this context; 'He gave *it to* His only begotten Son'" (*A Course in Miracles,* vol. 1, pp. 28–29, emphasis added). "The statement 'Vengeance is Mine, sayeth the Lord' is a misperception by which one assigns his own 'evil' past to God.... God does not believe in retribution" (Ibid., p. 32). "The Apostles often misunderstood [the crucifixion]... and out of their own fear they spoke of the 'wrath of God' as His retaliatory weapon.... These are some of the examples of upside-down thinking in the New Testament.... If the Apostles had not felt guilty, they never could have quoted me as saying, 'I come not to bring peace but a sword.' This is clearly the opposite of everything I taught" (Ibid., p. 87).	The revision of John 3:16 completely changes the meaning of the text. The statement "God so loved the world, that he gave his only begotten Son" (KJV) shows *God* as the Giver and the "Son" as the direct object: Jesus Christ is "what" was given. In the Course's rendering of the verse, the direct object is "the world" instead of Jesus, and it was given *to* God's "Son." Since the Course defines the "Son" as each of us, the consequence of this revision is that instead of the world being given Jesus Christ, we are given to the world. Moreover, this passage affirms that everlasting life comes from believing on "Him" [Jesus Christ]. In Course theology, the "Him" whom each person should believe on is *oneself,* since each person is God's "Son." The Bible says, "All Scripture is God-breathed" (2Ti 3:16), and records that the apostolic preaching should be received "not as the word of men, but as it actually is, the word of God, which is at work in you who believe" (1Th 2:13). Jesus put His stamp of approval on the OT Scriptures by calling them "the word of God" (Mk 7:13) that "cannot be broken" (Jn 10:35) and "must be fulfilled" (Lk 24:44). *A Course in Miracles* denies the full inspiration of Holy Scripture largely because the Bible refutes its teaching on creation, sin, righteousness, and judgment.

The Doctrine of God—*The Trinity*

Position	Support	Orthodox Response
***A Course in Miracles* supports the idea of monism (all reality is one).**	"In my own mind, behind all my insane thoughts of separation ... is the knowledge that all is one forever. I have not lost the knowledge of who I am because I have forgotten it. It has been kept for me in the Mind of God, Who has not left His thoughts. And I, who am among them, am one with them and one with Him" (*A Course in Miracles,* vol. 2, p. 92).	God is distinct from His creation; reality is plural, not "one." At the beginning of creation God divided light from darkness, the sea from the dry land, and mankind from all other creatures (Ge 1). God is spirit (Jn 4:24), but we are flesh. Repeatedly, God affirms that He is holy (Heb. *qadosh*; see Lev 11:44; 19:2; Isa 6:3), which means not just morally pure and supremely good but also separate in nature and unique in being. God is unlike mankind ethically ("You thought I [God] was altogether like you. But I will rebuke you," Ps 50:21); He absolutely distinguishes sin from righteousness (Isa 5:20; Eze 3:20).

The Doctrine of God—*The Trinity (cont.)*

Position	Support	Orthodox Response
It also supports Pantheism (God is in all) and Panentheism (all are a part of God).	"God is in everthing I see" (*A Course in Miracles,* vol. 2, p. 45). "God is still everywhere and in everthing forever. And we are a part of Him" (Ibid., p. 92). "Whenever you question your value, say: *'God Himself is incomplete without me'*" (Ibid., vol. 1, p. 165). "The recognition of God is the recognition of yourself. There is no separation of God and His creation" (Ibid., p. 136).	The Bible teaches that God is omnipresent, meaning that His being and Spirit are accessible at all points of the universe (see Ps 139:8). Yet His presence throughout the universe does not mean that His being *is* the physical universe. The Creator is *not* identified with the creation (Ro 1:20–23), and worship of any created thing is considered idolatry (Ex 20:2–5). God does not view such worship as an act of homage to one of His manifestations. God did not make the universe out of Himself (creation *ex Deo*) or existent material (creation *ex hules*), but instead out of nothing (creation *ex nihilo*)—see Pss 33:6, 9; 148:5; Jer 51:15; Heb 11:3. Although God is not far from humankind (Ac 17:27), our sins have caused a spiritual separation from Him (see Isa 59:1–2).

The Doctrine of Jesus Christ—*The Deity and Humanity of Christ*

Position	Support	Orthodox Response
Jesus and those who accept Him are equal.	"Equals should not be in awe of one another because awe implies inequality. It is therefore an inappropriate reaction to me. An elder brother is entitled to respect for his greater experience, and obedience for his greater wisdom.... There is nothing about me that you cannot attain" (*A Course in Miracles,* vol. 1, p. 5). "My mind will always be like yours, because we were created as equals. It was only my decision that gave me all power in Heaven and earth. My only gift to you is to help you make the same decision" (Ibid., pp. 70–71).	Jesus is both God and man, possessing two natures simultaneously. Thus, Jesus is equal to us in terms of our *essential* humanity, but He does not possess sinful desires, susceptibility to temptation, or mortality, which are the common experience of believers right now. (Sin is a temporary but nonessential attribute of humanness.) And since Jesus is also God, He is not equal to us as regards His deity. Jesus said, "You are of this world; I am not of this world" (Jn 8:23). Although the NT refers to Jesus as our "brother" (Heb 2:11–17), before the incarnation Jesus was God the Son, the eternal Word who created the universe (Jn 1:1–3). At the crossroads of history He took on a mortal, human nature (Jn 1:14) and came "in human likeness" (Php 2:7). At His resurrection Jesus retained His human nature as man and His divine nature as God, and His physical body was changed from mortal to immortal (1Co 15). Only Jesus, God the Son, possesses *two* natures in one person. By contrast, all other human beings have only one nature, a human nature.

The Doctrine of Jesus Christ—*The Deity and Humanity of Christ (cont.)*

Position	Support	Orthodox Response
Jesus should not be understood as a sacrificial lamb for our sins.	"I have been correctly referred to as 'the lamb of God who taketh away the sins of the world,' but those who represent the lamb as blood-stained do not understand the meaning of the symbol. Correctly understood, it is a very simple symbol that speaks of my innocence.... Innocence is incapable of sacrificing anything, because the innocent mind has everything and strives only to protect its wholeness" (*A Course in Miracles,* vol. 1, p. 33).	The Course would deny that Jesus died for us, paying the penalty for our sins in His own body on the cross (1Pe 2:24). According to the Course, the physical body and death and sin are all illusions; hence, God cannot judge or penalize anyone for wrongdoing. The Course denies any need for sacrifice or vicarious suffering by Jesus Christ, on the grounds that people are *already* sinless and perfect beings. The Bible never portrays the body, death, sin or God's judgment as illusory but rather as fundamental realities. For example, Scripture affirms unequivocally that "we were reconciled to him [God] through the death of his Son" (Ro 5:10), not by the "*apparent* death of his Son"! Nowhere does it state that mankind needs no reconciliation to God to start with.
The "Son of God" is not Jesus Christ, but rather our own true identity as a thought extended in the mind of God.	"The Sonship is the sum of all that God created" (*A Course in Miracles,* vol. 1, p. 2). "In the creation, God extended Himself to His creations and imbued them with the same loving will to create. You ... have also been created perfect. There is no emptiness in you" (Ibid., p. 14). "God and His creations are completely dependent on each other. He depends on them *because* He created them perfect.... God is lonely without His Sons, and they are lonely without Him" (Ibid., p. 19, italics in original). "You are the holy Son of God Himself. And with this holy thought you learn as well that you have freed the world.... All power is given unto you in earth and Heaven. There is nothing that you cannot do" (Ibid., vol. 2, pp. 353–54). The student is asked to affirm, "Your Son ... is but what I really am in truth. He is the Son You love above all things. He is my Self as You created me. It is not Christ that can be crucified" (*A Course in Miracles,* vol. 2, p. 441).	The Bible states clearly that Jesus is God's only begotten Son (Jn 1:18; 3:16; 1Jn 4:9). The term "only begotten Son of God" is applied only to Jesus in the New Testament and never to believers (Jn 3:18). The term "Son of God" refers to Jesus Christ throughout the NT (e.g., Mt 3:17; 14:33; 16:16), and only Jesus Christ is *the* Son of God. However, the words "sons" (plural) and "children of God" are applied to Jesus' followers several times (Ro 8:14; 9:8; 1Jn 5:2). Christians are not "sons of God" by nature, but instead come into this relationship through adoption (Ro 8:15; Gal 4:5–7; Jn 1:12). Unlike Jesus, who is eternally the Son of God (Ps 2:7; Heb 1:2, 4), we obtain a derivative relationship *through faith*: "You are all sons of God through faith in Christ Jesus" (Gal 3:26). The Course concept that the "Son of God" is an extension of God's thought that is both omniscient and fallible is contradictory.

The Doctrine of Jesus Christ—*The Deity and Humanity of Christ (cont.)*

Position	Support	Orthodox Response
The Word of God could not really become flesh.	"The Bible says, 'The word (or thought) was made flesh.' Strictly speaking, this is impossible, since it seems to involve the translation of one order of reality into another" (*A Course in Miracles*, vol. 1, p. 141).	The Course claims that only one "order of reality" exists: God and His thoughts. The Bible affirms that the physical universe *does* exist as a real creation. The NT says that "the Word became flesh and made his dwelling among us" (Jn 1:14), without reservation or equivocation, and dealt with the apostasy of gnostic cults from the start. "Every spirit that does not acknowledge Jesus is not from God. This is the spirit of the antichrist, which you have heard is coming and even now is already in the world" (1Jn 4:3).
Jesus is no more the Christ than anyone else.	"Is he [Jesus] the Christ? O yes, along with you. . . . Jesus became what all of you must be" (*A Course in Miracles*, vol. 3, p. 83). "Christ waits for your acceptance of Him as yourself, and of His Wholeness as yours" (Ibid., vol. 1, p. 187).	Jesus' own followers, who heard His teaching directly, did not believe that "the Christ" might be anyone at all. After his conversion, the apostle Andrew found his brother Simon Peter and told him, "'We have found the Messiah' (that is, the Christ)" (Jn 1:41–42). At the close of the first century, the apostle John wrote, "Who is the liar? It is the man who denies that Jesus is the Christ. Such a man is the antichrist—he denies the Father and the Son" (1Jn 2:22). If the apostles believed everyone could equally be the Christ, passages such as these, which point to Jesus alone, are hard to explain.
Jesus is but a man who found Christ in other people.	"The name of *Jesus* is the name of one who was a man but saw the face of Christ in all his brothers and remembered God. So he became identified with *Christ*, a man no longer, but at one with God. The man was an illusion, for he seemed to be a separate being, walking by himself, within a body that appeared to hold his self from Self, as all illusions do" (*A Course in Miracles*, vol. 3, p. 83). "Jesus remains a Savior because he saw the false without accepting it as true. And Christ needed his form that He might appear to men and save them from their own illusions" (Ibid.).	Jesus never made these claims. When Peter acknowledged, "You are the Christ, the Son of the living God" (Mt 16:16), Jesus did not reply, "Yes, and so are you!" When the woman at the well said, "I know that Messiah" (called Christ) "is coming," Jesus replied, "I who speak to you am he" (Jn 4:25–26). He did not say, "We are each the Christ." The word "Christ" is a Greek translation of the Hebrew term "Messiah." The OT predicted that the Messiah would be born in Bethlehem (Mic 5:2), before A.D. 33 (Dan 9:24–27), as a descendant of King David (Mt 22:42; 2Sa 7:12, 16; Ps. 132:11). Obviously, the term "Christ," or "Messiah," cannot apply to all people everywhere. Even after His resurrection, the apostles identified Jesus alone as the Christ. "As his custom was, Paul went into the synagogue, and on three Sabbath days he reasoned with them from the Scriptures, explaining and proving that the Christ had to suffer and rise from the dead. 'This Jesus I am proclaiming to you is the Christ'" (Ac 17:2–3).

The Doctrine of Jesus Christ —*The Resurrection of Christ*

Position	Support	Orthodox Response
The resurrection of Jesus should not be understood as a literal, physical return from the dead.	"... the resurrection is the symbol of sharing because the reawakening of every Son of God is necessary to enable the Sonship to know its wholeness" (*A Course in Miracles*, vol. 1, p. 87). "It [the resurrection] is a reawakening or rebirth: a change of mind about the meaning of the world" (Ibid., vol. 3, p. 65). "A slain Christ has no meaning. But a risen Christ becomes the symbol of the Son of God's forgiveness on himself; the sign he looks upon himself as healed and whole" (Ibid., vol. 1, p. 396).	According to the Course, the body does not exist and death does not exist. Thus, Jesus could not have been raised from the dead in any real sense. Yet the Bible repeatedly teaches that "Christ died for us" (Ro 5:8) and that "Christ was raised from the dead" (Ro 6:4). In John 2:19–21, as Jesus predicts His death and resurrection, the apostle John remarks that Jesus was speaking of His body. The physical nature of Jesus' resurrection was part of the apostolic message. On the Day of Pentecost, Peter said that the messianic psalms of King David "spoke of the resurrection of the Christ, that he was not abandoned to the grave, nor did his body see decay" (Ac 2:31). The reality that Christ "died for our sins" and subsequently "was raised on the third day" is the heart of the gospel (1Co 15:3–4). When Jesus appeared to "Doubting Thomas" and the other apostles to show His pierced hands, feet, and side (Jn 20:26–29), it is clear that He was showing His physical body and that this was not a visionary experience. Jesus plainly said, in anticipation of false ideas about His resurrection, "Why are you troubled, and why do doubts rise in your mind? Look at my hands and my feet. It is I myself! Touch me and see; a ghost does not have flesh and bones, as you see I have" (Lk 24:38–39). This unmistakable language shows that Jesus had a fleshly body, a literal death, and a physical resurrection.

The Doctrine of the Holy Spirit

Position	Support	Orthodox Response
The Holy Spirit is the voice of God inside every person. The Holy Spirit was created by "God" at the time man gained the illusion of separation from God. The Holy Spirit tells us that we have made "mistakes" or errors, but never says we have sinned.	"Jesus is the manifestation of the *Holy Spirit*, Whom he called down upon the earth after he ascended into Heaven.... The Holy Spirit, being a creation of the One Creator ... is eternal and has never changed.... The Holy Spirit abides in the part of your mind that is part of the Christ Mind. He represents your Self and your Creator, Who are one" (*A Course in Miracles*, vol. 3, p. 85, italics in original). ". . . the Holy Spirit is part of you. Created by God, He left neither God nor His creation. He is both God and you, as you are God and Him together" (Ibid., vol. 1, p. 312). "The Holy Spirit is the Christ Mind which is aware of the knowledge that lies beyond perception. He came into being with the separation as a protection, inspiring the Atonement principle at the same time" (Ibid., p. 68). "The Holy Spirit dispels it [guilt] simply through the calm recognition that it has never been" (Ibid., p. 223). "The Holy Spirit cannot punish sin. Mistakes He recognizes, and would correct them all as God entrusted Him to do. But sin He knows not, nor can He recognize mistakes that cannot be corrected" (Ibid., p. 377).	The Holy Spirit is God, the third Person of the Triune Godhead. The Holy Spirit is called "God" (Ac 5:3–4) and identified in the NT as Yahweh (Ac 28:25–27, quoting Isa 6:9–10; also Heb 10:15–17, quoting Jer 31:33–34). These references to the Spirit as deity, and to "the eternal Spirit" (Heb 9:14), show that the Holy Spirit always existed. The members of the Godhead are not eternal merely from now on, but have existed from eternity past. The Holy Spirit was not "created" at a point in time. The Holy Spirit is not "both God and you," but is only God. The Bible says, "The Spirit of God lives in you" (i.e., in Christians—Ro 8:9; 1Co 3:16). It never says, "The Spirit of God *is* you." Finally, the Holy Spirit was sent by God to "convict the world of guilt in regard to sin and righteousness and judgment" (Jn 16:8). The Holy Spirit is sent to convince us that sin and judgment are real and divinely established. The Course denies this, yet it is the Holy Spirit as the author of Scripture (Eph 3:2–5; 2Pe 1:21) who affirms the reality of sin and judgment to come. Part of the work of the Holy Spirit is to "contend" with mankind (Ge 6:3) to lead people to repentance (Ro 2:4).

The Doctrine of Man and Sin

Position	Support	Orthodox Response
Ultimately, sin does not exist, and each person is perfectly guiltless and innocent. No one is sinful in any way.	"No one is punished for sins, and the Sons of God are not sinners" (*A Course in Miracles*, vol. 1, p. 88). "The Holy Spirit will never teach you that you are sinful" (Ibid., p. 423). "When you are tempted to believe that sin is real, remember this: If sin is real, both God and you are not" (Ibid., p. 377). "God's Son [each person] is not guilty. He deserves only love because he has given only love ... [and] having never sinned, he has no need of salvation" (Ibid., pp. 220–21).	The Bible says that sin is a universal problem that affects all people. "For there is not a just man on earth who does good and does not sin" (Ecc 7:20 NKJV). "For all have sinned and fall short of the glory of God" (Ro 3:23). Moreover, the Bible addresses those who deny the reality of sin: "If we claim to be without sin, we deceive ourselves and the truth is not in us" (1Jn 1:8). "If we claim we have not sinned, we make him out to be a liar and his word has no place in our lives" (1Jn 1:10). The Bible does not imply that sin has merely the illusion of reality. Rather, it says that God's law has come in some fashion to everyone "so that every mouth may be silenced and all the world held accountable to God" (Ro 3:19).

The Doctrine of Man and Sin (cont.)

Position	Support	Orthodox Response
Yet sin *appears* to exist. This illusion is a false idea or an insane thought caused by the ego.	"Sin is insanity. It is the means by which the mind is driven mad, and seeks to let illusions take the place of truth.... And yet what sin perceives is but a childish game. The Son of God may play he has become a body, prey to evil and to guilt, with but a little life that ends in death. But all the while his Father shines on him.... There is no sin" (*A Course in Miracles,* vol. 2, p. 409). "There is no stone in all the ego's embattled citadel more heavily defended than the idea that sin is real" (Ibid., vol. 1, p. 376). "The betrayal of the Son of God lies only in illusions, and all his 'sins' are but his own imagining. His reality is forever sinless. He need not be forgiven but awakened. In his dreams he has betrayed himself, his brothers and his God. Yet what is done in dreams has not been really done" (Ibid., p. 327).	While sin is declared to be both real and universal, its nature is described in Scripture as the transgression of God's law, or lawlessness (1Jn 3:4); as "wrongdoing" (1Jn 5:17); as neglect of our biblical duties (Jas 4:17); as acts that stem from unbelief (Ro 14:23). The word "sin" is associated or equated with many other terms in the Bible: transgression, trespass, wickedness, evil, iniquity, abomination, disobedience, defilement, filthiness, backsliding, and rebellion. Moreover, the Bible is very specific in naming particular sins: murder, theft, blasphemy, adultery, sorcery, idolatry, violence, pride, fornication, deceit, and covetousness. The Bible does not treat sin as an error to be corrected, or as an illusion that does not exist. Rather, sin is a wrongful act and condition of mankind that requires repentance, remission, and forgiveness. "Without the shedding of blood there is no forgiveness," so "now he [Jesus Christ] has appeared once for all at the end of the ages to do away with sin by the sacrifice of himself" (Heb 9:22, 26). Scripture does not say that the remedy for sin is achieved by "waking up," but by repentance and confession: "If we confess our sins, he is faithful and just and will forgive us our sins and purify us from all unrighteousness" (1Jn 1:9). "He who conceals his sins does not prosper, but whoever confesses and renounces them finds mercy" (Pr 28:13).
The Course proposes that sin does not exist; therefore God will not punish people for purportedly sinning.	"Sin is defined as 'lack of love.' Since love is all there is, sin in the sight of the Holy Spirit is a mistake to be corrected, rather than an evil to be punished" (*A Course in Miracles,* preface). "It is essential that error not be confused with sin, and it is this distinction that makes salvation possible. For error can be corrected, and the wrong made right. But sin, were it possible, would be irreversible" (Ibid., vol. 1, p. 374). "The betrayal of the Son of God lies only in illusions, and all his 'sins' are but his own imagining. His reality is forever sinless. He need not be forgiven but awakened. In his dreams he has betrayed himself, his brothers and his God. Yet what is done in dreams has not been really done" (Ibid., p. 327).	The Bible addresses the contrast between calling an action "sin" and calling it an "error." A broken vow (an unkept promise) is sin, not an error: "When you make a vow to God, do not delay in fulfilling it.... Do not let your mouth lead you into sin. And do not protest to the temple messenger, 'My vow was a mistake.' Why should God be angry at what you say and destroy the work of your hands?" (Ecc 5:4–6). The Course's claim that error must "not be confused with sin" because "error can be corrected" and thus salvation is possible runs directly contrary to the purpose of Jesus' incarnation. The angel told Joseph, "You are to give him the name Jesus, because he will *save* his people from their sins" (Mt 1:21)—sins, not errors.

The Doctrine of Salvation

Position	Support	Orthodox Response
To partake of the Atonement, you must recognize your original state; then all that you were will be restored unto you.	"I am in charge of the process of Atonement, which I undertook to begin. When you offer a miracle to any of my brothers, you do it to *yourself* and me. The reason you come before me is that I do not need miracles for my own Atonement, but I stand at the end in case you fail temporarily. My part in the Atonement is the canceling out of all errors that you could not otherwise correct. When you have been restored to the recognition of your original state, you naturally become part of the Atonement yourself" (*A Course in Miracles,* vol. 1, p. 6). "The purpose of the Atonement is to restore everything to you; or rather, to restore it to your awareness" (Ibid., p. 9).	According to the Course, man's original state is perfection. Participating in the "Atonement" means undoing the misbelief that we are separated from God and are sinful, imperfect, or physical, limited beings within a body. The Course refers to "the process of Atonement" as something that occurs within our experience (namely, arriving at a state of awareness). In contrast, the Christian concept of atonement stems from the OT. The word "atonement" is used to translate the Hebrew words *kippur* (noun) and *kapar* (verb), which mean "to cover or conceal" the sin of man, lawfully accomplished by the offering of blood by the priest. "In this way the priest will make atonement for them, and they will be forgiven" (Lev 4:20). This verse is also translated with the word "reconcile," since the act of covering sin reconciles humans to God. Although sacrifices were offered daily, the Jews were commanded to celebrate a Day of Atonement (Yom Kippur) once a year: "Because on this day atonement will be made for you, to cleanse you. Then, before the LORD, you will be clean from all your sins" (Lev 16:30). In the NT, atonement, propitiation, and reconciliation are intertwined with the substitutionary death of Jesus Christ. In Christ we now receive "atonement" (Ro 5:11 KJV) or "reconciliation" (NIV). Through the blood of Jesus we obtain "propitiation" (Ro 3:25 KJV) or "a sacrifice of atonement" (NIV). It is Jesus who is the "propitiation for our sins" (1Jn 2:2; 4:10 KJV) or "atoning sacrifice" for us (NIV). Atonement does not open our eyes to our own perfection, but instead covers our sins before God.

The Doctrine of Salvation (cont.)

Position	Support	Orthodox Response
God did not allow His Son to die on the cross for our salvation.	"If the crucifixion is seen from an upside-down point of view, it does appear as if God permitted and even encouraged one of His Sons to suffer because he was good.... Yet the real Christian should pause and ask, 'How could this be?' Is it likely that God Himself would be capable of the kind of thinking which His Own words have clearly stated is unworthy of His Son?" (*A Course in Miracles,* vol. 1, p. 32). "Persecution frequently results in an attempt to 'justify' the terrible misperception that God Himself persecuted His Own Son on behalf of salvation. The very words are meaningless.... In milder forms a parent says, 'This hurts me more than it hurts you,' and feels exonerated in beating a child. Can you believe our Father really thinks this way? It is so essential that all such thinking be dispelled that we must be sure that nothing of this kind remains in your mind. I was not 'punished' because you were bad. The wholly benign lesson the Atonement teaches is lost if it is tainted with this kind of distortion in any form" (Ibid.). "Sacrifice is a notion totally unknown to God" (Ibid., p. 33).	It is clear in the NT that Jesus Christ died on the cross for the sins of mankind. "For Christ died for sins once for all, the righteous for the unrighteous, to bring you to God. He was put to death in the body but made alive by the Spirit" (1Pe 3:18). According to the OT, it was the good will of God the Father to sacrifice Jesus Christ for us: "But he was pierced for our transgressions, he was crushed for our iniquities; the punishment that brought us peace was upon him, and by his wounds we are healed" (Isa 53:5). At Pentecost Peter told the Jews that it was God's will to offer up Jesus for us: "This man was handed over to you by God's set purpose and foreknowledge; and you, with the help of wicked men, put him to death by nailing him to the cross. But God raised him from the dead, freeing him from the agony of death, because it was impossible for death to keep its hold on him" (Ac 2:23–24). The Course emulates the ideas of Peter *before* the resurrection. When Jesus told His disciples that He must go to Jerusalem and be killed, Peter rebuked Him and said this must not happen. Jesus replied, "Get behind me, Satan! You are a stumbling block to me; you do not have in mind the things of God, but the things of men" (Mt 16:21–23).
Forgiveness occurs when you realize your brother cannot sin against you.	"Forgiveness recognizes what you thought your brother did to you has not occurred. It does not pardon sins and make them real. It sees there was no sin. And in that vow are all your sins forgiven" (*A Course in Miracles,* vol. 2, p. 391).	Jesus once told a parable of a slave who owed ten thousand talents to a king. The king suspended the debt temporarily, but when the slave refused to forgive a much smaller debt, the king withdrew his suspension and penalized the slave in full (Mt 18:23–35). Jesus' warning, "This is how my heavenly Father will treat each of you," establishes the reality and the consequences of sin.
The reason for Christ's crucifixion was to induce people to love one another.	"The message of the crucifixion is perfectly clear: *'Teach only love, for that is what you are.'* If you interpret the crucifixion in any other way, you are using it as a weapon for assault rather than as the call for peace for which it was intended" (*A Course in Miracles,* vol. 1, p. 87).	"For the message of the cross is foolishness to those who are perishing, but to us who are being saved it is the power of God.... For what I received I passed on to you as of first importance: that Christ died for our sins according to the Scriptures, that he was buried, that he was raised on the third day according to the Scriptures" (1Co 1:18; 15:3–4).

The Doctrine of Rewards and Punishment

Position	Support	Orthodox Response
Hell does not exist.	"The Holy Spirit teaches thus: There is no hell. Hell is only what the ego has made of the present" (*A Course in Miracles,* vol. 1, p. 281).	Scripture teaches that there will be eternal punishment for the wicked and the unrepentant. "The Son of Man will send out his angels, and they will weed out of his kingdom everything that causes sin and all who do evil. They will throw them into the fiery furnace, where there will be weeping and gnashing of teeth" (Mt 13:41–42; see also vv. 49–50). "If anyone's name was not found written in the book of life, he was thrown into the lake of fire" (Rev 20:15).
The Second Coming and final judgment are not meant to punish sinners, but to heal the mind, rectify mistakes, and dispel the illusions we have believed in.	"Judgment is not an attribute of God.... The Last Judgment is generally thought of as a procedure undertaken by God. Actually it will be undertaken by my brothers with my help. It is a final healing rather than a meting out of punishment, however much you may think that punishment is deserved" (*A Course in Miracles,* vol. 1, pp. 29–30). "Christ's Second Coming, which is sure as God, is merely the correction of mistakes, and the return of sanity" (Ibid., vol. 2, p. 439). "The Final Judgment on the world contains no condemnation. For it sees the world as totally forgiven, without sin and wholly purposeless" (Ibid., p. 445). "The Second Coming means nothing more than the end of the ego's rule and the healing of the mind" (Ibid., vol. 1, p. 58).	Judgment is a basic attribute of God. "The LORD is a God of judgment" (Isa 30:18 KJV). This is fundamental to God's nature as a moral lawgiver: "He has established his throne for judgment. He will judge the world in righteousness; he will govern the peoples with justice" (Ps 9:7–8). The Second Coming of Christ will be as literal and physical as His first coming was. "This same Jesus, who has been taken from you into heaven, will come back in the same way you have seen him go into heaven" (Ac 1:11). The Second Coming is the return of *Jesus,* not simply the arrival of a spirit or a thought in our minds (Jn 14:3; Php 3:20; 1Th 2:19; 3:13; 5:23). When Jesus returns, He will bring God's punishment upon the wicked: "... the Lord Jesus is revealed from heaven in blazing fire with his powerful angels. He will punish those who do not know God and do not obey the gospel of our Lord Jesus. They will be punished with everlasting destruction and shut out from the presence of the Lord and from the majesty of his power" (2Th 1:7–9). Jesus referred to this coming as the "day of judgment" (Mt 10:15; 11:22–24; 12:36—see also 2Pe 3:7). In light of these and many other Scriptures that forewarn of the vengeance, everlasting destruction, and perdition that will accompany the day in which God calls all people to account, the claims of the Course must be rejected as totally unbiblical.

INTERESTING AND DISTINCTIVE BELIEFS

Position	Support	Orthodox Response
Time is an illusion.	"In order to understand the teaching-learning plan of salvation, it is necessary to grasp the concept of time that the course sets forth.... The instant the idea of separation entered the mind of God's Son, in that same instant was God's Answer given. In time this happened very long ago. In reality it never happened at all. The world of time is the world of illusion. What happened long ago *seems* to be happening now" (*A Course in Miracles*, vol. 3, p. 4, emphasis added). "We have covered the illusion of time already" (Ibid., p. 6). "... time does not really exist" (Ibid., vol. 1, p. 5). "There is no past or future, and the idea of birth into a body has no meaning either once or many times" (Ibid., vol. 3, p. 57).	The Bible never indicates time is an illusion. The word "time" occurs 620 times in the King James Version, but the word "illusion" never, nor is there any indication that time is not a real process. Because God ordained the sun, moon, and stars to designate "seasons and days and years" (Ge 1:14), and because biblical prophecy often puts time in human language (e.g., seven years) while never indicating that it is artificial, the indication is that time is not illusory.
Space is an illusion.	"... you think you live in space, where concepts such as 'up' and 'down' are meaningful. Ultimately, space is as meaningless as time. Both are merely beliefs" (*A Course in Miracles*, vol. 1, p. 11).	"And when Jesus came to the place, he looked up and saw him, and said to him, 'Zacchaeus, make haste and come down, for today I must stay at your house'" (Lk 19:5 NKJV). If "up" and "down" are meaningless, why does the Bible use the words so often?

What your eyes see is an illusion.	"With eyes closed, think of all the horrors in the world that cross your mind. Name each one as it occurs to you, and then deny its reality. God did not create it, and so it is not real. Say, for example:
	
	   'God did not create that war, and so it is not real.'
	
	   'God did not create that airplane crash, and so it is not real'" (*A Course in Miracles*, vol. 2, p. 23).
	
	"Nothing the body's eyes seem to see can be anything but a form of temptation" (Ibid., p. 105).
	
	"... your idea of what seeing means is tied up with the body and its eyes and brain. Thus you believe that you can change what you see by putting little bits of glass before your eyes. This is among the many magical beliefs that come from the conviction that you are a body, and the body's eyes can see" (Ibid., p. 157).
		The Bible never treats the material world as an illusion that is "not real" and must be denied. When God judged the Egyptians at the Red Sea for putting the Israelites into bondage, this event was to be seen and remembered by the people of Israel: "Only be careful, and watch yourselves closely so that you do not forget the things your eyes have seen or let them slip from your heart as long as you live" (Dt 4:9).
		
		Moreover, God's actions in history comprise events that are worth recalling, since they prove that God is not simply a philosophical speculation but an active agent in human affairs. "He is your praise; he is your God, who performed for you those great and awesome wonders you saw with your own eyes" (Dt 10:21).

Position	Support	Orthodox Response
The physical world does not exist.	"The world you see is an illusion of a world. God did not create it, for what He creates must be eternal as Himself" (*A Course in Miracles,* vol. 3, p. 81). "The world will end in an illusion, as it began.... It will not be destroyed nor attacked nor even touched. It will merely cease to seem to be" (Ibid., p. 35). "There is nothing outside you. That is what you must ultimately learn" (Ibid., vol. 1, p. 358). "The world you see has nothing to do with reality. It is of your own making, and it does not exist" (Ibid., vol. 2, p. 23).	"In the beginning God created the heavens and the earth" (Ge 1:1). He *created*, not *appeared to create*. The physical, material world of creation is not ultimate, but it is real. The fact that only God has always existed and is uncreated does not imply or require that the material universe be illusory or nonexistent. The universe is also dependent on God for its continuing existence, but dependency does not imply nonexistence. "By the word of the LORD were the heavens made, their starry host by the breath of his mouth.... He spoke, and it came to be; he commanded, and it stood firm" (Ps 33:6, 9). "By faith we understand that the universe was formed at God's command, so that what is seen was not made out of what was visible" (Heb 11:3). The universe "stood firm" after its creation. The Course's claim that the universe "has nothing to do with reality" is really a gnostic denial of God's activity in creation itself. At its most rudimentary level, a denial of the reality of the physical universe means denying the reality of the body and the flesh (which the Course insists are illusory). This invites one of the strongest rebukes in Scripture: "Beloved, do not believe every spirit, but test the spirits to see whether they are from God; because many false prophets have gone out into the world.... Every spirit that does not confess Jesus is not of God; and this is the spirit of the antichrist, of which you have heard that it is coming, and now it is already in the world" (1Jn 4:1, 3 NASB). The Course falls under this warning because it echoes the spirit of Antichrist, denying the incarnation of Jesus Christ.

8

Eckankar

FACTS AND HISTORY

Facts	
Topic	*Current Facts*
Membership	Current membership numbers are not reported by Eckankar, but in 1988 there were 127 centers in the United States and 284 centers worldwide in more than 100 countries. Major ECK seminars often attract 2,000 to 6,000 people. Eckankar's international headquarters is in Minneapolis.
Worship	ECK members receive monthly lessons for individual study. ECK Satsang classes are also available for those who want to study in groups. Worship services are about an hour long. Classes focus on reading ECK writings, leading discussions on ECK topics, and singing special music. ECK holds numerous weekend seminars each year in the United States, Canada, and other countries. Each seminar has five instructional sessions. Members are expected to make a $125 donation to attend the seminar, with nonmembers paying $15 per session (according to an Eckankar representative, November 7, 1994).
Leaders of Eckankar	Paul Twitchell (1965–1971) Darwin Gross (1971–1981) Harold Klemp (1981–) Leaders of Eckankar are called ECK Masters.
Publications	*Mystic World* (Quarterly publication for members only) *Eckankar Journal* (One issue per year) Also a variety of other printed materials and audio tapes, including *The Golden Heart*; *ECKANKAR—The Key to Secret Worlds*; *Soul Travelers of the Far Country*; *The Secret Teachings*; *The Spiritual Notebook*; *The Far Country*; *The Shariyat-Ki-Sugmad*; *Eckankar Dictionary*; *The Tiger's Fang*; and *Awakened Imagination*.
General statement of beliefs	Eckankar believes that God exists in two parts, the Light and Sound, known as ECK. This is held to be the sustaining force of all life and the equivalent of the Holy Spirit. Eckankar teaches that it is possible to experience the Light and Sound through the proper use of spiritual exercises. Spiritual exercise is important as the initiator of Soul Travel and for achieving spiritual growth and a deeper appreciation for one's past lives. A key spiritual exercise is the singing of the word *hu,* which is supposedly the name of God. Adherents believe in karma and reincarnation and hold that ECK helps to purify a person of karma. They emphasize a cooperative relationship with God. Humans are considered a spark of God sent to earth to gain spiritual experience and to serve others.

History

Topic	History
Paul Twitchell **1965–1971**	Paul Twitchell founded Eckankar, Religion of the Light and Sound of God, in 1965. Born in Kentucky, Twitchell was strongly influenced by the teachings of Sant Mat Master Kirpal and L. Ron Hubbard. In 1965 Twitchell declared himself the "Living ECK Master" and publicized his religious views by establishing Soul Travel workshops in San Francisco. He died in 1971.
Darwin Gross **1971–1981**	Upon Twitchell's death, Darwin Gross became the leader of Eckankar as the only living ECK Master. Gross married Twitchell's widow, Gail, but later they were divorced. In 1981 Gross established Harold Klemp as Living ECK Master, and in 1984 Gross left Eckankar.
Harold Klemp **1981–present**	Harold Klemp is the present Living ECK Master and therefore the movement's spiritual leader. Born in Wisconsin, Klemp became an ECKist in the 1960s. He has written several books, and in 1990 he supervised the completion of the Temple of ECK in Chanhassen, Minnesota. As ECK Master, Klemp is the main speaker at various ECK seminars around the world. Klemp's Eckankar books include *The Golden Heart, Soul Travelers of the Far Country*, and *The Secret Teachings*. Klemp claims to be the Mahanta, the inner or spiritual form of the Living ECK Master. As Mahanta, Klemp purportedly gives inner guidance to Eckankar's members through dreams, Soul Travel, and spiritual exercises.

THEOLOGY

The Doctrine of Revelation		
Position	*Support*	*Orthodox Response*
Eckankar's main scripture is called the Shariyat-Ki-Sugmad. Additional instructional materials are available for achieving spiritual advancement.	"The Shariyat-Ki-Sugmad is the scripture of Eckankar. The original copy is located in the spiritual city of Agam Des, which can only be reached in the 'soul body'" (*Encyclopedia of American Religions*, p. 955). Eckankar members receive monthly lessons, called discourses, which they are encouraged to study on their own. Currently 14 years of ECK discourses are available (*Eckankar Membership*, p. 2).	The Judeo-Christian Scriptures and the God who inspired them stand in sharp contrast to Eckankar. God repeatedly commanded His servants to leave authoritative, written records: "Write down these words, for in accordance with these words I have made a covenant with you and with Israel" (Ex 34:27). "When he takes the throne of his kingdom, he is to write for himself on a scroll a copy of this law, taken from that of the priests, who are Levites" (De 17:18). "Go now, write it on a tablet for them, inscribe it on a scroll, that for the days to come it may be an everlasting witness. These are rebellious people, deceitful children, children unwilling to listen to the LORD's instruction" (Isa 30:8–9). "Write in a book all the words I have spoken to you" (Jer 30:2). Moreover, we are warned not to go beyond that written record: "Now, brothers, I have applied these things to myself and Apollos for your benefit, so that you may learn from us the meaning of the saying, 'Do not go beyond what is written.' Then you will not take pride in one man over against another" (1Co 4:6). These examples demonstrate the difference between God's open, exoteric manner of communicating His will and the hidden, esoteric form of Eckankar's teaching.
Knowledge of God comes through contact with the Light and Sound of God. God becomes known to people through Light and Sound.	"Often called the Holy Spirit, the Light and Sound are twin aspects of God. Known in Eckankar as the ECK, It sustains all life" (*What Is Eckankar?*, p. 1). "This Sound stands for all that the Supreme Being is, and what IT does in all worlds. It is through Light and Sound that the universal Spirit can manifest Itself to the human consciousness" (*Eckankar: The Key to Secret Worlds*, p. 96).	Knowledge of God comes through His self-revelation contained in the Scriptures and in the person of Jesus Christ as recorded in the Scriptures. "You diligently study the Scriptures because you think that by them you possess eternal life. These are the Scriptures that testify about me" (Jn 5:39). "In the past God spoke to our forefathers through the prophets at many times and in various ways, but in these last days he has spoken to us by his Son, whom he appointed heir of all things, and through whom he made the universe" (Heb 1:1–2). "No one has ever seen God, but God the One and Only, who is at the Father's side, has made him known" (Jn 1:18). Moreover, the God of the Bible has revealed Himself in three distinct persons who make up the Godhead: the Father, the Son, and the Holy Spirit. The Holy Spirit is a person, rather than an "it," as

The Doctrine of Revelation (cont.)

Position	Support	Orthodox Response
... continued		Jesus made clear: "But the Counselor, the Holy Spirit, whom the Father will send in my name, will teach you all things and will remind you of everything I have said to you" (Jn 14:26).
The Bible is filled with esoteric meanings.	"According to the Gospels, Jesus said, 'Come, follow me.' But few knew what he was saying, that he wanted them to go with him into the worlds beyond" (*Eckankar: The Key to Secret Worlds*, p. 4).	The Bible is not an esoteric book, but rather God's revelation to mankind. While it contains numerous examples of dreams, visions, prophecies, and parables, it also offers explanations of these events. Jesus spoke to the masses in parables, but to His disciples He made His meaning clear: "He did not say anything to them without using a parable. But when he was alone with his own disciples, he explained everything" (Mk 4:34). The disciples in turn recorded those meanings. John summed up the Scriptures' intent: "I write these things to you who believe in the name of the Son of God so that you may *know* that you have eternal life" (1Jn 5:13 emphasis added).
The Bible has been edited and changed many times. Christianity, too, has been altered from its original form.	"Christianity has gone through many changes, and the Bible has seen many edits. As a result, the words spoken by Jesus sometimes bear little resemblance to what appears in the scriptures today" (*Eckankar: Ancient Wisdom for Today*, p. 107).	This betrays a major misunderstanding of the nature of manuscript evidence and manuscript transmission. The New Testament is historically more reliable than any ancient piece of literature. The entire NT, except possibly for John's writings, were written within a generation of the death of Christ or were contemporaneous with the events, issues, and persons they discuss. Portions of extant copies of the NT date within a generation of the actual writing. Scholars are in general agreement that the manuscripts have no major deviations that invalidate any biblical doctrine and that almost all scribal errors are in minor details such as spelling or word order. The Greek text of the NT is evaluated at being 99.9 percent accurate. The actual writings of the apostles and their companions were verbally inspired by God and without error. The few scribal problems in no way detract from this truth.

The Doctrine of Revelation (cont.)

Position	Support	Orthodox Response
The principles of Eckankar are taught to Eckists mainly by the living Eck Master. Other spiritual teachers who live in other planes of existence also impart spiritual knowledge.	"The secret knowledge of Eckankar includes much information about the spiritual travelers that has been lost to the world. [Spiritual travelers] are concerned with the welfare of those in the lower spiritual planes.... They see that all beings, on all planes, keep functioning in concurrence with divine law" (*Eckankar: The Key to Secret Worlds*, p. 55).	"The secret things belong to the LORD, our God, but the things revealed belong to us and to our children forever" (Dt 29:29). All occult or secret knowledge is less than the knowledge we have through Christ, "in whom are hidden [*occulted*] all the treasures of wisdom and knowledge" (Col 2:3).
Revelation can also come through dreams.	"The ultimate purpose of dreams is to bring the individual closer to the Light and Sound of God. The Mahanta can communicate in a dream with the new student who has not yet been able to open their conscious mind to the Inner Master" (*Eckankar: Ancient Wisdom for Today*, p. 35).	While the Bible records many instances of God's using dreams to reveal His purpose to mankind, not all dreams originate with Him. Note this warning rebuke: "'I am against those who prophesy false dreams,' declares the LORD. 'They tell them and lead my people astray with their reckless lies, yet I did not send or appoint them. They do not benefit these people in the least,' declares the LORD" (Jer 23:32). So dreams can also be evil, enticing a person away from God and not closer to Him.

The Doctrine of God—*The Trinity*

Position	Support	Orthodox Response
God is an impersonal "IT." Eckists call God the great SUGMAD, having both no attributes and all attributes. **An ancient name for this "Originator of Life" is allegedly "HU."**	"SUGMAD— A sacred name for God, the source of all life. IT is neither masculine nor feminine" (*Eckankar: Ancient Wisdom for Today*, p. 11). "Sugmad, IT: The formless, All-embracing, impersonal, infinite, the Ocean of Love and Mercy; from IT flows all life, all truth, all reality.... IT remains formless, impersonal, all pervading.... it has an inside called Nirguna, which is to say IT has no qualities and nothing can be said or thought about IT, and an outside called Saguna which is to say that IT may be considered as eternal reality, consciousness and joy" (*Eckankar Dictionary*, p. 137). "HU is an ancient name for God. It's a love song to God" (*A Love Song to God: HU*, p. 1).	When asked His name by Moses, God is recorded as replying, "'I AM WHO I AM' [YAHWEH]. This is what you are to say to the Israelites: 'I AM has sent me to you'" (Ex 3:14). The Bible leaves no room for ambiguity regarding the name of God. Yahweh is God's covenant name, not HU. God is essentially personal and cannot be confused with an impersonal force, whether from *Star Wars* or Eckankar. Unlike the Hindu concept of Nirguna, the God of the Bible is not without attributes. "The LORD, the LORD, the compassionate and gracious God, slow to anger, abounding in love and faithfulness, maintaining love to thousands, and forgiving wickedness, rebellion and sin" (Ex 34:6–7). Nor does God possess all attributes (Saguna): God cannot lie, be tempted with evil, or change. "God is light; in him there is no darkness at all" (1Jn 1:5). For this reason our God can be trusted.

The Doctrine of God—*The Trinity (cont.)*

Position	Support	Orthodox Response
Everything is part of the SUGMAD.	"Those whose inner vision is open will see all creation in God, meaning all of the divine drama, and God in all creation" (*Eckankar: The Key to Secret Worlds*, p. 34). "Therefore God looks upon all as the whole, as unity, throughout space and time, going out of and returning to the divine fountainhead" (Ibid., p. 34).	God's ethical and moral holiness is also an essential part of His unique Being. "Holy, Holy, Holy is the LORD Almighty" (Isa 6:3). This means it is impossible to see the totality of God's ethical perfection in either fallen mankind or demons, both of which are part of creation. God's presence throughout the universe (immanence) is logically distinct from the error of God's identity *as* the universe (pantheism).
God has very little, if anything, to do with the affairs of this earthly life.	"Therefore, we come to the understanding that God is unconcerned about what goes on in this world" (*Eckankar: The Key to Secret Worlds*, p. 33).	The God of the Bible is intensely concerned for and involved in His creation. "He is before all things, and in him all things hold together" (Col 1:17). From the creation in Genesis to the final judgment of Revelation and the commencement of eternity, God is in control and interactive. He said, "I make known the end from the beginning, from ancient times, what is still to come. I say: My purpose will stand, and I will do all that I please" (Isa 46:10). He also will demand a strict account of how each one of us conducts our earthly life: "Each of us will give an account of himself to God" (Ro 14:12).
Each person is Truth itself.	"... the secret of the ages, the simplest of all things [is] that each of us is Truth, itself. We are the living Truth, the very embodiment of God" (*Eckankar: The Key to Secret Worlds*, p. 49).	The statement that each of us is truth is at best ignorance and at worst sheer arrogance. History demonstrates suitably the capacity of human beings to lie and deceive and to be vulnerable to lies and deception. Jesus, calling Himself "the way and the truth and the life," said, "No one comes to the Father except through me" (Jn 14:6). This is in sharp contrast to mankind: "The LORD saw how great man's wickedness on the earth had become, and that every inclination of the thoughts of his heart was only evil all the time" (Ge 6:5). The Bible says that God actually hates those who possess "haughty eyes, a lying tongue, hands that shed innocent blood" (Pr 6:17).
The concept of Trinity	"... the chief qualities of the SUGMAD: The isness, nowness, and hereness—the trinity of the Supreme Being of all the universes" (*Eckankar: The Key to Secret Worlds*, p. 108). "Most important of all is that the heart of the doctrine of the unity of God is simply the trinity of wisdom, charity, and freedom" (Ibid., p. 151).	Because Eckankar does not have a personal God, it cannot have a biblical concept of the Trinity. Eckankar's "trinity" consists of attributes or qualities of its deity. However, we have seen that Eckankar defines its deity as having no attributes (Nirguna) at the same time it possesses some attributes (Saguna)—a contradiction. Moreover, one cannot have a fundamentally impersonal entity give rise to personal qualities such as "wisdom" and charity.

The Doctrine of Jesus Christ—*The Deity of Christ*

Position	Support	Orthodox Response
Jesus is merely one great religious teacher among many.	"Holy writings contain the inner experiences of these prophets, saints, and founders of religions: Buddha, Krishna, Christ, and Mohammed" (*Eckankar: The Key to Secret Worlds*, p. 7).	Jesus is the only one who proved His authority to found a true religion in that He rose from the dead.
There is no one right religion or unique savior of mankind.	"I am aware that there are many approaches to the SUGMAD, for nobody has a monopoly on any path. No teacher, living or past, can give us the actual understanding of Truth" (*Eckankar: The Key to Secret Worlds*, p. 49).	This is opposed by the biblical claims for Jesus Christ. "Salvation is found in no one else, for there is no other name under heaven given to men by which we must be saved" (Ac 4:12). Eckankar's assertion is contradicted by its offer to provide a living Eck master to guide us into truth.
Jesus was not the Word made flesh. The Word is the Sound of God.	"Although It is not understood by the Western church, the Sound is actually the voice of the SUGMAD. The Greeks called it the logos.... Often It is known as the Word, as spoken about in the Bible, or God making ITSELF known" (*Eckankar: The Key to Secret Worlds*, p. 97).	The Bible is clear about just who the Word is. In speaking of Jesus Christ, the apostle John said: "The Word became flesh and made his dwelling among us. We have seen his glory, the glory of the One and Only, who came from the Father, full of grace and truth" (Jn 1:14). God did indeed make Himself (not Itself) known through Jesus, who is "the radiance of God's glory and the exact representation of his being, sustaining all things by his powerful word" (Heb 1:3).

The Doctrine of Jesus Christ—*The Humanity of Christ*

Position	Support	Orthodox Response
Jesus was a follower of Eckankar and was like many other human religious teachers.	"We are living in an age which has become the effect of cosmic consciousness spreading to us through the orthodox savants: Jesus, Buddha, Zoroaster, St. Paul, Lao-tzu, and Emerson to name a few. These were in reality following the principles of Eckankar" (*Eckankar: The Key to Secret Worlds*, p. 23).	As has already been demonstrated, the principles and teachings of Eckankar are remote from the teachings of Jesus and the New Testament. Jesus Christ stands alone as "the way and the truth and the life. No one comes to the Father except through me" (Jn 14:6).
Jesus cannot give us an understanding of truth.	"No teacher, living or past, can give us the actual understanding of Truth. It is wholly dependent upon the individual to make his way to Truth.... each of us is truth itself" (*Eckankar: The Key to Secret Worlds*, p. 49).	Both human history and the Bible demonstrate that "the heart is deceitful above all things and beyond cure. Who can understand it?" (Jer 17:9). Truth, by its very definition, must be true, and this fact creates a serious problem for Eckists if they insist on making each human being a personification of truth. Jesus himself amply demonstrated understanding: "Everyone who heard him was amazed at his understanding and his answers" (Lk 2:47). He also exhibited the ability to make others

The Doctrine of Jesus Christ—*The Humanity of Christ (cont.)*

Position	Support	Orthodox Response
. . . continued		understand scriptural truth: "Then he opened their minds so they could understand the Scriptures" (Lk 24:45). Jesus also made it plain that people must depend on God and not on themselves to find Him, who is "the way and the truth and the life. No one comes to the Father except through me" (Jn 14:6).

The Doctrine of the Holy Spirit

Position	Support	Orthodox Response
The concept of the Holy Spirit	"Often called the Holy Spirit, the Light and Sound are twin aspects of God. The Eck (Holy Spirit) helps us purify ourselves of karma (sin), making it possible for us to accept the full love of God in this lifetime" (*What Is Eckankar*, pp. 1–2). "Most religions speak of the Holy Spirit. It connects each of us with God. You can experience the Holy Spirit as God's Light and Sound. It is the Voice of God speaking to all creation" (*What You Need to Know About the Light and Sound of God*, p. 1). "The Eck is the essence of the SUGMAD, or God. It flows from the Creator down into the lower worlds and then returns again to the Source. The Holy Spirit, Holy Ghost, Logos, the Word, Divine Spirit, the Bani, and the Vadan are a few of these names" (*Eckankar: Ancient Wisdom for Today*, pp. 93–94).	The Holy Spirit of God is not an impersonal force such as light or sound is, but is the third person of the Triune God. Impersonal light or sound even as sublimely used as "God's voice" is not at all consistent with a biblical understanding of the Holy Spirit. Light and sound cannot be "grieved" as the Holy Spirit can (Eph 4:30).

The Doctrine of Man and Sin

Position	Support	Orthodox Response
We are all sparks of God.	"We learn that each of us is Soul, a spark of God sent to this world to gain spiritual experience. And as we unfold spiritually, we learn to express the love of God through service to others" (*What is Eckankar*, p. 1).	The Bible affirms that man is made in God's image but nowhere asserts that the essense of man's being (created spirit) is made of the same substance as that of the Creator (uncreated spirit).

The Doctrine of Man and Sin (cont.)

Position	Support	Orthodox Response
The true nature of man is Soul.	"The Eckist . . . believes that each person **is** Soul and that It is the essential and permanent center of our being" (*Soul Travel and the Spiritual Exercises of Eckankar*, p. 1). "Soul, or Tuza, is the individual consciousness of the whole man, that part of him which is the true awareness of the divine power within himself" (*Eckankar: The Key to Secret Worlds*, p. 18).	The Bible teaches that man is spirit, soul, and body.
Man is composed of five main parts.	"The true component parts of man are actually the various bodies in which he is sheathed during his sojourn in the lower worlds. [1] The first part is the flesh, which we know as the Physical body. . . . This is the body that is visible to the eyes, gets hurt, becomes ill, and experiences death. . . . "[2] The next body of man is a more subtle body. . . . It is commonly known to the Western student of spiritual matters as the Astral body. It has a lighter and finer quality than the Physical body, and it is needed to encase Soul while on the Astral Plane. . . . It is called the Astral body simply because, when seen, it sparkles like stars. . . . "[3] Inside the Astral body and quite different from it is the Causal body. . . . It is so named because it represents that body which collects the causes of those effects that we may find disturbing in our outer life. . . . Often called the seed body, it is the sheath in which we find planted the causes of any karma that we might be serving out in this life. . . . "[4] The next sheath around soul is that which we know as the Mental body. . . . Often we think of this body as the reactive mind, or what is known to the psychologists as the subconscious. . . . It keeps a perfect record of every experience that Soul has, running through all the countless ages of Its existence on every plane in the universes. . . . It is the last body that man drops before entering into the Soul Plane. . . . "[5] The last of the bodies is Soul, or Spirit. . . . It is the real man, the spark of	The Bible teaches that man is composed of no more than three essential parts, two of which are immaterial. They are spirit, soul, and body (1Th 5:23). Another evangelical view proposes two parts on the grounds that spirit and soul are the same. In no sense can the five-part view of Eckankar be reconciled with Scripture.

The Doctrine of Man and Sin (cont.)

Position	Support	Orthodox Response
... continued	that divine being we know as the SUGMAD, or God.... all things in existence in all universes are entirely dependent on Spirit for their life and activity. It is in the Soul that all consciousness resides.... Spirit cannot contact any of the material worlds without intermediate instruments which correspond to the particular planes on which It must abide" (*Eckankar: The Key to Secret Worlds*, pp. 75–79).	
Each person has lived a number of times (reincarnation). We have perhaps even lived as a plant or animal.	"We evolve in consciousness through many different forms of life, even in plant and animal kingdoms, before we take human form" (*Eckankar: Ancient Wisdom for Today*, p. 46).	Reincarnation has been dealt with in the New Age Section. Incorporate and add to following. The idea that plant and animal life are evolving consciousnesses runs counter to Scripture. In Isaiah 44:13–19, it is clear that plants are not sentient. There is no evidence in the Bible that human souls either pre-exist or return to earth in another life after death. "Man is destined to die once, and after that to face judgment" (Heb 9:27). Further, "If anyone is in Christ, he is a new creation; the old has gone, the new has come!" (2Co 5:17). There is therefore no need to be "perfected" in reincarnation. Zechariah 12:1 speaks of "the LORD, who stretches out the heavens, who lays the foundation of the earth, and who forms the spirit of man within him." This tells us the spirit does not exist until the man's physical shell is formed to house it—a concept that runs counter to the idea of reincarnation.
Wrong things are merely productions of mental habits that have been passed from generation to generation.	"All social habits, religions, politics, and dogma are based on mental habits, set in grooves, and handed down through generations. These mental habits are rigid and inflexible and are often the cause of wars which kill millions of people. Mental habits often become the masters of races of people. We might say the whole human race is a slave to mental habits" (*Eckankar: The Key to Secret Worlds*, p. 89).	Man is born fallen and therefore contains within himself all the necessary motivations to do evil (Jer 17:9). Since Eckankar has spiritual dogma and is therefore a religion, it falls under the same criticism that it levels against others. And if that statement is correct, then Eckankar must also be a product of generational mental conditioning.
Man is truly "guilty" of nothing.	"Eckankar teaches that Soul is a happy being. It is not guilty of anything" (*Eckankar: Ancient Wisdom for Today*, p. 19).	The Bible says that "all the world" is "guilty before God" (Ro 3:19 KJV). Jesus warned us not to "be afraid of those who kill the body but cannot kill the soul. Rather, be afraid of the One who can destroy both soul and body in hell" (Mt 10:28). One who is not guilty would not be in danger of being destroyed. Though some souls are at peace with God, many are not.

The Doctrine of Man and Sin (cont.)

Position	Support	Orthodox Response
Present-day chaos and man's suffering are caused by the failure to study the methods of soul travel.	"The neglect to study the methods of separation of Soul from body by our spritual and political leadership is one of the main causes of present-day chaos and man's suffering throughout the ages" (*Eckankar: The Key to Secret Worlds*, p. 7).	The Bible teaches that human troubles are the result of sin and not a failure to study soul travel. Numerous passages demonstrate this, among them John 5:14, in which Jesus tells an invalid, "See, you are well again. Stop sinning or something worse may happen to you." Elsewhere, Jesus said, "Everyone who sins is a slave to sin" (Jn 8:34). Further, "there will be trouble and distress for every human being who does evil: . . . but glory, honor and peace for everyone who does good" (Ro 2:9–10). Merely being separated from the body in and of itself does not deal with sin. The soul still has the problem apart from the blood of Christ, as the Bible states: "Every living soul belongs to me [God], the father as well as the son—both alike belong to me. The soul who sins is the one who will die" (Eze 18:4).
All that is wrong can be grouped into five deadly passions.	"[The five passions] bring us only into harsh struggles against the lower worlds, the valley of death, and an endless circle of births and deaths. . . . "[1] . . . lust, is any normal function which has been allowed to grow into an abnormal demand. . . . [2] anger . . . Its purpose is to stir up strife, cause confusion, and scatter the attention to keep us from concentrating. . . . [3] greed . . . [Its] purpose is to enslave us to the material things of life and to cloud the mind to the higher values of Spirit. . . . [4] attachment . . . It means attachment to something, or an infatuation with another person. . . . [5] vanity . . . It completely deceives us by making us self-satisfied" (*Eckankar: The Key to Secret Worlds*, pp. 90–93).	While we agree that lust, greed, unrighteous anger, vanity, and unhealthy attachments are wrong, the Bible's ultimate statement on sin encompasses three things: "For all that is in the world, the lust of the flesh, and the lust of the eyes, and the pride of life, is not of the Father, but is of the world" (1Jn 2:16 KJV). As for such passions bringing us into "an endless circle of births and deaths," the Bible declares that "man is destined to die once, and after that to face judgment" (Heb 9:27).
The origin of all bad mental habits is Desire.	". . . desire is the source of all pain. When we break down desire, it is found to be avarice, greed, gluttony, appetite, and preference. . . . Desire stirs up the five perversions of the mind, which are actually its brood, and helps enslave the Soul. . . . The end of all desires is the beginning of immortality" (*Eckankar: The Key to Secret Worlds*, p. 155).	Christians can agree that evil desires are the cause of much conflict (Jas 4:1–2). However, the Eckists err in condemning all forms of desire. There can be good desires as well as bad ones: ". . . eagerly desire spiritual gifts" (1Co 14:1). Moreover, only the dead achieve total desirelessness.

The Doctrine of Salvation

Position	Support	Orthodox Response
People cleanse themselves of bad mental habits primarily through soul travel.	"What can Soul Travel do for you? . . . When filled with the excitement and joy which comes with these spiritual experiences, you are more able to change the habits of the past" (*Eckankar: Ancient Wisdom for Today*, pp. 18–19).	Foundational changes to human nature come from an encounter with the risen Savior, Jesus Christ, by trusting His gospel and being spiritually "born again" (see Jn 3:3), not by dubious, transient spiritual experiences such as soul travel or astral projection.
Reaching God, or higher states of consciousness, is also achieved primarily through soul travel.	"Its [Soul Travel's] purpose is mainly to enable Soul to leave the physical body, travel through the higher spiritual worlds, and eventually arrive at Its ultimate destination—the Ocean of Love and Mercy, the true heaven, wherein dwells the SUGMAD, God" (*Eckankar: The Key to Secret Worlds*, p. 2).	The Bible is clear that no one has access to God except through His chosen mediator. "For there is one God and one mediator between God and men, the man Christ Jesus" (1Ti 2:5). Jesus said, "I am the way and the truth and the life. No one comes to the Father except through me" (Jn 14:6). We reach God through a Person, not a practice.
Besides soul travel, one must do everything in the name of the great SUGMAD to escape the cycle of karma and reincarnation.	"Therefore, whatever we do must be done in the name of the SUGMAD. This is the only way to escape from karma in this life. . . . the way to live without creating karma is to act always in the name of the SUGMAD" (*Eckankar: The Key to Secret Worlds*, p. 142).	The Bible says, "And whatever you do, whether in word or deed, do it all in the name of the Lord Jesus, giving thanks to God the Father through him" (Col 3:17).
Initiations to higher levels of spiritual development can only be approved by the Living Eck Master.	"The Living Eck Master is the only one who can approve an initiation for an ECKist" (*Eckankar: Ancient Wisdom for Today*, p. 99).	Their "Master" has no grounds for assuming authority to determine who grows spiritually and who doesn't. The Bible says such decisions are God's alone. "Being confident of this, that he who began a good work in you will carry it on to completion until the day of Christ Jesus" (Php 1:6).
Forgiveness of sins cannot come just by asking for it.	"Our mistakes or sins of the past cannot be absolved at the last minute simply by request" (*ECKANKAR: Ancient Wisdom for Today*, p. 44).	It is not the prerogative of Eckankar to define the conditions to be met for the forgiveness of sins. The Bible says, "Everyone who calls on the name of the Lord will be saved" (Ac 2:21).
Soul travel might be said to be the very cornerstone of spiritual advancement for Eckists.	"The importance of this study [Soul Travel] is evident from the fact that omniscience can be gained through the release of the Soul from the bondage of the flesh. . . . The method of voluntarily withdrawing Soul from the body constitutes the highest technique and is the main occupation of the true seeker after truth" (*Eckankar: The Key to Secret Worlds*, p. 7).	Claiming that a finite person can gain an attribute such as omniscience that solely belongs to deity is both blasphemous and illogical. The fact that the Eckankar organization has lost several lawsuits suggests that its members do not possess omniscience.
Participating in the Sound of God is necessary if one is to become free of karma and reincarnation.	"Without participation in the Sound wave, none can escape the net of karma and reincarnation, or even be truly free and experience ultimate ecstasy" (*Eckankar: The Key to Secret Worlds*, pp. 101–2).	The claim that freedom and ecstasy come for humans from an impersonal source contradicts the biblical statement that only Jesus' teaching makes us truly free. "Then you will know the truth, and the truth will set you free" (Jn 8:32).

The Doctrine of Rewards and Punishment

Position	Support	Orthodox Response
Reincarnation and karma	"Karma and reincarnation are primary beliefs in Eckankar. We build up karma as a result of the spiritual law of cause and effect. The Eck (Holy Spirit) helps us purify ourselves of karma (sin), making it possible for us to accept the full love of God in this lifetime" (*What Is Eckankar?*, pp. 1–2). "If karma has not been paid up by the time of death, then two things can happen: one can pay off in the Astral or whatever world he goes to upon leaving this body, or he can return here for payment.... If a person finds himself filled with karmic debt concerning this physical life, then he must come back here" (*Eckankar: The Key to Secret Worlds*, p. 137). "When you achieve the exalted state of Self-Realization, you'll still be held accountable for your actions in your daily life. However, you will have worked off the karma built up from past lives. And when you finish your mission in this life, unless you choose to come back to this plane to teach or to serve, you need not return" (*Eckankar: Ancient Wisdom for Today*, pp. 39–40).	There is no biblical evidence that human souls return to earth or to an astral world to pay off karmic debt. The concept of karma presupposes that an impersonal force (the "law of karma") would know what personal beings do—which contradicts its nature as impersonal—or has any reason to demand retribution or give reward. An impersonal force can act upon human beings (as gravity and heat do), but the ability to judge human behavior is the domain of sentient beings. The Bible reserves this prerogative to God. Moreover, judgment requires a judge. "For he has set a day when he will judge the world with justice by the man he has appointed" (Ac 17:31). Justice also requires moral standards of behavior that apply to all humanity and are absolute. The error of reincarnation is that it seeks a moral code and an inescapable retribution without a moral lawgiver. It plunges into mysticism and illogic at the very point where reason demands a personal and just God. Further, it does not deal with the sinful nature of mankind. Only the biblical God can be both just and compassionate, as He alone knows all contingencies. Although Eckankar professes belief in the conscious existence of the soul after death, this concept cannot arise from its doctrine of ultimate reality. If ultimate reality (Sugmad) is impersonal, then our own personalities must be invalidated or regarded as illusory.
The ultimate reward is to become a co-manager with God.	"Eckankar teaches that our destiny is to become a Co-worker with God.... This differentiates Eckankar from Buddhism or Hinduism, which describe their final goal as a dissolution of the individual into God" (*Eckankar: Ancient Wisdom for Today*, pp. 22–23).	

The Doctrine of Rewards and Punishment (cont.)

Position	Support	Orthodox Response
Heaven, as most people think of it, is a misunderstanding of the astral plane of existence.	"When the physical body dies, Soul continues to exist on the other planes of God. Soul may stay on these other planes for a day, a thousand years, or more. . . . For many, this in-between time is heaven. The Astral Plane, for example, has sections which resemble all of the heavens described in the major religious traditions. You might find Saint Peter and the pearly gates, or the happy hunting grounds, or even visit the palace of Zeus, or Jupiter. On the Astral Plane you find what you expect, what you hope for, or what you fear" (*Eckankar: Ancient Wisdom for Today*, p. 48).	Equating the astral plane with heaven, Eckankar says it is what one expects and different for each individual. This is a weak, subjective view of what the Bible treats as an objectively real, wonderful place. Jesus said He went ahead to prepare a place for us (Jn 14:2). The apostle Paul was torn between leaving the real and its objective reality and going to that place Jesus went to prepare: "For to me, to live is Christ, and to die is gain. . . . I am torn between the two: I desire to depart and be with Christ, which is better by far" (Php 1:21–23). If this meant merely going to be in a place of his own imagining, he would be leaving objective reality and going to an inferior, subjective one. The objective reality of heaven is grounded in the objective reality of its Maker.

INTERESTING AND DISTINCTIVE BELIEFS

Position	Support	Orthodox Response
Spiritual advancement comes by performing various spiritual exercises such as singing the word "HU" (allegedly an ancient name for God).	"When you sing HU and sit in quiet contemplation, you might also perceive the inner Light and Sound.... As you sing the name of God, with love, for twenty minutes a day, the bindings and bands that constrain Soul will begin to unwind.... As these bindings are released, Soul rises in spiritual freedom" (*A Love Song to God: HU*, p. 3).	The only spiritual benefit to be gained from singing comes from that which glorifies and is directed to the true God (Ps 149:1; Col 3:16). Since Hu is a false god, singing its praises will only serve to perpetuate idolatry and bring condemnation on the souls who do this.
Eckankar teaches more than a hundred spiritual exercises designed to bring spiritual advancement.	"Soul Travel is accomplished by practicing the Spiritual Exercises of Eckankar on a daily basis. Similar to prayer, these spiritual exercises help you open your heart to Divine Spirit, the Light and Sound of God. Eckankar teaches over one hundred different exercises..." (*Soul Travel and the Spiritual Exercises of Eckankar*, pp. 1–2).	Eckankar is just one of a variety of spiritual exercises in the Surat/Shabd (light/sound) Yoga tradition. Others include the Divine Light Mission, MSIA, and Radha Soami. Each one offers a different technique for contacting the "divine" current of sound or light, yet none lead to the Creator.
Eckists hold to an interesting theory as to why babies have a soft spot on their heads.	"The top of the head is the point at which the human self merges with Spirit. Very young children have a soft spot at this place, where the opening has not closed.... As the spot closes, the child grows more worldly in outlook and expression. Those wishing to be initiated into the Supreme Consciousness, or that of the inner kingdom, must become as little children. This means that the opening must remain at the top of the head, like the soft spot of a baby" (*Eckankar: The Key to Secret Worlds*, pp. 29–30).	The "soft spot" on the top of the baby's head facilitates the birthing process. Christians see this as the intricate and masterful design of the Creator. The Eckist theory is biblically unwarranted, and they force the words of Jesus Christ (see Mt 19:13–15) into an alien context. Jesus was not speaking of adult souls leaving through the cranium, but of having the inherent trust that children display toward their earthly father extended to our heavenly Father.
Man creates his own realities whether he knows he is doing so or not.	"The chief delusion of man is his conviction that there are causes at work in his life other than his own states of consciousness. All that happens to him, all that is done by him, comes to him as a result of his states of consciousness. This is true of his state of spiritual consciousness, for he is all that he thinks and desires and loves, all that he believes is true and consents to happen to him" (*Eckankar: The Key to Secret Worlds*, p. 5).	The biblical teaching on ethics is that true and objective evil exists and results in great pain being inflicted on us from outside—by other people and by Satan. To say otherwise is to damage the very heart of compassion, which is a bulwark of Christian ethical thought. The implication of the Eckist position is that the six million Jews who were mutilated, tortured, and murdered by Hitler created that horror themselves. This is truly abhorrent to the believing Christian.

9

The Family / Children of God

NOTE: Due to the sexually explicit and profane nature of The Family's literature, some of the words in the following charts have been edited down to only their first letter.

FACTS AND HISTORY

Facts	
Topic	*Current Facts*
Membership	The Family (formerly known as the Children of God) is an extremely secretive group that does not usually release membership information. Former members monitoring the group estimate that there are 9,000–15,000 full-time members worldwide and about 5,000 "TSers" (Tithe Supporters) who, though not living in Family communes, give the group financial support.
Worship	Full-time members live in communes called "Homes." Once or twice a week they hold "Inspirations" (song and testimony meetings) and attend "lesson-sharing meetings." During these meetings confessions are made, members are rebuked for sins, and demons are cast out of those accused of being possessed or oppressed by the devil. "Sunday Fellowships," usually in the afternoon, consist of songs, testimonies, and communion. Worship usually includes singing "revolutionary songs" (folk songs urging members to greater sacrifice and dedication) and selected "loving up Jesus" tunes. Services are marked by the lifting up of hands and speaking in tongues. Ex-members report that at one time the Sunday communions often evolved into "come-unions" (nude dances and orgies). The founder, David Berg, promoted such events: "Do You have Come-union? . . . I often get something new in communion, the fact that in our Family we are one body, all the way!—Sexually as well. . . . LOVE IS GOING TO BE MANIFEST SOMEHOW IN THE FLESH—usually ultimately in sex. . . . DO WE HAVE COMPLETE FULL COMMUNION? . . . Communion in the flesh as well as the spirit?" (*DO* 781:72, 84, 86, "The Lord's Supper").
Leaders of The Family	1968–94 David "Moses" Berg was the undisputed leader of the Family. However, many of his responsibilities were taken over by Karen Zerby, his secretary since 1969. Berg is reported to have died in November 1994. 1980s– Karen Zerby has been in charge of all publications and the leadership structure since the mid-eighties and since Berg's death has become the leader of the movement. 1990s– Steve Kelly and Grant Montgomery (a.k.a. Paul Papers and Gary) began to take on more leadership as Zerby began to encounter blindness, reportedly owing to trachoma. As of 1994, Zerby's degree of blindness had reached 90 percent.
Publications	The Family produces numerous publications and cassette tapes for internal and public distribution. Those for the general public include (1) "Heaven's Magic" music tapes; (2) children's videos; and (3) *World News Digest* (newspaper reprints). Material strictly for internal use includes (1) numerous doctrinal booklets; (2) "Mo Letters" (talks and writings by Berg, abbreviated here as ML); (3) "Mo Volumes" (Mo Letters compiled in book form); and (4) "Mama Letters" (talks and writings of Zerby, which are given ML numbers, as if they were Mo Letters, but are also numbered separately as Mama Letters). [Abbreviations of publications are used in this chapter as follows: ML (Mo Letters); DO (Disciples Only); DFO (Disciples and Friends Only); LTA (Leadership Trainees); GP (General Public); GN (GoodNews).]

Facts (cont.)	
Topic	*Current Facts*
General statement of beliefs	A former high-ranking member states, "The Family has produced a professional looking Statement of Beliefs and has gone to pains to make it sound as orthodox as possible, carefully wording the text to hide their real teachings from evangelical Christians. In reality, they promote an unbelievable pantheon of pseudo-Christian heresies." Family members believe that (1) the Holy Spirit is a sexy, near-naked woman (God the Father's wife); (2) Christ is a creation of God; (3) Christ was conceived through sex between the angel Gabriel and Mary; (4) Christ freely fornicated with his female disciples and may have possibly even contracted venereal diseases; and (5) Christ has orgies in heaven. Family members may freely fornicate and commit adultery as long as they "do it in love" ; they have extolled "Flirty Fishing" (using sex to gain new members) as the best method of witnessing. Necromancy (contacting the dead) is also practiced.

History

Topic	*History*
David Brandt Berg	Born in California in 1919, David Berg was raised in a Christian environment. His grandfather and mother were traveling evangelists. In 1944 Berg married Jane Miller, and they had four children: Linda, Paul, Jonathan, and Faith. Much information about the family comes from Linda (called "Deborah"), who left the group in 1978 and wrote a book about her experiences (Deborah Davis, *The Children of God: The Inside Story,* 1984).
	Berg became the pastor of a Christian Missionary Alliance church in Valley Farms, Arizona, in 1949, but left abruptly in 1951. Some members of his personal family believe Berg was fired because of a sex scandal, although Berg consistently denied this. In any case, he became embittered toward the established church.
	Throughout the 1950s Berg allegedly searched for the perfect church, eventually settling into the Los Angeles-based American Soul Clinic, a missionary organization founded by Fred Jordan. Although Berg spent the next few years "serving God" by publically promoting Jordan's gospel broadcasts, his personal life was reportedly far from Christian, including adultery and incest (see *Urgent Warning* tract by No Longer Children Ministry, p. 2).
	In 1967 Berg moved to Huntington Beach, California, where in 1968-69 he took over a coffee house run by Teen Challenge (a national youth ministry founded by Assemblies of God minister David Wilkerson). Gaining popularity through his anti-church and anti-establishment sermons, Berg and his followers, then known as Teens for Christ, fled California in 1969 due to what they called "persecution." That same year Berg left his wife to live with a young new disciple named Karen Zerby (renamed "Maria"). Berg claimed in a "prophecy" that God ordained the replacing of his wife ("the old church") with Maria ("the new church"). Thus began Berg's use of prophetic utterances to justify his teachings and practices. (Berg's example and subsequent teachings on sex quickly led to unrestrained sexual promiscuity in the group.)
	After wandering around the United States for eight months—during which time a newspaper reporter dubbed them the Children of God (COG)—they settled at the Texas Soul Clinic (TSC) in Thurber, Texas. They soon started new communities across the country, beginning with Los Angeles. That same year Berg received a "spirit helper" (a gypsy king from the 1200s named Abrahim) allegedly sent by God, an event that marked the beginning of blatant occultism in the COG. The group eventually started being targeted by ex-members, angry parents of followers, and legal authorities. This "persecution" eventually caused the COG to go underground and assume a variety of names including The Family of Love, Heaven's Magic, and The Family. During a short period of time (from the late 1970s to the late 1980s) they all but completely disappeared from America and took up residence in numerous foreign countries. Even there, however, they drew angry protests and police raids over charges of child abuse, child pornography, and pedophilia.

History (cont.)	
Topic	**History**
. . . continued	The 1990s have seen Berg and his followers resurface in the United States as "The Family." Although the group still teaches heretical doctrines, their new *public* image is so attractive that they were invited to sing for President Bush at a White House ceremony during the 1992 Christmas season and for President Clinton in 1994.
	The Family has recently linked up with groups such as Scientology, the Jehovah's Witnesses, and the Moonies to form the International Federation of Religions and Philosophical Minorities, an organization designed to defend the rights of "New Religious Movements" and share information about those supposedly attacking religious freedom (such as counter-cult ministries).

THEOLOGY

The Doctrine of Revelation		
Position	*Support*	*Orthodox Response*
Whenever the Bible contradicts the Mo Letters, Berg states that Scripture is nothing but the outdated opinions of fallible, bigoted, and mistaken men.	"**. . . some of the parts of the Bible are no longer up to date!** . . . They're the rules God's people **used** to live by, not the rules they're supposed to live by **today**!" (*ML* 242:38—*DO*, "Old Bottles").	Asserting that parts of the Bible are no longer applicable today contradicts 2 Timothy 3:16–17: "All Scripture is God-breathed and is useful for teaching, rebuking, correcting and training in righteousness, so that the man of God may be thoroughly equipped for every good work."
	"A LOT OF THINGS THAT PAUL SAID WERE RIGHT FOR HIS TIME AND HIS DAY, BUT THEY DON'T NECESSARILY BIND US TODAY" (*ML* 635:70—*DFO*, "Grace vs. Law").	We can also be assured of Scripture's relevancy in contemporary society because God, the author of the Bible, is unchanging (Mal 3:6; Heb 6:17–18; Jas 1:17).
	"I DON'T AGREE WITH ALL THAT PAUL SAID. . . . he is probably sorry for some of the things he said" (*ML* 635:60—*DFO*, "Grace vs. Law").	The apostle Paul and all the other biblical writers did not simply put down whatever came to them. They transcribed Holy Scripture by divine inspiration. Peter wrote, "No prophecy of Scripture came about by the prophet's own interpretation. For prophecy never had its origin in the will of man, but men spoke from God as they were carried along by the Holy Spirit." (2Pe 1:20–21).
	"**NOT ALL OF PAUL'S WRITINGS WERE ALWAYS NECESSARILY TOTALLY IN THE SPIRIT. . . . IF ANY OF YOU WANNA STRING ME UP FOR HERESY FOR THAT, YOU'LL BE JUST LIKE ALL THE REST OF THE G———— ORTHODOXISTS**. . . . for God's Sake, don't hand me anymore of that s— about the Apostle Paul. . . . Paul was no more divinely inspired, nor infallible, than we are by His Spirit" (*ML* 76:49, 51—*LTA* "Dear Rahel").	

Position	Support	Orthodox Response
The true teachings of the Bible have been buried beneath men's false interpretations of the text. Only Berg, through the Mo Letters, can rightly uncover these lost truths.	"... the true Plan and Foundation of God as outlined in the Bible has been almost totally buried under the rubble of Churchianity and the traditions of man.... WHY WE NEED THE MO LETTERS.... If we sweep away all this churchy garbage and get back down and delve underneath to find the foundations, then we can see the Plan.... TO REDISCOVER THE TRUE FOUNDATION, it takes an archeologist who comes and clears away the rubble! He digs out the Bible from under all the trash and reveals it to you as it really is and really was.... I am your archeologist. WITH EVERY [MO] LETTER I'M CLEARING AWAY THE CHURCH RUBBLE" (*ML* 329:11, 12–15—*GP*, "The Word—New and Old [MT 13:52]").	The health and vitality of God's church depend on the continued perspecuity, or clarity and understandability, of Scripture. Claiming that the clear teachings of the Bible have been obscured by carnal traditions of organized denominations is a common ploy used by cult leaders to assert their authority and propound their teachings. However, 1 John 2:27 states that the Holy Spirit is our teacher and helps us discern truth from error. Also, Jesus promised that those who are truly following Him will hear His voice as He leads and guides them (Jn 10:27–28).
Berg is a new prophet of God with new truths that must be believed. **Those who reject Berg or his letters reject God as well.**	"YOU HAVE GOT TO BELIEVE IN THE LORD AND IN ME, that I am a new prophet of a new day of a whole lot of new things that Paul never even thought about!" (*ML* 635:67—*DFO*, "Grace vs. Law"). "'He that doesn't receive David doesn't receive Me', the Lord said! (Tongues:) 'Blessed are the words & blessed is the tongue that I have given David!'" (*DO* 1412:2, "Aphrodite!—Goddess of Love!").	Berg has repeatedly stated that he is the greatest prophet of God on earth, but his saying so does not make it so. His self-exalting prophecies are false. Berg fails every scriptural criterion for determining whether someone is a true prophet, and his vulgar and blasphemous teachings disqualify him from the role of a true Christian teacher.
The Bible is superseded by the revelations that have come to Berg.	"IT'S A DAMNABLE DOCTRINE OF CHURCH DEVILS TO CONFINE ALL THE TRUTH AND REVELATIONS OF GOD strictly to the Bible.... WHAT GOD HAS GIVEN ME is filling in some of the remaining details of Biblical truth" (*ML* 329: 22, 24—*GP*, "The Word—New and Old [MT 13:52]"). "If God has spoken at all and shown me these things at all ... it is His Words for today and it supercedes anything else that has ever been given, if it is different" (*ML* 635:70—*DFO*, "Grace vs. Law"). "MOST OF OUR KIDS DON'T KNOW THE OLD BIBLE DOCTRINES.... BUT SOME OF THESE PEOPLE HAVE HAD THEIR RESERVATIONS AND THEIR DOUBTS ... especially those of strong churchy Biblical backgrounds. Therefore some of the things that I have said are going to raise questions in their minds and I'm sure the Devil is going to supply them with lots of Scriptures and say, 'Well now, but, the Bible says so and so ...'" (*ML* 635: 55, 57—*DFO*, "Grace vs Law").	Jesus said, "Until heaven and earth disappear, not the smallest letter, not the least stroke of a pen, will by any means disappear from the Law until everything is accomplished" (Mt 5:18). He also promised that His own words would not "pass away" (Mt 24:35). The prophet Isaiah wrote, "The grass withers and the flowers fall, but the word of our God stands forever" (Isa 40:8).

The Doctrine of Revelation (cont.)

Position	Support	Orthodox Response
God is the author of the "Mo Letters" ("Word of God") written by Berg to his followers. They include his dreams, spiritual experiences, thoughts, and interpretations of the Bible.	"**THE MO LETTERS By Father Moses David**.... **AUTHOR:** God by His Spirit ..." (*The Mo Letters*, vol. V, credits page). "That is contempt, absolute contempt for the Word of God, to put that [a non-Mo Letter] up alongside the MO Letters.... <u>I GIVE THE KIDS SOMETHING GOD HAS GIVEN</u>" (*ML* 352:41, 58—DO, "The Uneager Beaver").	It is quite impossible that God authored the Mo Letters because they contradict in numerous places what God has already said in Scripture.
When Berg is drunk, he can more easily receive and impart revelations from God.	"<u>WHEN I GET DRUNK I YIELD TO GOD'S SPIRIT</u>.... if you get intoxicated, why, it just makes you even <u>more</u> free in the <u>spirit</u>" (*ML* 525:54—LTO, "The One That Got Away Part II: Jesus & Sex!"). "<u>DON'T YOU UNDERSTAND? WINE OPENS THE GATE OF REVELATION</u>! And if you give me a little <u>more</u> wine, I give you a lot more <u>revelation</u>.... I have to have wine to open my mouth to give you some more revelation" (*DFO* 796:8, "The Mystery of Otano!").	Drunkenness is a sin (Ro 13:13; Gal 5:21; 1Co 5:11), and Christians are explicitly told not to get drunk (Eph 5:18). Consequently, the "revelations" Berg received while drunk could not have come from God.

The Doctrine of God—*The Trinity*

Position	Support	Orthodox Response
Berg's dreams, also directly from God, are published through the Mo Letters.	"... when I dictate a dream ... I give it exactly the way I got it, and usually in the long run it always comes out that God gives the interpretation.... the Lord begins to add the meaning, the understanding" (*ML* 352:50–51—DO, "The Uneager Beaver").	Many of Berg's dreams, as we shall see, are not only vulgar but blasphemous. As such, they cannot be accepted as vehicles through which God would impart divine truths.

The Doctrine of God—*The Trinity (cont.)*

Position	Support	Orthodox Response
Berg believes that God created everything out of Himself, or His energy, yet also believes that God is still a personal God. Consequently, Berg and his group have a somewhat pantheistic view of God (that is, all is God and God is all). They are not strictly pantheistic, however, because they also teach that God is somehow a personal being.	"HINDUISM & THE INDIAN RELIGIONS TEACH THAT ALL THINGS ARE GOD, that everything is God really.... I never really argued too much with that particular theory of the Oriental religions because it was too close to the Truth" (*DO* 1854:14, "More on TM & the Unified Field"). "... God's marvellous creation of the Earth, Sun, Moon, & stars.... In a sense, they're <u>part</u> of God. God is in it all & everywhere.... God is in everything & everything is in God & everything is a part of God & God is part of everything!" (*GN* 15—*DFO* 1308: 69, "The Constellation of Daniel").	God is not one with all that is. Nor is He "part" of all that is. Genesis 1 draws a distinction between God and creation. This is demonstrated in many other Bible verses, including Isaiah 40:22; 42:5; Jeremiah 27:5; and Acts 17:23–24.
The orthodox definition of the Trinity is false. Jesus did not always exist, so He is not the eternal God, but only a part of God. The Holy Spirit, being female, is not God, but the Mother Goddess, God's wife.	"I don't even believe in the Trinity. You can't find that word in the Bible.... I believe in the <u>Father</u> and I believe in the <u>Son</u>, Jesus, and I believe in the <u>Holy Ghost</u>" (*DFO* 631:130, "Islam"). "If you want to call it Trinity, all right, but I don't believe in it in some ways.... You would think that Jesus just always was, just like God, but in a sense He was not until He was made man, although He was in the beginning and He was a part of God." "THE HOLY TRINITY: <u>FATHER</u>, <u>MOTHER</u> and <u>SON</u>!" (*DFO* 723, "The Goddess of Love," caption to drawing).	The orthodox Christian concept of the Trinity is of the Triune God manifesting Himself in three persons, yet being one God; belief in the Trinity is a vital part of the Christian faith. For Jesus to literally be God, one *does* have to believe that He "just always was, just like God" the Father. It is not enough to say you believe in the Father, Son, and Holy Spirit, but assign them vastly different roles and positions in the Godhead. To dissect the one Triune God into completely separate and unequal beings of Father, Mother, and Child is a heretical concept.
God the Father is a being who spiritually indulges in sex with believers.	"God has such thrills and intoxications of the Spirit in store for you.... you'll enjoy the very wonders of **total** intimacy with a **sexy naked God** Himself in a **wild orgy** of the **Spirit** as His **totally** surrendered Bride.... **WE HAVE A SEXY GOD AND A SEXY RELIGION WITH A VERY SEXY LEADER WITH AN EXTREMELY SEXY YOUNG FOLLOWING!**" (*ML* 286: 23, 32—*GP*, "C'mon Ma, Burn Your Bra!").	God is not a "sexy" being because God is neither male nor female. God is a spirit (Jn 4:24), and a spirit does not have flesh and bones (Lk 24:39). Scripture states explicitly that God is not a man (Nu 23:19; 1Sa 15:29; Hos 11:9).
Like God the Father, God the Son (Jesus) is a being who enjoys sex orgies with Christians in heaven.	"the Lord says: .... thou shalt be as one that is drunken with Me and one that doth **revel in My love**. (Mo sees a wine-drinking sex orgy with the Lord and others and laughs.)" (*ML* 152:16—*GP*, "A Psalm of David").	Such a concept of Jesus is not only repugnant and blasphemous, but contrary to what Scripture teaches. Fornication and sexual impurity are sinful (Ac 15:29; Ro 13:13; 1Co 6:9; 1Th 4:3). Hebrews 13:4 says that God will judge fornicators.

The Doctrine of Jesus Christ—*The Deity of Christ*

Position	Support	Orthodox Response
Jesus has not always existed. He was created sometime before the world was created.	"... here in the 14th verse of the third Chapter of Revelation, Jesus Himself... says <u>He</u> is the <u>Beginning</u> of the <u>Creation</u> of God! <u>So what was Jesus & what is Jesus?— A creation of God</u>.... He must've been created <u>before</u> the creation of the Heavens & the Earth" (*DO* 2359: 14–15, 18, "Vespers: Psalm 2:6–8").	In Revelation 3:14 (NASB) the word "beginning" does not mean "first-created" of creation. The Greek word *arche* literally means source or origin. What the verse is actually saying, then, is that Jesus is the source, or origin, of God's creation. In other words, Jesus is the one from whom all creation springs.

The Doctrine of Jesus Christ—*The Humanity of Christ*

Position	Support	Orthodox Response
Berg originally taught that Jesus was conceived through sexual intercourse between Mary and God the Father.	"Which was the more remarkable... the more intimate experience for Mary?— When Gabriel stood there merely making an announcement to her, or when the Lord Himself came in unto her, & had intercourse with her, held her in His arms & gave her such a spiritual orgasm that produced His Own Son!" (*DO* 998:18, "Listen"). "<u>GOD HIMSELF HAD SEX WITH MARY TO HAVE JESUS</u>.... God Himself took human form & literally f—— Mary to make her pregnant with Jesus!" (*DFO* 999:111, "The Devil Hates Sex").	This statement is blasphemous in the extreme. Nothing in Scripture suggests that Jesus was conceived through sex between Mary and God Himself. Jesus was miraculously conceived in the womb of the virgin Mary through the overshadowing power of the Holy Spirit: "His mother Mary was pledged to be married to Joseph, but before they came together, she was found to be with child through the Holy Spirit" (Mt 1:18). Further, "an angel of the Lord appeared to him [Joseph] in a dream and said, 'Joseph son of David, do not be afraid to take Mary home as your wife, because what is conceived in her is from the Holy Spirit'" (v. 20).
Berg's view of Jesus' conception has evolved over the years. He now believes that Jesus was conceived through sex between Mary and the angel Gabriel.	"... why couldn't God have used the angel Gabriel to f—— Mary.... Gabriel supplied the sperm, Mary supplied the egg & God supplied the Spirit.... **'HE CAME IN UNTO HER'**, & that expression's only used in having sex throughout the Bible" (*DFO* 1566:6, "Answers to Your Questions!—No. 8"). "Gabriel was a spirit, an angel of God. He is already, in a sense, a part of God, or a representation of God.... the angel came 'in unto her' is a term, a phrase used in the Bible only for sexual intercourse.... since the wording is so specific that He did come 'in unto her'; He in other words had sexual intercourse with her.... It was the Angel <u>Gabriel</u> that 'came in unto' her.... I did that this morning with you. I came in unto you when we had sexual intercourse" (*DO* 1854:42, 43, 45, 48, "More on TM & the Unified Field!").	This teaching is unbiblical (see above).

The Doctrine of Jesus Christ—*The Humanity of Christ (cont.)*

Position	Support	Orthodox Response
Berg was told through a vision that Jesus constantly fornicated with His female disciples.	"THAT'S THE ONLY TIME I EVER HAD A VISION OF CHRIST.... Maria & I were making love. I exploded in the spirit speaking loudly in tongues with a message that would shock most of the world about Jesus & Mary & Martha, with whom I saw Him in that moment.... why should Jesus have been considered sinful to have enjoyed sex with Mary & Martha?—Which He <u>did</u> according to what I saw in my vision" (*DFO* 1237:30, 46, "Houris of Heaven"). "... the Lord had sex with Mary and Martha and probably Mary Magdalene the harlot!" (*ML* 569:183—*DO*, "Afflictions"). "JESUS AND MARY WERE ENJOYING SEX WITHOUT SIN!" (*ML* 651:45—*DFO*, "Little Nuggets").	Berg's preoccupation with sex is apparent in these particular quotes. Because fornication is sinful (Ac 15:29; Ro 13:13; 1Co 6:9; 1Th 4:3), it would have been impossible for Jesus, who died sinless (1Pe 1:19; 2Pe 3:14), to have engaged in fornication.
Jesus probably caught a venereal disease because of His sexual promiscuity.	"NOW I'M GOING TO TELL YOU SOMETHING THAT'S GOING TO BE HARD FOR YOU TO BELIEVE.... I think it's a direct revelation of God—and I believe the Scriptures confirm it.... 'we have not an high priest who <u>cannot</u> be touched with the <u>feeling</u> of our <u>infirmities</u>.'... Are you beginning to realise what that means?... at sometime or other Jesus knew what it was like to be <u>sick</u>.... HOW COULD HE POSSIBLY HAVE BEEN TEMPTED IN ALL POINTS LIKE AS WE ARE UNLESS AT SOMETIME HE SUFFERED DISEASES?... HE MAY HAVE EVEN CONTRACTED A DISEASE FROM MARY MAGDALENE, WHO HAD BEEN A KNOWN PROSTITUTE, and several other women that were prostitutes that followed Him, or Mary and Martha.... One of these days they're probably going to say, 'Well, they even believe that Jesus had venereal disease!'... IF HE'D NEVER SUFFERED THEIR SEXUAL DISEASES HE COULD NEVER REALLY HAVE FULL COMPASSION ON THEIR SUFFERINGS" (*ML* 569:28, 29, 33, 48, 51, 52, 55—*DO*, "Afflictions").	Berg's assertion that Jesus would need to experience a sexual disease in order to have compassion on those with such afflictions is not only logically flawed, but also biblically unsound. We do not need to go through other people's experiences to feel genuine compassion for them. If such were the case, no one could really have compassion because no two people can experience life in exactly the same way, in the same order, at the same time, and with the same people. Jesus was able to know men's thoughts and feelings (Mt 9:4; 12:25; Lk 6:8; 9:47; Jn 4:17–18). Consequently, He would be able to have compassion on people with sexual diseases, without experiencing a sexual disease, because He would be able to know their exact thoughts and feelings.

The Doctrine of the Resurrection

Position	Support	Orthodox Response
Jesus Christ rose bodily from the grave.	"'SPIRIT HATH NOT FLESH AND BONE AS YOU SEE ME HAVE!' They <u>recognised</u> Jesus when they first saw Him" (*GP* 818:45, "Sex in Heaven").	This is an orthodox statement.

The Doctrine of the Holy Spirit

Position	Support	Orthodox Response
The Holy Spirit is the naked, sexy wife of God the Father.	"I ALWAYS DID THINK OF GOD AS OUR HEAVENLY FATHER AND HIS SPIRIT OF LOVE AS OUR HEAVENLY MOTHER.... His beautiful Holy Spirit, God's Spirit-Queen of Love.... the Heavenly Lover and Mother-God, the Queen of Love.... AND SHE'S DRESSED SO APPROPRIATELY!—Pearls for purity, hearts for Love—and nudity for Truth!" (DFO 723:3, 6, 11, 14, "The Goddess of Love"). "THESE SCRIPTURES IN THE OLD TESTAMENT USING 'SHE' AND 'HER' referring to His Spirit of Wisdom in Prov. 3:13–18; 4:5–9; 7:4; 8:1–36 and 9:1–12 have always been noted by Bible authorities as being some of the descriptions of the Holy Spirit in the Old Testament" (DFO 723:20, "The Goddess of Love"). "GOD THE FATHER, GOD THE SON, JESUS, AND GOD THE HOLY SPIRIT MOTHER.... SHE, AS PART OF THE GODHEAD, is even spoken of here as having always been with Him [God] from Eternity" (DFO 723:5, 27, "The Goddess of Love").	Nothing in the Bble supports such wild assertions about the identity of the Holy Spirit. The verses quoted by Berg use the terms "she" and "her" in a figurative sense, in much the same way one speaks of a car or a country as a "her." No one would assume that the object being spoken of is actually a woman or having feminine gender. This kind of figurative speech is common in Hebrew and many other languages. Using Berg's line of reasoning, we would have to assume that every human soul—including men's—are feminine. King David wrote, "My soul shall make her boast in the LORD" (Ps 34:2 KJV). This can hardly mean that his body and mind were masculine, but his soul was feminine. Berg's writings are replete with this kind of superficial understanding of the Scriptures. It should also be noted that in John 14, 15, and 16, the masculine words "He" and "Him" are applied to the Holy Spirit.
Berg claims that in one of his spiritual experiences, he went to heaven and had sex with the Holy Spirit/Mother.	"I THEN TURNED RESPECTFULLY & REVERENTLY TOWARD THE BEAUTIFUL QUEEN MOTHER OF ALL HEAVEN.... I didn't know exactly what to do, but She solved the problem for me immediately by throwing Her own arms about me & warmly, lovingly kissing & caressing & hugging me.... AND I IMMEDIATELY EXPLODED IN A TREMENDOUS ORGASM OF THE SPIRIT as I felt as though my whole body were inside of Her!" (DO 2115:25, 26, "Our Audience with the King of Kings!")	At least three people in the Bible speak of an experience of heaven: Isaiah (Isa 6:1–13), Paul (2Co 12:1–10), and John (Rev 4:1ff.). Isaiah and John both experienced the angels saying, "Holy, holy, holy," declaring the moral virtue of God. All three men came away with humble feelings about the heavenly experiences. These experiences were quite different from what Berg claimed for himself.

The Doctrine of Man and Sin

Position	Support	Orthodox Response
Everyone is a sinner because of Adam's transgression in the Garden of Eden. Only through faith in Jesus and His death can people receive righteusness.	"Man was created innocent by his Maker, but through the temptation of Satan he voluntarily transgressed and fell from his sinless and happy state, in consequence of which all Mankind are now sinners, and are absolutely unable to attain to righteousness without the saving power of Jesus Christ" (Our Statement of Faith, p. 1, sec. 4, "The Fall of Man").	This is an orthodox statements.

The Doctrine of Salvation

Position	Support	Orthodox Response
Salvation is by grace through faith alone, apart from works.	"You cannot save yourself no matter <u>how</u> good you try to be.... THERE'S NOTHING YOU CAN DO TO GET IT [salvation] EXCEPT JUST <u>RECEIVE</u> IT BY <u>FAITH</u>!" (*Growing in Love*, "Born Again—Are You?" p. 10)	This is an orthodox statement.
Since salvation is obtained apart from works, the only "law" that needs to be followed is Christ's "law of love." Someone can do whatever one pleases as long as it is done in love.	"<u>WE DO NOT HAVE TO KEEP THE TEN COMMANDMENTS</u>!... We now only have to keep <u>God's law</u> of <u>love</u>.... We are totally, utterly <u>free</u> of the old Mosaic law.... Now <u>all</u> things are lawful to us in <u>love</u>, praise God! As long as it's done in <u>love</u> it keeps God's <u>only Law</u> of <u>Love</u>!" (*ML* 592:29, 30—*DFO*, "God's Only Law of Love").	This statement is only orthodox in part. Although the Ten Commandments have been superseded by the law of grace (or law of love), they have not been abolished. Instead, the law of grace serves as an ultimate means of fulfilling the law of Moses. Jesus said He came not to abolish the law but to fulfill it (Mt 5:17). The whole purpose of the law is to point us toward Jesus Christ (Gal 3:24) so that through our relationship with Him we will be able to fulfill the perfect law of love by keeping His New Covenant commandments (Jn 13:34; 14:15; Rev 14:12).
For Christians, sins (acts that are not in accordance with Christ's "law of love") fall into two categories: (1) things that Christians believe are sins; and (2) anything Berg believes is a sin. (NOTE: To discern something as sin, one must first discover what is wrong and right. This knowledge is gained through reading Mo Letters. In reality, then, there is only one category of sins—whatever Berg calls a sin.)	"'<u>WHATSOEVER IS NOT OF FAITH IS SIN</u>'. (Rom. 14:23.) 'Happy is he that condemneth not himself in that thing which he alloweth'. (Rom. 14:22.).... In other words, if you have such strong <u>faith</u> in the <u>Spirit</u> and in the <u>Word</u> that you <u>know</u> what you're doing is right... <u>you</u> can do things that some <u>other</u> Christians can't even do" (*ML* 604: 2, 5—*DFO*, "Doubts!"). "<u>GOD'S ONLY LAW IS LOVE</u>, and if what you're doing you're doing in <u>love</u> and you're not hurting any innocent party, then it is perfectly legal for you.... now hurting <u>guilty</u> parties, that's something we can't avoid. (... <u>SAY A MAN WAS MAKING LOVE WITH ONE OF US AND HIS WIFE HADN'T GIVEN HIM THE LOVE THAT WE CAN GIVE HIM</u>... she's not innocent, she's guilty.... So if she isn't giving him <u>love</u> then it's all right if he gets it from somewhere <u>else</u>.) And it's her <u>own</u> fault and <u>she's</u> the guilty party" (*ML* 648:7–8, 9—*GP*, "Is <u>Love</u> Against the Law"). "<u>IF YOU PERSIST IN YOUR DEFIANT & FLAGRANT DISOBEDIENCE TO GOD & HIS WORD & ME</u> after the first & second admonition... you should then be cast out of the Home & the Family" (*DFO* 1022:8, "Desertion").	There appears to be a hidden agenda behind Berg's interpretation of the law of Moses and the law of love. By abolishing all restrictions he opens a door for him and his followers to do anything and everything they wish. Even something defined in Scripture as "sinful" will be acceptable because God's law of grace and love excuses the action. This is called antinomianism—a position that Paul refuted in Romans 6:1–4. Moreover, even if all things were now intrinsically acceptable, the law of love would actually prevent us from doing anything that would cause offense or stumbling to a fellow believer (Rom 14:21). Berg is also inconsistent in this view. He first maintains that *anything* can be done as long as it is done in love, but then states that his followers are committing sins worthy of excommunication if they disobey him. It is a classic example of someone wanting his cake and eating it too.

The Doctrine of Salvation (cont.)

Position	Support	Orthodox Response
Those who do not get a chance to accept Jesus Christ in this life will be able to accept Him and be saved in the afterlife.	"Some people are lost already & already condemned, He says, but I don't believe they're going to be lost <u>forever</u>. I think He's going to reclaim'm & reconstitute'm & regenerate'm—if not <u>now</u>, in the <u>next</u> life!" (*DFO* 1092:62, "Here & Now for Then & There").	Hebrews 9:27 says that "man is destined to die once, and after that to face judgment." Also, Paul preached that "now" is the day of salvation (2Co 6:2). In other words, there is no future realm of existence in which someone can achieve salvation.
Everything and everyone will be saved. The result will be several classes of saved people. All, however, will fall into one of two categories: (1) those who are saved *before* dying; and (2) those who are saved *after* dying.	"<u>NOTHING'S GOING TO BE LOST & NOTHING WASTED</u>, & everything finally saved, including everybody! But it won't be all the same, there'll be different classes" (*DFO* 1092:107, "Here & Now for Then & There"). "<u>GOD'S GOT ALL KINDS OF CLASSES EVEN AMONGST THE SAVED</u>" (*DFO* 1092:60, "Here & Now for Then & There").	Jesus said that on the day of judgment many will be told to depart from God's presence (Mt 7:23). He warned that the way to destruction is "broad" and that the way to eternal life is actually narrow (Mt 7:13). There are no class distinctions among those who are saved. We are all one in Christ (Gal 3:28), for God is no respecter of persons (Ac 10:34–35).
Those who fall into the first category are an "elite" group. They will be heaven's "first-class citizens." As such, they will receive a "special" reward. For example, disciples of The Family will have a far higher status than regular church members (and even in this elite group there will be different classes and rewards).	"<u>THERE WILL BE PEOPLE WHO ARE SAVED & IN A SPECIAL RELATIONSHIP WITH GOD CALLED SALVATION</u>, who <u>chose</u> His control & who <u>chose</u> His will, who <u>chose</u> to obey Him, & they will be <u>Heaven's first-class citizens</u>!" (*GN* 15—*DFO* 1308:120, "The Constellation of Daniel"). "<u>WE'RE THE ELITE, WE'RE ACCEPTING IT ALL VOLUNTARILY NOW</u>, & Him & His will, . . . So we're going to get a <u>special</u> reward" (*DFO* 1092:63, "Here & Now for Then & There").	Although Luke 6:35 and 12:47–48 indicate that there may be different levels of reward in heaven, there is no biblical evidence of different classes of citizens. On the contrary, all who receive eternal life will be thankful because it is by grace that anyone receives this gift. Revelation 22:3 states that all who receive eternal life are the everlasting servants of God and not an elite group. (See also above.)
The "elite" group of Christians (those who accept Christ while alive) will dwell in the New Jerusalem (also known as "Space City"), a huge, pyramid-shaped city at present concealed inside the moon. God, who lives in the apex of this pyramid, will eventually bring Space City down to Earth.	"GOD'S GREAT HEAVENLY <u>SPACE CITY</u> WILL THEN <u>DESCEND</u> FROM ABOVE TO THE BEAUTIFUL, RECREATED, GARDEN-OF-EDEN-LIKE <u>NEW EARTH</u>! —And God Himself will dwell <u>with</u> us. . . . This great Space City is <u>1,500 miles long</u>, <u>1,500 miles wide</u> & <u>1,500 mile high</u>—The greatest space vehicle ever created, the most wonderful Spaceship ever conceived, built by the <u>Lord</u> & on its way down to Earth now! (Rev. 21:All!)" (*Growing in Love*, "Would You Like To Know Your Future?: Here It Is!" p. 95). "**AND GUESS WHAT SHAPE THIS HEAVENLY CITY IS?—A <u>PYRAMID</u>!** . . . This is probably what the ancient Egyptians were trying to copy or imitate with <u>their</u> pyramids" (Ibid., p. 121).	Nothing in Scripture identifies heaven as a pyramid-shaped spaceship. The book of Revelation is apocalyptic literature, which means it is filled with a great deal of symbolism, figurative speech, and metaphorical language. The entire book of Revelation cannot legitimately be taken literally. There are various interpretations of the city of Revelation 21 and the measurements found there. Even if the description is meant to be taken literally, heaven would be not a pyramid but a cube. Berg is the only person we know of who has made the outlandish statement that the city exists now and is hidden inside the moon.

The Doctrine of Rewards and Punishment

Position	Support	Orthodox Response
Those of the elite group will enjoy sexual orgies in Space City.	"There's <u>sex</u> in <u>Heaven</u>!" (*GP 818:52*, "Sex in Heaven"). "There's going to be sex in the Millennium, did you know that? There's going to be sex in heaven!... you can still f— away in Heaven too, thank the Lord, & never get tired!" (*DO 919:15*, "Sex Jewels").	Jesus said that in heaven we are like the angels who neither marry nor are given in marriage (Lk 20:35). Because the Bible condemns sex outside of marriage and also states that adulterers won't be allowed into heaven (1Co 6:9; Eph 5:5), extramarital "free sex" will be excluded there.
While Berg describes all those who accept Jesus while on earth as first-class citizens of heaven, he warns that the majority of church members (due to their lack of service to God in this present life) and Family disciples who disobey will be looked down on as second-class citizens of heaven.	"<u>THERE MAY BE MORE CLASSES THAN THAT</u> if some people inside the City are even going to be in everlasting shame & contempt because of their minor disobediences—even major ones—even though saved. You might say they're the <u>second-class</u> citizens of Heaven.... <u>SO WATCH OUT, BELOVED, DO YOUR BEST & FOLLOW GOD</u>, obey Him, love Him" (*GN* 15—*DFO* 1308:121, 123, "The Constellation of Daniel"). "Even some of you who are saved will nevertheless be ashamed because you didn't serve the Lord as you should, & will suffer shame & everlasting contempt even in Heaven" (*GN* 15—*DFO* 1308:66, "The Constellation of Daniel").	The Bible says there is only one hope to which all Christians are called (Eph 4:4). Also see the Doctrine of Salvation section, pp. 130–1.
The second category of saved people are those who will respond to the gospel preached to them in hades after they are dead. Before they can enter heaven, however, they may have to be purged of their sins in a purgatory-like setting. Even then, they may suffer shame in heaven for their pre-death denial of The Family's doctrines and for the way they may have spoken against or otherwise mistreated members of The Family.	"Those who really didn't deserve much but punishment, I think He's [God] even going to make them into some kind of useful—if not a citizen—at least a slave in the Kingdom" (*ML* 1092:81, "Here & Now for There & Then"). "<u>THE LORD DOESN'T SAY THERE'S NOT GOING TO BE ANY TEARS IN HEAVEN</u>.... He says, 'God shall <u>wipe away</u> all tears from their eyes!' (Re. 21:4). A lot of people are going to have tears, but the Lord's going to comfort'm & wipe away the tears. <u>AND A LOT OF PEOPLE ARE GOING TO BE SORRY THEN</u>, a lot of these church people who wouldn't believe us & even persecuted us are going to be plenty sorry then & ashamed & even in contempt in the Halls of Heaven—Hang their heads in shame, they're hardly going to want to <u>look</u> at anybody! <u>BUT THEY'RE GOING TO BE D— THANKFUL TO BE THERE AT ALL</u> considering how unbelieving & rebellious & disobedient & contemptuous they were here on Earth in relation to <u>us</u>! They're going to be very thankful even to be our <u>slaves</u> or <u>servants</u> or down in the basement shining shoes, whatever!" (*DFO* 1092:110–12, "Here & Now for There & Then").	There is no biblical evidence for the idea of coming to salvation while in hades or enduring a purgatory. Christians who die go immediately into the presence of the Lord (Lk 23:43; 2Co 5:8). Those without God are viewed in the Scriptures as damned. The parable of the rich man and Lazarus suggests that ungodly persons are punished in hades (Lk 16:19–31). Although some have interpreted 1 Peter 3:18–22 to refer to a second chance, the passage really means that Christ preached through Noah to those who rejected the message of God and are now awaiting final judgment. Another passage appealed to is Ephesians 4:9, but this verse refers to the ascending and descending of Christ, first down into the earthly plane and then back to the heavenly realm. The passage says nothing of people in hell being preached to or being saved.

The Doctrine of Rewards and Punishment (cont.)

Position	Support	Orthodox Response
Those who do *not* accept the gospel when it is preached in hades will have to suffer for their sins and be purged in the lake of fire. They will eventually "learn their lesson," but because they didn't accept the gospel when it was first offered to them after death, they technically will never be saved. They will simply be "salvaged." Their reward will be to live on the glorified, perfected earth outside Space City.	". . . those outside who had rebelled against Him—although reconciled & now obeying & now fulfilling His will & honouring Him & worshipping Him & now following Him & doing His will outside—will be second-class citizens [not to be confused with 'second-class citizens of heaven']" (*GN* 15—*DFO* 1308:120, "The Constellation of Daniel"). ". . . some who <u>were</u> real bad & did have to go to Hell, to the Lake of Fire, but who <u>learned</u> their lessons there . . . were sorry for their sins & were forgiven & <u>released</u> by the Lord to live on the beautiful New Earth!" (*Growing in Love*, "Here's Heaven," pp. 126–27). "<u>THE LAKE OF FIRE IS WHERE THE WICKED GO TO GET PURGED</u> from their sins, or at least purged out enough to let them eventually come and live outside the City!" (*ML* 686:138—*GP*, "Out of this World").	The Christian doctrine of eternal conscious punishment for the wicked does not have an escape clause. The lake of fire (hell) is a place of *eternal* punishment (Rev 20:10–14). It is not a place of purging, but of judgment against sin and one's failure to accept Christ as Savior (Mt 7:23; Mk 9:43, 45, 47; 2Pe 2:9). Hell is where God's wrath will be poured out on the ungodly forever (Mt 25:46; Rev 14:10).
People who are not too bad will be allowed to bypass the purging process and go directly to live outside Space City.	"<u>THE NEW EARTH WILL HAVE PEOPLE LIVING ON IT WHO WERE NOT <u>BAD</u> ENOUGH TO GO TO <u>HELL</u>, BUT WHO, EVEN THOUGH THEY WERE PRETTY <u>GOOD</u>, DIDN'T GET <u>SAVED</u> THROUGH JESUS & SO COULDN'T GET INTO <u>HEAVEN</u>" (*Growing in Love*, "Here's Heaven," p. 126).	The Bible makes no mention at all of a middle ground of existence between heaven and hell where "good" unsaved people will dwell for eternity. Scripture speaks of only two groups: the saved and the unsaved (Mt 25:32–46).
Some spirits have been purged or are at present being purged by wandering on earth as ghosts.	"<u>VARIOUS DEPARTED SPIRITS ARE SOME-TIMES CONFINED IN CERTAIN PLACES LIKE HAUNTED HOUSES</u> . . . because of their past sins, & they have to stay there & suffer & be punished & see the result & consequences of their damnable dirty deeds. . . . They have to suffer the consequences after death, even in this World or in the next World, or in Hell" (*GN* 15—*DFO* 1308:66, "The Constellation of Daniel").	After death men undergo one thing in reference to sin—judgment (Heb 9:27). Those who are in Christ, their sins having been washed away by His death, will be given life. Those who have not been forgiven through Christ will be sentenced to death (Ro 6:23).

Position	Support	Orthodox Response
Satan and his demons will eventually be salvaged and released from the lake of fire after being purged of their evil.	"ONLY THE <u>MOST</u> WICKED OF ALL, SUCH AS SATAN, THE ANTICHRIST, HIS FALSE PROPHET & THEIR MOST ARDENT FOLLOWERS, will <u>remain</u> in the Lake of Fire to be punished & purged of their diabolical rebelliousness... until such a time as they, too, may have learned their lessons sufficiently for God to forgive them" (*Growing in Love*, "Would You Like To Know Your Future?" p. 95). "'<u>EVEN THE DEVIL!' IN THE END!</u>... He's going to be cast in the Lake of Fire with the Beast & the False Prophet & all those rascals.... it's going to be <u>hot</u> for them when the Lord turns up the heat, & they are going to <u>repent</u>!" (*DFO* 1092:102, "Here & Now for Then & There"). "<u>SOME PRETTY HARD CHARACTERS ARE GOING TO HOLD OUT TO THE BITTER END</u>, but I think God's even going to prove His almighty power by eventually conquering <u>them</u>... even the Devil & all his demons! <u>NOW THAT MAY BE STRETCHING IT A BIT & A BIT HARD FOR YOU TO BELIEVE</u>, but if God's going to salvage <u>mankind</u> in Universal Reconciliation, why not stretch it a bit further to the rebellious <u>spirits</u>?... why not give the rebellious <u>angels</u> another chance?" (*DFO* 1092:104–5, "Here & Now for Then & There").	Revelation 20:10 states that the devil, the anti-Christ, the false prophet, and all their followers will be cast into the lake of fire and be tormented (not purged) "day and night for ever and ever."
Berg departed from his usual stand in *DO 2142,* stating that Satan, the demons, and the most evil of humans would never be salvaged, but would instead be annihilated. No *official* change of doctrine, however, has taken place.	"I DON'T BELIEVE IN THIS ETERNAL TORTURE DOCTRINE.... I think it would be more merciful if they were just <u>annihilated</u>.... I DON'T KNOW WHETHER YOU COULD EVER REHABILITATE OR CONVERT <u>SOME</u> OF THOSE GUYS, like the Devil & the Antichrist... & some of the worst characters in history & the cruelest tyrants & whatnot.... They can be thankful they're just going to be annihilated.... So I stand corrected" (*DO* 2142:7–10, "Judah On Pearly Gate & the Doctrine of Annihilation").	The doctrine of annihilation for the wicked undercuts a plain and straightforward interpretation of the Bible (see p. 334). Some argue that annihilation is the result of God's punishment and that such a result is what should be considered eternal. But from a contextual, linguistic, and grammatical standpoint, it is not some result of punishment but rather the punishment itself that endures "for ever and ever."

Position	Support	Orthodox Response
The most reliable translation of the Bible is the King James Version.	"WHY WE USE THE KING JAMES VERSION.... It was translated by fundamentalists during a time when... the English language was in its purest, most beautiful form.... It has become the most widely used in the world today.... the KJV is an outstandingly, almost supernaturally, accurate translation.... The KJV is powerful and convicting (Heb 4.12). Quote a verse to someone in modern English or in a revised version, then quote someone the same verse from the KJV and compare the reactions. We believe the KJV was inspired!" (*The Revolution For Jesus*, pp. 35–36).	The goal of the translators of the King James Version of 1611, as expressed in the original preface, was "to deliver Gods booke vnto Gods people in a tongue which they vnderstand" (*sic*). All translations are removed from inspiration in that God only inspired the Hebrew, Aramaic, and Greek writing of the OT and NT. Therefore, although the modern Version of the King James Version continues to express the poetic beauty of a great literary age, it would be impossible to ascribe to it the qualities of inspiration. Several newer translations better fulfill today the goal that the original KJV stated in its preface.
Blacks and Jews are a curse to the world because they themselves are cursed by God. Only Jews and Blacks within The Family should be given equality and respect. **(Before he died, Berg altered his view slightly regarding Blacks' being a result of a "curse of Ham.")**	"THE WORLD IS ABSOLUTELY TURNED UPSIDE DOWN BY THE DEVIL & HIS FORCES & LARGELY THROUGH THE G———— JEWS & THEIR STOOGES, THE NEGROES!... They've been a curse to the World almost ever since God created them, & nearly everything that's evil in the World has happened through them!" (*DO* 1222:70, "The Troublemakers—and the Solution!"). "THE BLACKS HAVE BEEN CURSED EVER SINCE NOAH CURSED HAM" (*DO* 1222:72, "The Troublemakers—and the Solution!"). "'AH, HE'S NOT ONLY AN ANTI-SEMITE, HE'S A RACIST!'—Yes, I'm an anti-Semite, because God is! Yes, I'm a racist, because God is!" (*DO* 1222:110, "The Troublemakers—and the Solution!"). "WHEN IT COMES TO CHRISTIANS, BE THEY JEW OR GENTILE OR GREEK OR BLACK OR WHITE... I DON'T CARE.... There's no difference. But let me tell you, outside the fold, outside of the Christian Body of Jesus Christ.... they are devils" (*ML* 1222:73, "The Troublemakers—and the Solution!").	Racial hatred has no place in Christianity. It stands in direct opposition to everything God represents. We are told to love our neighbor (Lk 10:27–28), our neighbor being anyone whom we may meet in need. The Lord is no respecter of persons (Ac 10:34–35). Additionally, no one should have racial prejudice because all of us are related through Adam and Eve, the parents of mankind (Ge 3:20).
Astrology is not only true, but also biblical and from God.	"I'M CONVINCED OF THE TRUTH OF ASTROLOGY, HOW IT AFFECTS OUR LIVES.... How else was God going to get personalities distributed?" (*GN* 15—*DFO* 1309:36, "Astronomical Fakery!"). "WE'VE USED ASTROLOGY AS A WITNESS WITH A LOT OF PEOPLE" (*GN* 15—*DFO* 1310:41, "Body Clocks & Astrology").	Astrology is an occultic practice forbidden by God (Isa 47:13–15; Dt 4:19).

Position	Support	Orthodox Response
Berg, who called himself "sex-crazed," could not stop talking about sex. Consequently, most of his writings are about sex. For years Berg and his followers indulged their sexual cravings, but former followers now report that recent policies implemented by Karen (Maria) Zerby have curtailed sexual free-for-alls in favor of well-regulated hour long times of sexual "sharing."	"I've tried everything & everybody, but after all these years I still want more [sex]! So if you're as sex-crazed as I am personally, I can offer you no hope of a cure" (*DFO* 1125:15, 16, "Gypsy Joys"). "I don't <u>always</u> talk about sex, just <u>most</u> of the time!" (*DO* 919:22, "Sex Jewels"). "<u>MAYBE SOME OF YOU ARE GETTING BORED WITH SO MUCH TALK ABOUT SEX</u>! It's a neverending source of wonder to me.... I'm wild about sex & I tell the World about it!" (*DO* 919:45, "Sex Jewels"). "<u>AFTER ALL THESE YEARS OF CONSTANT SEXUAL ACTIVITY & MANY WOMEN LATER</u> I've finally given up & decided there's no cure for sex! I keep wanting more every day & I'm constantly yielding to my sexual appetite for more women & more sex, & have finally come to the conclusion that the only thing I can do about it is to constantly satisfy that craving with more!—More, more, more!—Hallelujah!" (*DFO* 1125:16, "Gypsy Joys").	Berg fits the description of someone who is intoxicated with the "fleeting pleasures of sin" (Heb 11:25 NRSV). An obsession with sex falls under the condemnation of biblical passages almost too numerous to mention (Mt 5:28; Ac 15:29; Ro 8:7; 13:13; 1Co 6:9, 18; 2Co 12:21; Eph 5:3; Col 3:5; 2Ti 2:22; 1Th 4:3; Heb 13:4; 1Jn 2:16).
Berg expresses himself through profanity and X-rated language. Many of Berg's writings cannot be quoted here owing to their extremely offensive nature.	"F—ing is <u>no</u> sin! It was <u>commanded</u> by God.... <u>THEY SAY YOU SHOULDN'T USE SUCH NAUGHTY WORDS</u>.... But you <u>understand</u> it, don't you?" (*GP* 818:3–4, "Sex in Heaven"). "Just lookin' at you girls I can hardly keep my hands off you! The Lord gave us that hunger when we see you to want to get ahold of you & love you & kiss you & f—ya! PTL!"(*GN* 9—*DFO* 1281:9, "The Test of Faith").	Berg's writings are clearly profane and contrary to the manner in which Christians are instructed to communicate. Colossians 3:8 and 4:6 and Titus 2:8 reveal that Christian speech should be wholesome and godly and able to impart grace to the hearers.
Polygamy and adultery are only two of many practices that have resulted from Berg's self-confessed obsession with sex.	"<u>I'M NOT SELFISH WITH MY WIVES, I GIVE THEM AWAY RIGHT AND LEFT</u> & share them with others who need help & need wives" (*DO* 919:37, "Sex Jewels"). "<u>WE BELIEVE IN SHARING</u> . . . in coming home and sleeping with the same mate nearly every night, but often after we've been out sleeping awhile with somebody else!" (*ML* 570:50—*DFO*, "Nuns of Love"). "Adultery is something gone out of style, you might say, with the Mosaic Law" (*ML* 648:41—*GP*, "Is Love Against the Law?").	God's original plan for marriage included only one man and one woman (Ge 2:21–25). Nowhere in Scripture does God actually sanction polygamy. The sin of adultery is so serious Jesus cited it as a legitimate reason for divorce (Mt 19:9). God will judge adulterers (Heb 13:4), and they will not inherit the kingdom of God (1Co 6:9).

Position	Support	Orthodox Response
Berg at one time forbade only sodomy. Prior to 1986–87, he allowed and promoted the following activities:	"'We don't have very many No-No's.... (sodomy) is about the only <u>sexual</u> one we have" (*DO* 1323:3, "Excommunication Rules & Procedures").	The Bible places a number of restrictions on sexual activity. In short, sexual expression of love is a gift that is only to be shared within the confines of marriage (Heb 13:4).
(1) Sex between children	**"WE WANTED TO ADD A WORD ABOUT THE CHILDREN'S <u>SEX</u> & <u>LOVE LIFE</u> TOO**. We have not really interfered.... Rubin [age 6] & Jonas [age 8 1/2] both have their little lovers among other little sisters who visit sometimes" (*Family News International No. 50*, p. 34).	Scripture forbids these sexual practices (see references in previous pages). The most obvious passages are those relating to marriage and fornication because people whom Berg encourages to engage in sex would be unmarried (for example, children and teens).
(2) Sex among teenagers	"<u>I THINK THE TEENAGE YEARS WERE WHEN I NEEDED SEX THE MOST!</u> Isn't it ridiculous though, that it's just at the age when you need sex the most that it's the most forbidden?... I hope all of our young kids have plenty of sex. I hope they won't have all those frustrations... from sex deprivation.... why did the <u>Lord</u> make you <u>able</u> to have <u>children</u> at the age of 11, 12 & 13 if you weren't supposed to have <u>sex</u> then?" (*DO* 902:1, 5–6, "Child Brides").	In addition to the biblical injunctions toward adultery, a special word must be said about incest and sex between adults and children. First, these practices are simply illegal. Because Christians are to be subject to the ruling authorities (Ro 13), the laws are reason enough to abstain from such conduct. Second, incest and adult-child sex are specifically prohibited in Leviticus 18:9–17. Disobeying God in these matters can produce not only physical injury but also severe emotional trauma.
(3) Incest and adult-child sex. (Adult-child sexual contact is now forbidden in The Family, owing to concern over the potential for legal action against the group.)	"'<u>WHAT ABOUT INCEST?</u>'... we'll just have to tell the kids that it's not prohibited by <u>God</u>, but you'd better watch out.... <u>IT IS THE MOST DANGEROUS FORM OF SEX & THE MOST PROHIBITED BY</u> THE SYSTEM! [the world outside the Family].... <u>I DON'T KNOW WHAT THE HELL AGE HAS GOT TO DO WITH IT</u>" (*DFO* 999:20–21, 23, "The Devil Hates Sex"). "<u>I'M TALKING ABOUT NATURAL NORMAL GODLY LOVE AS MANIFESTED IN SEX</u>, as far as I'm concerned for whomever!— There are no relationship restrictions or age limitations in His Law of <u>Love</u>" (*DFO* 999:110, "The Devil Hates Sex").	
(4) Pornographic videos. These videos portrayed sex acts, three-way lesbian encounters, masturbation, nude dances, and stripteases, some including girls as young as age three doing sexually provocative dances.	"<u>CAMERAMAN</u>... <u>BE NOT AFRAID OF THEIR FACES</u>.... Our kids' <u>faces</u> are their <u>credentials</u>.... You should seldom get further away than <u>waist-up</u>... unless they've got pretty bare legs, that you want to show off & be sexy!" (*DO* 979:16, 18–19, "Mugshots"). "<u>BE SURE NOT TO FOOLISHLY LABEL ANY OF THE TAPES</u> themselves inside with such curiosity-arousing investigation-inspiring & perhaps even illegal titles such as 'Love Tape' or "So & so strips' or any other sexy titles" (*DO* 979:62, "Mugshots").	Pornography is a sin against God and assaults the dignity of women. From a biblical standpoint it is condemned as adultery (Mt 5:28) and lust (1Jn 2:16). From a moral-ethical standpoint, evidence suggests that pornography perverts the sexual desires of men and is a factor in motivating violent crimes against women.

Position	Support	Orthodox Response
(5) Orgies	"We have a little orgy now & then, we don't publicise it or do it in front of reporters, although we have had it in front of a few guests! As long as it's all in the Family, why not?" (*DO* 919:29, "Sex Jewels").	Such sexual conduct runs directly contrary to multiple passages in Scripture that deal with sexual impurity, fornication, and adultery.
(6) "Flirty Fishing" (FFing). This tactic of seducing strangers in order to try to convert them, was widely practiced until 1987, when a Family member died of AIDS. Berg banned FFing except where high government officials or financially helpful people are concerned.	"THAT'S THE WHOLE BASIC DOCTRINE OF FFING, THAT SEX PROVES LOVE. . . . these girls are willing to go to bed with these men to prove they <u>love</u> them. . . . SEX PROVES LOVE, TRUE LOVE!—TRUE LOVE IS PROVEN BY SEX! That's one of the major ways to prove it, either by f——— or dying. . . . That's the whole idea of FFing, if by <u>sex</u> you can prove there is <u>Love</u>, thereby you prove there is <u>God</u>, because God <u>is</u> Love. If you can prove to these men through <u>sex</u> that you <u>love</u> them, therefore you prove that Love exists" (*DFO* 999:126, 133, "The Devil Hates Sex"). ". . . why do you think I would encourage your having sex with total strangers to win them to the Lord, if we weren't having perfect sexual freedom at <u>home</u>?" (*DO* 919:30, "Sex Jewels").	This practice amounts to little more than prostitution, which is condemned in Leviticus 21:9, 14; Proverbs 6:26; 23:27; and 1 Corinthians 6:16. It is also implicitly condemned in any passages dealing with adultery and fornication.
Spirits of the departed return to possess us and help us. Berg himself claimed to be possessed by Abrahim, a gypsy king from the 1200s who spoke through him and guided him.	"PEOPLE DO COME BACK & ARE HELPFUL TO SOMEONE, LIKE ABRAHIM IS TO ME. He is with me all the time, virtually <u>incarnated</u> in me. . . . I never go any place without him. He travels with me. . . . <u>I'm</u> his vehicle <u>now</u> just like <u>his</u> body was <u>before</u>" (*ML* 794:1—*DFO*, "Where Do Babies Come From?").	Communication with the dead is an occultic form of divination called necromancy. The practice is strongly condemned in Scripture (Ex 7; 8; 22:18; Lev 19:26, 31; 20:6, 27; Dt 18:9–12; Isa 8:19).
Berg claimed to have sex frequently with pagan "goddesses" from the spirit world and encouraged his followers to do the same.	". . . like all those other **goddesses I've made love to in the Spirit**. . . . In each case, the one I was making love to would suddenly turn into one of these strange and beautiful goddesses" (*MO* 224:3—*LTA*, "The Goddesses"). "Some of those goddesses are pretty strange. . . . every time they come—& they <u>come</u> all right, & make <u>me</u> come too. . . . <u>I DON'T KNOW WHY I ALWAYS HAVE SO MUCH EXPERIENCE WITH SO MANY FEMALE SPIRITS</u>. . . . I'm sure there are many fine handsome male spirits at your disposal, girls, so if you'd like to meet some of them just pray. . . . Meet the gods while I meet the goddesses!" (*DFO* 1237:14, 16, 22, "Houris of Heaven").	If what Berg described really happened, it appears that he encountered a succubus, regarded in occultic literature as a demonic entity who takes the form of a female in order to have intercourse with a man while he sleeps. The "male" counterpart to a succubus is known as an incubus. Scripture consistently refers to these entities as gods and goddesses. However, there is only one God (Isa 43:10; 1Ti 2:5). Whatever Berg was describing may very well be demonic.

10

Freemasonry

FACTS AND HISTORY

Facts	
Topic	*Current Facts*
Membership	As of 1990, the Masonic Lodge had a U.S. membership of 4,000,000 and worldwide membership of 6,000,000 (*The Secret Teachings of the Masonic Lodge*, p. 323). Membership is marked by various degrees through which one may pass. Also available are numerous affiliate organizations with specific memberships: youth—Demolay; women—Eastern Star; relatives—Job's Daughters.
	To become a Mason, one must go through the Blue Lodge, which is the parent or mother Lodge of Freemasonry. The Blue Lodge consists of three degrees: (1) the Entered Apprentice; (2) the degree of Fellow Craft; and (3) The Master Mason Degree. Each of these degrees serve as initiatory stepping stones into the deeper mysteries of Freemasonry
	After completing these degrees, one is a full Mason and may either stop or progress further along the Freemasonry route with a choice of two branches: the Scottish Rite, consisting of 30 degrees; or the York Rite, which consists of the Chapter degree (which has four levels), the Council degree (three levels), and the Commandery degree (which also has three levels, the final two being honorary).
Worship	Freemasonry has no worship services because it is not a church per se, but rather a fraternal organization. Masonic gatherings are more like club meetings, which may involve a number of issues such as Masonic-sponsored community projects, current events, or Lodge business. Yet Masonry has all the trappings and nomenclature of a deeply religious organization: the meeting place is a "temple" that has an "altar" and a "sacred book"; "prayers" are spoken by a "chaplain"; rituals are performed.
Leaders of Freemasonry	Freemasonry has never had one authoritative leader. Masons are led by the laws and regulations of Freemasonry itself. Each separate Lodge (meeting place) elects its own officers. Even so, all lodges worldwide have the same symbols, degrees, and teachings. Grand Lodges, which are a combination of more than one Lodge, also have elected officers. All Freemasons are bound through obedience to the ancient mystery "truths" that are gradually revealed as they advance in rank (degree).
Publications	Freemasonry is a secret fraternity—that is, it does not publicize its Lodge rituals or its sacred beliefs. The three most authoritative works on Freemasonry are *Coil's Masonic Encyclopedia* by Henry Coil, *Mackey's Revised Encyclopedia of Freemasonry* by Albert Mackey, *Morals and Dogma* by Albert Pike.
General statement of beliefs	Masons will often claim publicly that they are not part of a religion, but authoritative Masonic writings give Freemasonry the character of a religion. "Freemasonry may rightfully claim to be a religious institution. . . . We open and close our Lodges with prayer; we invoke the blessing of the Most High upon all our labors; we demand of our neophytes a profession of trusting belief in the existence and the superintending care of God" (*Mackey's Revised Encyclopedia of Freemasonry*, 2:847).
	Other literature written by Masonic authorities shows that the religion being promoted

Facts (cont.)	
Topic	*Current Facts*
... continued	through Freemasonry is incompatible with Christianity. Freemasonry denies the Trinity, the deity of Christ, salvation by grace through faith, the uniqueness of the Bible, and a number of other Christian beliefs. Masonry also promotes involvement with the occult as a means of achieving higher degrees of "truth."

History

Topic	*Current Facts*
Roots of Masonry	The roots of Freemasonry extend at least as far back as the Middle Ages. The guildsmen and craftsmen of that time were called Masons. For protection and credibility, these persons formed primitive trade unions (lodges). The content and purpose of this form of Masonry, called operative Masonry, began to change when the lodges were opened up to whoever sought membership. New members, including politicians, clergymen, and scientists, gradually began to formulate various rituals and doctrines to accompany some of the symbols already in use by the working masons (usually tools of the trade). It was at this point that occultism also began to be brought into the lodges. Eventually the various "grades" workers went through in learning their craft were replaced by degrees of advancement in esoteric knowledge. The eventual result of these changes is modern Masonry—also known as "speculative Masonry" because it speculates as to the true meanings behind the original symbols used in operative Masonry.
Modern Freemasonry	Modern Freemasonry dates to 1717, when several members of four lodges met at London's Goose and Gridiron Tavern to form the first Grand Lodge. By 1723 the organization had adopted James Anderson's *Constitutions* as a guide. Anderson's work clearly reflected a divergence from the Old Charges of operative Masonry, which had been in use since the fourteenth century. The Old Charges were distinctively Christian in tone and, according to *Fraternal Organizations* by Alvin J. Schmidt, dealt primarily with three issues: (1) God and religion, (2) the craft of masonry, and (3) regal duty. The *Constitutions*, however, omitted the Trinitarian formula and "spoke of a 'religion in which all men agree'" (*Fraternal Organizations*, p. 121). In 1738 Anderson produced another accepted document titled "The Old Charges of the Free and Accepted Masons." By that year, operative Masonry had evolved into accepted Masonry. It continued to evolve until, by the second half of the eighteenth century, it had become speculative Masonry, which interpreted "the symbols and artifacts of operative masonry in an allegorical, religious manner" (Ibid.). For example, whereas operative Masons built stone edifices, speculative Masons seek to build spiritual edifices. The first Masonic Lodge was established in the United States on April 13, 1733. In the United States it yielded great influence. In fact, many scholars believe that Freemasonry helped inspire the American Revolution (see for example, *Revolution and Freemasonry, 1680 to 1800* by Bernard Fay). There is also evidence that Freemasonry was influential in the formation of the U.S. Constitution. It has even been theorized that the designs on the back of American currency can be linked to Masonic signs and symbols (see *Fraternal Organizations*, p. 122). The popularity of Freemasonry has made it a model for hundreds of other fraternal societies. As far back as 1927, for instance, nearly all of the 800 fraternal orders of that time had adopted Masonic-like symbols, signs, passwords, rituals, oaths, obligations and degrees (Ibid.).

The Doctrine of Revelation

Position	Support	Orthodox Response
All non-Masons are in spiritual darkness and can arrive at the light of truth only through Masonry.	"[The Masonic initiate] has long been in darkness, and now seeks to be brought to light" (Malcom C. Duncan, *Masonic Ritual and Monitor*, n.d., p. 29).—A/W	A Christian already has the light of life (Jn 8:12) because God has rescued him from the dominion of darkness and brought him into the kingdom of His Son (Col 1:13). For the Christian to claim still to be in darkness is to lie and not to live by the truth (1Jn 1:6).
Light is obtainable only through Masonry because Masonry is of divine origin and, as such, is the true religion.	"Masonry is of divine origin" (J. Blanchard, *Scottish Rite Masonry Illustrated* [*The Complete Ritual of the Ancient and Accepted Scottish Rite*], 1:453).—A/W "[E]very Masonic Lodge is a temple of religion; and its teachings are instructions in religion. . . . reward is the knowledge of the True God. . . . Masonry is a worship. . . . It is the universal, eternal immutable religion, such as God planted it in the heart of universal humanity" (*Liturgy of the Ancient and Accepted Scottish Rite of Freemasonry for the Southern Jurisdiction of the United States*, Part Two, pp. 167, 198–99).—A/W	Jesus Christ is the Light of the world (Jn 1:4; 8:12; 9:5; 12:35–36). Unless Masonry teaches this truth, it cannot be the true religion, for it denies that "the true light that gives light to every man" has come into the world (Jn 1:9).
The Bible is affirmed, and even revered, by Masons, but not as the infallible and inerrant Holy Word of God. Scripture is nothing more than a symbol of the will of God. It is no more divine or inspired than any other "holy" book of other religions.	". . . the Bible, so rich in symbolism, is itself a symbol. . . . It is a sovereign symbol of the Book of Faith, the Will of God as man has learned it in the midst of the years. . . . Thus, by the very honor which Masonry pays to the Bible, it teaches us to revere every book of faith . . . joining hands with the man of Islam as he takes oath on the Koran, and with the Hindu as he makes covenant with God upon the book that he loves best" (Joseph Fort Newton, *The Bible in Masonry*, p. 5).	The Bible is the inspired Word of God (2Pe 1:20–21), written by men who had "the Spirit of Christ in them" (1Pe 1:11). The purpose of this God-breathed revelation is not merely to be a symbol of God's will, but to make people wise for salvation through faith in Christ and to train and equip people for a life of righteousness and good works (2Ti 3:15–16).
The Bible is not to be taken literally. Its contents are not divine.	"The prevailing Masonic opinion is that the Bible is only a symbol of Divine Will, Law, or Revelation, and not that its contents are Divine Law, inspired, or revealed. So far, no responsible authority has held that a Freemason must believe the Bible or any part of it" (Henry Wilson Coil, *Coil's Masonic Encyclopedia*, p. 520).—A/W	God's Word is truth, not a symbol of truth (Jn 17:17).
The Bible cannot be properly understood except by Masons.	"The Hebrew books were written only to recall to memory the traditions; and they were written in Symbols unintelligible to the Profane [non-Masons]" (Albert Pike, *Morals and Dogma*, pp. 744–45).—A/W	The truth of God is knowable and intelligible to all who will allow the Spirit of God to reveal God's truth to them (Jn 8:31–32; 14:26; 15:26; 16:13; 1Co 12:3).

The Doctrine of God—*The Trinity*

Position	Support	Orthodox Response
The God of Freemasonry is most often referred to as the "Great Architect of the Universe" (G.A.O.T.U.).	"Great Architect of the Universe, in Thy name we have assembled and in Thy name we desire to proceed in all our doings" (Raymond Lee et al., *Tennessee Craftsmen or Masonic Textbook*, p. 1). —A/W	God is referred to by many names in the Bible—e.g., I Am, the Lord, Yahweh (Ex 3); God Almighty, El Shaddai (Ge 17:3)—both as God's revelation of His name and in prayers addressed to God—Lord, God of Israel (1Ki 8:23). The real concern is what the names used for God reveal about His nature—who He is and what He has done.
The gods worshipped in all other religions, including the God of Christianity, are referred to as Baalims, or false gods. Hence, Masons of whatever religious tradition are to abandon personal beliefs about God in favor of the all-encompassing God of Freemasonry.	"Masonry, . . . around whose altars the Christian, the Hebrew, the Moslem, the Brahman, the followers of Confucius and Zoroaster, can assemble as brethren and unite in prayer to the one God who is above *all* the Baalim" (Albert Pike, *Morals and Dogma of the Ancient and Accepted Scottish Rite of Freemasonry*, p. 226). —A/W ". . . every religion and every conception of God is idolatrous, in so far as it is imperfect, and as it substitutes a feeble and temporary idea in the shrine of that Undiscoverable Being [of Masonry]" (Ibid., p. 516).—A/W	There is only one true God (Isa 44:6; Jn 17:3); He has revealed Himself in and through the person of Jesus (Jn 1:18; 14:9; 17:6; Col 1:15). God can be known, named, and approached (Heb 4:16; 10:22).
The one true God, the G.A.O.T.U., is actually present in every religion but is clouded by the particulars of a religion.	"God is equally present with the pious Hindoo [sic] . . . the Jew . . . the Mohammedan . . . and the Christian in the church" (Robert I. Clegg, rev. *Mackey's Revised Encyclopedia of Freemasonry*, 1:409–10).	Not all people can claim to be the children of God, because Jesus said that some are the children of the Devil (see Jn 8:44). "If anyone does not have the Spirit of Christ, he does not belong to Christ" (Ro 8:9).
This G.A.O.T.U. is to be chosen over the inferior God of Christianity. Masons of all religions are expected to unite under worship of the Masonic God, who is actually unapproachable and unknowable.	"Men have to decide whether they want a God like the ancient Hebrew Jahweh, a partisan, tribal God, with whom they can talk and argue and from whom they can hide if necessary, or a boundless, eternal universal, undenominational, and international, Divine Spirit, so vastly removed from the speck called man, that He cannot be known, named, or approached" (Henry Wilson Coil, *Coil's Masonic Encyclopedia*, pp. 516–17).—A/W	The God of the Bible is not a limited tribal deity, especially as portrayed by Henry Coil. In the book of Joshua we encounter for the first time Yahweh's being referred to as the "God in heaven above and on the earth below" (Jos 2:11). This early statement of God's universality came from the mouth of a Gentile and not from a member of one of the tribes of Israel. The quote by Wilson should allow any Mason who also claims to be a true Christian to see that it is impossible to maintain this double allegience with integrity.
God is not necessarily Triune.	"Masonry holds and teaches that with all and above all there is God, not essentially a Christian triune God" (G. A. Kenderdine, *New Age* magazine, as quoted in J. W. Acker, *Strange Altars: A Scriptural Appraisal of the Lodge*, p. 37).—A/W	The words *triune* and *Trinity* are not found in the Bible. They are terms used in Christian theology to summarize the revelation that the true God has given of Himself: one God (Dt 6:4) but three distinct persons (e.g., Jn 14:26; 2Co 13:14).

The Doctrine of God—*The Trinity (cont.)*

Position	Support	Orthodox Response
Masonry neither confirms nor denies the doctrine of the Trinity, but relegates it to a class of beliefs that are of little importance.	"To every Mason, WISDOM or INTELLIGENCE, FORCE or STRENGTH, and HARMONY, or FITNESS and BEAUTY, are the Trinity of the attributes of God. With the subtleties of Philosophy concerning them Masonry does not meddle, nor decide as to the reality of the supposed Existences which are their Personifications: nor whether the Christian Trinity be such a personification, or a Reality of the gravest import and significance" (Albert Pike, *Morals and Dogma of the Ancient and Accepted Scottish Rite of Freemasonry*, p. 525).—A/W	God is triune not in terms of characteristics or traits but because each person is identified as God (2Cor 1:3; Jn 20:28; Ac 5:3–4) and each person does the work of God (Eph 1:17 with 3:9; Col 1:16; Ge 1:2).
Any references to a specific nature of God (e.g., God being triune) must always be avoided.	"No phrase or terms should be used in a Masonic service that would arouse sectarian feelings or wound the religious sensibilities of any Freemason" (*Proceedings of the Grand Lodge of Texas*, December 22, 1920).—A/W	The Christian is to invoke the name of the true God only (Ps 50:14–15; Jn 4:24; 15:16).
Any conception of monotheism, including Christian monotheism, is incompatible with Freemasonry. This includes Christian monotheism.	"Monotheism . . . violates Masonic principles, for it requires belief in a specific kind of Supreme Deity" (Henry Wilson Coil, *Coil's Masonic Encyclopedia*, p. 517). —A/W	The Christian faith is predicated on Judaism's Torah. In the Torah we read the great Shema statement of Israel, "Hear, O Israel: The LORD our God, the LORD is One" (Dt 6:4). This is repeated by the Lord Jesus in Mark 12:29 and restated by the apostle Paul in 1 Corinthians 8:6. Monotheism is the absolute foundation of any true knowledge of God.

The Doctrine of Jesus Christ—*The Deity/Humanity of Christ*

Position	Support	Orthodox Response
Jesus was simply a great teacher of morality, similar to all other religious figures. If someone wishes to apply divinity to him or to another figure, that is acceptable.	"It [Masonry] reverences all the great reformers. It sees in Moses, the Law giver of the Jews, in Confucius and Zoroaster, in Jesus of Nazareth, and in the Arabian Iconoclast, Great Teachers of Morality, and Eminent Reformers, if no more: and allows every brother of the Order to assign to each such higher and even Divine Character as his Creed and Truth require" (Albert Pike, *Morals and Dogma of the Ancient and Accepted Scottish Rite of Freemasonry*, p. 525).—A/W "It has been found that every act in the drama of the life of Jesus, and every quality assigned to Christ is to be found in the life of Krishna" (J. D. Buck, *Symbolism or Mystic Masonry*, p. 119).	To teach that Jesus was a mere man and that His deity is a manmade doctrine runs counter to Scripture. The Masons' teachings about Jesus Christ are not compatible with the teachings of Christian Scriptures— that Jesus is the Christ, the eternal Son of God, who came into human flesh (Mt 16:16; Jn 1:1–2, 14, 17; Col 1:19; 2:9).

The Doctrine of Jesus Christ—*The Deity/Humanity of Christ (cont.)*

Position	Support	Orthodox Response
Jesus was not God. Belief in Jesus as God is a manmade doctrine.	"[Christian] Theologians first made a fetish of the Impersonal Omnipresent Divinity; and then tore the Christos from the hearts of all humanity in order to deify Jesus, that they might have a god-man peculiarly their own" (J. D. Buck, *Symbolism or Mystic Masonry*, p. 57).—A/W	The belief that Jesus achieved Christ-consciousness, in a way that we all can do, is a New Age teaching. Scripture makes clear that Jesus at birth was the Christ (Lk 2:11) and is still the Christ who will come again as the judge of all humanity (Tit 2:13; Rev 22:12).
The "Christ" is not a title reserved for Jesus. "Christ" is a higher consciousness that resides in all men. It can be achieved through Masonry.	"[I]n deifying Jesus, the whole humanity is bereft of Christos as an eternal potency within every human soul, a latent (embryonic) Christ in every man. In thus deifying one man, they have orphaned the whole humanity [of its divinity]" (R. Swineburne Clymer, *The Mysticism of Masonry*, p. 47)— A/W	The Greek title *Christos* is the equivalent to the Hebrew *Moshiach* or the English *Messiah* and means one anointed for God's purpose. Prophecies about the coming Messiah can be found throughout the Old Testament (e.g., Ps 22 and Isa 53). They are very specific in giving His credentials even to the point of naming the city (Bethlehem) where He would be born (see Mic 5:2). Jesus is the only Messiah-Christ who fits the criteria laid out in the Bible.

The Doctrine of Jesus Christ—*The Humanity of Christ*

Position	Support	Orthodox Response
Masons are taught to accept all religions and are allowed to believe that Jesus Christ is just a man.	"We do not tell the Hebrew that the Messiah whom he expects was born in Bethlehem nearly two thousand years ago. . . . And as little do we tell the sincere Christian that Jesus of Nazareth was but a man like us, or His history but the unreal revival of an older legend. To do either is beyond our jurisdiction. Masonry, of no one age, belongs to all time; of no one religion, it finds its great truths in all" (Albert Pike, *Morals and Dogma of the Ancient and Accepted Scottish Rite of Freemasonry*, p. 524).—A/W	Jesus said, "If you do not believe that I am the one I claim to be, you will indeed die in your sins" (Jn 8:24). Jesus proclaimed His divinity and was accused by His Jewish hearers of blasphemy, that is, of a man proclaiming himself to be God. It is illogical to praise Christianity for its "great truths" if it is fundamentally flawed in the one doctrine—the deity of Christ—that gives cohesiveness and clarity to all else it teaches. Pike paradoxically claims to have no jurisdiction to make the statements he has already made.
God did not manifest Himself in Jesus Christ.	"God never manifested himself to be seen of men. Creation is his manifestation" (J. D. Buck, *Symbolism or Mystic Masonry*, p. 276).	Colossians 2:9 says that in Christ "all the fullness of the Deity lives in bodily form." Theophanies—or manifestations of God comprehensible to humans—are found throughout the Bible, as in the accounts of the burning bush (Ex 3), the Shekina glory (e.g., Ex 25:22; Lev 16:2; 2Sa 6:2) or the commander of the LORD's army (Jos 5:13–15).

The Doctrine of Jesus Christ—*The Resurrection of Christ*

Position	Support	Orthodox Response
Christ is rarely mentioned in Masonic ceremonies, and in particular, His resurrection is ignored.	"In a well-ordered lodge, Jesus is never mentioned except in vague, philosphical terms. Prayers are never prayed in His name, and when scriptures are quoted in the ritual, all references to Him are simply omitted" (Jim Shaw, *The Deadly Deception*, p. 76). Shaw, a 33rd Degree Mason, is past Master of all Scottish Rite bodies.	Since they exclude proper reference to Jesus in biblical quotes, omit the use of His name in prayer, and deny His deity, it stands to reason that Masonic rituals and writings would ignore His resurrection. The teaching of Jesus' resurrection victory over death is at the heart of the Christian faith (e.g., 1Co 15:14–17).

The Doctrine of the Holy Spirit

Position	Support	Orthodox Response
The Holy Spirit is actually a type of universal agent.	"There is a Life-Principle of the world, a universal agent, wherein are two natures and a double current, of love and wrath. This ambient fluid penetrates everything. It is a ray detached from the glory of the Sun, and fixed by the weight of the atmosphere and the central attraction. It is the body of the Holy Spirit, the universal Agent, the Serpent devouring his own tail" (Albert Pike, *Morals and Dogma of the Ancient and Accepted Scottish Rite of Freemasonry*, p. 734).—A/W	Scripture clearly teaches that the Holy Spirit is deity (Ge 1:2; Pss 51:11; 139:7; Isa 63:10; Acts 1:2; 2Co 3:17; 2Th 2:13; 1Ti 3:16).
The concept of the Holy Spirit, as well as of the Father and the Son, is actually a modification of Hebrew philosohpy.	"In the KABALAH, or the Hebrew traditional philosophy, the Infinite Deity, beyond the reach of the Human Intellect, and without Name, Form, or Limitation, was represented as developing Himself ... in ten emanations or out-flowings, called SEPHIROTH. ... Here is the origin of the Trinity of the Father, the Mother or Holy Spirit, and the Son or Word" (Albert Pike, *Morals and Dogma of the Ancient and Accepted Scottish Rite of Freemasonry*, p. 552).—A/W	God is portrayed in the Bible as complete and unchanging. His immutability is found throughout the Scriptures. "I the LORD do not change" (Mal 3:6). The eternality of God argues against His "developing Himself." The word *Trinity* is not found in the Bible but serves to explain the doctrine that is found there. A compilation of Scriptures leads to the conclusion that God exists as three co-equal Persons in one Being. The doctrine is derived from the Scriptures alone and is not the product of any outside source.

The Doctrine of Man and Sin

Position	Support	Orthodox Response
Although man is basically good, he exists in an imperfect state marked by weaknesses (i.e., sins). The goal is to reach a better state of character. These two states are illustrated by what the Lodge calls the Rough and Perfect Ashlars. The Perfect Ashlar is obtained primarily through self-effort.	"By the Rough Ashlar we are reminded of our rude and imperfect state by nature; by the Perfect Ashlar, of that state of perfection at which we hope to arrive by a virtuous education, by our own endeavors, and by the blessing of God" (Raymond Allen et al., *Tennessee Craftsmen or Masonic Textbook*, p. 13).—A/W "Nor does Masonry teach that human nature is a depraved thing, like the ruin of a once proud building. Many think that man was once a perfect being but that through some unimaginable moral catastrophe he became corrupt unto the last moral fiber of his being, so that, without some kind of supernatural or miraculous help from outside him, he can never [be saved]" (H. L. Haywood, *The Great Teachings of Masonry*, p. 138).—A/W	In relation to a holy and sinless God, man is corrupt (Ge 6:5; 8:21; Isa 6:5; Ro 7:14ff.). Mankind is not inherently good, but has inherited the sinful nature of Adam (Ge 5:3; Ro 5:12ff.) and is sinful from the moment of conception (Ps 51:5). People cannot become righteous before God by self-effort (Ro 7:18–20; Gal 2:15–16).

The Doctrine of Salvation

Position	Support	Orthodox Response
Salvation is obtained apart from Christ through good works alone.	"[If your life is] without soil or blemish, you will be received at the pearly gates of heaven and there be presented with the pure white robe of righteousness" (Raymond Allen et al., *Tennessee Craftsmen or Masonic Textbook*, p. 61).—A/W "Perform the duties of your respective stations . . . and you will receive from your Almighty Father an inheritance incorruptible and undefiled, that fadeth not away" (Ibid., p. 126).—A/W	Many passages of Scripture make clear that salvation is only by God's grace through faith in Jesus Christ (Ac 16:31; Ro 3:22ff.; Eph 2:8–9; Tit 3:4–7).
The Masonic teaching of salvation by works is well illustrated from the ritual of the Entered Apprentice Degree.	"The Lamb has in all ages been deemed an emblem of innocence. By the lambskin, therefore, the Mason is reminded of that purity of life and conduct which is so essential to his gaining admission to the Celestial Lodge above, where the Supreme Architect of the Universe presides" (*Louisiana Masonic Monitor*, pp. 44–45).	"Therefore no one will be declared righteous in his sight by observing the law; rather, through the law we become conscious of sin" (Ro 3:20). "Know[ing] that a man is not justified by observing the law, but by faith in Jesus Christ . . ." (Gal 2:16). "It is by grace you have been saved, through faith—and this not from yourselves, it is the gift of God—not by works so that no one can boast" (Eph 2:8–9).

The Doctrine of Salvation (cont.)

Position	Support	Orthodox Response
Part of the Masonic plan of salvation includes the ultimate realization that we are not only basically good, but divine.	"[T]he great secret of Masonry [is] that it makes a man aware of that divinity within him" (Joseph Fort Newton, *The Builders: A Story and Study of Freemasonry*, p. 284).—A/W "[Masonry's purpose is] to reach the spiritual and divine within himself" (Henry C. Clausen, *Clausen's Commentaries on Morals and Dogma*, p. 157).—A/W	Man is not divine. God is Creator; man is creature. It was Satan's temptation of man to "be like God" that led to sin (Ge 3:5). God alone is God (Isa 45:5), and He condemns all efforts on man's part to achieve divinity (Ge 11; Isa 14:12ff.).

The Doctrine of Rewards and Punishment

Position	Support	Orthodox Response
Masonry promises its members that if they pursue obedience to the Lodge and good works, they will dwell with the G.A.O.T.U. for eternity.	"Let us imitate the good man in his virtuous and amiable conduct, in his unfeigned piety to God, in his inflexible fidelity to his trust, that we may welcome death as a kind messenger sent from our Supreme Grand Master to translate us from this imperfect to that all perfect and glorious Lodge above, where the Supreme Architect of the Universe presides" (*Masonic Monitor of the Degrees of the Entered Apprentice, Fellow Craft and Master Mason*, p. 68).—A/W	The Bible commends us to imitate the good conduct of others (1Co 11:1; Heb 6:12), but not in order to earn an eternal reward. Salvation is by faith alone.
Although Masonic literature mentions afterlife rewards, it says nothing about afterlife punishment.	According to evangelicals John Weldon and John Ankerberg, "Hell is not mentioned in any of the rituals or ceremonies of the three degrees of the Blue Lodge, the ten degrees of the York Rite, or the thirty degrees of the Scottish Rite" (*The Secret Teachings of the Masonic Lodge*, p. 153).	The biblical doctrine of hell and eternal punishment is taught by Jesus (Mt 5:22; 25:41; Mk 9:43) and in other Scriptures (Jas 3:6; 2Pe 2:4).

Position	Support	Orthodox Response
Masonry is a fraternal order that requires its members to swear oaths of secrecy about its inner workings and rituals. Breaking Masonic vows will allegedly bring catastrophe into one's life.	"The average Mason, as well as the modern student of Masonic ideals, little realizes the cosmic obligation he takes upon himself when he begins his search for the sacred truths of Nature as they are concealed in the ancient and modern rituals. He must not lightly regard his vows, and if he would not bring upon himself years and ages of suffering he must cease to consider Freemasonry solely as a social order only a few centuries old" (Manly Hall, *The Lost Keys of Freemasonry, or The Secret of Hiram Abiff*, p. 11). "Every Mason knows that a broken vow brings with it a terrible penalty.... When a Mason swears that he will devote his life to [Masonry]... and then defiles his living temple... he is breaking a vow which imposes not hours but ages of misery" (Ibid., p. 68).	Christians are not opposed to taking oaths (Nu 30:2), but they are to be taken seriously (Dt 23:21–23) and not treated frivolously. In most instances no oath is necessary; a simple yes or no will suffice (Mt 5:33–37).
The punishment for breaking certain vows is death, and it is believed that this punishment will be inflicted by God.	"[Masonic penalties] refer in no case to any kind of human punishment... to any kind of punishment which is to be inflicted by human hand.... if he violates his vows or betrays his trust he is worthy of such penalty, and that if such penalty were inflicted on him it would be just and proper. 'May I die,' said the ancient, 'if this be not true, or if I keep not this vow.' Nor may any man put me to death, nor is any man required to put me to death, but only, if I so act, then would I be worthy of death. The ritualistic penalties of Freemasonry, supposing such to be, are in the hands not of men, but of God, and are to be inflicted by God, and not by men" (*Mackey's Revised Encyclopedia of Freemasonry*, 2:723).—A/W	Since Masonry doesn't represent the God of the Bible, He would have no part in punishing someone for violating an oath taken to uphold a false system of religious thought. All punishmnent for sin takes place on the cross of Christ or at the Great White Throne of Judgement of unbelievers in the future (see Col 1:20; Rev 20:11).
It has been asserted that Freemasonry is racist in that blacks are not allowed to join. Because those of African descent are barred from Freemasonry, such persons have established their own Lodges, known as Prince Hall Masonry. Many white Masons do not recognize black Masonry as legitimate.	"The Committee believes that in view of the existing social conditions in our country, it is advisable for the official and organized activities of white and colored Freemasons to proceed in parallel lines, but organically separate and without mutually embarrassing demands or commitments" ("Report on Negro Freemasonry by the M. W. Grand Lodge of Massachusetts," November 25, 1946, as reprinted in Donn A. Cass, *Negro Freemasonry and Segregation*, p. 134). "Regardless of the way and manner that Negro Freemasonry arose in America it is today regarded as spurious and illegitimate" (Delmar Duane Darrah, *History and Evolution of Freemasonry*, as quoted in *Fraternal Organizations*, pp. 124–25).	A Christian is not to be racist in any way and certainly not in terms of membership in an organization. Christians are to show love and respect to all people (Lk 6:27–31) and recognize that in Christ all are one (Gal 3:28). Therefore they are committed to do good to all people (Gal 6:10). Also, the Bible is insistent that all come from Adam (Ge 2:7), all come from Eve (Ge 3:20), all come from Noah (Ge 9:18) and that all are of one blood (Ac 17:26).

11

Jehovah's Witnesses

FACTS AND HISTORY

Facts	
Topic	***Current Facts***
Membership	The 1999 Service Year Report of Jehovah's Witnesses Worldwide reported that a total of 5,912,492 "peak" (active, baptized) Witnesses spent about 1.1 billion hours evangelizing in 234 countries (*Watchtower*, January 1, 2000).
Worship	Services are conducted in a building called "Kingdom Hall." The meetings are led by laypeople appointed as elders; congregations do not have full time pastors. Members typically attend meetings three days per week. On Sunday there is a two-part service that consists of a public talk and the *Watchtower* Study—a study in which the entire congregation together, including all age groups, reviews in a question-and-answer format the previous week's study in *The Watchtower*. During the week Witnesses also attend a book study one evening and two instructional classes (the Theocratic Ministry School and the Service Meeting) on another evening. The latter are designed to instruct Witnesses in doctrine and prepare them for door-to-door witnessing.
Presidents of the Watchtower Society	1884–1916 Charles T. Russell 1916–1942 Joseph F. Rutherford 1942–1977 Nathan H. Knorr 1977–1992 Frederick W. Franz 1992– Milton G. Henschel
Publications	The organization's primary publications are two semi-monthly magazines: (1) *Awake!*, which targets mostly "unbelievers" and focuses on nonbiblical subjects such as current events and news stories; and (2) *The Watchtower*, which is the Society's "chief means of instructing members in doctrine and practice" (*Jehovah's Witness Literature*, p. 155). Circulation per issue as of May 1994 was, for *Awake*, 12,990,000 in 74 languages, and for *The Watchtower*, 16,100,000 in 116 languages. Once or twice a year the Witnesses publish books that either promote basic doctrines, serve as instructional guides to living, or examine various books of the Bible. These materials are also used to arouse the interest of nonmembers. In 1961 the Jehovah's Witnesses released their own translation of the Bible, *The New World Translation of the Holy Scriptures* (which had been previously published in a multivolume set from 1950 to 1960). By 1993, over 60 million copies of the NWT had been published in nine European languages and Japanese. Members are encouraged to study the Watch Tower Bible in conjunction with the other Watch Tower publications and discouraged from studying the Bible by itself.

Facts (cont.)

Topic	Current Facts
General statement of beliefs	Jehovah's Witnesses consider their organization the only true Christian organization. They also view themselves as God's righteous people who are persecuted by governments and traditional Christian groups ("apostate Christendom"). Witnesses believe that the truths of Scripture were lost through an apostasy that occurred centuries ago; then God used C. T. Russell to bring to light and restore many of the Christian teachings that had been lost. A few of Russell's doctrines have been kept, others have been modified over the years, and some have been discarded altogether. Jehovah's Witnesses deny many of the cardinal doctrines of historic Christianity: the Trinity, the deity of Christ, the physical resurrection of Christ, and the personality of the Holy Spirit. They also deny a conscious eternal punishment for the wicked, the immortality of the soul, and the substitutionary atonement of Christ.

History

Topic	History
Charles Taze Russell, 1884–1916	The Jehovah's Witnesses sprang from a Bible study in Allegheny, Pennsylvania, that was organized in 1870 by Russell and others interested primarily in studying about Christ's return. In 1876 the Bible class elected Russell their "pastor." In 1879, after leaving his job as assistant editor of a small monthly magazine, Russell founded his own periodical: *Zion's Watch Tower and Herald of Christ's Presence*. It evolved into what is now known as *The Watchtower—Announcing Jehovah's Kingdom*. In 1884 Russell founded, and installed himself as president of, Zion's Watch Tower Tract Society, which eventually added the Watch Tower Bible and Tract Society of New York, Inc. The organization moved its headquarters to its present location in Brooklyn, New York, in 1909. At that time Russell's sermons were printed in newspapers as advertisements throughout the world. Under Russell, the organization experienced tremendous growth. Its members, then called "Bible Students," were led exclusively through Russell's writings and sermons. His series of six books titled *Studies in the Scriptures* (a seventh volume was added after his death) are the studies from which modern Witnesses have drawn some of their beliefs. Although Russell claimed to be a biblical scholar, he received no formal training. Nor was he ever ordained as a pastor by a legitimate church. His career was marked by legal entanglements, a widely publicized divorce, questionable business practices, and charges of perjury.
Joseph Franklin Rutherford, 1916–1942	Judge Joseph Franklin Rutherford became president of the organization in 1917 after a three-month power struggle that followed the death of Russell on October 31, 1916. The group of Bible Students grew rapidly under Rutherford's leadership. He was a very charismatic leader who attacked traditional Christian groups through numerous radio shows, recordings, books, and other publications. Because of his opposition to military service, Rutherford served a term in a federal penitentiary in 1918 for violation of the Espionage Act, but the charges were dropped after the war. This imprisonment enabled him to return to his followers in 1919 as a victim-hero. In 1931 the name Jehovah's Witnesses was adopted to separate Rutherford's followers from traditional Christian groups and Russellite splinter groups. Rutherford was primarily responsible for starting the door-to-door preaching for which Witnesses are now so well known. During his presidency, *The Golden Age* periodical that is now known as *Awake!* was introduced.

History (cont.)	
Topic	*History*
Nathan H. Knorr, 1942–1977	After Rutherford died in 1942, Nathan H. Knorr became president of the Watch Tower Society. In 1943 Knorr founded the Watchtower Bible School of Gilead to train full-time ministers for missionary work in foreign countries. In 1950 the Society began to release portions of *The New World Translation of the Holy Scriptures*.
Frederick William Franz, 1977–1992	Upon Knorr's death in 1977, Frederick William Franz was named the Watch Tower's president. His term saw the well-known crackdown on dissident Witnesses in 1980 that culminated in the expulsion of Franz's nephew, Raymond Franz, from the organization. Frederick Franz died on December 22, 1992, at the age of 99.
Milton G. Henschel, 1992–	To this point there are no indications of new directions or significant changes in the Witnesses' Society under Henschel's leadership.

THEOLOGY

The Doctrine of Revelation		
Position	*Support*	*Orthodox Response*
The Bible is divinely inspired and accurately transmits God's thoughts and will to mankind.	". . . the Bible does not contain only true history. *Everything* it says is true" (*You Can Live Forever in Paradise on Earth*, 1982, p. 55).	This is an orthodox statement.
Only the Watch Tower Society can correctly interpret the Bible because it is an organizational book that cannot be properly understood by individuals without the help of the organization through which God works (that is, the Watch Tower Society).	". . . the Bible is an organizational book and belongs to the Christian congregation as an organization, not to individuals, regardless of how sincerely they may believe that they can interpret the Bible. . . . the Bible cannot be properly understood without Jehovah's visible organization in mind" (*Watchtower*, October 1, 1967, p. 587). "God has not arranged for that Word to speak independently or to shine forth life-giving truths by itself. . . . It is through his organization God provides this light" (Ibid., May 1, 1957, p. 274). "Unless we are in touch with this channel of communication that God is using, we will not progress along the road to life, no matter how much Bible reading we do" (Ibid., December 12, 1981, p. 27). "Let us face the fact that no matter how much Bible reading we have done, we would never have learned the truth on our own" (Ibid., December 1, 1990, p. 19).	Such a claim, which substitutes the organization for the Bible, means that no Christians in any age had access to scriptural truth until the Watch Tower Society began its work. Moreover, this claim relegates the direct help of the Holy Spirit in illuminating the text to either a minor or nonexistent role. This directly contradicts John 16:13 and 1 John 2:27. Moreover, Ephesians 1:17–18 states that the Spirit will provide wisdom and illumination to the revelation of God in the Bible. First Corinthians 2:12 says, "We have not received the spirit of the world but the Spirit who is from God, that we may understand what God has freely given us." Paul indicates that one stands approved of God through diligent study of the Scriptures (2Ti 2:15). If Paul the apostle needed to be judged by the Scriptures by the Bereans (Ac 17:11), surely the teachings of the Watch Tower should be judged by the Word of God.

The Doctrine of Revelation (cont.)

Position	Support	Orthodox Response
The *New World Translation of the Holy Scriptures* is the best translation of the Bible and should be used when there is disagreement between translations.	"The endeavor of the New World Bible Translation Committee has been to avoid this snare of religious traditionalism" (*New World Translation of the Christian Greek Scriptures*, 1950, p. 6). "Outstanding among Bibles is the *New World Translation of the Christian Greek Scriptures*.... Accuracy, uniformity, clarity, and up-to-date language mark this excellent work. Bible study aids without equal make this an indispensable help to sincere searching students of God's Word" (*What Has Religion Done for Mankind*, 1951, p. 351).	Biblical scholars and translators have never considered the New World Translation of the Holy Scriptures one of the better translations. It is dogged by special pleading and mistranslations in numerous verses in order to substantiate the aberrant teachings of the Watch Tower. Dr. Robert H. Countess, in his doctrinal dissertation titled "The Jehovah's Witnesses' New Testament," said the translation "has been sharply unsuccessful in keeping doctrinal considerations from influencing the actual translation.... It must be viewed as a radically biased piece of work. At some points it is actually dishonest. At others, it is neither modern nor scholarly" (p. 91). Greek scholar Bruce Metzger has stated that "the Jehovah's Witnesses have incorporated in their translation of the New Testament several quite erroneous renderings of the Greek" ("Jehovah's Witnesses and Jesus Christ," *Theology Today*, April 1953, p. 74).

The Doctrine of God—*The Trinity*

Position	Support	Orthodox Response
The Trinity is not a true doctrine.	"Never was there a more deceptive doctrine advanced than that of the trinity" (*Reconciliation*, 1928, p. 101). "... to worship God on his terms means to reject the Trinity doctrine. It contradicts what the prophets, Jesus, the apostles, and the early Christians believed and taught. It contradicts what God says about himself in his own inspired Word" (*Should You Believe in the Trinity?* 1989, p. 31). "Nowhere in the Scriptures is even any mention made of a trinity" (*Let God Be True*, 1946 [1952 rev.], p. 111). "... the word 'trinity' does not appear in the Bible" (*You Can Live Forever in Paradise on Earth*, 1982, p. 39).	Many Jehovah's Witness doctrines expressed in theological words are not explicitly found in the Bible either (for example, theocracy, disfellowshipping, Governing Body). Even the name *Jehovah* is not found in the Bible. The term was created when the Hebrew consonants for God's name (YHWH) were blended with the vowels from *Adonai* (another name for God that means Lord). The name *Jehovah* was introduced by Raymundus Martini, a Spanish monk of the Dominican Order, in his book *Puegeo Fidei*, in 1270. (Evidence found in *Aid to Bible Understanding*, 1971, p. 884.)

The Doctrine of God—*The Trinity (cont.)*

Position	Support	Orthodox Response
Trinitarians believe in three gods.	"**IS THERE A TRINITY?** . . . The doctrine, in brief, is that there are three gods in one: 'God the Father, God the Son, and God the Holy Ghost,' all three equal in power, substance and eternity" (*Let God Be True*, 1946 [1952 rev.], p. 100). ". . . sincere persons who want to know the true God and serve him find it a bit difficult to love and worship a complicated, freakish-looking, three-headed God" (Ibid., p. 102).	The Jehovah's Witnesses typically describe the Trinity as being three gods, a pagan three-headed God, or a freakish-looking monster. The arguments they use against the orthodox view are often based on misrepresentations of the Trinity concept. Consequently, the first step in refuting the Jehovah's Witness opinion that the Trinity is false is to demonstrate that their concept of the Trinity is incorrect. Orthodox Christianity defines the Trinity not as three gods or a three-headed God, but rather as one God who, within His nature, eternally exists as three distinct perons—namely, Father, Son, and Holy Spirit.
The Christian doctrine of the Trinity was borrowed from ancient paganism.	". . . the Trinity is not a Bible teaching. Actually, long before Jesus walked the earth gods were worshiped in groups of three, or trinities, in places such as ancient Egypt and Babylon" (*You Can Live Forever in Paradise on Earth*, 1982, pp. 40–41). "The origin of the trinity doctrine is traced back to the ancient Babylonians and Egyptians and other ancient mythologists" (*Let God Be True*, 1946 [1952 rev.], p. 101).	The Christian doctrine of the Trinity is considerably different from pagan deities, which, although sometimes paired in twos or threes, are always separate beings with differing abilities. No pagan triad of gods is analogous to the Christian Trinity. One might ask whether the fact that Islam, a false religion, believes in only one God means that the Jehovah's Witnesses belief in only one God is false. The obvious answer the Jehovah's Witness will give is no. A Christian can point out that in the same way, a pagan belief in "triads" does not mean the Christian Trinity is a false teaching.
Satan originated the doctrine of the Trinity.	"Satan is the originator of the trinity doctrine" (*Let God Be True*, 1946 [1952 rev.], p. 101).	Because the orthodox doctrine of the Trinity is based on Scripture and involves more than just countering the Jehovah's Witnesses point of view, see Appendix A, "Orthodox Christian Doctrine."

The Doctrine of Jesus Christ—*The Deity of Christ*

Position	Support	Orthodox Response
Jesus Christ, before becoming a man, was Michael the Archangel, the first and greatest creation of Jehovah God.	"Christ was first of God's creations **Col. 1:15;**[1] **Rev. 3:14**[2]"(*Jehovah's Witnesses in the 20th Century*, 1979 [1989 ed.], p. 13). ". . . he [the Word] was created before all the other spirit sons of God, and that he is the only one who was directly created by God" (*You Can Live Forever in Paradise on Earth*, 1982, p. 58). ". . . the Son of God was known as Michael before he came to earth" (*Reasoning from the Scriptures*, p. 218).	1. Colossians 1:15–17: The Greek text indicates that Jesus is being referred to as an heir, the first in rank, and, hence, prior to all creation and superior over it as the Lord. The passage uses *prototokos* (first-born or first-bearer), rather than *protoktistos* (first-created). See, for example, Jeremiah 31:9, where Ephraim is called God's "firstborn son." Genesis 41:51–52, however, states that Manasseh was literally the firstborn, not Ephraim. Obviously, "firstborn" does not always mean literally "first" born or "first" created. Also, in the New World Translation of Colossians 1:15–17, the word "other" appears four times. There is no basis for this in either the Greek text or in the rest of the translation. 2. Revelation 3:14: The Greek text refutes the Witnesses interpretation of this verse. The word translated "beginning" (*arche*) does not require a literal interpretation. It often connotes the idea of something being "the origin" or the "active cause" of something. So in this passage Jesus is being referred to as the source, or "origin," of all creation. Nowhere in the Bible is Jesus spoken of as being a creation of God. He is, in fact, described as the Creator of all that exists (Jn 1:3; Col 1:16). He is also said to be the same "yesterday and today and forever" (Heb 13:8).
Jesus was a spokesman for God before His birth.	". . . before being born on earth as a man Jesus had been in heaven as a mighty spirit person. . . . he served in heaven as the one who spoke for God" (*You Can Live Forever in Paradise on Earth*, 1982, p. 58).	See the evidence cited for "Diety of Christ" in Appendix A. Moreover, John 1:18 presents Christ as the one who fully explains God because He is the one and only God (NIV).
While on earth, Jesus was not God, only a perfect man.	". . . when God sent Jesus to earth as the ransom, he made Jesus to be what would satisfy justice, not an incarnation, not a god-man, but a perfect man" (*Should You Believe in the Trinity?* 1989, p. 15).	Jesus was God in the flesh. In Scripture He is called God (Jn 20:28; Heb 1:8–9; Tit 2:13), honored as God (Jn 5:23), and prayed to as God (Ac 7:59).
After Jesus died, He was resurrected with His original identity as Michael the Archangel restored.	"Read carefully the following Bible account: 'War broke out in heaven: Michael [who is the resurrected Jesus Christ] and his angels battled with the dragon'" (*You Can Live Forever in Paradise on Earth*, 1982, p. 21).	Michael, on his own authority, was unable to rebuke Satan (Jude 9), yet in Mark 9:25 Jesus Himself, while in a lower estate as man, rebukes Satan. Furthermore, Hebrews 2:5 says an angel can't rule the world, yet Luke 1:32–33 and Revelation 19:16 portray Christ as the one who will reign supreme. Thus Jesus and Michael cannot be the same being.

The Doctrine of Jesus Christ—*The Deity of Christ (cont.)*

Position	Support	Orthodox Response
Jesus is not the almighty God.	"Well, did Jesus ever say that he, was God? No, he never did. Rather, in the Bible he is called 'God's Son.' And he said: 'The Father is greater than I am.' (John 10:34–36;14:28) Also, Jesus explained that there were some things that neither he nor the angels knew but that only God knew. (Mark 13:32) Further, on one occasion Jesus prayed to God, saying: 'Let, not *my* will, but *yours* take place.' (Luke 22:42) If Jesus were the Almighty God, he would not have prayed to himself, would he? In fact, following Jesus' death, the Scripture says: 'This Jesus God resurrected.' (Acts 2:32) Thus the Almighty God and Jesus are clearly two separate persons. Even after his death and resurrection and ascension to heaven, Jesus was still not equal to his Father.—1 Corinthians 11:3; 15:28" (*You Can Live Forever in Paradise on Earth*, 1982, pp. 39–40).	John 10:34–36: Jesus was actually making Himself equal to God by saying He was the Son of God (see Jn 5:17–18). John 14:28: Jesus used the word "greater," not the word "better." The former speaks of the Father's greater position (in heaven), not greater nature. "Better" would have referred to the Father's nature. Mark 13:32: Jesus, as the God-man, had two natures: human and divine. When Jesus functioned in His humanity, He voluntarily *chose* not to exercise the attributes present in His divine nature (such as omniscience). On other occasions, when exercising attributes such as omniscience (Mt 9:4), He would operate in the sphere of His divine nature. Luke 22:42: Submission does not make the one in submission inferior in nature to the one in authority (for example, the relationship between wives and husbands). Acts 2:32: Scripture teaches that Jesus raised Himself from the dead (Jn 2:19–20), that the Father raised Jesus (Col 2:12), and that the Holy Spirit raised Jesus (Ro 8:11). In other words, the Triune God resurrected Jesus. First Corinthians 11:3; 15:28: While on earth, Christ honored God the Father. "Head of" means deserving of honor. Also, although all three persons of the Trinity are equal in dignity and deity, the Father is functionally above the other members in the Trinity.
Jesus is "a god," a lesser God than Jehovah God.	"At John 1:1, which refers to Jesus as 'the Word,' some Bible translations say: 'In the beginning was the Word, and the Word was with God, and the Word was God.' But notice, verse 2 says that the Word was 'in the beginning *with* God.' And while men have seen Jesus, verse 18 says that 'no man hath seen God at any time.' (*Authorized* or *King James Version*) So we find that some translations of verse 1 give the correct idea of the original language when they read: 'The Word was with God, and the Word was divine,' or was 'a god,' that is the Word was a powerful godlike one. (*An American Translation*) Clearly, Jesus is not Almighty God. In fact, Jesus spoke of his Father as 'my God' and as 'the only true God.'—John 20:17; 17:3" (*You Can Live Forever in Paradise on Earth*, 1982, p. 40).	John 1:1: The New World Translation of 'a god' rather than God is not a legitimate translation from the Greek. For a full discussion, see either Roy B. Zuck's "Open Letter to a Jehovah's Witness" (*Moody Monthly*, n.d.), pp. 8–11, or James W. Sire's *Scripture Twisting* (Downers Grove, Ill.: InterVarsity Press, 1980), pp. 161–63.

The Doctrine of Jesus Christ—*The Humanity of Christ*

Position	Support	Orthodox Response
Jesus was the equal of a perfect Adam.	"Jesus was the equal of the perfect man Adam" (*You Can Live Forever in Paradise on Earth*, 1982, p. 63).	Stating that Jesus is an equal to Adam contradicts the teachings in the Bible that Jesus is God.
Jesus did not become the Christ until He was baptized.	"Jesus came to John to be baptized! On that occasion he was anointed with holy spirit and became the Messiah, or Christ.—Luke 3:1, 2, 21–23" (*You Can Live Forever in Paradise on Earth*, 1982, p. 138).	This statement is contradicted by Luke 2:25–32. Simeon, who had been searching for the Messiah, declares that the child Jesus is the Messiah ("your salvation"). Also, the angel announcing Jesus' birth declared, "A Savior has been born to you; he is Christ the Lord" (Lk 2:11). So Jesus was the Messiah before He was baptized by John.
Jesus was not immortal before He was resurrected.	"The first one described in the Bible as rewarded with the gift of immortality is Jesus Christ. That he did not possess immortality before his resurrection by God is seen from . . . Romans 6:9" (*Insight on the Scriptures,* vol. 1; 1988, p. 1189).	Jesus in His divine nature is immortal, but in His humanity was subject to death. Romans 6:9 merely states that Jesus died and was resurrected never to die again. John 5:26 indicates that Jesus had life within His very nature just as the Father has life within Himself.

The Doctrine of Jesus Christ—*The Resurrection of Christ*

Position	Support	Orthodox Response
Jesus was resurrected in a spirit form.	"Jesus Christ . . . was the first to be raised as a spirit person. (1 Peter 3:18)" (*You Can Live Forever in Paradise on Earth*, 1982, p. 172).	1 Peter 3:18: ". . . [being] put to death in the body but made alive by the Spirit" does not require the meaning that Jesus Christ was raised as a spirit rather than in a physical body. Even if the phrase were "in the Spirit," the sense would be that He was raised in the sphere of the Holy Spirit, not that He was raised a spirit being. The teaching that He was raised a spirit is totally contrary to Christ's words to Thomas in Luke 24:39: "a ghost [spirit, KJV] does not have flesh and bones, as you see I have."
Jesus was not resurrected in the same physical body in which He died.	"Jesus thus gave up his fleshly body in sacrifice for humankind. . . . Having given up his flesh for the life of the world, Christ could never take it again and become a man once more. For that basic reason his return could never be in the human body that he sacrificed once for all time" (*You Can Live Forever in Paradise on Earth*, 1982, p. 143).	Offering His life for the sins of men has nothing whatsoever to do with somehow leaving His body on the earth for humanity. He merely died in the flesh; there is no requirement that He abandon that body. In fact, in the resurrection He takes it again (Ac 2:22–31). Also, Colossians 2:9 states that in Christ "all the fullness of the Deity lives [present tense] in bodily form."

The Doctrine of the Holy Spirit

Position	Support	Orthodox Response
The holy spirit is God's active force, not a personal being. Through this "force" God accomplishes His purposes.	"A comparison of Bible texts that refer to the holy spirit shows that it is spoken of as 'filling' people; they can be 'baptized' with it; and they can be 'anointed' with it.... None of these expressions would be appropriate if the holy spirit were a person" (*Reasoning from the Scriptures*, 1985, p. 380). "From God there goes forth an invisible active force by means of which he gets his will done.... He sends it forth to accomplish what is holy. So it is correctly called 'holy spirit'" (*Holy Spirit*, 1976, p. 11).	The Bible describes the Holy Spirit as a person. Personal pronouns are always used in reference to the Holy Spirit (Jn 14:16–17; 15:26; 16:13–14), the Holy Spirit is called a "witness" (Ac 5:32), and specific speech is attributed to the Holy Spirit (Ac 8:29; 10:19–20; 11:12; 13:2). Acts that can be accomplished only by a personal being are attributed to the Holy Spirit. The Holy Spirit feels love and grief (Ro 15:30; Eph 4:30/Isa 63:10), has a mind with which to intercede (Ro 8:27), possesses knowledge (1Co 2:11), can be lied to (Ac 5:3), can be insulted (Heb 10:29), can teach (Jn 14:26), can bear witness (Jn 15:26), can hear (Jn 16:13), and can make value judgments (Ac 15:28). The Bible also applies personal descriptive titles to the Holy Spirit, such as Helper (Jn 14:26 NASB). Note this statement in a *Watchtower* article affirming the personhood of Satan: "... can an unintelligent force carry on a conversation with a person? Also, the Bible calls Satan a manslayer, a liar, a father.... and a ruler. Only an intelligent person could fit all those descriptions" (*Awake!* December 8, 1973, p. 27). The criteria used in this article for personal attributes can also be applied to the Holy Spirit. If the *Watchtower* were consistent, it would have to acknowledge the personality of the Holy Spirit, yet it refuses to do so. The *Watchtower* arguments against the personality of the Holy Spirit are weak. For example, the fact that Scripture speaks of the Holy Spirit's filling a person does not mean the Holy Spirit cannot be a person. The *Watchtower* considers demons personal beings yet holds that such entities can fill someone via demonic possession. The *Watchtower* employs a different set of rules when dealing with the Holy Spirit. To say that God sends out an active force, which can be called "holy spirit" because it accomplishes a holy task, is to read a great deal into the biblical texts. If the *Watchtower* view were true, one would expect to find at least a few biblical passages describing a "holy active force." Such is not the case.

The Doctrine of Man and Sin

Position	Support	Orthodox Response
When Adam sinned, his punishment was death. His disobedience also passed sin and death to all humanity. Everyone is a condemned sinner because of Adam.	"... by the disobedience of Adam sin became active and he was sentenced to death, and condemnation resulted to all his offspring. Hence all were born sinners" (*Life*, 1929, p. 194).	This is an orthodox statement.
When a person dies, he or she completely ceases to exist. There is no consciousness after death.	"The dead are shown to be 'conscious of nothing at all' and the death state to be one of complete inactivity. (Ec 9:5, 10; Ps 146:4).... In both the Hebrew and the Greek Scriptures, death is likened to sleep, a fitting comparison not only because of the unconscious condition of the dead but also because of the hope of an awakening through the resurrection" (*Insight on the Scriptures*, vol. 1, 1988, p. 597). "... when a person is dead he is completely out of existence. He is not conscious of anything" (*You Can Live Forever in Paradise on Earth*, 1982, p. 88).	In context, Ecclesiastes 9:5 and Psalm 146:4 are discussing awareness relating to a person's earthly knowledge and participation in earthly events. The verses are not discussing lack of consciousness in the realm of the dead. According to Luke 16, people are conscious after they die. In Matthew 17:3 Moses appeared and spoke with Jesus even though he had died centuries earlier.
A man does not *have* a soul; he *is* a soul. A soul is a combination of a body and the "life force" that only Jehovah God can impart.	"Gen. 2:7: 'Jehovah God proceeded to form the man out of dust from the ground and to blow into his nostrils the breath of life, and the man came to be a living soul.' (Notice that this does not say that man *was given* a soul but that he *became* a soul, a living person.)" (*Reasoning from the Scriptures*, 1985, p. 375). "... 'man came to be a living soul'; hence man *was* a soul, he did not *have* a soul as something immaterial, invisible, and intangible residing inside him" (*Insight on the Scriptures*, vol. 2, 1988, pp. 1005–6).	Numerous passages indicate that man is composed of distinct parts called body, soul, and spirit (Ps 131:2; 142:3; Mt 10:28). Genesis 2:7 does not purport to state that man *is* a living soul, but is only declaring that man was animated to life.
The concept of an immortal "soul" came into apostate Christendom through pagan philosophy.	"How, then, did this belief about an immortal soul find its way into the teachings of Christendom's churches? Today it is frankly acknowledged that this has come about through the influence of pagan Grecian philosophy" (*Is This Life All There Is?* 1974, p. 43).	This statement is entirely untrue. Belief in an immortal soul existing separate from the body was held by Hebrews long before Grecian philosophy would have been able to influence Christian thought. Genesis 35:18 (NASB) speaks of a woman's "soul" departing; 1 Kings 17:21 recounts how Elijah asked God to let the soul of a child return to him. Such descriptions also appear in the New Testament (Mt 10:28; Ac 20:10; Rev 6:9–11).

The Doctrine of Salvation

Position	Support	Orthodox Response
Jesus' death paid only for Adam's sin, not for the sins of all humanity.	"... he [God] could not set aside the judgment that he had entered against Adam. He could, however, be consistent ... by permitting another to pay the debt of Adam and thereby to open the way for Adam and his offspring to be released from sin and death" (*Life*, 1929, p. 199). "To redeem or ransom man from the grave means that God will provide a means of satisfaction of the judgment against Adam" (Ibid., p. 206).	Jesus' death paid not only for Adam's sin, but also for our sins (1Co 15:3; Gal 1:4; Heb 9:28; 1Pe 2:24).
By clearing away the penalty of Adam's sin, Christ opened the way (gave us the opportunity) to work for salvation.	"It is for the reward of eternal life that every last person on earth should now be working. Are you?" (*Watchtower*, August 15, 1972, p. 492). "To get one's name written in that book of life will depend upon one's works, whether they are in fulfillment of God's will and approved by his Judge and King" (Ibid., July 1, 1947, p. 204). "Jesus Christ identified a first requirement when he said in prayer.... This means everlasting life, their *taking in knowledge* of you.... Many have found the second requirement more difficult. It is to *obey God's laws*.... A third requirement is that we *be associated with God's channel*, his organization.... To receive everlasting life in the earthly Paradise we must identify that organization and serve God as part of it. The fourth requirement ... requires that prospective subjects of his Kingdom support his government by *loyally advocating his Kingdom rule to others* [that is, preaching door-to-door]" (Ibid., February 15, 1983, pp. 12–13). "Jehovah God will justify, declare righteous, on the basis of their own merit all perfected humans who have withstood that final, decisive test of mankind [the release of Satan from bondage after the 1000-year reign of Christ]" (*Life Everlasting—In Freedom of the Sons of God*, 1966, p. 400).	The Jehovah's Witnesses gravely misunderstand salvation. First, salvation is a gift, not a reward (Ro 5:15–16; 6:23; Eph 2:8). Second, works do not produce salvation (Ro 4:1–4); they are the natural by-product of salvation (Jas 2:14–18). Regarding Jesus' words about knowledge, the *Watchtower* has misquoted and changed what Jesus actually said. In John 17:3 Jesus simply states that eternal life is knowing God—in other words, coming to a realization of who God is. Nowhere does Jesus equate salvation with an ongoing process of gaining knowledge. As for having to obey God's law, these statements are only half true. Scripture instructs us to keep Jesus' commandments (Jn 14:15, 21; 15:10; 1Jn 2:3; 3:22–24; 2Jn 6). At the same time, however, we know that because of sin and the weakness of our flesh, no one can keep the whole law (Jas 2:10). Consequently, although it is in and of itself holy (Ro 7:12; 1Ti 1:8), the law has become a curse to mankind because it points out sin (Gal 3:13). But Christ kept the law perfectly (Mt 5:17), and therefore His righteousness is imputed to us through faith apart from the law (Ro 3:28); in this way the law is fulfilled in us (Ro 8:3–4). No one is justified by the law (Ro 3:20; Gal 2:16; 3:11), and those who seek justification through the law will actually be severed from Christ (Gal 5:3–4). Christ, according to the Bible, is actually the end of the law (Ro 10:4). We are not under law, but under grace (Ro 6:14).

The Doctrine of Rewards and Punishment

Position	Support	Orthodox Response
There are two classes of Christians: the "little flock" and the "great crowd." The former are born-again children of God; only they can participate in the annual memorial service (communion), and they alone will go to heaven. The latter ("other sheep") will live in "Paradise" on earth after "unbelievers" are destroyed through either the Great Tribulation or Armageddon. (The "little flock" will be taken to heaven before the Tribulation.)	"The Bible shows that only a limited number of persons, a 'little flock,' will go to heaven.... The rest of faithful humankind will live on earth as the subjects of these rulers" (*Watchtower*, February 15, 1984, p. 9). "... these dedicated, baptized 'other sheep' of the 'great crowd' have not been begotten to be God's spiritual sons, with a heavenly inheritance" (*Holy Spirit*, 1976, p. 157). "... at the celebration of the memorial of Christ's death, only those who make up 'the Israel of God' should partake of the emblems of bread and wine.... the vast international company of 'other sheep,' who do not partake, will enjoy everlasting life on the Paradise earth" (*WT*, March 15, 1983, p. 9).	Nowhere does Scripture speak of two classes of Christians. All are one in Christ (Gal 3:28), and all share one future hope (Eph 1:18; 4:4; Col 1:5). The "other sheep" referred to by Jesus in John 10:16 are not a class of second-class Christians who will not inherit heaven. In context, Jesus is referring to Gentile believers who would one day join Jewish believers to form one body of Christians. This is clear from the fact that Jesus was addressing Jews, who in other verses are called "the lost sheep of Israel" (Mt 10:6; 15:24). Those who followed Christ were called His sheep (Mt 10:16; 26:31; Jn 10). Consequently, when Jesus referred to "other sheep," He must have been referring to non-Jewish people who would become believers and create one body of Christ (Eph 2:11–22).
Salvation for the "little flock" will include sharing in Jesus' divine nature and joining with Him in heaven to become "the Christ." In fact, they will be gods.	"... what is meant by 'Christ in you?'... Jesus was anointed with the Holy Spirit (Acts 10:38), and thus we recognize him to be the Christ—the anointed.... the saints of this Gospel age are an anointed company [1 John 2:27].... together with Jesus, their chief and Lord, they constitute Jehovah's Anointed—the Christ.... *the Christ* (the Anointed) is 'not one member, but many'.... Jesus is anointed to be the Head or Lord over the Church... and unitedly they constitute the *promised 'Seed'*—the Great Deliverer" (*Studies in the Scriptures, Series 1*, "The Divine Plan of the Ages," 1886 [1908 ed.], pp. 81–82). "... we are begotten of a divine nature.... Jehovah is thus our father.... we are divine beings—hence all such are Gods.... Now we appear like men, and all die naturally as men, but in the resurrection we will rise in our true character as Gods" (*Watchtower*, December 1881, p. 3 [1919 repr., p. 301]). "... the titles, Mighty God, and Everlasting Father... are very appropriate to Our Lord Jesus.... the same titles are applicable to the Church as his body" (*Watchtower*, November 1881, p. 10 [1919 repr., pp. 297–98]).	The Bible consistently identifies Jesus as the Christ (Mt 1:17; 16:16, 20; Lk 2:11; 4:41; Ac 3:20; 9:22; 17:3). The claim that the "anointed" ones of the Jehovah's Witnesses will actually become part of the Christ is a clear fulfillment of Jesus' warning that many false teachers will come saying they are the Christ (Mt 24:5, 23). Over against the teachings about the ability of the anointed class to become gods are Scriptures such as Isaiah 43:10 and 1 Timothy 2:5, which declare that there is only one God. To say that the titles of Christ found in Isaiah 9:6 can be applied to the church is both unwarranted and blasphemous. The *Watchtower*'s view of Jesus, coupled with its view of the anointed class, actually makes Jehovah's Witnesses polytheists because they believe there exists more than one God.

The Doctrine of Rewards and Punishment (cont.)

Position	Support	Orthodox Response
There is no conscious eternal punishment for the wicked. All "unbelievers" will be annihilated.	"The fiendish concepts associated with a hell of torment slander God and originate with the chief slanderer of God (the Devil)" (*Reasoning from the Scriptures*, 1985, p. 175).	In reality, the concept of hell comes from the Bible (Mt 25:46; Rev 14:11; 19:20; 20:10).

INTERESTING AND DISTINCTIVE BELIEFS

Position	Support	Orthodox Response
Jesus was crucified on a stake (a single verticle pole) rather than on a cross. Christendom's depiction of Christ on a cross has pagan origins.	"Jesus most likely was executed on an upright stake without any crossbeam" (*Watchtower*, August 15, 1987, p. 29). "... in a very subtle way, through the influence of a sun-worshiping ruler [Constantine], the non Christian cross came to be accepted by professed Christians.... the Greek word *stau-rous* (translated 'cross'... denotes, primarily, an upright pale or stake" (*Awake!* November 8, 1972, p. 28).	The Jehovah's Witnesses present a half-truth to make their case. The Greek word *stauros*, translated "cross" in English versions of the Bible, was used to refer to a number of different wooden structures including both a stake *and* a structure with a crossbeam. How then can we be sure that Jesus was crucified on a *stauros* that was a cross? In John 20, Thomas refuses to believe in the resurrected Christ unless he can see "the print of the nails" (plural) in Jesus' hands. If Jesus were crucified on a stake, the soldiers would have used only one nail. Only if Jesus were crucified on a cross could "nails" have been used. Until 1931 the *Watchtower* consistently pictured Christ as having been crucified on a cross (*The Harp of God*, 1921, p. 114) and often used the cross in its publications as part of a logo (see *Watchtower* magazines prior to 1931).
Participation in war and military service of any kind is strictly forbidden. In fact, any form of patriotism—such as saluting the flag, voting, and involvement in politics—is wrong. Such actions demonstrate an allegiance to men rather than to God.	"... each [JW] minister claims exemption... from military training and service. He is already... a 'soldier of Christ Jesus'.... he is not authorized by his Commander in Chief Jehovah God, to engage in carnal warfare of this world.... he cannot desert the forces of Jehovah to assume the obligations of a soldier in any army of this world without being guilty of desertion and suffering the punishment meted out by Almighty God" (*Let God Be True*, 1946 [1952 rev.], p. 238). "... we view the flag salute as an act of worship" (*School and Jehovah's Witnesses*, 1983, p. 13). "... Jehovah's Witnesses take no part whatsoever in political activities" (*United in Worship of the Only True God*, 1983, p. 166).	It cannot be demonstrated from Scripture that Christians must forsake military duty. Neither Jesus nor John the Baptist, when given the opportunity, listed leaving military duty as a requirement to bring forth fruits worthy of repentance (Lk 3:14; Mt 8:10). Nothing in the Bible would prohibit such acts as voting or saluting the flag. Scripture commands us to have respect and reverence for the government because it is an authority that God has allowed to be placed over us (Ro 13; 1Pe 2:13–14).

Position	Support	Orthodox Response
Birthday parties, Valentine's Day, Mother's Day, Father's Day, and other holidays are all unbiblical celebrations that must be avoided. Even holidays such as Christmas and Easter are not celebrated because they are pagan holidays.	"... birthday celebrations tend to give excessive importance to an individual.... Jehovah's Witnesses do not share in birthday festivities (the parties, singing, gift giving, and so forth).... We take no part in Christmas parties, plays, singing, exchanging of gifts, or in any other such activity that is associated with Christmas... **New Year's Day**.... **Valentine's Day**.... Jehovah's Witnesses for conscientious reasons do not take any part in these holiday activities" (*School and Jehovah's Witnesses*, 1983, pp. 18, 19, 20, 21). "... nowhere in the Bible do we find that parents are to be worshiped, or that there should be a Father's Day and a Mother's Day kept in their honor. Worship belongs exclusively to Jehovah" (*Awake!* May 8, 1956, p. 25). "Christendom's chief holiday, Easter, therefore finds no support at all in the Bible. It is of pagan origin" (*The Truth that Leads to Eternal Life*, 1968, p. 148).	The number of harmless activities outlawed by the Jehovah's Witnesses is an indication of the high degree of control under which the average member is made to live. To equate the celebration of birthdays, Mother's Day, or Father's Day with some kind of worship is absurd. Such celebrations are merely days set aside for expressions of gratitude and love. As for Easter and Christmas, it is true that these holy days coincide with pagan holidays. However, the reason that Christians began celebrating events such as Jesus' resurrection and Jesus' birth on pagan holidays was to divert attention from pagan lies to truths of God.
Blood transfusions, for adults and children, are strictly prohibited by Jehovah God. Receiving a blood transfusion puts one in danger of losing the possibility of salvation.	**"Blood Transfusions: Does the Bible's prohibitions include human blood?** Yes.... Acts 15:29 says to 'keep abstaining from ... blood'.... (Compare Leviticus 17:10, which prohibited eating 'any sort of blood.')... **Is a transfusion really the same as eating blood?** ... consider a man who is told by the doctor that he must abstain from alcohol. Would he be obedient if he quit drinking alcohol but had it put directly into his veins?" (*Reasoning from the Scriptures*, 1985, pp. 72–73). "Jehovah's Witnesses do not reject blood for their children due to any lack of parental love.... They know that if they violate God's law on blood and the child dies in the process, they have endangered that child's opportunity for everlasting life.... resorting to blood transfusions even under the most extreme circumstances is not truly lifesaving. It may result in the immediate and very temporary prolongation of life, but that at the cost of eternal life for a dedicated Christian" (*Blood, Medicine and the Law of God*, 1961, pp. 54–55).	Acts 15:28–29 addresses eating blood, not having blood transfused into the body for life-saving purposes. Dr. Ron Rhodes cogently states that eating blood "is not the same as a blood transfusion.... A transfusion treats the blood not with disrespect but with reverence. And a transfusion replenishes the supply of essential, life-sustaining fluid that has in some way been drained away.... A transfusion uses blood for the same purpose that God intended—as a life-giving agent in the bloodstream" (*Reasoning from the Scriptures with the Jehovah's Witnesses,* p. 389). In their Alcohol analogy, the Watchtower fails to see the obvious—that alcohol is not blood, nor is alcohol already an intricate part of man's physical make-up. We have already seen that the Watchtower misunderstands the nature of salvation. Its assertion that a blood transfusion would result in one's loss of eternal life again shows how confused Jehovah's Witnesses are when it comes to salvation. Romans 8:38–39 demonstrates that nothing whatsoever can separate us from God's love—including a blood transfusion.

Position	Support	Orthodox Response
Christ returned invisibly in 1914 and began setting up His kingdom. Part of the "sign" of His presence was the start of World War I.	"Christ's return does not mean that he literally comes back to this earth. Rather, it means that he takes Kingdom power toward this earth and turns his attention to it.... Bible evidence shows that in the year 1914 C.E. God's time arrived for Christ to return and begin ruling.... Christ's return is invisible.... Christ himself gave a visible 'sign' by which we may know that he is invisibly present.... **'NATION WILL RISE AGAINST NATION'**.... Surely you have seen this part of the 'sign' being fulfilled since 1914! In that year World War I began" (*You Can Live Forever in Paradise on Earth*, pp. 147, 150).	The Jehovah's Witnesses' belief in an invisible return of Christ is not rooted in the Bible, but in a failed prediction made by the Watchtower's founder, Charles Taze Russell. According to Russell, Jesus had returned to earth and set up His invisibly present kingdom toward the end of 1874 (later changed by Rutherford to 1914). According to Acts 1:9–11, Jesus ascended from His disciples in a bodily and visible form. Afterward an angel appeared to assure Jesus' followers that He would return in the same manner (that is, physically and visibly). Revelation 1:7 indicates that when Jesus returns, every eye will see Him. Note that the Greek word *horao* means to "see, catch sight of, notice *of sense perception*" (*Greek-English Lexicon of the New Testament* by William Arndt and F. Wilbur Gingrich, p. 581) or "to see with the eyes" (*Thayer's Greek-English Lexicon of the New Testament*, p. 451).
Jehovah's Witnesses consider themselves God's "prophet" on earth. As such, they have given numerous false prophecies, most of them dealing with the end of the world.	"... does Jehovah have a prophet to help them, to warn them of dangers and to declare things to come?... These questions can be answered in the affirmative. Who is this prophet?... This 'prophet' was not one man, but was a body of men and women.... Today they are known as Jehovah's Christian witnesses.... Of course, it is easy to say that this group acts as a 'prophet' of God. It is another thing to prove it. The only way that this can be done is to review the record. What does it show?" (*Watchtower*, April 1, 1972, p. 197). "... the 'battle of the great day of God Almighty' (Rev. 16:14), which will end in A.D. 1914 with the complete overthrow of earth's present rulership, is already commenced" (*Studies in the Scriptures*, Series 2, 1889, [1906 ed.] p. 101). "... we may confidently expect that 1925 will mark the return of Abraham, Isaac, Jacob and the faithful prophets of old, particularly those named ... in Hebrews chapter eleven, to the condition of human perfection" (*Millions Now Living Will Never Die*, 1920, pp. 89–90). "... the Lord's provided instrument for most effective work in the remaining months before Armageddon" (*Watchtower*, September 15, 1941, p. 288).	As these quotes indicate, the Jehovah's Witnesses have, on more than one occasion, proven themselves to be false prophets by making predictions in the name of the Lord that did not come to pass. Deuteronomy 18:21–22 asks, "You may say to yourselves, 'How can we know when a message has not been spoken by the LORD?' If what a prophet proclaims in the name of the LORD does not take place or come true, that is a message the LORD has not spoken. That prophet has spoken presumptuously. Do not be afraid of him."

Position	Support	Orthodox Response
. . . continued	"Proof is now submitted that we are now living at 'the end of the days', and we may expect to see Daniel and the other mentioned princes any day now!" (*Consolation*, May 17, 1942, p. 13). "According to this trustworthy Bible chronology six thousand years from man's creation will end in 1975, and the seventh period of a thousand years of human history will begin in the fall of 1975" (*Life Everlasting—In Freedom of the Sons of God*, 1966, p. 29).	

12
Mind Science Groups

CLASSIFICATION AND CONNECTION

The Three Major Branches of Mind Science

Three major religious-educational groups are so closely related in their philosophical and theological beliefs that they can properly be classified together under the single heading "Mind Science" (MS).

These three groups are Christian Science **(CS)**, Religious Science **(RS)**, and Unity School of Christianity **(USC)**.

All three groups can be considered metaphysical in nature. This means that they have a strong focus on explaining reality and analyzing (philosophically) the structure and origin of the world. Although Mind Science groups are not compatible in all areas, their core beliefs are virtually the same.

Most Mind Science groups would support the following statements:

- Sin, death, sickness, and evil do not exist.
- God is impersonal and can be understood as All within All.
- The material world is an illusion or a lower form of spirit.
- Jesus was just a man who best demonstrated metaphysical truth.
- The Christ is a divine idea, the higher self in everyone; Jesus is not the Christ.
- Jesus did not suffer, die, or resurrect himself bodily.
- Our group possesses a more complete and superior form of spiritual knowledge.

Specific Mind Science groups conform with one another in general metaphysical concepts because all of these groups originate from the same basic sources. Consider how these groups are very closely related:

Christian Science uses many of the ideas espoused by P. P. Quimby, a self-proclaimed mesmerist and "mental healer" of the early nineteenth century. It is known now that Mary Baker Eddy plagiarized some of the material from *Science of Man*, a book by P. P. Quimby, and also from *The English Reader*, a book by Lindley Murray (Walter R. Martin, *Kingdom of the Cults*, 1985 ed., pp. 128–30).

About thirty years after the founding of Christian Science, Charles and Myrtle Fillmore created the **Unity School of Christianity**. Both Charles and Myrtle were strongly influenced by Emma Curtis Hopkins, at one time the editor of Mary Baker Eddy's *Christian Science Journal*.

In a similar fashion, **Religious Science** was founded on concepts connected with and parallel to the writings of Mary Baker Eddy, Charles Fillmore, and P. P. Quimby (Todd Ehrenborg, *Mind Sciences*, p. 41). The founder of Religious Science was Ernest Holmes, a high school dropout who became interested in metaphysics at a young age and who later incorporated his own philosophy of Mind Science into "The Institute of Religious Science and School of Philosophy, Inc."

Christian Science originated near Boston, Massachusetts, in 1879. Its "revelation" is titled *Science and Health with Key to the Scriptures*, published in its first edition in 1875.

Unity School of Christianity was incorporated in 1914, although its founders, the Fillmores, published their views on metaphysics as early as 1889. In 1920 a headquarters was established in Jackson County, Missouri.

Religious Science started in 1917. Based in Los Angeles, the headquarters are better known as the Institute for Religious Science. The chief textbook accepted by Religious Scientists is *The Science of Mind*, published in 1926.

Minor groups that can be classified under Mind Science include Divine Science and New Thought.

I am indebted to Todd Ehrenborg for work on this chart on Mind Sciences.

Facts	
Topic	*Current Facts*
Membership	**(CS)**—The Christian Science leadership does not publish its membership statistics, but it is widely held that the number has suffered a net loss since the 1950s (*Christian Science Journal,* September 1992, pp. 26–27). Present membership figures are estimated at between 180,000 and 250,000 people worldwide (*CRI Journal,* Spring-Summer 1994, p. 42).
	(RS)—Religious Science is the fastest growing Mind Science group, with a membership of about 60,000 (*Orange County Register,* March 21, 1991, E-1).
	(USC)—Unity School of Christianity has a membership of about 100,000. Every month at least one new Unity study group is formed somewhere worldwide (Todd Ehrenborg, *Mind Sciences,* p. 62).
Worship	**(CS)**—Church services are led by two readers, one reading from the Bible and the other from *Science and Health with Key to the Scriptures.* The Church of Christ Scientist trains and certifies "Practitioners," who are paid by members to counsel and bring metaphysical healing where needed by correcting a patient's understanding (that he or she is not really sick).
	(RS)—Typical worship services involve the teaching of positive thinking, positive affirmations and metaphysical truth as a means to gain health, wealth, and prosperity.
	(USC)—Unity School services are similar to those of Religious Science.
Founders and leaders (length of leadership)	**(CS)**—Mary Baker Eddy (1866–1910)
	(RS)—Ernest Holmes (1917–1960)
	(USC)—Charles and Myrtle Fillmore (1889–1931)
General statement of beliefs	**(CS)** Mrs. Eddy claimed she founded Christian Science to "reinstate primitive Christianity and its lost element of healing" (*Church Manual,* 89th ed., p. 17).
	(RS) "The Science of Mind is not a special revelation of any individual; it is, rather, the culmination of all revelations. We take the good wherever we find it, making it our own, insofar as we understand it. The realization that Good is Universal, and that as much good as any individual is able to incorporate in his life is his to use, is what constitutes the Science of Mind and Spirit. We have discussed the nature of The Thing as being Universal Energy, Mind, Intelligence, Spirit-finding conscious and individualized centers of expression through us—and that man's intelligence is this Universal Mind, functioning at the level of man's concept of it. This is the essence of the whole teaching" (Ernest Holmes, *The Science of Mind,* p. 35).
	(USC) "Unity promises unlimited health, happiness, and prosperity to all who study its philosophy for living, 'to help people realize their spiritual nature, so that they can apply spiritual principles to their daily experiences to live happy, healthy and more productive lives.' . . . Unity claims to be the *recovery* of the real truths of *primitive* Christianity. . . . It teaches 'that there is good in every religion.' . . . They claim no strict creed or dogma for subscription, but they consistently teach the system of belief that is described in the thirty articles of faith listed in *Unity's Statement of Faith.* They emphatically teach a basic metaphysical worldview that includes panentheism, monism, dualism, reincarnation, mysticism, the occult, and healing and wholeness through metaphysics" (Todd Ehrenborg, *Mind Sciences,* p. 61).

The Doctrine of Revelation

Position	Support	Orthodox Response
While Religious Science and Unity teach that their revelations come from a variety of spiritual sources, Christian Science claims that the revelation of Mrs. Eddy is the only source that can lead a person to heaven.	**(RS)** "The Science of Mind is not a special revelation of any individual; it is, rather, the culmination of all revelations" (*The Science of Mind,* Ernest Holmes, p. 35). **(USC)** "... spiritual principle is embodied in the sacred books of the world's living religions. Christians hold to the Bible as the supreme exponent of spiritual principle. They believe that the Bible is the greatest and most deeply spiritual of all Scriptures, though they realize that other Scriptures such as the Zend-Avesta and the Upanishads, as well as the teachings of Buddha, the Koran, and the Tao of Lao-tse and the writings of Confucius, contain expressions of eminent spiritual truths" (*What Unity Teaches,* Unity School of Christianity, p. 4). **(CS)** "THERE IS NO OTHER WAY INTO THE KINGDOM OF HEAVEN EXCEPT THROUGH THE PRACTICE OF CHRISTIAN SCIENCE AS IT WAS DIVINELY REVEALED TO MRS. EDDY" (*Christian Science Journal* 98, no. 4, April 1980, p. 186).	There are at least 22 books that claim to be from God, yet only the Bible (66 books in one volume) is able to support this claim with internal and external evidence. All other claims must stand up to the enormous credentials of this "Book of Books." When its credentials are matched against any other so-called revelation, the Bible's qualifications as a divine revelation tower over them all. The Bible well demonstrates its reliability and trustworthiness through the science of textual criticism. It also speaks authoritatively and claims to be complete and final. Therefore, another revelation is not to be expected or even needed. Other so-called revelations contain numerous internal and external contradictions with historical fact. This automatically cancels their claim to divine inspiration. The many sources used by RS and USC do not even agree with one another and are contradictory. For example, the polytheism of Hindu Scriptures can never be reconciled with the fierce monotheism of the Koran. Not only are Mrs. Eddy's writings filled with historical, logical, and factual errors, but there is abundant documentation that Mrs. Eddy plagiarized much of her metaphysical material from a variety of sources
Mind Science Groups maintain various views concerning the Bible. Christian Science finds the Bible and its doctrines unimportant. Unity believes the Bible is necessary only for those who are limited in their relationship to God. Religious Science suggests the Bible is ineffective because no one can establish a revelation for another.	**(CS)** "The material record of the Bible ... is no more important to our well being than the history of Europe and America" (*Miscellaneous Writings,* 1896 ed., p. 170). **(USC)** "... Scripture may be a satisfactory authority for those who are not themselves in direct communion with the Lord" (*Unity Magazine* 7, October 1896, p. 400). **(RS)** "REVELATION—becoming consciously aware of hidden things. Since the mind that man uses is the same Mind that God uses, the One and Only Mind, the avenues of Revelation can never be closed. But no man can receive the Revelation for another" (*The Science of Mind,* p. 630).	The MS groups cast disdain on the literal, or normal, reading of the Bible and claim that one needs a "superior Metaphysical" interpretation of it to understand its true, "deeper" meaning. This approach to the Bible forces upon it a worldview that is foreign to its fundamental culture, origin, and authorship. The Bible itself in many places (such as 1Sa 15) states that it must be taken as normal communication between God and men, not as some special, mystical language that needs a secondary interpretation (see 2Co 4:2; Isa 8:20; Pr 30:5–6 cf. Rev 22:18–19; Dt 4:2, etc.). The Bible is a self-interpreting book, not needing another, external, authoritative worldview to explain it properly.

The Doctrine of God—*The Trinity*

Position	*Support*	*Orthodox Response*
All the Mind Science groups make the Triune God out to be a trinity of attributes or roles.	**(CS)** "Life, Truth, and Love constitute the triune Person called God,—that is, the triply divine Principle, Love. They represent a trinity in unity, three in one, —the same in essence, though multiform in office: God the Father-Mother; Christ the spiritual idea of sonship; divine Science or the Holy Comforter. These three express in divine Science the threefold, essential nature of the infinite. They also indicate the divine Principle of scientific being, the intelligent relation of God to man and the universe" (*Science and Health with Key to the Scriptures*, pp. 331–32). **(RS)** "Father, Son, and Holy Ghost is the Christian Trinity. It is the Thing, the Way it Works, and What it Does. The Thing is Absolute Intelligence; the Way It Works is Absolute Law; and What It Does, is the result manifestation. The action of the Thing Itself is What the Bible calls 'The Word' . . . Absolute Intelligence" (*The Science of Mind*, p. 80). **(USC)** "The Father is Principle, the Son is that Principle revealed in the creative plan, the Holy Spirit is the executive power of both the Father and Son carrying out the creative plan" (*Metaphysical Bible Dictionary,* Unity School of Christianity, p. 629).	The God of the Bible is clearly described as a personal being, never an impersonal Principle. He manifests a subject-object relationship with His Son Jesus Christ (e.g., Mt 3:17) and with us (e.g., Ex 3:14). He regularly manifests traits of personality (1Sa 15:29; Mt 6:10; Ge 6:6, etc.). He claims to be a personal Spirit and is described with personal pronouns (Jn 4:24; Heb 11:6). The one God of the Bible is described as three eternal, distinct persons manifesting themselves as Father (Php 2:11), Son (Col 2:9), and Holy Spirit (Ge 1:2), all with one-and-the-same divine nature. Claiming the God of the Bible is impersonal is reading something into the text that is plainly not there. The only way the Mind Sciences can create a God so foreign to the Bible is to resort to other so-called authorities.
God lives within us; we are an expression of this impersonal God.	**(CS)** "All is infinite Mind and its infinte manifestation, for God is All-in-All. . . . Spirit is God, and man is His image and likeness. Therefore, man is not material; he is spiritual" (*Science and Health with Key to the Scriptures,* pp. 468:9–15). **(RS)** "God is not a person, God is a Presence personified in us" (*The Science of Mind*, p. 308). **(USC)** "Fill yourself with the Trinity, and become its avenue of expression" (Charles Fillmore, *Christian Healing,* p. 19).	Monism (all is one) is never taught in the Bible, but rather comes from Hinduism, which is based on the idea that all is divine. God is separate from His creation and is not pantheistic or panentheistic (Eph 4:6; Heb 1:2, 12; 2Pe 3:10). He is transcendent (above and distinct from creation), yet immanent (active within creation) at the same time. The biblical view combines these two truths as compatible with each other (Isa 57:15; Eze 11:22–23; Acts 17:22–31).

The Doctrine of Jesus Christ—*The Deity and Humanity of Christ*

Position	Support	Orthodox Response
Jesus and Christ are not the same person. Jesus is the man, while Christ is the spiritual idea or element of God.	**(CS)** "Jesus is the human man, and Christ is the divine idea, hence the duality of Jesus the Christ" (*Science and Health with Key to the Scriptures*, p. 473). **(CS)** "By these sayings Jesus meant, not that the human Jesus was or is eternal, but that the divine idea or Christ was and is . . . not that the corporeal Jesus was one with the Father, but that the spiritual idea, Christ, dwells forever in the bosom of the Father . . . not that the Father is greater than Spirit, which is God, but greater, infinitely greater, than the fleshly Jesus, whose earthly career was brief" (Ibid., pp. 333–34). **(RS)** "JESUS—the name of a man. Distinguished from the Christ. The man Jesus became the embodiment of the Christ, as the human gave way to the Divine Idea of Sonship" (*The Science of Mind*, p. 603). **(RS)** "Christ is not limited to any person, nor does he appear in only one age. He is as eternal as God. He is God's idea of Himself, His own Selfknowingness" (Ibid., p. 363). **(USC)** "The Bible says that God so loved the world that He gave His only begotten Son, but the Bible does not here refer to Jesus of Nazareth the outer man; it refers to the Christ, the spiritual identity of Jesus, whom he acknowledged in all his ways, and brought forth into his outer, until even the flesh of his body was lifted up, purified, spiritualized, and redeemed. Thus he became Jesus Christ, the Word made flesh. And we are to follow in this perfect state and become like him, in each of us is the Christ, the only begotten Son. We can through Jesus Christ, our Redeemer and example, bring forth the Christ within us, the true self of all men, to be made perfect even as our Father in Heaven is perfect as Jesus Christ commandeth His followers to be" (*Unity Magazine* 57, no. 5, p. 464; vol. 72, no. 2, p. 8). **(USC)** "By Christ is not meant the man Jesus" (Ibid., vol. 72, no. 2, p. 146).	"Who is the liar? It is the man who denies that Jesus is the Christ. Such a man is the antichrist—he denies the Father and the Son. No one who denies the Son has the Father" (1Jn 2:22–23; see also 4:3). The MS position is based on an ancient Gnostic heresy of the first century that tried to rob Jesus Christ of the identity of the God-Man that He Himself claimed and proved to be. The epistle of 1 John was written against this heresy and adequately refutes it. Jesus personally claimed many times to be the Christ (Mt 26:63–65; Mk 14:61–64; 15:2; Lk 4:21; Jn 4:21–26, etc.). Others claimed that He was the Christ (Jn 11:27; 20:31; Mt 16:16–20; Ac 2:36; 9:22; 17:3; 18:5, etc.). One must acknowledge Jesus as the Christ in order to be saved (Jn 11:25–27; Mt 16:13–20). Many Scriptures show Christ doing things that a divine "idea" could never do (Lk 2:11; Ro 7:4; 1Co 1:23; 10:16; Ac 3:18; 26:23, etc.). The MS view is based on ignorance of the fact that "Jesus" is the personal name of the Christ (Mt 1:21), whereas "Christ" is His official name that denotes His title or office (Mt 16:16). "Christ" is the Greek equivalent of the Hebrew word *mashiach*, meaning "the Anointed One" or "Messiah." Messiah and Christ are titles that refer to the same person, Jesus.

The Doctrine of Jesus Christ—*The Humanity of Christ*

Position	Support	Orthodox Response
Jesus was merely a man who became an example for us. He was a trailblazer whose purpose was to show us the way to attain the nature of Christ.	**(CS)** "Jesus demonstrated Christ; he proved that Christ is the divine idea of God the Holy Ghost, or Comforter, revealing the divine Principle, Love, and leading into all truth" (*Science and Health with Key to the Scriptures*, p. 332:19). **(RS)** "To think of Jesus as being different from other men is to misunderstand His mission and purpose in life. He was a way-shower and proved His way to be a correct one" (*The Science of Mind*, p. 367). **(USC)** "The difference between Jesus and us is not one of inherent spiritual capacity, but in difference of demonstration of it. Jesus was potentially perfect, we have not yet expressed it" (*What Unity Teaches*, Unity School of Christianity, p. 3).	Jesus was fully human, but claimed to be fully God (Col 2:9) at the same time, being one person with two natures (Php 2:6–11). The Mind Science position ignores much Scripture. Jesus claimed to be much more than an example or a "way-shower." It is inconsistent to accept some of His claims and not others. Jesus claimed to be "the way" (Jn 14:6). There is a big difference between being merely a "way-shower" and actually being "the Way," like the difference between the road sign that tells of the destination and the road that actually leads there.

The Doctrine of Jesus Christ—*The Resurrection of Christ*

Position	Support	Orthodox Response
The resurrection of Jesus and, in fact, of all people has to do with the spiritualization of the consciousness, the transformation of a person from this realm to another, more spiritual one. Unity School of Christianity teaches this concept, but proposes that a process of continual incarnations is often necessary before one can gain immortality.	**(CS)** "RESURRECTION. Spiritualization of thought; a new and higher idea of immortality, or spiritual existence; material belief yielding to spiritual understanding" (Glossary of *Science and Health with Key to the Scriptures*, p. 593:9). **(RS)** "The physical disappearance of Jesus after His resurrection was the result of the spiritualization of His consciousness. This so quickened His mentality that His body disintegrated and His followers could not see Him because He was on another plane. Planes are not places; they are states of consciousness" (*The Science of Mind*, p. 104). **(USC)** "We believe that the dissolution of spirit, soul and body caused by death, is annulled by rebirth of the same spirit and soul in another body here on earth. We believe the repeated incarnations of man to be a merciful provision of our loving Father to the end that all may have opportunity to obtain immortality through regeneration as did Jesus" (*Unity Statement of Faith*, Article 22).	Jesus actually died physically on the cross (Mt 27:50–60; Ro 5:6; 8:34), and this was verified by many eyewitnesses (Gal 1:1–11; 2Pe 1:16; 1Co 15:5–6). His physical, personal resurrection from the dead is also verified by historical facts and eyewitness testimony (Mt 28:9, 16–17; Lk 24:13–15, 28–35, 51, etc.) and confirmed by as many as 15 post-resurrection appearances (Ac 1:3, 9; 1Co 15:6–8). Without these basic twin facts of history, Christianity would be based on the greatest hoax of history (1Co 15:1–4, 14–19; Gal 2:20–21). The bodily resurrection of Jesus is an essential belief for personal salvation (Ro 10:9). The Mind Sciences "metaphysical Spiritualization" of these historical facts is subjective, nonverifiable, and useless.

The Doctrine of the Holy Spirit

Position	Support	Orthodox Response
The Holy Spirit is not an actual person, but rather a characterization of God, a feminine quality, or a spiritual truth.	**(CS)** "HOLY GHOST. Divine Science; the development of eternal Life, Truth, and Love" (*Science and Health with Key to the Scriptures*, p. 588). **(RS)** "The Holy Ghost signifies the feminine aspect of the Divine Trinity. It represents the divine activity of the higher mental plane" (Ernest Holmes, *What Religious Science Teaches*, p. 65). **(USC)** ". . . the very Spirit of truth, is lying latent within us each and every one" (H. Emilie Cady, *Lessons in Truth*, p. 8).	The Holy Spirit is described as the eternal third person of the Triune God. He is referred to with personal pronouns (Jn 14:16–17; 16:7–14) and is described in terms of personality. He manifests characteristics of a divine person and is called God, equal in power, attributes, and nature with the Father and the Son (Isa 6:8–10 with Ac 28:25–27; Mt 3:16; 28:18; Lk 1:35, etc.). The Mind Sciences bring man up to God's level and God down to man's level. This kind of thinking creates a logical absurdity.

The Doctrine of Man and Sin

Position	Support	Orthodox Response
Man has the power to remove the idea of sin, and hence the authority to forgive himself, although in truth we have nothing to forgive ourselves of.	**(CS)** "To get rid of sin through Science, is to divest sin of any supposed mind or reality, and never to admit that sin can have intelligence or power, pain or pleasure. You conquer error by denying its verity" (*Science and Health with Key to the Scriptures*, p. 339). **(RS)** "As we correct our mistakes, we forgive our own sins" (*The Science of Mind*, p. 633). **(USC)** "Jesus was able to say, 'All authority is given to me in Heaven and on earth', we too can say truthfully that this authority has been given to us" (Charles Fillmore, *Christian Healing*, p. 26).	"If we claim to be without sin, we deceive ourselves and the truth is not in us. If we confess our sins, he is faithful and just and will forgive us our sins and purify us from all unrighteousness. If we claim we have not sinned, we make him out to be a liar and his word has no place in our lives" (1Jn 1:8–10). The Mind Sciences attempt to redefine sin to minimize its seriousness. Their remedy for sin is to correct ignorant thinking or wrong ideas about sin's seriousness. God's remedy is for us to acknowledge and confess our sin to Him (Ps 32:5; 38:18) and accept His payment for it that we can never make for ourselves (Ro 3; Jas 2:10; Heb 9:11–22).
Mind Science groups do not believe that sin is real, or that people commit sinful acts. Death and disease are also vehemently denied.	**(CS)** "Here also is found . . . the cardinal point in Christian Science, that matter and evil (including all inharmony, sin, disease, death) are unreal" (*Miscellaneous Writings*, p. 27). **(RS)** "SIN—We have tried to show that there is no sin but a mistake, and no punishment but a consequence. The Law of cause and effect. Sin is merely missing the mark" (*The Science of Mind*, p. 633). **(USC)** "THERE IS NO SIN, SICKNESS, OR DEATH" (*Unity Magazine* 47, no. 5, p. 403).	Sin is universal and very real because all people sin (Ro 3:23), and sin separates us from God (Ro 6:23). Jesus Christ came into the world to save sinners (1Ti 1:15). Only God can forgive sin (Mt 9:6). Man is a sinner in action and nature (Jer 17:9; Mk 7:21–23; Ro 5:12–21). Whatever does not proceed from faith is sin (Ro 14:23), transgression of God's law is sin (Jas 2:11), all lawlessness is sin (1Jn 3:4), and any wrongdoing is sin (1Jn 5:17). Sin, evil, disease, and death are very real in history and our experience. To attempt to redefine or deny them does not help us deal with them but rather compounds their negative effects on us. Sadly, like Hinduism, the monistic worldview of MS necessitates this denial of plain sensory data and leaves the adherent with no workable means of dealing with real life struggles.

The Doctrine of Man and Sin (cont.)

Position	Support	Orthodox Response
Man is actually a spiritual being. Man is sinless, perfect, and a part of the divine essence.	**(CS)** "Man is not matter—made up of brains, blood, bones, and other material elements.... Man is spiritual and perfect; and because of this, he must be so understood in Christian Science.... Man is incapable of sin, sickness, and death, inasmuch as he derives his essence from God" (*Science and Health with Key to the Scriptures*, p. 475). **(RS)** "There is that within every individual which partakes of the nature of the Universal Wholeness and—in so far as it operates is God. That is the meaning of the word Immanuel, the meaning of the word Christ. There is that within us which partakes of the nature of the Divine Being, and since it partakes of the nature of the Divine Being, we are divine" (*The Science of Mind,* pp. 33–34). **(USC)** "Never say, I don't know; I can't understand. Claim your Christ understanding at all times and declare: I am not under any spell of human ignorance. I am one with Infinite Understanding" (Charles Fillmore, *Christian Healing*, pp. 106–7).	Man is both a physical and spiritual being (Ge 1:26–27; 2:7; 5:1, 3). Man's track record proves that he is imperfect and separated from God (Ro 5:12–21). He is also a sinner by nature (Jer 17:9) and by choice (Ro 7:14–25). Man is not and could never be divine in nature (Nu 23:19; Hos 11:9). He was given a human nature (Ac 14:14–15) stamped with the spiritual image of God (Ge 9:6). Satan is the one who tempted mankind with divine qualities (Ge 3:4–5; Isa 14:14–15), and God judges all people who claim them (Eze 28:19; Ro 1:23–25).

The Doctrine of Salvation

Position	Support	Orthodox Response
All people will gain salvation, and in fact, we are already saved; therefore we do not need to ask God for salvation.	**(CS)** "Man as God's idea is already saved with an everlasting salvation" (*Miscellaeous Writings,* p. 261). **(RS)** "We need fear nothing in the Universe. We need not be afraid of God. We may be certain that all will arrive at the final goal, that not one will be missing. Every man is an incarnation of God. The soul can no more be lost than God could be lost" (*The Science of Mind,* p. 383). **(USC)** "Being 'born-again' or 'born from above' is not a miraculous change that takes place in man; it is the establishment of that which has always existed as the perfect man idea of divine Mind" (Charles Fillmore, *Christian Healing,* p. 24).	The Bible does not teach universal salvation but that some people will reject God's love and forgiveness and be lost by their own choice (Mt 7:15–23; 24:45–46; Jn 5:28–29). Some sin will not be forgiven because of lack of repentance (Mt 12:30–32). Universal salvation would be an unjust reward that a perfect, holy, and righteous judge could not allow. The God of the Bible will in no wise let the guilty go unpunished but will execute righteous punishment (Ex 34:7). All those who reject Jesus Christ and His gospel will be punished by God in eternity (2Th 1:8–9; Rev 19:20; 20:15). Salvation is a gift from God that must be received by grace through faith in the person and work of Jesus Christ (Jn 3:36; Eph 2:8–9).

The Doctrine of Salvation (cont.)

Position	Support	Orthodox Response
Actually, for us to reach enlightenment (the divine state) we need to purify our minds and work out our own salvation.	**(CS)** "Final deliverance from error, whereby we rejoice in immortality, boundless freedom, and sinless sense, is not reached through paths of flowers nor by pinning one's faith without works to another's vicarious effort" (*Science and Health with Key to the Scriptures,* p. 22). **(RS)** "What more can life demand of us that we do the best that we can and try to improve? If we have done this, we have done well, and all will be right with our souls both here and hereafter. This leaves us free to work out our own salvation—not with fear, or even with trembling—but with peace and in quiet confidence" (*The Science of Mind,* pp. 383–84). **(USC)** "Unity teaches that the eternal life taught and demonstrated by Jesus is not gained by dying but by purifying the body until it becomes the undying habitation of the soul" (Charles Fillmore, *Unity Magazine,* July 1922, vol. 58, no. 49).	Only Jesus Christ can save a person, because no human person could ever do enough to earn or deserve eternal life (Eph 2:8–9; Lk 7:37–48). God's remedy for sin, as stated throughout the Bible, is for us to trust in His means to remove it, never our own useless efforts. Philippians 2:12 says, "Work out your salvation," which means (v. 13) that God makes it possible for us to act. The apostle Paul is here urging believers to show evidence of the salvation they already have. While we are each responsible for our own actions as believers, we can never merit eternal life by our own efforts (Ro 3:22–24; 9:16; Tit 3:5–7). Salvation is totally a gift from God appropriated by trusting in Jesus Christ's work of atonement (Ro 5). We must receive Christ and His gift (Jn 1:12; Rev 3:20) and become adopted as children of God through faith in Him (Gal 4:5; Eph 1:5).

The Doctrine of Rewards and Punishment

Position	Support	Orthodox Response
Heaven and hell exist only in our own minds. We can create a heavenly experience for ourselves, or we can subject ourselves to a mental hell. But heaven and hell do not really exist objectively.	**(CS)** "The sinner makes his own hell by doing evil, and the saint his own heaven by doing right" (*Science and Health with Key to the Scriptures,* 1914 ed., p. 266). **(RS)** "God neither punishes nor rewards. Such a concept of God would create an anthropomorphic dualism, a house divided against itself.... In the long run, no one judges us but ourselves, and no one condemns us but ourselves.... If we make mistakes, we suffer. We are our own reward and our own punishment" (*The Science of Mind,* p. 383). **(USC)** "Both [heaven and hell] are states of mind, and conditions, which people experience as a direct outworking of their thoughts, beliefs, words, and acts" (*Metaphysical Bible Dictionary,* p. 271).	The Bible describes heaven and hell as places of conscious existence after death, not just states of mind. Hell is described as a place of separation from the blessings and presence of God, a place of punishment for all who reject God's means of salvation, Jesus Christ and His gospel (Da 12:2; Mt 8:11–12; 13:42, 50; 1Th 4:14, etc.). Heaven is described as a place of eternal fellowship with the personal Triune God of the Bible, a place with the absence of pain, sin, sorrow, and death, a place to enjoy His rewards forever (Mt 25:34, 37; Jn 3:5, 16, 18, 21; Rev 21–22). Unfortunately, some will choose not to dwell there (Rev 14:9–11; 19:20; 22:15).

INTERESTING AND DISTINCTIVE BELIEFS

Position	Support	Orthodox Response
(CS) Disease does not really exist except as we give it reality. To heal sickness, one must truly believe sickness does not exist.	"The cause of all so-called disease is mental, a mortal fear, a mistaken belief or conviction of the necessity and power of ill-health" (*Science and Health with Key to the Scriptures*, p. 377:26ff.). "The sick are not healed merely by declaring there is no sickness, but by knowing that there is none" (Ibid., p. 447).	The monistic worldview (all is one) of MS entails denying many vivid realities that our daily existence continually confirms. The dualistic approach that calls spirit good and matter evil perverts the natural order of things. The biblical worldview that explains the entrance of sin into the universe of a holy God is far superior and true to life as we find it. The distinction between a holy Creator God (who is both transcendent and immanent) and His finite creation (Isa 45:18) more adequately solves the problem that sin and sickness appear to come from a good God. Man was given a free moral choice and, because he chose rebellion, sin and disease came into the world. The MS view of disease also does not adequately provide a useful way of dealing with it.
(RS) The individual is progressively evolving into a higher form of spiritual consciousness.	"We are all in the process of spiritual evolution, but here is certainty behind us, certainty before us and certainty with us at every moment" (Ernest Holmes, *What Religious Science Teaches*, p. 89). "So we shall view eternity from the higher standpoint, as a continuity of time, forever and ever expanding, until time, as we now experience it, shall be no more. Realizing this, we shall see in everyone a budding genius, a becoming God, an unfolding soul, an eternal destiny" (*The Science of Mind*, p. 387).	This idealistic assertion runs contrary to the enormous evidence in history, experience, and Scripture that clearly demonstrates that mankind is gradually growing worse rather than better. The Bible teaches the multiplication of the effects of sin and its consequences over time (Ex 20:5; 34:7). It teaches that the world will grow increasingly worse until God Himself culminates history with the personal return in Jesus Christ (Mt 24–25). Then He will judge the world in righteousness and truth and set up His millennial kingdom of peace (Rev 20).
(USC) The *Second Coming* is not to be understood as the physical return of Christ, but rather the transformation of the subconscious of all mankind.	"We believe the second coming of Jesus Christ is *now* being fulfilled, that His spirit is quickening the whole world" (*Unity Statement of Faith*, Article 24). "The first coming of Christ is the receiving of truth in the conscious mind, and the second coming is the awakening and regeneration of the subconscious through the superconsciousness of Christ-Mind" (Charles Fillmore, *The Twelve Powers of Man*, p. 1).	The second coming of Christ is promised to be personal, visible, audible, and bodily (Rev 1:7–8; 19:6–16; 1Th 4:13–18; 1Co 15:51–52). Jesus taught that it would be a literal event in history (Mt 24:37; Lk 17:28–30). It will come unexpectedly (2Pe 2:10–12), and no one knows its date (Mt 24:36). It will be the central, catalytic event of eschatology. It will be accompanied by discernible signs (Mt 24:3–14). The purpose of Jesus' second coming is to complete what was begun at His first coming: the redemption of individuals, the glorification of the church, and the liberation of the created order from sin's enslaving effects (Rev 21:1–7).

13

New Age Movement

FACTS AND HISTORY

Facts	
Topic	*Current Facts*
Five points of belief for many New Age Groups	The New Age movement, as such, is just that—a movement, not a centralized cult with a well-defined leadership. Dealing with the New Age movement is problematic because it is very diverse and complex. As soon as you quote someone as being a spokesman for the movement, someone else from either inside or outside the movement will cry foul.
	Numerous groups could be considered New Age (such as Theosophy, Scientology, Eckankar, Church Universal and Triumphant, Silva Mind Control), and so could many individuals (such as J. Z. Knight, who channels a supposed 35,000-year-old spirit named Ramtha). Although few would agree on everything considered to be New Age, most New Age groups adhere to five points of "doctrine":
	1. **Monism**: The concept that all things are made of essentially the same spiritual substance and at a certain level are merged into the oneness of the all.
	2. **Pantheism**: The idea that all is God (*pan* = all, *theos* = God).
	3. **Reincarnation**: The belief in the preexistence of the soul—that is, that it returns to physical existence repeatedly until it achieves the most refined and highest state of the Great Oneness of the universe. This can also be described as Spiritual or Cosmic Evolution.
	4. **Enlightenment** (personal and societal): The notion that through a change of consciousness about one's own divinity and the monistic "oness of all" an evolutionary step of spiritual progression can be achieved by an individual and, eventually and incrementally, by the collective society. This should result in an understanding that we have secret or esoteric knowledge contained in our subconscious self—or what Carl Jung called the "collective unconscious of the human race"—that can allow us to manipulate energy and matter by our thoughts and thereby achieve health and wealth.
	5. **Spiritism**: The belief that there are spirits that can be contacted both of dead humans and extraterrestrial sources that provide us with insight into ethics and the meaning of life on earth.
Background of the New Age Movement	
	This movement comes on the heels of secular humanism, atheism, and nihilistic thought that engulfed Western civilization during the last 150 years. It started in a populous way with Darwinian evolutionary naturalism in the middle of the 19th century. The idea that man is nothing more than an animal who started in a primordial slime pit left little in the way of affirmation of personhood. This worldview offered no ultimate hope or destiny for the human race beyond the grave. This vacuum of hope, ultimate purpose, and meaning to life left the West in a state of despair and open for any philosophy or cosmology that

Background of the New Age Movement (cont.)

purported to deal with the age-old fear of death and the angst of nonexistence. The transition between a naturalistic humanism and a more "cosmic humanism" perhaps began with atheistic thinkers such as Julian Huxley, who said, "Man is that part of reality in which and through which the cosmic process has become conscious and has begun to comprehend itself. His supreme task is to increase that conscious comprehension and apply it as fully as possible to guide the course of events." Because the Bible was rejected, there was no longer a "big picture" provided for mankind to give human life purpose and meaning and an ultimate destiny. Meaning and purpose had to be fabricated out of sheer romantic existentialist imagination and willpower. Huxley retained the naturalistic while trying to sneak in a mystical notion of the "big picture" once provided to Western Civilization by a knowledge of the God of the Bible.

Historical Roots	It has been frequently stated that New Age thought is anything but new. It can be traced back 2,000 years to the first-century Gnostics and mystery cults of New Testament times. Even before that, however, this "secret doctrine," or occultism, was evident in Babylon, taking many circuitous stops along the way through all the great empires of the world—Egyptian, Persian, Greek, and Roman. In the 19th century a movement known as Transcendentalism arose. This movement, essentially mystical and existentialist at its root, was fueled by the writings of Ralph Waldo Emerson and other famous authors. Emerson, an ordained minister, taught about a mystical "oversoul" that is the "force" within all nature and human personality. He believed it was brought into existence by human consciousness and therefore subject to it. Also, in 1875, Helena Petrovna Blavatsky (1831–1891) and Colonel Henry Steel Olcott (1832–1907) founded the Theosophical Society, which now has headquarters in Wheaton, Illinois. Blavatsky, Olcott, and their successors Annie Besant (1847–1933), Guy Ballard (1878–1939), and Alice Bailey (1880–1949) provided the seminal concepts and first articulated them as New Age. Bailey is credited with having coined the phrase "New Age" in her numerous writings. These influences helped provide an early foundation for the Eastern mystics and gurus who would come to America and win many converts during the 1960s.

Freudian psychology, with its atheistic and naturalistic philosophical base, and the school of thought developed by Freud's friend Carl Gustav Jung were also gaining respectability and ascendancy during the early twentieth century. Freud represented ultimate metaphysical hopelessness in his naturalism. However, this was countered by Jung's irrational mystical hope (a hearkening back to Emersonian romanticism) and his espousal of the "collective unconscious" and the potential for life to exist beyond the grave in a very mystical framework. These two approaches to reality were the forces that led many in the United States and Western Europe to venture down the New Age path. |
| **Contemporary Expressions** | The late 1950s saw the emergence of the "Beat" movement and the bohemian writers who influenced it, such as Jack Kerouac. This movement foreshadowed the rise of the Hippie counterculture of the '60s and all its emphasis on rejecting the established norms of society. Christianity was seen as the established religion and was therefore targeted by this movement as something to rebel against. Maharishi Mahesh Yogi first came to the United States in 1959, bringing his teaching of Transcendental Meditation. He was virtually unknown until the popular English rock group, the Beatles, began to promote his ideas. They took a pilgrimage to India with him, and by this brought many fans to an awareness of Hinduistic New Age thought. The Beatles later rejected their affiliation with him, but George Harrison joined the Hare Krishna cult and continued to promote the reincarnationist and Eastern religious message in his music even after leaving the group. His song "My Sweet Lord," by referring to both, brought the message that worshiping Krishna and Christ were equivalent practices.

In 1965, federal policies toward immigration from the Orient were changed, and a new wave of immigrants from Asia appeared in America, bringing pantheistic ways of thought. This only helped buttress the rise of such thinking already gaining a following in the West.

Also during the late sixties, the musical *Hair* become popular through film, music, and stage. It produced a mystical-messianic song based on an astrological theme. A top-hit song from the musical announced that "This is the dawning of the Age of Aquarius." The |

musical advocated Indian Kama Sutra, rebellion against established norms, and relative ethics as the solution to social strife and racial hatred. *Hair* and the giant music event and counterculture gathering in New York State called Woodstock became the cultural symbols of a generation that believed all religions and nations should be one and that traditional Christianity doesn't have the answers to life's basic questions.

With the ending of the Vietnam War in the early seventies, the counterculture baby-boomers cut their hair, donned business suits, and took their places in the economic and political arenas. They did not leave behind the utopian dream of building a one-world society based on spiritual monism and its attendant relative ethics, but they became pragmatic in how they should go about implementing it. Before long, it was not uncommon for prominent figures and public officials to express New Age ideas. For instance, in May 1988 U.S. President Ronald Reagan's wife, Nancy, disclosed she had been consulting an astrological fortune teller in order to plan her husband's itinerary. During the '90s, Hillary Rodham Clinton, wife of U.S. President Bill Clinton, spoke of consulting the dead spirit of former First Lady Eleanor Roosevelt.

The rise of mystical New Age thought was championed by author Marilyn Ferguson in her 1980 book *The Aquarian Conspiracy*. It chronicled the many aspects of culture, such as business and religious thought, that are converging in a conspiracy of shared values that include meditation and a sense of the oneness of all. "We have had a profound paradigm shift about the Whole Earth. We know it now as a jewel in space, a fragile water planet. And we have seen that it has no natural borders. It is not the globe of our school days with its many-colored nations" (p. 407). The book served as a manifesto for many involved in the New Age worldview and was often used as a sociology textbook on college campuses.

The 1980s and '90s brought much expression of Eastern thought in the entertainment industry, such as the pantheistic theme of the "light and dark side of the force" in the *Star Wars* movies, the mystical evolutionary leaps of the *Star Trek* television series, and occultic mysticism and magic in the films *Willow* and *The Dark Crystal*. There also emerged New Age magazines such as *New Age Journal; Yoga Journal; East-West Journal; New Realities; Whole Life Times; Body, Mind and Spirit;* and *Fate*. Dozens of New Age newsletters were published by psychics and trance channelers. Franchise bookstores featured "New Age" sections, major music stores featured "New Age" music, although the term is often used more as a marketing vehicle for musical groups who offer mellow tones and new techniques rather than promoting New Age ideas.

Many entertainers have been outspoken in expressing various Eastern and New Age beliefs, including Richard Chamberlain, Helen Reddy, Tina Turner, David Carradine, Marsha Mason, Phillip Michael Thomas, Christy Jenkins, Mike Farrell, Priscilla Presley, Lisa Marie Presley, Kirstie Alley, John Travolta, Linda Evans, Paul Horn, and Joyce DeWitt. At an Oscar awards ceremony of the Motion Picture Academy, actor Richard Gere led a "collective meditation" in which he claimed to be "beaming energy" toward the Tibetans and the Dalai Lama, who is looked up to as a spiritual leader by many New Agers. Perhaps the most prominent entertainer in the movement is American actress Shirley Maclaine, whose book and TV mini-series entitled *Out On A Limb* document her spiritual conversion to New Age thinking. The series featured for the first time on television a person's going into a trance on television and allowing a spirit to possess a person's body and speak through it.

This pervasive resurgence of New Age paganism takes many forms, including cartoons on television and children's movies. Examples are *Captain Planet, He-Man and the Masters of the Universe, The Teenage Mutant Ninja Turtles, The Power Rangers, The Lion King,* and *Pocahontas*. The '90s have seen a proliferation of "psychic hotlines," promoted by celebrities through various mass media.

The Doctrine of Revelation

Position	Support	Orthodox Response
There are many spirits in the astral plane that are willing to converse with humans. This is accomplished when the body is surrendered over to the disincarnate entity through vacating the mind and will by means of a self-induced trance. These spirits may or may not be those of human beings. Some may be from animals or even other planets.	"Trance channeling is primarily an information source. The source of this information is a vast reservoir of knowledge called the Universal Mind or the Akashic Records. The Universal Mind is comparable to C. G. Jung's theory of the collective unconsciousness. Mr. Jung states in this theory that all of mankind's evolved higher systems of thought (i.e., art, philosophies, technology, etc.) survive throughout all time and space. In a state of altered consciousness, Kevin is able to tap into the vast reservoir of the Universal Mind. Subject materials . . . are expounded upon by the levels of intelligence to flow through Kevin while he is in the channeling state" (From psychic Kevin Ryerson's letter to prospective clients, as quoted in *Out on a Broken Limb,* by F. LaGard Smith, p. 52).	The Bible clearly prohibits spiritism of any kind. No one is supposed to contact a disincarnate spirit directly or go through another person as a medium to do so (Dt 18:9–22). Fallen angels (see 2Pe 2:4; Jude 6) have an evil nature (see Mt 25:41; 2Co 11:15). They can lie about their origin and impersonate any type of being for the sake of deception and malice. Satan is their master (see Ge 3:1–14).

The Doctrine of God—*The Trinity*

Position	Support	Orthodox Response
Most New Agers hold the monistic view that all matter and energy are made of the same basic substance. This substance is spirit.	"Both Science and the teachings of Buddha tell us of the fundamental unity of all things. This understanding is crucial if we are to take positive and decisive steps on the pressing global concerns with the environment" (The Dalai Lama, *My Tibet*). "I Pledge Allegiance to the soil . . . / one ecosystem / in diversity / under the sun— / With joyful interpenetration for all" (Gary Snyder, New Age poet). *"I am That, Thou art That, All This is That, That alone is, and there is nothing else but That"* (Maharishi Mahesh Yogi, *The Science of Being and Art of Living*, p. 33). *"I am he as you are he as you are me and we are all together"* (From the song "I am The Walrus" by John Lennon and Paul McCartney, ©1967 Northern Songs Ltd).	The God of the Bible is transcendent and separate from His creation. "As the heavens are higher than the earth, so are my ways higher than your ways and my thoughts than your thoughts" (Isa 55:9). "I am the LORD, who has made all things, who alone stretched out the heavens, who spread out the earth by myself" (Isa 44:24). God created the universe *ex nihilo*—out of nothing. God's creatures, whether human or animal, are not created from "spirit." The Bible states that mankind was formed by God "from the dust of the ground and breathed into his nostrils the breath of life, and the man became a living being" (Ge 2:7). The "spirit," or intelligent, animating part of man, was later added by God to the physical shell. Mineral substances do not possess a "spirit," which by definition must reflect soul, will, and intellect. Rocks are not "alive." "All flesh is not the same: Men have one kind of flesh, animals have another, birds another and fish another" (1Co 15:39). This demonstrates differences in God's creation, rather than everything being fashioned from one substance, misnamed "spirit" by New Agers.

The Doctrine of Jesus Christ—*The Trinity (cont.)*

Position	Support	Orthodox Response
All that exists (matter, energy, space, and spirit) is divine.	"Slowly, there is dawning upon the awakening consciousness of humanity, the great paralleling truth of God, Immanent—divinely pervading all forms, conditioning from within all kingdoms in nature, expressing innate divinity through human beings and—2,000 years ago—portraying the nature of that divine immanence in the Christ. Today, as an outcome of this unfolding divine presence, there is entering into the minds of men everywhere a new concept, that of 'Christ in us, the hope of glory.' (Colossians 1:27). There is a growing and developing belief that Christ is in us as He was in the Master Jesus, and this belief will alter world affairs and mankind's entire attitude to life" (Rudolf Steiner, *The Reappearance of the Christ in the Etheric,* p. 36).	To say that "all is god" is similar to the statement that "everything is important." Because of the equalizing or leveling nature of these statements, it would be just as true to say that nothing is god or that nothing is important. The God of the Bible is a unique, nonanalogous being, separate and distinct from His creation. Isaiah 46:9 says, "I am God, and there is none like me." Exodus 9:14 states, "This time I will send the full force of my plagues against you and against your officials and your people, so you may know that there is no one like me in all the earth."

The Doctrine of Jesus Christ—*The Deity and Humanity of Christ*

Position	Support	Orthodox Response
The person of Jesus is defined differently by respective teachers. One popular approach is to see Him as having been a master of Eastern mysticism by virtue of His having traveled to India during the years of His youth and young manhood. *The Aquarian Gospel of Jesus The Christ* **(ca. 1907) is widely read in New Age circles as the product of trance channeling. Because Jesus is a God-man like every other human being, there is no distinct, transcendent attribute of deity involved in His being.**	"Men call me Christ and God has recognized the name; but Christ is not a man. The Christ is universal love, and love is king. This Jesus is but a man who has been fitted by temptations overcome, by trials multiform, to be the temple through which the Christ can manifest to men. . . . Look to the Christ within who shall be formed in every one of you, as he is formed in me" (Attributed to Jesus the Christ, as communicated by Levi Dowling, who was commissioned by the "Goddess Visel" to tell the story of the "Aquarian Jesus"—quoted in Leo Dowling and Eva Dowling, *The Aquarian Gospel Of Jesus The Christ,* p. 8).

"The Indian sage and Jesus often met and talked about the needs of nations and of men; about the sacred doctrines, forms and rites best suited to the coming age" (Ibid., p. 56).

"It is I who am the light which is above them all. It is I who am the All. From me did the all come forth, and unto me did the all extend. Split a piece of wood and I am there. Lift up the stone and you will find me there" ("The Gospel of Thomas," James M. Robinson ed., *The Nag Hammadi Library,* p. 126—as cited by Doug Groothuis, *Unmasking the New Age,* p. 28). | Those in the New Age Movement who separate Jesus from the word "Christ" do not understand the origin of the word and its use as a title. It is from the Greek *Kristos,* which is the word used for the Hebrew *Moshiach,* which in English is translated "Messiah" or "Christ." The word "Messiah" means "anointed one" and connotes the meaning of being specially set apart by God for a specific purpose. Jesus didn't *become* the Christ or the Messiah, but in His humanity *was* such from the moment of His conception in Mary's womb. Jesus was anointed for His purpose "from the creation of the world" (Rev 13:8). To use mediums to gain knowledge of the years of Christ's youth is an abomination before God (see Dt 18:9–22; 29:29; Lev 19:26, 31). God would never use a means that He Himself has outlawed to share mysteries not covered by His Word, the Bible. There is no evidence anywhere except in the spiritistic writings of the New Age mediums for Jesus ever to have traveled as far as India.

Jesus is the unique God-man in that He was, and remains, the only begotten of the Father. "In the beginning was the Word, and the Word was with God, and the Word was God. . . . The Word became flesh |

The Doctrine of Jesus Christ—*The Deity and Humanity of Christ (cont.)*

Position	Support	Orthodox Response
. . . continued		and made his dwelling among us. We have seen his glory, the glory of the One and Only, who came from the Father, full of grace and truth" (Jn 1:1, 14). Unlike any other man before or after, Jesus possessed the attributes of deity. He alone among mankind has a nature in Him that is eternal (Jn 8:58; 17:5), omnipresent (Mt 18:20), omniscient (Mt 16:21; Lk 6:8; 11:17; Jn 4:29), and omnipotent (Mt 28:20; Mk 5:11–15; Jn 11:38–44).

The Doctrine of Man and Sin

Position	Support	Orthodox Response
Evil does not exist.	"But where is the place of evil in this scheme then?" "It doesn't exist. That's the point. Everything in life is the result of illumination or ignorance. Those are the two polarities, not good and evil. And when you are totally illuminated such as Jesus Christ or Buddha, or some of those people, there is no struggle any longer" (Trance channeler Kevin Ryerson, talking with Vassy, a Russian mystic, about good and evil—quoted in Shirley Maclaine, *Dancing in the Light,* 1985, p. 247).	In contrast to the denial of evil, the God of the Bible has both defined and drawn sharp distinctions between good and evil. When Adam disobeyed God in Eden and acquired a guilty conscience, God said, "The man has now become like one of us, knowing good and evil" (Ge 3:22). The wickedness of man continued to grow and grieve the Creator: "The LORD saw how great man's wickedness on the earth had become, and that every inclination of the thoughts of his heart was only evil all the time" (Ge 6:5). God abhors evil: "You are not a God who takes pleasure in evil; with you the wicked cannot dwell" (Ps 5:4). "The face of the LORD is against those who do evil, to cut off the memory of them from the earth" (Ps 34:16). The ability to discern good and evil is also linked to maturity: "But solid food is for the mature, who by constant use have trained themselves to distinguish good from evil" (Heb 5:14).
One should not resist evil.	"You must not resist what you call evil" (The spirit "John" speaking through Trance channeler Kevin Ryerson—as quoted in Shirley Maclaine, *Dancing in the Light,* p. 256).	While God does not want His people taking personal revenge for wrongdoing (see Mt 5:39), He does expect His people to oppose evil in themselves and in society. "Therefore put on the full armor of God, so that when the day of evil comes, you may be able to stand your ground" (Eph 6:13). "Submit yourselves, then, to God. Resist the devil, and he will flee from you" (Jas 4:7). "Be self-controlled and alert. Your enemy the devil prowls around like a roaring lion looking for someone to devour. Resist him, standing firm in the faith, because you know that your brothers throughout the world are undergoing

The Doctrine of Man and Sin (cont.)

Position	Support	Orthodox Response
		the same kind of sufferings" (1Pe 5:8–9). "Learn to do right! Seek justice, encourage the oppressed. Defend the cause of the fatherless, plead the case of the widow" (Isa 1:17). "This is what the Lord says: Do what is just and right. Rescue from the hand of his oppressor the one who has been robbed" (Jer 22:3). Numerous other Bible passages offer examples of God's people speaking out and taking action against evil. Human experience demonstrates that rampant evil, if allowed to go unchecked, will eventually destroy a society.
Good and evil arise from the same source, so what we mistakenly consider evil is actually also good.	Commenting on the movie version of his book, *The Serpent And The Rainbow,* the author hoped that the movie would "have had a more explicit statement that voodoo is good, that Haiti will teach you that good and evil are one" (Anthropologist Wade Davis, *Seattle Times,* January 31, 1988).	Voodoo is occultic in nature, and God condemns occultic practices: "When you enter the land the Lord your God is giving you, do not learn to imitate the detestable ways of the nations there. Let no one be found among you who sacrifices his son or daughter in the fire, who practices divination or sorcery, interprets omens, engages in witchcraft, or casts spells, or who is a medium or spiritist or who consults the dead. Anyone who does these things is detestable to the Lord, and because of these detestable practices the Lord your God will drive out those nations before you. You must be blameless before the Lord your God" (Dt 18:9–13). Good and evil are not one. They are diametric opposites. To say that good and evil originate in the same source violates a key principle of logic—something cannot be both "A" and "non A" at the same time.

The Doctrine of Man and Sin (cont.)

Position	Support	Orthodox Response
Everyone chooses one's own karmic destiny before incarnating into a physical body at birth. Although in standard New Age parlance no absolute definition is allowed for the terms "evil" or "good," they are used anyway to define and modify the word "karma." Bad karma derives from bad actions in this or a previous life. Karma determines what events will occur in our existence through various (re)incarnations. All human souls are constantly recycled in one incarnation after another. When a creature dies, its soul waits to be sent into another fetus in the womb. The circumstances of its birth and life are dictated by the laws of karma, which are impersonal and exacting.	"I found . . . that reincarnation had become part of New Age thought systems" (Shirley Maclaine, *Out on a Limb*, p. 350). "Realize that it is not easy to find a being who has not formerly been your mother, or your father, your brother, your sister or your son or daughter" (Hammalawa Saddhatissa, *Buddhist Ethics: The Path to Nirvana*, p. 83—as cited by Ralph Rath, *The New Age Christian Critique*, p. 52). "According to the doctrine of Karma, future happiness is a direct result or continuation of the maintaining of satisfactory standard of conduct in the present. The best that can be done to gain secure and lasting well being is to cut down the evil actions and increase the good ones" (Ibid., pp. 21, 45—as cited by Rath, *The New Age Christian Critique*, p. 52).	There is no evidence from the Bible that human souls either preexist or return to earth in another life after death. "Man is destined to die once, and after that to face judgment" (Heb 9:27). Jesus said, "It is finished," on the cross, indicating that He had paid for our sins and debts to God in full (Jn 19:30). That phrase was used on receipts in the Roman Empire to indicate satisfaction of a debt. When Christ's righteousness is attributed to a person, God considers the person—that is, a believer—to have no further spiritual debts required of him because he is in Christ. "If anyone is in Christ, he is a new creation; the old has gone, the new has come" (2Co 5:17). There is therefore no need to be "perfected" in reincarnation. Further, "This is the word of the LORD concerning Israel. The LORD, who stretches out the heavens, who lays the foundation of the earth, and who forms the spirit of man within him, declares . . ." (Zec 12:1). This tells us that the spirit is formed within us and does not exist until our physical shell is formed to house it. This contradicts the idea of reincarnation.

The Doctrine of Rewards and Punishment

Position	Support	Orthodox Response
The early church used its power to subvert the truth of reincarnation and to keep the Western world ignorant of the reality of multiple lives.	"I read that Christ's teachings about reincarnation were struck from the Bible during the Fifth Ecumenical Council meeting in Constantinople in the year 553" (Shirley MacLaine, *Out on a Limb,* p. 205—cited in Doug Groothuis, *Confronting the New Age,* p. 103). "Since the espousal of reincarnation and karma by the wisest spiritual and philosophical sages, the people of the East have remained in awe of the relentless revolutions of the wheel of life. Not so their counterparts in the Western Hemisphere where reincarnation was buried 14 centuries ago. The conspiring undertakers were the Church and the State, fearful that their authority could be challenged by a doctrine that made individuals responsible for their own salvation. Since A.D. 553, when the monstrous 'restoration' of rebirth was denounced by Emperor Justinian, the faithful have been taught to believe in eternal life while ignoring immortality's spiritual sister, reincarnation" (Joe Fisher, *The Case for Reincarnation*—quoted in *The New Age Catalog,* p. 106).	Historically, the New Testament canon was finalized in the 4th century, not the sixth as some allege. There were no "stricken" texts that dealt with reincarnation. Some apocryphal texts were stricken early on by both Jewish scribes and Christian authorities. These texts were rejected by the early church fathers because they were inconsistent with the rest of the Scriptures and contained doctrines that Jesus and the apostles never taught. In fact, many of the NT letters and the gospel of John were written in response to Gnosticism, the spiritual forebear of the New Age movement. The NT manuscripts extant from the 1st, 2d, and 3d centuries show no signs of a reincarnationist bent.

INTERESTING AND DISTINCTIVE BELIEFS

Position	Support	Orthodox Response
Since there is no ultimate Creator who is the final court of appeal in matters of right and wrong, every person is left to decide for oneself what is acceptable behavior. Even murder may be seen as acceptable in some circumstances by some people in the New Age movement.	"If you believe you are going to be reincarnated, and that you are going to live again, how can murder be a wrong?" (Trance channeler JZ Knight [Ramtha], on ABC News' *20/20,* January 22, 1987).	God inspired Moses to write the Ten Commandments, which include an injunction against murder. "You shall not murder" has been one of the legal foundations of Christian civilization and most other societies and has served as a bulwark against barbarism. To say that murder may be justified on a metaphysical basis, such as the doctrine of reincarnation, is to allow for cruel anarchy and destruction to rule in the affairs of men.

Position	Support	Orthodox Response
Our planet is about to ascend to a higher level of evolutionary positioning. Only a certain percentage of human beings will be willing and able to accept the necessary changes needed to affect the earth's advancement. People who resist the process and remain skeptical of this advancement will be irradicated. The entire human species will take the next step in evolution and realize its own divinity through self-realization and self-actualization (experience). This transformation is already under way.	"Nature will soon enter her cleansing cycle. Those who reject the Earth changes with an attitude of 'it can't happen here' will experience the greatest emotion of fear and panic, followed by rage and violent action. These individuals, with their lower vibratory rates, will be removed during the next two decades" (The spirit "Ashur" speaking in the book, *Practical Spirituality,* pp. 15–20, as cited by David Allen Lewis in *Prophecy 2000,* p. 299). "As you have learned to abort a genetically defective child who will inevitably be a monstrous human, so we have learned to abort a monstrous planetary civilization which gains its evolutionary technologies of transcendence and misuses them for self-annihilation. . . . Evolution is good but it is not nice. Only the good can evolve. Only the God-centered will survive to inherit the powers of a Universal Species. . . . Now, as we approach the quantum shift from creature-human to co-creative human —the destructive one fourth must be eliminated from the social body. . . . We will use whatever means we must to make this act of destruction as quick and painless as possible to the one half of the world who are capable of evolving" (Barbara Marx Hubbard, *Revelation: The Book of Co-Creation,* pp. 29, 56, 60, 62).	The New Age movement's penchant for relative ethics and its intolerance for those who object to its aims could play a role in the cultural preparation for the last days prior to the return of Christ. The Bible predicts an age of tribulation that will feature barbarism on a scale unheard of in human history. These are the perilous times cited by the apostle Paul: "But mark this: There will be terrible times in the last days. People will be lovers of themselves, lovers of money, boastful, proud, abusive, disobedient to their parents, ungrateful, unholy, without love, unforgiving, slanderous, without self-control, brutal, not lovers of the good, treacherous, rash, conceited, lovers of pleasure rather than lovers of God—having a form of godliness but denying its power. Have nothing to do with them" (2Ti 3:1–5). This condition of man will culminate in a horrific time of tribulation predicted in Revelation 20:4: "I saw the souls of those who had been beheaded because of their testimony for Jesus and because of the word of God." This shows that the universal peace mankind seeks will not come from man himself but only by the intervention of God. Jesus will return, and only then will there be a "new age" of universal peace and harmony.
Crystals can be used as a vehicle for our own energy that will allow or cause our desires to come to pass.	"The crystal is only the tool used to focus or amplify your own energy and intent. . . . To program hold the crystal in your right (activitating) hand while visualizing white light travelling from your brain center down your arm into the crystal. Use a 'seed phrase' such as 'balanced energy' or 'better communication' instead of a long drawn out thought. Once the crystal is programmed it will be sending out your intent twenty-four hours a day, seven days a week, without your conscious awarness. Wearing the crystal will have the most noticable results, as well as increasing your general vitality and energy level. You'll definitely get what you ask for so be conscious of the ramifications of what you program" (Ann E. Zilinskas in *Heartland Journal,* May-June 1988).	The use of crystals for the purpose of changing either the future or present circumstances, especially when coupled with a worded incantation such as "balanced energy," is a clear violation of the biblical ban on the casting of spells. "Let no one be found among you who sacrifices his son or daughter in the fire, who practices divination or sorcery, interprets omens, engages in witchcraft, or casts spells, or who is a medium or spiritist or who consults the dead. Anyone who does these things is detestable to the LORD, and because of these detestable practices the LORD your God will drive out those nations before you. You must be blameless before the LORD your God" (Dt 18:10–13).

14

Reorganized Church of Jesus Christ
of Latter-day Saints

FACTS AND HISTORY

Facts	
Topic	*Current Facts*
Membership	In December 1994 the Reorganized Church of Jesus Christ of Latter-day Saints (RLDS) reported 248,431 members worldwide in 27 nations (RLDS Public Relations Office).
Worship	Services are usually held on Sunday morning and evening along with a Wednesday night testimony meeting. Sunday morning services are similar to many Protestant churches, with congregational readings and responses, singing, and preaching.
Presidents of the RLDS	Joseph Smith, Jr. 1830–1844 (Period of fragmentation and reorganization) 1844–1860 Joseph Smith III 1860–1914 Frederick M. Smith (son of Joseph Smith III) 1915–1946 Israel A. Smith (son of Joseph Smith III) 1946–1958 W. Wallace Smith (son of Joseph Smith III) 1958–1978 Wallace B. Smith (son W. Wallace Smith) 1978–
Publications	The RLDS has two main publications: (1) *Saints Herald,* a monthly magazine that contains articles and testimonies, letters from readers, news from both local congregations and the RLDS headquarters, book reviews, and weekly worship helps including themes, Scriptures, and hymns; and (2) *Restoration Witness,* a bimonthly magazine for renewing the faith of members and helping them to share the RLDS gospel with others. It includes personal testimonies and articles.
General statement of beliefs	The RLDS church considers itself a Christian denomination: "The Reorganized Church of Jesus Christ of Latter-day Saints centers its life in basic affirmations of the Christian faith. The church is Christian in its belief and practice" (*Who Are the Saints?* rev. ed., 1985, p. 7). Actually, the RLDS either denies or compromises many essential doctrines of historic Christianity, including the personhood of the Holy Spirit, the authority of Scripture (by relegating it to a position below other sacred writings and the authority of the church's prophet-president), the vicarious atonement of Christ, and eternal punishment for the lost. Nevertheless, there is great latitude for belief in the RLDS. The church has thousands of members who believe that the standard books of Scripture are completely reliable and authentic in what they claim to be. Other members are of a more liberal bent, believing that the Scriptures generally convey spiritual truths even though their authorship and authenticity may be doubtful. It appears that much of the church administration inclines toward a neoorthodox or liberal theology.

History	
Topic	*History*
Joseph Smith, Jr., 1830–1844	See the history of the Church of Jesus Christ of Latter-day Saints in chapter 5.
Period of fragmentation and reorganization, 1844–1860	Joseph Smith was murdered in prison in 1844. "Dissensions within the church became more pronounced now that its leader was dead. The church divided into factions. The largest group moved westward to the Great Salt Lake Valley under the direction of an influential church leader, Brigham Young. Smaller factions scattered in all directions. "During the 1850's what was to become the Reorganized church began to emerge. This group was established in 1860 with the succession of Joseph Smith III, son of the slain founder" (*Who Are the Saints?* rev. ed., 1987, p. 12).
Joseph Smith III, 1860–1914	"Joseph Smith III served as president of the Reorganization for 54 years, dying in office in 1914. . . . His main doctrinal contributions were a flat denial—in spite of several associates' eyewitness testimony—that Joseph Smith had ever been involved in polygamy, and the principle that general officers are properly designated by revelation rather than chosen by committee or the body. He united the scattered, sometimes quarrelling branches, and established the groundwork for an authoritarianism that has been growing ever since" (Robert McKay, *An Introduction to the RLDS Church*, p. 6). During this period, the church grew to more than 70,000 worldwide. Joseph Smith III designated his son, Frederick M. Smith, as his successor.
Frederick M. Smith, 1915–1946	"Fred M. is best remembered for the 'Supreme Directional Control' controversy, which was not so much a departure from his father's policies as an attempt to move them ahead more quickly than the people were then willing to tolerate. He was also the first Smith prophet to receive higher education, and brought an element of intellectual skepticism into the church that has since borne unpleasant fruit. Frederick was succeeded by his brother Israel A. Smith" (Robert McKay, *An Introduction to the RLDS Church*, p. 6).
Israel A. Smith, 1946–1958	"Although Israel wasn't so very different from Fred M., he was well-liked, and was able to patch the church back together. He is remembered as a 'gentle monarch,' although how much of this perception is accurate, and how much is simply reaction to Fred M.'s heavy-handed policies, is open to question" (Robert McKay, *An Introduction to the RLDS Church*, p. 6).
W. Wallace Smith, 1958–1978	"A third son of Joseph III, W. Wallace Smith, succeeded Israel A. Smith in 1958. By now much of what Frederick M. Smith had tried to initiate was in place, and Wallace openly brought theological liberalism into the church. Under his leadership traditional RLDS dogmas began to be seriously questioned by church leaders, and in fact several papers, originally secret, openly denied such formerly cherished beliefs as the Reorganization being the 'only true church' and the historicity of the Book of Mormon. In 1978 W. Wallace Smith retired, appointing his son Wallace B. Smith to the presidency" (Robert McKay, *An Introduction to the RLDS Church*, pp. 6–7).
Wallace B. Smith, 1978–	"Wally B. Smith, a popular president, has continued his father's theological liberalism. In 1984 he presented a revelation to the World Conference admitting women to the priesthood office" (Robert McKay, *An Introduction to the RLDS Church*, p. 7). This revelation, which was accepted by a majority of the members, catalyzed many "fundamentalist" RLDS who were unhappy with the perceived drift toward liberalism on the part of the church administration. In 1994, Wallace B. Smith dedicated the second RLDS temple. The 35-million-dollar building, with a 300-foot-high spiral steeple, has become a rallying point for the RLDS and a center for pursuing the RLDS dream of establishing peace, or "Zion," throughout the world. At the 1994 conference the church lifted its long-standing practice of "close communion," which restricted the sacrament to baptized members. Nonmembers are now welcome to partake. Finally, in November 1994, after much preliminary discussion, Wallace B. Smith and the First Presidency proposed a new name for the RLDS Church, the "Community of Christ," which reflects their desire to gain recognition and unity with mainline and ecumenical Christendom.

The Doctrine of Revelation

Position	Support	Orthodox Response
Three "Standard Books" are authoritative and considered Scripture: the Book of Mormon [BOM], the Doctrine and Covenants [D&C], and the Inspired Version of the Holy Scriptures [IV]. Inspired Documents issued by the current president of the church are added to the D&C, after approval (by "common consent") of the membership at World Conferences.	"We have three books of scripture: • The Holy Scriptures, which includes the Old Testament and the New Testament. • The Book of Mormon, an additional revelation of how God ministers to people through the Lord Jesus Christ. • The Doctrine and Covenants, a record of guidance to the church through modern prophets" (*Communications Division Brochure*, 1991).	The initial revelation of God was limited to the 39 books of the Old Testament. Jesus indicated these were authoritative by quoting from them, and He referred to the Hebrew canon as "the word of God" (Jn 10:35). He also affirmed its perpetuity and integrity (Mt 5:17–18). By contrast, Jesus never referred to apocryphal writings as the "word of God" or as possessing divine authority. The authoritative writings of the New Testament era were limited to those written by apostles who were with Christ when He was on earth or by men recognized as authoritative by the apostles. This would exclude writings after the first century A.D. Even if God were to give additional canonical revelation, it would have to be consistent with His prior revelations. This would eliminate the writings of Joseph Smith, since many of these writings contradict the teachings of the Bible. Further, Joseph Smith also issued *false* revelations, saying "Thus saith the Lord," which the RLDS Church has not added to its canon (such as failed prophecies). A coherent doctrine of Scripture should not accept any revelations from a false prophet into the canon of sacred text.
The RLDS rejects plenary verbal inspiration.	"The Standard Books are authoritative guides. But we do not claim that every word of every one of them is divinely dictated so as to be entirely free from error" (*Joseph Smith's "New Translation" of the Bible*, 1970, p. 20). "The idea of plenary inspiration was accepted for a long time by a great majority of Christians.... The Bible does indeed contain the word of God.... But the theory... no longer stands the test of careful scrutiny" (*Saints Herald*, December 15, 1967, cited in *Exploring the Faith*, 1987, p. 241). The belief "that scripture *is* itself the revelation of God... and completely free of error except for the incidental errors of transmission... is virtually impossible to maintain in the face of a knowledge of the processes through which the scriptures have reached their present form" (*Exploring the Faith*, 1987, pp. 240–41).	It is impossible to justify the distinctive RLDS scriptures (Smith's revisions in the IV, BOM, and D&C) as the Word of God, infallible, or inerrant. The distinctive RLDS scriptures are uninspired and errant writings. The RLDS church does not acknowledge the Bible's representation of itself and its nature. Jesus declared that the Scripture is "the word of God" (Mk 7:13; Jn 10:35); that its affirmations "cannot be broken" (Jn 10:35); that it "must be fulfilled" (Mk 14:49; see Lk 24:49); and that the message of the apostles is "actually... the word of God, which is at work in you who believe" (1Th 2:13).

The Doctrine of Revelation (cont.)

Position	Support	Orthodox Response
Inspiration extends only to the concepts conveyed, not to the words in which these concepts are expressed.	"We use the term inspiration to describe how a person responds to revelatory experience.... There can be no such thing as 'pure' scripture. When you and I read scripture or hear someone else read it, we sift it through the filter of our own life experiences" (*Who Are the Saints?* rev. ed., 1987, pp. 15–16).	The doctrine of biblical inspiration is expressed in 2 Timothy 3:16: "All Scripture is God-breathed...," The Greek word *theopneustos* literally means "God-breathed" or "breathed (out) by God," indicating its divine origin and development. Inspiration as such is predicated of the Scripture (*graphe*, the writings), not of the hearer or receiver, as the RLDS church contends. Other texts corroborate this concept, such as 2 Peter 1:20–21: "... you must understand that no prophecy of Scripture came about by the prophet's own interpretation. For prophecy never had its origin in the will of man, but men spoke from God as they were carried along by the Holy Spirit."
	"The Bible is not a book of God's words; it is instead a record of human experience with God.... The Bible does indeed reserve for us special revelations through which we can become aware of God. These revelations are not in themselves the word of God, but they are words *about* God" (*Exploring the Faith*, 1987, p. 228).	That we bring our own presuppositions and life experiences with us when we read the Bible in no way invalidates the character of Scripture as propositional revelation. The biblical doctrine of the sovereignty and providence of God assures us that God would have (and in fact, has) chosen the human authors of His word to convey His message as He intended, even compensating for their "filters" and innate predispositions.
	"The scripture is not itself the revelation of God; rather, it is the record made by someone who perceives that God has acted and revelation has occurred.... Sacred writings and formulated statements of doctrine are neither the substance nor the reality of revelation. They are records of the divine acts in which the revelation was given" (Ibid., p. 236).	B. B. Warfield, writing in 1915, anticipated the RLDS concepts in pointing out that although the colored glass of a cathedral window may indeed stain the light from heaven, it is also true that the architect *intended* for the window to be made of stained glass. Likewise, the providence of God prepared the birth, training, attitudes, and inclinations of the writers of Scripture, so that when His message was committed to parchment, it would also convey to the church that which He intended ("Inspiration," *International Standard Bible Encyclopedia*, 1915, 3:1480–81).
	"Therefore when we confess that the scriptures are the word of God, we do not mean that the words of the record are literally the words of God. They refer instead to the actions of God and they are the words about God.... [T]o identify the word of God with the words which are used to interpret and communicate the experience [that is, the Bible] ascribes to those words a finality and inerrancy which does not exist" (Ibid., p. 241).	

The Doctrine of Revelation (cont.)

Position	Support	Orthodox Response
The authority of Scripture is contingent and dependent on an outside source of authority.	F. Henry Edwards presented this idea when he said that one of the reasons that the revelations in the Doctrine and Covenants are authoritative is that "they have been approved by the church" (*The Edwards Commentary on the Doctrine and Covenants*, 1986, p. 280). "Scripture has both external and internal authority. We use and respect scripture because the church says it is important.... This is authority in an external sense. If scripture elicits a positive response from us—a decison to change our lives for the better—then we can say that it has internal authority or meaning for us" (*Who Are the Saints?* rev. ed., 1985, p. 15).	The orthodox view is not that the canon of Scripture receives authority because people hope that it is inspired, but that it is recognized by the people of God because it is inspired and thus has inherent authority. The fact that the Bible comes from God means that the authority of God rests within the inspired text. The internal testimony of the Holy Spirit, along with the verification of the Bible in the life of the church causes Christians to recognize the authoritative Word from God.
The *Inspired Version* purports to be "a more correct version of the Bible," replacing parts that were lost through human deceit and scribal error. The RLDS leadership supports the authority of this book among church members and of some (but not all) of its contents.	"A prophecy regarding Smith's forthcoming 'New Translation' of the Bible, spoken by Jesus Christ: '... the Scriptures shall be given even as they are in mine own bosom, to the salvation of mine own elect'" (Joseph Smith, Jr., RLDS D&C 34:5b). "Thou shalt ask, and my Scriptures shall be given as I [Jesus Christ] have appointed, and they shall be preserved in safety" (Ibid., 42:15a). "As concerning the manner of translation and correction, it is evident... that it was done by direct revelation from God" (Preface to the first edition of the IV, 1867). "We do not consider it infallible.... we do not consider anything that passes through human hands to be infallible" (Joseph Smith III, in the Temple Lot suit, *Abstract of Evidence*, pp. 491–94; cited in *Exploring the Faith*, 1987, p. 241). "It is clear that many changes [introduced by Joseph Smith, Jr.] are indeed additions to the original text, reflecting 19th century concerns and theological positions, and elaborating the thought of the original writer.... it may also be held upon formidable grounds that a number of passages have been weakened in meaning by the changes introduced.... The Inspired Version is not to be regarded as an accurate textual revision, restoring the 'pure' text of the original" (*Position Papers*, 1967, pp. 26–27).	The *raison d'etre* of the Inspired Version (or the "Joseph Smith Translation") is that the original text of Scripture was corrupted by unfaithful Jews in pre-Christian times and later on by the Roman Catholic Church. Smith claimed to be "restoring" an ancient text. Yet the Hebrew text of the Old Testament has a lineage of transmission (recopying) separate from the Christian manuscript tradition. Moreover, the widespread distribution of Scripture—as well as its translation into other languages and dialects, its use in lectionaries, and tens of thousands of citations by Jewish commentators and early Christian leaders—make Smith's claim of a secret corruption untenable. The *Position Papers* are correct in saying that many of the changes are additions to the original text or even weaken it, although some members believe that Joseph Smith's modern additions could be "inspired" anyway.

The Doctrine of Revelation (cont.)

Position	Support	Orthodox Response
The Book of Mormon is accepted as a witness to Jesus Christ. Like the Bible, it is not *itself* the Word of God, but *contains* the Word of God. It is not considered infallible or final. Many church leaders doubt that it is a record of true history, but many other members believe it *is* an authentic record of ancient America.	"Like the Bible, the Book of Mormon is a collection of books—fifteen in all—whose central testimony is of Jesus Christ. Fourteen of these books include the story of a colony of people called Nephites who left Jerusalem in 586 B.C. and traveled across the ocean to another land. The remaining book is about another colony, the Jaredites, who migrated from the Tigris-Euphrates Valley at the time of the building of the Tower of Babel" (*Who Are the Saints?* p. 17). "The historicity of the book [of Mormon] cannot be proven. . . . We are aware of those who point out that much of its social thought and ethic is the Puritan thought and ethic of early 19th century New York State. The development of its Christology, doctrines of the atonement, the Trinitarian concepts are not found in the New Testament but in the development of medieval theology. . . . But to assent that the validity of either the Restoration movement or the Book of Mormon depends upon the truth or error of any of the above arguments is to miss the purpose of both" (*Presidential Papers,* 1979, p. 29). "If we can be secure enough to share the added witness of Jesus Christ contained in the Book of Mormon rather than recounting the details of its history, the book may become a valuable resource to many Christians who are not members of the Restoration church. The sin of our kind has always been to raise secondary questions to the level of primary significance. Let us not sin against the witness of Jesus Christ that we find in the Book of Mormon by judging its worth on the shallow basis of rational interpretation of historical events" (Ibid., p. 31).	If the Book of Mormon is not genuine history, then it cannot be a "witness to Jesus Christ" any more than other works of sacred fiction such as *Pilgrim's Progress, Ben-Hur,* or *The Robe.* Fictional works can be *inspirational,* but they cannot be *inspired.* Also, the Bible says, "A truthful witness does not deceive, but a false witness pours out lies" (Pr 14:5). How can the Book of Mormon be a faithful witness for Christ if it tells lies about past events? There are many reasons to believe that the Book of Mormon is a product of the nineteenth century rather than the ancient text it purports to be. Therefore it fails in its principal claim, namely, to provide additional first-century eyewitnesses of the ministry and resurrection of Jesus Christ. (See chapter 5 for some of the major difficulties in the Book of Mormon. Although the RLDS version is different from the LDS version in its method of dividing chapters and verses, the actual text or wording of the two versions is virtually identical, and thus the criticisms of the Book of Mormon in that section will also apply here.) The *Presidential Papers* seem to regard historicity and factuality as "secondary questions," beneath the "primary significance" of its message about Jesus Christ. They fail to recognize that any so-called witness it brings to Jesus is lost if the witnesses were not real to begin with.
The Doctrine and Covenants are a collection of revelations given to the presidents of the church. The "inspired documents" in the D&C contain the word of God to the church, but may be revoked if needed.	"The Doctrine and Covenants is a compilation of documents the church accepts as inspired statements representing 'the mind and will of God' and as a standard of church law and practice. The documents date back to 1828 and cover the period from then until the present. One of the specific functions of the prophet-president is to present in written form what he perceives as God's will for the church. The documents are presented to the various councils and quorums of the church and to the World Conference for consideration. After a formal vote, approved sections are printed as additions to the Doctrine and Covenants" (*Who Are the Saints?* p. 18).	Although the D&C purportedly contains the mind of God, the RLDS concept allows that some revelations in it may be revoked or rescinded (for example, sections 107, 109, and 110, removed to the appendix in 1970). Theologies represented in other passages of the D&C are denied in current RLDS literature, such as the claim that this is "the only true and living church upon the face of the whole earth, with which I the Lord am well pleased" (D&C 90:4b, 5a). The RLDS D&C also contains internal contradictions; for example, one section says whoremongers, sorcerers, and liars shall inherit the lake of fire, or the second death (63:5b), while another section says

The Doctrine of Revelation (cont.)

Position	Support	Orthodox Response
... continued		that these same people shall inherit "telestial glory" and be ministered to by the Holy Spirit (D&C 76:7f, 7o), but only apostates and the "sons of perdition" will suffer in the lake of fire (76:4e).
The inspiration of Scripture is not unique, nor is it restricted to prophets or apostles.	"There is a second sense in which the Scriptures are open. Alan Richardson writes: "'The inspiration of the Holy Spirit . . . did not cease when the New Testament books were all written, or when the canon of the New Testament was finally drawn up; there is a wide range of Christian literature from the second to the twentieth century which can with propriety be described as inspired by the Holy Spirit in precisely the same formal sense as were the Books of the Bible.'"—*Christian Apologetics,* p. 207. ". . . The scriptures do not and cannot constitute the whole revelation of God. Neither one book, nor three, nor any finite number could compass that revelation" (*Exploring the Faith,* 1987, p. 243). "Canonization does not imply limiting the spirit of revelation to those materials only which are identified as 'scripture.' . . . Plainly put, we do not understand scriptures to be 'divine' while all other writings are 'human'" (Ibid., pp. 244–45).	The Christian belief in the Bible as *uniquely* inspired, or given by God in a way unlike all other human writings, originates in the nature of the Hebrew OT canon; in the way Jesus treated that canon; in the special promises Jesus made to His apostles; and in the apostles' own view of the Scriptures. The Holy Spirit still illumines or enlightens people to understand the Scriptures, but He does not inspire people to write new Scripture. Christianity does not assert that God is incapable of communicating with humanity through nature ("natural revelation"), personal answers to prayer, inner convictions, pastoral counseling, or even semi-miraculous circumstances. We do not declare that all forms and degrees of revelation or communication from God have ceased; rather, we claim that all *normative* revelation has ceased, which is "special revelation" given by God to all humankind.
The scriptures of other cultures contain special revelation.	"'For I command all men, both in the east, and in the west, and in the north, and in the south, and in the islands of the sea, that they shall write the words which I speak to them. . . . and I shall also speak to *all nations of the earth,* and they shall write it. — II Nephi 12:65–69 (emphasis added).'" "The testimony of the Book of Mormon is that God does not intend to deprive any people of the world of the blessings of scriptures which are indigenous to them" (*Exploring the Faith,* 1987, p. 204).	The implication here is that God has revealed Himself to other major people groups through their indigenous scriptures, and therefore the scriptures of other religions may also be revelations from God—for example, the Qur'an; Hindu, Buddhist, and Taoist scriptures; or Zoroastrian and Sikh scriptures. It is a false and unbiblical assumption that God has spoken authoritatively through all the religions of the world (except through general revelation). The other religions lead people to embrace a false God and deny the Christian message.

The Doctrine of Revelation (cont.)

Position	Support	Orthodox Response
God's final revelation (beyond Scripture) is the person of Christ.	"In a sense, all scripture is commentary on the revelation in Christ. Christian faith declares that Jesus Christ is the 'Last Word.' . . . He is the one against whom all claims to revelation and truth must be measured. (See Hebrews chapter 1.) . . . "Once again, we confess that God is revealed not in abstract truth or religious tenets but through concrete acts. The gospel is not primarily a message about Jesus or a set of doctrinal propositions. It is Jesus himself, the Word or action of God made flesh. This is the central revelation without which all other claim to revelation is incoherent" (*Exploring the Faith,* 1987, p. 240).	These statements sound convincing, but they express inadequate theology. First, the church divorces "the revelation in Christ" from the Scriptures that provide the content of that revelation. Claiming that Christ is the central standard measuring everything else, the statements deny that the Bible, which tells us what Christ did and said, can be trusted without reservation when it records Christ's words and actions. This inherent contradiction highlights the problem of denying biblical infallibility while affirming Jesus' infallibility. If the Scriptures have erred in describing Christ, how can we affirm faith in Jesus' own infallibility? Second, if Jesus is God's final and ultimate revelation, has He erred in describing Scripture as infallible?

The Doctrine of God—*The Trinity*

Position	Support	Orthodox Response
The historic creeds of the early church should not be presented as something everyone ought to believe.	"It would be idolatrous on our part to attempt to take any one definition [among the historic Christian creeds] and lift it to status as a dogmatic statement which everyone should believe" (*Exploring the Faith,* 1987, p. 37).	This fails to resolve the issue of whether the early Christian definitions of faith, such as the Apostles' Creed or the Nicene Creed, represent truth or contain falsehood. If the creeds contain statements of truth, why would it be "idolatrous" to ask people to believe the truth? The RLDS church urges belief in the Scriptures, yet they claim to contain errors, so it is difficult to explain their reluctance at this point.
There is one eternal God, who is Father, Son, and Holy Spirit.	"Father, Son, and Holy Ghost are one God" (*Statement of Faith and Belief,* item #3, "Holy Spirit"). The "Father, Son, and Holy Ghost are one God, infinite and eternal, without end" (RLDS D&C 17:5h). "Christ the Son, and God the Father, and the Holy Spirit . . . is one Eternal God" (RLDS BOM, Alma 8:104).	This is an orthodox statement.
There are three separate manifestations within the Trinity.	"Our affirmations about God apply equally to Jesus Christ and the Holy Spirit. We experience God through these three distinct manifestations. At the same time, though, we affirm our belief that there is but one God in these three" (*Latter Day Saint Churches and Their Beliefs,* p. 8).	This statement gives the appearance of orthodoxy, but the term "manifestations" seems less concrete than the doctrine as defined in the historic creeds.

The Doctrine of God—*The Trinity (cont.)*

Position	Support	Orthodox Response
The RLDS church is not modalistic.	"... our understanding of the nature of God must apply to Jesus Christ and the Holy Spirit as well as to the Creator. However, some degree of separation must be made" (*Who Are the Saints?* pp. 7–8).	This is a correct statement as long as the separation is not of essence but only of personal reponsibilities or functions within the Trinity. (Note, however, that this quotation contrasts Jesus and "creator.")
The terms "person," "function," "aspect," and "manifestation" may be used as synonyms when referring to the members of the Godhead.	"... the early church leaders came to understand what they described as a 'tri-unity' in the Godhead.... when speaking about God or Christ or the Holy Ghost, they were simply talking about different aspects of the same God. "When we speak about God, of course, all analogies break down. For God is not really like anything else that we can ever experience. But to think of the three functions or aspects or persons in the Godhead as being one God is something like recognizing that the substance which is chemically described as H_2O may be experienced as a solid (ice), a liquid (water), or a gas (steam or water vapor). These are not three different substances, but rather three aspects of the same substance" (*Exploring the Faith*, 1987, pp. 56–57).	There is a wide difference between the concept of personhood, which implies personality and a center of self-consciousness and will, and the concepts of function (operation), aspect (perspective), and manifestation (appearance), which do not carry the idea of essential personhood. Indeed, some of these terms deny personhood. For example, if A is a function of B and B is a personal entity, A would be an attribute or quality exhibited by person B but not a distinct person in one's own right. Despite its affirmation of the personal nature of God elsewhere, the church's nomenclature tends to compromise this belief. The idea of a "tri-unity" or Trinity is acknowledged as correct, but is not a focal point of RLDS theology.

The Doctrine of God—*Attributes of God*

Position	Support	Orthodox Response
God is not limited to any physical shape.	"To say that God is a person is neither to limit him to a shape, nor to affirm that he has no shape" (*Exploring the Faith*, 1970 ed., p. 21).	While this statement is logically true (i.e., affirming personhood does not imply affirming a form for that person), it is also true that because God in essence is spirit, rather than matter (Jn 4:24), God the Father cannot have a shape or form. Therefore the RLDS statement results in ambiguity.

The Doctrine of God—*Attributes of God (cont.)*

Position	Support	Orthodox Response
God is omnipotent, omnipresent, and unchanging.	"We believe in God the Eternal Father; source and center of all love and life and truth, who is almighty, infinite, and unchanging" (*Statement of Faith and Belief,* 1970, item 1, p. 283). "Contrary to what many Christians believe, omnipotence (which means 'all-powerful') is not concerned with sheer power.... If God wanted to exercise sheer brute force, God could do absolutely anything; but because God is love, divine power is seen in divine love.... That God is 'almighty' simply means that God is free and able to deal with creation in terms of the divine purpose for it. There is no difference between what God wills to do and what God can do" (*Exploring the Faith,* 1987, p. 24). "God is all powerful and can do whatever God wills to do" (Ibid., p. 162). In regard to omnipresence, "we simply mean that God may be everywhere in the universe at once, and is not limited to being in one place at one time as we are" (Ibid., p. 24). "The Lord's quality of changelessness is best perceived as we are able to understand God's faithfulness and persistence to bring to fruition 'the works, and the designs, and the purposes of God [which] cannot be frustrated'" (Ibid., p. 25).	This represents the orthodox position, although the RLDS description of God's attribute of changlessness (or immutability) is weak. Immutability refers not only to God's faithfulness and purposes but also to His nature or being. The RLDS description of God's omnipresence in the 1987 edition of *Exploring the Faith* is far superior to that in the 1970 edition.

The Doctrine of God—*God as Creator*

Position	Support	Orthodox Response
God as Creator is both transcendent to the world and immanent within it.	"The Christian doctrine of creation boldly places God outside the world as creator. Another way of saying this is to state that God is *transcendent* to the world.... Although God identifies with the created world, the world is not God and God is not it.... [Yet] in spite of God's separation from the world in terms of transcendence due to the difference between creator and creation, God is also immanent within that world" (*Exploring the Faith,* 1987, p. 18).	These are orthodox statements.

The Doctrine of God—*God as Creator (cont.)*

Position	Support	Orthodox Response
Creation occurred *ex nihilo*, not out of preexisting substance.	"The Christian affirmation that God is creator means that nothing pre-exists God, nothing exists independently from God, and therefore, nothing can exist eternally and universally which is in rebellion against God's purposes within the universe. Therefore, we do not believe in the view of creation which asserts that God is the great artist who took an already existing raw material and molded the world out of it. We also do not accept the theory of creation which conceives of God as having created all things out of His own personal substance. The Christian faith simply asserts that God created all things from nothing" (*Presidential Papers,* 1979, p. 4).	This statement is biblical and orthodox, but it appears to contradict an older writing, namely, section 90 in the RLDS D&C, which says, "Man was also in the beginning with God. Intelligence, or the light of truth, was not created or made, neither indeed can be" (90:5a) and "The elements are eternal" (90:5e).
The church supports theistic evolution, as opposed to creationism or atheism, to account for the origin of life.	"It is just as incorrect for creationists to deny the theories of evolution because of their scripture-based faith position as it is for atheists to use scientific arguments to disprove the scriptures or any other item of faith.... The realms of faith and science do not intermix, and neither one can offer any kind of proof about the other" (*Exploring the Faith,* 1987, p. 13).	God never limits His authority or communication to purely "spiritual" matters such as salvation, faith, or hope. Biblical revelation was concerned with such things as the conduct of war, sanitation, diet, sexual behavior, property ownership, future events, and the ancient history of man. The Bible is just as authoritative when it speaks on the origin of life as when it speaks on the origin of sin. Jesus addressed this objection when He told Nicodemus, "I have spoken to you of earthly things and you do not believe; how then will you believe if I speak of heavenly things?" (Jn 3:12). If God has spoken about the origin of life as an object of purposive creation, and has recorded it in Holy Scripture, this is authoritative proof. The reluctance of the skeptic or the evolutionist to *accept* the Scriptures as proof does not mean that God has not spoken or that His word is not valid wherever it touches on earthly matters.

The Doctrine of Jesus Christ—*The Deity of Christ*

Position	Support	Orthodox Response
Jesus is uniquely God incarnate.	"We believe in Jesus Christ, the Only Begotten Son of God, who is from everlasting to everlasting; through whom all things were made; who is God in the flesh, being incarnate by the Holy Spirit for the salvation of all humankind" (*Statement of Faith and Belief*, 1969, item 2, p. 283). "Christ is the incarnation of God in the flesh. No other person or group of persons can presume to have such revelatory power or honor" (*Exploring the Faith,* 1987, p. 155). "Some theologians . . . would affirm that Jesus remains but one son from among the many. However, the testimony of the scriptures does not leave us with this alternative. . . . God was in Christ in a way not found in other human life" (Ibid., pp. 31–32).	These are orthodox statements.
Some RLDS leaders believe in a "cosmic Christ."	"The Temple for us RLDS . . . will be the central symbol of the cosmic Christ incarnating or coming in us. . . . Why limit the Spirit of Christ to a single body, human or divine? As a Reorganized Christian, I reject the notion that Divinity has a body just like mine, along with the idea that Christ has a specific gender, race, or nationality. Jesus of Nazareth was a Jew who lived in ancient Palestine. But I do not believe Jesus of Nazareth is the fullness of Christ. Neither is the resurrected Jesus encountered by Saul on his way to Damascus. . . . God wears many faces" (*Temple Foundations,* 1991, pp. 51–52).	There are several things wrong with this statement. First, the Bible never speaks of a "cosmic Christ" either directly or thematically. The "cosmic Christ" concept is borrowed from liberal and New Age theology. Second, while it is true that God in essence is spirit (Jn 4:24), it is not true that divinity has *no* body. The person of Jesus Christ is God incarnate (an idea affirmed in other RLDS writings). "He appeared in a body" (1Ti 3:16). In Jesus "all the fullness of the Deity lives in bodily form" (Col 2:9). Third, Jesus of Nazareth, who still is alive, is indeed "the fullness of Christ." The universal Christian church is the "body of Christ" by virtue of spiritual union *with* Him, not by virtue of ontological identity *as* Him.
Jesus did not commit any sin, but He may have wanted to.	Jesus is seen as one who on earth was "being tempted as we also are tempted, being able to sin and perhaps even wanting to do so, nevertheless resisting sin altogether" (*Exploring the Faith,* 1987, p. 124).	Because the Bible affirms that the "thought of foolishness is sin" (Pr 24:9 KJV) and that sin also can exist in the mind or heart (Mt 5:28), it is precarious to assert that Christ might have wanted to sin but that His desire to commit sin is not sinful in and of itself.

The Doctrine of Jesus Christ—*The Deity of Christ (cont.)*

Position	Support	Orthodox Response
The Sonship of Jesus does not imply that He was created.	"... for us, the father/son relationship implies that one existed before the other. In the scriptures, however, we understand that 'in the beginning... the Son was with God, and the Son was of God. The same was in the beginning with God.' (John 1:1–2)... In the instance of Jesus, however, the Son was the Son in the beginning,... So when we talk about the Father/Son relationships in the Godhead, we are not talking about priority or about procreation" (*Exploring the Faith,* 1987, p. 57).	This represents the orthodox position, but it should be noted that the citation of John 1:1 comes from the Inspired Version (the Joseph Smith translation), which is not supported by any Greek text. In fact, the IV adds three full clauses, signified by the ellipsis points, and changes the final clause from "the Word was God" (KJV, NASB, NIV, NRSV, and every known Greek text) to "the Son was of God" (IV only).

The Doctrine of Jesus Christ—*The Humanity of Christ*

Position	Support	Orthodox Response
Jesus was perfectly human.	"Jesus, who was in all respects human, was at the same time Eternal God (Philippians 2:5–8)" (*Exploring the Faith,* 1987, p. 19).	This is an orthodox statement.
The incarnation of Christ displays the truth about us and is intended to teach us the sacramental nature of the physical universe.	"He [Christ] is the revelation of the perfect human, so that we can see the truth about ourselves and all humanity. Christ is the revelation of the nature of the universe, so that we can see the sacramental meaning of all creation. Everything that is has a holy purpose" (*Exploring the Faith,* 1987, p. 157). "Acknowledging the sacramental nature of all creation, we recognize that there is no part which is to be despised, no creation which is not good, and no labor which is menial" (RLDS First Presidency, unpublished thematic materials for "Communities of Joy" presentation, 1993; cited in *Communities of Joy,* 1994, p. 70). "It is our Christian affirmation that all things are spiritual" (*Exploring the Faith,* 1987, p. 201).	The statements that Christ came so we could "see the truth about ourselves" and "see the sacramental meaning of all creation" are speculative and vague. Neither statement is affirmed clearly in Scripture, which does state clearly why Jesus came to earth. (For example, "The Son of Man did not come to be served, but to serve, and to give his life as a ransom for many" [Mk 10:45].) We do not deny that the Incarnation fulfilled several purposes of God and that it teaches us many things, but it is better to focus on clear statements of Scripture than on speculations. "The sacramental nature of all creation" is an undeveloped concept and can remain orthodox only within limits. If everything has a "holy purpose," what about cancer, random violence, crippling accidents, or personal sin? Some conditions and circumstances are the after-effects of the Fall or part of the divine curse on the ground (Ge 3:17–19). It is orthodox to confess God's sovereignty in the midst of a fallen world; it is precarious to assert that all creation is sacramental or that "all things are spiritual," since God still recognizes a difference between the holy and the unholy (see Ro 12:1; 1Co 3:16–17; 10:20–22; 2Co 6:14–7:1; Heb 12:14).

The Doctrine of Jesus Christ—*The Humanity of Christ (cont.)*

Position	Support	Orthodox Response
The Definition of Chalcedon represents true theology about the divine and human nature of Jesus Christ.	"A series of councils occurred, among them being one held in A.D. 451 which produced the Creed of Chalcedon. It declared that Jesus Christ was: "'at once complete in Godhead and complete in manhood, truly God and truly man . . . of one essence with the Father as regards his Godhead, and at the same time of one essence with us as regards his manhood, in all respects like us, apart from sin.' ". . . What is most surprising to us today is that, taken as a whole, all scriptures contained in the Bible, the Book of Mormon, and the Doctrine and Covenants, lend support to these positions taken by the early church fathers in the fifth century" (*Exploring the Faith,* 1987, pp. 39–40).	The Definition of Chalcedon is an orthodox statement of Christian belief. However, the Book of Mormon repeatedly and contradictorily states that Jesus is the Father, or is both "the Father and the Son" (or is merely the Son), whereas the Definition and the other ecumenical creeds properly distinguish the Father from the Son. Therefore the claim that the Book of Mormon is consistent with the church fathers or the early creeds is suspect. At the same time, we recognize that the RLDS church does not teach that Jesus is the Father and Son; it teaches that He is the Son only. On this point the church is orthodox.
The church acknowledges the virgin birth of Christ.	"The Apostles' Creed affirms, 'born of the Virgin Mary,' in order to establish once and for all that Jesus was actually born of a woman" (*Exploring the Faith,* 1987, p. 39). Jesus "was the Son in the beginning, and did not need to wait until he would be born of the Virgin Mary on earth" (Ibid., p. 57).	This is compatible with historic orthodoxy. However, we note in passing that the doctrine of the virgin birth is barely mentioned in the church's doctrinal study of basic beliefs, *Exploring the Faith*. That the authors emphasize that Jesus was "actually born of a woman" but not the word "Virgin" may indicate a preference for naturalism, but the evidence is too scanty to draw any firm conclusions.

The Doctrine of Jesus Christ—*The Resurrection of Christ*

Position	Support	Orthodox Response
Jesus rose from the dead and appeared bodily to others.	"We join all Christians in the belief that Jesus Christ arose from the tomb and that he lives. . . . That he arose from the dead is part of the evidence that Jesus was God in the flesh" (*Exploring the Faith,* 1987, p. 247). ". . . if he had not risen and shown himself in bodily form—the Christian gospel might very well not have been known to us today" (Ibid., p. 252).	These are orthodox statements. However, one focal issue of the Christian faith today is whether the resurrection body of Jesus was a temporary copy of the body that died (as the Jehovah's Witnesses claim) or was the *same* body, transformed and made immortal (the orthodox view). This issue also concerns what happened to the corpse of Jesus in the tomb. Did it decay and disintegrate, or did it come back to physical life? The RLDS statements do not address these questions.

The Doctrine of Jesus Christ—*The Resurrection of Christ (cont.)*

Position	Support	Orthodox Response
The nature of Christ's resurrected body is vague and inaccessible to us today.	"It is really useless to try to argue whether or not Jesus' resurrection was a 'spiritual' or 'physical' event. Either term, or both terms together, may well be inadequate to describe how he arose from the dead.... we cannot define with any real accuracy what resurrection in Christ means" (*Exploring the Faith,* 1987, p. 47).	Because Jesus Himself said His resurrection body was made of "flesh and bones" (Lk 24:39) and invited the apostles to feel and touch Him (Jn 20:26–29), it is hard to see how the Resurrection could be interpreted as anything less than a *physical* event. The physical realities of a missing corpse and an empty tomb occurred because Jesus' body was raised to life, and in this body He was repeatedly seen by His disciples (Ac 1:3). It was also *spiritual* (not spirit) in that in raising Jesus from the dead, the Holy Spirit imbued His body with glorious new powers (Ro 8:11; 1Co 15:42–44).
The best proof of Jesus' resurrection lies in personal experience rather than historical evidence.	"Perhaps the greatest proof of the Resurrection is to be seen in the lives of those who have actually believed in it.... Unlike some other fables or myths, the resurrection story has meaning to those who understand it because they know Jesus and his power of life" (*Exploring the Faith,* 1987, p. 46).	It is true that the Holy Spirit provides inner conviction of the truth of the resurrection of Jesus Christ. This is in harmony with the lines of the well-loved song, "You ask me how I know he lives? He lives, within my heart." Nevertheless, proofs of history are not to be superseded by personal experience. Is human experience thousands of years later really a "greater proof" than the Scripture, written by the apostles and other eyewitnesses of Jesus' resurrection?

The Doctrine of Holy Spirit

Position	Support	Orthodox Response
Sometimes RLDS literature refers to the Holy Spirit in impersonal terms as an energy or force.	"... the God of the Hebrews ... was now newly-experienced as life-giving energy" (*Exploring the Faith,* 1987, p. 53). "They experienced him as the generating, sustaining, redeeming and sanctifying force of the church" (Ibid., p. 54). "... the divine energy which raised him [Jesus] from the dead was a power without limits" (Ibid., p. 251).	Terms such as "energy" or "force" diminish recognition of the Holy Spirit as a personal being. For example, to refer to Satan as a "life-destroying energy" or a "debilitating force" would suggest that Satan was an evil principle, not a spirit being. Although RLDS writings elsewhere attribute self-direction and personal features to the Holy Spirit, some of their terminology implies that the Holy Spirit is not a personal entity. When believers are filled with the Holy Spirit, they do receive "power" (Ac 1:8; Lk 24:49), but the person of the Holy Spirit is distinct from the power He gives.

The Doctrine of Holy Spirit (cont.)

Position	Support	Orthodox Response
The Holy Spirit is more commonly understood as the presence of God.	"In the Holy Spirit, we feel the presence, love, and energy of God" (*Exploring the Faith,* 1987, p. 84). "The Holy Spirit, the abiding Comforter, is not merely a force, but a presence. The early Christians spoke of this as 'the mind of Christ' which dwelt within them" (Ibid., p. 89). "We believe in the Holy Spirit who is the living presence of the Father and the Son" (Ibid., p. 63).	The orthodoxy of these statements depends on whether the speaker ultimately views the person of the Holy Spirit to be distinct from the persons of God the Father and God the Son. If the Holy Spirit does not retain distinct personhood in His own right, many statements of Scripture are compromised. The RLDS church appears to be moving from a binitarian to a trinitarian theology, but has not fully completed this transition.
The Holy Spirit is personal and possesses "personality."	"The Holy Spirit is not simply power: the Holy Spirit is person, and therefore is also intelligence and personality. The Holy Spirit is not less than we are, and therefore is not subject to our direction. On the contrary, we know that the Holy Spirit is the personality, the power, and the intelligence of God at work" (*Exploring the Faith,* 1987, p. 83).	Although this is better than an impersonalist view of the Holy Spirit, by saying that "the Holy Spirit is the personality, the power, and the intelligence of God at work," the RLDS leadership does not distinguish the person of the Holy Spirit from the person of the Father. Thus, if the Holy Spirit is the "personality of God at work," the Holy Spirit is a synonym for the operative activity of God the Father. Although one can distinguish God's personal activity on earth from His quiescent attributes, there is still only one person in view. The RLDS has not satisfactorily ascribed separate personhood to the Holy Spirit.
The Holy Spirit gives life to the church, which is an organism, not just an organization.	"The church is enlightened, directed, sustained and empowered by the Holy Spirit. Without this Spirit the whole body ceases to be a living organism" (*Exploring the Faith,* 1987, p. 160).	This is an orthodox statement.

The Doctrine of Man and Sin

Position	Support	Orthodox Response
The fall of man is traceable to Adam and Eve and pervades all of humankind. The essence of sin is self-will in ignoring or opposing the will of God, and it affects all persons except children or the mentally retarded.	"In following the dictates of pride and in declaring independence from God, humanity loses the power to fulfill the purposes of creation and becomes the servant of sin, whereby persons are divided within themselves and estranged from God and their neighbors. This condition, experienced by our ancestors who first came to a knowledge of good and evil, is shared by all who are granted the gift of accountability" (*Statement of Faith and Belief*, Item 6, "Humanity," 1987, p. 284). "Our sin is to have the potential for communion with God, and to simply shrug it off. This sin is original with us, and yet continues into every generation, in our deliberate preference for our own will over against the will of God. This trouble began in the Garden of Eden when Adam said, in effect, 'My will, not thine, be done'" (*Exploring the Faith*, 1987, p. 108).	These are orthodox statements.
The "soul" is the union of spirit and body. Thus the "redemption of the soul" referred to in Scripture is the reuniting of spirit and body or, in other words, is synonymous with the coming resurrection.	"The spirit and the body is the soul of man. And the resurrection from the dead is the redemption of the soul" (RLDS D&C 85:4a, b; cited in *Exploring the Faith*, 1987, p. 254).	The RLDS acceptance of a dichotomous view of man (composed of two parts) is well within the bounds of historic orthodoxy. However, its definition of the *soul* as being "the spirit and the body" is inadequate. At death the spirit leaves the body (Jas 2:26; Ecc 12:7); therefore the "soul" could not exist between death and the resurrection, if the RLDS definition is valid. Its definition allows the *spirit* to survive death, but after it leaves the body, there is no more *soul*. Yet the Bible teaches that the soul does exist after death (Mt 10:28; Ac 2:27; Rev 6:9–10) and is an immaterial component of mankind.
The essence of sin is pride and independence from God.	"... pride, the source from which all other sins spring" (*Exploring the Faith*, 1987, p. 107). "At the core of our being is self-assertion. Under the Spirit of God, our self-assertion is part of being human. But when it becomes rebellion, the will to be separate from God is sin" (Ibid., p. 109). "There is a popular idea held by well-meaning people that God judges and condemns sin— but never the sinner. This casual view of sin fails to acknowledge it as rebellion against God. It is not something external to the sinner, for sin is a part of the sinner. God's judgment on a person's sin is a judgment upon that person. But it is while we were yet in sin that God has loved us" (Ibid., p. 271).	This statement is correct as far as it goes, in that it defines sin as willful independence of and rejection of God. The RLDS church also recognizes that sin consists in both outward acts and inward disposition. It seems that "pride" is defined as or equated with self-assertion. It should be noted that the RLDS church fails to define sin in terms of violating or transgressing the law of God. Not only are classical biblical definitions absent—such as "sin is lawlessness" (1Jn 3:4)—but also biblical synonyms are absent, such as "trespass," "transgression," "unrighteousness," "iniquity," and even "missing the mark." Also absent are any references to God's law in this context; therefore there is no recognition of unintentional sin or "sins of ignorance" (on which, see Lev

The Doctrine of Man and Sin (cont.)

Position	Support	Orthodox Response
. . . continued		4:1–35; Nu 15:24–29; Ac 3:17, for example). By contrast, since there are many references to sin's being a rejection of God's will, the RLDS understanding does encompass all active rebellion to God's will, law, and plan for us.
Mortality is not a consequence of the Fall.	"Some people . . . do not understand what it means to be mortal, or why God chose mortality as a fitting form for our life here. They become victims of poor theology which tells them that mortality is equal to sin. Orthodox theology tells us that human conception is sinful: that to be born mortal is to be 'conceived in sin.' Thus 'the Fall' is usually equated with our humanity" (*Exploring the Faith,* 1987, p. 121).	*Mortality* is not synonymous with *humanity*. To be mortal is to be subject to death and able to die; this is not essential to being human. God did not "choose mortality"; He chose humanity by which we could glorify Him. Mortality, or death, is a consequence of sin, as is stated variously in Scripture. "When you eat of it," God told Adam, "you will surely die" (Ge 2:17). "As sin entered the world through one man, and death through sin, and in this way death came to all men" (Ro 5:12). "The wages of sin is death" (Ro 6:23). Further, orthodox theology does not say that "human conception is sinful." Adam and Eve were commanded prior to the Fall to fill the earth with their offspring (Ge 1:28). Connecting the Fall with sexual knowledge is not a new teaching, but it does not accord with traditional Christian belief. Finally, orthodox theology has never equated the transgression of Adam (the Fall) with our humanity. Adam and Eve were human before the Fall; according to Scripture, their sin brought on death as a penalty or consequence for disobedience (see Ro 5:12–21).
Certain portions of RLDS scriptures hold that the fall of Adam and Eve was necessary for mankind to reproduce, but this concept is expressly denied today.	"And Eve, his wife, heard all these things and was glad, saying, Were it not for our transgression, we never should have had seed, and never should have known good and evil" (Ge 4:11, IV). "And as Enoch spake forth the words of God, the people trembled and could not stand in his presence. And he said unto them, Because that Adam fell, we are; . . ." (Ge 6:48–49, IV). "Now, behold, if Adam had not transgressed, he would not have fallen; but he would have remained in the garden of Eden. . . . They would have had no children; . . . Adam fell, that men might be . . ." (RLDS BOM, 2 Nephi 1:111, 113, 115). "The human body is made by God. Its properties for the reproduction of the human race were God-given" (*Exploring the Faith,* 1987, p. 121).	Although it does not overtly retract these statements from the Inspired Version and the Book of Mormon, the church is correct to deny them. The capacity for reproduction is natural and not a consequence of sin or the Fall.

The Doctrine of Man and Sin (cont.)

Position	Support	Orthodox Response
RLDS scripture affirms the preexistence of spirits in heaven with God before coming to earth. This doctrine is not taught by the church today.	"And I, the Lord God, had created all the children of men, and not yet a man to till the ground, for in heaven created I them, and there was not yet flesh upon the earth" (Ge 2:6, IV). "And the Lord said unto Cain, Why art thou wroth? Why is thy countenance fallen? . . . Thou shalt be called Perdition, for thou wast also before the world" (Ge 5:9, 10, IV). "And he [God] called upon our father Adam, by his own voice, saying, I am God; I made the world, and men before they were in the flesh" (Ge 6:52, IV). Speaking to the elders of Kirtland, Ohio: "Ye were also in the beginning with the Father" (RLDS D&C 90:4b). "Man was also in the beginning with God. Intelligence, or the light of truth, was not created or made, neither indeed can be. . . . Every spirit of man was innocent in the beginning" (Ibid., 90:5a, 6b). D&C gives permission to marry and bear children, "that it [the earth] might be filled with the measure of man, according to his creation before the world was made" (Ibid., 49:3c).	The church is correct to deny these teachings. However, it does not reject the "revelations" themselves, either individually as sections of the D&C or collectively as a whole.

The Doctrine of Salvation

Position	Support	Orthodox Response
The initiative for our salvation originated with God. The sacrifice that saves us is "the sacrifice of self."	"It is God and God alone who offers sacrifice, and the sacrifice which God offers is the sacrifice of self. God's mercy and love are not purchased by anything Jesus or anyone else may have done. It is God who is merciful, it is God who is love" (*Exploring the Faith*, 1987, p. 43).	It is true that the initiative for our salvation originated with God, and the Father was not persuaded to forgive us (contrary to His will) by the death of Jesus. It is also true that Jesus' death on the cross should not be seen as a human effort to buy salvation from God, but rather as a part of God's own actions: "God was reconciling the world to himself in Christ" (2Co 5:19). Other aspects of RLDS thought are confusing because it is unclear whether the triune God or God the Father is in view. The Bible is equally clear that "we were reconciled to him [God the Father] through the death of his Son" (Ro 5:10). It is God the Son, Jesus Christ, who was the sacrifice; the RLDS phrase "sacrifice of self" is vague, not specifying the victim, the place, or the manner.

The Doctrine of Salvation (cont.)

Position	Support	Orthodox Response
Jesus did not die as a substitute for man, taking on Himself the punishment we deserved. His death did not appease an angry God.	"Some religionists have attempted to explain the atonement in a 'bookkeeping' kind of manner, using such terms as debts and indebtedness, redemption and payment. Some would make it appear that God was 'satisfied' by Jesus' 'substitution' for us, or by Jesus having utilized his 'moral influence' to persuade God to accept us once again. Any of these attempts to explain the Atonement fall short.... Nor was Jesus offered as a sacrifice to placate an angry God, or to substitute for us in our rightful punishment" (*Exploring the Faith,* 1987, pp. 42–43).	The language of indebtedness, redemption, and payment comes directly from the New Testament. Denying the vicarious, substitutionary death of Christ betrays a fatal misunderstanding of Jesus' atonement: "the wages of sin is death" (Ro 6:23), but the Son of Man came "to give his life as a ransom for many" (Mt 20:28). "You were bought at a price" (1Co 6:20; 7:23). Jesus "gave himself as a ransom for all men" (1Ti 2:6); "... the church of God, which he bought with his own blood" (Ac 20:28). False prophets deny "the sovereign Lord who bought them" (2Pe 2:1). Christ is worshiped with these words: "you were slain, and with your blood you purchased men for God" (Rev 5:9). "In him we have redemption through his blood, the forgiveness of sins, in accordance with the riches of God's grace" (Eph 1:7). We are literally Jesus' "purchased possession" (Eph 1:14 KJV).
The chief significance of the blood of Jesus is that it shows us our need to be pure and spotless before God.	"References to 'the lamb' and 'spilt blood' are sometimes puzzling and even repulsive to some. We need to keep in mind that Old Testament customs were not pagan rights [rites] offered to appease a God of wrath. The implications of such early sacrifices were that those who offered gifts to God should be without spot or blemish.... When Jesus himself replaces the sacrificial lamb, he demonstrates in the clearest possible way what it means to be without spot or blemish in one's life" (*Exploring the Faith,* 1987, p. 44).	The significance of the blood of Jesus is not primarily in what it *shows* us about our needs, but what it *provides* us before the throne. The Bible says that "without the shedding of blood there is no forgiveness" of sins (Heb 9:22) and that "it is the blood that maketh an atonement for the soul" (Lev 17:11 KJV). This principle is dramatically emphasized in Leviticus and restated clearly in the book of Hebrews. Every key verse in Hebrews relating to Jesus' blood is missing from the RLDS description. "He did not enter by means of the blood of goats and calves; but he entered the Most Holy Place once for all by his own blood, having obtained eternal redemption" (Heb 9:12).

The Doctrine of Salvation (cont.)

Position	Support	Orthodox Response
Most of humanity will be saved and enter one of the "three degrees of glory."	According to D&C, Jesus Christ "saves all the works of his hands, except those sons of perdition, who deny the Son after the Father has revealed him; wherefore he saves all except them" (RLDS D&C 76:4h-i). Since the "sons of perdition" are those who have "denied the Holy Spirit, after having received it" (76:4d), clearly a majority of humankind will be saved. *Celestial* glory is reserved for the obedient ones "who received the testimony of Jesus, and believed on his name, and were baptized... that by keeping the commandments, they might be washed and cleansed from all their sins, and receive the Holy Spirit" (76:5b-c). In this place, they receive "the fullness of the Father" (76:6b). The glory of the *terrestrial* kingdom is for those "who were blinded by the craftiness of men" (76:6d) and "were not valiant in the testimony of Jesus" (76:6g). In this place, they "receive of the presence of the Son, but not of the fullness of the Father" (76:6f). Finally, *telestial* glory is for those who "received not the gospel," including "liars, and sorcerers, and adulterers, and whoremongers, and whoever loves and makes a lie" (76:7a, b, o). After a period of punishment, they receive the ministry of the Holy Spirit, "but where God and Christ dwell they can not come" (76:7v).	Several passages of Scripture indicate that most of humanity will be lost, not redeemed. The primary text is Jesus' own words: "Enter through the narrow gate. For wide is the gate and broad is the road that leads to destruction, and many enter through it. But small is the gate and narow the road that leads to life, and only a few find it" (Mt 7:13–14). Elsewhere, Jesus was asked, "Lord, are only a few people going to be saved?" and He replied, "Make every effort to enter through the narrow door, because many, I tell you, will try to enter and will not be able to" (Lk 13:23–24). The rest of this passage shows that Jesus' answer was yes, few will be saved. Further, the Bible affirms that the world in general is under deception (1Jn 5:19; Rev 12:9) and that only through Jesus can people be saved (Jn 10:7–9; 14:6; Ac 4:12), while judgment will come on those who do not know God or Jesus Christ (2Th 1:8–9). Since God calls "many" to salvation, but only "few" are finally chosen (Mt 20:16; 22:14), there is adequate warrant to reject the RLDS claim. Finally, the Bible clearly states that liars, sorcerers, adulterers, and whoremongers who die in their sins will inherit the lake of fire (Rev 21:8), not "telestial glory." Ironically, another passage of the D&C affirms that people in these same categories will enter the lake of fire (D&C 63:5b).
Justification occurs because of the atonement of Christ accompanied by human obedience to God's initiative.	Under the Old Testament provisions, "Israel, then, could be considered righteous (or justified) because of the faithfulness of both God *and* the chosen people. The Apostle Paul used remarkably similar imagery in describing the sacrifice (Atonement) of Jesus Christ.... With the blood of Jesus Christ 'covering' the sins of the entire world, all of humanity would be offered the possibility of being considered righteous (or justified), this time because of God's faithfulness in sending the Only Begotten *and* the response of believing obedience by all people" (*Temple Foundations*, 1991, p. 70; emphasis in original). "Therefore ye are justified of faith and works, through grace, to the end the promise might be sure to all the seed " (Ro 4:16, IV).	This concept of justification is foreign to the New Testament. "We maintain that a man is justified by faith apart from observing the law" (Ro 3:28). This is restated in different ways: "God credits righteousness [justification] apart from works" (Ro 4:6). Our faith *appropriates* justification, which we receive immediately. The claim that the apostle Paul teaches that people are justified due to God's faithfulness *and* man's response is found nowhere in the biblical text. In fact, even the Inspired Version argues against this, for Joseph Smith's rendering of Romans 3:28 says, "Therefore we conclude that a man is justified by faith alone without the deeds of the law." Also, in verse 24 the IV says we are "justified only by this grace." Nevertheless, Joseph Smith did not understand the contradiction he

The Doctrine of Salvation (cont.)

Position	Support	Orthodox Response
...continued		was creating when he rewrote Romans 4:16 to say that man is justified "of faith and works." A careful study of Romans 3:19–5:11 and Galatians 2:15–3:14 discloses the error of this thinking.
Persons who have never heard the gospel of Christ will have an opportunity to receive it after death. Those who would have believed in Christ and followed Him, had they known of Him on earth, can receive it in the spirit world and will inherit celestial glory.	"Joseph Smith, Jr.... had a vision in which he saw the celestial kingdom. In his vision, he saw his parents and his brother, Alvin, who had died some twelve years previously. Joseph marveled that Alvin should have 'obtained an inheritance in that kingdom [since] he had departed this life before the Lord [had] restored the church and had not been baptized for the remission of sins.' Joseph heard the Lord say in the vision, "'All who have died without a knowledge of this gospel, who would have received it if they had been permitted to tarry, shall be heirs of the celestial kingdom of God; also all that shall die henceforth without a knowledge of it, who would have received it with all their hearts, shall be heirs of that kingdom.' "It was apparently clearly intended to be an eternal principle" (*Exploring the Faith*, 1987, p. 117). "... mortal death [does not] rob individuals of their opportunity to hear the gospel, to accept Jesus Christ, and to be the recipient of our Lord's saving and redeeming work.... Every soul has a chance—not a second chance, but a first chance, whether in this life or the life beyond—to hear the gospel without being denied that opportunity due to national or cultural or racial or religious bias" (Ibid., p. 118).	The vision being referred to took place in 1834, and it contradicts the information from the following "revelation" Joseph Smith claimed he received in 1832: "Verily, verily, I say unto you, They who believe not on your words, and are not baptized in water, in my name, for the remission of their sins, that they may receive the Holy Ghost, shall be damned, and shall not come into my Father's kingdom, where my Father and I am" (D&C 83:12a). It also contradicts D&C 76:6c, which says that those "who received not the testimony of Jesus in the flesh, but afterwards received it" when they heard the gospel in the spirit world, would inherit *terrestrial* (not celestial) glory. Moreover, it appears that the church has allowed one of Joseph Smith's visions, which was never added to the D&C by common consent of the church, to possess greater weight than other revelations that *are* in its canon of sacred, authoritative text.

The Doctrine of Salvation (cont.)

Position	Support	Orthodox Response
People can come to God through Jesus even if they don't know Jesus or are not Christians.	"Perhaps an important key to our understanding [of the unknowableness of Christ] comes with a saying of Jesus: 'I am the way, the truth, and the life; no man cometh unto the Father, but by me.... He that hath seen me hath seen the Father' (John 14:6, 9). This particular scripture has been much used in evangelism efforts, often with an understanding that the Christian—or Restoration—way is the *only* valid way to know God.... But if we accept the idea that 'not to know is to know,' then we must allow ourselves to be open to other interpretations.... When Jesus says he is 'the way,' is he saying his private path to God is the only way anyone can ever hope to get to heaven or experience salvation? Is he saying that he alone holds the secret formula to unlock the mysteries...? No. As A. M. Watts has written: "... 'When Jesus says "no one comes to the Father but by me," he is stating that ultimately no one comes to God except through God.... To affirm that God was in Christ reconciling the world to Godself is not ground for believing that people of other religious traditions are all wrong. To affirm such an arrogant principle is not the way to affirm Christ'" (*Temple Foundations,* 1991, pp. 142–43).	Not all RLDS members believe this error, but some do. The closer the church moves toward ecumenism, the more likely it is to promote this thinking. First, note that a self-contradictory statement, "not to know is to know," is used to cast doubt on the inspired words of Jesus, who is God incarnate. The idea of "knowing" and coming to Christ is interpreted in light of a pagan catch-phrase; rather, the pagan phrase should be interpreted in light of what Jesus has said. Second, observe the wording of John 14:6b: "No one comes to the Father except through me." The restrictive language is intentional. Jesus did not say, "All who come to the Father come through me," which is more compatible with inclusivism. Third, the New Testament teaching that in this age, faith in Jesus Christ is "the only way anyone can ever hope to get to heaven" does not rest on John 14:6 alone, but on many statements by Jesus and the apostles. It is also implicit in several biblical principles.

The Doctrine of Rewards and Punishment

Position	Support	Orthodox Response
Eventually all human society will become transformed to the obedience of God and Christ.	The community of Jesus' disciples "is committed to make the word of God a tangible reality in the midst of society. By this means they will leaven society itself until the day will come when 'the kingdoms of this world are become the kingdom of our Lord, and of his Christ' (Revelation 11:15). This is the end toward which history moves" (*Exploring the Faith,* 1987, pp. 156–57).	This statement is orthodox as long as we recall that this global transformation will not be fulfilled apart from the personal, literal return of Jesus Christ to earth (Ac 1:11; Rev 1:7; 19:15–17). Further, the same passage and book quoted by the RLDS, proclaiming the universal reign of Christ over the earth, also describes God's punitive and endless punishment of the wicked (Rev 11:18; 14:9–11; 21:8). These conditions are compatible with Jesus' universal reign of truth.

The Doctrine of Rewards and Punishment (cont.)

Position	Support	Orthodox Response
Certain RLDS teachings hint at universalism.	"God draws persons into the community based upon faith in Jesus Christ. This fellowship cannot be content until every person has been drawn into its circle of love and care for every concern of each one. It can never be at rest until humankind is truly 'one body' according to the eternal purpose of God" (*Presidential Papers*, 1979, p. 14).	Ordinarily, several of these statements can be accepted as within the range of orthodoxy. However, since the RLDS church does not address the doctrine of endless punishment for the lost (not even for Satan), and since it redefines the term "eternal judgment" so that it fails to refer to a future period of reward and punishment, it contains possible hints at universalism.
	"...the Body of Christ [is] God's universal community, into which all people are to be drawn" (Ibid., p. 15).	The Bible does state that Christ shall rule sovereignly over all creation (1Co 15:24–28; Rev 11:15), that every knee will one day bow to Christ (Php 2:9–11), and that everything will be put "under his feet" (Heb 2:5; see vv. 5–8). However, the Bible also recognizes that the subjugation and punishment of all rebels to His dominion——that is, Satan, the demons, and the unregenerate——are part of that sovereignty (Mt 25:41–46; Rev 19:19–20:3; 20:7–15). Nowhere does Scripture predict, require, or permit the conversion or repentance of anyone cast into hell or the lake of fire.
	"We believe in eternal judgment.... This judgment is exercised through persons as they are quickened by the Holy Spirit to comprehend the eternal implications of divine truth.... The principle of eternal judgment acknowledges that Christ is the judge of all human aspiration and achievement, and that he summons persons to express the truth in decision until all things are reconciled under God" (*Statement of Faith and Belief,* Item 18 "Eternal Judgment," p. 287).	The RLDS description of "eternal judgment" as a quality or type of judging, primarily exercised by people thinking with godly values, is unscriptural and weak. Although this term appears once in Hebrews 6:2, the Bible often refers to "judgment to come" (Ac 24:25), the "judgment" (Mt 12:42), the "day of judgment" (Mt 11:22; 12:36), the fiery "day of judgment and destruction" (2Pe 3:7), a coming "day of God's wrath, when his righteous judgment will be revealed" (Ro 2:5), and a time when "we will all stand before God's judgment seat" (Ro 14:10; see also 2Co 5:10). It is well-known that the word *judgment* is also translated *condemnation* or *damnation,* and many passages speak of eternal, unending condemnation or punishment for sinners.
	"But even the whole of creation anticipates the marvelous day when we shall all be redeemed, and answer the end of our creation. When that redemption comes, not only will all humankind have joy, but also the living forms which God has created" (*Exploring the Faith,* 1987, pp. 262–63).	

INTERESTING AND DISTINCTIVE BELIEFS

Position	Support	Orthodox Response
The classic "Restoration" views of universal apostasy and a necessary restoration of priesthood authority, the Restored Gospel, and the True Church of Christ—common to the Mormon (LDS) church—are being abandoned by the contemporary RLDS church.	"This quest [of God to bring mankind into His presence] has evolved... from Reformation to Restoration; and through the development of the Restoration from its separatist tendencies to the present insights that the Restoration is a process.... When we are honest about our own personal and corporate history, we realize that the apostasy and the Restoration were not events that happened one time in history but rather are processes continually at work among us" (*Presidential Papers*, 1979, p. 28). "It is not possible for us to say that one person or group is in apostasy and another is not" (*Exploring the Faith*, 1987, p. 147). "We assume that because we are the Church of Jesus Christ and have authority... no other authority to represent God exists outside our own communion. Such a view is not in harmony with our tradition" (Ibid., p. 149).	The RLDS recognition that there was no worldwide apostasy, as the LDS and the early RLDS churches claimed, is a welcome step. Jesus promised that the gates of Hades would never prevail against His church (Mt 16:18), assuring us of its continual (not intermittent) preservation. Further, Ephesians 3:21 says that the church glorifies Christ "throughout all generations, for ever and ever," which could not be the case if the church were absent or apostate for several centuries. Yet the RLDS church still views itself as Restorationist, "restoring" something that was allegedly lost to the church. Its former claim to exclusive priesthood authority now seems to be withdrawn, though the theological errors that allow for a human "Melchisedec" and "Aaronic" priesthood have never been publicly explained, exposed, or repudiated. These "priesthood offices" remain in the RLDS Church.
The church wishes to minimize doctrinal beliefs and special distinctives in favor of general Christian mission and outreach.	"Over and over again the cry is heard from church members to identify what is distinctive about the church. This concern is often raised in the context of defining doctrinal differences. Today, however, the church is faced with questions of purpose more than concerns about unique doctrines and structures of belief" (*Communities of Joy*, 1994, p. 16).	Minimizing doctrinal issues is understandable if a church is likely to be torn over theological conflicts. This is especially so when a church is in theological transition. However, training in sound doctrine is vital to the growth and discernment of Christian believers (1Ti 4:13; 2Ti 2:15; 4:2–3; Tit 1:9). If the RLDS leaders believe the church has erred in the past, it would be advisable to openly acknowledge this and take steps to formally repudiate past doctrinal errors.

15

Rosicrucianism

FACTS AND HISTORY

Facts	
Topic	*Current Facts*
Membership	Several organizations exist in the United States that adhere to the teachings of Rosicrucianism. The largest group, used in this chart as being representative of Rosicrucianism, is the Ancient and Mystical Order of the Rosae Crucis (AMORC), with headquarters in San Jose, California. In 1990 this order claimed more than 250,000 members worldwide (J. Gordon Melton, *Encyclopedia of American Religions,* p. 770). According to a 1994 AMORC pamphlet, the organization has members in over 100 countries (AMORC, p. 16). AMORC maintains that it is not a religion or a church, but rather a fraternity. Consequently, one must pay a one-time registration fee to join and quarterly membership dues thereafter. These dues vary from country to country.
Worship	There are no worship services of any kind in Rosicrucianism. Involvement consists of personal study through a "system of instruction and guidance for exploring the inner self and discovering the universal laws that govern all human endeavor" (AMORC, p. 3). Members often compare the order to a "university" that provides "several colleges of study, teachings structured to build upon each other, and degrees of attainment" (Ibid., p. 19). Each degree is composed of weekly lessons called monographs (6–8 pages long), which serve as the basis of home-study (Ibid., p. 21). Members are asked to spend "roughly one and a half hours of one evening each week" in the study of their monographs, which consist of ideas, experiments and exercises designed to help the member learn "how to *listen, recognize,* and *respond* to inner guidance" (Ibid., p. 12). Rosicrucianism, like Freemasonry, has Lodges. At a Lodge, members participate in "mystical convocations, lectures, meetings, conventions and other various activities" (Ibid., p. 25).
Publications	Several publications are produced by AMORC. *The Rosicrucian Digest,* AMORC's official publication, is sent free to members. In 1991, it had a circulation of 40,000. It can be found in various public libraries. *On Park,* a newsletter that contains up-to-date information concerning the staff and activities of Rosicrucian Park (the San Jose headquarters), is also sent free to members. For a nominal charge members may subscribe to *Rosicrucian Forum,* "an open question and answer periodical dealing with current topics of interest from around the world, as well as subject matter from Rosicrucian teachings" (AMORC, p. 26). This publication had a circulation of 10,700 as of 1991. A selection of books, audio cassettes, video tapes, and gifts are also available.
General statement of beliefs	Rosicrucianism is a complex blending of doctrines taken from "the diverse mystical traditions of ancient Greece, China, India and Persia" (AMORC, p. 15). As such, it is an eclectic religious system that contradicts every essential tenet of Christianity.

History

Topic	History
H. Spencer Lewis 1915–1939 **Ralph M. Lewis 1939–1987** **Gary L. Stewart 1987–1990** **Christian Bernard 1990–present**	The founder of the Ancient and Mystical Order of the Rosae Crucis (AMORC) was H. Spencer Lewis. The order was built on a tradition of Rosicrucianism that can be traced organizationally to the Renaissance era and that was based on the study and dissemination of esoteric doctrines connected with the ancient Gnostic-oriented mystery religions. As early as 1909 attempts were made to found the organization in America as Lewis met with the French members of the International Rosicrucian Council in Toulouse. After going through their rituals of initiation, he returned to America and began holding the first regular meetings of the Society in New York City in 1915. This particular group rose in ascendancy above other groups wishing to use the name "Rosicrucian" on the strength of massive advertising campaigns throughout the nation and the world. These campaigns enabled the group to become firmly entrenched in the minds of the general public as the main Rosicrucian body. Lewis borrowed heavily from other occult groups and authors, as did other Rosicrucian writers. Vast portions of the apocryphal and highly imaginative *Aquarian Gospel of Jesus Christ* turned up (sometimes verbatim) in Levi Dowling's book *Mystic Life of Christ*. The Ordo Templis Orientis (O.T.O.), at one time headed by notorious black magician and sometime Satanist Aleister Crowley, was also included as a source for the symbols and definitions employed by AMORC. An example of this is the very symbol that gives AMORC its name: the Rose Cross. It was taken from *Equinox III,* a periodical of Crowley's. A major rift, which continues today, began with Lewis's conflict with the older Fraternitas Rosae Crucis, which in 1928 challenged Lewis and AMORC's right to use the name "Rosicrucian." Lewis retaliated with a personal attack on the validity of credentials held by R. Swinburne Clymer, accusing him of receiving his M.D. from a diploma mill. The Rosicrucians of San Jose continue to be in conflict with the Rosicrucians of Oceanside, California, over who properly owns or deserves the appellation "Rosicrucian." The Rosicrucians are in a sense naturalistic as opposed to being truly supernatural in their worldview. They believe in a closed system of immutable laws that was developed and put into place by their god. Their god is much more like the god of the deists than the God of the Bible. They would see themselves as students and practitioners of divine laws or mysteries that, when mastered, enable them to secure internal and external benefits such as peace of mind, happiness, and material wealth. These benefits derive from imaging, which involves using one's imagination to draw or attract these things to the student. Lessons containing various rituals, experiments, and techniques are sent through the mail. If these are followed and confidentiality is maintained, then the results are said to follow. The movement claims a historical continuity from the days of the ancient Pharaohs, specifically, Thutmosis III, who founded a school of philosophy in 1489 B.C. Amenhotep IV of Egypt and Solomon are said to be two other early people involved with Rosicrucianism. Other historical figures claimed by AMORC include Isaac Newton, Sir Francis Bacon, Benjamin Franklin, and Rene Descartes. The fraternity supposedly works on 180-year cycles, the most recent of which began in 1909. The top position in AMORC is called the Grand Emperor, and this position was held by Spencer Lewis's son, Ralph M. Lewis, from 1939 to 1987. The Grand Emperor, as the head of the Grand Lodge, has jurisdiction over North America, Africa, the British Commonwealth, and the following nations of Europe: France, Germany, Switzerland, and Sweden. After Ralph Lewis died, Gary L. Stewart became the Grand Emperor. Three years later he was removed from office by the order's board amid charges of misconduct. A man named Christian Bernard succeeded Stewart as Grand Emperor.

THEOLOGY

The Doctrine of Revelation		
Position	*Support*	*Orthodox Response*
"Truth" is obtainable solely through the teachings found in Rosicrucianism. This is not to say that the ultimate sources of revelational "truths" are contained in Rosicrucian teachings themselves, although many of them are to be found there.	"Through our teachings you will gain specific knowledge of metaphysics, mysticism, philosophy, psychology, parapsychology and science not taught by conventional educational systems or traditional religions. This profound wisdom, carefully preserved by mystery schools for centuries, is transmitted today through the Rosicrucian Order" (AMORC, p. 3).	To trust revelations from the spirit world in the form of other scriptures is dangerous, given the nature of reality posited by the Bible. The Scriptures reveal the existence of supernatural, malevolent beings (fallen angels or demons) capable of swaying the thoughts and actions of human beings through oppression if not possession. See the account of King Saul in 1 Samuel 16; also see the accounts of God's permitting a "lying spirit" to deceive an evil king's prophets (1Ki 22) and the Gerasene demoniac (Mk 5). This means that we cannot put any ultimate spiritual confidence in ourselves, the Rosicrucian's "Great White Brotherhood," or spirits from the "astral plane."
The greater goal of Rosicrucianism is to help the members look within for the answers to life's questions. Rosicrucianism's main goal is to attune individuals to the "inner" self, or higher consciousness, from which all truth may be obtained. Rosicrucianism teaches that all people are psychic and can bring these abilities to the surface. These psychic abilities in turn provide revelations of "truth." Whatever someone eventually "knows" or "feels" is what is true.	"The answers [to life's questions] have been and always will be within you.... The key to successfully meeting these challenges [of life] and the purpose of the Rosicrucian teachings is to learn how to find the answers within yourself. Inspiration, energy, and even specific answers to all challenges of life are available when one learns the proper techniques" (AMORC, p. 5). "[E]veryone has psychic faculties.... It is only ignorance, prejudice, and superstition that keep these natural functions in the dark. Yet, once awakened through understanding, and **practiced** through the experiments in the Rosicrucian teachings, your psychic faculties can be one of the greatest powers within you" (Ibid., p. 11). "The Rosicrucian teachings help you to accomplish this [gaining peace] through numerous exercises and experiments designed to discipline your five physical senses and awaken the deeper psychic sense, often left dormant within you" (Ibid., p. 10).	In contrast to the the claim that the answers to life's questions lie within us, Scripture says, "The heart is deceitful above all things and beyond cure" (Jer 17:9). Further on mankind's self-deception: "The Lord saw how great man's wickedness on the earth had become, and that every inclination of the thoughts of his heart was only evil all the time" (Ge 6:5). To believe that truth is not absolute and universally binding on all has disastrous consequences. What happens if the "truth" that individuals find within themselves contradicts objective reality around them? If it does and they consistently act out their "reality" oblivious to everyone around them, they will eventually become antisocial or appear insane.
The Bible is not the Word of God.	"Do the Rosicrucians accept the Bible as the 'Word of God' from cover to cover? Answer: Certainly not, and more particularly not in the extremely narrow interpretation of some people who think that the book we now have with us is the only genuine one ever given to humanity" (Max Heindel, *The Rosicrucian Philosophy in Questions and Answers*, pp. 154–55).	Second Timothy 3:16 states that "all Scripture is God-breathed" (NIV) or "inspired by God" (NASB).

The Doctrine of Revelation (cont.)

Position	Support	Orthodox Response
The Bible is at best one of many holy books given to humanity, and even then it has been intentionally edited and changed.	"At most, it [the Bible] could only be one of the *books* of God, for there are many other sacred writings which have a claim to recognition" (Max Heindel, *The Rosicrucian Philosophy in Questions and Answers*, p. 155). "A number of books [originally in the Bible] were thrown aside as apocryphal, and altogether words were wrenched out of their original meaning to conform to the superstition of the age" (Ibid.).	On what basis and authority do the Rosicrucians claim that the Bible is not the only Word of God? To say that there are other books of God is to be oblivious to the historical inaccuracies and false statements found in many of the supposed "holy texts" such as the Koran and the Book of Mormon. Other so-called holy texts are based on fanciful speculation, assertions, and conjecture rather than objective history. The Bible proves its trustworthiness through its predictive nature and its objective relationship to known data regarding archaeology and cultural and physical anthropology.
Writers of the Bible transcribed only what they could have known as true for the time in which they lived. Today a new Bible is needed.	"... the various persons who wrote the Bible and who were thus prophets and seers, but only in so far as that was possible at their time and age. A new era will require a new Bible, a new word" (Max Heindel, *The Rosicrucian Philosophy in Questions and Answers*, p. 157).	Orthodox Chrisianity asserts that the Bible represents the eternal Word of God and as such it will be relevant to all generations. There is never a need for an amended or expanded version of the Bible. The apocryphal literature and other so-called biblical writings were rejected first by the rabbinical tradition and then by the early church fathers because they lacked coherence with the inspired writings that preceded them. The New Testament requires that all writings be the words of Christ or the apostles, who were intimately acquainted with Him. The Bible condemns occult activity in Deuteronomy 18. See also 29:29, which states that "the secret things belong to the LORD our God, but the things revealed belong to us and to our children forever." Therefore the Rosicrucian's contention that only those who are in the occult can rightly interpret the Bible is specious and spiritually dangerous. Moreover, God has called occultic things abominable and detestable. Finally, to say that important spiritual truths have been withheld from us by our Creator and are not present in His Word, the Bible, is to impugn the character of God as being unloving and capricious. To say that the Rosicrucians have "truths" missed by all other ancient records is arrogant and historically suspect. The Bible states that God has both defined and revealed truth. As Creator, He has the sole right to establish both absolute truth and an objective standard to judge all "truth" claims, especially those pertaining to things spiritual. Jesus Christ said of God the Father, "Your word is truth" (Jn 17:17).
Although the Bible is severly marred and is not divine, it still contains a great deal of truth. But that truth is visible only to those in the occult who can rightly interpret the Bible's symbolism and find its esoteric truths.	"We do not contend for the Divinity of this Book [the Bible] or hold that it is the Word of God from cover to cover; we recognize the fact that it is a poor translation of the originals and that there are many interpolations which have been inserted at different times to support various ideas, but, nevertheless, the very fact that so much truth has been massed into such a small compass is a source of constant wonder to the occultist, who knows what that Book really is and has the key to its meaning" (Max Heindel, *The Rosicrucian Philosophy in Questions and Answers*, p. 149). "[I]n the Bible the pearls of occult truth are hidden in what are often hideous garments. The occultist who has fitted himself to possess these pearls has received the key, and sees them plainly" (Ibid., p. 156).	
Rosicrucianism alone holds the key to understanding the nature of God.	**"The teaching of Rosicrucianism is the Key that the Church has lost.** .... The Church has muddled the mind of Man for ages" (KHEI, *Rosicrucian Fundamentals*, pp. 147–48).	

The Doctrine of God—*The Trinity*

Position	Support	Orthodox Response
There exists a Universal Substance that is called Spirit. It is the pool from which everything is formed. Aeons ago, this cosmic pool somehow formed the Absolute, also known as the Creator essence from which everything else, including man, sprang. Actual personal contact with the Absolute is impossible. The Absolute produced the Supreme Being in the form of Power, Word, and Motion. This Supreme Being is known as the Great Architect of the Universe (G.A.O.T.U.).	"Therefore Spirit is the UNIVERSAL SUBSTANCE. It is the Cosmic Ocean in which all things from Universes and Solar systems to Man are but its crystallized forms.... As the ABSOLUTE exists, it must be Spirit.... The ABSOLUTE is the One Existent, beyond exact comprehension, impossible of tangible manifestation to mortals, conceived as... ROOT OF EXISTENCE.... From the ABSOLUTE proceeded the Supreme Being at the beginning of the Day of Cosmic Manifestation, under the Threefold Aspects of—Power, Word, Motion.... This SUPREME BEING is the one known... as the 'GREAT ARCHITECT OF THE UNIVERSE'" (KHEI, *Rosicrucian Fundamentals*, pp. 6–7).	Genesis 1 and John 1 both tell us that in the beginning God alone was in existence. Also see Psalm 90:2. God was not a "produced" entity. He is the ultimate Producer, as these Scriptures also indicate. The Christian position is that God created the universe *ex nihilo*, or from nothing. The Creator is unique, separate, and distinct from His creation (Isa 45:5, 18, 22).
From the G.A.O.T.U. proceed seven "Great Logoi," which together inhabit what is called the First Cosmic Region. The "Great Logoi" then diffused into "Hierarchies" and spread throughout six more cosmic regions. In the highest realm, the Seventh Cosmic Region, reside the Gods of the various solar systems. The God of Earth also dwells there. This God, like all other gods, expresses itself in triune aspect—will, wisdom, and activity.	"From the Supreme Being proceed what are known as the Seven Great Logoi. The Supreme Being and the Seven Great Logoi occupy what is known as the First Cosmic Region.... In the First Cosmic Region the Seven Great Logoi bring into manifestation and direct what are known as 'HIERARCHIES' which diffuse and differentiate in sevenfold progression through the succeeding Regions.... We find in the seventh Cosmic Region, in its highest sub-division, the Gods of the various Solar Systems... [including] the God of our own Solar System.... Our God, as well as the Gods of all other solar systems, expresses in triune aspect—WILL, WISDOM AND ACTIVITY" (KHEI, *Rosicrucian Fundamentals*, pp. 7–8).	Isaiah 44:24 states, "This is what the LORD says—your Redeemer, who formed you in the womb: I am the LORD, who has made all things, who alone stretched out the heavens, who spread out the earth by myself." "Before me no god was formed, nor will there be one after me" (Isa 43:10). "I am the first and I am the last; apart from me there is no God" (Isa 44:6). "You are my witnesses. Is there any God besides me? No, there is no other Rock; I know not one" (Isa 44:8). The Rosicrucian notion of plural "Gods of the various Solar Systems" is an affront to the one true God of the Bible.

The Doctrine of God—*The Trinity (cont.)*

Position	Support	Orthodox Response
There is only one soul that exists—God—and each of us has a portion of this soul residing within our physical bodies. We are not individuals, but rather a part of the divine soul that is manifested outwardly through individual bodies and the various things each of us learns during our earthly existence.	"The Rosicrucians believe and have always believed that there is but one soul in the universe, and that is the universal soul or the universal consciousness of God. . . . a segment, or essence, of that universal soul resides in each being that possesses soul. And this essence is never separated from the universal soul or is never an entity in such a sense as to make it independent and individual. The soul expression of each person. . . through the medium of the physical body and through the channel of our education and comprehension of things, may be quite different and thereby give us those characteristics or traits of personality which we interpret as individuality" (H. Spencer Lewis, *Rosicrucian Questions and Answers with Complete History*, p. 237).	Genesis 1 and John 1 both tell us that in the beginning God alone was in existence. Also see Psalm 90:2. God was not a "produced" entity. He is the ultimate Producer, as these Scriptures also indicate. The Christian position is that God created the universe *ex nihilo*, or from nothing. The Creator is unique, separate, and distinct from His creation (Nu 23:19; Isa 15:29; 55:8; 45:5, 18, 22). Also, Genesis tells us that God breathed the breath of life into Adam and at that point man became a living soul. This clearly shows that the soul of man is distinct and separate from the Creator who preceded him. The Bible also portrays God as *owning* all souls, not *being* all souls (Eze 18:4). The soul of man is *given* by God through His role as Creator (Ecc 12:7).
"God" is one with everything that is. What we see, including ourselves, are manifestations of the different vibrations of the same "Spirit."	"Yet God, the Initiates and ourselves are all of one Substance, *undivided, indivisible,* but differentiated in vibrational status" (KHEI, *Rosicrucian Fundamentals*, p. 155).	To say that we are a part of God contradicts God's self-revelation—that He is separate and distinct (transcendent) from His creation (Isa 15:29; 55:8; Nu 23:19). The Bible views us as being interconnected because God sustains His creation (see Col 1:17). When God ultimately judges the human race at the Great White Throne of Judgment (Rev 20), millions of human souls will be sent to eternal punishment in the lake of fire. Therefore, to say that all souls are part of God is to have God damning Himself. God did pronounce judgment on Himself once—at Calvary, where He became the substitutionary atonement for souls that were not Him.
The Father, Son, and Holy Ghost are three differentiated forms of the one "Spirit" that evolved through a period of time (Saturn, Sun, and Moon respectively) in ancient history and then progressed onward to a higher state of existence.	"In the stream of Virgin Spirits [a mode of the Universal Principle of Life] differentiated from the Body of God and entering the dip into Matter. . . those who constituted the Humanity of the Saturn Period are now the LORDS OF MIND, and THE HIGHEST INITIATE OF THAT PERIOD is the lofty Being we term the FATHER. . . . the HIGHEST INITIATE OF THE SUN PERIOD IS 'THE SON' or 'CHRIST'. . . . the same stream continued through the Moon Period. . . . its HIGHEST INITIATE WAS THE HOLY SPIRIT—JEHOVAH as He was called when known as the Race Deity of the Hebrews" (KHEI, *Rosicrucian Fundamentals*, p. 149).	The Christian teaching is that God exists as three co-equal, co-eternal, perfect Persons within one infinite, omnipotent, omnipresent, and omniscient being. To say that the Father, the Son, and the Holy Spirit were once human or "material" in their essence is to deny the Christian doctrine of the triunity and immutability of the Godhead. To relate growth in the Father, Son, and Holy Spirit to various periods of time denoted by astrological symbols is blasphemous. To call them initiates as though they ever had need of some sort of perfection or evolution within their being is also blasphemous. "Jesus Christ is the same yesterday and today and forever" (Heb 13:8). "I the LORD do not change" (Mal 3:6).

The Doctrine of God—*The Trinity (cont.)*

Position	Support	Orthodox Response
God is universal mind, intelligence, and infinite power that can be accessed from within man himself. God is not a transcendent Person, but rather an impersonal force of intelligence, external and internal to the individual human, that can be tapped into through meditation and ritual. It is not the personal, all-mighty objective God of the Bible who manifested himself fully in Jesus Christ.	"To Rosicrucians, there is but one God, ever living, ever present, without limiting attributes or definite form or manifestation—it is the God of our Hearts, a phrase found throughout our ritual and meditation practices. The God which we conceive, of which we can be conscious, sooner or later manifests in that strange intimacy within us. In ancient rituals we find this as part of the Rosicrucian pledge: 'Man is God and Son of God, and there is no other God but Man.' But this has a mystical meaning and is not to be taken literally. The Rosicrucian concept of God is essentially a universal mind, intelligence and infinite power. The concept is not dogmatic. The Rosicrucians expound the principle that God is wholly a subjective experience and thus a personal interpretation. Consequently, the Rosicrucian refers to the 'God of My Heart'" (*Rosicrucian Manual*, 17th ed., 1963, p. 170)	The God of the Bible, in contrast to the "God" of Rosicrucianism, has self-consciousness (Ex 3:14; Isa 45:5; 1Co 2:10) and self-determination (Job 23:13; Ro 9:11; Eph 1:9; Heb 6:17). He has revealed Himself to mankind through direct intervention into human history. He has revealed Himself through numerous theophanies as recorded in the Old Testament, through the predictive words of His prophets, and finally through the incarnation of the Second Person of the Triune God in Jesus of Nazareth (1Ti 3:16). Human subjective experience is to be evaluated by His objective, written revelation (2Ti 3:16–17; Jn 17:17). Contrary to Rosicrucian doctrine, actual, personal contact with God is indeed possible, for He has chosen to make it so (Jn 14:9; Ex 33:11). Isaiah 44:24 states, "This is what the LORD says—your Redeemer, who formed you in the womb: I am the LORD, who has made all things, who alone stretched out the heavens, who spread out the earth by myself." Isaiah 43:10 states further "Before me no god was formed, nor will there be one after me." Isaiah 44:6, 8 say, "I am the first and I am the last; apart from me there is no God.... You are my witnesses. Is there any God besides me? No, there is no other Rock; I know not one." The Rosicrucian notion of "Gods of the various Solar Systems" is an affront to the one true God of the Bible.

The Doctrine of Jesus Christ—*The Deity of Christ*

Position	Support	Orthodox Response
Jesus was not the Son of God.	"In studying this Trinity, first let it be clearly understood that the word 'Son' does not mean Jesus.... at that Baptism [by John] Jesus became Jesus the Christ " (KHEI, *Rosicrucian Fundamentals*, p. 149, 152).	Jesus was (and is) indeed the Second Person of the Triune God, the Logos, who was called the Son of God because He is the only begotten of the Father. It was because of the Incarnation that He was called the Son of God (see Lk 1:35).

The Doctrine of Jesus Christ—*The Humanity of Christ*

Position	Support	Orthodox Response
Jesus Christ was not born miraculously of a virgin.	"Jesus, highly advanced as he was... had a purely natural birth, with natural parents, Mary and Joseph" (KHEI, *Rosicrucian Fundamentals*, p. 151).	Jesus was born of a virgin named Miriam or Mary in the English (see Isa 7:14 and Mt 1:23).
The soul essence of Jesus had been incarnated several times prior to his birth as Jesus of Nazareth. Because of his advanced state, he was able to be used by "the Christ."	"This Man Jesus had been known to ancient history by many names throughout many previous incarnations in each of which He had advanced to such a point that in the incarnation by the name of Jesus He had beome so highly spiritualized that His physical, etheric, and astral vehicles could be utilized by... the CHRIST... for its work upon the Earth" (KHEI, *Rosicrucian Fundamentals*, p. 151).	The Rosicrucians show a dismal understanding of the word "Christ" and its origins. It is a title coming from the Greek *Kristos*, which is the word used for the Hebrew *Moshiach*, in English translated Messiah or Christ. "Messiah" means "anointed one" and connotes the meaning of being specially set apart by God for a specific purpose. Jesus didn't *become* the Christ or Messiah, but in His humanity *was* the Christ or Messiah from the moment of His conception in Mary's womb. Jesus was anointed for His purpose "from the creation of the world" (Rev 13:8).
Christ did not come to die for sins, but to be a vehicle for the "Christ" and serve as an impetus for all humanity. He bridged the gap between the physical world and God.	"Christ, when He took the vital body and the dense body of Jesus, was thus furnished with a complete chain of vehicles bridging the gap between the World of Life Spirit and the dense Physical World.... He [Jesus] submitted gladly, that his brother humanity might receive the gigantic impetus which was given to its development by the mysterious sacrifice on Golgotha" (Max Heindel, *The Rosicrucian Cosmo-Conception*, pp. 381–82).	In Matthew 1:20, an angel of the Lord appeared to Joseph and said, "Joseph son of David, do not be afraid to take Mary home as your wife, because what is conceived in her is from the Holy Spirit. She will give birth to a son, and you are to give him the name Jesus, because he will save his people from their sins." The salvation of His people occurred when that same person died some 33 years later on the cross at Calvary. First Thessalonians 4:14 states, "We believe that Jesus died and rose again and so we believe that God will bring with Jesus those who have fallen asleep in him." After His resurrection from the dead, which showed God's approval of His sacrifice and role as Savior, Jesus departed from His disciples on the Mount of Olives. As on prior occasions, angelic voices gave the testimony of heaven regarding the continuity of the person of the Savior: "Men of Galilee,... why do you stand here looking into the sky? This same Jesus, who has been taken from you into heaven, will come back in the same way you have seen him go into heaven" (Ac 1:11). It was Jesus who was announced to Joseph, Jesus who died on the cross and was raised from the dead as the Savior, and Jesus who departed with an angelic prophecy of His return. None of these Scriptures refers to Him as a separate personage known as "the Christ." Jesus clearly identified His divinity and His unique role as Messiah throughout the Gospels. It is presumptuous of the Rosicrucians to put such an imaginary spin on the baptism of Christ and His eternal, divine nature. Indeed, they fail the apostle Paul's remonstrance, "Do not go beyond what is written" (1Co 4:6).
Jesus was not the Christ. "The Christ," a separate entity, entered Jesus' body, which Jesus vacated at his baptism. "The Christ" left Jesus at the crucifixion.	"The Christ spirit which entered the body of Jesus when Jesus himself vacated it, was a ray from the cosmic Christ" (Max Heindel, *The Rosicrucian Philosophy in Questions and Answers*, p. 181). "Jesus and Jesus Christ... are thus two entirely distinct and separate entities or Egos" (KHEI, *Rosicrucian Fundamentals*, p. 154). "The Christos... occupied the Vehicles of the Man Jesus, until the Crucifixion of the latter on Golgotha.... [H]e cried out with a loud voice AND GAVE UP THE GHOST, according to St. Mark xv-37.... In John xix-30 we are told that 'he bowed his head and GAVE UP THE GHOST' (the Christos)" (Ibid., p. 152).	

The Doctrine of Jesus Christ — *The Resurrection of Christ*

Position	Support	Orthodox Response
Everyone actually has three bodies with which they operate in the various realms: (1) the "dense" [physical] body, to operate in the physical world; (2) the "vital" [invisible] body, to operate in the etheric, or spiritual plane; and (3) the "desire" body, to operate in the realm of emotion. All three of these bodies that belonged to the man Jesus were taken over by "the Christ."	"In order to function in the dense Physical World it is necessary to have a dense body.... we must have a vital body before we can express life, grow, or externalize the other qualities peculiar to the Etheric Region" (Max Heindel, *The Rosicrucian Cosmo-Conception*, p. 57).	The Christian Church has held two differing views on the nature of man: trichotomous and dichotomous. The former holds that there are two immaterial parts to man, the latter that there is only one. Both assert the basic dichotomy of the material part of man (Greek: *soma*) and the immaterial (Greek: *psyche, pneuma,* Hebrew: *ruach*). Trichotomists point to the mention of "spirit" and "soul" in the same sentence, as in Hebrews 4:12 and 1 Thessalonians 5:23. Dichotomists point out that "soul" and "spirit" are used interchangeably in many passages and that "souls" are seen in heaven. Neither group would liken what they teach to the Rosicrucian view that there are three distinct bodies given to everyone that operate on different planes of existence. The orthodox position is one of a total enmeshing or merging of the immaterial and material natures so as to be considered indistinguishable until the time a person dies.
The exact nature of who or what visited the disciples is difficult to determine in Rosicrucian writings. At one point it is suggested that after the dense body was destroyed, "the Christ," not Jesus, appeared to the disciples in a vital body. The same source, however, states that it was Jesus who reacquired his vital body and taught the disciples the truths that "the Christ" had left behind.	"After the destruction of the dense body, Christ appeared among His disciples in the vital body, in which He functioned for some time. The vital body is the vehicle which He will use when He appears again, for He will never take another dense body" (Max Heindel, *The Rosicrucian Cosmo-Conception*, p. 381). "Upon the death of the dense body of Christ Jesus, the seedatom was returned to the original owner, Jesus of Nazareth, who for some time afterward, while functioning in a vital body which he had gathered temporarily, taught the nucleus of the new faith which Christ had left behind" (Ibid., pp. 408–9).	It is certain that the resurrected body of Jesus was not basically spiritual in nature, because He told Thomas to touch Him and see that "a ghost does not have flesh and bones, as you see I have" (Lk 24:39). The body of Jesus was able to eat fish and engage in normal human activities such as talking and walking—activities that require a physical body at least similar to if not exactly like the bodies we have at present.

The Doctrine of the Holy Spirit

Position	Support	Orthodox Response
The Holy Spirit is called Jehovah, but this is not the Jehovah that Christians recognize. The Rosicrucian Jehovah is the highest evolved angel that proceeded from something called Virgin Spirits, which are supposedly embodiments of the Universal Life Principle that sprang from God.	". . . the same Stream [of Virgin Spirits] continued through the Moon Period places its evolved Humanity as what are now termed ANGELS, and its HIGHEST INITIATE WAS THE HOLY SPIRIT—JEHOVAH as He was called when known as the Race Deity of the Hebrews" (KHEI, *Rosicrucian Fundamentals*, p. 149).	The Holy Spirit is the Third Person of the Triune God and therefore holds all the attributes of deity. As such, He is not an angelic being, for He would be a created being, a mere creature, if He were.
The affairs of this life are governed by a group of "persons," some of whom are incarnated in physical bodies and others of whom are on the "cosmic plane" awaiting incarnation. This group is known as either the Great White Brotherhood or the Great White Lodge. The members of this group are given attributes of deity such as omniscience and infallibility. While never assembling all together as a tribunal, they nevertheless communicate their judgments and decisions on a psychic level through some form of telepathy.	"The Great White Brotherhood and The Great White Lodge have no visible organization. They never come together in one united session; their members are never assembled in one meeting; they have no Temple known by their names; and they have no earthly rituals, physical organization laws, or earthly form as a Brotherhood or Lodge. That is why it is often said, in mystical writings, that the real Rosicrucian Brotherhood is an invisible organization" (*Rosicrucian Manual*, AMORC, p. 148). "For the Masters of The Great White Lodge always know what you will do in the future as well as what you have done in the past, and they would not initiate anyone who would be capable of falling from grace. If the Great Masters did not have such knowledge, they would not be infallible in their judgment, and if they were not infallible in Cosmic knowledge, they would not be the Great Masters" (Ibid., p. 149).	God alone is omniscient. Other beings, human or angelic, do not share the glory and attributes of the Creator. "I am the LORD; that is my name! I will not give my glory to another or my praise to idols" (Isa 42:8). One of the glories of God is His omniscience, found in such Scriptures as Acts 15:18 and Psalm 139:16. The fact that God alone is all-knowing is clearly demonstrated through Jesus' words about His second coming: "No one knows about that day or hour, not even the angles in heaven, nor the Son, but only the Father" (Mt 24:36).

The Doctrine of Man and Sin

Position	Support	Orthodox Response
Everyone existed prior to being born on earth.	*"Every one of us is an individual spirit, which existed before the bodies we call races and will exist after they have ceased to be"* (Max Heindel, *The Rosicrucian Philosophy in Questions and Answers*, p. 195).	The Bible does not teach pre-existence of the soul. First Corinthians 15:46–47 states, "The spiritual did not come first, but the natural, and after that the spiritual. The first man was of the dust of the earth." Genesis 2:7 says, "The LORD God formed the man from the dust of the ground and breathed into his nostrils the breath of life, and the man became a living being." God first formed the body out of the clay, then breathed life into the body, which became a living soul (*nephesh* in Hebrew, *pneuma* in Greek). There is no reason to believe the process was altered for all subsequent men, the only difference being the physical forming of the body in the womb. Zechariah 12:1 sheds further light on this subject: "This is the word of the LORD concerning Israel. The LORD, who stretches out the heavens, who lays the foundation of the earth, and who forms the spirit of man within him. . . ." This tells us that the spirit is formed within a person but does not exist until the person's physical shell is formed to house it.
Everything in reality is "spirit." What we see is spirit substance crystalized. Since God and man are from the same substance, man and God are actually of the same nature.	"Rosicrucians teach that MATTER is the external manifestation of an internal or invisible 'PRINCIPLE.' That 'Principle' is SPIRIT. . . . MATTER may be termed the external manifestation of SPIRIT substance, in other words, CRYSTALLIZED SPIRIT. . . . The ABSOLUTE and Man, both being spirit, are therefore of the same substance. . . . Man is thus Divinity incarnated in Humanity" (KHEI, *Rosicrucian Fundamentals*, pp. 5–6).	The God of the Bible makes it plain that He is transcendent and separate from His creation. "As the heavens are higher than the earth, so are my ways higher than your ways and my thoughts than your thoughts" (Isa 55:9). "I am the LORD, who has made all things, who alone stretched out the heavens" (Isa 44:24). God, being Himself uncreated, created all things and existed before them. He is eternally an infinite, unmade, uncreated Being; humans will forever be made of created infinite substance.
Man is divine by nature. However, this truth has been forgotten. Rosicrucianism is designed to help man rediscover this truth.	"[T]he Rosicrucian Order is in existence today and has been for centuries, offering people a way to realize their own infinitely powerful and divine nature" (*AMORC*, p. 7).	The Rosicrucians hold to a form of monism and pantheism in that they believe man is God and all is made up of one divine substance. To say that "all is god" is equivalent to saying that "everything is important." If all things are equal or on the same level, it would be just as true to say that "nothing is god" or that "nothing is important." The God of the Bible is a unique, nonanalogous being, separate and distinct from His creation. Isaiah 46:9 says, "I am God, and there is none like me." Exodus 9:14 states, "This time I will send the full force of my plagues against you, . . . so you may know that there is no one like me in all the earth."

The Doctrine of Salvation

Position	Support	Orthodox Response
The Astral World, also known as Purgatory, is a place where one goes between incarnations. In the Astral World one is purged of unnecessary earthly desires.	"Here in the Astral World EVERY HUMAN BEING HAS TO GO THROUGH AN INDIVIDUAL PERGATORY. This purgative state or condition lasts until the individual has learned fully the illusion of desire" (KHEI, *Rosicrucian Fundamentals,* p. 95).	Because Jesus paid for all of our sins, there is no need for purgatory. Nothing can be added to the finished work of Christ on the cross. On the cross He proclaimed *tetelestai*—"it is finished!"—which in the ancient Roman world was used as a statement on bills of lading meaning "paid in full." To suggest that we can add anything to our salvation by somehow suffering or being purged of desire is an ascetic Greek concept not found in the Bible.
Reincarnation is a true doctrine that was actually taught by Jesus the Christ.	"Reincarnation solves the problem of Life's apparent injustices and inequalities.... Reincarnation—IS a FACT in Nature... IS taught by Jesus and the Bible... IS the truth with the greatest number of adherents... IS NOT antagonistic to the teachings of ANY TRUE Church" (KHEI, *Rosicrucian Fundamentals,* pp. 107, 108–9). "Reincarnation IS taught, not by the Church, although the early Christian Fathers DID teach it as evidenced by their writings, but by JESUS and the BIBLE.... In Matthew xvii-12, 13, Jesus distinctly states the identity of John the Baptist as the reincarnate Elias" (Ibid., p. 105).	It is untenable to assert that Elijah could be reincarnated, because he never died! Elijah was caught up to heaven while still existing in his physical body (see 2Ki 2:11). For reincarnation to be the meaning behind the words of Christ concerning Elijah and John, Elijah would have had to been absent from his physical body and reincarnated into the physical body of John the Baptist. This is inconsistent with the biblical text. Josephus wrote in his works that the Jews of his day expected Elijah to descend to earth in the same physical body in which he was taken to heaven. Luke 1:17 states that John the Baptist came in the "spirit and power of Elijah," and this is the key to understanding what Jesus meant in referring to John as Elijah. It was this spiritual empowerment by God that Elisha (Elijah's protégé) was referring to when he asked for "a double portion" of Elijah's spirit (see 2Ki 2:9–18). It is equally untenable to assert that the early church fathers believed in reincarnation and that the teaching was somehow struck from the canon by future generations. Historically, the New Testament canon was not finalized until the fourth century, and there were no "stricken" texts that dealt with reincarnation. There were apocryphal texts, having nothing to do with reincarnation, taken out early on by both Jewish scribes and Christian authorities. These texts were rejected by the early church fathers because they were inconsistent with the rest of the Scriptures and contained doctrines that Jesus and the apostles never taught. In fact, many of the New Testament letters and the Gospel of John were written in response to Gnosticism, the spiritual forebear of the New Age movement.

The Doctrine of Salvation (cont.)

Position	Support	Orthodox Response
Jesus died in order to help those who are somewhat "bogged" down in their cycles of rebirth.	"Not all are in need of salvation. Christ knew that there is a very large class who do not require salvation… but just as surely… there are 'sinners' who have become 'bogged' in matter and cannot escape without a rope. Christ came to save them" (Max Heindel, *The Rosicrucian Cosmo-Conception,* p. 402).	To say that Christ did not come to die for sins is, in essence, to call Him a liar: He Himself stated that this was His purpose. He said, "For even the Son of Man did not come to be served, but to serve, and to give his life as a ransom for many" (Mk 10:45). The Rosicrucians also ignore the words of Paul, who said, "Christ died for our sins according to the Scriptures" (1Co 15:3). Paul also said, "Here is a trustworthy saying that deserves full acceptance: Christ Jesus came into the world to save sinners—of whom I am the worst" (1Ti 1:15). Jesus Christ's mission is well documented.

The Doctrine of Rewards and Punishment

Position	Support	Orthodox Response
There is neither reward nor punishment. All that occurs is simply an endless cycle of reaction to impersonal laws governing all that exists.	"The inquirer should get away from the idea of punishment. There is no such thing as punishment. Whatever happens to a man is in consequence of immutable, invariable laws, and *there is no personal God who gives rewards or punishments as he sees fit, according to an inscrutable will or any other such method*" (Max Heindel, *The Rosicrucian Philosophy in Questions and Answers,* p. 121).	Reincarnation is not scriptural. The Bible says that there is one punishment for sin and that consists of being eternally separated from God (see Mt 25:41), the Giver of "every good and perfect gift" (see Jas 1:17). The biblical position is that Jesus paid for all sins committed by every human being past, present, and future (Heb 10:10; 13:8; 1Jn 2:2). No man has been justified before God by any law (see Gal 2:16; 3:11), whether it came from the God of the Old Testament or from some guru or cult leader teaching a supposed law of karmic progression. If Jesus died for our sins—which He did—there is no need for us to suffer to pay for them. To suggest otherwise is to insult the Spirit of grace by saying that Jesus didn't suffer enough on the cross where He cried, *"Eloi, Eloi, lama sabachthani?"* or "My God, my God, why have you forsaken me?" (Mt 27:46).
Anything that may resemble punishment between reincarnations is actually a purging of the self of evil tendencies that hinder progression.	"The Rosicrucians know that the soul-personality of man is ever progressing and ever evolving to a higher and higher standard of pureness…. Man may be punished in various ways for his transgressions, but such punishment is to enable him to purge himself of his evil tendencies and rise to a higher standard" (H. Spencer Lewis, *Rosicrucian Questions and Answers with Complete History,* p. 268).	Reincarnation is not scriptural. Without an absolute standard for evil, such as provided by God in the Bible, one is left with an uncertain and relative understanding of what evil is. It is hard to determine just what is meant by "evil" in Rosicrucian writings. The Bible says that all who are loved by God as His children will be chastised by Him on occasion (see Dt 8:5; Heb 12:6; and Rev 3:19). Chastisement is the act of bringing unpleasant circumstances to bear

The Doctrine of Rewards and Punishment (cont.)

Position	Support	Orthodox Response
. . . continued		for the purpose of changing a person's character, and therefore behavior, for the better. It may feel like punishment, but it is not in the strictest sense judicial punishment for wrongdoing. Chastisement occurs when a loving father administers a spanking or some other unpleasantness so as to teach a lesson about behavior that could result in very serious consequences. God only chastises His own children who are His by grace through their faith in Jesus Christ; He does not chasten those who don't belong to Him. Not all people are the children of God, and those who are not are therefore free of chastisement, since God does not consider Himself their Father. Wicked people can live their whole lives without much discomfort, but they should not take great pleasure in this.
No one can be damned because the process of evolving goes on forever.	". . . no human or other form of life can ever be lost, damned, or destroyed. . . . Life itself being a part of the ALL-LIFE, must go on unfolding, expanding and growing, or as we say, evolving to higher and higher states of consciousness" (KHEI, *Rosicrucian Fundamentals*, p. 90).	The Bible teaches that there will be a final judgment of each soul that has been created by God. The final judgment for the believer occurs at the *bema* seat of judgment, where rewards are given out for faithful service to the Lord (see 1Co 3:10–15). At this judgment there is no condemnation (Ro 8:1). The unbeliever appears at the Great White Throne judgment that occurs at the end of the millennial reign of Christ (see Rev 20:11). This judgment leads to the execution of an eternal sentence of hell, or the lake of fire, for those who have sinned against the image of God in their own souls represented by their conscience (see Ro 2:12–16). This applies to all who don't know God through trusting in the gospel of Jesus Christ (see Rev 20:10–15).

INTERESTING AND DISTINCTIVE BELIEFS

Position	Support	Orthodox Response
Pain and disease can be eliminated by following the teachings of Rosicrucianism.	"It is possible . . . for man or woman to live to such a ripe old age without disease or pain that eventually the body just gradually weakens and . . . goes to sleep . . . . [T]he proper way to live to prevent disease and pain, and the proper way to remedy the cause of any disease or pain naturally and properly is thoroughly taught by the organization" (H. Spencer Lewis, *Rosicrucian Questions and Answers With Complete History*, pp. 241–242).	The definition of disease is found in the word itself. Disease or illness is where the body functions "without ease." For the body to eventually weaken and die is for the body to be diseased. To admit to death the Rosicrucians offer no final solution to the physical ailments which even the strongest of us eventually succumb to. The body doesn't function well six feet under in the grave. Death is the ultimate form of disease and can only be cured by God. The last enemy that will be destroyed by God alone through Jesus Christ is death (see 1 Cor 15:26).
Blasphemy of the Holy Spirit is the abuse of "sex energy." Such abuse is defined as premarital sex, or sex within marriage if done for the purpose of sensual gratification rather than procreation.	"[T]he Holy Spirit is the creative energy in nature, the sex energy is its reflection in man, and misuse or abuse of that power is the sin that is not forgiven, but must be expiated in impaired efficiency of the vehicles, in order to teach us the sanctity of the creative force. . . . Occult science teaches that the sex-function should *never* be used for sense gratification, but for propagation *only*. Therefore, an aspirant to the higher life would be justified in refusing coition with the marriage partner unless the object were the begetting of a child, and then only if both parties were in perfect health—physically, morally and mentally—as otherwise the union would be likely to result in the generation of a feeble or degenerate body" (Max Heindel, *The Rosicrucian Cosmo-Conception*, pp. 468, 471). "Speaking generally, the Holy Spirit is the creative power of God. . . . By that all that is has been brought into being, and it is a ray from that attribute of God which is used by men for perpetuation of the race. When that is abused, that is to say, when it is used for sense gratification, whether in solitary or associated vice, with or without the legal marriage, that is the sin against the Holy Spirit. That sin, we are told, is not forgiven; it must be expiated" (Max Heindel, *The Rosicrucian Philosophy in Questions and Answers*, pp. 220–21).	Blasphemy of the Holy Spirit is never defined explicitly in the Scriptures. This has led to a number of definitions being put forward. Perhaps the best of these is one that can be derived contextually. In Matthew 12 Jesus was warning the Pharisees about an unforgivable sin while they were accusing Him of performing miracles by the power of the devil. This has led many to conclude that blasphemy of the Holy Spirit is the ascribing of Jesus' miraculous works to the devil. Some have said that it is likely that this unforgivable sin was only able to be committed during the physical lifetime of Jesus on the earth. Jesus never said anyone had committed this terrible sin but only warned about its possibility. On the basis of His words we can certainly say blasphemy has to do with speaking against (or evil of) the Holy Spirit. Some have said that the unforgivable sin is a person's dying without the blessing of the Holy Spirit's confirmation of the gospel in his life. We can be sure that dying in unbelief toward Christ will assure the same results as if one had committed the unpardonable sin. It has nothing whatever to do with sexual matters. The Christian view of sex is at great variance with that of the Rosicrucians. The Christian view is not limited to affirming the procreative or reproductive function of sex. Rather, it also affirms the aspect of pleasure attached to sexuality. This begins in Genesis with God's pronouncement that what He created was good. The New Testament principle is one of mutuality in regard to pleasure. We are told that the marriage bed is pure (see Heb 13:4). God is the Creator of physical sexuality and the pleasure attached to it.

16

Unification Church

FACTS AND HISTORY

Facts	
Topic	**Current Facts**
Membership	Accurate figures for the Unification Church are difficult to obtain. Estimates put American membership of the church at between 5,000 and 10,000 with much larger memberships in Japan and Korea. Though some have referred to members of the church as "Moonies" because they follow the teachings of the Rev. Sun Myung Moon, they prefer to be known as Unificationists.
Worship	Unification Church worship services are usually held on Sunday at 11 A.M. They consist of prayer, Unification Holy Songs, traditional hymns, and Bible reading. Sermons by Moon have usually been delivered at Unification Training Headquarters in Tarrytown, New York. A special pledge service is held at 5 A.M. each Sunday and the first day of each month.
Leaders	1954– The Rev. Sun Myung Moon is the head of all Unification churches.
	1995– Tyler O. Hendricks becomes the president of the Unification Church of America (*Unification News,* May 1995, p. 1.)
	1998– Hyun Jin Moon, Sun Myung Moon's son, becomes international vice president of the Family Federation for World Peace and Unification (FFWPU) and the Holy Spirit Association for the Unification of World Christianity (HSA–UWC) (*Today's World,* July 1998, p. 4).
	1999– Sun Jo Hwang becomes international president of FFWPU and HSA–UWC (*Today's World,* June 1999, p. 2).
Publications	The Unification Church publishes a newspaper about its work (*Unification News*) and a monthly magazine (*Today's World*). Moon founded *The Washington Times,* a daily newspaper, and he has supported the publication of many books from Unification-sponsored conferences.
General statement of beliefs	Moon's teachings represent a mixture of Korean folk custom, Taoism, Neo-Confucianism, and ideas learned from some sectarian Christian groups that flourished in Korea in the 1940s. Most doctrines of orthodox Christianity are denied or distorted by the Unification Church. Moon's purpose is to unite all religions and all humans under his messianic leadership.
History	
Topic	**History**
The Rev. Sun Myung Moon	Born as Yong Myung Moon on January 6, 1920, in Pyungan Buk-do, Korea, Sun Myung Moon founded the Holy Spirit Association for the Unification of World Christianity in Seoul in 1954. Moon, who was raised in a Presbyterian church, claims that when he was sixteen he received a vision in which Jesus Christ said his mission on earth had been left uncompleted. Jesus had "spiritually" redeemed man, but was arrested and crucified before He could "physically" redeem man; Moon said he was selected to complete the latter part of the unfinished

History (cont.)

Topic	History
	mission. Moon arrived in Los Angeles on December 11, 1971, to begin the restoration of America (see *Day of Hope in Review,* Part 1, 1972, 1974; ed. David S. C. Kim, 1974).
	Moon claims frequent supernatural experiences, including visitations to the spirit world to battle Satan, and trips to heaven to talk with Buddha, Jesus, and God the Father. Moon also claims that his wedding day in 1960 is the fulfillment of the biblical marriage supper of the Lamb (Moon, "Children's Day" sermon in Tarrytown, NY, August 4, 1974, p. 10).
	In 1992 Moon officially announced that he was the Messiah. "God chose me to be the Messiah and during this time He has been performing His work of salvation. I have fulfilled my mission as the Lord of the Second Advent, Savior, and the True Parent.... Those who accept this will be blessed" (Moon, "The Reappearance of the True Parents and the Ideal Family," sermon, July 7, 1992, and reprinted in *Today's World,* September 1992, p. 6).
	The beliefs of the Unification Church are presented in *Divine Principle,* its basic spiritual text. The current edition is based on the teachings that Moon gave in the early years of the church.
	Moon became famous through his support of Richard Nixon during the Watergate crisis, at which time the Unification Church was targeted as a cult (*New York Times,* November 30, 1973). Moon was convicted on income tax charges in the early 1980s and served a prison sentence in Danbury, Connecticut ("Moon Held Guilty of Tax Fraud," *Christianity Today,* June 18, 1982, p. 59). Moon claims that he was an innocent victim of religious bigotry.

THEOLOGY

The Doctrine of Revelation

Position	Support	Orthodox Response
The Bible is not inerrant or the final authority. It is an incomplete revelation that has been largely misunderstood. Consequently, God has had to reveal the correct interpretation of the Bible through Sun Myung Moon. God has also revealed new truths through Moon in his role as Messiah.	"... we cannot believe in the verbal inspiration or infallible authority of the Bible as a guide to either faith or morals.... the Scriptures as a whole are inspired because some passages are literary masterpieces, some parts are spiritually elevating, some of its ideas are magnificently true" (Young Oon Kim, *Unification Theology,* 2d ed., 1987, p. 26). "The Bible does not proclaim itself to be the final revelation" (Ibid., p. 28). "The New Testament was given as a textbook for the teaching of truth to the people of 2,000 years ago, people whose spiritual and intellectual standards were very low, compared to that of today.... new truth must appear" (*Divine Principle,* 2d ed., p. 131). "... the Bible is not the truth itself but a textbook teaching us the truth" (Ibid.). "With the fullness of time, God has sent His messenger to resolve the fundamental questions of life and the universe. His name is Sun Myung Moon.... he came in contact with many saints in Paradise and with Jesus, and thus brought into light all the heavenly secrets through his communion with God" (Ibid., p. 16).	Moon has in effect made the Bible a worthless document. The Bible itself claims to be verbally inspired (2Pe 1:21), infallible (Ps 119:160; Pr 30:5–6), and authoritative (Mt 4:4; 2Ti 3:16–17). Furthermore, God assures us that His Word is applicable to all generations (Isa 40:8; 1Pe 1:25). This is possible because God's Word is "living and powerful" (Heb 4:12 NKJV). Jesus said that nothing in God's Word would pass away until all that must happen has happened (Mt 5:18). Also, if God is unchanging (Mal 3:6), then the Bible—which is the perfect expression of God's revelation in written form—must also be unchanging. By impuning the authority and relevance of Scripture, Moon has effectively set himself up as the ultimate authority for his followers. Moon's assertion that Scripture was written for the spiritually and intellectually inferior people of the past indicates a lack of knowledge and understanding not only about the Bible, but also about those who lived during the early centuries of the

The Doctrine of Revelation (cont.)

Position	Support	Orthodox Response
... continued	"The *Principle* is not the word of man, but the Word of God" ("On Prayer and the Spirit World," sermon, MS–3, p. 8). "What do we mean when we say that the *Divine Principle* is revealed? We believe that God revealed to Reverend Moon the fundamental core of his teachings.... *Divine Principle's* convincing interpretations of the Heart of God and the ultimate purpose of history can bring people closer to God's love and offers a clear direction for human destiny. Thus, *Divine Principle* provides the essential elements of Unity for all faiths" (*Unification Theology*, 2d ed., pp. 39–40).	Christian era. Some of the most articulate and godly men in history lived during the first few centuries after Christ's earthly sojourn—for example, Jesus' apostles, Paul, Justin Martyr, Athanasius, and Tertullian.

The Doctrine of God—*The Trinity*

Position	Support	Orthodox Response
God is not a Trinity. God exists only as the Father.	"Unificationists believe that there is only one God, God the Father" (Young Oon Kim, *Unification Theology*, 1987, p. 181).	The orthodox Christian doctrine of the Trinity can be demonstrated from a number of verses.
All creation is a part of the one God. Creation is actually God's Body or outward form.	"He [God] is reflected ... in the whole creation, which is His Body or outward form" (Young Oon Kim, *Unification Theology*, 1987, p. 41). "God the infinite Spirit created finite humans in His image as a way for Him to become incarnate" (Ibid., p. 46). "Since God must live in everything that is created ... God must have the same nature as the rest of His creation" (Moon, "Where God Resides and His Course," sermon, (March 19, 1978, p. 9). "If man did not exist then God would vanish. There is no way that God could continue alone, and without man the universe would have no value" ("Happy Unification Church Members," sermon, May 22, 1977).	This view seems to be almost pantheistic (God is all), or panentheistic (God is in all). Both clearly contradict the Bible, which repeatedly demonstrates a vast difference between God the Creator and creation. God is as distinct from creation as a carpenter is from a bench he has built. The first few chapters of Genesis, for example, systematically show God as being above and beyond creation, not a part of it. Romans 1 also makes a distinction between the creature and the Creator.
Male and female duality is the unifying thread of all reality. Even God and creation can be labeled as male and female.	"Before creating the universe, God existed as the internal masculine subject, and He created the universe as His external feminine object.... Since God is the masculine subject of internal character we call Him 'Our Father,' emphasizing His masculine nature" (*Divine Principle*, 2d ed., p. 25). "God is the subject who consists of the dual characteristics of essential character and essential form.... He is a subject consisting of the dual characteristics of masculinity and femininity" (Ibid., p. 25).	The Bible does not portray God as having a dual nature, especially one consisting of maleness and femaleness. God is neither male nor female; God is spirit (Jn 4:24). Moon's belief in a dual God probably stems from his familiarity with Eastern philosophy and religions. Duality plays a major role in several Eastern religions such as Taoism, which teaches that all reality consists of one substance that is dual in nature (that is, light/dark, positive/negative, male/female).

The Doctrine of God—*The Trinity (cont.)*

Position	Support	Orthodox Response
There are several trinities: the first— God, Adam, and Eve—failed to materialize because of the Fall; the second was a spiritual one consisting of God, Jesus, and the Holy Spirit. The third trinity will occur when Christ becomes the True Parent both spiritually and physically.	"... Adam and Eve was to form a trinity... as the True Parents of mankind,... centered on God.... due to the fall... [they] formed trinities centered on Satan.... God must work to have all fallen men born anew through the True Parents of mankind, Jesus and the Holy Spirit.... But because of the undue death of Jesus, he and the Holy Spirit have fulfilled only the mission of spiritual True Parents, by forming the spiritual Trinity centered on God.... Christ must come again in flesh in order that he may become the True Parent both spiritually and physically, by forming the substantial Trinity centered on God" (*Divine Principle,* 2d ed., pp. 217–18).	Nowhere does Scripture hint at such concepts. These ideas come from Moon's personal revelations of truth and have no historical or biblical foundation.

The Doctrine of Jesus Christ—*The Deity of Christ*

Position	Support	Orthodox Response
Jesus was not equal to God the Father.	"Jesus was a human leader anointed by God to carry out the messianic mission, realizing God's reign on earth. So we cannot say that he is equal to God" (Young Oon Kim, 1987, *Unification Theology,* p. 181).	The Bible often and in many ways puts Jesus on a level equal with God the Father. Jesus is prayed to (Ac 7:59), accepts the same level of honor that the Father is given (Jn 5:23), and perfectly expresses all that the Father is (Jn 14:9). Jesus is called the exact representation of God (Heb 1:3). Jesus Himself said that equality with God was something He did not have to grasp for because it was already His (Php 2:6).
Jesus was not God in the flesh.	"Jesus, on earth, was a man no different from us except for the fact that he was without original sin.... it becomes clear that Jesus is not God Himself" (*Divine Principle*, 2d ed., p. 212). "He [Jesus] can by no means be called God Himself. The relationship between God and Jesus can be compared to that between the mind and body.... Jesus, being one body with God, may be called a second God (image of God), but he can by no means be God Himself" (Ibid., pp. 210–11).	Jesus is called God several times in the Bible (Isa 9:6; Jn 1:1; 1:18 NASB; 20:28; Heb 1:8–9; Tit 2:13).
Christianity has mistakenly made Jesus into God.	"After his crucifixion, Christianity made Jesus into God" (Sun Myung Moon, *Christianity in Crisis*, p. 12).	The Christian belief in Christ's deity is founded on the clear reading of Scripture (see above).

The Doctrine of Jesus Christ—*The Humanity of Christ*

Position	Support	Orthodox Response
Jesus was not born of a virgin. He was the son of Mary and Zacharias (the husband of Mary's cousin Elizabeth and the father of John the Baptist).	"As soon as the young girl [Mary] heard that she had been chosen to give birth to the Son of God, she 'went with haste and entered the house of Zacharias' (Luke 1:39). By giving herself to the aged priest, Mary would prove that she was truly a hand-maiden of the Lord. Such an act of total surrender, far from being considered immoral in the ancient world, revealed the highest degree of spiritual dedication" (Young Oon Kim, *Unification Theology*, 1987, p. 172). "Jesus' father was Zachariah" (Moon, "True Parents' Day is My True Son's Day," sermon, April 18, 1996, p. 13).	If Mary had indeed committed this act of fornication and adultery, both she and Zacharias would have deserved stoning per the Law of Moses (Lev 20:10). Jesus Christ was miraculously conceived by the power of the Holy Spirit in the womb of the virgin Mary (Isa 7:14; Mt 1:18–25).

The Doctrine of Jesus Christ—*The Resurrection of Christ*

Position	Support	Orthodox Response
Jesus was not physically resurrected from the dead.	"Like most liberal Protestants, Unificationists believe that Jesus' resurrection was spiritual and not physical" (*Unification Theology*, 2d ed., p. 151). "(was Jesus' physical body resurrected?) No." ("On the Restoration and Judment," sermon, MS–4, 1965, p. 9). "... but resurrection does not mean that dead bodies will rise again" (Moon, "Jesus and the Second Coming" in *God's Warning to the World*, 1985, p. 136).	In John 2:19–22, Jesus indicated that He would be raised physically from the dead He assured His followers in Luke 24:38–39 that He was physically resurrected. Colossians 2:9 states that Christ *at present* has divinity dwelling within him "bodily."

The Doctrine of the Holy Spirit

Position	Support	Orthodox Response
The Holy Spirit is a female spirit, the True Mother, the Second Eve.	"There must be a true mother—she is the Holy Spirit" (*Divine Principle*, 2d ed., p. 215). "... the Holy Spirit is a female Spirit; this is because she came as the True Mother, that is, the second Eve" (Ibid.). "The Holy Spirit who worked with Jesus was the element of the original Eve. In God there is the esence of male and the essence of female. These essences were given to Adam and Eve as representative of the Word of God. When they moved away from God, these essences returned to God. When Jesus came, the male element of essence was given to him as the male Word of God. But there was no woman on earth to whom the female	The Bible nowhere presents the Holy Spirit as a female personage. The Holy Spirit can be neither male nor female.

The Doctrine of the Holy Spirit (cont.)

Position	Support	Orthodox Response
. . . continued	element could be given. So when Jesus was working in spirit after his crucifixion, this female element of God worked with him as the Holy Spirit" (Moon, "On Prayer and the Spirit World," sermon, MS–3, p. 20.)	

The Doctrine of Man and Sin

Position	Support	Orthodox Response
An evil force impels man to do wrong.	"Men, without exception, are inclined to repel evil and to pursue goodness. But men, unconsciously driven by an evil force, repel the goodness desired by their original minds and perform evil acts which they do not really want to do. In Christianity, this evil force is known as 'Satan'" (*Divine Principle*, 2d ed., p. 65).	Man is inherently evil (Ps 58:2–3; Ecc 9:3; Jer 17:9). His heart continually shuns God and seeks to do wrong (Ge 6:5; Ps 14:3; Isa 53:1–3; Jn 3:19; Ro 3:11–12). Paul the apostle went so far as to call men "slaves" to sin (Ro 6:6, 17, 20).
The Fall resulted from sexual intercourse between Satan and Eve, and then between Eve and Adam.	". . . the angel [Lucifer] ventured to seduce her despite his knowledge that such an act was in direct contradiction to God's will. Eve responded to Lucifer's advances. Their action is called. . . the spiritual fall. . . . After the spiritual fall came the physical fall of Adam and Eve. . . . Once Eve realized that she had sinned with Lucifer, she longed to recover God's favor. Since she now realized that Adam was her true partner, she tempted him to unite with her. God wanted Adam and Eve to become husband and wife only when they had reached the proper level of spiritual maturity. . . . Because they united prematurely, and therefore without God's blessing, they transgressed his will" (*Unification Theology*, pp. 103–4). "Eve's fall consisted of two kinds of illicit love affairs. The first one was the spiritual fall through love with the archangel. The second was the physical fall through love with Adam" (Moon, *Divine Principle,* 2d ed., p. 241).	This belief is Moon's own twist on a doctrine known as the "serpent seed" doctrine, which also teaches that men fell because Eve had sex with Satan. Nothing in Genesis suggests that such an occurrence took place. Scripture does not state that God intended that Adam and Eve marry only after they had reached a certan level of maturity. Genesis 2:23–24 states that Eve was given to Adam immediately after she was created. Moreover, the Fall occurred as a result of Satan's deceiving Eve, not seducing Eve (Ge 3:1–6; 1Ti 2:13–14).

The Doctrine of Salvation

Position	Support	Orthodox Response
Jesus' death actually prevented Him from successfully completing His mission.	"Jesus did not come to die on the cross" (*Divine Principle*, 2d ed., p. 143). "Jesus' crucifixion was the result of the ignorance and disbelief of the Jewish people and was not God's predestination to fulfill the whole purpose of Jesus' coming as the Messiah" (Ibid., p. 145).	Jesus' explicit purpose for coming was first to preach the gospel of God's kingdom (Mk 1:38; Lk 4:43) and then to die (Jn 12:27) so that He could draw all people to Himself (Jn 3:14; 12:32). The crucifixion had been part of God's sovereign plan since before Creation (Eph 3:11; 1Pe 1:20).

The Doctrine of Salvation (cont.)

Position	Support	Orthodox Response
. . . continued	"Unification Principle diametrically contradicts the Fundamentalist view that Jesus' sole mission was to atone for the sins of mankind by dying on the cross" (*Unification Theology*, p. 145). "Here, we have come to understand that the greatest factor leading to the crucifixion of Jesus was the failure of John the Baptist" (*Divine Principle*, p. 162).	Through dying, Jesus took away people's sins (1Jn 3:5). By doing so He destroyed the works of the devil (1Jn 3:8). Jesus repeatedly told His disciples what would occur (Mt 16:20–21; 26:2; Lk 18:31–33). Because Moon's Unification Principle "diametrically contradicts" the view that Jesus' sole mission was "to atone for the sins of mankind by dying," it also contradicts the Bible.
Salvation is a process based on works, which leads us to our future resurrection.	". . . when we repent of our sins, making ourselves better and better, day by day, we are coming closer to resurrection" (*Divine Principle*, 2d ed., p. 170). "Many Christians believe that simply to have faith means they will be saved. Faith alone is not enough" (Leaders' Speech [Questions and Answers] at Rowlane Farmhouse in England, March 16, 1972, p. 13).	Salvation is a gift of God (Eph 2:8–10) that comes through faith in the person and finished work of Jesus Christ (Ro 10:9). Although we can grow in God's grace and become more conformed to the image of Christ (Ro 8:29), we cannot make ourselves intrinsically "better and better." Man is inherently evil (Ps 58:2–3; Jer 17:9). The Lord accepts us only because of Jesus' death on the cross (Col 1:20–22).
Salvation is possible through Moon (the Lord of the Second Advent) and his wife. They are the modern Adam and Eve, the "True Parents" of humanity. Moon fulfills the Second Coming promised in the New Testament.	"The second coming of the Messiah will be highlighted by the work of the True Parents. It will be the most brilliant new age, the final consummation of the work of God. The True Parents will be the mediators between God and man and all men shall be saved, becoming the direct children of God and true parents of mankind" (Moon, "True Parents' Day From the Historical Point of View," talk, April 18, 1977, p. 13). ". . . mankind has been awaiting the arrival of the original seed and prototype, which is the Messiah. The Messiah means True Parents; True Parents means perfect man and perfect woman" (Moon, "Thirtieth Anniversary of the Unification Church," talk, May 1, 1984, p. 6). "Are True Parents absolutely neccessary? Without them, the world has no hope for salvation, no way to turn. . . . " (Moon, "True Parents and I," talk, June 15, 1986, p. 7).	Jesus warned His followers that many false Christs and false prophets would arise after His departure and that they should not be followed (Mk 13:21–22; Mt 24:24–26). Furthermore, Moon could not be another Messiah, for the Bible states that there is only one mediator between God and men, the man Christ Jesus (1Ti 2:5).

The Doctrine of Rewards and Punishment

Position	Support	Orthodox Response
Physical death is not a consequence of sin.	". . . Unification theology does not think of man's physical death as a curse placed upon Adam because of the Fall. The Bible does not imply that physical death is divine punishment. Death should be thought of as a natural process. Everybody must die" (*Unification Theology*, p. 109). "God created man to grow old and turn to dust; this would occur even if man had not fallen" (*Divine Principle,* 2d ed., p. 168).	The Bible states very clearly that death is a consequence of sin. "Sin entered the world through one man, and death through sin, and in this way death came to all men" (Ro 5:12). "For the wages of sin is death" (Ro 6:23). See also 1 Corinthians 15:56. The certainty of death for man began at the fall of Adam and Eve (Ge 2:16–17; Ro 5:14, 17).
Everyone will eventually obtain salvation (universalism).	"God's complete truimph necessarily involves universal restoration and unlimited salvation. Even Satan and his hosts of supporters must be not only disarmed but also reunited with God" (*Unification Theology*, p. 236). "The ultimate purpose of God's providence of restoration is to save all mankind. Therefore, it is God's intention to abolish Hell completely, after the lapse of the period necessary for the full payment of all indemnity" (*Divine Principle*, 2d ed., p. 190). "[The Bible infers that Satan will be cast out forever. Will he be restored completely?] Moon, 'Of course. But it will take almost an eternity for it to happen'" ("On Satan, the Fall, and Evil," talk, MS–6, p. 4). Having said above that Satan will require almost an eternity for restoration, Moon said thirty years later: "As of last March 21, God gave the final order to Satan. Before the order, Satan asked for forgiveness, and declared his will to return before God to support the recreation of the original garden of love. He confessed all this by himself and asked for forgiveness before True Parents [Moon and wife]," (Moon, "Prayer and Declaration of the Liberation of the Cosmos," May 14, 1999, in *Today's World,* June 1999, p. 12). Following is Lucifer's statement to God: "I am offering this to God. God, I am very sorry. How could I dare to ask for Your forgiveness? Although I knew that history would end some day, I wasn't able to see either the direction or my original position to which I must go. I was always anxious because there was no one who radically, formally made determination to lead me strongly. How could I dare to go to the position where I am told to go? I will	Jesus said, "Wide is the gate and broad is the road that leads to destruction, and many enter through it. But small is the gate and narrow the road that leads to life, and only a few find it" (Mt 7:13). He also said that on the day of judgment many will be told to depart from His presence into everlasting torment: "Depart from me, you who are cursed, into the eternal fire prepared for the devil and his angels" (Mt 25:41). "They will go away to eternal punishment" (Mt 25:46). Also see Revelation 14 and 20. These scenes of everlasting punishment spoken of by Jesus indicate just the opposite of what Sun Myung Moon teaches.

The Doctrine of Rewards and Punishment (cont.)		
Position	*Support*	*Orthodox Response*
. . . continued	return as I would carry the punishment given by God. What more could I say about the countless day that I sinned by ignoring God's long sigh [sic] although I saw it? God! God! I am very sorry" (Message from the Spirit World, in Dr. Sang Hun Lee, *Lucifer; A Criminal Against Humanity,* Chap. 5, Sun Moon University, February 10–March 21, 1999).	

INTERESTING AND DISTINCTIVE BELIEFS

Position	*Support*	*Orthodox Response*
Jesus failed in His mission, and Moon is greater than Jesus.	"Jesus and his disciples and all the rest failed to carry out their missions" (Moon, sermon titled "The True Path of Restoration," talk, January 11, 1972, p. 5). "Is there any other religious leader in Korea or history who has achieved what I have achieved? Did Jesus achieve what I have achieved? Why do you follow me around? Because you have tasted the honey" (Moon, "Unite, the Kingdom of Heaven Is at Hand," talk, March 5, 1989, p. 4).	Although Jesus phrased the reason for His coming in multiple ways (for example, to call sinners to repentance, to do the will of the Father, to bear witness to the truth, to fulfill the law and the prophets), the chief purpose He stated many times was to die for our sins, thus making a way of salvation. He came "to give his life as a ransom for many" (Mt 20:28), to "save his people from their sins" (Mt 1:21), not "to judge the world, but to save it" (Jn 12:47). Jesus fulfilled His mission in His death and resurrection. The apostles focused on the ascension and exaltation of Jesus, now seated on the right hand of God the Father, as proof that Jesus' mission was complete (Ac 2:32–36, 3:20–26, 10:40–43). Jesus was delivered to death "by God's set purpose and foreknowledge" (Ac 2:23), and "this is how God fulfilled what he had foretold through all the prophets, saying that his Christ would suffer" (Ac 3:18). He called the death of Christ part of "God's secret wisdom," designed by the Holy Spirit for the salvation and glorification of humankind (1Co 2:7–8).
Koreans will one day be the Third Israel.	". . . the Korean people will become the 'Third Israel'. . . . many spiritual signs regarding the Lord coming again in Korea are appearing" (*Divine Principle*, 2d ed., pp. 521, 529). "Therefore, the nation of the East where Christ will come again would be none other than Korea" (Ibid., p. 520).	There are basically two orthodox views on the identity of the Israel of God. One holds that national Israel is still, in some special way, God's chosen people (dispensationalism). The other view regards all believers as spiritual Israel (covenant theology). There are a number of complexities and nuances in each of these positions. Neither, however, leaves room for Israel to be equated with ethnic Koreans. There is no biblical support for such a view.

Position	Support	Orthodox Response
Moon believes that God needs to be liberated and that he alone can accomplish this.	"You thought God was almighty and all-perfect, but actually He has a weakness: without us even God cannot be perfected" (Moon, "The Ideal World of Subject and Object," talk, February 13, 1977, p. 5). "What would be the most simple description of Reverend Moon's goal and mission? If I were asked that question, I would immediately answer, 'To liberate God, to Save God'" (Moon, "Restoration From the Origin and Rebirth Are for Myself," talk, September 20, 1992, p. 6). "I [Moon] know I am the only person on earth who truly knows God and can comfort Him. . . . God has now said I have done enough and He told me to relax, because He has been comforted by me, but that is the one command from God that I am defying." (Moon, "The Stony Path of Death," talk, April 27, 1980, p. 5).	The Bible declares that God is omnipotent (Rev 19:6) and almighty (Ge 17:1; 35:11; Ex 6:3). Nothing is impossible with God (Mt 19:26; Lk 1:37), nor too difficult for Him (Jer 32:27). God's knowledge and ways are unsearchable (Ro 11:33), and His understanding is infinite (Ps 147:5). All God's works and deeds are perfect (Dt 34:12; Ps 18:30). Since God existed prior to creation, and since the universe is kept from dissolution solely by the word of His power (Col 1:17; Heb 1:3), God obviously does not "need" anything to sustain Him. This is clearly stated in Scripture: "He is not served by human hands, as if he needed anything, because he himself gives all men life and breath and everything else" (Ac 17:25). The idea that God is imperfect, weak, and suffering is totally unscriptural. Biblical statements that God is grieved by man's sins (for example, Ge 6:6; Jdg 10:16) do not indicate a psychological weakness or emotional defect in God; rather, they describe God's deep moral revulsion and antipathy toward sin and His full understanding of its consequences. The works of Moon do not "comfort" God, because sin still has judicial consequences. Only the blood of Jesus Christ, who was without sin, can atone for and cover our sins (1Jn 4:10).
Unificationists use Holy Salt to sanctify their possessions.	"All items purchased for individual, family, or center purposes—groceries, clothing, furniture, vehicles, etc., should be purified with Holy Salt when brought into the center or home" ("Use of Holy Salt," in Chung Kwak, ed., *The Tradition*, 1985 and 1993, p. 53). "Stand in the center of the room facing north (toward the direction of north) with Holy Salt in your right hand. Follow the same basic prayer included in the section *Using Holy Salt*: 'Prayer,' substituting appropriate words where necessary" (Ibid.). "So whenever we buy anything from the grocery store or any stores of the world, we bring them home and sanctify those things before using them, with our holy salt, of course. . . . when we move into a new house we sanctify the whole place" (Moon, "The Seven Day Fast," talk, October 20, 1974, p. 3).	This custom is possibly a carryover from Old Testament priestly traditions (Lev 2:13; Ezr 6:9), but these traditions have no purpose or place under the new covenant. Moreover, in Old Testament times, salt was used only on sacrificed animals, not physical objects. Sacramental objects, such as "holy water" or incense, are often carried over into Christian worship by people who do not understand that they were only temporarily instituted for the people of Israel under the Levitical priesthood. Because that priesthood has been changed and superseded by the priesthood of Christ (Heb 7:12, 18–24), its ordinances and rituals have been abolished.

Position	Support	Orthodox Response
Moon can supernaturally match couples to be married.	"I rely upon my intuition that enables me to see everything about each man and woman, like special 'X-ray eyes.' You believe that I have that ability, don't you, and you have confidence that I am a champion at matching people?" (Moon, "True Way of Life," talk, July 1, 1984, p. 8). "I have a special 'antenna' which never fails. When I feel a match is bad, it is always bad. That is not because I want it to be bad; it is simply the truth" (Moon, "Ideal Family and Ideal World," talk, June 6, 1982, p. 11).	"Intuition" or discernment is only meaningful if Moon knows something about the couples themselves. However, in practice Moon is presented with tens of thousands of names of total strangers, whom he usually matches up on the basis of differing ethnic background. Divergent ethnicity is the main factor used in matching candidates for marriage. Often these couples do not speak a common language. Although members may reject Moon's choice, the great majority accept his selections. Because so many of Moon's beliefs are unorthodox, there is no reason to think that his intuition comes from the Holy Spirit. It is more likely that Moon makes this claim to calm the fears of followers who anticipate marriage to a total stranger from another country.
Korean will be the language of heaven.	"... the heavenly ceremonies will all be conducted by Koreans, so if you don't know Korean, you will be lost" (Moon, "History of the Providence Through Restoration by Indemnity," talk, February 10, 1981, p. 12). "What language would you want God to speak? It must be the language which God had to use to make Himself understood by His most beloved one. That is, God would want to use the language of the True Parents who have nothing to do with the fall and sin" ("Important Person," talk, June 10, 1973, MS–377, p. 3).	Just as some religious movements in the West focus on Britain or America as the true Israel (British Israelism, Anglo-Israelism, Mormonism) and Shakespearean English as supreme, so also there are Eastern cults that focus on Korea as the true Israel and the Korean language as supreme. The book of Revelation shows that in heaven, a multitude "from every tribe and language and people and nation" will stand before the throne of God, offering Him praise (Rev 5.9, see also 7.9). No mention is made of which language is spoken in worship. All languages have strengths and weaknesses, and it is noteworthy that God chose the contrasting languages of Hebrew and Greek to convey the Scriptures, perhaps in part to show that His people are not limited to one language alone.

Position	Support	Orthodox Response
Moon believes that the death of his son Heung Jin in 1984 was allowed by God to offset a satanic attack on Korea or Moon himself.	"If the sacrifice of Heung Jin Nim had not been made, either of two great calamities could have happened. Either the Korean nation could have suffered a catastrophic setback, such as an invasion from the North; or I myself could have been assassinated. Since special indemnity was paid that protected me in Korea at the Kwangju rally—Satan's specific target day—he hit Heung Jin Nim instead, at the same exact hour" (Moon, "Let Us Go Over the Hill," February 7, 1984, p. 9).	Heung Jin Nim died from injuries suffered in a car-truck collision near Poughkeepsie, New York. We do not usually refer to a fatal auto accident as a "sacrifice" to God. A true sacrifice requires that the death accomplishes expiation or atonement for sin, and that the sacrificial victim act as a representative or a substitute for the sins of others. Most important, God the Father must require and recognize the validity of the sacrificial offering. In Heung Jin Nim's case, nothing in biblical prophecy or teaching required his death. The sacrifice of Jesus is sufficient for the sins of "the whole world" (1Jn 2:2), and "he is able to save completely" (Heb 7:25) by making "for all time one sacrifice for sins" (Heb 10:12). Thus Heung Jin's death was not a sacrifice by biblical standards. It is purely speculation that Heung Jin's death somehow saved Korea from a communist invasion or his father from assassination.
Jesus allegedly spoke to Moon from the spirit world by channeling.	"You should all now acquire the book that has been conveyed [by Dr. Sang Hun Lee] from the spirit world and study deeply about Lucifer and the profound contents of the spirit world" (Moon, "Declaration and Celebration of True Parents' Cosmic Victory and 37th True Day of All Things," June 14, 1999, Seoul, Korea: quoted in *Today's World,* June 1999, p. 4). "A letter presented by Jesus to True Parents, May 22, 1998: "Father, my name is Jesus. Though I am not worthy, you have given me so much love, concerned yourself for my sake, and prayed for me so often. . . . my wife is a woman who is far better than I deserve. Truly, I am awestruck. From this point on, my wife and I will uphold your will and work to make an offering of our lives as a beautiful family. I will attend Heung Jin Nim, offer my prayers and hard work. . . . Father, please forgive this sinner (in the sense that the responsibility was not fulfilled). . . . Jesus, who was born in Nazareth of Judea sends this letter from the spiritual world to Father" (*Life in the Spirit World and on Earth: Messages From the Spirit World,* Dr. Sang Hun Lee, New York: Family Federation for World Peace and Unification, 1998, pp. 141–142).	The alleged communication is unfortunate for Moon because such communication is forbidden by God (Lev 19:31; 20:27; Dt 18:9–14; 1Sam 28:6–25 with 1Ch 10:13–14; Isa 8:19) and is full of inaccurate information about Jesus, the sinless man (2Co 5:21; Heb 4:15), who is also God incarnate (Jn 1:1, 14, 18; 8:58; 20:28; Ro 9:5; Tit 2:13), succeeded in His mission to give His life for the ungodly (Heb 2:9, 14) and to save those who believe in Him (Ro 3:21–26). Moreover, the so-called message from the spirit world says that Jesus was born in Nazareth of Judea. Nazareth is in the Galilee, not Judea, and Jesus was born in Bethlehem, not in Nazareth (Mt 2:1–6, 19–13).

17

United Pentecostal Church

FACTS AND HISTORY

	Facts
Topic	*Current Facts*
Membership	The United Pentecostal Church International (UPC), based in Hazelwood, Missouri, reported 1.5 million constituents worldwide in 1991. More than 3,635 UPC churches in the United States and Canada were attended by some 500,000 members that included about 7,500 active ministers. The UPC also has nine Bible colleges, an orphanage, a rehabilitation center for boys, and a ministry for substance abuse. The foreign missionary budget for 1987 was about $12 million, according to the *Dictionary of Pentecostal and Charismatic Movements* (p. 863).
Worship	UPC services, as in other Pentecostal churches, usually last from one to three hours and include a sermon along with music and singing. One evangelical missionary has described UPC services as being quite moving: "United Pentecostals really seem to enjoy their meetings. The emotionally charged atmosphere of their church services offers a feeling of joy, of fiesta, and of the sensational (miracles, tongues, healings) that thrills, excites, and lifts these humble believers from the dreariness and drudgery of daily life.... Then there is freedom in their meetings—liberty to pray aloud, to pray all at once, to stand and shout, and to interject an 'amen,' 'hallelujah,' 'praise the Lord,' as they wish.... this liberty is often mentioned by both pastors and members as a major factor in the appeal of their meetings" (*Dynamic Religious Movements*, p. 234).
Leaders (called general superintendents)	1945–1951 Howard A. Goss 1951–1967 Arthur T. Morgan 1967–1968 Oliver F. Fauss 1968–1977 Stanley W. Chambers 1977– Nathaniel A. Urshan
Publications	Word Aflame Press, the UPC's publishing house in Hazelwood was founded in 1945. It produces tracts, church supplies, flyers, and Sunday school materials; it had also published more than 90 books by 1980. The UPC currently produces seven national periodicals, including the *Pentecostal Herald* and the *Global Witness*.
General statement of beliefs	At first glance the UPC seems orthodox. Members believe that only one God exists, Jesus rose bodily from the dead, and there is a literal heaven and hell. Additionally, they hold views about the Bible, eschatology, and standards of outward holiness (for example, loving your neighbor as yourself, honesty, not swearing) that are common to many evangelicals. What separates United Pentecostals from orthodox Christians are their concepts of God and their belief that to be saved one must be baptized in Jesus' name only and speak in tongues. The group also enforces stricter standards of holiness than those found in most evangelical churches, including the length of one's hair (men's short, women's long), abstinence from watching television, and a prohibition against women wearing makeup or jewelry.

History

Topic	History
Howard A. Goss, 1945–1951	The United Pentecostal Church was formed in 1945 through a merger of two Pentecostal groups: the Pentecostal Church, Incorporated (PCI), and the Pentecostal Assemblies of Jesus Christ (PAJC). This merger capped several years of turmoil and doctrinal debate that started shortly after the Pentecostal movement began early in the century. Howard A. Goss, the first general superintendent of the UPC, had been associated with Charles Parham, who in 1900 founded Bethel Bible College in Topeka, Kansas. The seeds of the Pentecostal movement were planted at Bethel that year when Parham's students convinced him that speaking in tongues was the initial evidence of the baptism of the Holy Spirit. (The students began speaking in tongues on January 1, 1901.) Although the Pentecostal movement didn't actually gain worldwide recognition until the Azusa Street Revival in 1906–9, Parham, who died in 1929, is considered one of the movement's most important early leaders. In 1906 Goss was appointed field director of the Texas revivals, and even though he resigned after Parham was arrested for a moral offense, he remained a leader among the Pentecostals and established churches in Texas and Arkansas. Goss became one of the prime movers in organizing the Assemblies of God denomination in 1914. A year earlier, the birth pangs of the UPC began when R. E. McAllister asserted that the singular "name" of the Father, Son, and Holy Spirit in Matthew 28:19 was Jesus and that, consequently, baptism should be done in the name of Jesus only and not in the three names of the Trinity. In 1914, Frank Ewert, another well-known Pentecostal, began teaching that the name of the one true God was Jesus. He soon began rebaptizing numerous Pentecostals in Jesus' name only. (Howard Bell, a Pentecostal minister who endorsed Ewert, eventually rebaptized Goss.) Such actions quickly led to a rift between Pentecostals that culminated in forcing all "oneness" ministers out of the Assemblies of God. The displaced ministers responded by forming their own organizations, which either folded or merged with one another. The formation of the UPC in 1945 made it the largest of the "Jesus Only" or "Oneness" Pentecostal denominations.
Arthur T. Morgan, 1951–1967	Arthur T. Morgan was elected general superintendent of the UPC after Goss died in 1951. During his term a larger UPC headquarters was purchased (1952) and expanded (1954). He died in 1967.
Oliver F. Fauss, 1967–1968	Oliver F. Fauss was elected to fill Morgan's position on a temporary basis.
Stanley W. Chambers, 1968–1977	Stanley Chambers was elected general superintendent in 1968. His term saw the construction of a brand new two-story headquarters for the UPC in 1970.
Nathaniel A. Urshan, 1977–	The UPC is currently led by Nathaniel A. Urshan, the son of an early Oneness leader named A. D. Urshan. The UPC continues to thrive and gain converts under its current leaderhip.

THEOLOGY

The Doctrine of Revelation

Position	Support	Orthodox Response
The Bible is the only source of doctrine. It is God's Word.	The Preamble of the Articles of Faith of the United Pentecostal Church states, "The Bible is the only God-given authority which man possesses; therefore, all doctrine, faith, hope, and all instruction for the church must be based upon, and harmonize with, the Bible" (*Meet the United Pentecostal Church International*, p. 46).	These are orthodox statements.
	"In every United Pentecostal church pulpit the Word of God is honored and proclaimed to be infallible, the message of eternal life, to be believed and obeyed" (Ibid., p. 107).	
	"The Bible is the inspired Word of God, giving a true history of the creation of heaven, earth, and humanity and containing a correct prophecy of the ages to come regarding heaven, earth, and the destiny of humanity. Moreover, there is no salvation outside of what is taught in its pages" (*The Apostles Doctrine*, p. 4).	

The Doctrine of God—*The Trinity*

Position	Support	Orthodox Response
There is only one God.	"Biblical Christianity strongly held to the truth of one God . . . to allow more than one God would be to contradict God's Word and be idolatry, false doctrine, and polytheism" (*The P.A.S.T.O.R.S. Course: Theology, Book Two of Five*, p. 54).	These are orthodox, monotheistic statements.
	"There is only one God (Deuteronomy 6:4). He is the Creator of heaven and earth, and of all living beings. He has revealed Himself to humanity as the Father (Creator), in the Son (Savior), and as the Holy Ghost (indwelling Spirit)" (*The Apostles Doctrine*, p. 4).	

The Doctrine of God—The Trinity (cont.)

Position	Support	Orthodox Response
United Pentecostals call their theology "Oneness" because they believe a plurality of persons does not exist within God's nature. In other words, God exists only as one "person."	"God is absolutely and indivisibly one. . . . His eternal nature contains no essential distinctions or divisions. . . . Any plurality associated with God is only a plurality of attributes, titles, roles, manifestations, modes of activity, or relationships to man" (*Essential Doctrines of the Bible*, p. 7). "In contrast to trinitarianism, Oneness asserts that (1) God is indivisibly one in number with no distnction of persons . . ." (*Meet the United Pentecostal Church International*, p. 66). "The Oneness doctrine can be presented succinctly in two propositions: (1) there is one indivisible God with no distinction of persons; (2) Jesus Christ is all the fulness of the Godhead incarnate. All titles of the Deity can be applied to Him and all aspects of the divine personality are manifest in Him" (*Essentials of Oneness Theology*, p. 8).	This is an ancient heresy known by a number of different names, including Modalism, Monarchianism, and especially Sabellianism—after Sabellius, a third-century teacher who prominently championed this doctrinal position. The orthodox position is that the God of the Bible exists as three distinct persons—Father, Son, and Holy Spirit—who are one essence or being sharing all attributes of deity including eternality, infinitude, uncreated spirituality, omniscience, omnipresence, and omnipotence. The doctrine of the Trinity is derived from Scriptures that clearly show different entities (The Father, The Son, and The Holy Spirit) that are all ascribed all the characteristics of both individual personhood (intellect, emotions, and will) and a divine nature.
The doctrine of the Trinity is not mentioned in Scripture. Oneness doctrine restores the biblical doctrine of God that was held by the apostles.	"Trinitarians sometimes explain that the Old Testament monotheistic passages merely speak of perfect agreement and unity among the trinity, excluding a plurality of false deities but not a plurality of persons in the true God. This view would allow outright polytheism, however, for many distinct deities could exist in perfect harmony. Neither testament uses the word trinity or associates the word three or the word persons with God in any significant way" (*Meet the United Pentecostal Church International*, p. 58). "The Oneness doctrine is important because it upholds biblical Christianity in at least three specific ways: (1) It restores biblical terms and patterns of thought on the subject of the Godhead . . ." (Ibid., p. 67).	Often those who reject the Trinity do so partly on the grounds that the term is not found in the Bible. It is true that the word *Trinity* (Latin *trinitas*, three in one) is not found in Scripture, since it arose from a theological attempt to explain the biblical teaching. This doctrine derives from the combination of Scripture passages that present the idea that three persons simultaneously exist within the monotheistic God. Several passages implicitly allow for the doctrine (Ge 1:26–27; 11:5–9; Ps 2:7; Isa 6:8, 9), while various passages explicitly teach the idea (Mt 3:16–17; 28:19; Jn 17:1–5; 2Co 13:14). The attempt to identify these different persons as merely roles played by one person does an injustice to the One God. The three persons are described as distinct from one another and possessing personal attributes, yet in union with one another in one essence. "Roles" or "natures" do not communicate, love, will, or express emotion, but a "person" does. When the Father and the Son communicate, there is a demand for the two persons to be involved, not two natures. Only persons can express intellect, emotion, and will.

The Doctrine of God—*The Trinity (cont.)*

Position	Support	Orthodox Response
God consists of Jesus only, who is the Father. God is not three distinct persons.	"The term *Father* refers to God Himself— God in all His deity" (*The Oneness of God: Series in Pentecostal Theology,* vol. 1, p. 98).	The confusion arises in the definition and understanding of personhood versus nature. A person can be described as self-aware and aware of others who are also self-aware, having an intellect, being volitional (having a will), and capable of emotional thought and sensibilities or feelings. A nature is different from a person as it describes the parameters and essence of personal qualities or attributes. The human nature is finite in its intellectual comprehension, whereas God is infinite. The same can be said of all aspects of personality shared by God and mankind. This understanding helps to explain how man can be made in the image of God and yet can never legitimately hope to be God. Nature can also describe character. God's nature is contrasted with fallen human nature in that God is good and man is evil. Jesus shared man's nature in the personhood sense, but not in character, as He was without sin.
The Father, Son, and Holy Spirit, rather than being three distinct persons within the Godhead, are actually titles that describe the multiple roles played by God as He has progressively revealed Himself to mankind.	"The Bible certainly speaks of the Father, Son, and Holy Ghost, but not as three distinct persons.... the titles of Father, Son, and Spirit describe God's multiple roles and works.... The terms can also be understood in God's revelation to humanity: *Father* refers to God in family relationship to humanity; *Son* refers to God in flesh; and *Spirit* refers to God in activity. For example, one man can have three significant relationships or functions—such as administrator, teacher, and counsellor— and yet be one person in every sense of the word" (*Meet the United Pentecostal Church International,* pp. 60–61).	The idea that God role plays or assumes modes of function—acting as the Father at one moment, the Holy Spirit at another, and the Son at another time—is why the Oneness groups are called modalists.
The Trinitarian concept that Jehovah God of the Old Testament consists of the Father, the Son, and the Holy Spirit is wrong.	"It has been stated by some that LORD, or Jehovah in the Old Testament, is inclusive of three personalities (Father, Son, Holy Ghost). This concept should be avoided for two reasons. First, because scripture plainly declares 'to us there is one Lord ... Jesus Christ' (I Cor. 8:6).... Secondly ... when scripture speaks of 'one Lord,' it so obviously means a mathematical one" (*The P.A.S.T.O.R.S. Course: Theology, Book Two of Five,* p. 99).	Again, the confusion arises over the definitions of personhood and nature. The existence of more than one person in the Godhead is arrived at by examining the revelation of God in the Bible and allowing it to speak for itself without having to find an analogy or similar situation in the creation. It is admitted that the harmoniously shared essence of One Eternal Being by three persons is nonanalogous. This is simply to say that God is other than His creation and therefore is totally transcendent and unique in His essential existence.

The Doctrine of God—*The Trinity (cont.)*

Position	Support	Orthodox Response
Trinitarianism inevitably leads to tritheism (belief in three Gods).	"Despite the protests of trinitarians, their doctrine inevitably leads to a practical form of tritheism" (*The Oneness of God: Series in Pentecostal Theology,* vol. 1, p. 288).	The orthodox faith has always embraced monotheism and condemned tritheism. The Athanasian Creed: "And the Catholic faith is this: That we worship one God in Trinity, and Trinity in Unity; neither confounding the persons, nor dividing the substance. For there is one Person of the Father; another of the Son; and another of the Holy Ghost. But the Godhead of the Father, and of the Son, and of the Holy Ghost, is all one; the Glory equal, the Majesty co-eternal. . . . So the Father is God: the Son is God: and the Holy Ghost is God. And yet there are not three Gods: but one God."
The doctrine of the Trinity is unbiblical.	"The doctrine of the Trinity is not a New Testament formulated doctrine" (*The P.A.S.T.O.R.S. Course: Theology, Book Two of Five,* p. 110). "Neither testament uses the word *trinity* or associates the word *three* or the word *persons* with God in any significant way" (*Meet the United Pentecostal Church International,* p. 58).	Scriptural examples abound of divine persons interacting and being aware of one another's existence. Jesus refers to Himself and His Father as providing two witnesses (persons who can speak, not natures that cannot speak) for the authentication of His ministry (Jn 5:31–32; 8:16–18). This complies with the Mosaic injunction that everything be confirmed by at least two witnesses. For just a divine nature and a human nature to bear witness would be tantamount to saying in court that your body and your mind, or your physical nature and your nonphysical soul nature, will give two distinct testimonies. The Father is shown to have sent the Son (see Jn 3:17; Gal 4:4; 1Jn 4:10). This shows that Jesus not only existed, before His earthly life, in eternity with the Father, but that there was an interaction in eternity between the Father and the Son before there ever was a human nature of Jesus. Perhaps most significant is the fact that the Father loves and shows approval of the Son (see Jn 3:35; 17:23–26). People or persons can show love, but natures can't.

The Doctrine of God—*The Trinity (cont.)*

Position	Support	Orthodox Response
The 20th-century Pentecostal revival that gave birth to the UPC restored truths that were previously hidden. These truths, regarding the name and nature of Jesus Christ, are now taught in the UPC. The UPC also teaches that Oneness theology was taught by the early church until corrupt Christendom eventually repressed the teaching and "misplaced" (deliberately destroyed) the documentation that would prove that church fathers taught Oneness theology.	"With the coming of the Holy Spirit, the Word of the Lord became a new book. Truths which had been hidden for many years were made clear. In the year 1914 came the revelation on the name of the Lord Jesus Christ.... God marvelously confirmed our message as the gospel was preached in its fulness. The power which was hidden in the name of Jesus began to be revealed" (*Highlights in Church History*, pp. 62–63). "... very little is known about these groups [oneness and other groups deemed heretical] of people. Suppressed, ostracized and persecuted greatly, the things they stood for have been, as a whole, conveniently 'misplaced,'..." (*Their Story: 20th Century Pentecostals* as quoted in Keith Tolbert, *The Views of Church History Within the United Pentecostal Church International*, p. 6).	Jesus said that heaven and earth would pass away but not His words. He also said that not "one jot or one tittle" of His law would disappear until all things are fulfilled in it (Mt 5:18 KJV). The UPC would have to contend that all things were somehow fulfilled in order to believe that God allowed His truth to be tampered with. It is a very low view of God's ability to maintain His truth and therefore an insult to God to hold this position. Jude 3 says that "the faith" was "once for all delivered to the saints." This means that God delivered all the essentials to the faith at one time and doesn't intend to allow them to be "misplaced." The idea that there are missing documents that would prove their case is an illogical argument from silence.

The Doctrine of Jesus Christ—*The Deity of Christ*

Position	Support	Orthodox Response
Jesus is God manifested in the flesh. He is truly God and truly man.	"One cannot overemphasize the supreme deity of Christ" (*The P.A.S.T.O.R.S. Course: Theology, Book Two of Five*, p. 114). "Jesus Christ is the incarnation of the one God" (*Meet the United Pentecostal Church International*, p. 58). "Jesus is God with us, the eternally blessed God, the image of the invisible God, God manifest in the flesh, our God and Savior, and the express image of God's substance" (Ibid., p. 59). "Jesus is both God and man at the same time" (Ibid., p. 63).	These are orthodox statements.

Position	Support	Orthodox Response
Jesus is God. He is both the Son and the Father.	"If there is only one God and that God is the Father (Malachi 2:10), and if Jesus is God, then it logically follows that Jesus is the Father" (*The Oneness of God: Series in Pentecostal Theology,* vol. 1, p. 66). "*Jesus is the Father incarnate.* 'His name shall be called ... The mighty God, The everlasting Father' (Isaiah 9:6). . . . 'I and my Father are one' (John 10:30). . . . 'He that hath seen me hath seen the Father' (John 14:9)" (*Meet the United Pentecostal Church International,* p. 59).	These statements makes a charade or farce out of the prayers of Christ and the statements made by God the Father throughout the Gospels. Natures don't pray or talk to one another but self-aware persons do. The person Jesus was addressing in the garden of Gethsemane when He asked the cup to be taken from Him was the person of His Father (see Mt 26:39).
Jesus, the *man*, was God only because the perfect expression, or thoughts of God the Father (Logos/Word), came to dwell in Jesus. In a sense, God the Father was actually in Christ.	"Jesus is not just a part of God, but *all* of God is resident in Him" (*The Oneness of God: Series in Pentecostal Theology,* vol. 1, p. 57). "God the Father dwelt in the man Christ. . . . The divine nature of Jesus Christ is the Holy Spirit . . . which is the Spirit of the Father" (*Essential Doctrines of the Bible,* p. 8). ". . . the deity of Jesus is none other than the Father Himself" (*The Oneness of God: Series in Pentecostal Theology,* vol. 1, p. 115).	Isaiah 9:6 teaches that Jesus, as the prophesied coming Messiah, would be "Everlasting Father," or more acurately, "Father of eternity." In the ancient mind, one who owned a property could be called the "father of the property," thus Christ would be the Father of eternity or the Creator of the Ages, as Hebrews 1:2 and 11:3 point out. So a reference to "Father" does not prove that He is the "God and Father of our Lord Jesus Christ" (2Co 1:3). John 10:30 and 14:9 show that because Jesus exists as the second person of the indivisible being known as God, He can make the statements from that vantage point. The context "No one comes to the Father except through me" (Jn 14:6) seems to suggest a more mediatorial position in which Jesus is the perfect representation of the Father to men. But the idea that Christ had a dual personality is unscriptural. In *Lectures in Systematic Theology,* Henry C. Thiessen writes, "Christ's personality resides in His divine nature, because the Son did not unite with a human person but with a human nature." In *Jesus Christ Our Lord,* John Walvoord writes, "Christ at the same moment has seemingly contradictory qualities. He can be weak and omnipotent, increasing in knowledge and omniscient, finite and infinite. . . . There is evidence that human nature developed and with it a human self consciousness came into play" (pp. 116, 118). It was the Logos, whom the Father sent, that did all of this and not the Father Himself.

The Doctrine of Jesus Christ—*The Humanity of Christ*

Position	Support	Orthodox Response
The divinity of God the Father united with the human body that was formed in the Virgin Mary's womb. Hence, Jesus was not only divine, but also human.	"Jesus, the Son, received a set of chromosomes from God, the Father. The single cell which encased these tiny bands which would help determine His characteristics had been the glorious image through which God ruled the universe.... This cell ... united with another single cell in the womb of Mary, and thus the Son of man was conceived" (*The P.A.S.T.O.R.S. Course: Theology, Book Two of Five*, p. 101).	This is an orthodox statement.
The Word mentioned in John 1:1 is not a reference to Jesus before His incarnation. The term *Word* describes only the mind of God, or a thought in the mind of God.	"The Word is God's self-revelation, self-expression, or self-disclosure. Before the Incarnation, the Word was the unexpressed thought, plan, or mind of God. In the beginning, the Word was with God, not as a separate person but as God Himself—pertaining to and belonging to God much like a man and his word. In the fullness of time God put flesh on the Word; He revealed Himself in flesh" (*Meet the United Pentecostal Church International*, p. 64).	In John 1:1–5 the Word is said to be "with God" and indeed "was God." The language allows for no other conclusion than that the person spoken of is someone who can be said to be in some way alongside of or "with" the person of God while being God at the same time. The doctrine of the Trinity is the only logical explanation of this passage.
Because Jesus was both God the Father and man, His two natures could interact with each other. This interaction is seen when Jesus is praying to the Father. It is not one person praying to another; it is Jesus' human nature conversing with His divine nature.	"While Jesus was both God and man at the same time, sometimes He acted from the human viewpoint and sometimes from the divine viewpoint. As Father, He sometimes spoke from His divine self-consciousness; as Son He sometimes spoke from His human self-conciousness" (*Essential Doctrines of the Bible*, p. 9).	Self-aware *persons* communicate with one another, not *natures*.

The Doctrine of Jesus Christ—*The Resurrection of Christ*

Position	Support	Orthodox Response
Jesus Christ was raised bodily from the grave.	"Of all the great truths of God's Word, there is none so meaningful to the human as the resurrection of Jesus Christ.... The resurrection is the culminated result of Christ's death and burial—and completes what is called the Gospel" (*The P.A.S.T.O.R.S. Course: Christology, Book Three of Five*, p. 55).	This is an orthodox statement.

The Doctrine of the Holy Spirit

Position	Support	Orthodox Response
The Holy Spirit is the Father, rather than a person distinct *from* the Father.	"The Bible identifies the Father and the Holy Spirit as one and the same being. The title of Holy Spirit simply describes what the Father is.... The Holy Spirit is literally the Father of Jesus, since Jesus was conceived by the Holy Spirit" (*Meet the United Pentecostal Church International*, p. 61).	Jesus *asked* the Father to send the Holy Spirit to the believers (Jn 14:16, 26; 15:26). This action clearly speaks of the three persons interacting with each other. The Holy Spirit proceeds from both the Father and the Son (Jn 14:26; 15:26; Ac 2:33; Heb 9:14).
Because the Holy Spirit (the Father that was in Jesus) was also Christ Himself (that aspect of Him that was divine), then the Holy Spirit is also Jesus.	"The Holy Spirit is literally the Spirit that was in Jesus Christ" (*Meet the United Pentecostal Church International*, pp. 59–60). "When Christ in reference to the Holy Ghost, promised 'another comforter' (Jn. 14:16), they did not understand this to be another person. The 'another' was the Spirit of the divine Christ that would dwell in them, as opposed to His physical bodily presence,... "Christ defines Himself as 'the truth' (Jn. 14:6), then goes on to define the Holy Ghost as 'the Spirit of truth' (Jn. 14:17). He further states.... 'I will not leave you comfortless: I will come to you' (Jn. 14:17, 18). He here asserts that he (Christ) will return in spirit form and be their comforter" (*The P.A.S.T.O.R.S. Course: Pneumatology, Book Three of Five*, p. 2).	"Jesus Christ is the same yesterday and today and forever" (Heb 13:8). This tells us that His nature has been the same throughout His eternal existence. Another direct statement about His eternal nature is that "God is love" (1Jn 4:8). The Greek word for "love" here is *agape,* a self-sacrificing and outgoing concern *for another.* This means that Jesus is eternally unselfish and selflessly concerned with a person outside of Himself. How can this be if He was the only person who existed before other persons were created? He would have been just the opposite of *agape* in self-absorbed narcissism. The doctrine of the Trinity resolves this issue: The persons of the Triune God loved one another throughout all eternity past.

The Doctrine of Man and Sin

Position	Support	Orthodox Response
Through Adam, every person is born in sin and is condemned to physical as well as spiritual death (separation from God) because of Adam.	"... every single individual born onto earth is born with the curse of sin already upon them.... With the fall of Adam, this curse of sin has come upon the entire race" (*The P.A.S.T.O.R.S. Course: Soteriology, Book Four of Five*, p. 6). "All men, regardless of race, are utterly guilty before God" (Ibid., p. 7).	These are orthodox statements.

The Doctrine of Salvation

Position	Support	Orthodox Response
Christ's death atoned for the sins of the world and is effective for those who accept Him as their Lord and Savior.	"The gospel . . . is the good news of the coming of Jesus Christ and what He has accomplished. . . . through the shedding of His blood in His sacrificial death, the full payment for the penalty of sin has been provided. . . . Christ's death at Calvary was the ultimate sacrifice for the sins of the world, and effects salvation for all who accept Him" (*The P.A.S.T.O.R.S. Course: Soteriology, Book Four of Five*, p. 15).	This is an orthodox statement.
We must take three steps to obtain salvation. We must (1) have faith and repentance; (2) be baptized with water in the name of Jesus only (because Jesus is the name of God—Father, Son, and Holy Ghost—and Matthew 28:19 tells us to baptize in the name [singular] of the Father, Son, and Holy Ghost); and (3) receive the Holy Spirit, which is evidenced by speaking in tongues.	(1)— "The necessity of believing in order to receive salvation is repeatedly emphasized throughout scripture. . . . Repentance has always . . . been a requirement for approaching God" (*The P.A.S.T.O.R.S. Course: Soteriology, Book Four of Five*, pp. 38, 42). (2)—". . . scripture portrays repentance and baptism as being inextricably bound together in the process of remitting sins (Mk. 16:16, Lk. 24:47, Acts 2:38)" (Ibid., p. 61). ". . . the curse of sin stems from a dual source. First, from birth, the sinner carries the curse of sin which is come upon the whole race from Adam. . . . Secondly, he carries the curse of sin because of his committed sins. . . . when one repents, he repents of sins committed. . . . When one is baptized, he is removed from the curse of his inherited Adamic family—and born (of the water) into a new family" (Ibid., pp. 60–61). "Christian baptism is to be administered 'in the name of Jesus.' This means to invoke the name Jesus orally at water baptism" (*The New Birth: Series in Pentecostal Theology*, vol. 2, p. 156). ". . . the fact is emphatically clear in scripture that the entirety of the Godhead . . . has one name and one name only, and that one name is JESUS" (*The P.A.S.T.O.R.S. Course: Soteriology, Book Four of Five*, p. 49). "Christ himself declared, 'I am come in my Father's Name.' . . . He also laid claim to the same name Jehovah. . . . Concerning the name of the Holy Ghost, suffice it to quote Christ: 'But the Comforter which is the Holy Ghost, whom the Father will send in my name . . .' (Jn. 14:26)" (Ibid., pp. 51, 52). "Today, just as in the New Testament, believers speak with new tongues when they receive the Holy Ghost and enter into the body of Christ" (*Meet the United Pentecostal Church International*, p. 53).	Evangelical Christianity has always contended that faith is the means through which one is justified. Repentance—turning from sin—is merely the counterpart of faith—turning toward God. Baptism is in the name of the triune God—Father, Son, and Holy Spirit. Baptism in the name of Jesus—which is mentioned in the book of Acts—is only a statement of identification with the risen Lord. The *Didache*, a manual of the faith dating from the late first century A.D., has both the trinitarian baptismal formula and mention of baptism in the name of Jesus. The name of the Father and Son and Holy Ghost would be YAHWEH, not Jesus, and is equivalent to the Greek *Kurios*, or "Lord," in the New Testament. Jesus is *Kurios*. The reception of the Holy Spirit occurs at salvation but in no way is speaking in tongues viewed in the New Testament as a necessary result of this indwelling. Speaking in tongues occurs only three places in the book of Acts and in each instance serves as a sign of God's movement among a new group of people in the ancient world, not as evidence of personal salvation.

The Doctrine of Rewards and Punishment

Position	Support	Orthodox Response
Those who are saved will not be damned, but instead dwell with God for all eternity. Those who reject salvation through Jesus Christ will suffer eternal conscious punishment in hell.	"All whose names are not found written in the book of life will be cast into the lake of fire" (*Meet the United Pentecostal Church International*, p. 54). "Physical death is not cessation of the soul-mind, but is rather separation of the soul-mind from the body. The second death (spiritual) is separation of the spirit from God. Neither incorporates the idea of annihilation" (*The P.A.S.T.O.R.S. Course: Pneumatology, Book Three of Five*, p. 14).	These are orthodox statements.
Those who do not believe Oneness theology are either completely lost or not fully saved.	"Sincere profession based on a faulty concept of Christ is not enough; one must believe and obey the gospel.... Where does this leave those who have a certain degree of faith in Christ but have not obeyed the full gospel?... such people are pre-Pentecost believers, not part of the apostolic church.... they need to be led to further truth.... they are in the conception stage and have not yet had the new birth" (*The New Birth: Series in Pentecostal Theology*, vol. 2, pp. 313–14).	The Bible does not allow for a person to be partially saved. Either one is in Christ and justified by His blood or one is unregenerate and perishing. There is no halfway or in-between state, anymore than one could partially drown or be a "little bit pregnant." You are either born of the Word of God or you are not. "For you have been born again, not of perishable seed, but of imperishable, through the living and enduring word of God" (1Pe 1:23).

INTERESTING AND DISTINCTIVE BELIEFS

Position	Support	Orthodox Response
To retain salvation, one must remain holy through a variety of standards.	"**Holiness is essential to salvation**. Hebrews 12:14 is just as strong, as true, and as relevant to salvation as the words, 'You must be born again.' After the new birth experience, a conflict arises.... This battle is a battle for holiness, and we must win it in order to be saved" (*In Search of Holiness: Series in Pentecostal Theology*, vol. 3, p. 11). ". . . remember that a bad attitude will keep you out of heaven just as surely as any violation of outward holiness" (Ibid., p. 62).	Isaiah 64:6 says, "All our righteous acts are like filthy rags" in God's eyes. Our righteousness, or justification before God, comes by His grace through faith and not through works (Eph 2:8–9). Our right standing before God is based on the gift of Christ's righteousness imputed to us that cannot be earned (see Ro 4:5–6; Tit 3:5; Eph 2:4–5). John puts it this way: "My dear children, I write this to you so that you will not sin. But if anybody does sin, we have one who speaks to the Father in our defense—Jesus Christ, the Righteous One. He is the atoning sacrifice for our sins" (1Jn 2:1–2). Our staying saved is the work of Christ on our behalf; it is foolish and insulting to the Spirit of grace to haughtily imagine that our righteousnesses will be more important than Christ's in keeping us saved.
UPC standards for holiness are rigid, with restrictions covering television sets, cosmetics, and other commonplace things. For example, on the basis of 1 Corinthians 11:12–16, women are not allowed to cut their hair.	"We wholeheartedly disapprove of our people indulging in any activities which are not conducive to good Christianity and godly living, such as theaters, dances, mixed bathing, women cutting their hair, make-up, any apparel that immodestly exposes the body, all worldly sports and amusements; and unwholesome radio programs and music. Furthermore, because of the display of all these evils on television, we disapprove of any of our people having television sets in their homes" (*Articles of Faith of the United Pentecostal Church International*, pp. 9–10).	Various denominations or congregations have set standards of behavior to define external evidence of sanctification, some of which change according to the culture and the times. Many of these restrictions or prohibitions should be left to a person's conscience and not dictated by church leadership. The apostle Paul never admonished people to separate from the ungodly of the world as a means of sanctification but just the opposite (see 1Co 5:9–10).
School students cannot participate in many common activities including sports, dances, and theatrical performances.	"We disapprove of school students attending shows, dances, dancing classes, theatres, engaging in school activities against their religious scruples, and wearing gymnasium clothes which immodestly expose the body" (*Articles of Faith of the United Pentecostal Church International*, p. 14).	Where the Word of God is silent, there is liberty in trusting that God's Spirit will lead us in His sovereignty. First John 2:27 states, "As for you, the anointing you received from him remains in you, and you do not need anyone to teach you. But as his anointing teaches you about all things and as that anointing is real, not counterfeit—just as it has taught you, remain in him."

Position	Support	Orthodox Response
It is ungodly for women to wear jewelry.	"Those who are really consecrated to God will not adorn themselves with jewelry. It is vanity—the opposite of humility" (*In Search of Holiness: Series in Pentecostal Theology,* vol. 3, p. 118). ". . . women believer's are admonished by both Peter and Paul to adorn themselves in 'modest apparel', abstaining from attempting to produce physical beauty by use of accoutrements of the world—i.e., jewelry, pearls, trinkets, etc. (I Tim. 2:9, 10, I Pet. 3:3–5)" (*The P.A.S.T.O.R.S. Course: Soteriology, Book Four of Five,* p. 66).	The apostle Paul asks, "Why should my freedom be judged by another's conscience?" (1Co 10:29). He also says, "Blessed is the man who does not condemn himself by what he approves" (Ro 14:22). All believers, including those in authority, are fallible and accountable directly to God (Ro 14:4). Disdaining beautification is as much a form of vanity and self-adulation—and therefore contrary to the Spirit of grace—as is an over-concern for achieving it. Although the apostle Peter said that a woman's beauty should not be outward *only,* he did not preclude or forbid the adornment of the body (1Pe 3:3).
Women cannot wear makeup because it is a heathen practice.	"Dye for the hair, paint for the face, and mascara for the eyes, makes the present society a strange mixture of artificiality and hypocrisy. The United Pentecostal Church has taken a position that all of these conditions are heathenistic in origin and date back to Queen Jezebel. . . . The scriptures give us a very decided understanding that the natural beauty of women . . . demands every aspect of reality and natural appearance" (*The P.A.S.T.O.R.S. Course: Soteriology, Book Four of Five,* p. 72).	Many conventions that are heathen in origin have been allowed in different times and cultures. The names of the months and the days of the week on the calendar all come from heathen or non-Christian sources, yet they are used by all without concern. The use of cosmetics extends back to ancient Egypt and elsewhere, predating Jezebel. Women in the most ancient of societies, including Israel, all used some form of makeup. There is no explicit biblical injunction against cosmetics per se.

18

Urantia Foundation

FACTS AND HISTORY

Facts	
Topic	*Current Facts*
Membership	The Urantia Foundation, founded in 1950 in Chicago, has no membership. Its sole purpose has always been to publish and disseminate the teachings contained in *The Urantia Book*, a 2,097-page collection of revelations received from about 1929 to 1942 (*The Origin of the Urantia Book*, p. 4) by an anonymous person who was supposedly in contact with "numerous supermortal (angel-like) beings" (*Introduction*, p. 9). The preferred method of spreading the doctrines contained in *The Urantia Book* is "quiet person-to-person dissemination" (*Encyclopedia of American Religions*, 3d ed., J. Gordon Melton, pp. 714–15). The Foundation is led by a board of trustees of five people who serve for life.
	From 1955 to 1989 an organization called the Urantia Brotherhood, "a voluntary and fraternal association of believers in the teachings of *The Urantia Book*," was closely associated with the Foundation (Letter dated May 9, 1978, as quoted in "Urantia... the Brotherhood, the Book," *SCP Journal*, August 1981, p. 1). When the Brotherhood and Foundation split, the Brotherhood reorganized under the name Fifth Epochal Fellowship, which in 1991 was shortened to simply "The Fellowship." Another organization committed to spreading the teachings of *The Urantia Book* is the Jesusonian Foundation based in Boulder, Colorado.
Worship	No worship services are conducted by Urantia-oriented groups; but there *are* Urantian "funeral services." Although adherents often meet to discuss what they have learned, these sessions are not considered services or church gatherings. Literature originally published by the Urantia Brotherhood refers to itself as "a social group which has a religious objective" ("A Brotherhood—Not a Church or a Sect," by William S. Sadler, *The Urantian: A Journal of Urantia Brotherhood*, March 1976, as quoted in "Urantia... the Brotherhood, the Book," *SCP Journal*, August 1981, p. 3).
	When a Urantia-oriented group, called a society, meets on a regular basis, the meetings are usually held on Sunday. During these gatherings a creedal statement is read, but there are no other rites, no rituals, and no clergy. Each meeting is designed simply to discuss the various "truths" being learned from *The Urantia Book*. Since the mid-1970s, several thousand Urantia Book readers believe they have been contacted by supermortal intelligences with additional revelations about mankind, divine truth, and the future.
Presidents of the Urantia Foundation	1950– William Sadler Jr. (son of Dr. William Sadler) Warren H. Kulieke Alven Kulieke Dr. Meredith Sprunger John Hales Martin W. Myers Patricia Sadler Mundelius

Facts (cont.)

Topic	Current Facts
Publications	The Urantia Foundation publishes *The Urantia Book* (first published in 1955) and *Urantia News... from Urantia Foundation*. Circulation figures for the Urantia Foundation's newsletter are unavailable. As of 1995, more than 250,000 copies of the book were in print in three languages. It is noteworthy that *The Urantia Book* in particular interacts with the Bible a great deal and devotes much attention to reinterpreting the meaning of many concepts and facts presented in Scripture. (See under the various Theology topics.)
General statement of beliefs	Literature from the Urantia Foundation and kindred groups contains a number of lofty claims about *The Urantia Book* (hereafter *UB*). The *UB* allegedly answers many of life's most peplexing questions, including the following: Why do evil and suffering exist? Is there intelligent life on other planets? What is heaven like? Who is Jesus? What did he teach? Where is he now? What is God's purpose for your life? (*Introduction*, p. 1).
	The *UB* offers answers to these and other thought-provoking questions, but none of them are consistent with the teachings of the Bible. The book denies the orthodox doctrines of the Trinity, the uniqueness and true deity of Jesus, His virgin birth through Mary, His sacrificial death for our sins, His physical resurrection from the dead, and other teachings. It is no surprise that the *UB* declares, "Modern culture must become spiritually baptized with a new revelation of Jesus' life and illuminated with new understanding of his gospel of eternal salvation" (*UB*, p. 2084).

History

The story of how *The Urantia Book* came into being was long shrouded in secrecy by the Urantia Foundation. The board of trustees made a pledge not to reveal its human author or means of transmission. So the particulars of its origin remained largely unknown until the discoveries of Martin Gardner as recounted in 1991 in the journal *The Skeptical Inquirer*. Gardner greatly expanded on his findings in his 1995 book *Urantia: The Great Cult Mystery*.

The history of the *UB* begins in the 1920s with a psychiatrist and former Seventh-day Adventist named William S. Sadler (1875–1969), who also served as a lecturer in pastoral psychiatry and counseling at McCormick Theological Seminary in Chicago. The Urantia Foundation now has its headquarters in Sadler's former home.

The "official" story from the Urantia Foundation is that a group of people met in Sadler's home in the 1920s to discuss "psychological and medical topics" (Meredith J. Sprunger, *The Origin of the Urantia Book*, p. 3). This group called itself the Forum. Communication was somehow established between the Forum and superhuman, celestial personalities known as the "the revelators" (Sprunger, p. 3; *UB*, p. 1109). These "revelators" are the true authors of the *UB*.

To impart the contents of the *UB*, the revelators made contact with one of the members of the Forum through his "Thought Adjuster," a fragment of God supposedly indwelling all people. According to the *UB*, the Thought Adjuster is an "impersonal entity" (pp. 31, 1203), yet it is "conscious" (pp. 431, 1204–8) and has "volition" (p. 1183). The identity of the contactee was never to be disclosed. Meredith Sprunger, a past president of the Urantia Foundation, admits that there are "numerous missing links in the story of how this revelation came to appear in written English" (Sprunger, p. 4). Inquirers are told the *UB* should be judged on its merits rather than on the human vehicle or manner of its arrival.

Most of the members of the Forum never knew the contactee's identity. At the meetings Dr. Sadler would read typewritten manuscripts from the revelators. Forum members would write out questions for Dr. Sadler, who would relay them to the contactee. Written responses to the questions would appear later. As to the manner of communication, the members were told that it "in no way parallels or impinges upon" psychic phenomena such as automatic writing, telepathy, clairvoyance, or trance mediumship.

Slight details of the story can be found in a book by William Sadler, *The Mind at Mischief: Tricks and Deceptions of the Subconscious and How to Cope With Them* (New York: Funk & Wagnalls, 1929). Sadler said that since 1911 he had been present at about 250 instances of a man's (while supposedly sleeping) being "used as a sort of clearing house for the coming and going of alleged extra-planetary personalities" and beings "en route from one universe to another." The entities presented an advanced philosophy that Sadler deemed both scientific and "essentially Christian." Sadler was then having a stenographer take down the messages from these entities while the man slept.

More of the puzzle was revealed in 1975 in a Fawcett paperback by Harold Sherman, *How to Know What to Believe*. Sherman and his wife joined the Forum in 1941 and attended until 1947. Sherman (who died in 1987) revealed much about the inner workings of the early Forum meetings, though he disguised the names of all the participants, including the name of the *UB* itself. Martin Gardner in 1991 identified the sleeping contact to be Wilfred Custer Kellogg (1876–1956), Sadler's brother-in-law.

Kellogg was raised a Seventh-day Adventist, which explains much of the Adventist influence in the *UB*. He and his wife moved in with the Sadlers in 1912, which gave Dr. Sadler ample opportunity to observe his brother-in-law's nocturnal revelations. Kellogg was a member of the Forum inner circle from the beginning, and various factors make identifying him as the contact credible. The 196 Urantia papers were composed, edited, and revised between 1929 and 1939, at which time the "revelators" asked that the book be published.

The *UB* is divided into four parts, preceded by a 17-page foreword that offers definitions of terms. Part 1 addresses the nature of the universe and of deity. Part 2 discusses "local universes" and the planets we travel to after death. Part 3 gives the history of earth (or "Urantia"), including the evolution of life, religion, and the soul. Part 4 offers a revision of the life and teachings of Jesus Christ. In February 1995, following a lawsuit filed by the Urantia Foundation against people who were republishing the *UB*, a federal district court declared that the *UB*'s copyright renewal was invalid and the book is now legally in the public domain.

THEOLOGY

The Doctrine of Revelation

Position	Support	Orthodox Response
There have been five epochs or periods when earth (Urantia) has been given divine revelation. *The Urantia Book* is the fifth such revelation.	The first "revelation" was the materialization of 100 beings from 100 different planets to Mesopotamia 500,000 years ago, who served as staff assistants to Caligastia (who later became the Devil). After 300,000 years, 60 of them fell away (*UB*, pp. 741–42, 758, 1007).	In *none* of these epochs is the Bible called a revelation from God. The only scripture it recognizes is *The Urantia Book* itself. Figures such as Adam and Melchizedek are depicted as aliens from other planets. True revelation cannot come from mythical beings whose history cannot be corroborated.
	The second "revelation" was when Adam and Eve materialized on earth from the planet Jerusem 38,000 years ago. They provided truth for 100 years until their "default" in following Lucifer (Ibid., pp. 828, 840, 1007).	In each of the first four cases, the data supposedly "revealed" by these celestial beings were lost to mankind. Even with regard to Jesus, the *UB* claims that the apostles distorted His message, so that His "revelation" was mangled as well. By contrast, the Bible affirms that God takes sovereign initiative in disclosing His nature, law, will, and grace to mankind. God says of His word "from my mouth: It will not return to me empty, but will accomplish what I desire and achieve the purpose for which I sent it" (Isa 55:11).
	The third "revelation" came in 1980 B.C. when Machiventa Melchizedek materialized in Palestine. The Melchizedeks were a class of beings and the "offspring" of Michael of Nebadon and his spirit consort (Ibid., pp. 384–85, 1007–8, 1015).	
	The fourth "revelation" occurred when Michael of Nebadon entered the son of Joseph and Mary and was incarnated on August 21, 7 B.C., as Jesus Christ (Ibid., pp. 1008, 1309–17, 1346).	God's word is preserved by His power. "I tell you the truth, until heaven and earth disappear, not the smallest letter, not the least stroke of a pen, will by any means disappear from the Law until everything is accomplished" (Mt 5:18).
	The fifth "revelation" occurred in 1931–1935 and some time later, with the coming of the Urantia Papers. This is "the most recent presentation of truth to the mortals of Urantia. These papers... [are] a composite presentation by many beings" (Ibid., p. 1008).	

The Doctrine of Revelation (cont.)

Position	Support	Orthodox Response
All revelation is fallible and incomplete, and the people who receive it are generally resistant to change. Belief in a final, infallible revelation is cultic.	"Evolutionary religion makes no provision for change or revision. . . . its followers believe it is The Truth; 'the faith once delivered to the saints' must, in theory, be both final and infallible. The cult resists development because real progress is certain to modify or destroy the cult itself" (*UB*, p. 1006). "But no revelation short of the attainment of the Universal Father can ever be complete. All other celestial ministrations are no more than partial, transient, and practically adapted to local conditions in time and space" (Ibid., p. 1008).	*The Urantia Book* fails to distinguish between developing or *progressive* revelation and *contradictory* revelation. The Old Testament makes provision for change, such as predicting that God will issue a new covenant with His law written on our hearts (Jer 31:31–34). This is not the same as a contradictory "revelation." Revelation is an act of God, not the guesswork of men (Jer 1:9; 2Pe 1:21). While revelation in Scripture is not *exhaustive* (e.g., not all the miracles of Jesus are recorded), it is nevertheless authoritative and inspired, even to its selection of words (see Mk 12:26; Gal 3:16).
Moses could not have written the Pentateuch. The book of Genesis and other books credited to Moses were composed around 500 B.C., as was most of the Old Testament.	"The Old Testament account of creation dates from long after the time of Moses; he never taught the Hebrews such a distorted story" (*UB*, p. 837). "The Hebrews did little writing until about 900 B.C., and having no written language until such a late date, they had several different stories of creation. . . . almost a thousand years after Moses' sojourn on earth the tradition of creation in six days was written out and subsequently credited to him. . . . the contemporary Hebrews of around 500 B.C. did not consider these writings to be divine revelations" (Ibid., p. 838).	The belief that the Hebrews had no written language in Moses' day (the Graf-Wellhausen theory) was common when *The Urantia Book* was allegedly being channeled. Since the 1930s, archaeological findings have yielded inscriptions in Hebrew and related Semitic languages dating back to 1500 B.C. Also, the *UB* itself says Moses was an educated man whose mother was from "the royal family of Egypt," so he could at least have written in Egyptian! Moreover, the Pentateuch claims Mosaic authorship. "Moses then wrote down everything the LORD had said. . . . Then he took the Book of the Covenant and read it to the people" (Ex 24:4, 7). Jesus affirmed that the Law came from Moses (Mt 19:8) and stated that "he wrote about me" (Jn 5:46).

The Doctrine of Revelation (cont.)

Position	Support	Orthodox Response
Although the Bible has much truth, it also contains many errors and false claims about God.	In the *UB,* Jesus tells the apostle Nathaniel, "The Scriptures are faulty and altogether human in origin. . . . Many of these books were not written by the persons whose names they bear" (*UB,* p. 1767). "Nathaniel, never permit yourself for one moment to believe the Scripture records which tell you that the God of love directed your forefathers to go forth in battle to slay all their enemies—men, women, and children. Such records are the words of men, not very holy men, and they are not the word of God" (Ibid., p. 1768). Jesus warns Nathaniel of "this erroneous idea of the absolute perfection of the Scripture record and the infallibility of its teachings. . . . Many earnest seekers after the truth have been, and will continue to be, confused and disheartened by these doctrines of the perfection of the Scriptures" (Ibid.).	Jesus never discredited the Old Testament. In fact, the strongest argument we have for the inerrancy of Scripture comes from Jesus' own statements. Jesus spoke of the Scriptures in the highest terms. He said the Scriptures "cannot be broken" (Jn 10:35), that they "must be fulfilled" (Lk 24:44), and that they contain "the command of God" (Mt 15:3) and are "the word of God" (Mk 7:13; Jn 10:35). Jesus said God was the author of Genesis 2:24 (Mt 19:4–5). For Jesus, the Scriptures were the final way to resolve doctrinal questions ("What is written in the Law?"—Lk 10:26) or resist demonic temptation ("Away from me, Satan! For it is written. . ."—Mt 4:10). In the Sermon on the Mount, Jesus upheld the validity of the written word (Mt 5:17).
The apostle Paul misrepresented Jesus' teachings.	"Paul, in an effort to utilize the widespread adherence to the better types of the mystery religions, made certain adaptations of the teachings of Jesus so as to render them more acceptable to. . . prospective converts" (*UB,* p. 1337). "Paul's theory of original sin, the doctrines of hereditary guilt and innate evil and redemption therefrom, was partially Mithraic in origin, having little in common with Hebrew theology. . . or Jesus' teachings. Some phases of Paul's teachings regarding original sin and the atonement were original with himself" (Ibid., p. 1339). "In his last years Abner denounced Paul as the 'clever corrupter of the life teachings of Jesus of Nazareth, the Son of the living God'" (Ibid., p. 1832).	If the apostle Paul were so unreliable, why did Luke (author of Acts) and Peter speak so highly of him? The latter half of Acts shows Paul faithfully proclaiming the gospel. The apostles in Jerusalem endorsed Paul's ministry (Ac 11; 13; 15). Peter wrote, "Our dear brother Paul also wrote you with the wisdom that God gave him," even though Paul's letters contain "some things that are hard to understand, which ignorant and unstable people distort, as they do the other Scriptures, to their own destruction" (2Pe 3:15–16). By these words Peter affirms Paul's letters as inspired Scripture. This Urantia attack on Paul also does not account for God's sovereignty. God is both able and willing to protect His word from distortion (Dt 29:29; Ps 111:7–8; Pr 30:5–6).

The Doctrine of Revelation (cont.)

Position	Support	Orthodox Response
Even *The Urantia Book* contains errors and will need revision.	"We full well know that, while the historic facts and religious truths of this series of revelatory presentations will stand on the records of the ages to come, within a few short years many of our statements regarding the physical sciences will stand in need of revision in consequence of additional scientific developments and new discoveries. These new developments we even now foresee, but we are forbidden to include such humanly undiscovered facts in the revelatory records. Let it be made clear that revelations are not necessarily inspired. The cosmology of these revelations is *not inspired*" (*UB,* p. 1109, italics in original). "Truth may be but relatively inspired, even though revelation is invariably a spiritual phenomenon. While statements with reference to cosmology are never inspired, such revelations are of immense value in that they at least transiently clarify knowledge" (Ibid.).	In these quotations, *UB* divides its revelation into three categories: historic facts, religious truths, and statements on cosmology and physical science. The *UB* views the first two as true and correct, but its scientific statements as uninspired or even false. It says its *cosmology* is "never inspired," but does *not* make similar disclaimers with regard to its statements on theology or history. Science in the *UB* is indeed errant. It claims that our part of the galaxy was created 875 billion years ago (p. 652); modern science estimates the age of the entire universe at 15–20 billion years. The *UB* says there are now 11 planets in the solar system (pp. 656–58); astronomers know of only nine. The *UB* gives the Sun a surface temperature of 6000° F and an internal temperature of 35,000,000° F (p. 463); in fact, the solar surface is about 10,000° F and its core about 27,000,000°. F. Martin Gardner's book *Urantia* contains two chapters on its scientific errors.

The Doctrine of God—*The Trinity*

Position	Support	Orthodox Response
The Urantia Book claims to be monotheistic, yet it makes numerous references to other Gods, Deities, and Creators in the universe. It also misquotes the Bible to promote polytheism.	"God is one God; he is alone and by himself; he is the only one. And this one God is our Maker and the last destiny of the soul" (*UB,* p. 1448). However, ". . . throughout the central creation of the Gods, the Father acts, and creature personality appears. Then does the presence of the Paradise Deities fill all organized space" (Ibid., 91). ". . . the spirits of the Gods even now indwell you, hover over you, and inspire you to true worship" (Ibid., p. 304). "In the persons of the Supreme Creators the Gods have descended from Paradise to the domains of time and space" (Ibid., p. 1278). "Do you not recall how the Scriptures begin by asserting that 'In the beginning the Gods created the heavens and the earth'?" (Ibid., p. 1598). "The Gods are my caretakers; I shall not stray; Side by side they lead me in the beautiful paths and glorious refreshing of life everlasting. I shall not, in this Divine Presence want for food nor thirst for water" (Ibid., p. 552).	The terms "Gods," "Deities," and "Creators" appear hundreds of times in *The Urantia Book.* The *UB* teaches that there are 700,000 "local universes," each with its own "Michael" or Creator Son, who is a God to that universe and who rules with a spirit "consort." Although the *UB* recognizes a chief God (the Paradise Father), it agrees that there are gods below him. Yet the *UB* professes to be monotheistic. The *UB* is like Mormonism, which also claims to be monotheistic. Mormonism says there is only one God over *this* universe. But the Bible is clear that God created *all* that exists (Col 1:16; Rev 4:11), not simply all that we can see. Further, God says there are no beings *like* Him (Isa 46:9), and there are no other Gods *with* Him or *beside* Him (Isa 43:10; 44:6). "God is one and there is no other but him" (Mark 12:32). The *UB* revision of Genesis 1:1 ("In the beginning God created the heavens and the earth") and Psalm 23 ("The LORD is my shepherd, I shall not be in want") to refer to "Gods" (plural) is an attempt to revise the Bible to teach polytheism.

The Doctrine of God—*The Trinity (cont.)*

Position	Support	Orthodox Response
The traditional doctrine of the Trinity is false.	"One of the greatest sources of confusion on Urantia concerning the nature of God grows out of the failure of your sacred books clearly to distinguish between the personalities of the Paradise Trinity and between Paradise Deity and the local universe creators and administrators" (*UB,* p. 60). "The Eternal Son is the original and only-begotten Son of God. He is God the Son, the Second Person of Deity and the associate creator of all things.... Paul confused Jesus, Creator Son of the local universe, with the Second Person of Deity, the Eternal Son of Paradise" (Ibid., pp. 73, 1144). "Not since the times of Jesus has the factual identity of the Paradise Trinity been known on Urantia... until its presentation in these revelatory disclosures. But though the Christian concept of the Trinity erred in fact, it was practically true" (Ibid., p. 1145).	The *UB* takes biblical references to Jesus Christ and the Holy Spirit and divides them to form two or more identities for each one. Thus the *UB* posits an Eternal Son which it calls the only-begotten Son of God, Second Person of the Trinity—and a secondary being *created* by the Eternal Son, which it identifies as Jesus Christ. Likewise, the book posits an Infinite Spirit (God the Spirit, Third Person of the Trinity, though even this is a created being); a secondary being it made, a "local universe Mother Spirit" which humans misidentify as the Spirit of God; and the "Holy Spirit," which is the Daughter Spirit's "circuit" (travels in space) and influence. The result of this revisionism is that Jesus Christ and the Holy Spirit are reinterpreted as secondary creatures, both brought into existence at a point in time, which, according to the *UB,* the Christian church mistakenly worships as truly God. The *UB* teaches that there are many Gods on par with, and above, Jesus.
God the Father continues to manifest himself as three more Gods who are coming into being, or, in the words of *The Urantia Book,* coming into "actualization." These other Gods are God the Supreme, God the Ultimate, and God the Absolute.	"Having achieved existential Deity expression of himself in the Son and the Spirit, the Father is now achieving experiential expression on hitherto impersonal and unrevealed deity levels as God the Supreme, God the Ultimate, and God the Absolute; but these experiential Deities are not now fully existent; they are in process of actualization" (*UB,* pp. 10–11). "The first three and past-eternal Deities of Paradise—the Universal Father, the Eternal Son, and the Infinite Spirit—are, in the eternal future, to be personality-complemented by the experiential actualization of associate evolutionary Deities—God the Supreme, God the Ultimate, and possibly God the Absolute" (Ibid., p. 13).	Orthodox Christianity and the Bible have never referred to the Father, the Son, and the Holy Spirit as "deities" or Gods. Christian theism is, by definition, monotheistic: We believe in one God (or deity) who exists in three Persons. Each Person is eternal and unchangeable in being and character, "who was, and is, and is to come" (Rev 4:8; see also 1:8). The claim that additional Gods (plural) come into existence through God's evolutionary experiences is self-refuting. If they come into existence, they cannot be God. The creature is not the Creator (Rom 1:25). It is also contradictory to refer to a possibly "impersonal" being which is not yet come into existence as Supreme, Ultimate, or Absolute.

Position	Support	Orthodox Response
The Urantia Book applies female terms to two members of its Trinity and to the deity that operates as the local "Holy Spirit": 1. **The Universal Father (or Paradise Father) is male.** 2. **The Eternal Son is also known as the Universal Mother, the Mother Son, and God the Mother. Together God the Father and God the Mother (Eternal Son) created the universe.** 3. **The Infinite Spirit is also known as the Paradise Mother Spirit and the Infinite Mother Spirit.** 4. **Below these are 700,000 "local universes," each with divine couples: a Creator Son (Michael) and a "local universe Mother Spirit" (a/k/a Daughter Spirit, or Mother Spirit), who functions as the Creative Consort to the Creator Son. The "circuits" (interplanetary travels) and personal influence of the Daughter Spirit constitute the Holy Spirit for that universe.**	"The monontia soul of an evolving mortal is really the son of the Adjuster action of the Universal Father and the child of the cosmic reaction of the Supreme Being, the Universal Mother" (*UB,* p. 1288). "The first act of the Inifinite Spirit is the inspection and recognition of his divine parents, the Father-Father and the Mother-Son" (Ibid., p. 90). "All soul-evolving humans are literally the evolutionary sons of God the Father and God the Mother, the Supreme Being" (Ibid., p. 1289). *(Also see the sections on Jesus Christ and the Holy Spirit below.)*	Although the idea of female deities fits well with modern feminism, it has no basis in biblical theology. "God is spirit" (Jn 4:24) and thus is neither gendered nor a sexual being. The Bible says God has no form and is not like any creature. However, though the Bible uses some female metaphors for God, as one who gave birth to Israel or who nurses her children, these metaphors are anthropomorphisms (that is, the application of human attributes to a Being who is not human). The difference is that the Bible presents *one* God, not two deities of different gender whose unions or parentage give rise to spirit offspring. This concept is more akin to paganism. Further, there is a logical ambiguity in referring to an "Eternal Son" who can *also* be called a "Mother Son" or "God the Mother." The Bible never translates female metaphors into an androgynous (bisexual) or basically female identity.

The Doctrine of God—*The Trinity (cont.)*

Position	Support	Orthodox Response
The apostolic Trinity was Father, Son, and Mother Spirit.	"The Christian concept of the Trinity, which began to gain recognition near the close of the first century after Christ, was comprised of the Universal Father, the Creator Son of Nebadon, and the Divine Minister of Salvington—the Mother Spirit of the local universe and creative consort of the Creator Son" (*UB*, pp. 1144–45).	The first-century church never had a doctrine of the Trinity as Father, secondary Son, and Mother Spirit. The theology of the first three centuries after Christ is widely known, and absolutely *no* Christian leaders taught that Jesus had a female "consort" spirit in heaven. To the contrary, all attempts to make Jesus a lesser God or to view Him as a "derived" deity with a beginning in time was condemned by the bishops and leaders from the very earliest days. Urantia teaching is similar to the heretical Gnostic teaching of the second and third centuries.

The Doctrine of Jesus Christ—*The Deity of Christ*

Position	Support	Orthodox Response
Jesus is not the Eternal Son of God. He is the offspring, so to speak, of the the Eternal Son and the Eternal Father. He is only one of many similar beings called Michael Sons. These entities are eventually paired with a Daughter Spirit that is generated by the Infinite Spirit. Each pair then goes through the "superuniverse" and creates a "local universe" complete with inhabitable planets on which an evolutionary cycle is started.	**Q:** "[You mean that] from the Eternal Father and the Son, you have the Michael Sons? And from the Eternal Spirit, you have one Daughter Spirit? Or, many Daughter Spirits?" **A:** "One Daughter Spirit for each Michael Son. They're to work in partnership" (May 10, 1995, interview with Jesusonian Foundation representative). **Q:** "So, then, Jesus is a Paradise Son, also called a Michael Son, which is one of many offspring of the Father and the original Eternal Son? And these Michael Sons go throughout the Universe and create a series of planets on which is begun the evolutionary cycle of that planet?" **A:** "Right. They create an entire local universe.... You have the Infinite Spirit, [who] creates a Daughter Spirit that works in partnership [with a corresponding Michael Son] and together they actually go out and create the universes. So, the Michael Son and the Daughter Spirit work together" (Ibid.).	The Bible contradicts the notion of many Christs by stating that all things were created through Jesus (see Jn 1:1–5) and that all things consist or are held together by Him (see Col 1:17). This means that everything that is in all the creation of God (this universe, dimension, or any other one that YAHWEH created) was created by the one and only Christ and is currently held together by Him. As Paul says in Acts 17:28, "In him we live and move and have our being."

The Doctrine of Jesus Christ—*The Deity of Christ (cont.)*

Position	Support	Orthodox Response
Jesus is *called* God in *The Urantia Book,* but ultimately Jesus was created at a point in time. Jesus is a "Creator Son" formed by the "Eternal Son"; he is not absolute deity. The Eternal Son above Jesus is also known as the Original Son.	"Our Creator Son [Jesus] is not the Eternal Son, the existential Paradise associate of the Universal Father and the Infinite Spirit. Michael of Nebadon is not a member of the Paradise Trinity" (*UB,* p. 366). "The primary or Creator Sons are brought into being by the Universal Father and the Eternal Son" (Ibid., p. 224). When the thoughts of the Universal Father and the Eternal Son join perfectly together, ". . . there flashes into full-fledged being a new and original Creator Son," who was created by "those divine creative potentials which united to bring this Michael Son into existence" (Ibid., p. 235). "Had the New Testament writer referred to the Eternal Son, he would have uttered the truth when he wrote: 'In the beginning was the Word, and the Word was with God, and the Word was God. All things were made by him, and without him was not anything made that was made.'. . . On your world, . . . this Original [Eternal] Son has been confused with a co-ordinate Creator Son, Michael of Nebadon" (Ibid., p. 74).	The Urantia view of Jesus ("Michael of Nebadon") is heretical for several reasons: (1) It denies His true deity, making Jesus a creature who came into being at a point in time; (2) it denies that Jesus is the Word of God referred to in John 1:1 and instead applies that title to a different entity; (3) it denies that Jesus is truly the Son of God, making Him instead a "son of the Son of God"; yet the Bible teaches unequivocally that Jesus is *the* Son of God, not *a* son of God; and (4) it denies that Jesus existed eternally, stating instead that Jesus/Michael came into existence at a point in the past; yet the Bible is clear that Jesus is truly eternal (see Mic 5:2; Jn 8:58; Col 1:16–17; Rev 22:13). Many sects which will occasionally call Jesus "God," but when it comes down to asking what they mean by this term, they will not credit Jesus Christ with absolute and true deity.
Jesus is one of 700,000 Creator Sons, each of whom presides over a different "local universe." Each Creator is named Michael. Our local universe is Nebadon, so Jesus is Michael of Nebadon. Jesus is not God the Son.	"I do not know the exact number of Creator Sons in existence, but I have good reasons for believing that there are more than seven hundred thousand" (*UB,* p. 235). "The Creator Sons are the makers and rulers of the local universes of time and space. These universe creators and sovereigns are of dual origin, embodying the characteristics of God the Father and God the Son. . . . These primary Paradise Sons are personalized as Michaels. As they go forth from Paradise to found their universes, they are known as Creator Michaels. . . . Sometimes we refer to the sovereign of your universe of Nebadon as Christ Michael" (Ibid., p. 234). "Our Creator Son is the personification of the 611,121st original concept of infinite identity of simultaneous origin in the Universal Father and the Eternal Son. The Michael of Nebadon is the 'only-begotten Son' personalizing this 611,121st universal concept of divinity and infinity" (Ibid., p. 366).	These are additional beliefs that make the Urantia Book a false and deceptive revelation. Continuing the list of points given above, we find that *The Urantia Book* (5) denies the uniqueness of Jesus Christ, inasmuch as it makes Him only one among 700,000 peers and equals; the Bible says that Jesus is God's "one and only Son" (Jn 3:16, 18); in Greek this word is *monogenes*, which means "unique or one-of-a-kind"; although parts of the *UB* claim that *each* of the 700,000 Michael Sons is an "only begotten Son," this certainly denies the basic meaning of one-of-a-kind; (6) the *UB* also denies the work of Christ in creation; the Bible declares that Jesus is the creator of *all* things in heaven and earth (Jn 1:3; 1Co 8:6; Col 1:16), and the Scripture does not limit His creative work to merely one part of the galaxy, as the *UB* contends; (7) it also denies the supremacy of Christ; Scripture declares that Jesus has supreme and final authority "in the heavenly realms, far above all rule and authority, power and dominion, and every title that can be given, not only in the present age but also in the one to come" (Eph 1:20–21).

The Doctrine of Jesus Christ—*The Deity of Christ (cont.)*

Position	Support	Orthodox Response
Jesus was incarnated ("bestowed") at least six separate times, as six different life forms on many different planets, before coming to earth.	"Michael of Nebadon had bestowed himself six times after the similitude of six differing orders of his diverse creation of intelligent beings. Then he prepared to descend upon Urantia in the likeness of mortal flesh" (*UB*, p. 1323). On Michael's fourth incarnation 450 million years ago, he appeared as "what you might denominate a private secretary, to twenty-six different master teachers, functioning on twenty-two different worlds" (Ibid., p. 1313).	The belief in intelligent life on other planets is basic to *The Urantia Book*. Its Jesus incarnated repeatedly. However, the Bible is silent about the habitation of other planets. Other than humans, the only other sentient creatures mentioned in Scripture are angels and demons. In the Incarnation, Jesus Christ as eternal God took on a human body and nature that He possesses even now (1Ti 2:5; 2Jn 7). Had Jesus incarnated *previously* as He did on earth, He would not have been "God with us" (Mt 1:23), but God-plus-aliens with us. Since the Bible portrays Christ as being solely God before taking on flesh, the theory of previous incarnations for Jesus must be false. Further, when Jesus became human, He also became mortal—that is, able to die. At the resurrection He became immortal—unable to die (1Co 15:53–54). This means that if Jesus had died and resurrected on other planets, He should have been immortal when He came here. If the manner of incarnation was similar, He would have had to dispense with not only His "other" physical body but His immortality as well.

The Doctrine of Jesus Christ—*The Humanity of Christ*

Position	Support	Orthodox Response
Jesus was both human and divine. But he was only divine in that his humanity was coupled with "the Christ," which imparted deity to Jesus.	"Throughout his entire experience he was truly both human and divine, even as he yet is. . . . while the human Jesus was recognized as having a religion, the divine Jesus (Christ) almost overnight became a religion. Paul's Christianity made sure of the adoration of the divine Christ, but it almost wholly lost sight of the struggling and valiant human Jesus of Galilee" (*UB*, p. 2092).	Jesus was "very God of very God" (as one creed puts it), and His goings forth were from eternity. He did not *become* God or have deity added to Him. He always was, and always will be, the Divine Creator (see Mic 5:2; Heb 13:8).

Position	Support	Orthodox Response
Jesus was conceived through natural relations between Joseph and Mary. He was not born miraculously of a virgin, and angelic appearances were the only supernatural events connected to the conception and birth of Jesus.	"Joshua ben Joseph [Jesus], the Jewish baby, was conceived and was born into the world just as all other babies before and since *except* that this particular baby was the incarnation of Michael of Nebadon.... The only supernatural event associated with the birth of Jesus was this announcement to Ardnon and his associates [i.e., the Chaldean magi] by the seraphim [angels] of former attachment to Adam and Eve" (*UB,* p. 1317). "Gabriel's announcement to Mary was made the day following the conception of Jesus and was the only event of supernatural occurrence connected with her entire experience of carrying and bearing the child of promise" (Ibid., p. 1347). "At first Joseph had doubts about the Gabriel visitation.... How could the offspring of human beings be a child of divine destiny?" (Ibid.). "Even the passage, 'a maiden shall bear a son,' was made to read, 'a virgin shall bear a son'" (Ibid., p. 1348).	Note a contradiction: On page 1317 the *UB* says the *only* supernatural event associated with Jesus' birth was the announcement of the angels to the magi (the *UB* says there was no "star"). But on page 1347 it says the *only* supernatural event Mary experienced in bearing Jesus was Gabriel's appearance to her. The denial that Mary was a virgin when she conceived Jesus smacks of liberal skepticism, which appears in large doses in the *UB*. Although the *UB* affirms that *some* of the miracles recorded in the Bible took place, it denies many others outright or reinterprets them as natural events. The key prophecy of Isaiah 7:14 ("Therefore the Lord himself will give you a sign: The virgin will be with child and will give birth to a son...") is said to have been distorted and applied to Jesus after His birth. The Hebrew word for "virgin" in this verse is *'alma* and can refer to a young woman of pre-childbearing age. When the Jews translated the OT into Greek about 250 B.C. (the Septuagint), they used the word *parthenos* to translate *'alma* in Isaiah 7:14, and *parthenos* means a true virgin. No ordinary pregnancy could qualify as a sign from God! Matthew's gospel records that Joseph "had no union with her until she gave birth to" Jesus (1:25). Luke also states that Mary was a virgin (1:27, 34). Other Old and New Testament allusions (Ge 3:15; Jn 8:41; Gal 4:4) also testify to Mary's virginity.
Jesus did not fulfill the Old Testament messianic prophecies, nor did he believe he was the Messiah. The messianic prophecies were applied to Jesus long after his death to make him *appear* to be the Messiah, such as Isaiah's prophecy of a virgin who would bear a son.	"He [Jesus] had thoroughly considered the idea of the Jewish Messiah and was firmly convinced that he was not to be that Messiah.... He knew he would never sit on the throne of David at Jerusalem.... Likewise he was certain he was never to appear as the Son of Man depicted by the Prophet Daniel" (*UB,* p. 1390). "And now he [Jesus] made his final decision regarding those Scriptures which his mother had taught him, such as: 'The Lord has said to me, "You are my Son; this day have I begotten you. Ask of me, and I will give you the heathen for your inheritance and the uttermost parts of the earth for your possession. You shall break them with a rod of iron; you shall dash them in pieces like a potter's vessel."' ... Jesus of Nazareth reached the conclusion that such utterances did not refer to him" (Ibid., p 1522).	*The Urantia Book* has to claim that the apostles were deluded about the messiahship of Jesus because this teaching runs throughout the New Testament. The very prophecies that the *UB* says Jesus allegedly did not believe in are applied to Jesus in the NT. For example, that Jesus would sit on the "throne of his father David" was spoken by the angel Gabriel to Mary (Lk 1:32). The phrase "You are my Son; today I have become your Father" (Ps 2:7) is applied to Jesus three times in the NT (Ac 13:33; Heb 1:5; 5:5). Peter's announcement that Jesus is the Messiah, and specifically that Jesus was descended from David and would sit on David's throne, was made on the Day of Pentecost when Peter was filled with the Holy Spirit (Ac 2:29–31). The claim that Jesus was not the Messiah also fails to observe that the Hebrew word

The Doctrine of Jesus Christ—*The Humanity of Christ (cont.)*

Position	Support	Orthodox Response
. . . continued	"Peter persisted in making the mistake of trying to convince the Jews that Jesus was, after all, really and truly the Jewish Messiah. Right up to the day of his death, Simon Peter continued to suffer confusion in his mind" (Ibid., p. 1552). "Most of the so-called Messianic prophecies of the Old Testament were made to apply to Jesus long after his life had been lived on earth. . . . many figurative passages found throughout the Hebrew scriptures were subsequently misapplied to the life mission of Jesus. Many Old Testament sayings were so distorted as to appear to fit some episode of the Master's earth life" (Ibid., pp. 1347–48).	"Messiah" is interchangeable with the Greek word "Christ," each of which means the Anointed One. The NT records that the apostle Andrew told his brother, "'We have found the Messiah' (that is, the Christ)" (Jn 1:41). We may safely say that every biblical statement that Jesus is the Christ is also an affirmation that Jesus is the Messiah. For example, "These are written that you may believe that Jesus is the Christ" (Jn 20:31). In light of these facts, the *UB* falls under the judgment of 1 John 2:22: "Who is the liar? It is the man who denies that Jesus is the Christ. Such a man is the antichrist—he denies the Father and the Son."
Jesus was not literally a descendant of David, nor was he the "son of David," as stated in the Bible.	"Joseph was not of the line of King David" (*UB*, p. 1347). "[T]he many genealogies of both Joseph and Mary . . . were constructed subsequent to Michael's [i.e., Jesus'] career on earth. . . . on the whole they are not genuine and may not be depended upon as factual" (Ibid., p. 1348). "David and Solomon were not in the direct line of Joseph's ancestry, neither did Joseph's lineage go directly back to Adam" (Ibid., p. 1344). "Was he [Jesus] or was he not of the house of David? His mother averred he was; his father had ruled that he was not. He decided he was not" (Ibid., pp. 1390–91).	That Jesus would be literally descended from David was predicted in the Old Testament (2Sa 7:12–16; Isa 11:1; Jer 23:5) and fulfilled as stated in the genealogies of Christ (Mt 1:1, 6; Lk 3:31). The New Testament affirms this in several other ways also. According to Luke 1:32, when the angel Gabriel announced the incarnation to Mary, he said, "The Lord God will give him the throne of his father David." Matthew and Mark record several people who called out to Jesus as the "Son of David," and He never corrected them (Mt 9:27; 15:22; Mk 10:47). The apostle Paul taught that Jesus was descended from David (Ac 13:22–23; Rom 1:3). Finally, Jesus Himself declared, "I am the Root and the Offspring of David, and the bright Morning Star" (Rev 22:16). The attempt of the *UB* to question Matthew's genealogy is disingenuous, since the Jews were very careful to maintain their genealogies. The *UB* says that Joseph was adopted by a man called Zadoc, but there is no biblical support for such an occurrence.

The Doctrine of Jesus Christ—*The Resurrection of Christ*

Position	Support	Orthodox Response
Jesus did not rise physically and bodily from the tomb. He was raised in a "morontia" body, as a being composed of neither flesh nor spirit.	"Let us forever clarify the concept of the resurrection of Jesus by making the following statements: "1. His material or physical body was not a part of the resurrected personality. When Jesus came forth from the tomb, his body of flesh remained undisturbed in the sepulchre. He emerged from the burial tomb without moving the stones before the entrance and without disturbing the seals of Pilate" (*UB,* p. 2021). "2. He did not emerge from the tomb as a spirit. . . . "3. He did come forth from this tomb of Joseph in the very likeness of the morontia personalities. "After the resurrected Jesus emerged from his burial tomb, the body of flesh in which he had lived and wrought on earth for almost thirty-six years was still lying there in the sepulchre niche, undisturbed and wrapped in the linen sheet" (Ibid.). The apostles' discovery of an empty tomb "led to the formulation of a belief which was not true: the teaching that the material and mortal body of Jesus was raised from the grave" (Ibid., p. 2023).	The resurrection of Jesus Christ is the keystone of the Christian faith. The Bible says, "If Christ has not been raised, your faith is futile: you are still in your sins" (1Co 15:17). The *UB* claims Christ is "risen," but raised nonphysically in a "morontia body," supposedly halfway between physical and spiritual. This claim is refuted by several lines of evidence. First, early Judaism believed in physical resurrection and Jesus never corrected this. The books of Job and Daniel teach a resurrection of the flesh (Job 19:26–27; Da 12:2–3). David predicted a resurrection of Jesus' body (Ps 16:8–11; Ac 2: 25–32). The Pharisees taught a physical resurrection (Ac 23:6–8), as did Jesus himself (Jn 6:25). Second, logically what *dies* must be what is *raised* again. The New Testament uses the words "rise again," "raised back," "raised again" and other terms besides "resurrection." Since it is the *body,* it must be the *body* that is raised back to life. The Bible confirms this in Isaiah 26:19; Matthew 27:52; and Acts 9:40. Third, Jesus took pains to teach that His body would be returned to life. "Destroy this temple," He said, "and I will raise it again in three days." Later the disciples realized that "the temple he had spoken of was his body" (Jn 2:19–21). Jesus told the disciples that His resurrected body was made of "flesh and bones, as you see I have" (Lk 24:39). Whatever a "morontia body" is, it is a replacement for "flesh and bones," not the *same* flesh and bones.
The resurrected Christ had no wounds in his hands or feet.	"When the Master had so spoken, he looked down into the face of Thomas and said, 'And you, Thomas, who said you would not believe unless you could see me and put your finger in the nail marks of my hands, have now beheld me and heard my words; and though you see no nail marks on my hands, . . . be not faithless but believing" (*UB,* p. 2043).	The marks on Jesus' hands, feet, and side clarify the nature of His resurrection. According to the Bible, Jesus *did* show the wounds from the cross to His disciples (Jn 20:20–29). These wounds prove that the body that was crucified is the same body that was returned to life, glorified, and made immortal (1Co 15:42–44). They prove that Jesus was not an apparition or a reincarnation into a different body.

Position	Support	Orthodox Response
The corpse of Jesus in the tomb rapidly disintegrated.	"The tomb of Joseph was empty, not because the body of Jesus had been rehabilitated or resurrected, but because the celestial hosts had been granted their request to afford it a special and unique dissolution, a return of the 'dust to dust,' without the interventions of the delays of time. . . . "The mortal remains of Jesus underwent the same natural process of elemental disintegration as characterizes all human bodies on earth except that, in point of time, this natural mode of disintegration was greatly accelerated, hastened to the point where it became well-nigh instantaneous" (*UB,* pp. 2023–24).	*The Urantia Book* claims the body of Jesus decayed, or rotted, quickly. The New Testament teaches differently. Peter on the Day of Pentecost said that King David, "spoke of the resurrection of the Christ, that he was not abandoned to the grave, nor did his body see decay" (Ac 2:31). Paul even contrasts the corpse of David with the corpse of Christ: "For when David had served . . . he fell asleep; he was buried with his fathers and his body decayed. But the one whom God raised from the dead did not see decay" (Ac 13:36–37). Moreover, Jesus had challenged the Jews by saying, "Destroy this temple, and I will raise it again in three days" (Jn 2:19). Since "the temple" was a metaphor for Jesus' body, it would make little sense for Jesus to say, in effect, "Destroy this temple and in three days it will disintegrate completely." Jesus intended to raise His body, not replace it.

The Doctrine of the Holy Spirit

Position	Support	Orthodox Response
There are many divine Spirits. The chief is the Infinite Spirits Third Person of Deity, also known as God the Spirit, the Conjoint Actor, or the Paradise Mother Spirit. The Infinite Spirit was created by the Universal Father (Father-Father) and the Eternal Son (Mother-Son). Next, the Infinite Spirit created 700,000 Creative Daughter Spirits, one for each "Creator Son." On our "local universe" (sector of the galaxy), the influences of one of these Creative Daughters is the Holy Spirit. Third, each person has a Spirit of Truth (a teaching spirit from Jesus/Michael) and a Thought Adjuster (another spirit being), which enter humans at six years at age. Christians have often confused all these as the Holy Spirit.	"The Third Source and center is known by numerous titles: the Universal Spirit,... the Infinite Mind, the Spirit of Spirits, the Paradise Mother Spirit, the Conjoint Actor" (*UB*, p. 92). "[T]hat very moment, the Infinite Spirit springs fullfledgedly into existence.... The first act of the Infinite Spirit is the inspection and recognition of his divine parents, the Father-Father and the Mother-Son" (Ibid., 90). "His coming into being completes the Father's liberation" (Ibid., p. 98). "In your sacred writings the term Spirit of God seems to be used interchangeably to designate both the Infinite Spirit on Paradise and the Creative Spirit of your local universe. The Holy Spirit is the spiritual circuit of this Creative Daughter of the Paradise Infinite Spirit. The Holy Spirit is a circuit indigenous to each local universe and is confined to the spiritual realm of that creation; but the Infinite Spirit is omnipresent" (Ibid., p. 95). "Since the bestowal of the Spirit of Truth, man is subject to the teaching and guidance of a threefold spirit endowment: the spirit of the Father, the Thought Adjuster; the spirit of the Son, the Spirit of Truth: the spirit of the Spirits the Holy Spirit" (Ibid., pp. 2061–62).	The Bible knows nothing of multiple Spirits. As *The Urantia Book* itself acknowledges, the Bible uses the term "Spirit of God" to refer to the Holy Spirit (1Co 12:3) and our Creator (Ge 1:2). However, one term is not being used to designate two different entities. Scripture is very clear that there is only "one and the same Spirit" (1Co 12:11). Christians know "one body and one Spirit... one Lord, one faith, one baptism, one God and Father" (Eph 4:4–6). The "Spirit of God" is not a term that covers many different spirits, as the *UB* teaches. The *UB* claims the Holy Spirit is the influence (not the person) of one of many "Creative Daughter Spirits," which are the product of an earlier created being, the Infinite Spirit. This teaching denies both the personality and the full deity of the Holy Spirit. The Bible teaches that the Holy Spirit is a personal being who acts, not just the work of a personal being. Further, the Holy Spirit is God (Ac 5:3–4) and thus is uncreated and has always existed.

The Doctrine of the Holy Spirit (cont.)

Position	Support	Orthodox Response
In each "local universe" of 1000 planets there is a Creator Son and a Creative Daughter Spirit (who later becomes a "local universe Mother Spirit"). She is co-creator of our local universe with the Creator Son (Jesus), and acts as a "consort" to him. The Mother Spirit creates certain spirits, and her circuits are the Holy Spirit in our world. She is equal to Jesus and is treated as equal to God the Father.	"When energy-matter has attained a certain stage in mass materialization, a Paradise Creator Son appears upon the scene, accompanied by a Creative Daughter of the Infinite Spirit" (*UB*, p. 358). "From Paradise come the [local] Universe Mother Spirits, the cocreators of local universes. . . . This [Creator] Son and his Spirit associate *are* your creator parents" (Ibid., pp. 162, 367). The local universes contain "the local universe Mother Spirits, the Holy Spirit of your world" (Ibid., p. 177). "The Universe Mother Spirit acts as the universe focus and center of the Spirit of Truth as well as of her own personal influences the Holy Spirit" (Ibid., p. 378). After Jesus' resurrection, "the triumphant Creator Son elevates the Universe Mother Spirit to cosovereignty and acknowledges the Spirit consort as his equal" (Ibid., p. 204). "The Father in heaven treats the Spirit Mother of the children of the universe as one equal to himself" (Ibid., p. 1471).	The concept of a "Daughter Spirit" or "Mother Spirit" who acts as Jesus' "consort" (i.e., sexual partner) who brings offspring into existence with him is as repulsive as it is unscriptural. The triune God alone made the heaven and earth (Ne 9:6; Isa 44:24). The Holy Spirit is never depicted as a female "consort" or "wife" to Jesus, nor does the Holy Spirit represent our "mother" or parent. In *The Urantia Book*, Jesus and the Holy Spirit are creatures made by higher deities, with 700,000 pairs just like them. They are then given creative powers, but were nevertheless brought into existence at a point in the past. According to the Bible, the Holy Spirit is God—not simply a "local" deity over part of the galaxy. In Acts 5:3–4, Peter equates the Holy Spirit with God. In Acts 28:25, Paul says, "The Holy Spirit spoke through Isaiah the prophet," yet Isaiah attributes those words to Yahweh (see Isa 6:9–10). Thus, the Holy Spirit is identified with the sacred covenant name of God. The Holy Spirit is also known as "the Spirit of God" (Ge 1:2; Mt 3:16), the Spirit of Yahweh (Isa 11:2; 61:1), "the Spirit of your Father" (Mt 10:20), and "the Spirit of adoption" (Rom 8:15 KJV). God never identifies a creature as being "equal to himself."
The members of the Godhead do not actually indwell believers. Neither the person of Christ nor the Holy Spirit ("Mother Spirit") lives within or directly contacts the human mind and soul.	"As individuals you do not personally possess a segregated portion or entity of the spirit of the Creator Father-Son or the Creative Mother Spirits; these ministries do not contact with, nor indwell, the thinking centers of the individual's mind as do the Mystery Monitors" (*UB*, p. 379).	According to the Bible, regenerate believers have the high privilege that God dwells within them (Rom 8:11; 1Co 14:25; Eph 4:6). Further, Jesus indwells believers (Rom 8:10; 2Co 13:5; Col 1:27; 1Jn 4:4) and the Holy Spirit indwells believers (Jn 14:17; Rom 8:9; 1Co 3:16; 6:19). This is not true of all people. Although God is omnipresent, by virtue of his *selective indwelling* He lives within Christian believers (see above), but does not live within unbelievers (Rom 8:9; 1Co 2:12; Eph 2:12; 2Jn 9; Rev 3:20).

The Doctrine of Man and Sin

Position	Support	Orthodox Response
Adam and Eve were not the first humans. The first humans were Andon and Fonta, who evolved from lower forms of life almost one million years ago. Adam and Eve came here from the planet Jerusem about 25,000 B.C.	"[A]fter almost nine hundred generations of development, covering about twenty-one thousand years from the origin of the dawn mammals, the Primates *suddenly* gave birth to two remarkable creatures, the first true human beings.... From the year A.D. 1934 back to the birth of the first two human beings is just 993,419 years" (*UB*, p. 707). "Andon and Fonta were the most remarkable pair of human beings that have ever lived on the face of the earth. This wonderful pair, the actual parents of all mankind, were in every way superior..." (Ibid., p. 711). "Adam and Eve arrived on Urantia, from the year A.D. 1934, 37,848 years ago.... At high noon and unannounced, the two seraphic transports, accompanied by the Jerusem personnel intrusted with the transportation of the biologic uplifters to Urantia, settled slowly to the surface of the revolving planet in the vicinity of the temple of the Universal Father" (Ibid., p. 828).	*The Urantia Book* expresses many views that run contrary to biblical history and evidence. The Bible presents Adam and Eve as direct creations by God, not as interplanetary travelers. "The Lord God formed the man from the dust of the ground and breathed into his nostrils the breath of life, and the man became a living being" (Ge 2:7). The man was Adam, and the name literally means "man" in Hebrew. Thus, Adam was formed on earth and was the first human being. Jesus confirmed this when He said that "at the beginning the Creator 'made them male and female'" (Mt 19:4), quoting Genesis 1 as authoritative about the origin of mankind. First Corinthians 15:45 says, "The first man Adam became a living being," and thus affirms that it was Adam who was the first man, not Andon.
Adam and Eve did not "fall" or commit a sin that had consequences on the rest of the human race, nor does man have a fallen or sinful nature that is passed from parent to child. Sin is an act of rebellion against the laws of one's "local universe" creator.	"There has been no 'fall of man.' The history of the human race is one of progressive evolution, and the Adamic bestowal left the world peoples greatly improved over their previous biologic condition" (*UB*, p. 846). "Adam and Eve did default, but no mortal subsequently born on Urantia has suffered in his personal spiritual experience because of these blunders" (Ibid., p. 761). "... sin is not transmitted from parent to child. Sin is the act of conscious and deliberate rebellion against the Father's will and the Sons' laws by an individual will creature" (Ibid., p. 2016). "Mankind was not consigned to agricultural toil as the penalty of supposed sin. 'In the sweat of your face shall you eat the fruit of the fields' was not a sentence of punishment pronounced because of man's participation in the follies of the Lucifer rebellion under the leadership of the traitorous Caligastia" (Ibid., pp. 751–52). "The Christian teachers perpetuated the belief in the fiat creation of the human race, and all this led directly to... the theory of the fall of man or superman which accounted for the nonutopian condition of society. These outlooks... were predicated upon a belief in retrogression rather than	*The Urantia Book*'s interpretation of the Fall is a product of nineteenth-century rationalism, which views the Bible alternately as *revelation* (when it agrees) or as *speculation* (when it disagrees). The doctrine of the sinfulness of mankind is especially obnoxious to the *UB*. The Bible affirms that death is a literal consequence of the sin of Adam and Eve. "The wages of sin is death" (Rom 6:23). Through the sin of Adam, many others were affected (Rom 5:12, 19). The great suffering and pain inflicted by humans on one another throughout history is obvious and empirical truth of the validity of the Bible on the sinfulness of man. The *UB* defines sin as rebellion "against the Father's will and the Sons' laws"—that is, the laws of the local universe Michael Sons (or creators). Although this has echoes of the biblical definition of sin as transgression of God's law (1Jn 3:4), it wedges polytheism into its definition. There are *not* many creators over other local universes (Rev 4:11). Moreover, the Bible also defines sin as a principle or inclination that dwells within mankind, not merely as an act of disobedience. "It is no longer I myself who do it, but it is sin living in me" (Rom 7:17). "Therefore do not let sin reign in your mortal body so that you obey its evil desires" (Rom 6:12).

The Doctrine of Man and Sin (cont.)

Position	Support	Orthodox Response
... continued	progression, as well as implying a vengeful Deity, who had vented wrath upon the human race in retribution for the errors of certain onetime planetary administrators" (Ibid., p. 838).	
The world is not fundamentally evil, and sin is not a major problem for man.	"Jesus led men to feel at home in the world; he... taught them that the world was not fundamentally evil.... Jesus did not share Paul's pessimistic view of humankind. The Master looked upon men as the sons of God.... He saw most men as weak rather than wicked, more distraught than depraved. But no matter what their status, they were all God's children and his brethren" (*UB*, p. 2093). "The doctrine of the total depravity of man destroyed much of the potential of religion for effecting social repercussions of an uplifting nature and of inspirational value. Jesus sought to restore man's dignity when he declared that all men are the children of God" (Ibid., p. 1091).	The Bible portrays the world as good in substance, but evil in that its inhabitants are alienated against God. "There is not a righteous man on earth who does what is right and never sins" (Eccl 7:20). "All of us have become like one who is unclean, and all our righteous acts are like filthy rags" (Isa 64:6). "If we claim to be without sin, we deceive ourselves and the truth is not in us" (1Jn 1:8). "The whole world is under the control of the evil one" (1Jn 5:19). Jesus viewed the world as basically lost, for He said, "This is the verdict: Light has come into the world, but men loved darkness instead of light because their deeds were evil" (Jn 3:19). "If the world hates you, keep in mind that it hated me first" (Jn 15:18).
All persons are indwelt by a "Thought Adjuster," also known as a Mystery Monitor. Thought Adjusters are spiritual beings, and are a fragment of God. By following their leading, we follow God, and we can become aware of other spirit beings around us.	"Adjusters reach their human subjects on Urantia, on the average, just prior to the sixth birthday" (*UB*, pp. 1186–87). "Man is spiritually indwelt by a surviving Thought Adjuster.... The indwelling Thought Adjusters are a part of the eternal Deity of the Paradise Father.... God lives in every one of his spirit-born sons" (Ibid., pp. 63, 62, 64). "The divine presence cannot, however, be discovered anywhere... so fully and so certainly as in your attempted communion with the indwelling Mystery Monitor, the Paradise Thought Adjuster. What a mistake to dream of God far off in the skies when the spirit of the Universal Father lives within your own mind! "It is because of this God fragment that indwells you that you can hope, as you progress in harmonizing with the Adjuster's spiritual leadings, more fully to discern the presence and transforming power of those other spiritual influences that surround you" (Ibid., p. 64).	The Bible portrays man as a unified human creature made of "spirit, soul and body" (1Th 5:23). Spirit and soul are intricately interrelated (Heb 4:12), but are definitely spoken of in the singular throughout Scripture when applied to a single person. For believers, only the Holy Spirit is said to indwell a person (e.g., "God's Spirit [singular] lives in you," 1Co 3:16). *The Urantia Book* regards the "Thought Adjuster" as an entity distinct from its own "Holy Spirit," allowing human beings to be indwelt by multiple spirit entities, allegedly from God. The only biblical cases of multiple spirits dwelling within one person occurs when one is indwelt by "evil spirits" (Mk 1:27; 3:11; 5:13; Ac 19:13), or "unclean spirits" (KJV), which can be cast out with authority in the name of Jesus Christ (Ac 8:7).

The Doctrine of Man and Sin (cont.)

Position	Support	Orthodox Response
Man's soul is embryonic in this life. After we die and are resurrected on other planets, our soul is "born" and progressively develops.	"During the mortal life in the flesh the soul is of embryonic estate; it is born (resurrected) in the morontia life and experiences growth through the successive morontia worlds" (*UB,* p. 744).	*The Urantia Book's* description of the soul as an "embryo" that isn't even born until after death seems like a subtle attempt to get man to ignore the seriousness of his condition. The Bible says that the soul can be "forfeited" (Mt 16:26), or "lost," and can conversely be "saved" (Jas 1:21) and "redeemed" (Ps 49:15). We need to give attention to our alienated condition before God in this life ("Seek the LORD while he may be found," Isa 55:6), because if we delay repentance until death, there will be no opportunity for repentance then (Heb 9:27).
The dead are unconscious between death and their "resurrection" on the "mansion worlds."	"All mortals of survival status... pass through the portals of natural death and, on the third period, personalize on the mansion worlds.... The passing of time is of no moment to sleeping mortals; they are wholly unconscious and oblivious to the length of their rest. On reassembly of personality at the end of an age, those who have slept five thousand years will react no differently than those who have rested five days" (*UB,* p. 341). "Between the time of planetary death or translation and resurrection on the mansion world, mortal man gains absolutely nothing aside from experiencing the fact of survival. You begin over there right where you leave off down here" (Ibid., p. 533). "This child of persisting meaning and surviving value is wholly unconscious during the period from death to repersonalization.... You will not function as a conscious being, following death, until you attain the new consciousness of morontia on the mansion worlds of Satania" (Ibid., p. 1234).	The doctrine that the dead, whether righteous or unrighteous, are unconscious between death and the resurrection is traditionally called "soul sleep." It means no one is punished nor consciously in the presence of the Lord until the resurrection. It bears notice that this is a key doctrine of Seventh-day Adventism and that both William Sadler and Wilfred Kellogg (the probable human channeler of *The Urantia Book*) were Adventists. The *UB* has a slight twist in that its resurrections occur on other planets; otherwise, there is a resemblance with the Adventist teachings on soul sleep. Several biblical passages show that humans are conscious after death. The unjust dead are kept by God "for the day of judgment, while continuing their punishment" (2Pe 2:9). This is also apparent in Jesus' parable of the unregenerate rich man (Lk 16:19–31). By contrast, Christians anticipate that when they are "absent from the body" (that is, disembodied), they are "present with the Lord" (2Co 5:8 KJV), and that even at death, separated from "the body" they are present "with Christ" (Php 1:22–23). The book of Revelation shows the martyrs of the Tribulation period, not yet resurrected, in communion with and rewarded by God (6:9–11). Finally, Christians are promised that we "will never die" and now possess "eternal life" (Jn 11:26; 5:24). If we went out of existence, even temporarily, this would nullify Christ's promise to His children in Scripture.

The Doctrine of Salvation

Position	Support	Orthodox Response
The death of Jesus was not in the plan of God.	"It was man and not God who planned and executed the death of Jesus on the cross.... the Father in Paradise did not decree, demand, or require the death of his Son" (*UB*, p. 2002).	The sacrificial death of Jesus Christ not only was predicted in the Bible but was also the intentional plan and good will of the Triune God (Isa 53:10). Jesus rebuked the apostle Peter for suggesting that He did not have to die (Mt 16:23). After His resurrection, Jesus reminded the disciples that His death was ordained in the Scriptures (Lk 24:25–26). Peter's perspective was altered by the time he proclaimed on the Day of Pentecost that Jesus was crucified "by God's set purpose and foreknowledge" (Ac 2:23).
The concept of sacrifice and atonement are actually repugnant to God.	"The barbarous idea of appeasing an angry God, of propitiating an offended Lord, of winning the favor of Deity through sacrifices and penance and even by the shedding of blood, represents a religion wholly puerile and primitive, a philosophy unworthy of an enlightened age of science and truth. Such beliefs are utterly repulsive to the celestial beings and the divine rulers who serve and reign in the universes. It is an affront to God to believe, hold, or teach that innocent blood must be shed in order to win his favor or to divert the fictitious divine wrath" (*UB*, p. 60).	The practice of sacrifice is rooted in the Old Testament, and it is God who says He has given it to the people of Israel: "For the life of a creature is in the blood, and I have given it to you to make atonement for yourselves on the altar; it is the blood that makes atonement for one's life" (Lev 17:11). Further, God is not "angry" with mankind for being human, but rather is angry for their sin. "The wrath of God is being revealed from heaven against all the godlessness and wickedness of men" (Rom 1:18). It would seem appropriate for God to be angry toward evil-doers. However, God's just anger is also joined with His deep mercy, so that "he loved us and sent his Son as an atoning sacrifice for our sins" (1Jn 4:10; see also Heb 2:17; 9:26).
The gospel of Jesus is the "brotherhood of man, fatherhood of God." Salvation means becoming aware that we are already children of God.	"A Creator Son did not incarnate... to reconcile [us] to an angry God but rather to win all mankind to the recognition of the Father's love and to the realization of their sonship with God" (*UB*, p. 1083). "Simon Zelotes asked, 'But, Master, are *all* men the sons of God?' And Jesus answered: 'Yes, Simon, all men are the sons of God, and that is the good news you are going to proclaim.'" (Ibid., p. 1585). "Salvation should be taken for granted by those who believe in the fatherhood of God.... Human salvation is *real*; it is based on two realities... the fact of the fatherhood of God and its correlated truth, the brotherhood of man" (Ibid., 2017). "Your mission to the world is founded on... the truth that you and all other men are the sons of God" (Ibid., p. 2043).	The New Testament makes an important distinction between recognizing God as our Father and the Creator of all humankind and the point when we become adopted children (Rom 8:14; Gal 4:5; Eph 1:5) through faith in Christ. The former is general and extends to all; the latter is particular and includes only some. In general, all humanity are the "offspring" of God (Ac 17:28–29), since God has created the spirits of all flesh (Nu 16:22; Mal 2:10). However, the Bible never says *all* men are sons of God. We achieve the status of son or daughter only through faith in Jesus Christ (Gal 3:26; Jn 1:12). Moreover, the Bible says that *before* people receive Jesus and become children of God, they are "by nature objects of wrath" (Eph 2:3) or are "disobedient" (Eph 5:6; see also Col 3:6). The relationship whereby God adopts us as His children is conditional, but open to any who will turn to Jesus (1Jn 5:1).

The Doctrine of Rewards and Punishment

Position	Support	Orthodox Response
Man is rewarded after death with life on other planets, with advancement dependent on how he has lived on earth [Urantia]. The final reward of our faith is to be united with our "Thought Adjuster" spirit being.	"The evolutionary planets are the spheres of human origin, the initial worlds of the ascending mortal career. Urantia is your starting point; here you and your divine Thought Adjuster are joined in temporary union. You have been endowed with a perfect guide; therefore, if you will sincerely run the race of time and gain the final goal of faith, the reward of the ages shall be yours; you will be eternally united with your indwelling Adjuster. Then will begin your real life, the ascending life, to which your present mortal state is but the vestibule. Then will begin your exalted and progressive mission as finaliters in the eternity which stretches out before you" (*UB*, p. 1225).	Although *The Urantia Book* does not proclaim typical reincarnationist doctrine, it does teach that there are multiple lives on different worlds for people to "ascend" to God. The Bible teaches that there is only one life or opportunity for humankind: "Man is destined to die once, and after that to face judgment" (Heb 9:27). After death, one is sent either to Hades to await the penal judgment of God (Lk 16:22ff.; Heb 10:27; Jude 7) or to the presence of the Lord Jesus (Php 2:21–23). The Bible allows no place for other lives in different worlds. The biblical doctrine of justification means we have not only "peace with God through our Lord Jesus Christ" but also "access" directly to God (Rom 5:1–2; Eph 2:18). There is no need for additional training experiences on other worlds to qualify us for fellowship and access to God, since the blood of Jesus gives us access to the Most Holy Place (Heb 9:8, 10:19). The reward and goal of our faith is not fellowship with a spirit being (which is not the Holy Spirit), but fellowship with God. The Urantian hope of being "united with your indwelling Adjuster" pales in comparison with the Christian hope expressed by Paul in Philippians 3:8–9.
The Christian concept of heaven is false. When the Bible writers referred to "heaven," they were not speaking of Paradise, the special dwelling place of God.	"The heaven conceived by most of your prophets was the first of the mansion worlds of the local system. When the apostle spoke of being 'caught up to the third heaven,' he referred to that experience in which his Adjuster was detached during sleep and in this unusual state made a projection to the third of the seven mansion worlds. Some of your wise men saw the vision of the greater heaven, 'the heaven of heavens,' of which the sevenfold mansion world experience was but the first; the second being Jerusem; the third, Edentia and its satellites; the fourth, Salvington and the surrounding educational spheres the fifth, Uversa; the sixth, Havona; and the seventh, Paradise" (*UB*, p. 553).	According to *The Urantia Book*, Paradise is the dwelling place of God, but heaven is not; rather, it is one of the "mansion worlds." Yet the Bible says many times that heaven is the dwelling place of God (1Ki 8:27, 30, 39; 2Ch 30:27), so the biblical writers were not referring to some lower realm on another planet. The apostle Paul was "caught up to the third heaven" (2Co 12:2), which he said was also being "caught up to paradise" (v. 4); thus, heaven and Paradise are regarded as one in the Bible.

The Doctrine of Rewards and Punishment (cont.)

Position	Support	Orthodox Response
Paradise is the location of the central heaven and can only be reached after hundreds or thousands of lives. The thief on the cross did not go to Paradise.	Jesus said to the repentant thief who died next to him, "Verily, verily, I say to you today, you shall sometime be with me in Paradise" (*UB*, p. 2009). "There is a long, long road ahead of mortal man before he can consistently and within the realms of possibility ask for safe conduct into the Paradise presence of the Universal Father. Spiritually, man must be translated many times before he can attain a plane that will yield the spiritual vision which will enable him to see even any one of the Seven Master Spirits" (Ibid., p. 62). "Very plainly Jesus explained that the kingdom of heaven was an evolutionary experience, beginning here on earth and progressing up through successive life stations to Paradise" (Ibid., p. 1603).	*The Urantia Book* describes "a long, long road" to gain the presence of God the Father in Paradise, but the Bible says that because of the blood of Jesus, we can directly approach God the Father even "behind the curtain" (Heb 6:19) and have "confidence to enter the Most Holy Place" (10:19), even to the very "throne of grace" (4:16). When Jesus died, the curtain of the temple was torn, symbolizing our access to God directly (Mk 15:38). There is no need for many life stations to achieve this privilege. Also, the Bible records Jesus' telling the thief, "I tell you the truth, today you will be with me in paradise" (Lk 23:43). The *UB* moved the comma to be *after* the word *today*, even though the introductory phrase "I tell you the truth," followed by a comma and a full independent clause, appears many times in the Gospels. Adding the word *sometime* in this passage is an unwarranted attempt to undercut Jesus' promise to the repentant sinner.
The dead are not "resurrected" on earth, but on other planets called the "mansion worlds."	"All mortals of survival status... pass through the portals of natural death and, on the third period, personalize on the mansion worlds.... In each local system of approximately one thousand inhabited planets there are seven mansion worlds.... They are the receiving worlds for the majority of ascending mortals" (*UB*, p. 341). "You will not function as a conscious being, following death, until you attain the new consciousness of morontia on the mansion worlds of Satania" (Ibid., p. 1234). "While some of your records have pictured these events as taking place on the planets of mortal death, they all really occur on the mansion worlds" (Ibid., p. 569). "On the mansion worlds the resurrected mortal survivors resume their lives just where they left off when overtaken by death.... you would hardly notice the difference except for the fact that you were in possession of a different body; the tabernacle of flesh and blood has been left behind on the world of [your] nativity" (Ibid., p. 532).	*The Urantia Book* teaches that, in the same way that it happened to Jesus, the dead are not resurrected, but replicated, or copied, into a different body. This difference is important because, in the *UB*, "resurrections" supposedly occur even while the body remains in its grave on earth. Jesus said, "Do not be amazed at this, for a time is coming when all who are in their graves will hear his voice and come out—those who have done good will rise to live, and those who have done evil will rise to be condemned" (Jn 5:28–29). We will come out of our graves. Also, the Bible says the dead are raised with physical bodies, not "morontia bodies," which are nonphysical. At the resurrection of the just, Jesus "will transform our lowly bodies so that they will be like his glorious body" (Php 3:21). Since believers will have a body like Jesus' and since His body is physical (Lk 24:39), their bodies will also be physical. Finally, since Jesus is returning to earth (Rev 19:11–19), the resurrected believers will also be with Him on earth, not on the "morontia" planets (Jn 14:3).

The Doctrine of Rewards and Punishment (cont.)

Position	Support	Orthodox Response
A few rebellious souls will be annihilated.	"The greatest punishment (in reality an inevitable consequence) for wrongdoing and deliberate rebellion against the government of God is loss of existence as an individual subject of that government. The final result of wholehearted sin is annihilation" (*UB*, p. 37). "That which mercy cannot rehabilitate justice will eventually annihilate" (Ibid., p. 241). "We await the flashing broadcast that will deprive these traitors of personality existence" and "will effect the annihilation of these interned rebels" (Ibid., p. 611).	The Bible teaches that the lost are not annihilated but are instead punished eternally. "Then they will go away to eternal punishment, but the righteous to eternal life" (Mt 25:46). In this verse "eternal" (Greek *aionios*) is the attribute of both life and punishment. If "eternal punishment" has an end or ceasing, then by the same token so might eternal life. Other passages talk about those who are cast into hell, "where the fire never goes out" (Mk 9:43), or those who are punished such that "the smoke of their torment rises for ever and ever" (Rev 14:11). The Bible speaks of "everlasting contempt" (Da 12:2) and "unquenchable fire" (Mt 3:12), and it thereby seems to exclude annihilation or extinction of consciousness. The *UB* teaching perhaps reflects the Seventh-day Adventist background of the *UB* channeler.

INTERESTING AND DISTINCTIVE BELIEFS

Position	Support	Orthodox Response
Paul wrote the epistle to the Hebrews.	"Paul also had a view of the ascendant-citizen corps of perfecting mortals on Jerusem, for he wrote: 'But you have come to Mount Zion and to the city of the living God, the heavenly Jerusalem, and to an innumerable company of angels, to the grand assembly of Michael, and to the spirits of just men being made perfect'" (*UB*, p. 539). "Paul learned of the existence of the morontia worlds and of the reality of morontia materials, for he wrote, 'They have in heaven a better and more enduring substance'" (Ibid., p. 542).	Note that in the first "quotation" from Paul's writings, the unnamed reference is a corruption of Hebrews 12:22–23. In the second quote, *The Urantia Book* states that Paul wrote the passage in Hebrews 10:34. However, in contradiction to this, the *UB* also states that Hebrews is one of the books of the New Testament that does *not* portray Paul's "personal religious convictions."
Paul did *not* write the epistle to the Hebrews.	"Almost the whole of the New Testament is devoted... to a discussion of Paul's religious experience and to a portrayal of his personal religious convictions. The only notable exceptions to this statement, aside from certain parts of Matthew, Mark, and Luke, are the Book of Hebrews and the Epistle of James" (Ibid., p. 2091).	

Position	Support	Orthodox Response
Satan, Lucifer, and the Devil are three separate entities.	"Very little was heard of Lucifer on Urantia owing to the fact that he assigned his first lieutenant, Satan, to advocate his cause on your planet. Satan was a member of the same primary group of Lanonandeks... he entered fully into the Lucifer insurrection. The 'devil' is none other than Caligastia, the deposed Planetary Prince of Urantia and a Son of the secondary order of Lanonandeks" (*UB,* p. 602). "The devil has been given a great deal of credit for evil which does not belong to him. Caligastia has been comparatively impotent since the cross of Christ" (Ibid., p. 610).	The Bible treats these three terms synonymously. For instance, in the temptation of Jesus in the wilderness, Jesus is tempted by the "devil" (Greek *diabolos;* Mt 4:1, 5, 8). Jesus says, "Away from me, Satan!" (v. 10), and then we are told that "the devil left him" (v. 11). In Mark's account of the parable of the sower, "Satan" snatches the seed on the roadside (4:15); in Luke's account, it is "the devil" (8:12). In Revelation 12:9 and 20:2, the terms are explicitly used together as synonyms. Isaiah 14:12 has the only reference to Lucifer (though the name is not used in some translations), and those who do not consider it a reference to the king of Babylon hold that it refers to Satan.
Demon possession has been impossible since the day of Pentecost.	"[T]he pouring out of the Spirit of Truth upon all flesh forever made it impossible for disloyal spirits of any sort or description ever again to invade even the most feeble of human minds. Since the day of Pentecost there never again can be such a thing as demoniacal possession" (*UB,* p. 864).	This passage appears to be ignorant of the accounts in the book of Acts. In Philip's ministry, "unclean spirits, crying with a loud voice, came out of many who were possessed" (Ac 8:7 NKJV). Paul cast out a spirit of divination from a woman in Philippi (Ac 16:18). In Acts 19:12, which recounts events occurring some 25 years after Pentecost, Luke records that "evil spirits left" people in Ephesus.
The story of the Twelve Tribes of Israel is false.	"There never were twelve tribes of the Israelites—only three or four tribes settled in Palestine" (*UB,* p. 1071).	A concordance to *The Urantia Book* will reveal the names of Judah, Levi, Zebulun, Gad, Dan, Ephraim, and Manasseh: seven of the 12 tribes. Granting that some of these are the names of people or places, there still needs to be some explanation for how these people got such names. The famous name is traceable to the historic figure behind the name. There is no reason for the *UB* to deny the historicity of the Bible in this regard.

Position	Support	Orthodox Response
Jesus did not found the Christian church as we know it. The church now existing is a perverted form of the teachings given by Jesus.	"When Jesus' immediate followers recognized their partial failure to realize his ideal of the establishment of the kingdom in the hearts of men... they set about to save his teaching from being wholly lost by substituting for the Master's ideal of the kingdom the gradual creation of a visible social organization, the Christian church" (*UB*, p. 1865). "The early Christians (and all too many of the later ones) generally lost sight of the Father-and-son idea embodied in Jesus' teaching of the kingdom, while they substituted therefore the well-organized social fellowship of the church. The church thus became in the main a *social* brotherhood which effectively displaced Jesus' concept and ideal of a *spiritual* brotherhood" (Ibid.). "Likewise, the Christian churches of the twentieth century stand as great, but wholly unconscious, obstacles to the immediate advance of the real gospel—the teachings of Jesus of Nazareth.... Jesus did not found the so-called Christian church, but he has, in every manner consistent with his nature, *fostered* it as the best existent exponent of his lifework on earth" (Ibid., p. 2085).	These sentiments ignore the clear statement of Jesus that "I will build my church, and the gates of Hades will not overcome it" (Mt 16:18). Thus, the church is not an inferior afterthought of the apostles, but something that Christ established and also promised to protect and uphold. Ephesians 5:25–32 says that Christ "loved the church and gave himself up for her" (v. 25) and that He currently "feeds and cares for it" (v. 29). Because Christ is sovereign head of the church (1:22–23), He effectively accomplished His will within it. This is not to say that the church is perfect or that everyone who professes to be a Christian and is a church member is truly a Christian. Jesus also said there would be many hypocrites within His flock (Mt 13:27–29). Yet, though they are within the church, they are not truly *of* the church, as 1 John 2:19 tells us. While there is some merit in distinguishing between visible Christendom and the invisible church or body of Christ, the *UB* goes too far in rejecting the church as a divinely appointed institution.
Blacks are inferior to whites. A half-million years ago, the Sangik family inexplicably produced children of six different colors, who became the ancestors of six colored races of man: red, yellow, blue, orange, green, and indigo. The modern Caucasian and Mongoloid races are descended from the earlier (primary) red, yellow, and blue races, while the Negroid races stem from the inferior (secondary) races.	"These Sangik children... [found that] their skins manifested a unique tendency to turn various colors upon exposure to sunlight. Among these nineteen children were five red, two orange, four yellow, two green, four blue, and two indigo. These colors became more pronounced as the children grew older, and when these youths later mated with their fellow tribesmen, all of their offspring tended toward the skin color of the Sangik parent" (*UB*, p. 722). "The Negroid—the secondary Sangik type, which originally included the orange, green, and indigo races. This is the type best illustrated by the Negro, and it will be found through Africa, India, and Indonesia wherever the secondary Sangik races located" (Ibid., p. 905). "Even such inferior races as the African Bushmen,..." (Ibid., p. 1132). "The green race was one of the less able groups of primitive men, and they were greatly weakened by extensive migrations.... The southern nation entered Africa, where they destroyed their almost equally inferior orange cousins" (Ibid., p. 724). "As the red men were the most advanced	The theory of racial supremacy was popular among social Darwinists of the 1930s, but is untenable today. Such terms as "backward," "inferior," and "racial deterioration" reveal the prejudices of the authors, who also apply such terms as "advanced" or "superior" to the white-skinned peoples (supposedly descendants of the blue race). The Bible knows nothing of racial supremacy. The Scripture says that in the church "there is neither Jew nor Greek, slave nor free, male nor female, for you are all one in Christ Jesus" (Gal 3:28). The principles of boasting in one's parentage are not consistent with any Christian virtues (Php 3:3–7).

Position	Support	Orthodox Response
. . . continued	of all the Sangik peoples, so the black men were the least progressive. . . . Isolated in Africa, the indigo peoples, like the red man, received little or none of the race elevation which would have been derived from the infusion of the Adamic stock. . . . Notwithstanding their backwardness, these indigo peoples have exactly the same standing before the celestial powers as any other earthly race" (Ibid., p. 725).	
	"The blue man most of all profited by these early social teachings, the red man to some extent, and the black man least of all. In more recent times the yellow race and the white race have presented the most advanced social development on Urantia" (Ibid., p. 763).	
	"The indigo race was moving south to Africa, there to begin its slow but long-continued racial deterioration" (Ibid., p. 871).	
Mankind should eliminate inferior and unfit races through a program of eugenics—that is, sterilization and selective breeding.	"These six evolutionary races are destined to be blended and exalted by amalgamation with the progeny of the Adamic uplifters. But before these peoples are blended, the inferior and unfit are largely eliminated. . . . The difficulty of executing such a radical program on Urantia consists in the absence of competent judges to pass upon the biologic fitness or unfitness of the individuals of your world races. Notwithstanding this obstacle, it seems that you ought to be able to agree upon the biologic disfellowshiping of your more markedly unfit, defective, degenerate, and antisocial stocks" (*UB*, p. 585).	The concept of eugenics is based on the theory of evolution and racial-ethnic superiority. But the Bible says man is created by God in God's image and likeness (Ge 1:27; Jas 3:9), regardless of skin color or ethnic background. It is only sin which makes mankind "defective," and there are no racial classes that are genetically prone to degeneracy or antisocial behavior. This theory was popular in Hitler's Germany in the 1930s and in the "racial cleansing" encountered in Bosnia and Kosovo in the 1990s, but is totally bereft of biblical or scientific support.
	". . . the people eagerly look forward to the day when announcement will be made that those who have qualified as belonging to the superior racial strains may proceed to the Garden of Eden and be there chosen by the sons and daughters of Adam as the evolutionary fathers and mothers of the new and blended order of mankind" (Ibid.).	
	"The church, because of overmuch false sentiment . . . has led to the unwise perpetuation of racially degenerate stocks which have tremendously retarded the progress of civilization" (Ibid., p. 1088).	
	". . . most worlds seriously address themselves to the tasks of race purification, something which the Urantia peoples have not even yet seriously undertaken. . . . It is the false sentiment of your partially perfected civilizations that fosters, protects, and perpetuates the hopelessly defective strains of evolutionary human stocks" (Ibid., p. 592).	

Position	Support	Orthodox Response
Mankind has 48 chromosomes ("trait determiners") in human reproductive cells.	"This number twelve, with its subdivisions and multiples, runs throughout all basic life patterns of all seven superuniverses.... On Urantia there are forty-eight units of pattern control—trait determiners—in the sex cells of human reproduction" (*UB*, p. 397).	Although the word "chromosomes" does not appear, it is evident that these are in mind as "units of pattern control" that determine the traits of offspring in human reproduction. In 1923, biologists erroneously believed there were 48 chromosomes in human cells, and this mistake appears in *The Urantia Book,* which originated in that era. The actual count of 46 chromosomes (23 pairs) was established in 1956. Moreover, when human sex cells (ova and sperm) reach maturity, the process of *meiosis* reduces the number of chromosomes to 23 per cell. This is a bad mistake for the supposedly celestial authors of the *UB* to have made!
The Urantia Book, **which professes to be written by direct inspiration of super-mortal and inter-planetary higher beings, contains many instances of plagiarism from authors such as Charles Hartshorne, Bertrand Russell, and Lewis Browne. No credit is ever given to the original authors.**	"1. Absolute perfection in all aspects. 2. Absolute perfection in some phases and relative perfection in all other aspects. 3. Absolute, relative, and imperfect aspects in varied association. 4. Absolute perfection in some respects, imperfection in all others. 5. Absolute perfection in no direction, relative perfection in all manifestations. 6. Absolute perfection in no phase, relative in some, imperfect in others. 7. Absolute perfection in no attribute, imperfection in all" (*UB*, p. 3). "His hopes of survival are strung on a figment of mortal imagination; his fears, loves, longings, and beliefs are but the reaction of the incidental juxtaposition of certain lifeless atoms of matter. No display of energy nor expression of trust can carry him beyond the grave. The devotional labors and inspirational genius of the best of men are doomed to be extinguished by death, the long and lonely night of eternal oblivion and soul extinction. Nameless despair is man's only reward for living and toiling under the temporal sun of mortal existence. Each day of life slowly and surely tightens the grasp of a pitiless doom which a hostile and relentless universe of matter has decreed shall be the crowning insult to everything in human desire which is beautiful, noble, lofty, and good" (Ibid., p. 1118).	"Absolute perfection in *all* respects. Absolute perfection in *some* respects, relative perfection in all others. Absolute perfection, relative perfection, and 'imperfection'... each in *some* respects. Absolute perfection in *some* respects, imperfection in all others. Absolute perfection in *no* respects, relative in all. Absolute perfection in *no* respects, relative in some, imperfection in the others. Absolute perfection in *no* respects, imperfection in all" (Charles Hartshorne, *Man's Vision of God,* 1941, p. 8). "... That Man is the product of causes which had no prevision of the end they were achieving; that his origin, his growth, his hopes and fears, his loves and his beliefs, are but the outcome of accidental collocations of atoms; that no fire, no heroism, no intensity of thought and feeling, can preserve an individual life beyond the grave; that all the labors of the ages, all the devotion, all the inspiration, all the noonday brightness of human genius, are destined to extinction in the vast death of the solar system, and that the whole temple of Man's achievement must inevitably be buried beneath the debris of a universe in ruins.... on him and all his race the slow, sure doom falls pitiless and dark. Blind to good and evil, reckless of destruction, omnipotent matter rolls on its relentless way; for Man, condemned today.... it remains only to cherish, ere yet the blow fall, the lofty thoughts that ennoble his little day" (Bertrand Russell, "A Free Man's Worship," 1903 essay).

Position	Support	Orthodox Response
... continued	"If the volume of a proton—eighteen hundred times as heavy as an electron—should be magnified to the size of the head of a pin, then, in comparison, a pin's head would attain a diameter equal to that of the earth's orbit around the sun" (Ibid., p. 477).	"Then, we have the proton... a thing 1800 times as heavy as the electron, but 1800 times smaller in size, so that if you should magnify it to the size of a pin's head, that pin's head would, on the same scale of magnification, attain a diameter equal to the diameter of the earth's orbit around the sun" (William F. G. Swann, *The Architecture of the Universe*, 1934, pp. 44–45).
	"Mithras was conceived as the surviving champion of the sun-god in his struggle with the god of darkness. And in recognition of his slaying the mythical sacred bull, Mithras was made immortal, being exalted to the station of intercessor for the human race among the gods on high" (Ibid., p. 1082).	"Mithras grew up to be the most strenuous champion of the sun-god in his war against the god of darkness, and the climax of his career was a life-and-death struggle with a mythical sacred bull. By finally slaying this bull... Mithras was exalted to the abode of the Immortals, and there he dwelt as the divine protector of all the faithful on earth" (Lewis Browne, *This Believing World*, 1926, p. 110).
	"The inhabitants of the Nile valley believed that each favored individual had bestowed upon him at birth, or soon thereafter, a protecting spirit which they called the ka. They taught that this guardian spirit remained with the mortal subject throughout life and passed before him into the future estate. On the walls of a temple at Luxor, where is depicted the birth of Amenhotep III, the little prince is pictured on the arm of the Nile god, and near him is another child, in appearance identical with the prince, which is a symbol of that entity which the Egyptians called the ka. This sculpture was completed in the fifteenth century before Christ. "The ka was thought to be a superior spirit genius which desired to guide the associated mortal soul into the better paths of temporal living but more especially to influence the fortunes of the human subject in the hereafter. When an Egyptian of this period died, it was expected that his ka would be waiting for him on the other side of the Great River. At first, only kings were supposed to have kas, but presently all righteous men were believed to possess them" (Ibid., p. 1215).	"In beginning the new and untried life after death, the deceased was greatly aided by a protecting guardian spirit called the *ka*, which came into being with each person, followed him throughout life, and passed *before* him into the life hereafter. On the walls of the temple of Luxor, where the birth of Amenhotep III was depicted in sculptured scenes late in the Fifteenth Century before Christ, we find the little prince brought in on the arm of the Nile-god, accompanied apparently by another child. This second figure, identical in external appearance with that of the prince, is the being called by the Egyptians the *ka*.2 He was a kind of superior genius intended especially to guide the fortunes of the individual *in the hereafter*, where every Egyptian who died found his ka awaiting him. It is of importance to note that in all probability the ka was originally the exclusive possession of kings, each of whom thus lived under the protection of his individual guardian genius, and that by a process of slow development the privilege of possessing a ka became universal among all the people" (James Henry Breasted, *The Dawn of Conscience*, 1933, pp. 49–50).

19

The Way International

FACTS AND HISTORY

Facts	
Topic	*Current Facts*
Membership	The Way International maintains that it is not a church, but an organization that facilitates home Bible studies. Consequently, the group claims no membership and discloses no statistics on adherents. Although The Way has probably never had more than 30,000 active followers at one time, it is probable that some 100,000 people have completed the group's Power for Abundant Living training course. The twelve-week series of classes is an essential part of The Way's program, and all new or prospective recruits go through the course. The Way is currently active in 50 countries.
Worship	The Way followers (called "Wayers") living in the same city meet at least once a week in private homes for fellowship, singing, "abundant sharing" (sending financial gifts to The Way headquarters), and recorded Bible teachings issued from the group's headquarters. Supernatural manifestations of the spirit, such as speaking in tongues and prophecy, are an indispensible part of the meetings. These intimate gatherings are called "Twig" meetings because The Way is structured after the parts of a tree.
	"Branch" gatherings usually comprise followers from several cities. Statewide meetings are "Limbs." Branch and Limb meetings occur less frequently than Twig meetings and are usually reserved for special announcements, group events, or the future planning of significant events. Once a year all followers meet at the annual "Rock of Ages" festival in New Knoxville, Ohio, where The Way headquarters is located. Followers are strongly encouraged to attend.
	Wayers receive their teachings primarily from the Sunday sermons given by the current president at the group's national headquarters. The sermons are circulated not only through audio tapes, but also through telephone hookups and video cassettes. Materials produced by The Way's founder, Victor Paul Wierwille, are also important for instruction. All the doctrinal positions of The Way have been defined by Wierwille.
Presidents of The Way	Victor Paul Wierwille 1942–1985 Loy Craig Martindale 1985–
Publications	Most of the printed material distributed by The Way International was produced by Wierwille. The Way's 36-hour taped instructional course titled *Power for Abundant Living* is offered to all potential recruits for a donation (fee) that has ranged from twenty to two hundred dollars. The recorded messages by Wierwille give the basic doctrines that initiates must adopt to stay in the group. A 370-page book with the course's title (sold only to those taking the classes) "sets forth in written form" the taped sessions. Numerous other courses using Wierwille's materials are also offered.
	In 1954 the organization launched *The Way Magazine*, a semi-monthly publication of news and teachings. Another periodical, *Heart*, comes in a newspaper format and is used as a recruiting aid. Way Productions distributes cassette tapes containing music performed by groups in The Way.

Facts (cont.)	
Topic	*Current Facts*
General statement of beliefs	Although members of The Way International consistently use Christian terminology and seem to affirm orthodox Christianity, they deny several key doctrines of the faith, including the Trinity, the deity of Christ, and the personality and deity of the Holy Spirit.
	After Wierwille's death in 1985, the movement encountered internal strife, which resulted in the formation of some splinter groups. This chart deals only with the main organization that has remained true to Wierwille's teachings and retains the name "The Way International."

History

Topic	*History*
Victor Paul Wierwille, 1947–1985	Born December 31, 1916, Victor Paul Wierwille received a master of theology degree from Princeton Theological Seminary in 1941 and became an ordained pastor of the Evangelical and Reformed Church that same year. He claimed that in 1942 God audibly promised to personally teach him the Word "as it had not been known since the first century" if he in turn would promise to teach these things to others (*Twenty-fifth Anniversary Souvenir Booklet*, p. 9). The Way considers 1942 the year of its founding although it was not officially incorporated until 1947 as the Chimes Hour Youth Caravan.
	In 1948 Wierwille was awarded a doctoral degree from Pike's Peak Seminary in Manitou Springs, Colorado, a correspondence school that had no faculty, no accreditation, and no resident instruction. Followers thereafter addressed him as "doctor."
	For the next three years Wierwille spent much of his time seeking "spiritual power" out of frustration over what he considered a lack of real spiritual life in the parishes he served. He said he found the "power" he was looking for when, through a chance meeting with the early charismatic leader J. E. Stiles, he learned how to breathe in the Holy Spirit and speak in tongues. This meeting allegedly took place on December 12, 1951, when the two men got stranded together during a blizzard in Tulsa, Oklahoma. (Meteorological records for the area indicate that only a half-inch of snow fell on December 8, and only six-tenths of an inch fell on December 20. No snow was recorded on December 12 or any other time during Wierwille's entire visit to Tulsa.)
	Seven years later, Wierwille resigned from the ministry of the Evangelical and Reformed Church, apparently to avoid being dismissed for making speeches that were "embarrassing" to the missionary program (Lee Steele, *The Toledo Blade Sunday Magazine*, March 26, 1972, p. 11).
	As time passed, Wierwille's teachings became a mixture of doctrines derived from diverse sources, including Stiles, George Lamsa, E. W. Bullinger, and E. W. Kenyon. His movement took the name The Way International in 1955. It remained quite small until Wierwille made his Power for Abundant Living classes available nationwide. The largest increase in membership occurred, however, as a result of the Jesus movement of the late sixties and early seventies. This growth prompted him in 1969 to begin the training of The Way missionaries known as WOW (Word Over the World) Ambassadors, and in 1970, the Way Corps (WOW's leadership training arm).
	As The Way grew, so did problems and criticism. Detractors raised serious questions about immorality in the movement as well as concerns over mass weddings, organized gun training, the formation of its own police force, and psychological manipulation of its members.

History (cont.)

Topic	History
Loy Craig Martindale, 1985–	After Wierwille died in 1985, dissension arose within the leadership. Chris Geer, a European leader, accused trustees Loy Martindale, Howard Allen, and Donald Wierwille of spiritual and moral error. These charges eventually led to a split into Geer and Martindale factions. At the same time, several thousand others left the movement, accusing leaders variously of authoritarianism, adultery, and teaching false doctrine. The defectors either drifted from the fellowship entirely or formed regional units similar to the Limb groups they had come from. Some were able to form national networks. Martindale became the leader of those who remained with The Way International.

THEOLOGY

The Doctrine of Revelation

Position	Support	Orthodox Response
The Bible is God's Word.	"... the Bible is the revealed Word and Will of God" (*Power for Abundant Living*, p. 5). "There is only one author of the Bible and that is God. There are many writers but only one author" (Ibid., p. 79).	These are orthodox statements.
The original Word of God had no errors.	"The original, God-given Word literally contained no errors or contradictions" (*Power for Abundant Living*, p. 79).	This is an orthodox statement.
No translation or version may properly be called the Word of God. Only the original documents were the Word of God.	"... no translation or version of the Bible may properly be called the Word of God.... When I refer to the Word of God, I do not mean a copy or a translation or a version; I mean that Word of God which was originally given by revelation to holy men" (*Power for Abundant Living*, pp. 127–28).	Such a position is unacceptable because it effectively renders God unable to communicate with us. The various translations and versions of the Bible extant conform to some 99 percent of what was contained in the original manuscripts. Consequently, it is quite proper to refer to today's Bibles as "the Word of God."
The Bible, as we have it today, is full of doctrinal errors, mistakes, and contradictions because people inserted chapter breaks, verse delineations, and grammatical changes.	"God cannot be blamed for the error in the division of verses or chapters" (*Power for Abundant Living*, p. 129). "Paragraphs are interpretations of what the translators think.... God gave the original Word. He is not at all responsible for the errors that men have introduced by their chapter headings or by their center references or by their paragraph markings" (Ibid., pp. 132–33). "Punctuation is another man-made trickery. If you want the Bible to say something to substantiate your theology, all you have to do is to manipulate the punctuation. The Word of God can be made to say something that it does not really say by just putting in a comma" (Ibid., p. 133).	It is true that the original manuscripts were not written in a chapter and verse format. Nor were there chapter headings or center references. All these were added to help Christians find their way in the Bible more easily. To label such Bible study helps as "errors" goes much too far. It is possible that Wierwille made this charge to point up the need for someone to correct the errors—a responsibility that only he would be qualified to undertake. Punctuation, as we know it in English, did not appear in the original texts. However, the grammatical construction of the Hebrew (OT) and Greek (NT) languages consistently help us to know where punctuation belongs. Punctuation is often

The Doctrine of Revelation (cont.)

Position	Support	Orthodox Response
. . . continued		obvious because there is only one sensible way to read a sentence. It is ironic that Wierwille would protest so strongly over punctuation because he himself would often rearrange punctuation to support false doctrines.
To understand God's Word, one must accept only the seven "church epistles" (Romans through 2 Thessalonians) and the personal epistles are authoritative—that is, directed specifically to the church. The rest of Scripture, although written for our learning, was not addressed to the church and therefore is not authoritative.	"Most people believe that the entire Bible—from Genesis to Revelation—is written to them. This is not true. Believing that the entire Word of God is written to everyone throughout history has caused confusion and contradiction. . . . That part which is addressed *to* us must be applied by us. All the rest of Scripture which does not have our name on it, which is not addressed to us, is *for* our learning. . . . In I Corinthians 10:32 God discloses His system of classification. . . . Give none offence, neither to the Jews, nor to the Gentiles, nor to the Church of God. God lists Jew, Gentile, the Church of God. . . . The entire Bible is addressed to one or the other of these three groups. Unless one understands to whom a passage or book or section is written, he will never be able to rightly divide the Word of Truth. . . . Romans was written after Pentecost, the day on which the Church of God was founded. . . . Those things written before the day of Pentecost are not addressed *to* us but are *for* our learning. . . . This is why the Word says in I Corinthians 10:11 that all Scripture before Pentecost is an admonition to those of us who belong to the Church of God. . . . So are the Gospels addressed to us? Not if the Word of God is right for Romans says that all Scripture before the day of Pentecost is for our learning and the Gospels obviously come before the founding day of the Church of God. . . . One of the greatest errors in the translation of the Bible was placing the four Gospels in the New Testament. . . . Jesus came to Israel, His own people. He was the prophet who fulfilled the law of the Old Testament; therefore, the Gospels complete the Old Testament. . . . The New Testament actually begins with the book of Romans, with Acts being the book of transition between the Old Covenant and the New. . . . the Epistles . . . are addressed specifically to the Church as are the personal Epistles like Timothy, Titus, and Philemon. Hebrews is not addressed to the Church. . . . James is addressed to the same Old-Testament minded believers. . . . James,	Wierwille quotes the following verses in support of his position (although he did not quote from the NIV): First Corinthians 10:31–33: "So whether you eat or drink or whatever you do, do it all for the glory of God. Do not cause anyone to stumble, whether Jews, Greeks or the church of God—even as I try to please everybody in every way. For I am not seeking my own good but the good of many, so that they may be saved." First Corinthians 10:11: "These things happened to them as examples and were written down as warnings for us, on whom the fulfillment of the ages has come." Neither of these passages supports Weirwille's view of biblical authority. To the contrary, verse 11 draws a direct connection between Old Testament believers and Christians. Wierwille states, "This is why the Word says in 1 Cor. 10:11 that all Scripture before Pentecost is an admonition to those of us who belong to the Church of God." The context of the passage is that of the wilderness wandering; Pentecost is not mentioned anywhere. Verse 32 declares a Christian's responsibility not to hinder anyone—Jew, Gentile, or Christian—in one's relationship with God. Only Luke among the four Gospels is addressed to a group or individual. "Theophilus" could be either one person or a group of Gentiles who love God. Luke 1:4 implies that Theophilus already believes in the Christian faith. In any case, these facts contradict Wierwille's position. The Gospels as well as the Old Testament, Hebrews, and James are all authoritative Scripture. "All Scripture is God-breathed and is useful for teaching, rebuking, correcting and training in righteousness" (2Ti 3:16). The Scripture spoken of here was what Timothy had learned from childhood, which must surely have embraced the Old Testament. Moreover, Paul draws on the authority of the Old Testament more than 100 times in his writings.

The Doctrine of Revelation (cont.)

Position	Support	Orthodox Response
	a servant of God and of the Lord Jesus Christ, to [to] the twelve tribes which are scattered abroad, greeting. Could God write the address any more directly?" (*Power for Abundant Living*, pp. 207–13, brackets and emphasis in original).	

The Doctrine of God—*The Trinity*

Position	Support	Orthodox Response
God the Father is the one and only true God.	"The Bible clearly teaches that Christianity is monotheistic. God, the Father of our Lord Jesus Christ, is the one and only true God whom Jesus Christ and his followers are to worship" (*Jesus Christ is not God*, inside front flap of book jacket).	This statement is only partially correct. Christianity is monotheistic, but the orthodox position is that this one God exists as a triune being of three equal persons: Father, Son, and Holy Spirit. Jesus is worshiped on numerous occasions in Scripture (Mt 2:11; 14:33; 28:9, 17; Jn 9:38; Heb 1:6).
Christians during the first three centuries of the church were not trinitarians.	". . . the trinity was not a part of Christian dogma and formal documents of the first three centuries after Christ" (*Jesus Christ is not God*, p. 12).	This statement is a half-truth. The doctrine of the Trinity was not *formally* set forth until the Athanasian Creed was drawn up in the latter half of the fourth century. Before that, however, Trinitarian thought had already been hinted at, if not clearly expressed, at the Council of Nicea (A.D. 325). This council was convened by the emperor Constantine to deal with a heresy termed Arianism (similar to what Jehovah's Witnesses believe about Jesus). The council eventually produced the Nicene Creed. The purpose of church councils was not to invent new doctrines, but to state clearly in a formal manner the doctrines that Christians already embraced. So although the Trinity had not been clearly thought out until the Athanasian Creed, its doctrinal building blocks were already being adhered to by Christians.

The Doctrine of God—*The Trinity (cont.)*

Position	Support	Orthodox Response
The concept of a triune God did not originate with Christians, but with pagans and their ancient religions.	"Long before the founding of Christianity the idea of a triune god or a god-in-three persons was a common belief in ancient religions. Although many of these religions had many minor deities, they distinctly acknowledged that there was one supreme God who consisted of three persons or essences. The Babylonians used an equilateral triangle to represent this three-in-one god.... The Hindu trinity was made up of the gods Brahma, Vishnu, and Shiva. The Greek triad was composed of Zeus, Athena, and Apollo.... ancient cultures also accepted this idea; cultures such as the Babylonian, Egyptian, Phoenician, Greek, Indian, Chinese, Japanese, Icelandic, Siberian and others" (*Jesus Christ is not God*, pp. 11–12).	This objection to the Trinity is common among anti-trinitarian cults, but all fail to recognize the vast difference between pagan "triad" deities and the Christian Trinity. Christian trinitarianism is unique. There is no historical evidence to suggest that Christians borrowed from pagan religions to form the doctrine of the Trinity.
Pagans brought the concept of the Trinity into Christianity.	"... historians of Church dogma and systematic theologians agree that the idea of a Christian trinity was not a part of the first century Church.... It gradually evolved and gained momentum in late first, second and third centuries as pagans, who had converted to Christianity, brought to Christianity some of their pagan beliefs and practices. Trinitarianism then was confirmed at Nicaea in 325 by Church bishops out of political expediency" (*Jesus Christ is not God*, pp. 25–26).	The main emphasis of the Nicene Creed is not the nature of the Trinity, but rather the nature of the Son and how He relates to the Father. Trinitarian concepts are expressed in the creed, but this was not the creed's main purpose. There is no historical support for the idea that the doctrine of the Trinity grew out of pagan concepts brought into the church.

The Doctrine of Jesus Christ—*The Deity of Christ*

Position	Support	Orthodox Response
Jesus Christ was not God. He was the Son of God, but nowhere in the Bible is He called God.	"JESUS CHRIST IS **NOT** GOD" (*Jesus Christ is not God*, p. 1). "The term 'Son of God' is used at least 50 times in the Bible; not one place is there 'God the Son.' To say that 'Son of God' means or equals 'God the Son' totally negates the rules of language, leaving it utterly useless as a tool of communication. In other words, I am saying that Jesus Christ is not God, but the Son of God" (Ibid., p. 5).	The Bible records several succinct statements of Christ through which He claims to be God. On these occasions His immediate audience understood His statements to be claims of deity (see Jn 8:57–59; 10:30–31; 17:5). In addition to Jesus' claims, biblical authors, under the inspiration of the Holy Spirit, identify Jesus as the one and only true God (see Col 2:9; Tit 2:13; 2Pe 1:1; Ro 9:5).

The Doctrine of Jesus Christ—*The Deity of Christ (cont.)*

Position	Support	Orthodox Response
Jesus did not exist before his birth in Bethlehem. He only existed with God in God's foreknowledge.	"Jesus Christ was not literally with God in the beginning" (*Jesus Christ is not God*, p. 5). "Where was Jesus Christ before he was born to Mary? Jesus Christ was with God in His foreknowledge. . . . I Peter 1:20: Who [Christ] verily was foreordained [Carefully note this word 'foreordained' in its context.] before the foundation of the world. . . . The word 'foreordained' is the Greek word *proginosko* which means 'to foreknow.' God foreknew Christ; Christ was in God's foreknowledge before the foundation of the world, but Christ was manifested when he was born. The same Greek word . . . is translated 'foreknow' in Romans 8:29" (Ibid., pp. 28–29, brackets in original). "God is eternal in contrast to Jesus whose beginning was his birth" (Ibid., p. 82).	Jesus must have existed before His conception and birth because John the Baptist—who was born before Jesus—said that Jesus was greater because Jesus existed first (Jn 1:15, 30). This is an obvious reference to Jesus' preexistent state. The foreordination mentioned in 1 Peter 1:20 refers to Christ's role as the Lamb. God foreordained the entirety of Christ's work of redemption before the creation of the world.
Jesus Christ did not create all things.	"The people who say that all things were created by Jesus Christ contradict the first verse of the Bible: 'In the beginning God created . . .'" (*Jesus Christ is not God*, p. 119).	This interpretation of Genesis is obviously based on a presupposition that Jesus is not God. John 1:3 states, "Through him all things were made; without him nothing was made that has been made." Jesus' role as creator is affirmed in Colossians 1:16.
Bible verses that seem to assert Christ's divinity were deliberately tampered with by unknowledgeable believers in previous centuries.	"Throughout the centuries following 325 A.D., unknowledgeable believers, because of previous teaching and believing, deliberately forged scriptures in support of the doctrine of God the Son by purposely tampering with manuscripts and by false translations" (*Forgers of the Word*, p. 3).	A number of Bible verses state plainly that Jesus Christ was God in the flesh. It appears that when faced with such evidence, Wierwille could only negate the passages by stating they were false insertions. He provided no historical evidence to support his view.
Hebrews 1:8 does not prove that Jesus is God.	"Every verse leading up to verse 8 in Hebrews 1 emphasizes the greatness of Christ. . . . thus the title of 'God.' It is only a formal title, used here to indicate his power and glory. Calling a person 'God' is not that unique in Oriental usage. . . . Jehovah called Moses a 'god.' Exodus 7:1. . . . The judges of Israel . . . were referred to as gods. Exodus 22:28. . . . children of the most high are also referred to as gods. Psalm 82:6" (*Jesus Christ is not God*, pp. 32–33).	In Exodus 7:1, Jehovah was not calling Moses a god. Jehovah said that He would make Moses appear as a god *to Pharaoh*. In other words, Pharoah would view Moses as a powerful deity once Jehovah began working through him. Psalm 82 has a noticeably sarcastic tone and does not portray the judges of Israel as true gods. The psalm indicates that although the judges could be called gods, it would not change the fact that they were really men and would die as such (v. 7). The psalm ends with an appeal to the true God (v. 8).

The Doctrine of Jesus Christ—*The Deity of Christ (cont.)*

Position	Support	Orthodox Response
John 20:28 does not prove that Jesus is God.	"... Thomas' addressing Jesus Christ as 'my Lord and my God.' It brings to light the precision of a figure of speech... called *hendiadys*.... Whenever two words are used but only one idea intended, it is the figure *hendiadys*. One of the two words expresses the fact and the other intensifies it.... When Thomas exclaimed 'My Lord and my God,' he was observing the resurrected Christ as 'my godly Lord.' The word 'Lord' expresses the fact and the word 'godly' intensifies 'lord' to the superlative degree" (*Jesus Christ is not God*, pp. 34–35).	Whether you view "God" as a term qualifying "Lord" or as a separate name, "Lord" is still a divine name. "Lord" is often used in the Bible as a divine name (see, for example, Mt 4:7; 22:37; Mk 12:29; Lk 1:68). If "Lord " is used here in the superlative degree, then this is surely an example of Jesus' being given a divine name. Wierwille does not account for the numerous Old Testament and New Testament passages in which the divine person is called both "God" and "Lord." It seems most reasonable to take Thomas' declaration of the risen Jesus as a new step of faith—that He is both Lord and God.
John 1:1 does not prove Jesus is God because it has been misinterpreted. There are actually three different "Words" being discussed in John 1:1 (contrary to the trinitarian view that only Jesus is the Word). The first mention of "Word" refers to the Father (God). The second mention refers to the revealed "Word" of God, which includes both Jesus and the Bible; the revealed Word was with God only in God's foreknowledge. The third mention again refers to God the Father.	"... John 1:1. This has been read and interpreted as follows: 'In the beginning was God the Father, God the Son, God the Holy Ghost. All three were with God, and all three were God.' But this is not what the verse says.... The question of John 1:1 is who is 'the Word' or what is 'the Word' (*logos*). Genesis 1:1 plainly states, 'In the beginning God....' God alone was from the beginning.... When John 1:1 says, '... and the Word was with God,' it refers to the manifested, revealed *logos*: (1) the written Word ... the Bible and (2) the created Word which is Jesus Christ. 'In the beginning was the Word [God] and the [revealed] Word was with God....' How was this revealed Word with God? The Word was with God in His foreknowledge.... The preposition 'with' in verses 1 and 2 of John 1 further confirms this whole truth.... *Pros* means 'together with and yet having distinct independence.'... The revealed Word was together *with* God and yet distinctly independent of Him.... verse 2 could literally read, 'The same [the written Word, which is the Bible, and the Word in the flesh, which is Jesus Christ] was in the beginning with God [in His foreknowledge]'" (*Jesus Christ is not God*, pp. 82–84, 86–87, brackets and emphasis in original).	The Greek text of John's gospel does not allow the concept of different kinds of "Words," but quite the opposite. The personal nature of "Word" is assumed or declared in every instance in John 1:1–14. The "Word" is a person. Wierwille emphasizes the phrase "the Word was with God," but the succeeding phrase, "the Word was God," poses problems for his interpretation. Either the written word (the Bible) or the incarnated Word (Jesus) is God; the text does not allow for both. The first option promotes idolatry; the second runs contrary to what Wierwille is trying to prove. The only other choice is to abandon any consistency in the meaning of the "Word"; once this is done, Wierwille is free to ascribe to the "Word" whatever meaning fits his assumptions.

The Doctrine of Jesus Christ—*The Humanity of Christ*

Position	Support	Orthodox Response
To impregnate Mary, God created a sperm that contained "soul-life." (See also under **The Doctrine of Man and Sin.**)	"God, in order to produce a sinless man and yet one who was of the line of Adam, had to provide a way whereby Jesus would have a human body derived from Adam and yet not have soul-life from Adam's sinful blood.... God created soul-life in the sperm that impregnated the ovum (egg) of Mary.... This created sperm carried only dominant characteristics and did what ordinarily any sperm would do to an egg" (*The Word's Way*, p. 161).	No sperm, with or without "soul-life," impregnated Mary. Jesus was miraculously conceived in the womb of the Virgin Mary by the power of the Holy Spirit (Mt 1:18 23).
Jesus must have been only a man. If Christ were God, He could not have redeemed us.	"... the male passover lamb was to be taken out from among the sheep. This is why Jesus Christ had to be a man. He had to be one of the flock. God could not have died for our sins" (*Jesus Christ is not God*, p. 78). "Our very redemption... is dependent on Jesus Christ's being a man and not God. Our passover... had to be a sheep from the flock. God would hardly qualify as one of our brethren, yet His Son could" (Ibid., p. 7).	Jesus had to be a man; otherwise, He could not have represented humanity. But Jesus also had to be God because no one can redeem the soul of another person (Ps 49:7–8). Consequently, our redemption is dependent on Jesus' being both God and man.
Although He was not God, Jesus lived a sinless life.	"The Bible clearly teaches that Jesus Christ was a man... whose life was without blemish and without spot" (*Jesus Christ is not God*, p. 79).	It is an orthodox statement to say that Jesus lived a sinless life. This could not have been accomplished, however, if He was not God in the flesh.

The Doctrine of Jesus Christ—*The Resurrection of Christ*

Position	Support	Orthodox Response
Jesus was crucified on a Wednesday and rose bodily from the grave on a Saturday.	"Jesus Christ literally fulfilled the law; He carried out the Word of God by being buried on Wednesday afternoon and being raised seventy-two hours later on Saturday afternoon" (*Power for Abundant Living*, p. 179).	Scholars disagree whether Jesus more likely rose on Saturday or on Sunday. The day is relatively unimportant. The crucial issue is whether He physically rose from the dead.
Speaking in tongues is infallible proof of the resurrection of Jesus.	"... we know that God raised Jesus Christ out from among the dead because we speak in tongues, which is the external manifestation in the senses world of the internal reality of Christ within. Speaking in tongues is our *absolute proof*, our present-tense evidence that God did raise Jesus from the dead!" (L. Craig Martindale, *April 1987 letter to all believers*, p. 1).	Speaking in tongues has nothing to do with proof of the resurrection of Jesus. In John 2:19–22 Jesus said He would rise from the grave. The rest of the New Testament testifies that He did so. Tongues is a gift of the Holy Spirit distributed to various people for the purpose of self-edification and, when coupled with interpretation, for the purpose of bringing a message to the church.

The Doctrine of the Holy Spirit

Position	Support	Orthodox Response
The "Holy Spirit" (with capital letters) is God the Father because He is holy and is also spirit. Hence, God the Father is the "Holy Spirit." There is also a "holy spirit" (without capital letters) that comes from God the "Holy Spirit." In other words, the "Holy Spirit" (God) is the giver of the "holy spirit."	"God is Holy and God is Spirit. The gift that He gives is holy spirit.... in the Greek manuscripts and texts the word *pneuma*, 'spirit,' is never capitalized. Therefore, when the word *pneuma* is translated 'Spirit' with a capital 'S' or 'spirit' with a small 's,' it is an interpretation.... it is understandable why so many people confuse the Giver, Holy Spirit, with the gift, holy spirit. The Giver is God who is Spirit, *pneuma*, and Holy, *hagion*.... Luke 11:13... how much more shall your heavenly Father give the Holy Spirit [*pneuma hagion*] to them that ask him? This verse clearly shows that *pneuma hagion* is the gift from God the Father, therefore, should be translated with a small 'h' and a small 's.'" (*Jesus Christ is not God*, pp. 127–28, brackets in original).	The Bible declares that there are three persons in the Trinity and that the Holy Spirit is God but has a different function from the Father. The use of masculine pronouns for the Spirit (as in Jn 16:13–14 and Eph 1:14), the continuation of the personal work of Christ (Jn 14:26; 15:26; 16:7), and the mention of the Spirit with the Father and the Son (Mt 28:19; 2Co 13:14; Eph 1:3–14) all point to the personal and unique work of the Holy Spirit.
Paul referred to the gift of the "holy spirit" when he spoke of "Christ in you, the hope of glory" (Col 1:27).	"The gift is holy spirit, *pneuma hagion*, which is an inherent spiritual ability, *dunamis*, power from on high. This gift is 'Christ in you, the hope of glory' with all its fullness" (*Receiving the Holy Spirit Today*, p. 5).	Colossians 1:27 does not refer to an impersonal power. Paul explicitly defines Christ's ability to personally dwell in us by the power of the Holy Spirit as a mystery that includes His death, burial, and resurrection (Ro 16:25; Eph 3:4, 9; 6:19; 1Ti 3:9). As part of God's eternal plan, this mystery will one day culminate in the glorification of the saints (1Co 15:51) and the establishment of the eternal kingdom (Rev 10:7).
The "holy spirit" is an impersonal power from on high that enables a Christian to serve God.	"The gift from The Holy Spirit, *the Giver*, is *pneuma hagion*, holy spirit, power from on high, spiritual abilities, enablements" (*Receiving the Holy Spirit Today*, p. 4). "Acts 2:4:... they were all filled with the holy ghost [*pneuma hagion*, the gift, power from on high], and began to speak with other tongues, as the Spirit [the *pneuma*, the Giver] gave them utterance" (Ibid., p. 10, brackets in original).	There is only one Holy Spirit mentioned in Scripture, and He is described as a personal entity who is God. The Holy Spirit is not the "Giver." John repeatedly states (Jn 14:26; 15:26; 16:7) that the Spirit is sent by the Father and the Son. Acts 2:4 does not point to the work of an impersonal force any more than Luke 4:1–13 does. Luke states that Jesus was led by the Holy Spirit. In Luke and Acts, the Holy Spirit expresses His personality and will.

The Doctrine of the Holy Spirit (cont.)

Position	Support	Orthodox Response
Every believer should operate the "manifestations" of the spirit listed in 1 Corinthians 12:7–10 (such as speaking in tongues, prophecy, and interpretation of tongues). Speaking in tongues is the external proof that the holy spirit has been imparted to a person.	"It is urgent, if we are going to have the power which Jesus Christ made available, that we study God's Word and begin evidencing the nine manifestations of the holy spirit" (*Power for Abundant Living*, p. 362). "Speaking in a tongue is the believer's external manifestation in the senses world of the internal reality and presence of the power of the holy spirit" (*Receiving the Holy Spirit Today*, p. 41). "One produces the fruit of the spirit by operating the manifestations of the spirit" (*Power for Abundant Living*, p. 279).	Not every Christian receives every gift of the Spirit. Paul indicated this in 1 Corinthians 12:29–30 by asking a series of rhetorical questions calling for "no" as the obvious answer: "Are all apostles? Are all prophets? Are all teachers? Do all work miracles? Do all have gifts of healing? Do all speak in tongues? Do all interpret?" (Or, "All are not apostles, are they?" and so on.) Tongues is not even ranked as first in importance. Paul said he would rather people prophesy than speak in tongues (1Co 14:5–6). He said that in church it would be better to speak five words with understanding than 10,000 words in tongues (v. 19). He also warned that all gifts, including tongues, are beneficial only as long as they are accompanied with love (1Co 13:1).

The Doctrine of Man and Sin

Position	Support	Orthodox Response
Man, in his original state, had a three-fold nature: body, soul, and spirit. These aspects of man are seen through the Bible's use of the words *formed, made,* and *created* when referring to the creation of man.	"... to understand the origin of man is Isaiah 43:7.... every one that is called by my name: for I have created him for my glory, I have formed him; yea, I have made him.... When God said *formed*, He meant *formed*. When He said *made*, He meant *made*. When He said *created*, He meant *created*.... In the beginning man was formed, made and created" (*Power for Abundant Living*, pp. 231–32).	It is acceptable within the pale of orthodoxy to view man as a threefold being who comprises body, soul, and spirit. This is known as the trichotomist view. However, the way Wierwille derives this doctrine from the biblical text is most unusual and without merit. The three Hebrew words translated for *created, formed,* and *made—bara, yatsar,* and *asah*—are simply different words that express the same concept. Nothing would indicate that each is used to refer to a different aspect of man's being.
The "body" was that which God *formed* from the dust of the earth.	"... God formed man of the dust of the ground.... The body of man was formed (*yatsar*) of the dust of the ground" (*Power for Abundant Living*, p. 233).	This is a true statement.

The Doctrine of Man and Sin (cont.)

Position	Support	Orthodox Response
The "soul" was the life-force that God breathed into mankind. He *made* man a living soul by giving him that which brought life to his body. The soul life is in the blood; and through conception one's soul is passed on to a child. God created "soul" (life) only once and passed it around to every living creature—including man.	"The soul in man is that which gives the body its life, its vitality.... The soul is nothing more and nothing less than that which gives life to a person's body.... As long as a person breathes, he has a soul" (*Power for Abundant Living*, pp. 233–34). "Leviticus 17:11: For the life of the flesh *is* in the blood.... The soul life is in the blood and is passed on when the sperm impregnates the egg.... the soul is passed on from one person to his progeny. If a person has no offspring, his soul is gone when he dies; it is no more" (Ibid., p. 237). "How many times did God create soul? The Bible says that (except for the birth of Jesus) God created it just once and that was when animals first came into being. God simply took the previously created soul life and gave it to man.... The soul life which was in Adam was carried on in his children.... To this day the same soul life continues in mankind which God originally put in Adam" (Ibid., pp. 244–45).	The Bible does not say that one's soul is passed on through the blood. It only states that life, survival, or existence is inseparable from the blood. A person would die without the regenerative process of blood circulating in the body. Nowhere does Scripture suggest that there is a kind of soul-life essence that circulates among humans and is passed from parent to child.
The "spirit" was that aspect of man which God created so that He and man could spiritually communicate. Communication was possible because the "spirit" placed in man was actually part of God Himself.	"God created within man His Spirit (*ruach*), His image.... It is that part of man which made it possible for God to talk to man and for man to communicate with God" (*Power for Abundant Living*, p. 239).	Man is wholistic. Man is flesh as well as spirit, and man was created in the image of God. There is nothing innately wrong with physical flesh. God created flesh and walked with human flesh and has on many occasions in the Bible communicated on the physical level.
When man fell, he lost his spirit. Unregenerate man is now a twofold being comprising only body and soul, just like animals.	"The spirit which God originally created in man was given on a condition.... In not fulfilling the conditions which God had prescribed, man became a two-fold being of just body and soul" (*Are the Dead Alive Now?* pp. 109–10). "Adam's mistake was cataclysmic.... The spirit disappeared. The reason the spirit was called dead is that it was no longer there.... From that very day Adam and Eve were just body and soul—as any other animal. Man, being body and soul, had to rely solely on his five senses" (*Power for Abundant Living*, p. 258).	Scripture often speaks of man having a spirit (Pss 51:10; 77:6; 142:3–4; 143:7; Pr 15:13; 20:27). In fact, Zechariah 12:1 says that God forms the spirit of each man within him, and Hebrew 4:12 speaks of God's Word being so powerful that it can divide the soul from the spirit. How could God's Word do this if man has no spirit? Our spirit is that which is intrinsically all that we are.

The Doctrine of Man and Sin (cont.)

Position	Support	Orthodox Response
When people are born again, they once again receive "spirit," which is actually a part of God Himself that He is only lending (for lack of a better expression) to Christians so that they can communicate with Him.	"... on the day of Pentecost, every believer for the first time could have the spirit from God born within, so man could again become a tripartite being of body, soul, and spirit. This anointing with spirit from God places the believer again in the position where God can communicate directly with tripartite man.... The *spirit* from God is *created* in the believer and at the end of natural life this created spirit must return to God *of whom it is a part*" (*Are the Dead Alive Now?* pp. 110–11, emphasis added).	God's ability to communicate with man is not dependent on whether man has the Spirit of God indwelling him. The Bible recounts a number of instances when God spoke to unbelievers. For example, God spoke to Abimelech, the Philistine king of Gerar (Ge 20:3). Also, God spoke in a miraculous way while Saul was traveling on the road to Damascus (Ac 9:3–6).

The Doctrine of Salvation

Position	Support	Orthodox Response
Salvation is by grace alone through faith alone in the finished work of Christ, who died on the cross for our sins.	"... salvation is not of works; it is by grace and grace alone" (*Power for Abundant Living*, p. 294). "You become a Christian by believing that God raised Jesus from the dead, by confessing Him as Lord in your life.... God laid on Jesus the iniquity of us all. You by your good works and efforts cannot save yourself.... If you confess with your mouth Jesus as your Lord, you are acting on your believing. You still have not done any works for your salvation" (*The New, Dynamic Church*, pp. 36–38).	These are true statements.

The Doctrine of Rewards and Punishment

Position	Support	Orthodox Response
At death, Christians do not immediately go to be with the Lord. They remain unconscious in the grave.	"Most Christians hold the belief that upon death those who belong to Christ are immediately received up into glory, commonly called Heaven or paradise, to appear before the Father. There they are alive and conscious and have a joyous existence with Him and their loved ones. Such a belief is contrary to the teachings in the Word of God" (*Are the Dead Alive Now?* p. 21). "The Word of God shows that new life to the dead comes with the return of Christ. Before Christ's coming, all those who have died remain in the grave in corruption and unconscious" (Ibid., p. 9).	This teaching is in direct opposition to what Paul the apostle says about desiring "to be away from the body and at home with the Lord" (2Co 5:8). Paul also states in Philippians 1:23 that it was his desire to depart this life and be with God. That the dead experience continued consciousness until the resurrection is clearly established in Scripture. The wicked are held in torment (2Pe 2:9), while the righteous are with God (Rev 6:9–11).
Luke 23:43 does not prove that Christians go to be with the Lord imediately after they die.	"Luke 23:43: And Jesus said unto him [the malefactor], Verily I say unto thee, To day shalt thou be with me in paradise. . . . The King James puts the comma before 'today'. . . . Why? Because one group teaches that the moment one dies, he goes to heaven. . . . If a man is going to heaven today, heaven must be available. . . . heaven is not available. . . . this verse talks about paradise—and paradise is not heaven. . . . Paradise is present in Genesis chapters 1 and 2. . . . Paradise is always a place upon earth. . . . Since paradise was non-existent on the day of the crucifixion, Jesus had to say to the malefactor that sometime in the future he would be with Him, not in heaven, but in paradise. Let us read the sentence with literal accuracy. . . . Verily, I say to you To day, thou shalt [the day is coming in the future when you are going to] be with me in paradise" (*Power for Abundant Living*, pp. 133–35, brackets in original).	Placing the comma in Luke 23:43 after the word "today" is senseless. Why would Jesus have had to tell the thief on the cross that he was speaking to him "today"? On what other day would Jesus have been speaking? Furthermore, the text grammatically supports putting the comma *before* today.
A Christian's final reward is to be together with Christ for all eternity.	"The great hope of the Christian Church is the return of Christ and our gathering together unto him" (*God's Magnified Word*, p. 227). "What a glorious hope! We will all be changed to have a body fashioned like unto Christ's. We will meet him in the air and 'so shall we ever be with the Lord,' according to I Thessalonians 4:17" (Ibid., p. 258).	These are true statements.

INTERESTING AND DISTINCTIVE BELIEFS

Position	Support	Orthodox Response
God never meant for Christians to live in poverty. It is the Lord's will that all Christians prosper.	". . . III John 2 tells us . . . The will of God is that we may prosper. He never meant for the Christian to be poverty-stricken and down-trodden in any segment of his life" (*Power for Abundant Living*, pp. 11–12).	This verse is not expressing God's will for every believer. John is expressing his personal desire for those to whom he is writing. Furthermore, he specifically says he is praying toward this end: "Dear friend, I pray that you may enjoy good health and that all may go well with you, even as your soul is getting along well" (3Jn 2). Christians often suffer poverty and ill health. In fact, some of the most godly people in church history endured such trials (Heb 11:36–38). A Christian's treasure is stored up in heaven, not on earth (Mt 6:19–21).
Contrary to what is said in Philippians 4:11, Christians should not be content in states of life that are difficult to endure (such as sickness, suffering, poverty).	". . . Philippians 4:11. . . . I have learned, in whatsoever state I am, *therewith* to be content. That is the King James rendition, and it is erroneous. This verse conveys the idea that, for example, if you are sick, you should just enjoy being sick—be content and at peace with your condition. If you are dying, be content that you are dying. . . . No, No! You see, this teaching that you have to be content with suffering is just a trick of the Adversary. . . . The accurate text of Philippians 4:11 reads: '. . . I have learned in whatsoever state I am, I am self-sufficient, self-adequate.' What a tremendous revelation!" (*God's Magnified Word*, pp. 11–12).	While it is true that *autarkes* can be literally translated "self-sufficient," Paul's use of the word is playing off the Stoic concept of prideful self-sufficiency. In Philippians 4:11–13 Paul informs his readers that he has experienced enough of the difficulty and abundance of life that he is able to cope with either suffering or prosperity. This ability was not from within himself, but "I can do everything through him who gives me strength." Paul did not even record his preference between poverty or prosperity. He learned contentment in either circumstance.
When people have their needs and wants in line, they will definitely receive what they pray for as long as they firmly *believe* that they will receive what they want and act upon that belief in a positive way. This is the "law of believing," and it is so powerful that even unbelievers will get what they want from God as long as they really *believe* they will receive it.	"After knowing what is available, how to receive, and what to do, a person then believes and finally acts upon his believing in a positive way" (*Power for Abundant Living*, p. 31). "Mark 11:21, 22. . . . And Jesus answering saith unto them, Have faith in God. The 'original' text read, '. . . Have the faith of God.' Observe verse 23. . . . whosoever shall say unto this mountain, Be thou removed. . . . he shall have whatsoever he saith. This is the great law in the Word of God.' . . . Whosoever . . . It does not say Christian or non-Christian; *whosoever* means *whosoever*" (Ibid., pp. 34–35). ". . . a high-caste Hindu, whose paralyzed arm was hanging limp . . . said to me, 'Will you pray for my arm?' However, he immediately added, 'But I do not believe in your Jesus.' What would you have done? I asked him if he believed God would deliver him. He said, '. . . God will heal me if you pray for me, but I do not believe in	The prayers of unbelievers are not answered (Pss 34:15–16; 145:19; Isa 1:15; Jn 9:31) because a wall of separation exists between them and God (Isa 59:2). Christians, too, if they are to receive from God, must pray in accordance with God's will (1Jn 5:14). Sometimes God simply says no, despite how hard people may believe they are going to receive a positive response (Jas 4:3). Even Paul received a negative answer from God after having prayed three times about a "thorn in my flesh" (2Co 12:7).

Position	Support	Orthodox Response
... continued	your Jesus.' So again I asked him, 'Do you believe God will set you free?' And he said, 'I believe God will heal me, but I do not believe in your Jesus.' I laid my hands on him and I prayed.... When I finished I said to him, 'Now lift your arm.' He began to put it up and suddenly he thrust up both of his arms.... He was totally set free" (Ibid., p. 30).	
Matthew 27:46 should read, "My God, my God, for this purpose was I kept" rather than "My God, my God, why have you forsaken me?"	"Matthew 27:46... *Eli, Eli, lama sabachthani?* that is to say, My God, my God, why hast thou forsaken me?... Jesus must have been doing God's will when He was dying upon the cross.... This verse contradicts the rest of the Word. What is the problem?... Jesus spoke Aramaic. These Aramaic words are left in this particular Scripture because the translators really did not know what to do with them. They let the verse set and added the English interpretation.... The word *eli* means 'my God,' but there is no Aramaic word like the word *lama*. There is a word lmna. *Lmna* is always a cry of victory, a declaration of 'for this purpose,' or 'for this reason.' The root of *sabachthani* is *shbk*. *Shbk* means 'to reserve,' 'to leave,' to spare' or 'to keep.'... Hanging on the cross at that crucial hour, Jesus came forth with this utterance.... 'My God, my God, for this purpose was I reserved, for this purpose was I spared'" (*Power for Abundant Living*, pp. 152, 154–55, brackets in original).	In this passage it appears that Jesus is calling out a cry from Psalm 22:1. The psalmist is asking why God has abandoned him. Both Matthew and Mark record an interpretation of the Aramaic phrase in reference to Jesus' experiencing the feeling of being forsaken by the Father. Even the root *Shbk* conveys the idea "to leave." Therefore the natural, uncontrived reading of the passage should be read, "My God, my God, why has thou forsaken me?" Wierwille is partly correct in recognizing that this event diverges radically from the rest of Scripture. This should not come as a surprise, because the Crucifixion is a unique event in history.
Jesus was crucified between four men, not two.	"Matthew 27:38: Then [after all that] were there two thieves crucified with him.... The King James says 'two thieves'; the Greek words are *duo lestai*... lestai is 'robbers.' The Greeks used an entirely different word for a thief, *kleptes*.... let us go to Luke 23:32. And there were also two other, malefactors [*kakourgoi*, malefactors, not robbers], led with him to be put to death.... The word 'malefactor' is the word *kakourgos*; the word 'robbers' is *lestai*. Luke uses an entirely different word because entirely different people are involved.... When Jesus was led out to be crucified, they led two malefactors with him. The soldiers crucified Jesus and the malefactors.... Both of the robbers reviled Jesus, but only one of the malefactors reviled Him.... According to the accurate Word of God, how many men were crucified with Jesus? Two malefactors plus two thieves makes four people.... there were four crucified with Jesus" (*Power for Abundant Living*, pp. 159, 161–63, brackets in original).	Different words and meanings are commonly reported among the four Gospels. Luke uses a more general term, "malefactor" or "evildoer," while Matthew is more precise and records the kind of evil committed. Surely it is possible that one of the thieves reviled Jesus and later, while watching His death, had a change of heart. It is also possible the Bible mentions only two of many people who were crucified on that day with Jesus.

Position	Support	Orthodox Response
Water baptism should not be practiced.	"Acts 1:4, 5.... John truly baptized with water; but ye shall be baptized with the Holy Ghost.... In other words, with the coming of the greater (holy spirit), the lesser (water) came to an end. This replacement was initiated on Pentecost" (*The Bible Tells Me So*, p. 134). "The records of baptism in Acts... do not mention water at all; thus to say that there is water involved in baptism can only be private interpretation. In Acts 2:38 Peter baptized 'in the name of Jesus Christ.' In Acts 8:16 people were 'baptized in the name of the Lord Jesus'.... Nowadays whenever the word 'baptize' is mentioned, water is immediately associated with it because of the influence of religious doctrines" (Ibid., pp. 135–36). "... water baptism was indeed instituted by God, but only for Israel and the kingdom, and then for only a limited period of time" (Ibid., p. 141).	Wierwille's statement that the records of baptism in Acts do not mention water at all is incorrect. Two separate accounts mention water, and in many other places water is implied. Acts 8:38 clearly states that the apostle Philip baptized the Ethiopian. The encounter between Peter and Cornelius recorded in Acts 10:44–48 also shows that many Gentiles first received the Spirit (given evidence in this passage through speaking in tongues) and then were baptized in water at the recommendation of Peter. Water baptism is also reported in other sections of the New Testament. Paul expressed his understanding of baptism in Romans 6:4: "We were therefore buried with him through baptism into death in order that, just as Christ was raised from the dead through the glory of the Father, we too may live a new life." As Christ died and was buried, so in baptism are we buried (under water) with him. First Peter 3:21 can only be interpreted to refer to water baptism.
The Lord's prayer (Mt 6:9) is not addressed to, or meant for, Christians.	"What about the Lord's prayer?... He taught it to His disciples, to Israel" (*Power for Abundant Living*, p. 215).	To state that the Lord's Prayer is not addressed to Christians is to deny the purpose of all the Gospels. These Gospels, including Matthew 6:9 and Luke 11:1–4, were written to give us the good news of Jesus Christ and to instruct believers, whether Jews or Gentiles. Even though Jesus' disciples were Jewish, these men were "followers" of Christ, not followers of Israel.
The New Testament was originally written in Aramaic, not Greek.	The Way believes that "Aramaic was the original language in which the New Testament was written" (*Twenty-fifth Anniversary Souvenir Booklet*, p. 17).	There is no evidence that the New Testament was written in Aramaic. There are some ancient traditions that Matthew wrote "the oracles" in Aramaic and that it was later translated into Greek. There is however much disagreement on exactly what was meant by Papias. No early Aramaic text of Matthew or of any of the remaining parts of the New Testament have been found. This and many other evidences lead one to know that at least a majority of the New Testament was written in Greek.

Position	Support	Orthodox Response
Tithing (giving 10 percent of one's income to the group) is the minimal amount that should be given. Tithing will always bring financial prosperity. Not tithing will cause ruin.	"... material prosperity always hinges upon tithing.... the tithe is a minimum external manifestation of an internal spiritual recognition that God is our basic source of supply and prosperity.... As long as the people tithed, they prospered.... When they withheld their tithe ... they became afflicted, oppressed, diseased and defeated... Malachi 3:7–12. Whatever our life's calling may be, we can prosper only as we return to God at least a tithe of all our increase" (*Christians Should Be Prosperous*, pp. 4–7).	It appears that even as he is willing to accept many passages written to Israel in regard to tithing, Wierwille is unwilling to accept that the Lord's Prayer is for believers. The Old Testament supports the tithing of income, and the practice continues among many orthodox believers. However, from Old Testament times until today, many believers who have given sacrificially to God have nevertheless suffered according to God's providence. Paul reveals in Philippians 4:10–13 that he had been in financial need so many times that he had learned to be content with very little.

APPENDIX A
Orthodox Christian Doctrine

The Doctrine of Revelation	
Position	*Support*
The doctrine of revelation defined	Revelation is God's supernatural act of self-communication and disclosure of Himself to humankind. In revelation the infinite God narrates a story about Himself to finite humans. Revelation is personal, since God has taken the initiative of revealing Himself to persons for the purpose of establishing a redemptive relationship with humankind. Moreover, these divine truths as recorded in the Bible are propositional—that is, they reveal the nature of God exclusively and objectively through the medium (words) of the Bible. These propositions generally assume the character of doctrine.
The importance of the doctrine	"In the study of all other sciences man places himself above the object of his investigation and actively elicits from it his knowledge by whatever method may seem most appropriate, but in theology he does not stand above but rather under the object of his knowledge. In other words, man can know God only in so far as the latter actively makes Himself known. . . . Without revelation man would never have been able to acquire any knowledge of God. And even after God has revealed Himself objectively, it is not human reason that discovers God, but it is God who discloses Himself" (Berkhof, *Systematic Theology*, p. 34).
God's revelation is personal.	**God reveals Himself by telling His name.** "Nothing is more personal than one's name. When Moses asked who he should say has sent him to the people of Israel, Jehovah responded by giving his name. Ex. 3:14 'I am who I am [or I will be who I will be]'" (Erickson, *Christian Theology*, pp. 178–79). **God reveals Himself by establishing a personal covenant relationship with His chosen people.** Genesis 17:7: "I will establish my covenant as an everlasting covenant between me and you and your descendants after you for the generations to come, to be your God and the God of your descendants after you." Exodus 6:7: "I will take you as my own people, and I will be your God. Then you will know that I am the LORD your God, who brought you out from under the yoke of the Egyptians."
God reveals Himself through various modes.	**Throughout history, God has revealed Himself through miraculous events, divine speech, and visible manifestations.** **1. Miraculous Events** ***The saving of Noah's family from the Flood*** Genesis 7:1: "The LORD then said to Noah, 'Go into the ark, you and your whole family, because I have found you righteous in this generation.'" ***The call of Abram*** Genesis 12:1: "The LORD had said to Abram, 'Leave your country, your people and your father's household and go to the land I will show you.'"

Position	Support
	Moses and the burning bush

Moses and the burning bush

Exodus 3:4: "When the Lord saw that he had gone over to look, God called to him from within the bush, 'Moses! Moses!' And Moses said, 'Here I am.'"

Gideon's fleece

Judges 6:39: "Then Gideon said to God, 'Do not be angry with me. Let me make just one more request. Allow me one more test with the fleece. This time make the fleece dry and the ground covered with dew.' That night God did so. Only the fleece was dry; all the ground was covered with dew."

2. Divine Speech

John's vision

Revelation 1:8: "'I am the Alpha and the Omega,' says the Lord God, 'who is, and who was, and who is to come, the Almighty.'"

Daniel's dream

Daniel 7:2: "Daniel said: 'In my vision at night I looked, and there before me were the four winds of heaven churning up the great sea.'"

Audible speech to Adam and Eve in the garden

Genesis 2:16–17: "And the Lord God commanded the man, 'You are free to eat from any tree in the garden; but you must not eat from the tree of the knowledge of good and evil, for when you eat of it you will surely die.'"

Audible speech to Samuel in the temple

1 Samuel 3:10: "The Lord came and stood there, calling as at the other times, 'Samuel! Samuel!' Then Samuel said, 'Speak, for your servant is listening.'"

Prophetic utterances

Deuteronomy 18:15–18: "The Lord your God will raise up for you a prophet like me from among your own brothers. You must listen to him. For this is what you asked of the Lord your God at Horeb on the day of the assembly when you said, 'Let us not hear the voice of the Lord our God nor see this great fire anymore, or we will die.' The Lord said to me: 'What they say is good. I will raise up for them a prophet like you from among their brothers; I will put my words in his mouth, and he will tell them everything I command him.'"

Even through the mouth of a donkey

Numbers 22:28–30: "Then the Lord opened the donkey's mouth, and she said to Balaam, 'What have I done to you to make you beat me these three times?' Balaam answered the donkey, 'You have made a fool of me! If I had a sword in my hand, I would kill you right now.' The donkey said to Balaam, 'Am I not your own donkey, which you have always ridden, to this day? Have I been in the habit of doing this to you?' 'No,' he said."

3. Visible Manifestations

Old Testament theophanies before the incarnation of Jesus Christ

Usually described as the angel of Yahweh

Genesis 16:7–9: "The angel of the Lord found Hagar near a spring in the desert; it was the spring that is beside the road to Shur. And he said, 'Hagar, servant of Sarai, where have you come from, and where are you going?' 'I'm running away from my mistress Sarai,' she answered. Then the angel of the Lord told her, 'Go back to your mistress and submit to her.'"

In the form of a man, as with Jacob

Genesis 32:30: "So Jacob called the place Peniel, saying, 'It is because I saw God face to face, and yet my life was spared.'"

The Doctrine of Revelation (cont.)

Position	Support
	Shekinah glory Exodus 24:15–16: "When Moses went up on the mountain, the cloud covered it, and the glory of the LORD settled on Mount Sinai. For six days the cloud covered the mountain, and on the seventh day the LORD called to Moses from within the cloud." **Jesus Christ, the unique manifestation of God, was an actual human, with all the human processes and experiences such as birth, pain, and death.** John 1:14: "The Word became flesh and made his dwelling among us. We have seen his glory, the glory of the One and Only, who came from the Father, full of grace and truth." John 14:9: "Jesus answered: 'Don't you know me, Philip, even after I have been among you such a long time? Anyone who has seen me has seen the Father. How can you say, "Show us the Father"?'"
Revelation is progressive; its final manifestation is Jesus Christ, the Son of God.	**The final manifestation of God's revelation is His Son, Jesus Christ.** Hebrews 1:1–2: "In the past God spoke to our forefathers through the prophets at many times and in various ways, but in these last days he has spoken to us by his Son, whom he appointed heir of all things, and through whom he made the universe." Ephesians 3:2–5: "Surely you have heard about the administration of God's grace that was given to me for you, that is, the mystery made known to me by revelation, as I have already written briefly. In reading this, then, you will be able to understand my insight into the mystery of Christ, which was not made known to men in other generations as it has now been revealed by the Spirit to God's holy apostles and prophets." Colossians 1:25–27: "I have become its servant by the commission God gave me to present to you the word of God in its fullness—the mystery that has been kept hidden for ages and generations, but is now disclosed to the saints. To them God has chosen to make known among the Gentiles the glorious riches of this mystery, which is Christ in you, the hope of glory."
The Bible communicates objective truths about God and His will.	1 Thessalonians 2:13: "And we also thank God continually because, when you received the word of God, which you heard from us, you accepted it not as the word of men, but as it actually is, the word of God, which is at work in you who believe."
The Bible, containing the 66 books of the Old and New Testaments, is the source of authority as it pertains to matters of faith and practice (*sola Scriptura*).	1 Corinthians 15:2–4: "By this gospel you are saved, if you hold firmly to the word I preached to you. Otherwise, you have believed in vain. For what I received I passed on to you as of first importance: that Christ died for our sins according to the Scriptures, that he was buried, that he was raised on the third day according to the Scriptures." Romans 3:2: "First of all, they have been entrusted with the very words of God." **The Old Testament attests to its own unique authority.** Deuteronomy 4:2: "Do not add to what I command you and do not subtract from it, but keep the commands of the LORD your God that I give you." Deuteronomy 12:32: "See that you do all I command you; do not add to it or take away from it." **The OT prophets are God's mouthpiece and record God's words.** Exodus 4:12: "Now go; I will help you speak and will teach you what to say." Exodus 24:4: "Moses then wrote down everything the LORD had said. He got up early the next morning and built an altar at the foot of the mountain and set up twelve stone pillars representing the twelve tribes of Israel." Jeremiah 30:2: "This is what the LORD, the God of Israel, says: 'Write in a book all the words I have spoken to you.'" Isaiah 30:8: "Go now, write it on a tablet for them, inscribe it on a scroll, that for the days to come it may be an everlasting witness."

The Doctrine of Revelation (cont.)

Position	Support
	The authority of the OT and Paul's writings are confirmed by Jesus and the apostle Peter.

Matthew 5:17: "Do not think that I have come to abolish the Law or the Prophets; I have not come to abolish them but to fulfill them."

John 17:17: "Sanctify them by the truth; your word is truth."

2 Peter 1:20–21: "Above all, you must understand that no prophecy of Scripture came about by the prophet's own interpretation. For prophecy never had its origin in the will of man, but men spoke from God as they were carried along by the Holy Spirit."

2 Peter 3:15–16: "Bear in mind that our Lord's patience means salvation, just as our dear brother Paul also wrote you with the wisdom that God gave him. He writes the same way in all his letters, speaking in them of these matters. His letters contain some things that are hard to understand, which ignorant and unstable people distort, as they do the other Scriptures, to their own destruction."

Although *graphe* (Scripture) as used in the New Testament always refers to the OT writings, there is ample evidence to conclude that the NT is equally inspired.

1 Timothy 5:18: "For the Scripture says, 'Do not muzzle the ox while it is treading out the grain,' and 'The worker deserves his wages.'"

"The first quotation corresponds to Deut. 25:4 but the second is not found in the O.T. However, it does occur in Lk. 10:7, thus indicating that Paul is quoting Luke's Gospel as *graphe*. Paul is equating Luke's writings on the same level as O.T. Scripture" (Wayne A. Grudem, "Scripture's Self-Attestation," in *Scripture and Truth*, ed. Carson and Woodbridge, pp. 48–49).

The NT attests to its own unique authority.

Galatians 1:8: "But even if we or an angel from heaven should preach a gospel other than the one we preached to you, let him be eternally condemned!"

1 Thessalonians 2:13: "And we also thank God continually because, when you received the word of God, which you heard from us, you accepted it not as the word of men, but as it actually is, the word of God, which is at work in you who believe."

2 Peter 3:2: "I want you to recall the words spoken in the past by the holy prophets and the command given by our Lord and Savior through your apostles."

1 Thessalonians 4:2: "For you know what instructions we gave you by the authority of the Lord Jesus." |
| **Biblical inspiration comes from the Holy Spirit.** | **The apostles verify that the words they speak are from the Holy Spirit.**

1 Corinthians 2:10: "But God has revealed it to us by his Spirit. The Spirit searches all things, even the deep things of God."

1 Corinthians 2:13: "This is what we speak, not in words taught us by human wisdom but in words taught by the Spirit, expressing spiritual truths in spiritual words."

John 17:8: "For I gave them the words you gave me and they accepted them. They knew with certainty that I came from you, and they believed that you sent me."

The Holy Spirit bears witness to the authority of the Word.

1 Thessalonians 1:5: "Our gospel came to you not simply with words, but also with power, with the Holy Spirit and with deep conviction. You know how we lived among you for your sake." |

The Doctrine of Revelation (cont.)	
Position	**Support**
The Bible's divine inspiration extends to the individual words of the original manuscripts, and all of its contents are equally inspired.	**All of Scripture is inspired by God.** *Theopneustos* literally means God-"spirated," denoting that Scripture is literally the product of God's creative breath (Elwell, *Evangelical Dictionary of Theology,* p. 145). 2 Timothy 3:16: "All Scripture is God-breathed and is useful for teaching, rebuking, correcting and training in righteousness." 2 Peter 1:20–21: "Above all, you must understand that no prophecy of Scripture came about by the prophet's own interpretation. For prophecy never had its origin in the will of man, but men spoke from God as they were carried along by the Holy Spirit." **The Bible is fully without error in all it teaches or affirms (inerrant) and is wholly trustworthy and reliable (infallible).** *It is rooted in God, who "cannot lie."* Numbers 23:19: "God is not a man, that he should lie, nor a son of man, that he should change his mind. Does he speak and then not act? Does he promise and not fulfill?" Titus 1:2: ". . . a faith and knowledge resting on the hope of eternal life, which God, who does not lie, promised before the beginning of time." John 3:33: "The man who has accepted it has certified that God is truthful." Hebrews 6:18: "God did this so that, by two unchangeable things in which it is impossible for God to lie, we who have fled to take hold of the hope offered to us may be greatly encouraged." *Jesus affirmed that Scripture will be fulfilled to its smallest detail and that it is inviolable and enduring.* Matthew 5:18: "I tell you the truth, until heaven and earth disappear, not the smallest letter, not the least stroke of a pen, will by any means disappear from the Law until everything is accomplished." John 10:35: "If he called them 'gods,' to whom the word of God came—and the Scripture cannot be broken . . ." Matthew 24:35: "Heaven and earth will pass away, but my words will never pass away." The grammatical construction of the second clause of this sentence (*ou me*) is a double negative asserting its negative emphasis. Scripture will *by no means* pass away (see also Luke 16:17). **Inerrancy extends to the words, tenses, and singular or plural form of nouns in Scripture.** On several occasions, the arguments of Christ and the biblical writers rested on specific words. The use of the word "gods" by the psalmist was the key to Jesus' rebuttal of the Jews' charge of blasphemy. John 10:34–35: "Jesus answered them, 'Is it not written in your Law, "I have said you are gods"? If he called them "gods," to whom the word of God came—and the Scripture cannot be broken . . ."' "The fact that the promise of God recorded in Genesis said 'seed' rather than 'seeds' was significant for the apostle Paul's argument to the Galatians" (Saucy, *Is the Bible Reliable?,* p. 75). Galatians 3:16: "The promises were spoken to Abraham and to his seed. The Scripture does not say 'and to seeds,' meaning many people, but 'and to your seed,' meaning one person, who is Christ."

The Doctrine of Revelation (cont.)

Position	Support
By virtue of the Bible's inspiration, its 66 books are recognized as canonical.	**The Early Christian Church recognized inspired books as canonical.** "The New Testament books did not become authoritative for the Church because they were formally included in a canonical list; on the contrary, the Church included them in her canon because she already regarded them as divinely inspired, recognizing their innate worth and generally apostolic authority, direct or indirect. . . . But what these councils did was not to impose something new upon the Christian communities but to codify what was already the general practice of those communities" (Bruce, *The New Testament Documents—Are They Reliable?*, 27). "The slowness in determining the final limits of the canon is testimony to the care and vigilance of early Christians in receiving books purporting to be apostolic. . . . In the most basic sense neither individuals nor councils created the canon; instead they came to perceive and acknowledge the self-authenticating quality of these writings, which imposed themselves as canonical upon the church" (Metzger, *The New Testament: Its Background, Growth, and Content*, p. 276).
Jesus Christ is the supreme revelation and climax of Old Testament disclosure; therefore the canon is closed.	**God has completed His revelation of Himself and His plans in Jesus Christ, so with the completion of the New Testament there is no need for additional written revelation.** Exodus 24:3–4: "When Moses went and told the people all the LORD's words and laws, they responded with one voice, 'Everything the LORD has said we will do.' Moses then wrote down everything the LORD had said. He got up early the next morning and built an altar at the foot of the mountain and set up twelve stone pillars representing the twelve tribes of Israel." Luke 1:3: "Therefore, since I myself have carefully investigated everything from the beginning, it seemed good also to me to write an orderly account for you, most excellent Theophilus." Luke 24:44: "He said to them, 'This is what I told you while I was still with you: Everything must be fulfilled that is written about me in the Law of Moses, the Prophets and the Psalms.'" Romans 16:25–26: "Now to him who is able to establish you by my gospel and the proclamation of Jesus Christ, according to the revelation of the mystery hidden for long ages past, but now revealed and made known through the prophetic writings by the command of the eternal God, so that all nations might believe and obey him. . . ." Hebrews 1:1–2: "God, who at various times and in various ways spoke in time past to the fathers by the prophets, has in these last days spoken to us by His Son, whom He has appointed heir of all things, through whom also He made the worlds" (NKJV). 1 John 4:1–3: "Dear friends, do not believe every spirit, but test the spirits to see whether they are from God, because many false prophets have gone out into the world. This is how you can recognize the Spirit of God: Every spirit that acknowledges that Jesus Christ has come in the flesh is from God, but every spirit that does not acknowledge Jesus is not from God. This is the spirit of the antichrist, which you have heard is coming and even now is already in the world." **Paul warned the Thessalonian believers of the circulation of false letters.** 2 Thessalonians 2:2–3: ". . . not to become easily unsettled or alarmed by some prophecy, report or letter supposed to have come from us, saying that the day of the Lord has already come. Don't let anyone deceive you in any way, for that day will not come until the rebellion occurs and the man of lawlessness is revealed, the man doomed to destruction." **The last book of the Bible warns against adding to or taking away from its prophecies.** Revelation 22:18–19: "I warn everyone who hears the words of the prophecy of this book: If anyone adds anything to them, God will add to him the plagues described in this book. And if anyone takes words away from this book of prophecy, God will take away from him his share in the tree of life and in the holy city, which are described in this book."

The Doctrine of the Trinity

Position	Support
The doctrine of the Trinity defined	"And the Catholic faith is this: That we worship one God in Trinity, and Trinity in Unity; neither confounding the persons, or dividing the substance. For there is one Person of the Father; another of the Son; and another of the Holy Ghost. But the Godhead of the Father, and of the Son, and of the Holy Ghost, is all one; the Glory equal, the Majesty co-eternal. So the Father is God: the Son is God: and the Holy Ghost is God. And yet there are not three Gods: but one God. The Father is made of none: neither created, nor begotten. The Son is of the Father alone: not made, nor created: but begotten. The Holy Ghost is of the Father and of the Son: neither made, nor created, nor begotten: but proceeding. And in this Trinity none is afore, or after another: none is greater, or less than another. But the whole three Persons are co-eternal, and co-equal. So that in all things, as aforesaid: the Unity in Trinity, and the Trinity in Unity, is to be worshiped" (The Athanasian Creed).
The importance of the doctrine	The doctrine of the Trinity reveals the perfect, loving relationship existing between the Father, Son, and Holy Spirit that makes eternal personality conceivable. God was and is complete in himself and therefore man's creation is an expression of God's complete loving personal nature and not a need to complete his personal nature. The reality of salvation is also dependent on the truth of the Triune God. Without the Trinity, there could be no incarnation, no atonement, and no mediator between God and man.
God is one being or essence.	**The Bible presents God as one indivisible being as to His essence. The Scriptures do not allow for any doctrine of many gods or for God to be composed of numerous separate essences.** Deuteronomy 6:4: "The LORD is our God, the Lord is one!" (NASB). Exodus 20:3: "You shall have no other gods before me." Deuteronomy 4:35: "You were shown these things so that you might know that the LORD is God; besides him there is no other." Isaiah 46:9: "I am God, and there is no other; I am God, and there is none like me." 1 Corinthians 8:6: "For us there is but one God, the Father, from whom all things came and for whom we live; and there is but one Lord, Jesus Christ, through whom all things came and through whom we live." Ephesians 4:3–6: "Make every effort to keep the unity of the Spirit through the bond of peace. There is one body and one Spirit—just as you were called to one hope when you were called— one Lord, one faith, one baptism; one God and Father of all, who is over all and through all and in all." James 2:19: "You believe that God is one" (NASB).
God is more than one person.	Even as the Bible presents God as one solitary being, it presents God as consisting of more than one person, or subsistence, in His essence. Whereas the Old Testament implicitly indicates that God is more than one person, the New Testament explicitly reveals these persons to be the Father, Son, and Holy Spirit—three persons who share equally and totally the essence of God's being. **Old Testament implications of a multipersonal God** The Hebrew word *Elohim* is a plural noun that allows, though it does not require, singular pronouns when referring to God. Genesis 1:1: "In the beginning God created the heavens and the earth." **The Lord speaks and refers to Himself as "Us."** Genesis 1:26: "Then God said, 'Let us make man in our image, in our likeness...'" Genesis 3:22: "And the LORD God said, 'The man has now become like one of us, knowing good and evil. He must not be allowed to reach out his hand and take also from the tree of life and eat, and live forever.'"

The Doctrine of the Trinity (cont.)

Position	Support
. . . continued	Genesis 11:7: "Come, let us go down and confuse their language so they will not understand each other."
	Isaiah 6:8: "Then I heard the voice of the LORD saying, 'Whom shall I send? And who will go for us?' And I said, 'Here am I. Send me!'"
The Trinity is revealed in the New Testament.	**The New Testament explicitly reveals the multipersonal God to be Father, Son, and Holy Spirit.**
	The Father is God.
	John 6:27: "Do not work for food that spoils, but for food that endures to eternal life, which the Son of Man will give you. On him God the Father has placed his seal of approval."
	1 Peter 1:2: ". . . who have been chosen according to the foreknowledge of God the Father, through the sanctifying work of the Spirit, for obedience to Jesus Christ and sprinkling by his blood: Grace and peace be yours in abundance."
	Ephesians 4:6: ". . . one God and Father of all, who is over all and through all and in all."
	The Son is God.
	John 1:1: "In the beginning was the Word, and the Word was with God, and the Word was God."
	John 1:18: "No one has ever seen God, but God the One and Only, who is at the Father's side, has made him known."
	John 8:58: "'I tell you the truth,' Jesus answered, 'before Abraham was born, I am!'"
	John 20:28: "Thomas said to him, 'My Lord and my God!'"
	See section on deity of Christ for more thorough look at the above passages as well as other arguments for the deity of Jesus Christ.
	The Holy Spirit is God.
	Acts 5:3–4: "Then Peter said, 'Ananias, how is it that Satan has so filled your heart that you have lied to the Holy Spirit and have kept for yourself some of the money you received for the land? Didn't it belong to you before it was sold? And after it was sold, wasn't the money at your disposal? What made you think of doing such a thing? You have not lied to men but to God.'"
	This verse equates lying to the Holy Spirit with lying to God.
	(See also the section on the personality and deity of the Holy Spirit.)
	Several times in the New Testament two or three persons of the Trinity are mentioned in conjunction.
	Christ identifies three persons in Christian baptism.
	Matthew 28:19: ". . . baptizing them in the name of the Father and the Son and the Holy Spirit. . . ."
	Jesus' baptism displays the oneness, threeness, and equality of three persons—hence, the Trinity of God.
	Matthew 3:16–17: "As soon as Jesus was baptized, he went up out of the water. At that moment heaven was opened, and he saw the Spirit of God descending like a dove and lighting on him. And a voice from heaven said, 'This is my Son, whom I love; with him I am well pleased.'"
	Paul names in one statement all three persons of the Trinity.
	2 Corinthians 13:14: "May the grace of the Lord Jesus Christ, and the love of God, and the fellowship of the Holy Spirit be with you all."

The Doctrine of the Deity of Christ

Position	Support
The deity of Christ: defined	"We believe . . . in one Lord Jesus Christ, the only-begotten Son of God, begotten of the Father before all the ages, Light of Light, true God of true God, begotten not made, of one substance with the Father, through whom all things were made" (Nicene Creed).
The importance of the doctrine	"He is the Son of God incarnate in our nature. In this doctrine there is sure and sufficient ground for all the great facts of Christian soteriology: atonement; justification by faith; regeneration by the Holy Spirit; a new and gracious spiritual life. A mere human Christ could not make an atonement for sin" (Miley, *Systematic Theology*, 2:5).
Jesus specifically claims that He Himself is God.	**The Bible records several succinct statements of Christ through which He claims to be God. On these occasions His audience understood His claims to be claims of deity.** John 8:57–59: "'You are not yet fifty years old,' the Jews said to him, 'and you have seen Abraham!' 'I tell you the truth,' Jesus answered, 'before Abraham was born, I am!' At this, they picked up stones to stone him." John 10:30–31: "'I and the Father are one.' Again the Jews picked up stones to stone him." John 17:5: "And now, Father, glorify me in your presence with the glory I had with you before the world began."
Jesus is specifically identified as God by biblical authors.	**In addition to His own claims to deity, biblical authors, under the inspiration of the Holy Spirit, identify Jesus Christ as the one and only true God.** John 1:1: "In the beginning was the Word, and the Word was with God, and the Word was God." John 1:18: ". . . God the One and Only, who is at the Father's side, has made him known." John 20:28: "Thomas said to him, 'My Lord and my God!'" Acts 20:28: "Be shepherds of the church of God, which he bought with his own blood." Romans 9:5: ". . . and from them is traced the human ancestry of Christ, who is God over all, forever praised! Amen." Colossians 1:15: "He is the image of the invisible God." Colossians 2:9: "For in Christ all the fullness of the Deity lives in bodily form." Titus 2:13: ". . . our great God and Savior, Jesus Christ." 2 Peter 1:1: ". . . through the righteousness of our God and Savior Jesus Christ."
Jesus existed eternally before the Creation.	**A crucial element of Christ's deity is His preexistence. The fact that Scripture declares His eternal preexistence with the Father demonstrates His deity.** John 1:1 and 1 John 1:1: "In the beginning . . ." and ". . . from the beginning." John 1:1–2: ". . . with God." John 17:5: ". . . before the world began." John 1:14: "The Word became flesh" (implying a previous existence).
Jesus participated in the Creation.	**The inspired authors of Scripture declare that Jesus Christ was the responsible agent of Creation.** Genesis 1:26: "Let us make man" (plurality demonstrating multiplicity of persons involved in the Creation event). Colossians 1:15: ". . . the firstborn over all creation." John 1:3; Colossians 1:16: All things were created "through" or "by" Him. John 1:10; 1 Corinthians 8:6: The world was created "through" Him. Colossians 1:16: All things were created "for him." Colossians 1:17: "In him all things hold together."

The Doctrine of the Deity of Christ (cont.)

Position	Support
Jesus is described as having divine attributes.	**Jesus Christ is identified by several biblical authors as having attributes that God alone possesses.** ***Eternal*** John 1:1: "In the beginning was the Word" (see also 8:58; 17:5). ***Omnipresent*** Matthew 28:20: "Surely I am with you always, to the very end of the age" (see also Eph 1:23). ***Omniscient*** John 16:30: "Now we can see that you know all things" (see also 21:17). ***Omnipotent*** John 5:19: "Whatever the Father does the Son also does." ***Immutable*** Hebrews 1:12: "But you remain the same, . . ." (see also 13:8).
Divine offices are attributed with Jesus.	**Certain offices are reserved for God alone. No persons or creatures can maintain these offices unless, of course, they are God.** ***Jesus is the Creator of all things.*** John 1:3: "Through him all things were made; without him nothing was made that has been made." Colossians 1:16: "For by him all things were created: things in heaven and on earth. . . ." ***He is the sustainer of all that is.*** Colossians 1:17: "He is before all things, and in him all things hold together."
Jesus possesses divine prerogatives.	**Certain activities and functions are impossible apart from supernatural intervention, yet Jesus regularly performs such "miracles" independent of any external, earthly force.** ***Jesus is able to forgive sins.*** Matthew 9:2: "Take heart, son; your sins are forgiven." Luke 7:47: "Her many sins have been forgiven." ***Jesus raises the dead.*** John 5:25: "A time is coming . . . when the dead will hear . . . and those who hear will live." John 11:25: "I am the resurrection and the life." ***Jesus executes judgment.*** John 5:22: "The Father judges no one, but has entrusted all judgment to the Son." ***Jesus saves.*** Luke 19:10: "For the Son of Man came to seek and to save what was lost." Romans 10:9: "That is you confess with your mouth, 'Jesus is Lord,' . . . you will be saved." Titus 3:5: ". . . he saved us."
Jesus is specifically identified with Yahweh, the God of the Old Testament.	**Jesus claimed to be the God who appeared to Moses in Exodus 3:14. The Jews clearly understood this, because their response was to try to stone Him.** John 8:58 : "Before Abraham was born, I am!"

The Doctrine of the Deity of Christ (cont.)

Position	Support
Jesus possesses divine names.	**The biblical authors identify Jesus by several specific names typically reserved for God alone.** ***Alpha and the Omega*** Revelation 22:13: "I am the Alpha and the Omega, the First and the Last, the Beginning and the End." ***I Am*** John 8:58: "'I tell you the truth,' Jesus answered, 'before Abraham was born, I am!'" ***Immanuel*** Matthew 1:23: "'The virgin will be with child and will give birth to a son, and they will call him Immanuel'—which means, 'God with us.'" ***Son of Man*** Matthew 9:6: "'But so that you may know that the Son of Man has authority on earth to forgive sins. . . .' Then he said to the paralytic, 'Get up, take your mat and go home.'" ***Lord*** Luke 1:43: "But why am I so favored, that the mother of my Lord should come to me?" ***Son of God*** John 10:36: "What about the one whom the Father set apart as his very own and sent into the world? Why then do you accuse me of blasphemy because I said, 'I am God's Son'?" ***God*** 2 Peter 1:1: "Simon Peter, a servant and apostle of Jesus Christ, To those who through the righteousness of our God and Savior Jesus Christ have received a faith as precious as ours. . . ."
Jesus accepts divine worship and honor.	**Jesus neither denies nor refuses the worship of men who recognize His deity. Likewise, biblical authors attribute to Him the worship that only God is worthy to receive.** Matthew 14:33: "Then those who were in the boat worshiped him, saying, 'Truly you are the Son of God.'" Matthew 28:9: "Suddenly Jesus met them. 'Greetings,' he said. They came to him, clasped his feet, and worshiped him." John 20:28–29: "Thomas said to him, 'My Lord and my God!'" (and Jesus did not correct him in his statement). Hebrews 1:6: "Let all God's angels worship him."

The Doctrine of the Humanity of Christ

Position	Support
The humanity of Christ defined	"We believe . . . in one Lord Jesus Christ . . . who for us men and for our salvation came down from the heavens, and was made flesh of the Holy Spirit and the Virgin Mary, and became man, and was crucified for us under Pontius Pilate, and suffered and was buried" (Nicene Creed).
	"Therefore, following the holy Fathers, we all with one accord teach men to acknowledge one and the same Son, our Lord Jesus Christ, at once complete in Godhead and complete in manhood, truly God and truly man, consisting also of a reasonable soul and body; of one substance with the Father as regards his Godhead, and at the same time of one substance with us as regards his manhood; like us in all respects, apart from sin; as regards his Godhead, begotten of the Father before the ages, but yet as regards his manhood begotten, for us men and for our salvation, of Mary the Virigin, the God-bearer; one and the same Christ, Son, Lord, Only-begotten, recognized in two natures, without confusion, without change, without division, without sepatation; the distinction of natures being in no way annulled by the union, but rather the characteristics of each nature being preserved and coming together to form one person and subsistence, not as parted of separated into two persons, but one and the same Son and Only-begotten God the Word, Lord Jesus Christ; even as the prophets from earliest times spoke of him, and our Lord Jesus Christ himself taught us, and the creed of the Fathers has handed down to us" (The Definition of Chalcedon, A.D. 451).
The importance of the doctrine	"Man is unable by his own moral effort to counter his sin, to elevate himself to the level of God. If there is to be fellowship between the two, they have to be united in some other way. This, it is traditionally understood, has been accomplished by the incarnation, in which deity and humanity were united in one person. If, however, Jesus was not really one of us, humanity has not been united with deity, and we cannot be saved" (Erickson, *Christian Theology*, p. 706).
Jesus had a human birth.	**The Bible describes the birth of Christ as a human delivery.**
	Matthew 2:1: "After Jesus was born in Bethlehem in Judea, during the time of King Herod, Magi from the east came to Jerusalem."
	The birth of Jesus is placed in the context of human history.
	Luke 2:4–7: "So Joseph also went up from the town of Nazareth in Galilee to Judea, to Bethlehem the town of David, because he belonged to the house and line of David. He went there to register with Mary, who was pledged to be married to him and was expecting a child. While they were there, the time came for the baby to be born, and she gave birth to her firstborn, a son. She wrapped him in cloths and placed him in a manger, because there was no room for them in the inn."
	Luke 2:11–12: "Today in the town of David a Savior has been born to you; he is Christ the Lord. This will be a sign to you: You will find a baby wrapped in cloths and lying in a manger."
	Luke traces Jesus' ancestry through His mother, Mary. This was Jesus' human bloodline.
	Usually the bloodline would be traced through the father's line. Since Mary conceived by the Holy Spirit, Jesus had no human father; His bloodline could only be traced through Mary. However, as the virgin-born son of Mary, Jesus had no right to the throne under Jewish law, for that right came only through the father.
	Luke 3:23, 38: "Now Jesus himself was about thirty years old when he began his ministry. He was the son, so it was thought, of Joseph, the son of Heli, . . . the son of Seth, the son of Adam, the son of God."
	Jesus was treated as a normal baby. His parents followed the rituals and customs of Jewish law.
	Luke 2:21: "On the eighth day, when it was time to circumcise him, he was named Jesus, the name the angel had given him before he had been conceived."

The Doctrine of the Humanity of Christ (cont.)

Position	Support
Jesus grew physically.	**The Scriptures indicate the development of Jesus from a child into adulthood at several stages of His life.**
	Luke 2:41–42. "Every year his parents went to Jerusalem for the Feast of the Passover. When he was twelve years old, they went up to the Feast, according to the custom."
	Here Luke records the only incident in Jesus' childhood from the time He was an infant to when He began His public ministry. We can assume that Jesus followed the traditional rituals and rights of passage of Jewish males.
	"In the perfections of his divine nature there could be no increase; but this is meant of his human nature, his body increased in stature and bulk, he grew in growing age; and his soul increased in wisdom and in all the endowments of a human soul" (*Matthew Henry's Commentary on the Whole Bible,* p. 1421).
	Luke 2:52: "And Jesus grew in wisdom and stature, and in favor with God and men."
	Jesus is now seen as a mature adult.
	At the age of 30, Joseph began serving the Pharoah of Egypt (Ge 41:46), David took the throne (2Sa 5:4), and Jesus began his public ministry.
	Luke 3:23: "Now Jesus himself was about thirty years old when he began his ministry. He was the son, so it was thought, of Joseph."
Jesus had a physical body.	**The Bible is explicit in stating that Jesus had a physical body.**
	Matthew 26:12: "When she poured this perfume on my body, she did it to prepare me for burial." Here Jesus, Himself, refers to His body.
	This expresses Christ's incarnation, God becoming man. God became flesh. The Greek word translated "flesh" is *sarx,* meaning the meat of an animal (as food) or the body as opposed to the soul. (See 4561 in *Strong's Exhaustive Concordance of the Bible.*)
	John 1:14: "The Word became flesh and made his dwelling among us. We have seen his glory, the glory of the One and Only, who came from the Father, full of grace and truth."
	Colossians 1:22: "But now he has reconciled you by Christ's physical body through death to present you holy in his sight, without blemish and free from accusation."
	Paul declares that the very essence of deity was present in totality in Jesus' human body.
	Colossians 2:9: "For in Christ all the fullness of the Deity lives in bodily form."
	1 Timothy 3:16: "He appeared in a body, was vindicated by the Spirit, was seen by angels, was preached among the nations, was believed on in the world, was taken up in glory."
	Christ shared in man's humanity to bridge the gap between man and God. (See "The importance of the doctrine" at the beginning of this section.)
	Hebrews 2:14: "Since the children have flesh and blood, he too shared in their humanity so that by his death he might destroy him who holds the power of death—that is, the devil."
	"John is here establishing the reality of the human nature of Jesus. He actually heard, saw and touched Jesus. Touch was thought by the Greeks to be the most basic and reliable of the senses, for it is a direct perception—no medium intervenes between the perceiver and the object perceived. Thus, when John speaks of having 'touched with our hands', he is emphasizing just how thoroughly physical was the manifestation of Jesus" (Erickson, *Christian Theology,* pp. 707–8).
	1 John 1:1: "That which was from the beginning, which we have heard, which we have seen with our eyes, which we have looked at and our hands have touched—this we proclaim concerning the Word of life."
	"John was particularly emphatic on this matter in his first letter, one of the purposes of which was to combat heresy which denied that Jesus had been genuinely human. . . . it is

The Doctrine of the Humanity of Christ (cont.)

Position	Support
... continued	apparent the 'flesh' is not used in the Pauline sense of humanity's orientation away from God, but in the more basic sense of physical nature" (Erickson, *Christian Theology,* p. 712). 1 John 4:2–3: "This is how you can recognize the Spirit of God: Every spirit that acknowledges that Jesus Christ has come in the flesh is from God, but every spirit that does not acknowledge Jesus is not from God."
Jesus had physical limitations.	**Jesus experienced the same physical limitations as other humans: hunger, thirst, weariness, pain, and death.** Matthew states that Jesus experienced the sensation of hunger. If Jesus was merely God, He would not need to eat. He would have felt no hunger. God is self-sustaining. He does not have a physical body that requires maintenance. Matthew 4:2: "After fasting forty days and forty nights, he was hungry." **Jesus experienced physical injury and pain, as demonstrated in His trial and crucifixion.** John 19:28: "Later, knowing that all was now completed, and so that the Scripture would be fulfilled, Jesus said, 'I am thirsty.'" Matthew 26:67: "They spit in his face and struck him with their fists." Matthew 27:26: "But he had Jesus flogged, and handed him over to be crucified." John 19:34: "Instead, one of the soldiers pierced Jesus' side with a spear, bringing a sudden flow of blood and water." **Peter, who was one of those closest to Jesus, states that Christ suffered.** 1 Peter 2:21: "To this you were called, because Christ suffered for you, leaving you an example, that you should follow in his steps." 1 Peter 3:18: "For Christ died for sins once for all, the righteous for the unrighteous, to bring you to God. He was put to death in the body but made alive by the Spirit." 1 Corinthians 15:3: "... that Christ died for our sins according to the Scriptures." Philippians 2:8: "And being found in appearance as a man, he humbled himself and became obedient to death—even death on a cross!"
Jesus shared with humanity an emotional nature.	**Jesus experienced all types of emotions such as anger, disgust, distress, loneliness and sorrow. He loved people and had compassion for them.** Mark 3:5: "He looked around at them in anger and, deeply distressed at their stubborn hearts, ..." John 2:13–16: "When it was almost time for the Jewish Passover, Jesus went up to Jerusalem. In the temple courts he found men selling cattle, sheep and doves, and others sitting at tables exchanging money. So he made a whip of cords, and drove all from the temple area, both sheep and cattle; he scattered the coins of the money changers and overturned their tables. To those who sold doves he said, 'Get these out of here! How dare you turn my Father's house into a market!'" Matthew 26:37–38: "He took Peter and the two sons of Zebedee along with him, and he began to be sorrowful and troubled. Then he said to them, 'My soul is overwhelmed with sorrow to the point of death. Stay here and keep watch with me.'" John 11:3: "So the sisters sent word to Jesus, 'Lord, the one you love is sick.'" **Some emotions do not necessarily show that Jesus was human, but He displayed some that can only be identified as human.** Anger is an emotion that God has expressed throughout history. His anger was evident in the destruction of Sodom and Gomorrah, in the destruction of the world by flood, and during the times when Israel turned from Him.

The Doctrine of the Humanity of Christ (cont.)

Position	Support
... continued	However, Jesus displayed some reactions that can only be identified as human. The faith of the centurion astonished Jesus as did the unbelief of the people in Nazareth. Luke 7:9: "When Jesus heard this, he was amazed at him, and turning to the crowd following him, he said, 'I tell you, I have not found such great faith even in Israel.'" Mark 6:6: "And he was amazed at their lack of faith." "One of Jesus' most human reactions occurred at the death of Lazarus. Seeing Mary and her companions weeping, 'Jesus was deeply moved in spirit and troubled'; he wept; at the tomb he was 'deeply moved again.' The description here is very vivid, for to depict Jesus 'groaning in the spirit,' John chose a term that is used of horses snorting (*embrimaomai*). Obviously, Jesus possessed a human nature capable of feeling sorrow and remorse as deeply as we do" (Erickson, *Christian Theology*, p. 709). John 11:33, 35, 38: "When Jesus saw her weeping, and the Jews who had come along with her also weeping, he was deeply moved in spirit and troubled.... Jesus wept.... Jesus, once more deeply moved, came to the tomb."
Jesus was called a man.	**Jesus was called a man by many different people. Both His friends and His enemies referred to Him as a man.** The Jewish leaders received Jesus as just a man. They knew His family and His background and did not believe they would know whence the Messiah would come. Under Jewish law, anyone claiming to be God was guilty of blaspheming the name of God. Leviticus 24:16 mandates stoning as the penalty for blasphemy. John writes that the Jews were going to stone Jesus for blasphemy, and indeed, they had no choice under the Mosaic Law if Jesus' claims were false. It is clear from this passage that the Jewish leaders considered Jesus a man. John 10:33: "'We are not stoning you for any of these,' replied the Jews, 'but for blasphemy, because you, a mere man, claim to be God.'" The words *man* and *men* are both from the Greek word *aner*. Peter used *aner* in addressing his Pentecost audience as "Men of Israel" and then in the same breath saying that "Jesus of Nazareth was a man accredited by God to you" (Acts 2:22). *Aner* is a primary word meaning a man, fellow, husband, sir; an individual male (435 in *Strong's Exhaustive Concordance of the Bible*). It is similar to the Greek word *anthropos*, which means man-faced or human being (444 in *Strong's*). Acts 2:22–23: "Men of Israel, listen to this: Jesus of Nazareth was a man accredited by God to you by miracles, wonders and signs, which God did among you through him, as you yourselves know. This man was handed over to you by God's set purpose and foreknowledge."
Jesus referred to Himself as a man.	John 8:40: "As it is, you are determined to kill me, a man who has told you the truth that I heard from God." The word used both times for *man* in this passage is the Greek word *anthropos*. Paul is stating that in the same way that death came through Adam, a human being, so the resurrection of the dead comes through Jesus, a human being. Paul ties the humanness of Jesus to the humanness of Adam. 1 Corinthians 15:21–22: "For since death came through a man, the resurrection of the dead comes also through a man. For as in Adam all die, so in Christ all will be made alive."

The Doctrine of the Resurrection of Christ

Position	Support
The doctrine defined	"We believe… in one Lord Jesus Christ… and was crucified for us under Pontius Pilate, and suffered and was buried, and rose again on the third day according to the Scriptures, and ascended into the heavens, and sitteth on the right hand of the Father, and cometh again with glory to judge living and dead, of whose kingdom there shall be no end" (Nicene Creed).
The importance of the doctrine	"It is the fundamental doctrine of Christianity.… In 1 Cor. 15:12–19 Paul shows that everything stands or falls with Christ's bodily resurrection. If Christ has not risen, preaching is vain (v. 14), the Corinthians' faith was vain (v. 14), the apostles were false witnesses (v. 15), the Corinthians were yet in their sins (v. 17), those fallen asleep in Jesus have perished (v. 18), and Christians are of all men most to be pitied (v. 19)" (Thiessen, *Lectures in Systematic Theology,* p. 243).
Jesus spoke of His own resurrection.	Matthew 12:40: "For as Jonah was three days and three nights in the belly of a huge fish, so the Son of Man will be three days and three nights in the heart of the earth." Mark 10:32–34: "They were on their way up to Jerusalem, with Jesus leading the way, and the disciples were astonished, while those who followed were afraid. Again he took the Twelve aside and told them what was going to happen to him. 'We are going up to Jerusalem,' he said, 'and the Son of Man will be betrayed to the chief priests and teachers of the law. They will condemn him to death and will hand him over to the Gentiles, who will mock him and spit on him, flog him and kill him. Three days later he will rise.'" John 2:19–22: "Jesus answered them, 'Destroy this temple, and I will raise it again in three days.' The Jews replied, 'It has taken forty-six years to build this temple, and you are going to raise it in three days?' But the temple he had spoken of was his body. After he was raised from the dead, his disciples recalled what he had said. Then they believed the Scripture and the words that Jesus had spoken." John 10:17–18: "The reason my Father loves me is that I lay down my life—only to take it up again. No one takes it from me, but I lay it down of my own accord. I have authority to lay it down and authority to take it up again. This command I received from my Father."
Christ's resurrection was the early church's central focus.	**Peter represents the earliest recorded preaching. In each of his sermons recorded in Acts, the physical resurrection of Jesus is the focus and reasoning behind the evangelistic call.** Acts 2:31–32: "Seeing what was ahead, he spoke of the resurrection of the Christ, that he was not abandoned to the grave, nor did his body see decay. God has raised this Jesus to life, and we are all witnesses of the fact." Acts 3:15: "You killed the author of life, but God raised him from the dead. We are witnesses of this." Acts 4:10: "Then know this, you and all the people of Israel: It is by the name of Jesus Christ of Nazareth, whom you crucified but whom God raised from the dead, that this man stands before you healed." Acts 4:33: "With great power the apostles continued to testify to the resurrection of the Lord Jesus, and much grace was upon them all." **Paul likewise focused on the resurrection and the credibility of the witnesses.** Acts 13:30–31, 34: "But God raised him from the dead, and for many days he was seen by those who had traveled with him from Galilee to Jerusalem. They are now his witnesses to our people.… The fact that God raised him from the dead, never to decay, is stated in these words: 'I will give you the holy and sure blessings promised to David.'" Acts 17:3: "… explaining and proving that the Christ had to suffer and rise from the dead. 'This Jesus I am proclaiming to you is the Christ,' he said." Acts 17:18: "A group of Epicurean and Stoic philosophers began to dispute with him. Some of them asked, 'What is this babbler trying to say?' Others remarked, 'He seems to be advocating foreign gods.' They said this because Paul was preaching the good news about Jesus and the resurrection."

The Doctrine of the Resurrection of Christ (cont.)

Position	Support
... continued	Acts 17:31–32: "'For he has set a day when he will judge the world with justice by the man he has appointed. He has given proof of this to all men by raising him from the dead.' When they heard about the resurrection of the dead, some of them sneered, but others said, 'We want to hear you again on this subject.'" Romans 1:4: "... and who through the Spirit of holiness was declared with power to be the Son of God by his resurrection from the dead: Jesus Christ our Lord." Romans 6:4–5: "We were therefore buried with him through baptism into death in order that, just as Christ was raised from the dead through the glory of the Father, we too may live a new life. If we have been united with him like this in his death, we will certainly also be united with him in his resurrection." First Corinthians 15:3–4: "For what I received I passed on to you as of first importance: that Christ died for our sins according to the Scriptures, that he was buried, that he was raised on the third day according to the Scriptures." Philippians 3:10: "I want to know Christ and the power of his resurrection and the fellowship of sharing in his sufferings, becoming like him in his death."
Jesus had a bodily resurrection.	**Jesus actually experienced death.** Mark 15:44–45: "Pilate was surprised to hear that he was already dead. Summoning the centurion, he asked him if Jesus had already died. When he learned from the centurion that it was so, he gave the body to Joseph." John 19:33–34: "But when they came to Jesus and found that he was already dead, they did not break his legs. Instead, one of the soldiers pierced Jesus' side with a spear, bringing a sudden flow of blood and water." **Jesus Himself claimed to still be in the flesh and corrected the disciples' view that He is a spirit.** Luke 24:39: "Look at my hands and my feet. It is I myself! Touch me and see; a ghost does not have flesh and bones, as you see I have." **The empty tomb pointed toward a physical continuity between Jesus' body before and after the resurrection.** Luke 24:22–23: "In addition, some of our women amazed us. They went to the tomb early this morning but didn't find his body. They came and told us that they had seen a vision of angels, who said he was alive." **After the resurrection Jesus continued to have experiences common to humanity.** *He could be touched.* Matthew 28:9: "Suddenly Jesus met them. 'Greetings,' he said. They came to him, clasped his feet and worshiped him." John 20:27: "Then he said to Thomas, 'Put your finger here; see my hands. Reach out your hand and put it into my side. Stop doubting and believe.'" *He could walk.* Luke 24:15: "As they talked and discussed these things with each other, Jesus himself came up and walked along with them." *He could eat.* Luke 24:41–43: "And while they still did not believe it because of joy and amazement, he asked them, 'Do you have anything here to eat?' They gave him a piece of broiled fish, and he took it and ate it in their presence."

The Doctrine of the Resurrection of Christ (cont.)

Position	Support
. . . continued	**After the resurrection Jesus had experiences uncommon to human experience.** *He experienced miraculous locomotion.* Luke 24:31: "Then their eyes were opened and they recognized him, and he disappeared from their sight." Luke 24:36–37: "While they were still talking about this, Jesus himself stood among them and said to them, 'Peace be with you.' They were startled and frightened, thinking they saw a ghost." Although these are uncommon experiences, there are other instances in Scripture when humans have miraculous locomotion. Jesus also experienced miraculous locomotion before the resurrection, such as walking on water. Therefore miraculous locomotion does not suggest a discontinuity between the pre-resurrection and post-resurrection bodies.
Problems relating to Jesus' appearances	**Jesus was not always recognized on the basis of physical appearance after the resurrection.** John 20:14–15: "At this, she turned around and saw Jesus standing there, but she did not realize that it was Jesus. 'Woman,' he said, 'why are you crying? Who is it you are looking for?' Thinking he was the gardener, she said, 'Sir, if you have carried him away, tell me where you have put him, and I will get him.'" **Many of the disciples were unable to believe that Jesus would be resurrected, and this unbelief may account for the inability to recognize Jesus.** John 20:24–25: "Now Thomas (called Didymus), one of the Twelve, was not with the disciples when Jesus came. So the other disciples told him, 'We have seen the Lord!' But he said to them, 'Unless I see the nail marks in his hands and put my finger where the nails were, and put my hand into his side, I will not believe it.'" Luke 24:31: "Then their eyes were opened and they recognized him, and he disappeared from their sight." **It appears that on several occasions Jesus' identity was intentionally concealed from people.** Luke 24:16: "They were kept from recognizing him." God's purpose and will were responsible for the lack of recognition. Therefore the lack of recognition does not signify a discontinuity between the pre-resurrection and post-resurrection bodies.
Results of Jesus' resurrection	**It attests to the deity of Jesus.** Romans 1:4: ". . . and who through the Spirit of holiness was declared with power to be the Son of God by his resurrection from the dead: Jesus Christ our Lord." **It makes redemption a reality.** Acts 5:30–31: "The God of our fathers raised Jesus from the dead—whom you had killed by hanging him on a tree. God exalted him to his own right hand as Prince and Savior that he might give repentance and forgiveness of sins to Israel." Romans 4:25: "He was delivered over to death for our sins and was raised to life for our justification." Romans 5:10: "For if, when we were God's enemies, we were reconciled to him through the death of his Son, how much more, having been reconciled, shall we be saved through his life!" Romans 8:34: "Who is he that condemns? Christ Jesus, who died—more than that, who was raised to life—is at the right hand of God and is also interceding for us." 1 Peter 1:3: "Praise be to the God and Father of our Lord Jesus Christ! In his great mercy he has given us new birth into a living hope through the resurrection of Jesus Christ from the dead."

The Doctrine of the Resurrection of Christ (cont.)

Position	Support
. . . continued	1 Corinthians 15:17–19: "And if Christ has not been raised, your faith is futile; you are still in your sins. Then those also who have fallen asleep in Christ are lost. If only for this life we have hope in Christ, we are to be pitied more than all men."
The resurrection provides additional blessing.	**Power for life and service** Ephesians 1:18–20: "I pray also that the eyes of your heart may be enlightened in order that you may know the hope to which he has called you, the riches of his glorious inheritance in the saints, and his incomparably great power for us who believe. That power is like the working of his mighty strength, which he exerted in Christ when he raised him from the dead and seated him at his right hand in the heavenly realms." Romans 6:4: "We were therefore buried with him through baptism into death in order that, just as Christ was raised from the dead through the glory of the Father, we too may live a new life." **The assurance of the believer's resurrection** Philippians 3:10–11: "I want to know Christ and the power of his resurrection and the fellowship of sharing in his sufferings, becoming like him in his death, and so, somehow, to attain to the resurrection from the dead." 1 Corinthians 15:13–14: "If there is no resurrection of the dead, then not even Christ has been raised. And if Christ has not been raised, our preaching is useless and so is your faith." 2 Corinthians 4:14: ". . . because we know that the one who raised the Lord Jesus from the dead will also raise us with Jesus and present us with you in his presence." 1 Thessalonians 4:14: "We believe that Jesus died and rose again and so we believe that God will bring with Jesus those who have fallen asleep in him."

The Doctrine of the Holy Spirit

Position	Support
The doctrine of the Holy Spirit defined	"We believe . . . in the Holy Spirit, the Lord and the Life-giver, that proceedeth from the Father, who with Father and Son is worshipped together and glorified together, who spake through the prophets" (Constantinopolitan Creed).
The importance of the doctrine	"But the Godhead of the Father, and of the Son, and of the Holy Ghost, is all one; the Glory equal, the Majesty co-eternal. . . . So the Father is God: the Son is God: and the Holy Ghost is God. . . . The Holy Ghost is of the Father and of the Son: neither made, nor created, nor begotten: but proceeding. . . . And in this Trinity none is afore, or after another: none is greater, or less than another. But the whole three Persons are co-eternal, and co-equal" (Athanasian Creed). In reflecting upon all the works accomplished by the Spirit, we see that everything we know or experience about God is actualized or energized by the Spirit. He makes the will of the Father and the sacrifice of the Son a reality in the lives of believers.
The Holy Spirit holds an equal position with the Father and the Son.	**The Holy Spirit is the Third Person of the Godhead and is mentioned in conjunction with the other persons of the Trinity.** Matthew 3:16–17: "As soon as Jesus was baptized, he went up out of the water. At that moment heaven was opened, and he saw the Spirit of God descending like a dove and lighting on him. And a voice from heaven said, 'This is my Son, whom I love; with him I am well pleased.'" John 14:16: "I will ask the Father, and he will give you another Counselor to be with you forever." Acts 10:38: ". . . how God anointed Jesus of Nazareth with the Holy Spirit and power, and how he went around doing good and healing all who were under the power of the devil, because God was with him."
The Holy Spirit possesses personal characteristics.	**The Holy Spirit has a personality, as expressed in bibilical references to His attributes.** *He is intelligent.* Isaiah 11:2: "The Spirit of the LORD will rest on him—the Spirit of wisdom and of understanding, the Spirit of counsel and of power, the Spirit of knowledge and of the fear of the LORD." Romans 8:27: "He who searches our hearts knows the mind of the Spirit, because the Spirit intercedes for the saints in accordance with God's will." 1 Corinthians 2:10–11: "But God has revealed it to us by his Spirit. The Spirit searches all things, even the deep things of God. For who among men knows the thoughts of a man except the man's spirit within him? In the same way no one knows the thoughts of God except the Spirit of God." *He can be grieved.* Isaiah 63:10: "Yet they rebelled and grieved his Holy Spirit. So he turned and became their enemy and he himself fought against them." Ephesians 4:30: "Do not grieve the Holy Spirit of God, with whom you were sealed for the day of redemption." Romans 15:30: "I urge you, brothers, by our Lord Jesus Christ and by the love of the Spirit, to join me in my struggle by praying to God for me." *He has a will.* 1 Corinthians 12:11: "All these are the work of one and the same Spirit, and he gives them to each one, just as he determines." *He can be reverenced.* Psalm 51:11: "Do not cast me from your presence or take your Holy Spirit from me."

The Doctrine of the Holy Spirit (cont.)

Position	Support
. . . continued	**He can be blasphemed.** Matthew 12:31: "And so I tell you, every sin and blasphemy will be forgiven men, but the blasphemy against the Spirit will not be forgiven." **He can be obeyed.** Acts 10:19–21: "While Peter was still thinking about the vision, the Spirit said to him, 'Simon, three men are looking for you. So get up and go downstairs. Do not hesitate to go with them, for I have sent them.' Peter went down and said to the men, 'I'm the one you're looking for. Why have you come?'" **He can be lied to.** Acts 5:3: "Then Peter said, 'Ananias, how is it that Satan has so filled your heart that you have lied to the Holy Spirit and have kept for yourself some of the money you received for the land?'" **He can be resisted.** Acts 7:51: "You stiff-necked people, with uncircumcised hearts and ears! You are just like your fathers: You always resist the Holy Spirit!" **He can become outraged.** Hebrews 10:29: "How much more severely do you think a man deserves to be punished who has trampled the Son of God under foot, who has treated as an unholy thing the blood of the covenant that sanctified him, and who has insulted the Spirit of grace?"
The deity of the Spirit is recognized in the divine names He bears.	**The Third Person of the Trinity is called by various names.** **Holy Spirit** Mark 3:29: "But whoever blasphemes against the Holy Spirit will never be forgiven; he is guilty of an eternal sin." Romans 15:13: "May the God of hope fill you with all joy and peace as you trust in him, so that you may overflow with hope by the power of the Holy Spirit." **Spirit of God** Genesis 1:2: "Now the earth was formless and empty, darkness was over the surface of the deep, and the Spirit of God was hovering over the waters." Matthew 3:16–17: "As soon as Jesus was baptized, he went up out of the water. At that moment heaven was opened, and he saw the Spirit of God descending like a dove and lighting on him. And a voice from heaven said, 'This is my Son, whom I love; with him I am well pleased.'" **Spirit of the Lord** Isaiah 11:2: "The Spirit of the LORD will rest on him—the Spirit of wisdom and of understanding, the Spirit of counsel and of power, the Spirit of knowledge and of the fear of the LORD." Isaiah 61:1: "The Spirit of the Sovereign LORD is on me, because the LORD has anointed me to preach good news to the poor. He has sent me to bind up the brokenhearted, to proclaim freedom for the captives and release from darkness for the prisoners." 2 Corinthians 3:17–18: "Now the Lord is the Spirit, and where the Spirit of the Lord is, there is freedom." **Counselor** John 14:16: "I will ask the Father, and he will give you another Counselor to be with you forever." John 14:26: "But the Counselor, the Holy Spirit, whom the Father will send in my name, will teach you all things and will remind you of everything I have said to you."

The Doctrine of the Holy Spirit (cont.)

Position	Support
... continued	***Spirit of Jesus*** Romans 8:9: "You, however, are controlled not by the sinful nature but by the Spirit, if the Spirit of God lives in you. And if anyone does not have the Spirit of Christ, he does not belong to Christ." Galatians 4:6: "Because you are sons, God sent the Spirit of his Son into our hearts, the Spirit who calls out, 'Abba, Father.'" ***Spirit of Truth*** John 15:26: "When the Counselor comes, whom I will send to you from the Father, the Spirit of truth who goes out from the Father, he will testify about me." John 16:13: "But when he, the Spirit of truth, comes, he will guide you into all truth. He will not speak on his own; he will speak only what he hears, and he will tell you what is yet to come." ***Spirit of Grace*** Hebrews 10:29: "How much more severely do you think a man deserves to be punished who has trampled the Son of God under foot, who has treated as an unholy thing the blood of the covenant that sanctified him, and who has insulted the Spirit of grace?" ***Good Spirit*** Psalm 143:10: "Teach me to do your will, for you are my God; may your good Spirit lead me on level ground." ***Spirit of Holiness*** Romans 1:4: "... and who through the Spirit of holiness was declared with power to be the Son of God by his resurrection from the dead: Jesus Christ our Lord." ***Spirit of Life*** Romans 8:2: "... because through Christ Jesus the law of the Spirit of life set me free from the law of sin and death." ***Spirit of Glory*** 1 Peter 4:14: "If you are insulted because of the name of Christ, you are blessed, for the Spirit of glory and of God rests on you." ***Spirit of Wisdom and Understanding/Counsel and Power/Knowledge and Fear of the Lord*** Isaiah 11:2: "The Spirit of the LORD will rest on him—the Spirit of wisdom and of understanding, the Spirit of counsel and of power, the Spirit of knowledge and of the fear of the LORD."
The deity of the Holy Spirit is recognized in His divine attributes.	**The Spirit is omniscient.** John 14:26: "But the Counselor, the Holy Spirit, whom the Father will send in my name, will teach you all things and will remind you of everything I have said to you." John 16:13: "But when he, the Spirit of truth, comes, he will guide you into all truth. He will not speak on his own; he will speak only what he hears, and he will tell you what is yet to come." 1 Corinthians 2:10: "But God has revealed it to us by his Spirit. The Spirit searches all things, even the deep things of God." **The Spirit is omnipresent.** Psalm 139:7–12: "Where can I go from your Spirit? Where can I flee from your presence? If I go up to the heavens, you are there; if I make my bed in the depths, you are there. If I rise on the wings of the dawn, if I settle on the far side of the sea, even there your hand will guide me, your right hand will hold me fast. If I say, 'Surely the darkness will hide me and

The Doctrine of the Holy Spirit (cont.)

Position	Support
. . . continued	the light become night around me,' even the darkness will not be dark to you; the night will shine like the day, for darkness is as light to you." **The Spirit is omnipotent.** Luke 1:35: "The angel answered, 'The Holy Spirit will come upon you, and the power of the Most High will overshadow you. So the holy one to be born will be called the Son of God.'" **The Spirit is eternal.** Hebrews 9:14: "How much more, then, will the blood of Christ, who through the eternal Spirit offered himself unblemished to God, cleanse our consciences from acts that lead to death, so that we may serve the living God!"
The deity of the Spirit is recognized in the works of God that He accomplishes.	**He was active in creation.** Genesis 1:2: "Now the earth was formless and empty, darkness was over the surface of the deep, and the Spirit of God was hovering over the waters." **He inspired the biblical writers.** 2 Peter 1:21: "For prophecy never had its origin in the will of man, but men spoke from God as they were carried along by the Holy Spirit." **He empowered the conception of Christ.** Luke 1:35: "The angel answered, 'The Holy Spirit will come upon you, and the power of the Most High will overshadow you. So the holy one to be born will be called the Son of God.'" **He teaches.** John 14:26: "But the Counselor, the Holy Spirit, whom the Father will send in my name, will teach you all things and will remind you of everything I have said to you." **He guides.** Romans 8:14: ". . . because those who are led by the Spirit of God are sons of God." **He commissions.** Acts 13:4: "The two of them, sent on their way by the Holy Spirit, went down to Seleucia and sailed from there to Cyprus." **He commands people.** Acts 8:29: "The Spirit told Philip, 'Go to that chariot and stay near it.'" **He intercedes.** Romans 8:26: "In the same way, the Spirit helps us in our weakness. We do not know what we ought to pray for, but the Spirit himself intercedes for us with groans that words cannot express." **He speaks.** John 15:26: "When the Counselor comes, whom I will send to you from the Father, the Spirit of truth who goes out from the Father, he will testify about me." **He works in the church.** 1 Corinthians 12:7: "Now to each one the manifestation of the Spirit is given for the common good." **He actualizes the presence of God.** Haggai 2:5: "This is what I covenanted with you when you came out of Egypt. And my Spirit remains among you. Do not fear." **He actualizes the kingdom of God.** Matthew 12:28: "But if I drive out demons by the Spirit of God, then the kingdom of God has come upon you."

The Doctrine of the Holy Spirit (cont.)

Position	Support
... continued	**He restrains evil.** 2 Thessalonians 2:6–7: "And now you know what is holding him back, so that he may be revealed at the proper time. For the secret power of lawlessness is already at work; but the one who now holds it back will continue to do so till he is taken out of the way." **He resurrected Christ.** 1 Peter 3:18: "For Christ died for sins once for all, the righteous for the unrighteous, to bring you to God. He was put to death in the body but made alive by the Spirit."
The deity of the Spirit is recognized in His involvement in the salvific process and the spiritual life of the believer.	**He convicts of sin.** John 16:8: "When he comes, he will convict the world of guilt in regard to sin and righteousness and judgment." **He regenerates.** John 3:5–6: "Jesus answered, 'I tell you the truth, no one can enter the kingdom of God unless he is born of water and the Spirit. Flesh gives birth to flesh, but the Spirit gives birth to spirit.'" **He gives eternal life.** Titus 3:5: "He saved us, not because of righteous things we had done, but because of his mercy. He saved us through the washing of rebirth and renewal by the Holy Spirit." **He brings the assurance of salvation.** Romans 8:26–27: "In the same way, the Spirit helps us in our weakness. We do not know what we ought to pray for, but the Spirit himself intercedes for us with groans that words cannot express. And he who searches our hearts knows the mind of the Spirit, because the Spirit intercedes for the saints in accordance with God's will." **He works in baptism.** 1 Corinthians 12:13: "For we were all baptized by one Spirit into one body—whether Jews or Greeks, slave or free—and we were all given the one Spirit to drink." **He indwells the believer.** Romans 8:9–11: "You, however, are controlled not by the sinful nature but by the Spirit, if the Spirit of God lives in you. And if anyone does not have the Spirit of Christ, he does not belong to Christ. But if Christ is in you, your body is dead because of sin, yet your spirit is alive because of righteousness. And if the Spirit of him who raised Jesus from the dead is living in you, he who raised Christ from the dead will also give life to your mortal bodies through his Spirit, who lives in you." Romans 8:13–14: "For if you live according to the sinful nature, you will die; but if by the Spirit you put to death the misdeeds of the body, you will live, because those who are led by the Spirit of God are sons of God."
The deity of the Spirit is recognized in the gifts He bestows on the church.	**The Spirit is the source of all gifts to the church.** 1 Corinthians 12:7–11: "Now to each one the manifestation of the Spirit is given for the common good. To one there is given through the Spirit the message of wisdom, to another the message of knowledge by means of the same Spirit, to another faith by the same Spirit, to another gifts of healing by that one Spirit, to another miraculous powers, to another prophecy, to another distinguishing between spirits, to another speaking in different kinds of tongues, and to still another the interpretation of tongues. All these are the work of one and the same Spirit, and he gives them to each one, just as he determines." 1 Corinthians 12:4: "There are different kinds of gifts, but the same Spirit." **The Spirit grants spiritual gifts to individual believers.** Romans 12:6–8: "We have different gifts, according to the grace given us. If a man's gift is prophesying, let him use it in proportion to his faith. If it is serving, let him serve; if it is

The Doctrine of the Holy Spirit (cont.)

Position	Support
	teaching, let him teach; if it is encouraging, let him encourage; if it is contributing to the needs of others, let him give generously; if it is leadership, let him govern diligently; if it is showing mercy, let him do it cheerfully."
	1 Corinthians 12:8–9: "To one there is given through the Spirit the message of wisdom, to another the message of knowledge by means of the same Spirit, to another faith by the same Spirit, to another gifts of healing by that one Spirit, to another miraculous powers, to another prophecy, to another distinguishing between spirits, to another speaking in different kinds of tongues, and to still another the interpretation of tongues."
	1 Corinthians 12:28–30: "And in the church God has appointed first of all apostles, second prophets, third teachers, then workers of miracles, also those having gifts of healing, those able to help others, those with gifts of administration, and those speaking in different kinds of tongues. Are all apostles? Are all prophets? Are all teachers? Do all work miracles? Do all have gifts of healing? Do all speak in tongues? Do all interpret?"
	Ephesians 4:12: ". . . to prepare God's people for works of service, so that the body of Christ may be built up."

The Doctrine of Man and Sin

Position	Support
The doctrine of man defined	"God is Spirit, the human soul is a spirit. The essential attributes of a spirit are reason, conscience, and will. A spirit is a rational, moral, and therefore also a free agent. In making man after his own image, therefore, God endowed him with those attributes which belong to his own nature as a spirit. . . . He belongs to the same order of being as God Himself, and is therefore capable of communion with his Maker" (Hodge, *Systematic Theology*, 2:96).
The importance of the doctrine	"With a moral lapse of the race and a common depravity, we need the redemptive mediation of Christ, and the offices of the Holy Spirit in our regeneration and spiritual life. . . . With these truths we require the truth of the divine Trinity. On a denial of the primitive lapse and moral ruin of the race, all these great truths may be dismissed" (Miley, *Systematic Theology*, 1:354).
Man was created in the image of God.	Genesis 1:26–27: "Then God said, 'Let us make man in our image, in our likeness, and let them rule over the fish of the sea and the birds of the air, over the livestock, over all the earth, and over all the creatures that move along the ground.' So God created man in his own image, in the image of God he created him; male and female he created them."
Man reflects some of God's characteristics.	Unlike the rest of God's creation, man has the unique and privileged capacity for rational, moral, and spiritual fellowship with his Creator. Man reflects, in a limited sense, the image of his infinite Creator through various means: **Dominion** Genesis 1:28: "God blessed them and said to them, 'Be fruitful and increase in number; fill the earth and subdue it.'" **Communication** Genesis 2:16, 18: "And the LORD God commanded the man, . . . The LORD God said, . . . " **Rational and moral decision making** Genesis 3:6: "When the woman saw that the fruit of the tree was good for food and pleasing to the eye, and also desirable for gaining wisdom, she took some and ate it. She also gave some to her husband, who was with her, and he ate it."

The Doctrine of Man and Sin (cont.)

Position	Support
The doctrine of sin defined	Original sin is best defined by John Calvin: "This is the inherited corruption, which the church fathers termed 'original sin,' meaning by the word 'sin' the depravation of a nature previously good and pure" (Calvin, *Institutes of the Christian Religion,* ed. McNeill, vol. 20, book 2, ch. 2, p. 246).
Sin and death entered the world through the willful disobedience of Adam (i.e., original sin).	**God commanded Adam not to eat of a certain tree in the garden, with a warning of the consequences.** Genesis 2:17: "But you must not eat from the tree of the knowledge of good and evil, for when you eat of it you will surely die." **Death, as the subsequent curse of Adam's sin, is described in Scripture in various ways:** ***The physical decay of all creation*** Genesis 3:17–19: "Cursed is the ground because of you, ... By the sweat of your brow you will eat your food until you return to the ground ...; for dust you are, and to dust you will return." Romans 8:20: "For the creation was subjected to frustration, not by its own choice, but by the will of the one who subjected it." ***The spiritual death of all humanity in relation to God*** Romans 3:23: "For all have sinned and fall short of the glory of God." (The word *sinned* is in the aorist tense in Greek, implying that the offense took place at some point in the past—i.e., Adam's fall.) Romans 5:12: "Therefore, just as sin entered the world through one man, and death through sin, and in this way death came to all men, because all sinned...." 1 Corinthians 15:22: "For as in Adam all die, so in Christ all will be made alive."
Spiritual death is demonstrated by man's inherent bondage to a "sin nature."	Romans 7:5: "For while we were in the flesh, the sinful passions, which were aroused by the Law, were at work in in the members of our body to bear the fruit for death" (NASB). Ephesians 2:3: "All of us also lived among them at one time, gratifying the cravings of our sinful nature and following its desires and thoughts. Like the rest, we were by nature objects of wrath."
Jesus Christ paid the just penalty for man's sin.	2 Corinthians 5:21: "God made him who had no sin to be sin for us, so that in him we might become the righteousness of God." 1 Peter 3:18: "For Christ died for sins once for all, the righteous for the unrighteous, to bring you to God. He was put to death in the body but made alive by the spirit." 1 John 2:2: "He is the atoning sacrifice for our sins, and not only for ours but also for the sins of the whole world." Colossians 2:14: "... having canceled out the certificate of debt consisting of decrees against us and which was hostile to us; and He has taken it out of the way, having nailed it to the cross" (NASB).
Redeemed man still struggles with sin, but he is no longer in bondage to it.	Romans 8:1–2: "Therefore, there is now no condemnation for those who are in Christ Jesus, because through Christ Jesus the law of the Spirit of life set me free from the law of sin and death." 1 Corinthians 10:13: "No temptation has seized you except what is common to man." 1 John 2:1: "My dear children, I write this to you so that you will not sin. But if anyone does sin, we have one who speaks to the Father in our defense—Jesus Christ, the Righteous One."

The Doctrine of Salvation

Position	Support
The doctrine of salvation defined	Man's sin has caused his complete condemnation and separation from God. "Salvation is the sum total of all God's work for man in delivering him from his lost condition in sin and finally presenting him in glory (as well as everything in between)" (Cook, *Systematic Theology in Outline Form*, p. 368).
The importance of the doctrine	It is in the doctrine of salvation that we as humans most experience God's justice and grace. His justice demands a penalty for sin that we are unable to satisfy. God pays the penalty His justice demands and provides life through the means of grace. Man is left in awe of God's love and his own sinfulness.
Jesus Christ's death on the cross provides atonement for sin.	Isaiah 53:4–5: "Surely he took up our infirmities and carried our sorrows, yet we considered him stricken by God, smitten by him, and afflicted. But he was pierced for our transgressions, he was crushed for our iniquities; the punishment that brought us peace was upon him, and by his wounds we are healed." Romans 5:8: "But God demonstrates his own love for us in this: While we were still sinners, Christ died for us." 1 Corinthians 15:3–4: "For what I received I passed on to you as of first importance: that Christ died for our sins according to the Scriptures, that he was buried, that he was raised on the third day according to the Scriptures." 2 Corinthians 5:21: "God made him who had no sin to be sin for us, so that in him we might become the righteousness of God." Colossians 1:21–22: "Once you were alienated from God and were enemies in your minds because of your evil behavior. But now he has reconciled you by Christ's physical body through death to present you holy in his sight, without blemish and free from accusation." 1 Timothy 2:5–6: "For there is one God and one mediator between God and men, the man Christ Jesus, who gave himself as a ransom for all men—the testimony given in its proper time." Hebrews 9:27–28: "Just as man is destined to die once, and after that to face judgment, so Christ was sacrificed once to take away the sins of many people; and he will appear a second time, not to bear sin, but bring salvation to those who are waiting for him."
Salvation involves the process of regeneration.	Regeneration is the instantaneous spiritual re-creation of a person when he or she comes to faith in Christ. 2 Corinthians 5:17: "Therefore, if anyone is in Christ, he is a new creation; the old has gone, the new has come!" Ephesians 2:4–5: "But because of his great love for us, God, who is rich in mercy, made us alive with Christ even when we were dead in trangressions—it is by grace you have been saved." Colossians 2:13: "When you were dead in your sins and in the uncircumcision of your sinful nature, God made you alive in Christ." Titus 3:4–5: "But when the kindness and love of God our Savior appeared, he saved us, not because of righteous things we had done, but because of his mercy. He saved us through the washing of rebirth and renewal by the Holy Spirit." 1 Peter 1:3, 23: "Praise be to the God and Father of our Lord Jesus Christ! In his great mercy he has given us new birth into a living hope through the resurrection of Jesus Christ from the dead.... For you have been born again, not of perishable seed, but of imperishable, through the living and enduring word of God."

The Doctrine of Salvation (cont.)

Position	Support
Conversion (repentance and faith)	"Conversion is that voluntary change in the mind of a sinner, in which he turns, on the one hand, from sin, and on the other hand, to Christ" (Strong, *Systematic Theology,* p. 289: quoted in Cook, *Systematic Theology in Outline Form,* p. 410).
	Scripture addresses the issue of conversion in various passages.
	Acts 2:37–38: "When the people heard this, they were cut to the heart and said to Peter and the other apostles, 'Brothers, what shall we do?' Peter replied, 'Repent and be baptized, every one of you, in the name of Jesus Christ for the forgiveness of your sins. And you will receive the gift of the Holy Spirit.'"
	Acts 8:22: "Repent of this wickedness and pray to the Lord. Perhaps he will forgive you for having such a thought in your heart."
	Acts 16:30–31: "He then brought them out and asked, 'Sirs, what must I do to be saved?' They replied, 'Believe in the Lord Jesus, and you will be saved—you and your household.'"
	Romans 5:1–2: "Therefore, since we have been justified through faith, we have peace with God through our Lord Jesus Christ, through whom we have gained access by faith into this grace in which we now stand. And we rejoice in the hope of the glory of God."
	Romans 10:9–10: "That if you confess with your mouth, 'Jesus is Lord,' and believe in your heart that God raised him from the dead, you will be saved. For it is with your heart that you believe and are justified, and it is with your mouth that you confess and are saved."
	2 Corinthians 7:9–10: "Yet now I am happy, not because you were made sorry, but because your sorrow led you to repentance. For you became sorrowful as God intended and so were not harmed in any way by us. Godly sorrow brings repentance that leads to salvation and leaves no regret, but worldly sorrow brings death."
	2 Timothy 2:25: "Those who oppose him he must gently instruct, in the hope that God will grant them repentance leading them to a knowledge of the truth."
	Hebrews 11:6: "Without faith it is impossible to please God, because anyone who comes to him must believe that he exists and that he rewards those who earnestly seek him."
Works are not a means of salvation.	Salvation is achieved solely by God's grace. Salvation is not achieved by keeping the Law of Moses to earn God's favor. There is nothing a sinner can do in and of himself to please God apart from trusting in God's mercy, which was realized in Christ's death on the cross. Works can serve as visible evidence of genuine belief.
	John 6:28–29: "Then they asked him, 'What must we do to do the works God requires?' Jesus answered, 'The work of God is this: to believe in the one he has sent.'"
	Romans 4:4–5: "Now when a man works, his wages are not credited to him as a gift, but as an obligation. However, to the man who does not work but trusts God who justifies the wicked, his faith is credited as righteousness."
	Galatians 2:21: "I do not set aside the grace of God, for if righteousness could be gained through the law, Christ died for nothing."
	Ephesians 2:8–9: "For it is by grace you have been saved, through faith—and this not from yourselves, it is the gift of God—not by works, so that no one can boast."
	Titus 3:4–5: "But when the kindness and love of God our Savior appeared, he saved us, not because of righteous things we had done, but because of his mercy. He saved us through the washing of rebirth and renewal by the Holy Spirit."
	James 2:14, 17–18: "What good is it, my brothers, if a man claims to have faith but has no deeds? Can such a faith save him? ... In the same way, faith by itself, if it is not accompanied by action, is dead. But someone will say, 'You have faith; I have deeds.' Show me your faith without deeds, and I will show you my faith by what I do."

The Doctrine of Salvation (cont.)

Position	Support
Results of salvation: (1) Union with Christ	**Union with Christ refers to the believer's position in Christ whereby Christ's life becomes the life of the Christian.** Romans 8:1: "Therefore, there is now no condemnation for those who are in Christ Jesus." 2 Corinthians 13:5: "Examine yourselves to see whether you are in the faith; test yourselves. Do you not realize that Christ Jesus is in you—unless, of course, you fail the test?" Galatians 2:20: "I have been crucified with Christ and I no longer live, but Christ lives in me. The life I live in the body, I live by faith in the Son of God, who loved me and gave himself for me." Colossians 1:27: "To them God has chosen to make known among the Gentiles the glorious riches of this mystery, which is Christ in you, the hope of glory."
Results of salvation: (2) Justification	**Justification refers to the legal transaction in which God is able to declare believers righteous because Christ endured their deserved punishment.** Romans 3:24–26: ". . . justified freely by his grace through the redemption that came by Christ Jesus. God presented him as a sacrifice of atonement, through faith in his blood. He did this to demonstrate his justice, because in his forbearance he had left the sins committed beforehand unpunished—he did it to demonstrate his justice at the present time, so as to be just and the one who justifies those who have faith in Jesus." Romans 4:25: "He was delivered over to death for our sins and was raised to life for our justification." Romans 5:9: "Since we have now been justified by his blood, how much more shall we be saved from God's wrath through him!" Romans 5:18: "Consequently, just as the result of one trespass was condemnation for all men, so also the result of one act of righteousness was justification that brings life for all men." 2 Corinthians 5:21: "God made him who had no sin to be sin for us, so that in him we might become the righteousness of God." Colossians 2:13–14: "When you were dead in your transgressions and the uncircumcision of your flesh, He made you alive together with Him, having forgiven us all our transgressions, having canceled out the certificate of debt consisting of decrees against us and which was hostile to us; and He has taken it out of the way, having nailed it to the cross" (NASB).
Results of salvation: (3) Reconciliation	**Reconciliation speaks of the restored relationship between the believer and God whereby God adopts those who come to Him through faith in Christ as His children.** Romans 5:10: "For if, when we were God's enemies, we were reconciled to him through the death of his Son, how much more, having been reconciled, shall we be saved through his life! Not only is this so, but we also rejoice in God through our Lord Jesus Christ, through whom we have now received reconciliation." 2 Corinthians 5:18–19: "All this is from God, who reconciled us to himself through Christ and gave us the ministry of reconciliation: that God was reconciling the world to himself in Christ, not counting men's sins against them. And he has committed to us the message of reconciliation." Colossians 1:19–22: "For God was pleased to have all his fullness dwell in him, and through him to reconcile to himself all things, whether things on earth or things in heaven, by making peace through his blood, shed on the cross. Once you were alienated from God and were enemies in your minds because of your evil behavior. But now he has reconciled you by Christ's physical body through death to present you holy in his sight, without blemish and free from accusation."

The Doctrine of Salvation (cont.)

Position	Support
Results of salvation: (4) Sanctification	**Sanctification refers to the process that God effects upon believers to make them holy.** 1 Corinthians 1:30: "But by His doing you are in Christ Jesus, who became to us wisdom from God, and righteousness and sanctification, and redemption" (NASB). 1 Corinthians 6:11: "And that is what some of you were. But you were washed, you were sanctified, you were justified in the name of the Lord Jesus Christ and by the Spirit of our God." 2 Corinthians 3:18: "And we, who with unveiled faces all reflect the Lord's glory, are being transformed into his likeness with ever-increasing glory, which comes from the Lord, who is the Spirit." 1 Thessalonians 4:3–4, 7: "It is God's will that you should be sanctified: that you should avoid sexual immorality; that each of you should learn to control his own body in a way that is holy and honorable.... For God did not call us to be impure, but to live a holy life." 2 Thessalonians 2:13: "But we ought always to thank God for you, brothers loved by the Lord, because from the beginning God chose you to be saved through the sanctifying work of the Spirit and through belief in the truth."
Results of salvation: (5) Glorification	**Glorification is the future event (occurring at the resurrection of believers) that will completely purify the believer, including his physical body. Corruption will be eliminated, and the believer's sin nature will be stripped away forever.** Romans 8:18–19: "I consider that our present sufferings are not worth comparing with the glory that will be revealed in us. The creation waits in eager expectation for the sons of God to be revealed." 1 Corinthians 15:42–44: "So will it be with the resurrection of the dead. The body that is sown is perishable, it is raised imperishable; it is sown in dishonor, it is raised in glory; it is sown in weakness, it is raised in power; it is sown a natural body, it is raised a spiritual body. If there is a natural body, there is also a spiritual body." Philippians 3:20–21: "But our citizenship is in heaven. And we eagerly await a Savior from there, the Lord Jesus Christ, who, by the power that enables him to bring everything under his control, will transform our lowly bodies so that they will be like his glorious body." Colossians 3:4: "When Christ, who is your life, appears, then you also will appear with him in glory." 1 Peter 5:1, 4, 10: "To the elders among you, I appeal as a fellow elder, a witness of Christ's sufferings and one who also will share in the glory to be revealed.... And when the Chief Shepherd appears, you will receive the crown of glory that will never fade away.... And the God of all grace, who called you to his eternal glory in Christ, after you have suffered a little while, will himself restore you and make you strong, firm, and steadfast."
The means and extent of salvation: (1) The Holy Spirit	**The Holy Spirit is the member of the Trinity who convicts sinners of sin and transforms believers through spiritual birth.** John 3:5–6: "Jesus answered, 'I tell you the truth, no one can enter the kingdom of God unless he is born of water and the Spirit. Flesh gives birth to flesh, but the Spirit gives birth to spirit.'" John 16:8–11: "When he comes, he will convict the world of guilt in regard to sin and righteousness and judgment: in regard to sin, because men do not believe in me; in regard to righteousness, because I am going to the Father, where you can see me no longer; and in regard to judgment, because the prince of this world now stands condemned."

The Doctrine of Salvation (cont.)

Position	Support
The means and extent of salvation: (2) The Word of God	**The Word of God is the instrument that the Holy Spirit uses to bring people to saving faith.** Romans 1:16: "I am not ashamed of the gospel, because it is the power of God for the salvation of everyone who believes: first for the Jew, then for the Gentile." Romans 10:17: "Faith comes from hearing the message, and the message is heard through the word of Christ." 1 Corinthians 1:18: "For the word of the cross is to those who are perishing foolishness, but to us who are being saved it is the power of God" (NASB). James 1:18: "He chose to give us birth through the word of truth, that we might be a kind of firstfruits of all he created."
The means and extent of salvation: (3) Salvation is available to all.	**Scripture indicates that Christ's work on the cross provides salvation for the whole world, regardless of race or any other factor. God invites everyone to trust His Son Jesus Christ.** John 1:29: "The next day John saw Jesus coming toward him and said, 'Look, the Lamb of God, who takes away the sin of the world!'" John 3:16: "For God so loved the world that he gave his one and only Son, that whoever believes in him shall not perish but have eternal life." Romans 3:29–30: "Is God the God of Jews only? Is he not the God of Gentiles too? Yes, of Gentiles too, since there is only one God, who will justify the circumcised by faith and the uncircumcised through that same faith." 1 Timothy 2:3–4: "This is good, and pleases God our Savior, who wants all men to be saved and to come to a knowledge of the truth." 1 Timothy 4:10: "For it is for this we labor and strive, because we have fixed our hope on the living God, who is the Savior of all men, especially of believers" (NASB). 2 Peter 3:9: "The Lord is not slow in keeping his promise, as some understand slowness. He is patient with you, not wanting anyone to perish, but everyone to come to repentance." 1 John 2:2: "He [Jesus Christ] is the atoning sacrifice for our sins, and not only for ours but also for the sins of the whole world."
The means and extent of salvation: (4) Salvation is effective for some.	**Although the death of Jesus Christ provides salvation to all people, it is effective only to those who receive it by faith.** John 1:12: "Yet to all who received him, to those who believed in his name, he gave the right to become children of God." John 3:18: "Whoever believes in him is not condemned, but whoever does not believe stands condemned already because he has not believed in the name of God's one and only Son." John 3:36: "Whoever believes in the Son has eternal life, but whoever rejects the Son will not see life, for God's wrath remains on him." Acts 13:48: "When the Gentiles heard this, they were glad and honored the word of the Lord; and all who were appointed for eternal life believed."

The Doctrine of Rewards and Punishment

Position	Support
The doctrine of reward and punishment defined	**The Apostles' Creed (The Old Roman Creed)** "I believe in God . . . And in Christ Jesus . . . "Whence he cometh to judge the living and the dead . . . "The resurrection of the flesh . . . "The life everlasting." **The Constantinopolitan Creed** "We believe in one God the Father All-sovereign, maker of heaven and earth, and of all things visible and invisible; "And in one Lord Jesus Christ, . . . ascended into the heavens, and sitteth on the right hand of the Father, and cometh again with glory to judge living and dead, of whose kingdom there shall be no end: . . . We look for a resurrection of the dead, and the life of the age to come."
The importance of the doctrine	"If we accept the truth of the Scriptures we must be loyal to their teaching on the question of future punishment, as on all others, and none the less so because of its fearful character, as on all others, and none the less so because of its fearful character. On no subject could the perversion of truth be more disastrous. While such perversion may neutralize the practical force of the truth, and induce a false sense of security, it is powerless to avert the doom of sin. Our only safety lies in the acceptance of the salvation in Christ Jesus" (Miley, *Systematic Theology,* 2:462).
The intermediate state of the righteous	**For the believers the existence after death is one of peace and rest in the presence of the Lord.** Luke 23:43: "Jesus answered him, 'I tell you the truth, today you will be with me in paradise.'" 2 Corinthians 5:8: "We are confident, I say, and would prefer to be away from the body and at home with the Lord." Philippians 1:23–24: "I am torn between the two: I desire to depart and be with Christ, which is better by far; but it is more necessary for you that I remain in the body." Revelation 14:13: "Then I heard a voice from heaven say, 'Write: Blessed are the dead who die in the Lord from now on.' 'Yes,' says the Spirit, 'they will rest from their labor, for their deeds will follow them.'"
The intermediate state of the wicked	**For the unrighteous the existence after death is one of torment and suffering.** Luke 16:23: "In hell, where he was in torment, he looked up and saw Abraham far away, with Lazarus by his side."
The second coming of Christ	**Jesus will come to take His people to Himself, forever to be with Him and to judge the world for rejecting Him.** 1 Thessalonians 4:16–17: "For the Lord himself will come down from heaven, with a loud command, with the voice of the archangel and with the trumpet call of God, and the dead in Christ will rise first. After that, we who are still alive and are left will be caught up together with them in the clouds to meet the Lord in the air. And so we will be with the Lord forever." Matthew 24:37–39: "As it was in the days of Noah, so it will be at the coming of the Son of Man. For in the days before the flood, people were eating and drinking, marrying and giving in marriage, up to the day Noah entered the ark; and they knew nothing about what would happen until the flood came and took them all away. That is how it will be at the coming of the Son of Man."

The Doctrine of Rewards and Punishment (cont.)

Position	Support
... continued	**Jesus Christ will return physically and visibly, in the clouds of heaven.** Acts 1:11: "'Men of Galilee,' they said, 'why do you stand here looking into the sky? This same Jesus, who has been taken from you into heaven, will come back in the same way you have seen him go into heaven.'" Matthew 24:30: "At that time the sign of the Son of Man will appear in the sky, and all the nations of the earth will mourn. They will see the Son of Man coming on the clouds of the sky, with power and great glory."
The resurrection of the body	**Resurrection is a physical bodily resurrection, like that of Jesus Christ.** 1 Corinthians 15:48–49: "As was the earthly man, so are those who are of the earth; and as is the man from heaven, so also are those who are of heaven. And just as we have borne the likeness of the earthly man, so shall we bear the likeness of the man from heaven." 1 John 3:2: "Dear friends, now we are children of God, and what we will be has not yet been made known. But we know that when he appears, we shall be like him, for we shall see him as he is." Romans 8:11: "And if the Spirit of him who raised Jesus from the dead is living in you, he who raised Christ from the dead will also give life to your mortal bodies through his Spirit, who lives in you."
The resurrection of the just	**Several Scriptures point toward the resurrection of the just and the gathering of believers who are alive at His coming.** 1 Corinthians 15:23: "But each in his own turn: Christ, the firstfruits; then, when he comes, those who belong to him." John 14:3: "And if I go and prepare a place for you, I will come back and take you to be with me that you also may be where I am." 1 Corinthians 15:51–53: "Listen, I tell you a mystery: We will not all sleep, but we will all be changed—in a flash, in the twinkling of an eye, at the last trumpet. For the trumpet will sound, the dead will be raised imperishable, and we will be changed. For the perishable must clothe itself with the imperishable, and the mortal with immortality." 1 Thessalonians 4:14–17: "We believe that Jesus died and rose again and so we believe that God will bring with Jesus those who have fallen asleep in him. According to the Lord's own word, we tell you that we who are still alive, who are left till the coming of the Lord, will certainly not precede those who have fallen asleep. For the Lord himself will come down from heaven, with a loud command, with the voice of the archangel and with the trumpet call of God, and the dead in Christ will rise first. After that, we who are still alive and are left will be caught up together with them in the clouds to meet the Lord in the air. And so we will be with the Lord forever."
The resurrection of the unjust	Daniel 12:2: "Multitudes who sleep in the dust of the earth will awake: some to everlasting life, others to shame and everlasting contempt."
All humans will experience a judgment.	Matthew 16:27: "For the Son of Man is going to come in his Father's glory with his angels, and then he will reward each person according to what he has done." 2 Corinthians 5:10: "For we must all appear before the judgment seat of Christ, that each one may receive what is due him for the things done while in the body, whether good or bad."

The Doctrine of Rewards and Punishment (cont.)

Position	Support
Believers will experience judgment but not condemnation.	John 5:24: "I tell you the truth, whoever hears my word and believes him who sent me has eternal life and will not be condemned; he has crossed over from death to life." Romans 8:1: "Therefore, there is now no condemnation for those who are in Christ Jesus, because through Christ Jesus the law of the Spirit of life set me free from the law of sin and death." Matthew 12:36: "But I tell you that men will have to give account on the day of judgment for every careless word they have spoken."
The standard of judgment	**All humans will be judged by the revelation that has been given to them.** Matthew 11:24: "But I tell you that it will be more bearable for Sodom on the day of judgment than for you." Romans 2:12: "All who sin apart from the law will also perish apart from the law, and all who sin under the law will be judged by the law." Entrance into heaven depends on the righteousness of Jesus alone. Romans 1:16–17: "I am not ashamed of the gospel, because it is the power of God for the salvation of everyone who believes: first for the Jew, then for the Gentile. For in the gospel a righteousness from God is revealed, a righteousness that is by faith from first to last, just as it is written: 'The righteous will live by faith.'"
The final state of the wicked	**There will be different levels of punishment.** Luke 12:47–48: "That servant who knows his master's will and does not get ready or does not do what his master wants will be beaten with many blows. But the one who does not know and does things deserving punishment will be beaten with few blows. From everyone who has been given much, much will be demanded; and from the one who has been entrusted with much, much more will be asked." Romans 2:12: "All who sin apart from the law will also perish apart from the law, and all who sin under the law will be judged by the law."
The punishment of the wicked is eternal.	**The Bible speaks of the eternal, non-annihilistic punishment of the wicked.** Matthew 25:41: "Then he will say to those on his left, 'Depart from me, you who are cursed, into the eternal fire prepared for the devil and his angels.'" Revelation 14:11: "And the smoke of their torment rises for ever and ever. There is no rest day or night for those who worship the beast and his image, or for anyone who receives the mark of his name." Mark 9:48: ". . . where 'their worm does not die, and the fire is not quenched.'" Matthew 25:46: "Then they will go away to eternal punishment, but the righteous to eternal life."
The reward of believers is eternal life.	**Eternal life is the gift of God that believers receive by faith and not through good works.** Matthew 25:46: "Then they will go away to eternal punishment, but the righteous to eternal life." John 3:16–18: "For God so loved the world that he gave his one and only Son, that whoever believes in him shall not perish but have eternal life. For God did not send his Son into the world to condemn the world, but to save the world through him. Whoever believes in him is not condemned, but whoever does not believe stands condemned already because he has not believed in the name of God's one and only Son." Romans 6:23: "For the wages of sin is death, but the gift of God is eternal life in Christ Jesus our Lord."

The Doctrine of Rewards and Punishment (cont.)

Position	Support
There will be levels of rewards in heaven.	**The Scripture gives examples of works that will bring rewards.** ***Evangelism*** Daniel 12:3: "Those who are wise will shine like the brightness of the heavens, and those who lead many to righteousness, like the stars for ever and ever." ***Hospitality*** Matthew 10:41–42: "Anyone who receives a prophet because he is a prophet will receive a prophet's reward, and anyone who receives a righteous man because he is a righteous man will receive a righteous man's reward. And if anyone gives even a cup of cold water to one of these little ones because he is my disciple, I tell you the truth, he will certainly not lose his reward." Matthew 25:37: "Then the righteous will answer him, 'Lord, when did we see you hungry and feed you, or thirsty and give you something to drink?'" ***Suffering for Christ's Name*** Matthew 5:11: "Blessed are you when people insult you, persecute you and falsely say all kinds of evil against you because of me. Rejoice and be glad, because great is your reward in heaven, for in the same way they persecuted the prophets who were before you." Romans 8:17: "Now if we are children, then we are heirs—heirs of God and co-heirs with Christ, if indeed we share in his sufferings in order that we may also share in his glory." ***Stewardship*** Matthew 6:20: "But store up for yourselves treasures in heaven, where moth and rust do not destroy, and where thieves do not break in and steal."

APPENDIX B
Creeds of the Church

The Apostles' Creed (The Old Roman Creed)

1. I believe in God Almighty [the Father almighty]
2. And in Christ Jesus, his only son, our Lord
3. Who was born of the Holy Spirit and the Virgin Mary
4. Who was crucified under Pontius Pilate and was buried
5. And the third day rose from the dead
6. Who ascended into heaven
7. And sitteth on the right hand of the Father
8. Whence he cometh to judge the living and the dead
9. And in the Holy Ghost
10. The holy church
11. The remission of sins
12. The resurrection of the flesh
13. The life everlasting.

(Bettenson, *Documents of the Christian Church*, pp. 23–24)

The Creed of Nicaea (Nicene Creed)

We believe in one God the Father All-sovereign, maker of all things visible and invisible;

And in one Lord Jesus Christ, the only-begotten Son of God, begotten of the Father before all the ages, Light of Light, true God of true God, begotten not made, of one substance with the Father, through whom all things were made, things in heaven and things on the earth; who for us men and for our salvation came down and was made flesh, and became man; suffered, and rose on the third day, ascended into the heavens, is coming to judge living and dead.

And in the Holy Spirit.
And those that say "There was when he was not.'"
  and, "Before he was begotten he was not,"
  and that, "He came into being from what-is-not,"
or those that allege, that the son of God is
  "of another substance or essence"
  or "created,"
  or "changeable"
  or "alterable"

these the Catholic and Apostolic Church anathematizes.

(Bettenson, *Documents of the Christian Church*, p. 25)

The Constantinopolitan Creed

We believe in one God the Father All-sovereign, maker of heaven and earth, and of all things visible and invisible;

And in one Lord Jesus Christ, the only-begotten Son of God, Begotten of the Father before all the ages, Light of Light, true God of true God, begotten not made, of one substance with the Father, through whom all things were made; who for us men and for our salvation came down from the heavens, and was made flesh of the Holy Spirit and the virgin Mary, and became man, and was crucified for us under Pontius Pilate, and suffered and was buried, and rose again on the third day according to the Scriptures, and ascended into the heavens, and sitteth on the right hand of the Father, and cometh again with glory to judge living and dead, of whose kingdom there shall be no end:

And in the Holy Spirit, the Lord and the Life-giver, that proceedeth from the Father, who with Father and Son is worshipped together and glorified together, who spake through the prophets:

In one holy Catholic and Apostolic Church:

We acknowledge one baptism unto remission of sins. We look for a resurrection of the dead, and the life of the age to come.

(Bettenson, *Documents of the Christian Church,* pp. 25–26)

The Athanasian Creed

And the Catholic faith is this: That we worship one God in Trinity, and Trinity in Unity; neither confounding the persons, or dividing the substance. For there is one Person of the Father; another of the Son; and another of the Holy Ghost. But the Godhead of the Father, and of the Son, and of the Holy Ghost, is all one; the Glory equal, the Majesty co-eternal.... So the Father is God: the Son is God: and the Holy Ghost is God. And yet there are not three Gods: but one God.... The Father is made of none: neither created, nor begotten. The Son is of the Father alone: not made, nor created: but begotten. The Holy Ghost is of the Father and of the Son: neither made, nor created, nor begotten: but proceeding.... And in this Trinity none is afore, or after another: none is greater, or less than another. But the whole three Persons are co-eternal, and co-equal. So that in all things, as aforesaid: the Unity in Trinity, and the Trinity in Unity, is to be worshiped.

(Miley, *Systematic Theology,* p. 228)

The Definition of Chalcedon

Therefore, following the holy Fathers, we all with one accord teach men to acknowledge one and the same Son, our Lord Jesus Christ, at once complete in Godhead and complete in manhood, truly God and truly man, consisting also of a reasonable soul and body; of one substance with the Father as regards his Godhead, and at the same time of one substance with us as regards his manhood; like us in all respects, apart from sin; as regards his Godhead, begotten, for us men and for our salvation, of Mary the Virgin, the God-bearer; one and the same Christ, Son, Lord, Only-begotten, recognized in two natures, without confusion, without change, without division, without separation; the distinction of natures being in no way annulled by the union, but rather the characteristics of each nature being preserved and coming together to form one person and subsistence, not as parted or separated into two persons, but one and the same Son and Only-begotten God the Word, Lord Jesus Christ; even as the prophets from earliest times spoke of him, and our Lord Jesus Christ himself taught us, and the creed of the Fathers has handed down to us.

(Bettenson, *Documents of the Christian Church,* pp. 51–52)

Bibliography

Works on Cults, Sects and Religious Movements	
	Note: This bibliography of recommended literature generally omits important reference works that occur in "Works Cited in the Text," below. Please consult both bibliographies for a more complete picture of significant sources and critical literature. Not all groups will be represented in the primary or secondary bibliography.
Primary Literature of the Cults, Sects and Religious Movements	*Association for Research and Enlightenment* Frejer, B. Ernest. *The Edgar Cayce Companion: A Comprehensive Treatise of the Edgar Cayce Readings.* Virginia Beach, VA: A.R.E. Press, 1995. Kittler, Glenn D., under the editorship of Hugh Lynn Cayce. *Edgar Cayce on the Dead Sea Scrolls.* New York: Paperback Library, 1970. Reed, Anne, under the editorship of Hugh Lynn Cayce. *Edgar Cayce on Jesus and His Church.* New York: Paperback Library, 1970. Sparrow, Lynn Elwell. *Edgar Cayce and the Born Again Christian.* Virginia Beach, VA: Edgar Cayce Foundation, 1985. Stearn, Jess. *Edgar Cayce—The Sleeping Prophet.* New York: Bantam Books, 1968. *Christadelphians* *God Is One Not Three: Bible Truth Contrasted with Church Error.* *Church of Jesus Christ of Latter-day Saints* Ludlow, Daniel H., ed. *Encyclopedia of Mormonism.* New York: Macmillan, 1992. *Church Universal and Triumphant* Lewis, James R., and J. Gordon Melton. *Church Universal and Triumphant in Scholarly Perspective.* Stanford, CA: Center for Academic Publication, 1994. (This work is *not* published by the Church Universal and Triumphant, but it is sufficiently favorable that it is sold through their public relations office.) Prophet, Elizabeth Clare. *The Chela and the Path: Meeting the Challenge of Life in the Twentieth Century.* Los Angeles: Summit University Press, 1977. Prophet, Elizabeth Clare, with Erin L. Prophet. *Reincarnation: The Missing Link in Christianity.* Corwin Springs, MT: Summit University Press, 1997. *Eckankar* Cramer, Todd, and Doug Munson, compilers. *Eckankar: Ancient Wisdom for Today.* Minneapolis: Eckankar, 1993. *Soul Travel and the Spiritual Exercises of Eckankar.* Minneapolis: Eckankar, 1992. Pamphlet. Twitchell, Paul. *The Flute of God.* Minneapolis: Eckankar, 1969. Twitchell, Paul. *The Key to Eckankar.* Minneapolis: Eckankar, 1968, 1985. *What Is Eckankar? Religion of the Light and Sound of God.* Minneapolis: Eckankar, 1993. Pamphlet.

Freemasonry

Interesting Facts About Freemasonry. Grand Rapids: Grand Lodge of Free and Accepted Masons of the State of Michigan, 1961.

Waite, Arthur Edward. *A New Encyclopedia of Freemasonry.* 2 vols. in 1. New York: Weathervane Books, 1970.

Jehovah's Witnesses

Jehovah's Witnesses: Proclaimers of God's Kingdom. Brooklyn: Watchtower Bible and Tract Society of New York, 1993.

Russell, Charles T. *The Divine Plan of the Ages.* Studies in the Scriptures, Series I. East Rutherford, NJ: Dawn Bible Students Association, 1916.

Mind Science Groups

Armor, Reginald. *Ernest Holmes: The Man.* Los Angeles: Science of Mind Publications, 1977.

The Basic Ideas of Science of Mind. Los Angeles: Science of Mind Publications, n.d.

"A Century of Christian Science Healing." Boston, MA: Christian Science Publishing Society, 1966.

Freeman, James D. *The Story of Unity.* Lee's Summit, MO: Unity School of Christianity, 1954.

Gottschalk, Stephen. *The Emergence of Christian Science in American Religious Life.* Berkeley: University of California Press, 1973.

Larson, Martin A. *New Thought, or a Modern Religious Approach: The Philosophy of Health, Happiness and Prosperity.* New York: Philosophical Library, 1985.

Peel, Robert. *Spiritual Healing in a Scientific Age.* San Francisco: Harper & Row, 1987.

Reorganized Church of Jesus Christ of Latter-day Saints

Judd, Peter A., and A. Bruce Lindgren. *An Introduction to the Saints Church.* Independence, MO: Herald Publishing House, 1976.

Koury, Aleah G. *The Truth and the Evidence.* Independence, MO: Herald Publishing House, 1965.

Ralstoon, Russell F. *Fundamental Differences Between the Reorganized Church and the Church in Utah.* Independence, MO: Herald Publishing House, 1960.

Statement on Objectives for the Church. Independence, MO: n.d.

Rosicrucians

Who and What Are the Rosicrucians: Facts at Your Finger Tips. San Jose, CA: Supreme Grand Lodge of AMORC, 1938, 1966.

United Pentecostal Church

Bernard, David K. *In the Name of Jesus.* Hazelwood, MO.: Word Aflame Press, 1992.

Bernard, David K. *Oneness and Trinity, A.D. 100-300.* Hazelwood, MO.: Word Aflame Press, 1991.

Bernard, David K. *The Oneness View of Jesus Christ.* Hazelwood, MO: Word Aflame Press, 1994.

Bernard, David K. *The Trinitarian Controversy in the Fourth Century.* Hazelwood, MO: Word Aflame Press, 1993.

Herrmann, Robert A. *Oneness, the Trinity and Logic.* Arnold, MD: Antioch Publishes the Word, 1984.

Reeves, Kenneth V. *The Godhead.* Granite City, IL: Privately published, 1967.

Rugger, Gary C. *Oneness—Trinity—Arian, Which One Does Scripture Teach?* Bakersfield, CA: Sarah's Christian Books, 1988.

Urantia Foundation

Bedell, Clyde. *Concordex of the Urantia Book.* 3d ed. Santa Barbara, CA: Clyde Bedell Estates, 1986.

Works on Cults, Sects and Religious Movements (cont.)

	McMullan, Harry. *Why I Believe the Urantia Book.* Oklahoma City: Asoka Foundation, 1993. Pamphlet.
	Melchizedek. Boulder, CO: Jesusonian Foundation, n.d. Pamphlet.
	Mysteries of Jesus Revealed. Boulder, CO: Jesusonian Foundation, n.d.
	Sprunger, Meredity J. *The Origin of "The Urantia Book."* Boulder, CO: Jesusonian Foundation, 1991. Pamphlet.
	The Urantia Book Is a 20th Century Revelation Integrating Science, Philosophy and Religion. Boulder, CO: Jesusonian Foundation, 1988. Pamphlet.
Secondary Literature Analyzing the Cults, Sects and Religious Movements*	Abanes, Richard. *American Militias.* Downers Grove, IL: InterVarsity Press, 1996.
	Aho, James. *The Politics of Righteousness: Idaho Christian Patriotism.* Seattle: University of Washington Press, 1990.
	Barkun, Michael. *Religion and the Racist Right: The Origins of the Christian Identity Movement.* Chapel Hill: University of North Carolina Press, 1994.
	Beckwith, Francis J., et al. *The Counterfeit Gospel of Mormonism.* Eugene, OR: Harvest House, 1998.
	Bowman, Robert M., Jr. *Jehovah's Witnesses.* Zondervan Guide to Cults and Religious Movements. Grand Rapids: Zondervan, 1995.
	Bowman, Robert M., Jr. *Jehovah's Witnesses, Jesus Christ, and the Gospel of John.* Grand Rapids: Baker Book House, 1989.
	Bowman, Robert M., Jr. *Understanding Jehovah's Witnesses: Why They Read the Bible the Way They Do.* Grand Rapids: Baker Book House, 1991.
	Bowman, Robert M., Jr. *Why You Should Believe in the Trinity: An Answer to Jehovah's Witnesses.* Grand Rapids: Baker Book House, 1989.
	Boyd, Greg. *Oneness Pentecostals and the Trinity.* Grand Rapids: Baker Book House, 1992.
	Braden, Charles S. *Christian Science Today: Power, Policy, Practice.* Dallas: Southern Methodist University Press, 1958.
	Braden, Charles S. *Spirits in Rebellion: The Rise and Development of New Thought.* Dallas: Southern Methodist University Press, 1963.
	Brodie, Fawn M. *No Man Knows My History: The Life of Joseph Smith.* 2d ed., revised and enlarged. New York: Alfred A. Knopf, 1971.
	Brumback, Carl. *God in Three Persons.* Cleveland, TN: Pathway Press, 1959. (A Trinitarian reply to Oneness Pentecostals regarding the Trinity and water baptism.)
	Dakin, Edwin Franden. *Mrs. Eddy: The Biography of a Virginal Mind.* New York: Charles Scribner's Sons, 1929.
	Ehrenborg, Todd. *Mind Sciences.* Zondervan Guide to Cults and Religious Movements. Grand Rapids: Zondervan, 1995.
	Enroth, Ronald, et al. *A Guide to Cults and New Religions.* Downers Grove, IL: InterVarsity Press, 1983.
	Gardner, Martin. *The Healing Revelations of Mary Baker Eddy: The Rise and Fall of Christian Science.* Buffalo, NY: Prometheus Books, 1993.
	Gardner, Martin. *Urantia: The Great Cult Mystery.* Amherst, NY: Prometheus Books, 1995.
	Gomes, Alan W. *Unmasking the Cults.* Zondervan Guide to Cults and Religious Movements. Grand Rapids: Zondervan, 1995.
	Haldeman, I. M. *Christian Science in the Light of Holy Scripture.* 5th ed. New York: Fleming H. Revell, 1909.
	Halverson, Dean C. "A Course in Miracles: Seeing Your Self as Sinless." *SCP Journal* 7, no. 1 (1987): 18–28.
	Harm, Frederick R. *How to Respond to the Science Religions.* St. Louis, MO: Concordia Publishing House, 1981.
	Higley, Dennis, and Rauni Higley. *What Is the Truth about Mormonism?* Sandy, Utah: Privately published, n.d.

Works on Cults, Sects and Religious Movements (cont.)

Hong, Nansook. *In the Shadow of the Moons: My Life in the Reverend Sun Myung Moon's Family.* Boston: Little, Brown, 1998.

Lane, David Christopher. *The Making of a Spiritual Movement: The Untold Story of Paul Twitchell and Eckankar.* Revised ed. Del Mar, CA: Del Mar Press, 1993.

Marquardt, H. Michael, and Wesley P. Walters. *Inventing Mormonism: Tradition and the Historical Record.* Salt Lake City: Smith Research Associates, 1994.

Martin, Walter. *The Kingdom of the Cults.* Minneapolis: Bethany House, 1985; revised ed. 1997 (ed. Hank Hanegraaff and Gretchen Passantino).

Martin, Walter. *The New Cults.* Santa Ana, CA: Vision House, 1980.

Mather, George A., and Larry A. Nichols. *Masonic Lodge.* Zondervan Guide to Cults and Religious Movements. Grand Rapids: Zondervan, 1995.

McDowell, Josh, and Don Stewart. *Understanding the Cults.* San Bernardino: Here's Life Publishers, 1982.

Milmine, Georgine. *The Life of Mary Baker G. Eddy and the History of Christian Science.* Editorial assistance by Willa S. Cather. 1909. Reprint, Grand Rapids: Baker Book House, 1971.

Passantino, Robert, and Gretchen Passantino. *Answers to the Cultist at Your Door.* Eugene, OR: Harvest House, 1981.

Penton, M. James. *Apocalypse Delayed: The Story of Jehovah's Witnesses.* Toronto: University of Toronto Press, 1985.

Reed, David A. *Blood on the Altar: Confessions of a Jehovah's Witness Minister.* Amherst, NY: Prometheus Books, 1996.

Rhodes, Ron. *New Age Movement.* Zondervan Guide to Cults and Religious Movements. Grand Rapids: Zondervan, 1995.

Sire, James W. *Scripture Twisting.* Downers Grove, IL: InterVarsity Press, 1980.

Todd Ehrenborg. *Speaking the Truth in Love to the Mind Sciences.* Privately published, 1990. (May be obtained at 19002 Yorba Linda Blvd., Yorba Linda, CA 92886.)

Sumner, Robert L. *Jesus Christ IS God! An Examination of Victor Paul Wierwille and His "Way International," a Rapidly Growing Unitarian Cult.* Murfreesboro, TN: Biblical Evangelism Press, 1983.

Van Gorden, Kurt. *Mormonism.* Zondervan Guide to Cults and Religious Movements. Grand Rapids: Zondervan, 1995.

Whalen, William J. *Christianity and American Freemasonry.* 3d ed. San Francisco: Ignatius Press, 1998.

White, James R. *Is the Mormon My Brother?* Minneapolis: Bethany House, 1997.

Williams, J. L. *Victor Paul Wierwille and the Way International.* Chicago: Moody Press, 1979.

Yamamoto, J. Isamu. *Unification Church.* Zondervan Guide to Cults and Religious Movements. Grand Rapids: Zondervan, 1995.

Works Cited in the Text

Alamo Christian Ministries

Works by Tony Alamo

The Arrangement.

The Authorities. Canyon Country, CA: Holy Alamo Christian Church, 1993. Pamphlet.

Conspiracy. Canyon Country, CA: Holy Alamo Christian Church, 1993. Pamphlet.

Cult Protection Racket. Canyon Country, CA: Holy Alamo Christian Church, 1993. Pamphlet.

Duped? Alma, AR: Holy Alamo Christian Churches Consecrated, [c. 1985]. Pamphlet.

Fugitive Pope. Van Buren, AR: Music Square Church, 1990. Pamphlet.

Genocide. Alma, AR: Alamo Christian Church, [c. 1985]. Pamphlet.

Give Caesar Tribute?

Works Cited in the Text (cont.)

Government Subversion Against Alamo.

Guilty by Association. Alma, AR: Tony and Susan Alamo Christian Foundation, 1983. Pamphlet.

The Heavenly Pharmacy. Canyon Country, CA: Holy Alamo Christian Church, 1993. Pamphlet.

Intolerance. Canyon Country, CA: Holy Alamo Christian Church, 1993. Pamphlet.

Judge or Be Judged.

Let's Sing It Right.

Messiah According to Bible Prophecy. Alma, AR: Holy Alamo Christian Church, 1992.

The Polygamists. Canyon Country, CA: Holy Alamo Christian Church, 1993. Pamphlet.

The Pope's Secrets. Alma, AR: Tony and Susan Alamo Christian Foundation, 1984. Pamphlet.

The Preacher. Canyon Country, CA: Holy Alamo Christian Church, 1993. Pamphlet.

Serpent.

The Set Up. Canyon Country, CA: Holy Alamo Christian Church, 1992. Pamphlet.

Signs of the Times.

Spiritual War.

Tony Alamo Asks . . . "Did You Know that Satan Needed a Church and Government?" Alma, AR: Alamo Christian Churches, n.d. Pamphlet.

"Tony Alamo Is Right!!!" Alma, AR: Holy Alamo Christian Church, Consecrated, [c. 1985]. Pamphlet.

Tony Alamo: My Side of the Story.

Hoffman, Bernie Lazar. *Tony Alamo's Answer to Rabbi Nuri.* Alma, AR: Tony and Susan Alamo Christian Foundation, n.d. Pamphlet. (Text and publication line reads, "Bernie Lazar Hoffman, aka Tony Alamo.")

The Weapon. Canyon Country, CA: Holy Alamo Christian Church, 1993. Pamphlet.

What Is Truth? Privately published, n.d.

You Be the Judge!! Alma, AR: Alamo Christian Churches, [1986?]. Pamphlet.

Other Materials

Board of Directors, with commentaries by Evangelist Tony Alamo. *Nailed!!* Van Buren, AR: Music Square Church, n.d. Pamphlet.

Association for Research and Enlightenment

Bro, Harmon Hartzell. *A Seer Out of Season: The Life of Edgar Cayce.* New York: Signet Books, 1989.

Bro, Harmon Hartzell. *Edgar Cayce on Religion and Psychic Experience.* New York: Paperback Library, 1970.

Furst, Jeffrey. *Edgar Cayce's Story of Jesus.* New York: Berkley Medallion Books, 1970.

Sugrue, Thomas. *There Is a River: The Story of Edgar Cayce.* New York: Dell Publishing, 1961. (A revised version of this book was issued by A.R.E. Press in 1997. References in the charts refer to the 1961 edition.)

Turner, Gladys Davis, and Mae Gimbert St. Clair, compilers. *Individual Reference File.* Revised ed. Virginia Beach: Association for Research and Enlightenment, 1976.

Christadelphians

Answering Your Questions About the Christadelphians. Privately published, n.d.

Baptism Essential to Salvation. Privately published, n.d.

Christ's Death and Your Salvation. Privately published, n.d.

Christadelphinians. "The Way Leaflet No. 8." Privately published, n.d.

God Is One Not Three. Privately published, n.d.

Herald of the Coming Age. Privately published, n.d.

Introducing the Christadelphians. Privately published, n.d.

"Jehovah's Witnesses Refuted by the Bible!" Privately published, n.d.

The Christadelphian Instructor. Privately published, n.d.

Works Cited in the Text (cont.)

	The Christadelphinian. Birmingham, AL, 1974.
	The Constitution of the Glendale Christadelphian Ecclesia. Glendale, CA: 1937, first printing 1939, amended 1972.
	"The Devil Defined." Privately published, n.d.
	What Your Decision for Christ Demands. Privately published, n.d.
Christian Identity Movement	"Doctrinal Statement of Beliefs" of the Christian Identity Church. Quoted in J. Gordon Melton, ed., *The Encyclopedia of American Religions: Religious Creeds* (Detroit: Gale Research, 1988), 624-26.
	Emry, Sheldon. *Heirs of the Promise*. Privately published, n.d.
	_____. *Who Killed Christ?* Privately published, n.d.
	Gayman, Dan. *The Seven Big Lies of Religion*. Privately published, n.d.
	Pike, Theodore Winston. *Israel: Our Duty, Our Dilemma*. Oregon City, OR: Big Sky Press, [c. 1984].
	Rittenhouse, Stan. *For Fear of the Jews*. Vienna, VA: Exhorters, 1982.
	Robb, Thom Arthur. Untitled pamphlet. Privately published, n.d.
	This Is Aryan Nations. Privately published, n.d.
	Lewis, David A. *Can Israel Survive in a Hostile World?* Green Forest, AR: New Leaf Press, 1994.
Church of Jesus Christ of Latter-day Saints	*A Chronology of Mormon Church Leaders 1830–1996*. Privately published, n.d.
	The Book of Mormon. Salt Lake City: Church of Jesus Christ of Latter-day Saints, 1986. (Books include 1 Nephi, 2 Nephi, Jacob, Enos, Jarom, Omni, Words of Mormon, Mosiah, Alma, Helaman, 3 Nephi, 4 Nephi, Mormon, Ether, Moroni).
	From *Come Unto Christ*. Quoted in *Teachings of Ezra Taft Benson*. Salt Lake City: Bookcraft, 1988.
	Gospel Principles. Salt Lake City: Corporation of the President of the Church of Jesus Christ of Latter-day Saints, 1978; revised periodically. (A study manual.)
	Hunter, Milton R., *The Gospel Through the Ages*. Salt Lake City, 1958.
	Millennial Star [or, *Latter-day Saints Millennial Star*]. Newspaper in Liverpool, England, published by the LDS Church since 1840.
	Stewart, John J. *Letter of LDS Presidency to Dr. Lowery Nelson*, July 17, 1947. Quoted in *Mormonism and the Negro*, 46–47. Oren, UT: Bookmark, 1960.
	Ludlow, Daniel H., ed. *Encyclopedia of Mormonism*. New York: Macmillan, 1992.
	McConkie, Bruce R., ed. *Mormon Doctrine*. Salt Lake City: Bookcraft, 1977.
	Smith, Joseph. The Pearl of Great Price. Salt Lake City: Church of Jesus Christ of Latter-day Saints, 1986. (Books include Selections from the Book of Moses, The Book of Abraham, Joseph Smith—Matthew, Joseph Smith—History, and The Articles of Faith of the Church of Jesus Christ of Latter-day Saints.)
	Salt Lake Tribune. Selected issues. Salt Lake City.
	Skousen, W. Cleon. *The First 2000 Years*. Salt Lake City: Bookcraft, 1979.
	Smith, Joseph Fielding. *Doctrines of Salvation*. Salt Lake City: Bookcraft, 1954.
	Smith, Joseph Fielding. *The Way to Perfection*. Salt Lake City: Bookcraft, 1931
	Smith, Joseph. The Doctrine and Covenants. Salt Lake City: Church of Jesus Christ of Latter-day Saints, 1986. (Various revelations given to Joseph Smith and many of his successors in the presidency of the church).
	Smith, Joseph, Jr. *History of the Church*. Salt Lake City: Deseret Book Co., 1978.
	Talmage, James E. *A Study of the Articles of Faith*. Salt Lake City: Church of Jesus Christ of Latter Day Saints, 1987.
	Teachings of the Prophet Joseph Smith. Salt Lake City: Deseret Book Co., 1973.
	Watt, George D. *Journal of Discourses*. 26 vols. Liverpool, England: 1854–1886.
	What the Mormons Think of Christ. Salt Lake City: Deseret Book Co., 1873.

Works Cited in the Text (cont.)

Church Universal and Triumphant	Prophet, Elizabeth Clare. *The Great White Brotherhood in the Culture, History, and Religion of America*. Colorado Springs: Summit University Press, 1976. Prophet, Elizabeth Clare. *The Lost Years of Jesus*. Livingston, MT: Summit University Press, 1984. "Interview: Elizabeth Clare Prophet." *Heart*. Vol. 3, no. 1 (Spring 1983): 58–65. (*Heart* magazine was published by Summit University Press in Westlake Village, California.) Prophet, Mark, and Elizabeth Clare Prophet. *Climb the Highest Mountain*. Colorado Springs: Summit Lighthouse, 1972. Prophet, Mark L., and Elizabeth Clare Prophet. *The Lost Teachings of Jesus*. Vol. 1, *Missing Texts, Karma and Reincarnation*. Livingston, MT: Summit University Press, 1986. *Profile: Elizabeth Clare Prophet—Teachings of the Ascended Masters*. Summit University Press, n.d. Pamphlet.
A Course in Miracles	*A Course in Miracles*. Vol. 1, *Text*. Tiburon, CA: Foundation for Inner Peace, 1975. *A Course in Miracles*. Vol. 2, *Workbook for Students*. Tiburon, CA: Foundation for Inner Peace, 1975. *A Course in Miracles*. Vol. 3, *Manual for Teachers*. Tiburon, CA: Foundation for Inner Peace, 1975. Melton, J. Gordon, Jerome Clark, and Aidan A. Kelly. *New Age Almanac*. Detroit: Gale Research/Visible Ink Press, 1991. "The Divine Miss W." *People*. March 9, 1992.
Eckankar	*Eckankar Membership*. Minneapolis: Eckankar, 1993. Pamphlet. *A Love Song to God: HU*. Pamphlet. Melton, J. Gordon. "Eckankar." In *Encyclopedia of American Religions*. 3d ed. Detroit: Gale Research, 1989. *Soul Travel and the Spiritual Exercises of Eckankar*. Pamphlet. Twitchell, Paul. *Eckankar Dictionary*. Las Vegas: Illuminated Way Press, 1973. _____. *Eckankar: The Key to Secret Worlds*. Menlo Park, CA: IWP Publishing, 1969. *What Is Eckankar?* Pamphlet. *What You Need to Know About the Light and Sound of God*. Pamphlet.
The Family/ Children of God	(The literature of The Family generally is in mimeograph or photocopied form and intentionally does not bear dates and places of location.) *Disciples and Friends Only (DFO)*. Privately published, n.d. *Disciples Only (DO)*. Privately published, n.d. *Family News International*. No. 50, p.34, n.d. *General Public (GP)*. Privately published, n.d. *Good News (GN)*. Privately published, n.d. *Growing in Love*. Privately published, n.d. *Leadership Trainees (LTA)*. Privately published, n.d. *Mo Letters (ML)*. Privately published, n.d. *MT*. Privately published, n.d. *Our Statement of Faith*. Privately published, n.d. *The Revolution For Jesus*. Privately published, n.d. "*Urgent Warning*." Tract by No Longer Children Ministry. Privately published, n.d.
Freemasonry	Acker, J. W. *Strange Altars: A Scriptural Appraisal of the Lodge*. St. Louis: Concordia Publishing House, 1959. Ankerberg, John, and John Weldon. *The Secret Teachings of the Masonic Lodge: A Christian Perspective*. Chicago: Moody Press, 1990.

Works Cited in the Text (cont.)

Blanchard, J. *Scotch [sic] Rite Masonry Illustrated.* Chicago: Ezra A. Cook Publications, 1957.

Buck, J. D. *Symbolism or Mystic Masonry.* Chicago: Ezra A. Cook Publications, 1925.

Cass, Donn. A. *Negro Freemasonry and Segregation.* Chicago: Ezra A. Cook Publications, 1977.

Clausen, Henry C. *Clausen's Commentaries on Morals and Dogma.* San Diego: Supreme Council, 33d Degree, Ancient and Accepted Scottish Rite of Freemasonry, Southern Jurisdiction of the U.S.A., 1976.

Clymer, R. Swineburne. *The Mysticism of Masonry.* CA: Philosophical Publishing Co., 1900.

Coil, Henry Wilson. *Coil's Masonic Encyclopedia.* New York: Macoy Publishing and Masonic Supply Company, 1961.

Darrah, Delmar Duane. *History and Evolution of Freemasonry.* Chicago: C. T. Powner, 1954.

Duncan, Malcom C. *Duncan's Masonic Ritual and Monitor, or Guide to the Three Symbolic Degrees.* Revised ed. Chicago: Ezra A. Cook Publications, 1960.

Hall, Manly Palmer. *The Lost Keys of Freemasonry, or The Secret of Hiram Abiff.* Richmond: Macoy, 1976.

Haywood, H. L. *The Great Teachings of Masonry.* Richmond: Macoy, 1971

Huckaby, G. C., compiler. *Louisiana Monitor of the Degrees of Entered Apprentice, Fellow Craft and Master Mason.* N.p.: Grand Lodge of the State of Louisiana, 1941.

Liturgy of the Ancient and Accepted Scottish Rite of Freemasonry for the Southern Jurisdiction of the United States. Washington, D.C.: Supreme Council, 33d Degree of the Ancient and Accepted Scottish Rite of Freemasonry of the Southern Jurisdiction of the U.S.A., 1982.

Mackey, Albert. *An Encyclopaedia of Freemasonry and Its Kindred Societies.* Revised ed. Edited by Edward L. Hawkins under the direction of William J. Hughan. Chicago: Masonic History Company, 1921.

Newton, Joseph Fort. "The Bible in Masonry." In *The Holy Bible, The Great Light in Masonry, Containing the Old and New Testaments.* Masonic ed. Philadelphia: A. J. Holman Co., 1957.

Newton, Joseph Fort. *The Builders: A Story and Study of Freemasonry.* Richmond: Macoy, 1951.

Pike, Albert. *Morals and Dogma of the Ancient and Accepted Scottish Rite of Freemasonry.* Charleston: Supreme Council of the Thirty-third Degree for the Southern Jurisdiction of the United States, Ancient and Accepted Scottish Rite, 1917.

Schmidt, Alvin J. *Fraternal Organizations.* Westport, CT: Greenwood Press, 1980.

Shaw, Jim, and Tom McKinney. *The Deadly Deception.* Lafayette, LA: Huntington House, 1988.

Jehovah's Witnesses	**Works by the Watchtower Society**

(Literature by Jehovah's Witnesses routinely is published without personal name authorship. In the following entries, the corporate author and publisher is the Watchtower Bible and Tract Society of New York, Inc. in Brooklyn, unless explicitly listed otherwise.)

Awake! Periodical published since 1919. (Originally entitled *The Golden Age,* it was renamed *Consolation* in 1937 and *Awake!* in 1946.)

Blood, Medicine and the Law of God. 1961.

Consolation. (See *Awake!* Above.)

Holy Spirit—The Force behind the Coming New Order. 1976.

Insight on the Scriptures. 2 vols. 1988.

Is This Life All There Is? 1974.

Jehovah's Witnesses in the 20th Century. Revised ed. 1989.

Let God Be True. 2d ed. 1952.

Life Everlasting—In Freedom of the Sons of God. 1966.

New World Bible Translation Committee. *New World Translation of the Christian Greek Scriptures*. 1950. (Revised several times subsequently and currently published as *New World Translation of the Holy Scriptures*.)

Reasoning from the Scriptures. 1985.

Should You Believe in the Trinity? 1989.

The Truth That Leads to Eternal Life. 1968. Brooklyn, NY, or Allegheny, PA: Watchtower Bible and Tract Society.

The Watchtower Announcing Jehovah's Kingdom. Periodical published since 1879. (Originally entitled *Zion's Watch Tower and Herald of Christ's Presence*, it was renamed three times, receiving its current title in 1939.)

What Has Religion Done for Mankind? 1951.

You Can Live Forever in Paradise on Earth. 1982.

Russell, Charles Taze. *Studies in the Scriptures*. 6 vols. Brooklyn: Watchtower Bible and Tract Society, 1886–1904. (This series was revised several times until 1917; a reprint of the 1916 edition is available from the Dawn Bible Students Association of East Rutherford, New Jersey.)

Rutherford, J. F. *Life*. 1929.

Rutherford, J. F. *Millions Now Living Will Never Die*. 1920.

Rutherford, J. F. *Reconciliation*. 1928.

Other Materials.

Reed, David A. *Jehovah's Witness Literature: A Critical Guide to Watchtower Publications*. Grand Rapids: Baker Books, 1993.

Mind Science Groups

Christian Science

Christian Science Journal. April 1980. Vol. 98, no. 4.

Eddy, Mary Baker G. *Manual of the Mother Church*. 89th ed. Boston: Trustees under the Will of Mary Baker G. Eddy, 1908.

_____. *Miscellaneous Writings 1883–1896*. Boston: Trustees under the Will of Mary Baker G. Eddy, 1896.

_____. *Science and Health with Key to the Scriptures*. Boston: First Church of Christ, Scientist, 1906.

Unity School of Christianity

Fillmore, Charles. *Christian Healing*. Kansas City, MO: Unity School of Christianity, 1909.

_____. *Metaphysical Bible Dictionary*. Unity Village, MO: Unity School of Christianity, 1931.

_____. *The Twelve Powers of Man*.

Cady, H. Emilie. *Lessons in Truth*. Kansas City, MO.: Unity School of Christianity, 1939.

Unity. Periodical published since 1891 by the Unity School of Christianity.

"Unity Statement of Faith." Unity Village: Unity School of Christianity, n.d.

What Unity Teaches. The Unity School of Christianity. Lee's Summit, MO: n.d.

Religious Science

Holmes, Ernest. *The Basic Ideas of Science of Mind*. Los Angeles: Science of Mind, 1971.

Holmes, Ernest, and Fenwicke L. Holmes. *What Religious Science Teaches*. Los Angeles: Institute of Religious Science, 1944.

Holmes, Ernest, with Maude Allison Lathem. *The Science of Mind*. Revised ed. New York: Dodd, Mead, 1938.

Other Materials

Ehrenborg, Todd. *Mind Sciences*. Zondervan Guide to Cults and Religious Movements. Grand Rapids: Zondervan, 1995.

Martin, Walter R. *The Kingdom of the Cults*. 3d ed. Minneapolis: Bethany House, 1985. (See especially chap. 6, "Christian Science" and chap. 11, "The Unity School of Christianity.")

Works Cited in the Text (cont.)

New Age Movement	Bailey, Alice A. *The Reappearance of the Christ*. New York: Lucis Publishing Co., 1937.
	The 14th Dalai Lama of Tibet and Galen Rowell. *My Tibet*. Berkeley: University of California Press, 1990.
	Dowling, Levi H. *The Aquarian Gospel of Jesus the Christ*. Marina Del Rey, CA: DeVoors & Co., 1907, 1964.
	The editors of *Body, Mind & Spirit* magazine. *The New Age Catalogue*. New York: Doubleday, 1988.
	Ferguson, Marilyn. *The Aquarian Conspiracy*. Los Angeles: J. P. Tarcher, 1980.
	Fisher, Joe. *The Case for Reincarnation*. New York: Bantam Books, 1985.
	Groothuis, Douglas R. *Unmasking The New Age*. Downers Grove, IL: InterVarsity Press, 1986.
	Hubbard, Barbara Marx. *Revelation: Our Crisis Is a Birth (The Book of Co-Creation)*. 2d ed. Novato, CA: Nataraj Publishing, 1993.
	MacLaine, Shirley. *Out on a Limb*. New York: Bantam Books, 1983.
	Robinson, James M., ed. "The Gospel of Thomas." *The Nag Hammadi Library in English*. San Francisco: HarperCollins, 1990.
	Saddhatissa, Hammalawa. *Buddhist Ethics: The Path to Nirvana*. London: Wisdom Publications, 1987.
	Smith, F. LaGard. *Out on a Broken Limb*. Eugene, OR: Harvest House, 1986.
	Yogi, Maharishi Mahesh. *The Science of Being and Art of Living*. New York: Signet Books, 1968.
	Zilinskas, Ann E. *Heartland Journal*. May–June 1988.
Reorganized Church of Jesus Christ of Latter-day Saints	Brown, Richard A. *Temple Foundations: Essays on an Emerging Concept*. Independence, MO: Herald Publishing House, 1991.
	Department of Religious Education, Reorganized Church of Jesus Christ of Latter-day Saints. *Position Papers*. 1968. Reprint, with introduction, "Items of Interest," index, and new pagination, Independence, MO: Cumorah Books, n.d.
	Edwards, F. Henry. *The Edwards Commentary on the Doctrine and Covenants*. Independence, MO: Herald Publishing House, 1986.
	Edwards, F. Henry. "Introduction." In *Joseph Smith's "New Translation" of the Bible*. Independence, MO: Herald Publishing House, 1970.
	The First Presidency, Reorganized Church of Jesus Christ of Latter-day Saints. *Presidential Papers*. 1979. Reprint, with critical introductory and explanatory material, plus index, Independence, MO: Cumorah Books, 1979.
	Kelley, Stephanie. "Reorganized Church of Jesus Christ of Latter-day Saints: Information Sheet," April 1992. Public news release.
	RLDS Communications Division brochure, 1991.
	Saints Herald. Periodical published by the RLDS Church since March 1860.
	Smith, Joseph, Jr., trans. The Book of Mormon. Independence, MO: Board of Publication of the Reorganized Church of Jesus Christ of Latter-day Saints, 1966.
	Smith, Joseph, Jr. *The Holy Scriptures, Containing the Old and New Testaments: An Inspired Revision of the Authorized Version*. Independence, MO: Herald Publishing House, 1944.
	Smith, Joseph, Jr. *Joseph Smith Tells His Own Story*. Independence, MO: Herald Publishing House, n.d. Originally published in the *Times and Seasons* (Nauvoo, IL), 3:726ff. (1842).
	[Smith, Joseph, Jr., and others.] Book of Doctrine and Covenants. Independence, MO: Herald Publishing House, 1970.
	Smith, Joseph III. *Abstract of Evidence*, pp. 491–94. Quoted in Alan Tyree, *Exploring the Faith* (1987), p. 241.
	Statement of Faith and Belief. Prepared by the Basic Beliefs Committee of the Reorganized Church of Jesus Christ of Latter Day Saints and issued by the First Presidency in 1969. Reprinted in Alan Tyree, ed., *Exploring the Faith* (1970, 1987).

	Times and Seasons. Newspaper in Nauvoo, Illinois. Vols. 1-6, July 1839–February 15, 1846.
	Tyree, Alan D., ed. *Exploring the Faith.* Independence, MO: Herald Publishing House, 1970; revised ed. 1987.
	Who Are the Saints? Revised ed. Independence, MO: Herald Publishing House, 1985.
	Young, Leonard M. *Communities of Joy: New Experiences in Congregational Living.* Independence, MO: Herald Publishing House, 1994.
Rosicrucianians	Heindel, Max. *The Rosicrucian Philosophy in Questions and Answers.* 2d ed. Oceanside, CA: Rosicrucian Fellowship, 1910.
	Heindel, Max. *The Rosicrucian Cosmo-Conception, or Mystic Christianity.* 1929. Reprint, Oceanside, CA: Rosicrucian Fellowship, 1974.
	Khei, [George Winslow Plummer]. *Rosicrucian Fundamentals: An Exposition of the Rosicrucian Synthesis of Religion, Science and Philosophy.* New York: Flame Press, 1920. Reprint, Kila, MT: Kessinger Publishing Co., 1997.
	Lewis, H. Spencer. *Rosicrucian Manual.* 21st ed. Vol. 8 of the Rosicrucian Library. San Jose, CA: Supreme Grand Lodge of AMORC, 1971.
	Lewis, H. Spencer. *Rosicrucian Questions and Answers with Complete History of the Rosicrucian Order.* Vol. 1 of the Rosicrucian Library. San Jose, CA: Supreme Grand Lodge of AMORC, 1929.
	Melton, J. Gordon. "Ancient Wisdom Family" (chap. 17) and "Rosicrucianism" (sect. 17). In *Encyclopedia of American Religions.* 3d ed. Detroit: Gale Research, 1989.
	The Ancient and Mystical Order of the Rosae Crucis (AMORC). San Jose, CA: Supreme Grand Lodge of AMORC, n.d.
Unification Church	**Works or Talks by Sun Myung Moon.**
	Divine Principle. Washington, D.C.: Holy Spirit Association for the Unification of World Christianity, 1973.
	"History of the Providence Through Restoration by Indemnity." February 10, 1981.
	"Ideal Family and Ideal World." June 6, 1982.
	"Let Us Go over the Hill." February 8, 1984.
	"The Ideal World of Subject and Object." February 13, 1977.
	Leader Speaks [Questions and Answers]. At Rowlane Farmhouse, England, March 16, 1982.
	On Prayer and The Spirit World. MS–3.
	"Restoration from the Origin and Rebirth for Myself." September 20, 1992.
	On Satan, the Fall and Evil. MS–6.
	"The Stony Path of Death." April 27, 1980.
	Textbook for World Peace. 1992.
	"Thirtieth Anniversary of the Unification Church." May 1, 1984.
	Today's World. Magazine, various issues.
	"True Parent's Day from the Historical Point of View." April 18, 1977.
	"True Parents and I." June 15, 1986.
	"The True Path of Restoration." January 11, 1972.
	"True Way of Life." July 1, 1984.
	"United, the Kingdom of Heaven Is at Hand." March 5, 1989.
	Other Materials
	"The Marriage of the Lamb." *Unification News,* August 1995.
	Divine Principle Outline and Study Guide.
	"Important Person." June 10, 1973. MS–377.
	Kim, Young Oon. *Unification Theology.* 2d ed. New York: Holy Spirit Association for the Unification of World Christianity, 1987.
	Kwak, Chung, ed. *The Tradition.* "Use of Holy Salt."

Works Cited in the Text (cont.)

United Pentecostal Church	Bernard, David K. *The New Birth*. Vol. 2 of Series in Pentecostal Theology. Hazlewood, MO: Word Aflame Press, 1984. Bernard, David K. *The Oneness of God*. Vol. 2 of Series in Pentecostal Theology. Hazelwood, MO: Word Aflame Press, 1983. Bernard, Loretta, and David Bernard. *In Search of Holiness*. Vol. 3 in Series in Pentecostal Theology. Hazlewood, MO: Word Aflame Press, 1981, 1988. Hesselgrave, David J. *Dynamic Religious Movements*. Grand Rapids: Baker Book House, 1978. *Their Story: 20th Century Pentecostals*. Quoted in Keith Tolbert, *The Views of Church History Within the United Pentecostal Church International*. N.p.: n.d. Thiessen, Henry C. *Lectures in Systematic Theology*. Revised ed. Grand Rapids: Wm. B. Eerdmans, 1989.
Urantia Foundation	Breasted, James Henry. *The Dawn of Conscience*. New York: Charles Scribner's Sons, 1933. Sadler, William S. *The Mind at Mischief: Tricks and Deceptions of the Subconscious and How to Cope with Them*. New York: Funk & Wagnalls, 1929. Sprunger, Meredith J. *Origins of the Urantia Book*. Boulder, CO: Jesusonian Foundation, 1988. Pamphlet. *The Urantia Book*. Chicago: Urantia Foundation, 1955.
The Way International	Martindale, L. Craig. April 1987 letter addressed "to all believers." *Twenty-fifth Anniversary Souvenir Booklet*. Wierwille, Victor Paul. *Are the Dead Alive Now?* Old Greenwich, CT: Devin-Adair Company, 1971. _____. *The Bible Tells Me So*. Vol. 1 of Studies in Abundant Living. New Knoxville, OH: American Christian Press, 1973. _____. *Christians Should Be Prosperous*. New Knoxville, OH: American Christian Press, [c. 1971]. _____. "Forgers of the Word." In Wierville, *Jesus Christ Is Not God*, "Bibliography." _____. *God's Magnified Word*. New Knoxville, OH: American Christian Press, 1977. _____. *Jesus Christ Is Not God*. New Knoxville, OH: American Christian Press, 1975. _____. *The New, Dynamic Church*. Vol. 2 of Studies in Abundant Living. New Knoxville, OH: American Christian Press, 1973 Wierwille, Victor P. *Power for Abundant Living*. New Knoxville, OH: American Christian Press, 1971. _____. *Receiving the Holy Spirit Today*. Van Wert, OH: The Way Inc., 1957. Reprint, New Knoxville, OH: American Christian Press, 1972. _____. *The Word's Way*. Vol. 3 of Studies in Abundant Living. New Knoxville, OH: American Christian Press, 1973.
Orthodox Christian Doctrine	Berkhof, Louis. *Systematic Theology*. 2d ed. Grand Rapids: Wm. B. Eerdmans, 1941. Bruce, F. F. *The New Testament Documents—Are They Reliable?* Downers Grove, IL: InterVarsity Press, 1967. Calvin, John. Institutes of the Christian Religion. Carson, D. A., and John D. Woodbridge, eds. *Scripture and Truth*. Grand Rapids: Baker Book House, 1992. Cook, W. Robert. *Systematic Theology in Outline Form*. N.p.: n.d. Elwell, Walter A., ed. *Evangelical Dictionary of Theology*. Grand Rapids: Baker book House, 1991. Erickson, Millard J. *Christian Theology*, 2d ed. Grand Rapids: Baker Book House, 1998. Hodge, Charles. *Systematic Theology*. Grand Rapids: Wm. B. Eerdmans, 1952. *Matthew Henry's Commentary on the Whole Bible*. Grand Rapids: Zondervan, 1961.